www.wadsworth.com

wadsworth.com is the World Wide Web site for Wadsworth Publishing Company and is your direct source to dozens of online resources.

At *wadsworth.com* you can find out about supplements, demonstration software, and student resources. You can also send e-mail to many of our authors and preview new publications and exciting new technologies.

wadsworth.com
Changing the way the world learns®

SECOND
EDITION

Western Civilization

A Brief History

Volume I: To 1715

Jackson J. Spielvogel
The Pennsylvania State University

WADSWORTH

THOMSON LEARNING

Australia • Canada • Mexico • Singapore • Spain
United Kingdom • United States

WADSWORTH

THOMSON LEARNING ™

History Publisher: *Clark Baxter*
Senior Development Editor: *Sue Gleason*
Assistant Editor: *Jennifer Ellis*
Senior Marketing Manager: *Diane McOscar*
Senior Print Buyer: *Mary Beth Hennebury*
Senior Production Editor: *Michael Burggren*
Permissions Editor: *Bob Kauser*
Interior Designer: *Norman Baugher*
Cover Designer: *Carole Lawson*
Copy Editor: *Bruce Emmer*
Production Service: *Jon Peck, Dovetail Publishing Services*

Maps: *MapQuest.com, Inc.*
Photo Researcher: *Sarah Evertson, Image Quest*
Compositor: *New England Typographic Service*
Printer/Binder: *Quebecor World Taunton*
Cover Printer: *Phoenix Color Corp.*

Cover Image: Master of Frankfort (15th c.). *Festival of the Archers,* c. 1493. Koniniijk Museum voor Schone Kunsten, Antwerp, Belgium. © Scala/Art Resource, NY

Photo Credits begin on page xxii which constitutes a continuation of the copyright page

Wadsworth/Thomson Learning
10 Davis Drive
Belmont, CA 94002-3098
USA

For more information about our products, contact us:
Thomson Learning Academic Resource Center
1-800-423-0563
http://www.wadsworth.com

International Headquarters
Thomson Learning
International Division
290 Harbor Drive, 2nd Floor
Stamford, CT 06902-7477
USA

UK/Europe/Middle East/South Africa
Thomson Learning
Berkshire House
168-173 High Holborn
London WC1V 7AA
United Kingdom

Asia
Thomson Learning
60 Albert Street, #15-01
Albert Complex
Singapore 189969

Canada
Nelson Thomson Learning
1120 Birchmount Road
Toronto, Ontario M1K 5G4
Canada

Library of Congress Cataloging-in-Publication Data

Spielvogel, Jackson J.
　　Western civilization : a brief history / Jackson J. Spielvogel.—2nd ed.
　　　　p.　cm.
　　Includes bibliographical references and index.
　　ISBN 0-534-58707-0 (comprehensive vol. : alk. paper)
　　ISBN 0-534-58708-9 (vol I. : alk. paper)
　　ISBN 0-534-58709-7 (vol II. : alk. paper)
　　ISBN 0-534-58710-0 (instructor's edition : alk. paper)
　　1. Civilization, Western—History.　I. Title.
CB245.S63　2001
909'.09821—dc21
2001026221

 This book is printed on acid-free recycled paper.

About the Author

*J*ACKSON J. SPIELVOGEL *is associate professor emeritus of history at The Pennsylvania State University. He received his Ph.D. from The Ohio State University, where he specialized in Reformation history under Harold J. Grimm. His articles and reviews have appeared in such journals as* Moreana, Journal of General Education, Catholic Historical Review, Archiv für Reformationsgeschichte, *and* American Historical Review. *He has also contributed chapters or articles to* The Social History of Reformation, The Holy Roman Empire: A Dictionary Handbook, Simon Wiesenthal Center Annual of Holocaust Studies, *and* Utopian Studies. *His work has been supported by fellowships from the Fulbright Foundation and the Foundation for Reformation Research. At Penn State, he helped inaugurate the Western civilization courses as well as a popular course on Nazi Germany. His book* Hitler and Nazi Germany *was published in 1987 (fourth edition, 2001). He is the co-author (with William Duiker) of* World History, *published in January 1994 (third edition, 2001). Professor Spielvogel has won five major university-wide teaching awards. During the year 1988–1989, he held the Penn State Teaching Fellowship, the university's most prestigious teaching award. In 1996, he won the Dean Arthur Ray Warnock Award for Outstanding Faculty Member, and in 1997, he became the first recipient of the Schreyer Institute's Student Choice Award for innovative and inspiring teaching.*

To Diane,
whose love and support
made it all possible

Brief Contents

Detailed Contents

✳ **CHAPTER 12**
Recovery and Rebirth: The Age of the Renaissance   235

✳ **CHAPTER 13**
The Age of Reformation   260

✳ **CHAPTER 14**
Discovery and Crisis in the Sixteenth and Seventeenth Centuries   280

Maps

Chronologies

Documents

We are grateful to the authors and publishers acknowledged here for their permission to reprint copyrighted material. We have made every reasonable effort to identify copyright owners of materials in the boxed documents. If any information is found to be incomplete, we will gladly make whatever additional acknowledgments might be necessary.

Photo Credits

Preface

We are often reminded how important it is to understand today's world if we are to deal with our growing number of challenges. And yet that understanding will be incomplete if we in the Western world do not comprehend the meaning of Western civilization and the role Western civilization has played in the world. For all of our modern progress, we still greatly reflect our religious traditions, our political systems and theories, our economic and social structures, and our cultural heritage. I have written this brief history of Western civilization to assist a new generation of students in learning more about the past that has helped create them and the world in which they live.

I began this project with two primary goals. First, I wanted to write a well-balanced work in which the political, economic, social, religious, intellectual, cultural, and military aspects of Western civilization would be integrated into a chronologically ordered synthesis. Second, I wanted to avoid the approach that is quite common in other brief histories of Western civilization—an approach that makes them collections of facts with little continuity from section to section. Instead, I sought to keep the story in history. Narrative history effectively transmits the knowledge of the past and is the form that best enables students to remember and understand the past. At the same time, I have not overlooked the need for the kind of historical analysis that makes students aware that historians often disagree in their interpretations of the past.

To enliven the past and let readers see for themselves the materials that historians use to create their pictures of the past, I have included in each chapter primary sources (boxed documents) that are keyed to the discussion in the text. The documents include examples of the religious, artistic, intellectual, social, economic, and political aspects of Western life. Such varied sources as a Roman banquet menu, advice from a Carolingian mother to her son, marriage negotiations in Renaissance Italy, the diary of a German soldier at Stalingrad, and a debate in the Reformation era all reveal in a vivid fashion what Western civilization meant to the individual men and women who shaped it by their activities.

Each chapter has a lengthy introduction and conclusion to help maintain the continuity of the narrative and to provide a synthesis of important themes. Anecdotes in the chapter introductions convey more

dramatically the major theme or themes of each chapter. Detailed chronologies reinforce the events discussed in the text while timelines at the end of each chapter enable students to see at a glance the major developments of an era. An annotated bibliography at the end of each chapter reviews the most recent literature on each period and also gives references to some of the older, "classic" works in each field. Extensive maps and illustrations serve to deepen the reader's understanding of the text. To facilitate understanding of cultural movements, illustrations of artistic works discussed in the text are placed next to the discussions. New to the second edition are focus questions and chapter outlines at the beginning of each chapter, which should help students to gain a quick overview and guide them to the main subjects of each chapter. A glossary of important terms and a pronunciation guide have also been added to the second edition.

As preparation for the revision of *Western Civilization: A Brief History,* I reexamined the entire book and analyzed the comments and reviews of colleagues who have found the book to be a useful instrument for introducing their students to the history of Western civilization. In making revisions for the second edition, I sought to build upon the strengths of the first edition and, above all, to maintain the balance, synthesis, and narrative qualities that characterized that edition. To keep up with the ever-growing body of historical scholarship, new or revised material has been added throughout the book on many topics, including, for example, civilization in Mesopotamia and Egypt; ancient Israel; Homer; Sparta; Aristotle's views of women; women in the Hellenistic world; Roman values and attitudes; literature in the late Roman Republic; late Roman Empire; women in early Christianity and the new Germanic kingdoms; the rise and spread of Islam; the Vikings; the Black Death; Catherine of Siena; Christine de Pizan; marriage and childbirth in Renaissance Italy; European discovery and expansion in the sixteenth and seventeenth centuries; Artemisia Gentileschi; Judith Leyster and Dutch realism; Louis XIV; limits of absolutism; nobility in the eighteenth century; female utopian socialists; the economy of Latin America; revolution of 1848 in Italy; Napoleon II; women and work in the nineteenth century; women and the Paris commune; Impressionism; Marie Curie; women reformers and the "new woman" in the nineteenth century; Asian response to imperialism; the history of

Canada; social repercussions of the Great Depression; movies in the 1920s and 1930s; new attitudes toward sexuality in the 1920s; history of the United States and Canada since 1945; decolonization; the women's liberation movement; and the war in Kosovo. Throughout the revising process, I also worked to craft a book that I hope students will continue to find very readable. New subheadings were added in many chapters in the second edition in order to facilitate the reader's comprehension of the content of the chapters.

To provide a more logical arrangement of the material, I have also made organizational changes in Chapters 1, 6, 14, 28, and 29. Chapters 9, 10, and 11 on the High Middle Ages were reorganized and condensed to form two new chapters entitled "The Recovery and Growth of European Society in the High Middle Ages" and "A New World of Cities and Kingdoms." Moreover, all "Suggestions for Further Reading" at the end of each chapter were thoroughly updated, and new illustrations were added to almost every chapter.

The enthusiastic response to the primary sources (boxed documents) led me to evaluate the content of each document carefully and add new documents throughout the text, including "The Twelve Tables," "West Meets East: An Exchange of Royal Letters," "British Victory in India," "Declaration of the Rights of Man and the Citizen," "A Leader of the Paris Commune," "Hesse and the Unconscious," and "Margaret Thatcher: Entering a Man's World." For the second edition, the maps have been revised where needed and, as in previous editions, are carefully keyed to all text references. New maps have also been added, including "The Columbian Exchange" and "The Holocaust."

Because courses in Western civilization at American and Canadian colleges and universities follow different chronological divisions, a one-volume edition and a two-volume edition of this text are being made available to fit the needs of instructors. Teaching and learning ancillaries include the following:

✻ For the Instructor

Instructor's Manual with Test Bank Prepared by Kevin Robbins, Indiana University Purdue University Indianapolis. This new Instructor's Manual contains chapter outlines, suggested lecture topics, and discussion questions for the maps and artwork as well as the primary source documents located in the text. World Wide Web sites and resources, video collections, suggested student activities, and secondary sources for lecture preparation are also included. Exam questions include essays, identifications, and multiple-choice questions. Available in two volumes.

ExamView Instructors can create, deliver, and customize tests and study guides (both print and online) in minutes with this easy-to-use assessment and tutorial system. ExamView offers both a Quick Test Wizard and an Online Test Wizard that guide the user step by step through the process of creating tests, while its unique "WYSIWYG" capability allows users to see the test they are creating on the screen exactly as it will print or display online. Tests of up to 250 questions using up to 12 question types can be built. Using ExamView's complete word processing capabilities, instructors can enter an unlimited number of new questions or edit existing questions. Available for Windows and Macintosh.

Full Color Map Acetate Package This package includes maps from the text and from other sources. More than 100 four-color images are provided in a handy three-ring binder. Map commentary is provided by James Harrison, Siena College.

Map Slides 100 full-color map slides.

Lecture Enrichment Slides Prepared by Dale Hoak and George Strong, College of William and Mary. These 100 slides contain images of famous paintings, statues, architectural achievements, and interesting photos. The authors supply commentary for each slide.

History Video Library A completely new selection of videos to go with the second edition. Over 50 titles to choose from, with coverage spanning from "Egypt: A Gift to Civilization" to "Children of the Holocaust." *CNN Today Videos* For *Western Civilization*, the perfect lecture launchers contain video clips ranging from one to five minutes long.

Sights and Sounds of History Video Uses focused video clips, photos, artwork, animations, music, and dramatic readings to bring history to life. The video segments average four minutes long and are available on VHS. These make excellent lecture launchers.

HistoryLink An advanced PowerPoint presentation tool containing text-specific lecture outlines, figures, and images that allows instructors to quickly deliver dynamic lectures. In addition, it provides the flexibility to customize each presentation by editing what we have provided or by adding one's own collection of slides, videos and animations. All of the map acetates and selected photos have also been incorporated into each of the lectures. In addition, the extensive Map Commentaries for each map slide are available through the "Comments" feature of PowerPoint.

✻ For the Student

Study Guide Prepared by James Baker, Western Kentucky University. Includes chapter outlines, chapter summaries, and seven different types of questions for each chapter. Available in two volumes.

Exploring the European Past: Text and Images   A completely customizable reader that brings to life the events, people, and movements that helped define Western civilization. Each reading begins with an introduction that sets the time and tone, followed by primary source and then secondary source documents, each with a series of critical thinking questions. Every reading is brought to life with visual resources presented on the Internet, including images of architecture, artifacts, photographs, artwork, and maps, as well as animations. To find out more, contact your local Thomson Learning sales representative.

Map Exercise Workbook   This workbook, prepared by Cynthia Kosso, Northern Arizona University, has been thoroughly revised including new easier to read maps. Over 20 maps and exercises ask students to identify important cities and countries and answer critical thinking questions. Available in two volumes.

MapTutor CD ROM   This interactive map tutorial helps students learn geography by having them locate geographical features, regions, cities, and sociopolitical movements. Each map exercise is accompanied by questions that test their knowledge and promote critical thinking. Animations vividly show movements such as the conquests of the Romans, the spread of Christianity, invasions, medieval trade routes, the spread of the Black Death, and more.

Document Exercise Workbook   Prepared by Donna Van Raaphorst, Cuyahoga Community College. A collection of exercises based on primary sources. Revised for this edition, it now contains a web component that points students to museums and other useful sites. Available in two volumes.

Journey of Civilizations CD ROM   This CD ROM takes the student on 18 interactive journeys through history. Enhanced with QuickTime movies, animations, sound clips, maps, and more, the journeys allow students to engage in history as active participants rather than as readers of past events. Available for Windows.

WebTutor   This customized online study supplement helps students succeed by taking the course beyond the classroom boundaries to a virtual environment. Professors can use *WebTutor* to provide virtual office hours, post their syllabi, set up threaded discussions, and track student progress with the quizzing material. For Students, *WebTutor* offers real-time access to a full array of study tools, including flashcards, practice quizzes and tests, online tutorials, exercises, discussion questions, web links, and a full glossary. Visit www.itped.com for a demonstration.

Magellan World History Atlas   This atlas helps integrate dozens of maps into the course.

Internet Guide for History, 3/e   Prepared by John Soares. This newly revised and up-to-date internet provides exercises by topic. It can be found on the web at http://history.wadsworth.com.

Western Civilization, Canadian Supplement   Prepared by Maryann Farkus, Dawson College. Discusses Canadian history and culture in the context of Western civilization.

Archer, Documents of Western Civilization   Contains a broad selection of carefully chosen documents. Available in two volumes.

InfoTrac® College Edition   Create your own collection of secondary readings from more than 900 popular and scholarly periodicals such as *Smithsonian*, *Historian*, and *Harper's* for four months. Students can browse, choose, and print any articles they want 24 hours a day.

Historic Times: The Wadsworth History Resource Center   A web site just for history students. Features links to museums, documents, and other web sites. Available at http://history.wadsworth.com.

❋ *Acknowledgments*

I would like to thank the many teachers and students who have used the first edition of *Western Civilization: A Brief History*. I am gratified by their enthusiastic response to a textbook that was intended to put the story back in history and capture the imagination of the reader. I especially thank the many teachers and students who made the effort to contact me personally to share their enthusiasm. I want also to thank Charmarie Blaisdell of Northeastern University for her detailed analysis of women's history; her suggestions were very valuable in preparing the second edition. A number of historians were asked to evaluate my original manuscript and review the first edition. I am grateful to the following for the innumerable suggestions that have greatly improved my work:

Dieter Buse,
   Laurentian University
Don R. Fisher,
   Albuquerque Technical-Vocational Community College
Stephen C. Govedich,
   Yavapai College
Robert E. Herzstein,
   University of South Carolina
Daniel W. Hollis III,
   Jacksonville State University
Paul W. Knoll,
   University of Southern California
Clayton Lehmann,
   University of South Dakota

Chris Oldstone-Moore,
  Augustana College
Matthew Redinger,
  Montana State University-Billings
Fiona Stoertz,
  Trent University

I am also grateful to the following reviewers who have helped me improve the second edition:

Marion Deshmukh,
  George Mason University
Kenneth R. Hall,
  Ball State University
Carolyn Malone,
  Ball State University
Loyce B. Miles,
  Hinds Community College
Wyatt Moulds,
  Jones Junior College
Dana L. Sample,
  Hampton University
Steven Seyer,
  Lehigh Carbon Community College
Rex A. Wade,
  George Mason University

The editors at Wadsworth Publishing Company—Thomson Learning have been both helpful and congenial at all times. Michael Burggren guided the overall production of the book with much insight. I especially wish to thank Clark Baxter, whose clever wit, wisdom, gentle prodding, and good friendship have added much depth to our working relationship. Sharon Adams Poore and Sue Gleason thoughtfully guided the preparation of outstanding teaching and learning ancillaries. Jon Peck, of Dovetail Publishing Services, was extremely cooperative and competent in the production of the book. Bruce Emmer, an outstanding copy editor, taught me much about the fine points of the English language. Sarah Evertson provided valuable assistance in obtaining permissions for the photographs and illustrations.

Above all, I thank my family for their support. The gifts of love, laughter, and patience from my daughters, Jennifer and Kathryn; my sons, Eric and Christian; and my daughters-in-law, Liz and Laurie, were enormously appreciated. My wife and best friend, Diane, contributed editorial assistance, wise counsel, humor, and the loving support that made it possible to complete yet another ambitious project. I could not have written the book without her.

Introduction to Students of Western Civilization

Civilization, as historians define it, first emerged between five thousand and six thousand years ago when people began to live in organized communities with distinct political, military, economic, and social structures. Religious, intellectual, and artistic activities also assumed important roles in these early societies. The focus of this book is on Western civilization, a civilization that for most of its history has been identified with the continent of Europe. Its origins, however, go back to the Mediterranean basin, including lands in North Africa and the Middle East, as well as Europe itself. Moreover, the spread of Europeans abroad led to the development of offshoots of Western civilization in other parts of the world.

Because civilized life includes all the deeds and experiences of people organized in communities, the history of a civilization must embrace a series of studies. An examination of Western civilization therefore requires us to study the political, economic, social, military, cultural, intellectual, and religious aspects that make up the life of that civilization and show how they are interrelated. In so doing, we need also at times to focus on some of the unique features of Western civilization. Certainly, science played a crucial role in the development of modern Western civilization. Although such societies as those of the Greeks, the Romans, and medieval Europeans were based largely on a belief in the existence of a spiritual order, Western civilization experienced a dramatic departure toward a natural or material view of the universe in the seventeenth-century Scientific Revolution. Science and technology have been important in the growth of modern and largely secular Western civilization, although antecedents to scientific development also existed in Greek, Islamic, and medieval thought and practice.

Many historians have also viewed the concept of political liberty, the fundamental value of every individual, and the creation of a rational outlook, based on a system of logical, analytical thought, as unique aspects of Western civilization. Of course, Western civilization has also witnessed the frightening negation of liberty, individualism, and reason. Racism, violence, world wars, totalitarianism—these too must form part of the story. Finally, regardless of our concentration on Western civilization and its characteristics, we need to take into account that other civilizations have influenced Western civilization and it, in turn, has affected the development of other civilizations.

In our examination of Western civilization, we need also to be aware of the dating of time. In recording the past, historians try to determine the exact time when events occurred. World War II in Europe, for example, began on September 1, 1939, when Hitler sent German troops into Poland and ended on May 7, 1945, when Germany surrendered. By using dates, historians can place events in order and in relation to one another and try to determine the development of patterns over periods of time.

If someone asked you when you were born, you would reply with a number, such as 1982. In the United States, we would all accept that number without question because it is part of the dating system followed in the Western world (Europe and the Western Hemisphere). In this system, events are dated by counting backward or forward from the birth of Jesus Christ (assumed to be the year 1). An event that took place four hundred years before the birth of Jesus would be dated 400 B.C. ("before Christ"). Dates after the birth of Jesus are labeled A.D. These letters stand for the Latin words *anno Domini*, which mean "in the year of the Lord." Thus an event that took place 250 years after the birth of Jesus is written A.D. 250, meaning "in the year of the Lord 250." It can also be written as 250, just as you would not give your birth year as A.D. 1982, but simply as 1982.

Historians also make use of other terms to refer to time. A decade is ten years, a century is one hundred years, and a millennium is one thousand years. The expression "fourth century B.C." refers to the fourth period of one hundred years counting backward from 1, the assumed date of the birth of Jesus. Since the first century B.C. would be the years 100 B.C. to 1 B.C., the fourth century B.C. would be the years 400 B.C. to 301 B.C. We could say, then, that an event in 350 B.C. took place in the fourth century B.C.

The phrase "fourth century A.D." refers to the fourth period of one hundred years after the birth of Jesus. Since the first period of one hundred years would be the years 1 to 100, the fourth period of one hundred years, or fourth century, would be the years 301 to 400. We could say, then, for example, that an event in 350 took place in the fourth century. In similar manner, the first millennium B.C. refers to the years 1000 B.C. to 1 B.C.; the second millennium A.D. refers to the years 1001 to 2000.

Some historians now prefer to use the abbreviations B.C.E. (for "before the Common Era") and C.E. (for "Common Era") instead of B.C. and A.D. This is especially true of world historians, who prefer to use terminology that is not so Western or Christian oriented. The dates remain the same, of course: 1950 B.C.E. and 1950 B.C. would be the same year. In keeping with current usage by many historians of Western civilization, this book will use the terms B.C. and A.D.

The dating of events can also vary from people to people. Most people in the Western world use the Western calendar, also known as the Gregorian calendar after Pope Gregory XIII, who refined it in 1582. The Hebrew calendar, by contrast, uses a different system in which the year 1 is the equivalent of the Western year 3760 B.C., considered by Jews to be the date of the creation of the world. The Western year 2000 is thus the year 5760 on the Jewish calendar. The Islamic calendar begins year 1 on the day Muhammad fled Mecca, which is the year 622 on the Western calendar. Thus the Western year 2000 is the year 1348 on the Islamic calendar.

SECOND
EDITION

Western Civilization

A Brief History
Volume I: To 1715

CHAPTER 1

The Ancient Near East: The First Civilizations

CHAPTER OUTLINE

- The First Humans
- Civilization in Mesopotamia
- Egyptian Civilization: "The Gift of the Nile"
- Conclusion

FOCUS QUESTIONS

- Where did the Neolithic agricultural revolution occur, and how did it affect the lives of men and women?
- What are the characteristics of civilization, and what are some explanations for why early civilizations emerged?
- How did geography contribute to the civilizations that arose in Mesopotamia and Egypt?
- What role did religion play in the civilizations of Mesopotamia and Egypt?
- What were the chief legacies of Mesopotamia and Egypt to later civilizations?

*I*N 1849, *a daring young Englishman made a hazardous journey into the deserts and swamps of southern Iraq. Moving south down the banks of the Euphrates River while braving high winds and temperatures that reached 120 degrees Fahrenheit, William Loftus led a small expedition in search of the roots of civilization. As he said, "From our childhood we have been led to regard this place as the cradle of the human race."*

Guided by native Arabs into the southernmost reaches of Iraq, Loftus and his small group of explorers were soon overwhelmed by what they saw. He wrote, "I know of nothing more exciting or impressive than the first sight of one of these great piles, looming in solitary grandeur from the surrounding plains and marshes." One of these piles, known to the natives as the mound of Warka, contained the ruins of Uruk, one of the first cities in the world and part of the world's first civilization.

Southern Iraq, known to ancient peoples as Mesopotamia, was one of the four areas in the world where civilization began. In the fertile valleys of the Tigris and Euphrates Rivers in Mesopotamia, the Nile in Egypt, the Indus in India, and the Yellow River in China, intensive agriculture became capable of supporting large groups of people. In these regions the first civilizations were born. The beginnings of Western civilization can be traced back to the ancient Near East, where people in Mesopotamia and Egypt developed organized societies and created the ideas and institutions that we associate with civilization. The later Greeks and Romans, who played such a crucial role in the development of Western civilization, were themselves nourished and influenced by these older societies in the Near East. It is appropriate, therefore, to begin our story of Western civilization in the ancient Near East with the early civilizations of Mesopotamia and Egypt. Before considering them, however, we must briefly examine humankind's prehistory and observe how human beings made the shift from hunting and gathering to agricultural communities and ultimately to cities and civilization.

◆ The First Humans

Historians rely primarily on documents to create their pictures of the past, but no written records exist for the prehistory of humankind. In their absence, the story of early humanity depends on archaeological and, more recently, biological information, which anthropologists and archaeologists use to formulate theories about our early past.

The earliest humanlike creatures—known as hominids—lived in Africa as long as three to four million years ago. Known as Australopithecines, they flourished in East and South Africa and were the first hominids to make simple stone tools.

A second stage in early human development occurred around 1.5 million years ago when *Homo erectus* ("upright human being") emerged. *Homo erectus* made use of larger and more varied tools and was the first hominid to leave Africa and to move into both Europe and Asia.

Around 250,000 years ago, a third—and crucial—stage in human development began with the emergence of *Homo sapiens* ("wise human being"). By 100,000 B.C., two groups of *Homo sapiens* had devel-

oped. One type was the Neanderthal, whose remains were first found in the Neander valley in Germany. Neanderthal remains have since been found in both Europe and the Middle East and have been dated to between 100,000 and 30,000 B.C. Neanderthals relied on a variety of stone tools and were the first early people to bury their dead.

The first anatomically modern humans, known as *Homo sapiens sapiens* ("wise, wise human being"), appeared in Africa between 200,000 and 150,000 years ago. Recent evidence indicates that they began to spread outside Africa around 100,000 years ago. Map 1.1 shows probable dates for different movements, although many of these are still controversial. By 30,000 B.C., *Homo sapiens sapiens* had replaced the Neanderthals, who had largely become extinct, and by 10,000 B.C., members of the *Homo sapiens sapiens* species could be found throughout the world. By that time, it was the only human species left. All humans today, be they Europeans, Australian aborigines, or Africans, belong to the same subspecies of human being.

❉ The Hunter-Gatherers of the Old Stone Age

One of the basic distinguishing features of the human species is the ability to make tools. The earliest tools were made of stone, and the term *Paleolithic* (Greek for "old stone") Age is used to designate this early period of human history (c. 2,500,000–10,000 B.C.).

For hundreds of thousands of years, humans relied on hunting and gathering for their daily food. Paleolithic peoples had a close relationship with the world around them, and over a period of time, they came to know which animals to hunt and which plants to eat. They did not know how to grow crops or raise animals, however. They gathered wild nuts, berries, fruits, and a variety of wild grains and green plants. Around the world, they hunted and consumed different animals, including buffalo, horses, bison, wild goats, and reindeer. In coastal areas, fish provided a rich source of food.

The hunting of animals and the gathering of wild plants no doubt led to certain patterns of living. Archaeologists and anthropologists have speculated that Paleolithic people lived in small bands of twenty to thirty people. They were nomadic (they moved from place to place) since they had no choice but to follow animal migrations and vegetation cycles. Hunting depended on careful observation of animal behav-

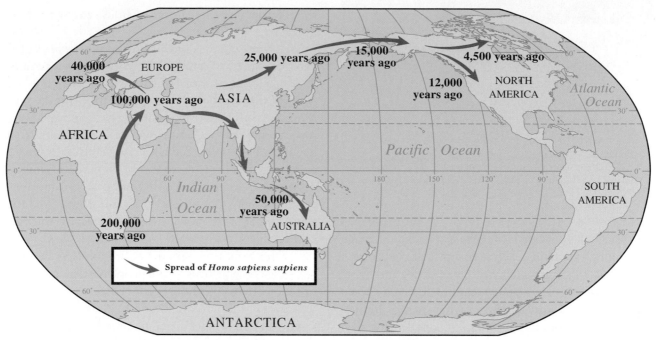

MAP I.I   **The Spread of *Homo sapiens sapiens*.**

ior patterns and required a group effort to achieve any real degree of success. Over the years, tools became more refined and more useful. The invention of the spear, and later the bow and arrow, made hunting considerably easier. Harpoons and fishhooks made of bone increased the catch of fish.

Both men and women were responsible for finding food—the chief work of Paleolithic people. Since women bore and raised the children, they generally stayed close to the camps, but they played an important role in acquiring food by gathering berries, nuts, and grains. Men hunted the wild animals, an activity that took them far from camp. Because both men and women played important roles in providing for the band's survival, scientists have argued that a rough equality existed between men and women. Indeed, some speculate that both men and women made the decisions that affected the activities of the Paleolithic band.

These groups of Paleolithic peoples, especially those who lived in cold climates, found shelter in caves. Over time, they created new types of shelter as well. Perhaps the most common was a simple structure of wood poles or sticks covered with animal hides. The systematic use of fire, which archaeologists believe began around 500,000 years ago, made it possible for the caves and human-made structures to have a source of light and heat. Fire also enabled early humans to cook their food, making it better tasting, longer lasting, and, in the case of some plants, such as wild grain, easier to chew and digest.

The making of tools and the use of fire—two important technological innovations of Paleolithic peoples—remind us how crucial the ability to adapt was to human survival. But Paleolithic peoples did more than just survive. The cave paintings of large animals found in southwestern France and northern Spain bear witness to the cultural activity of Paleolithic peoples. A cave discovered in southern France in 1994 contains more than 300 paintings of lions, oxen, owls, panthers, and other animals. Most of these are animals that Paleolithic people did not hunt, which suggests that they were painted for religious or even decorative purposes.

❊ *The Agricultural Revolution, c. 10,000–4000 B.C.*

The end of the last ice age around 10,000 B.C. was followed by what is called the Neolithic Revolution, the revolution that occurred in the New Stone Age (the word *Neolithic* is Greek for "new stone"). The name New Stone Age is misleading, however. Although Neolithic peoples made a new type of polished stone ax, this was not the major change that occurred after 10,000 B.C.

The real change was the shift from hunting animals and gathering plants for sustenance to producing food by systematic agriculture. The planting of grains

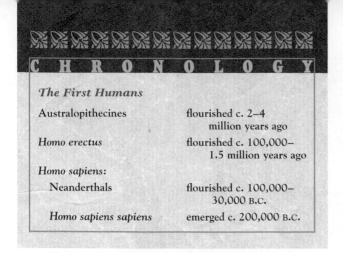

The First Humans

Australopithecines	flourished c. 2–4 million years ago
Homo erectus	flourished c. 100,000–1.5 million years ago
Homo sapiens:	
Neanderthals	flourished c. 100,000–30,000 B.C.
Homo sapiens sapiens	emerged c. 200,000 B.C.

and vegetables provided a regular supply of food, while the taming of animals, such as sheep, goats, cattle, and pigs, added a steady source of meat, milk, and fibers such as wool for clothing. Larger animals could also be used as beasts of burden. The growing of crops and the taming of food-producing animals created a new relationship between humans and nature. Historians like to speak of this as an agricultural revolution. Revolutionary change is dramatic and requires great effort, but the ability to acquire food on a regular basis gave humans greater control over their environment. It also enabled them to give up their nomadic ways of life and begin to live in settled communities.

Systematic agriculture probably developed independently between 8000 and 7000 B.C. in four different areas of the world. In each of these areas, different plants were cultivated: wheat, barley, and lentils in the Near East, rice and millet in southern Asia, millet and yams in western Africa, and beans, potatoes, and corn in the middle Americas. In the Near East as elsewhere, the Neolithic agricultural revolution needed a favorable environment. The upland areas above the Fertile Crescent (present-day northern Iraq and southern Turkey) were initially more conducive to systematic farming than the river valleys. This region received the necessary rainfall and was the home of two wild plant species (barley and wheat) and four wild animal species (pigs, cows, goats, and sheep) that humans eventually domesticated for their use.

The growing of crops on a regular basis gave rise to more permanent settlements, which historians refer to as Neolithic farming villages or towns. One of the oldest and most extensive agricultural villages was Çatal Hüyük, located in modern-day Turkey. Its walls enclosed 32 acres, and its population probably reached 6,000 inhabitants during its high point from 6700 to 5700 B.C. People lived in simple mudbrick houses that were built so close to one another that there were few streets. To get to their homes, people had to walk along the rooftops and then enter the house through a hole in the roof.

Archaeologists have discovered twelve cultivated products in Çatal Hüyük, including fruits, nuts, and three kinds of wheat. Artisans made weapons and jewelry that were traded with neighboring people. Religious shrines housing figures of gods and goddesses have been found at Çatal Hüyük, as have a number of female statuettes. Molded with noticeably large breasts and buttocks, these "earth mothers" perhaps symbolically represented the fertility of both "our mother" earth and human mothers. Both the shrines and the statues point to the growing role of religion in the lives of these Neolithic peoples.

The Neolithic agricultural revolution had far-reaching consequences. Once people settled in villages or towns, they built houses for protection and other structures for the storage of goods. As organized communities stored food and accumulated material goods, they began to engage in trade. People also began to specialize in certain crafts, and a division of labor developed. Pottery was made from clay and baked in a fire to make it hard. The pots were used for cooking and to store grains. Woven baskets were also used for storage. Stone tools became refined as flint blades were employed to make sickles and hoes for use in the fields. In the course of the Neolithic Age, many of the food plants still in use today began to be cultivated. Moreover, vegetable fibers from such plants as flax and cotton were used to make thread that was woven into cloth.

The change to systematic agriculture in the Neolithic Age also had consequences for the relationship between men and women. Men assumed the primary responsibility for working in the fields and herding animals, jobs that kept them away from the home. Women remained behind, caring for the children, weaving clothes, and performing other tasks that required much labor in one place. In time, as work outside the home was increasingly perceived as more important than work done at home, men came to play the more dominant role in society, a basic pattern that would persist until our own times.

Other patterns set in the Neolithic Age also proved to be enduring elements of human history. Fixed dwellings, domesticated animals, regular farming, a division of labor, men holding power—all of these are part of the human story. For all of our scientific and technological progress, human survival still depends on the growing and storing of food, an accomplishment of people in the Neolithic Age. The Neolithic Revolution was truly a turning point in human history.

STATUES FROM AIN GHAZAL. These life-size statues made of plaster and bitumen date from 6500 B.C. and were discovered in 1984 in Ain Ghazal, an archaeological site near Amman, Jordan. They are among the oldest statues of the human figure ever found. Archaeologists are studying the sculptures to try to understand their purpose and meaning.

Between 4000 and 3000 B.C., significant technical developments began to transform the Neolithic towns. The invention of writing enabled records to be kept, and the use of metals marked a new level of human control over the environment and its resources. Already before 4000 B.C., craftspeople had discovered that metal-bearing rocks could be heated to liquefy metals, which could then be cast in molds to produce tools and weapons that were more refined than stone instruments. Although copper was the first metal to be made into tools, after 4000 B.C., craftspeople in western Asia discovered that a combination of copper and tin created bronze, a much harder and more durable metal than copper. Its widespread use has led historians to call the period from around 3000 to 1200 B.C. the Bronze Age; thereafter, bronze was increasingly replaced by iron.

At first, Neolithic settlements were hardly more than villages. But as their inhabitants mastered the art of farming, more complex human societies began to emerge. As wealth increased, these societies began to develop armies and to build walled cities. By the beginning of the Bronze Age, the concentration of larger numbers of people in the river valleys of Mesopotamia and Egypt was leading to a whole new pattern for human life.

✽ The Emergence of Civilization

As we have seen, early human beings formed small groups that developed a simple culture that enabled them to survive. As human societies grew and developed greater complexity, a new form of human existence—called civilization—came into being. A civilization is a complex culture in which large numbers of human beings share a number of common elements. Historians have identified a number of basic characteristics of civilization, most of which were evident in ancient Mesopotamia and Egypt. These include (1) an urban revolution: cities became the focal points for political, economic, social, cultural, and religious development; (2) a distinct religious structure: the gods were deemed crucial to the community's success, and professional priestly classes, as stewards of the gods' property, regulated relations with the gods; (3) new political and military structures:

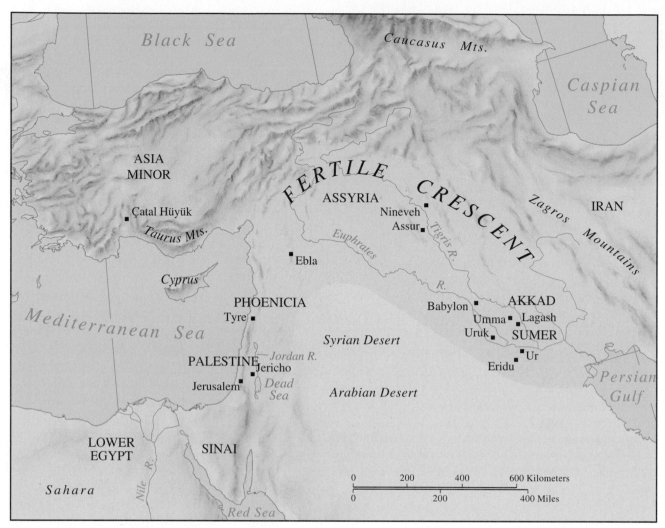

MAP I.2   The Ancient Near East.

an organized government bureaucracy arose to meet the administrative demands of the growing population while armies were organized to gain land and power; (4) a new social structure based on economic power: while kings and an upper class of priests, political leaders, and warriors dominated, there also existed a large group of free men (farmers, artisans, craftspeople) and at the very bottom, socially, a class of slaves; (5) the development of writing: kings, priests, merchants, and artisans used writing to keep records; and (6) new forms of significant artistic and intellectual activity: monumental architectural structures, usually religious, occupied a prominent place in urban environments.

Why early civilizations developed remains difficult to explain. One theory maintains that challenges forced human beings to make efforts that resulted in the rise of civilization. Some scholars have argued that material forces, such as the growth of food surpluses, made possible the specialization of labor and development of large communities with bureaucratic orga-

nization. But the area of the Fertile Crescent (see Map 1.2), in which Mesopotamian civilization emerged, was not naturally conducive to agriculture. Abundant food could be produced only with a massive human effort to carefully manage the water, an effort that created the need for organization and led to civilized cities. Some historians have argued that nonmaterial forces, primarily religious, provided the sense of unity and purpose that made such organized activities possible. Finally, some scholars doubt that we are capable of ever discovering the actual incentives that led to early civilization.

◆ Civilization in Mesopotamia

The Greeks spoke of the valley between the Tigris and Euphrates Rivers as Mesopotamia, the land "between the rivers." The region receives little rain, but the soil of the plain of southern Mesopotamia was enlarged and enriched over the years by layers of silt deposited by the two rivers. In late spring, the Tigris and Euphrates overflow their banks and deposit their fertile silt, but since this flooding depends on the melting of snows in the upland mountains where the rivers begin, it is irregular and sometimes catastrophic. In such circumstances, farming could be accomplished only with human intervention in the form of irrigation and drainage ditches. A complex system was required to control the flow of the rivers and produce the crops. Large-scale irrigation made possible the expansion of agriculture in this region, and the abundant food provided the material base for the emergence of civilization in Mesopotamia.

✳ *The City-States of Ancient Mesopotamia*

The creators of the first Mesopotamian civilization were the Sumerians, a people whose origins remain unclear. By 3000 B.C., they had established a number of independent cities in southern Mesopotamia, including Eridu, Ur, Uruk, Umma, and Lagash. As cities expanded in size, they came to exercise political and economic control over the surrounding countryside, forming city-states. These city-states were the basic units of Sumerian civilization.

Sumerian cities were surrounded by walls. Uruk, for example, occupied an area of approximately 1,000 acres encircled by a wall 6 miles long with defense towers located every 30 to 35 feet along the wall. City dwellings, built of sun-dried bricks, included both the small flats of peasants and the larger dwellings of the civic and priestly officials. Although Mesopotamia had little stone or wood for building purposes, it did have plenty of mud. Mudbricks, easily shaped by hand, were left to bake in the hot sun until they were hard enough to use for building. People in Mesopotamia were remarkably inventive with mudbricks, constructing some of the largest brick buildings in the world. Mudbricks are still used in rural areas of the Middle East today.

The most prominent building in a Sumerian city was the temple, which was dedicated to the chief god or goddess of the city and often built atop a massive stepped tower called a ziggurat. The Sumerians believed that gods and goddesses owned the cities, and much wealth was used to build temples as well as elaborate houses for the priests and priestesses who served the gods. Priests and priestesses, who supervised the temples and their property, had great power. The temples owned much of the city land and livestock and

served not only as the physical center of the city but also its economic and political center. In fact, historians believe that in the early stages of the city-states, priests and priestesses played an important role in ruling. The Sumerians believed that the gods ruled the cities, making the state a theocracy (government by a divine authority). Eventually, however, ruling power passed into the hands of worldly figures known as kings.

Sumerians viewed kingship as divine in origin; they believed kings derived their power from the gods and were the agents of the gods. As one person said in a petition to his king: "You in your judgment, you are the son of Anu [god of the sky]; your commands, like the word of a god, cannot be reversed; your words, like rain pouring down from heaven, are without number."[1] Regardless of their origins, kings had power—they led armies, initiated legislation, supervised the building of public works, provided courts, and organized workers for the irrigation projects on which Mesopotamian agriculture depended. The army, the government bureaucracy, and the priests and priestesses all aided the kings in their rule. Befitting their power, Sumerian kings lived in large palaces with their wives and children.

The economy of the Sumerian city-states was primarily agricultural, but commerce and industry became important as well. The people of Mesopotamia produced woolen textiles, pottery, and the metalwork for which they were especially well known. Foreign trade, which was primarily a royal monopoly, could be extensive. Royal officials imported luxury items, such as copper and tin, aromatic woods, and fruit trees, in exchange for dried fish, wool, barley, wheat, and the metal goods produced by Mesopotamian craftspeople. Traders traveled by land to the eastern Mediterranean in the west and by sea to India in the east. The invention of the wheel around 3000 B.C. led to carts with wheels that made the transport of goods easier.

Sumerian city-states contained three major social groups—nobles, commoners, and slaves. Nobles included royal and priestly officials and their families. Commoners included the nobles' clients who worked for the palace and temple estates and other free citizens who worked as farmers, merchants, fishers, scribes, and craftspeople. Probably 90 percent or more of the population were farmers. They could exchange their crops for the goods of the artisans in free town markets. Slaves belonged to palace officials, who used them mostly in building projects; temple officials, who used mostly female slaves to weave cloth and grind grain; and rich landowners, who used them for farming and domestic work.

THE "ROYAL STANDARD" OF UR. This series of panels is from the "Royal Standard" of Ur, a box dating from around 2700 B.C. discovered in a stone tomb from the royal cemetery of the Sumerian city-state of Ur. These scenes from the box depict the activities of the king and his court after a military victory. In the top panel, the king and his court drink wine while at the right a musician plays a bull-headed harp. The middle panel shows bulls, rams, and fish being brought to the banquet hall. The bottom panel shows booty from the king's victory.

✺ *Empires in Ancient Mesopotamia*

As the number of Sumerian city-states grew and the states expanded, new conflicts arose as city-state fought city-state for control of land and water. The fortunes of various city-states rose and fell over the centuries. The constant wars, with their burning and sacking of cities, left many Sumerians in deep despair, as is evident in the words of this Sumerian poem from the city of Ur: "Ur is destroyed, bitter is its lament. The country's blood now fills its holes like hot bronze in a mold. Bodies dissolve like fat in the sun. Our temple is destroyed, the gods have abandoned us, like migrating birds. Smoke lies on our city like a shroud."

Located on the flat land of Mesopotamia, the Sumerian city-states were also open to invasion. To the north of the Sumerian city-states lived the Akkadians. We call them a Semitic people because of the type of language they spoke (see Table 1.1). Around 2340 B.C., Sargon, leader of the Akkadians, overran the Sumerian city-states and established an empire that included most of Mesopotamia as well as lands westward to the Mediterranean. But the Akkadian empire eventually disintegrated, and its end by 2100 B.C. brought a return to the system of warring city-states until Ur-Nammu of Ur succeeded in reunifying most of Mesopotamia. But this final flowering of Sumerian culture collapsed with the coming of the Amorites. Under Hammurabi, the Amorites, or Old Babylonians, a large group of Semitic-speaking semi-nomads, created a new empire.

Hammurabi (1792–1750 B.C.) employed a well-disciplined army of foot soldiers who carried axes, spears, and copper or bronze daggers. He learned to divide his opponents and subdue them one by one. Using such methods, he gained control of Sumer and Akkad and reunified Mesopotamia almost to the old borders created by Sargon of Akkad. After his conquests, he called himself "the sun of Babylon, the king who has made the four quarters of the world subservient," and established a new capital at Babylon, north of Akkad.

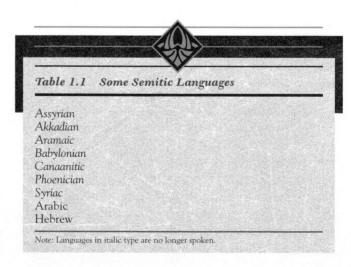

Table 1.1   Some Semitic Languages

Assyrian
Akkadian
Aramaic
Babylonian
Canaanitic
Phoenician
Syriac
Arabic
Hebrew

Note: Languages in italic type are no longer spoken.

The Code of Hammurabi

Hammurabi's code is the most complete, although not the earliest, Mesopotamian law code. It was inscribed on a stone stele topped by a bas-relief picturing Hammurabi receiving the inspiration for the law code from the sun god Shamash, who was also the god of justice. The law code emphasizes the principle of retribution ("an eye for an eye") and punishments that vary according to social status. Punishments could be severe. The following examples illustrate these concerns.

�֎ The Code of Hammurabi

25. If fire broke out in a free man's house and a free man, who went to extinguish it, cast his eye on the goods of the owner of the house and has appropriated the goods of the owner of the house, that free man shall be thrown into that fire.

129. If the wife of a free man has been caught while lying with another man, they shall bind them and throw them into the water. If the husband of the woman wishes to spare his wife, then the king in turn may spare his subject.

131. If a free man's wife was accused by her husband, but she was not caught while lying with another man, she shall make affirmation by god and return to her house.

196. If a free man has destroyed the eye of a member of the aristocracy, they shall destroy his eye.

198. If he has destroyed the eye of a commoner or broken the bone of a commoner, he shall pay one mina of silver.

199. If he has destroyed the eye of a free man's slave or broken the bone of a free man's slave, he shall pay one-half his value.

209. If a free man struck another free man's daughter and has caused her to have a miscarriage, he shall pay ten shekels of silver for her fetus.

210. If that woman has died, they shall put his daughter to death.

211. If by a blow he has caused a commoner's daughter to have a miscarriage, he shall pay five shekels of silver.

212. If that woman has died, he shall pay one-half mina of silver.

213. If he struck a free man's female slave and has caused her to have a miscarriage, he shall pay two shekels of silver.

214. If that female slave has died, he shall pay one-third mina of silver.

Hammurabi, the man of war, was also a man of peace. He followed in the footsteps of previous conquerors by assimilating Mesopotamian culture, with the result that Sumerian ways continued to exist despite the end of the Sumerians as a political entity. A collection of his letters, found by archaeologists, reveals that he took a strong interest in state affairs. He built temples, defensive walls, and irrigation canals; encouraged trade; and brought about an economic revival. After his death, however, a series of weak kings were unable to keep Hammurabi's empire united, and it finally fell to new invaders.

✍ THE CODE OF HAMMURABI

Hammurabi is best remembered for his law code, a collection of 282 laws. For centuries, laws had regulated people's relationships with one another in the lands of Mesopotamia, but only fragments of these earlier codes survive. Hammurabi's collection provides considerable insight into almost every aspect of everyday life there and provides us a priceless glimpse of the values of this early society (see the box above).

The Code of Hammurabi reveals a society with a system of strict justice. Penalties for criminal offenses were severe and varied according to the social class of the victim. A crime against a member of the upper class (a noble) was punished more severely than the same offense against a member of the lower class. Moreover, the principle of retaliation ("an eye for an eye, a tooth for a tooth") was fundamental to this system of justice. It was applied in cases where members of the upper class committed crimes against their social equals. For crimes against members of the lower classes, a money payment was made instead.

Hammurabi's code took the responsibilities of public officials very seriously. The governor of an area and city officials were expected to catch burglars. If they failed to do so, the officials in the district where the crime was committed had to replace the lost property. If murderers were not found, the officials had to pay a fine to the relatives of the murdered person.

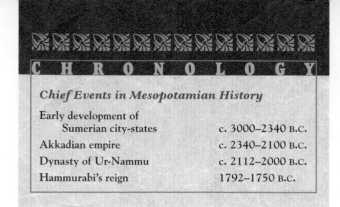

CHRONOLOGY

Chief Events in Mesopotamian History

Early development of Sumerian city-states	c. 3000–2340 B.C.
Akkadian empire	c. 2340–2100 B.C.
Dynasty of Ur-Nammu	c. 2112–2000 B.C.
Hammurabi's reign	1792–1750 B.C.

Soldiers were likewise expected to fulfill their duties for the order and maintenance of the state. If a soldier hired a substitute to fight for him, he was put to death, and the substitute was given control of his estate.

The law code also furthered the proper performance of work with what virtually amounted to consumer protection laws. Builders were held responsible for the buildings they constructed. If a house collapsed and caused the death of the owner, the builder was put to death. If the collapse caused the death of the son of the owner, the son of the builder was put to death. If goods were destroyed by the collapse, they had to be replaced and the house itself reconstructed at the builder's expense.

The number of laws in Hammurabi's code dedicated to land tenure and commerce reveals the importance of agriculture and trade in the Mesopotamian economy. Laws concerning land use and irrigation were especially strict, an indication of the danger of declining crop yields if the land were used incompetently. Commercial activity was also carefully regulated. Rates of interest on loans were watched closely. If the lender raised the interest rate after a loan was made, he lost the entire amount of the loan. The Code of Hammurabi even specified the precise wages of laborers and artisans, such as brickmakers and jewelers.

The largest number of laws in the Code of Hammurabi focused on marriage and the family. Parents arranged marriages for their children. After marriage, the parties involved signed a marriage contract; without it, no one was considered legally married. The husband provided a bridal payment, and the woman's parents were responsible for a dowry to the new husband.

As in many patriarchal societies, women possessed far fewer privileges and rights in marriage than men. A woman's place was in the home, and failure to fulfill her expected duties was grounds for divorce. If she was not able to bear children, her husband could divorce her, but he did have to return the dowry to the woman's family. If his wife tried to leave home to engage in business, thus neglecting her house, her husband could divorce her and did not have to repay the dowry. Furthermore, a wife who was a "gadabout, . . . neglecting her house [and] humiliating her husband," could be drowned. We do know that in practice not all women remained at home. Some worked in business and were especially prominent in the running of taverns.

Women were guaranteed some rights, however. If a woman was divorced without good reason, she received the dowry back. A woman could seek divorce and get her dowry back if her husband was unable to show that she had done anything wrong. In theory, a wife was guaranteed use of her husband's property in the event of his death. The mother could also decide which of her sons would receive an inheritance.

Sexual relations were strictly regulated as well. Husbands, but not wives, were permitted sexual activity outside marriage. A wife caught committing adultery was pitched into the river, although her husband could ask the king to pardon her. Incest was strictly forbidden. If a father committed incestuous relations with his daughter, he would be banished. Incest between a son and mother resulted in both being burned.

Fathers ruled their children as well as their wives. Obedience was duly expected: "If a son has struck his father, they shall cut off his hand." If a son committed a serious enough offense, his father could disinherit him, although fathers were not permitted to disinherit their sons arbitrarily.

❉ *The Culture of Mesopotamia*

A spiritual worldview was of fundamental importance to Mesopotamian culture. To the peoples of Mesopotamia, the gods were living realities who affected all aspects of life. It was crucial, therefore, that the correct hierarchies be observed. Leaders could prepare armies for war, but success really depended on a favorable relationship with the gods. This helps explain the importance of the priestly class and is the reason why even the kings took great care to dedicate offerings and monuments to the gods.

ℰ THE IMPORTANCE OF RELIGION

The Mesopotamians viewed their city-states as earthly copies of a divine model and order. Each city-state was sacred, linked to its god or goddess. Nippur, the earliest center of Sumerian religion, was dedicated to

Enlil, the god of wind. Moreover, located at the heart of each city-state was a temple complex. Occupying several acres, this sacred area consisted of a ziggurat with a temple at the top dedicated to the god or goddess who owned the city. The temple complex was the true center of the community. The main god or goddess dwelt there symbolically in the form of a statue, and the ceremony of dedication included a ritual that linked the statue to the god or goddess and thus supposedly harnessed the power of the deity for the city's benefit. Considerable wealth was poured into the construction of temples and other buildings used for the residences of priests and priestesses who helped the gods. Although the gods literally owned the city, the temple complex used only part of the land and rented out the remainder. The temples dominated individual and commercial life, an indication of the close relationship between Mesopotamian religion and culture.

The physical environment had an obvious impact on the Mesopotamian view of the universe. Ferocious floods, heavy downpours, scorching winds, and oppressive humidity were all part of the Mesopotamian climate. These conditions and the resulting famines easily convinced Mesopotamians that this world was controlled by supernatural forces and that the days of human beings "are numbered; whatever he may do, he is but wind," as *The Epic of Gilgamesh* put it. In the presence of nature, Mesopotamians could easily feel helpless, as this poem relates:

> *The rampant flood which no man can oppose,*
> *Which shakes the heavens and causes earth to tremble,*
> *In an appalling blanket folds mother and child,*
> *Beats down the canebrake's full luxuriant greenery,*
> *And drowns the harvest in its time of ripeness.*[2]

The Mesopotamians discerned cosmic rhythms in the universe and accepted its order but perceived that it was not completely safe because of the presence of willful, powerful cosmic powers that they identified with gods and goddesses.

With its numerous gods and goddesses animating all aspects of the universe, Mesopotamian religion was polytheistic. The four most important deities were An, Enlil, Enki, and Ninhursaga. An was the god of the sky and hence the most important force in the universe. Since his basic essence was authority, he was also viewed as the source or active principle of all authority, including the earthly power of rulers and fathers alike. Enlil, god of wind, was considered the second greatest power of the visible universe. In charge of the wind and thus an expression of the legitimate use of force, Enlil became the symbol of the proper use

of force on earth as well. Enki was god of the earth. Since the earth was the source of life-giving waters, Enki was also god of rivers, wells, and canals. More generally, he represented the waters of creativity and was responsible for inventions and crafts. Ninhursaga began as a goddess associated with soil, mountains, and vegetation. Eventually, however, she was worshiped as a mother goddess, a "mother of all children," who manifested her power by giving birth to kings and conferring the royal insignia of officialdom on them.

Human beings' relationship with their gods was based on subservience since, according to Sumerian myth, human beings were created to do the manual labor the gods were unwilling to do for themselves. Moreover, humans were insecure because they could never be sure of the gods' actions. But humans did make attempts to circumvent or relieve their anxiety by discovering the intentions of the gods; these efforts gave rise to the development of the arts of divination.

Divination took a variety of forms. A common form, at least for kings and priests who could afford it, involved killing animals, such as sheep or goats, and examining their livers or other organs. Supposedly, features seen in the organs of the sacrificed animals foretold events to come. One handbook predicted that if the animal organ had shape x, then the outcome of the military campaign would be y. Private individuals relied on cheaper divinatory techniques. These included interpreting patterns of smoke from burning incense or the pattern formed when oil was poured into water. The Mesopotamian arts of divination arose out of the desire to discover the purposes of the gods: if people could decipher the signs that foretold events, the events would be predictable, and humans could act wisely.

THE CULTIVATION OF NEW ARTS AND SCIENCES

The realization of writing's great potential was another aspect of Mesopotamian culture. The oldest Mesopotamian texts date to around 3000 B.C. and were written by the Sumerians, who used a cuneiform ("wedge-shaped") system of writing. Using a reed stylus, they made wedge-shaped impressions on clay tablets, which were then baked or dried in the sun. Once dried, these tablets were virtually indestructible, and the several hundred thousand that have been discovered have provided a valuable source of information for modern scholars. Sumerian writing evolved from pictures of concrete objects to simplified and

Pictographic sign c. 3100 B.C.	(sign)	(sign)	(sign)	(sign)	(sign)	(sign)	(sign)	(sign)	(sign)
Interpretation	star	?sun over horizon	?stream	ear of barley	bull's head	bowl	head + bowl	lower leg	?shrouded body
Cuneiform sign c. 2400 B.C.	(sign)	(sign)	(sign)	(sign)	(sign)	(sign)	(sign)	(sign)	(sign)
Cuneiform sign c. 700 B.C. (turned through 90°)	(sign)	(sign)	(sign)	(sign)	(sign)	(sign)	(sign)	(sign)	(sign)
Phonetic value*	dingir, an	u_4, ud	a	še	gu_4	nig_2, ninda	ku_2	du, gin, gub	lu_2
Meaning	god, sky	day, sun	water, seed, son	barley	ox	food, bread	to eat	to walk, to stand	man

* Some signs have more than one phonetic value, and some sounds are represented by more than one sign. Thus u_4 means the fourth sign with the phonetic value u.

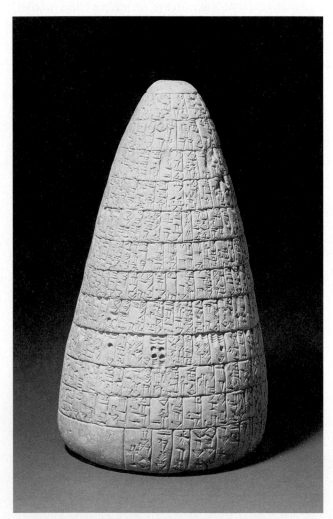

THE DEVELOPMENT OF CUNEIFORM WRITING. Pictured here is the cone of Uruinimgina, an example of cuneiform script from an early Sumerian dynasty. The inscription announces reductions in taxes. The table shows the development of writing from pictographic signs to the evolution of cuneiform script.

stylized signs, leading eventually to a phonetic system that made possible the written expression of abstract ideas.

Mesopotamian peoples used writing primarily for record keeping. They also produced monumental texts, documents that were intended to last forever, such as inscriptions etched in stone on statues and royal buildings. A large body of texts were prepared for teaching purposes. Schools for scribes were in operation by 2500 B.C. They were necessary because much time was needed to master the cuneiform system of writing. The primary goal of scribal education was to produce professionally trained scribes for careers in the temples and palaces, the military, and government. Pupils were male and primarily from wealthy families. Gradually, the schools became centers for culture because Mesopotamian literature was used for instructional purposes.

Writing was important because it enabled a society to keep records and maintain knowledge of previous practices and events. Writing also made it possible for people to communicate ideas in new ways, which is especially evident in Mesopotamian literary works. The most famous piece of Mesopotamian literature was *The Epic of Gilgamesh*, an epic poem that records the exploits of a legendary king of Uruk. Gilgamesh—wise, strong, and perfect in body, part man, part god—befriends a hairy beast named Enkidu. Together they set off in pursuit of heroic deeds. When Enkidu dies, Gilgamesh experiences the pain of mortality and embarks on a search for the secret of immortality. But his efforts fail (see the box on p. 13), and Gilgamesh remains mortal. The desire for immortality, one of humankind's great searches, ends

The Great Flood

The great epic poem of Mesopotamian literature, The Epic of Gilgamesh, includes an account by Utnapishtim (a Mesopotamian version of the later biblical Noah), who had built a ship and survived the flood unleashed by the gods to destroy humankind. This selection recounts how the god Ea advised Utnapishtim to build a boat and how he came to land his boat at the end of the flood. In this section, Utnapishtim is telling his story to Gilgamesh.

✷ The Epic of Gilgamesh

"In those days the world teemed, the people multiplied, the world bellowed like a wild bull, and the great god was aroused by the clamor. Enlil heard the clamor and he said to the gods in council, 'The uproar of mankind is intolerable and sleep is no longer possible by reason of the babel.' So the gods agreed to exterminate mankind. Enlil did this, but Ea [Sumerian Enki, god of the waters] because of his oath warned me in a dream. . . . 'tear down your house and build a boat, abandon possessions and look for life, despise worldly goods and save your soul alive. Tear down your house, I say, and build a boat. . . . then take up into the boat the seed of all living creatures. . . .' [Utnapishtim did as he was told and then the destruction came.]

"For six days and six nights the winds blew, torrent and tempest and flood overwhelmed the world, tempest and flood raged together like warring hosts. When the seventh day dawned the storm from the south subsided, the sea grew calm, the flood was stifled; I looked at the face of the world and there was silence, all mankind was turned to clay. The surface of the sea stretched as flat as a rooftop; I opened a hatch and the light fell on my face. Then I bowed low, I sat down and I wept, the tears streamed down my face, for on every side was the waste of water. I looked for land in vain, but fourteen leagues distant there appeared a mountain, and there the boat grounded; on the mountain of Nisir the boat held fast, she held fast and did not budge. . . . When the seventh day dawned I loosed a dove and let her go. She flew away, but finding no resting-place she returned. Then I loosed a swallow, and she flew away but finding no resting-place she returned. I loosed a raven, she saw that the waters had retreated, she ate, she flew around, she cawed, and she did not come back. Then I threw everything open to the four winds, I made a sacrifice and poured out a libation on the mountain top."

---

in complete frustration. Everlasting life, this Mesopotamian epic makes clear, is only for the gods.

Peoples in Mesopotamia also made outstanding achievements in mathematics and astronomy. In math, the Sumerians devised a number system based on 60, using combinations of 6 and 10 for practical solutions. Geometry was used to measure fields and erect buildings. In astronomy, the Sumerians made use of units of 60 and charted the heavenly constellations. Their calendar was based on twelve lunar months and was brought into harmony with the solar year by adding an extra month from time to time.

◆ Egyptian Civilization: "The Gift of the Nile"

Although contemporaneous with Mesopotamia, civilization in Egypt evolved along somewhat different lines. Of central importance to the development of Egyptian civilization was the Nile River. That the Egyptian people recognized its significance is apparent in this Hymn to the Nile (also see the box on p. 14): "The bringer of food, rich in provisions, creator of all good, lord of majesty, sweet of fragrance. . . . He who . . . fills the magazines, makes the granaries wide, and gives things to the poor. He who makes every beloved tree to grow. . . ."[3] Egypt, like Mesopotamia, was a river valley civilization.

The Nile is a unique river, beginning in the heart of Africa and coursing northward for thousands of miles. It is the longest river in the world. The Nile was responsible for creating an area several miles wide on both banks of the river that was fertile and capable of producing abundant harvests. The "miracle" of the Nile was its annual flooding. The river rose in the summer from rains in central Africa, crested in Egypt in September and October, and left a deposit of silt that created an area of rich soil. The Egyptians called this fertile land the "Black Land," because it was dark in

Significance of the Nile River and the Pharaoh

Two of the most important sources of life for the ancient Egyptians were the Nile River and the pharaoh. Egyptians perceived that the Nile River made possible the abundant food that was a major source of their well-being. This *Hymn to the Nile*, probably from the nineteenth and twentieth dynasties in the New Kingdom, expresses the gratitude Egyptians felt for the Nile.

✸ Hymn to the Nile

> Hail to you, O Nile, that issues from the earth and
>   comes to keep Egypt alive! . . .
> He that waters the meadows which Re created, in order
>   to keep every kid alive.
> He that makes to drink the desert and the place distant
>   from water: that is his dew coming down from
>   heaven. . . .
> The lord of fishes, he who makes the marsh-birds to go
>   upstream. . . .
> He who makes barley and brings emmer [wheat] into
>   being, that he may make the temples festive.
> If he is sluggish, then nostrils are stopped up, and
>   everybody is poor. . . .
> When he rises, then the land is in jubilation, then every
>   belly is in joy, every backbone takes on laughter,
>   and every tooth is exposed.
> The bringer of good, rich in provisions, creator of all
>   good, lord of majesty, sweet of fragrance. . . .

He who makes every beloved tree to grow, without lack of them.

The Egyptian king, or pharaoh, was viewed as a god and the absolute ruler of Egypt. His significance and the gratitude of the Egyptian people for his existence are evident in this hymn from the reign of Sesotris III (c. 1880–1840 B.C.).

✸ Hymn to the Pharaoh

> He has come unto us that he may carry away Upper
>   Egypt; the double diadem [crown of Upper and
>   Lower Egypt] has rested on his head.
> He has come unto us and has united the Two Lands;
>   he has mingled the reed with the bee [symbols of
>   Lower and Upper Egypt].
> He has come unto us and has brought the Black Land
>   under his sway; he has apportioned to himself the
>   Red Land.
> He has come unto us and has taken the Two Lands
>   under his protection; he has given peace to the Two
>   Riverbanks.
> He has come unto us and has made Egypt to live; he
>   has banished its suffering.
> He has come unto us and has made the people to live; he
>   has caused the throat of the subjects to breathe. . . .
> He has come unto us and has done battle for his
>   boundaries; he has delivered them that were robbed.

---

color from the silt and lush crops that grew on it. Beyond these narrow strips of fertile fields lay the deserts (the "Red Land").

Unlike the floods of Mesopotamia's rivers, the flooding of the Nile was gradual and usually predictable, and the river itself was seen as life enhancing, not life threatening. Although a system of organized irrigation was still necessary, the small villages along the Nile could make the effort without the massive state intervention that was required in Mesopotamia. Egyptian civilization consequently tended to remain more rural, with many small population centers congregated along a narrow band on both sides of the Nile. About 100 miles before it empties into the Mediterranean, the river splits into two major branches, forming the delta, a triangular-shaped territory called Lower Egypt to distinguish it from Upper Egypt, the land upstream to the south (see

Map 1.3). Egypt's important cities developed at the tip of the delta. Even today, most of Egypt's people are crowded along the banks of the Nile River.

The surpluses of food that Egyptian farmers grew in the fertile Nile valley made Egypt prosperous. But the Nile also served a unifying factor in Egyptian history. In ancient times, the Nile was the fastest way to travel through the land, making both transportation and communication easier. Winds from the north pushed sailboats south, and the current of the Nile carried them north. Often when they headed downstream (north), people used long poles or paddles to propel their boats forward.

Unlike Mesopotamia, which was subject to constant invasion, Egypt was blessed by natural barriers that fostered isolation, protected it from invasion, and gave it a sense of security. These barriers included the deserts to the west and east, the cataracts (rapids)

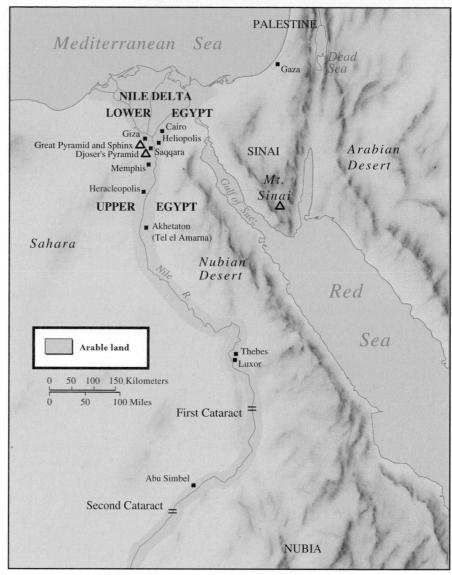

MAP I.3 Ancient Egypt.

on the southern part of the Nile, which made defense relatively easy, and the Mediterranean Sea to the north. These barriers, however, did not prevent the development of trade.

In essence, Egyptian geography and topography played important roles in the early history of the country. The regularity of the Nile floods and the relative isolation of the Egyptians created a sense of security that was accompanied by a feeling of changelessness. Egyptian civilization was characterized by a remarkable degree of continuity over thousands of years. It was certainly no accident that Egyptians believed in cyclical rather than linear progress. Just as the sun passed through its daily cycle and the Nile its annual overflow, Egyptian kings reaffirmed the basic, unchanging principles of justice at the beginning of each new cycle of rule.

❊ The Old and Middle Kingdoms

The basic framework for the study of Egyptian history was provided by Manetho, an Egyptian priest and historian who lived in the early third century B.C. He divided Egyptian history into thirty-one dynasties of kings. Using Manetho and other king lists, modern historians have divided Egyptian history into three major periods known as the Old Kingdom, the Middle Kingdom, and the New Kingdom. These were periods of long-term stability characterized by strong monarchical authority, competent bureaucracy, freedom from invasion, much construction of temples and pyramids, and considerable intellectual and cultural activity. But between the periods of stability were times of political chaos known as the Intermediate Periods, which were characterized by weak political

The Egyptians

Thinite Period or Early Dynastic (dynasties 1–2)	c. 3100–2700 B.C.
Old Kingdom (dynasties 3–6)	c. 2700–2200 B.C.
First Intermediate Period (dynasties 7–10)	c. 2200–2050 B.C.
Middle Kingdom (dynasties 11–12)	c. 2050–1652 B.C.
Second Intermediate Period (dynasties 13–17)	c. 1652–1567 B.C.
New Kingdom (dynasties 18–20)	c. 1567–1085 B.C.
Postempire (dynasties 21–31)	1085–30 B.C.

structures and rivalry for leadership, invasions, a decline in building activity, and a restructuring of society.

According to the Egyptians' own tradition, their land consisted initially of numerous populated areas ruled by tribal chieftains. Around 3100 B.C., the first Egyptian royal dynasty, under a king called Menes, united both Upper and Lower Egypt into a single kingdom. Henceforth the king would be called "king of Upper and Lower Egypt," and the royal crown would be a double diadem, signifying the unification of all Egypt. Just as the Nile served to unite Upper and Lower Egypt physically, kingship served to unite the two areas politically.

The Old Kingdom encompassed the third through sixth dynasties of Egyptian kings, lasting from around 2700 to 2200 B.C. It was an age of prosperity and splendor, made visible in the construction of the greatest and largest pyramids in Egypt's history. The capital of the Old Kingdom was located at Memphis, south of the delta.

Kingship was a divine institution in ancient Egypt and formed part of a universal cosmic scheme (see the box on p. 14): "What is the king of Upper and Lower Egypt? He is a god by whose dealings one lives, the father and mother of all men, alone by himself, without an equal."[4] In obeying their king, subjects helped maintain the cosmic order. A breakdown in royal power could only mean that citizens were offending divinity and weakening the universal structure. Among the various titles of Egyptian kings, pharaoh (originally meaning "great house" or "palace") eventually came to be the most common.

Although they possessed absolute power, Egyptian kings were supposed to rule not arbitrarily but according to set principles. The chief principle was called *Ma'at*, a spiritual precept that conveyed the idea of truth and justice, especially right order and harmony. To ancient Egyptians, this fundamental order and harmony had existed throughout the universe since the beginning of time. Pharaohs were the divine instruments who maintained it and were themselves subject to it.

Although theoretically absolute in their power, in practice Egyptian kings did not rule alone. Initially, members of the king's family performed administrative tasks, but by the fourth dynasty, a bureaucracy with regular procedures had developed. Especially important was the office of vizier, "steward of the whole land." Directly responsible to the king, the vizier was in charge of the bureaucracy, with its numerous departments, including police, justice, river transport, and public works. Agriculture and the treasury were the two most important departments. Agriculture was, of course, the backbone of Egyptian prosperity, and the treasury collected taxes, which were paid in kind. A careful assessment of land and tenants was undertaken to provide the tax base. For administrative purposes, Egypt was divided into provinces or nomes, as they were later called by the Greeks—twenty-two in Upper and twenty in Lower Egypt. A governor, called by the Greeks a nomarch, was head of each nome and was responsible to the king and vizier. Nomarchs, however, tended to build up large holdings of land and power within their nomes, creating a potential rivalry with the pharaohs.

Despite the theory of divine order, the Old Kingdom eventually collapsed, ushering in a period of chaos. Finally, a new royal dynasty managed to pacify all Egypt and inaugurated the Middle Kingdom, a new period of stability lasting from around 2050 to 1652 B.C. Several factors contributed to its vitality. The nome structure was reorganized. The boundaries of each nome were now settled precisely, and the obligations of the nomes to the state were clearly delineated. Nomarchs were confirmed as hereditary officeholders but with the understanding that their duties must be performed faithfully. These included the collection of taxes for the state and the recruitment of labor forces for royal projects, such as stone quarrying.

The Middle Kingdom was characterized by a new concern on the part of the pharaohs for the people. In the Old Kingdom, the pharaoh had been viewed as an inaccessible god-king. Now he was portrayed as the shepherd of his people with the responsibility to build public works and provide for the public welfare. As one pharaoh expressed it: "He [a particular god] created me as one who should do that which he had done, and to carry out that which he commanded should be done. He appointed me herdsman of this land, for he knew who would keep it in order for him."[5]

✳ *Society and Economy in Ancient Egypt*

Egyptian society had a simple structure in the Old and Middle Kingdoms; basically, it was organized along hierarchical lines with the god-king at the top. The king was surrounded by an upper class of nobles and priests who participated in the elaborate rituals of life that surrounded the pharaoh. This ruling class ran the government and managed its own landed estates, which provided much of its wealth.

Below the upper classes were merchants and artisans. Merchants engaged in active trade up and down the Nile as well as in town and village markets. Some merchants also engaged in international trade; they were sent by the king to Crete and Syria, where they obtained wood and other products. Expeditions traveled into Nubia for ivory and down the Red Sea to Punt for incense and spices. Egyptian artisans displayed unusually high standards of craftsmanship and beauty and produced an incredible variety of goods: stone dishes; beautifully painted boxes made of clay; wooden furniture; gold, silver, and copper tools and containers; paper and rope made of papyrus; and linen clothing.

By far, the largest number of people in Egypt simply worked the land. In theory, the king owned all the land but granted out portions of it to his subjects. Large sections were in the possession of nobles and the temple complexes. Most of the lower classes were serfs or common people who were bound to the land and cultivated the estates. They paid taxes in the form of crops to the king, nobles, and priests, lived in small villages or towns, and provided military service and forced labor for building projects.

✳ *The Culture of Egypt*

Egypt produced a culture that dazzled and awed its later conquerors. The Egyptians' technical achievements alone, especially visible in the construction of the pyramids, demonstrated a measure of skill unique to the world of that time. To the Egyptians, all of these achievements were part of a cosmic order suffused with the presence of the divine.

✳ SPIRITUAL LIFE IN EGYPTIAN SOCIETY

The Egyptians had no word for religion because it was an inseparable element of the world order to which Egyptian society belonged. The Egyptians possessed a remarkable number of gods associated with heavenly bodies and natural forces. Two groups, sun gods and land gods, came to have special prominence, hardly unusual in view of the importance of the sun, the river, and the fertile land along its banks to Egypt's well-being. The sun was the source of life and hence worthy of worship. A sun cult developed, and the sun god took on different forms and names, depending on his specific function. He was worshiped as Atum in human form and as Re, who had a human body but the head of a falcon. The pharaoh took the title of "Son of Re" because he was regarded as the earthly embodiment of Re. Eventually, Re became associated with Amon, an air god of Thebes, as Amon-Re.

River and land deities included Osiris and Isis with their child Horus, who was related to the Nile and to the sun as well. Osiris became especially important as a symbol of resurrection. A famous Egyptian myth told of the struggle between Osiris, who brought civilization to Egypt, and his evil brother Seth, who killed him, cut his body into fourteen parts, and tossed them into the Nile. Osiris's faithful wife Isis found the pieces and, with help from other gods, restored Osiris to life. As a symbol of resurrection and as judge of the dead, Osiris took on an important role for the Egyptians. By identifying with Osiris, one could hope to gain new life, just as Osiris had done. The dead, embalmed and mummified, were placed in tombs (in the case of kings, in pyramidal tombs), given the name of Osiris, and by a process of magical identification became Osiris. Like Osiris, they would then be reborn. The flood of the Nile and the new life it brought to Egypt were symbolized by Isis gathering all of Osiris's parts together and were celebrated each spring in the festival of the new land.

Later Egyptian spiritual practice began to emphasize morality by stressing Osiris's role as judge of the dead. The dead were asked to give an account of their earthly deeds to show whether they deserved a reward. Other means were also employed to gain immortality. Magical incantations, preserved in the *Book of the Dead,* were used to ensure a favorable journey to a happy afterlife. Specific instructions explained what to do when confronted by the judge of the dead. These

OSIRIS AS JUDGE OF THE DEAD. According to the *Book of the Dead*, after making a denial of offenses (the "negative confession"), the deceased experienced the "weighing of the heart." Shown here is a judgment scene from the *Book of the Dead* of Hunefer, a royal scribe who died around 1285 B.C. Hunefer's heart is placed on one side of a balance scale; on the other side is the feather of Ma'at, the goddess of truth. For Hunefer, heart and feather are of equal weight, so the god Anubis ushers him into the presence of Osiris, seated on his throne at the right. A "swallowing monster," a hybrid creature of crocodile, lion, and hippopotamus, stood ready at the scale to devour the deceased if he failed the test.

instructions had two aspects. The negative confession gave a detailed list of what one had not done:

> *I have not committed evil against men.*
> *I have not mistreated cattle.*
> *I have not blasphemed a god. . . .*
> *I have not done violence to a poor man. . . .*
> *I have not defamed a slave to his superior.*
> *I have not made anyone sick.*
> *I have not made anyone weep.*
> *I have not killed. . . .*
> *I have not caused anyone suffering. . . .*
> *I have not had sexual relations with a boy.*
> *I have not defiled myself. . . .*[6]

Later the supplicant made a speech listing his good actions: "I have done that which men said and that with which gods are content. . . . I have given bread to the hungry, water to the thirsty, clothing to the naked, and a ferry-boat to him who was marooned. I have provided divine offerings for the gods and mortuary offerings for the dead."[7] At first the Osiris cult was reserved for the very wealthy, who could afford to take expensive measures to preserve the body after death. During the Middle Kingdom, however, the cult became "democratized," open to all Egyptians who aspired to an afterlife.

THE PYRAMIDS

One of the great achievements of Egyptian civilization, the building of pyramids, occurred in the time of the Old Kingdom. Pyramids were not built in isolation but as part of a larger complex dedicated to the dead—in effect, a city of the dead. The area included a large pyramid for the king's burial, smaller pyramids for his family, and mastabas, rectangular structures with flat roofs, as tombs for the pharaoh's noble officials. The tombs were well prepared for their residents. The rooms were furnished and stocked with numerous supplies, including chairs, boats, chests, weapons, games, dishes, and a variety of foods. The Egyptians believed that human beings had two bodies, a physical one and a spiritual one, which they called the *ka*. If the physical body was properly preserved (that is, mummified) and the tomb furnished with all the various objects of regular life, the *ka* could return and continue its life despite the death of the physical body.

To preserve the physical body after death, the Egyptians practiced mummification, a process of slowly drying a dead body to prevent it from rotting. Special workshops, run by priests, performed this procedure, primarily for the wealthy families who could afford it. Workers first removed the liver, lungs, stomach, and intestines and placed them in four special jars. The priests also removed the brain by extracting it through the nose. They then covered the corpse with a natural salt that absorbed the body's water. Later, they filled the body with spices and wrapped it with layers of linen soaked in resin. At the end of the process, which took about seventy days, a lifelike mask was placed over the head and shoulders of the mummy, which was then sealed in a case and placed in its tomb in a pyramid.

The largest and most magnificent of all the pyramids was built under King Khufu. Constructed at Giza around 2540 B.C., this famous Great Pyramid covers 13 acres, measures 756 feet at each side of its base, and stands 481 feet high. Its four sides are almost precisely oriented to the four points of the compass. The interior included a grand gallery to the burial chamber, which was built of granite with a lidless sarcophagus for the pharaoh's body. The Great Pyramid still stands as a visible symbol of the power of Egyptian kings and the spiritual conviction that underlay Egyptian society. No pyramid built later ever matched its size or splendor. But an Egyptian pyramid was not just the king's tomb; it was also an important symbol of royal power. It could be seen for miles away as a visible reminder of the glory and might of the ruler, who was a living god on earth.

ART AND WRITING

Commissioned by kings or nobles for use in temples and tombs, Egyptian art was largely functional. Wall paintings and statues of gods and kings in temples served a strictly spiritual purpose. They were an integral part of the performance of ritual, which was thought necessary to preserve the cosmic order and hence the well-being of Egypt. Likewise, the mural scenes and sculptured figures found in the tombs had a specific function. They were supposed to aid the journey of the deceased into the afterworld.

Egyptian art was also formulaic. Artists and sculptors were expected to observe a strict canon of proportions that determined both form and presentation. This canon gave Egyptian art a distinctive appearance for thousands of years. Especially characteristic was the convention of combining the profile, semiprofile, and frontal views of the human body in relief work and painting in order to represent each part of the body accurately. The result was an art that was highly stylized yet still allowed distinctive features to be displayed.

Writing in Egypt emerged during the first two dynasties. The Greeks later labeled Egyptian writing hieroglyphics, meaning "priest carvings" or "sacred writings." Hieroglyphs were sacred characters used as

THE PYRAMIDS AT GIZA. The three pyramids at Giza, across the Nile River from Cairo, are the most famous in Egypt. Pyramids served as tombs for both the king and his immediate family. At the rear is the largest of the three pyramids, the Great Pyramid of Khufu. In the foreground is the smaller pyramid of Menkaure standing behind the even smaller pyramids for the pharaohs' wives.

picture signs that depicted objects and had a sacred value at the same time. Although hieroglyphs were later simplified into two scripts for writing purposes, they never developed into an alphabet. Egyptian hieroglyphs were initially carved in stone, but later the two simplified scripts were written on papyrus, a paper made from the papyrus reed that grew along the Nile. Most of the ancient Egyptian literature that has come down to us was written on papyrus rolls and wooden tablets.

✳ Chaos and a New Order: The New Kingdom

The Middle Kingdom came to an end in the midst of another period of instability. An incursion into the delta region by a people known as the Hyksos initiated this second age of chaos. The Hyksos, a Semitic-speaking people, infiltrated Egypt in the seventeenth century B.C. and came to dominate much of Egypt. However, the presence of the Hyksos was not entirely negative for Egypt. They introduced Egypt to Bronze Age technology by teaching the Egyptians how to make bronze for use in new agricultural tools and weapons. The Hyksos also introduced new aspects of warfare to Egypt, including the horse-drawn war chariot, a heavier sword, and the compound bow. Eventually, a new line of pharaohs—the eighteenth dynasty—made use of the new weapons to throw off Hyksos domination, reunite Egypt, establish the New Kingdom (c. 1567–1085 B.C.), and launch the Egyptians along a new militaristic and imperialistic path. During the period of the New Kingdom, Egypt became the most powerful state in the Middle East. The Egyptians occupied Palestine and Syria but permitted the local princes to rule under Egyptian control. Egyptian armies also moved westward into Libya.

The eighteenth dynasty was not without its own troubles, however. Amenhotep IV (c. 1364–1347 B.C.) introduced the worship of Aton, god of the sun disk, as the chief god and pursued his worship with great enthusiasm. Changing his own name to Akhenaton ("It is well with Aton"), the pharaoh closed the temples of other gods and especially endeavored to lessen the power of Amon-Re and his priesthood at Thebes. Akhenaton strove to reduce their influence by replacing Thebes as the capital of Egypt with Akhetaton ("dedicated to Aton"), a new city located near modern Tel el Amarna, 200 miles north of Thebes.

Akhenaton's attempt at religious change proved to be a failure. It was too much to ask Egyptians to give up their traditional ways and beliefs, especially since they saw the destruction of the old gods as subversive of the very cosmic order on which Egypt's survival and continuing prosperity depended. Moreover, the priests at Thebes were unalterably opposed to the changes, which diminished their influence and power. At the same time, Akhenaton's preoccupation with religion caused him to ignore foreign affairs and led to the loss of both Syria and Palestine. Akhenaton's changes were soon undone after his death by those who influenced his successor, the boy-pharaoh Tutankhamon (1347–1338 B.C.). Tutankhamon returned the government to Thebes and restored the old gods. The Aton experiment had failed to take hold, and the eighteenth dynasty itself came to an end in 1333 B.C.

The nineteenth dynasty managed to restore Egyptian power one more time. Under Rameses II (c. 1279–1213 B.C.), the Egyptians regained control of Palestine but were unable to reestablish the borders of their earlier empire. New invasions in the thirteenth century by the "Sea Peoples," as Egyptians called them, destroyed Egyptian power in Palestine and drove the Egyptians back within their old frontiers. The days of Egyptian empire were ended, and the New Kingdom itself expired with the end of the twentieth dynasty in 1085 B.C. For the next thousand years, despite periodical revivals of strength, Egypt was dominated by Libyans, Nubians, Persians, and finally Macedonians after the conquest of Alexander the Great (see Chapter 4). In the first century B.C., Egypt became a province in Rome's mighty empire.

✳ Daily Life in Ancient Egypt: Family and Marriage

Ancient Egyptians had a very positive attitude toward daily life on earth and followed the advice of the wisdom literature, which suggested that people marry young and establish a home and family. Monogamy was the general rule, although a husband was allowed to keep additional wives if his first wife was childless. Pharaohs were entitled to harems; the queen, however, was acknowledged as the Great Wife, with a status higher than that of the other wives. The husband was master in the house, but wives were very much respected and in charge of the household and education of the children. From a book of wise sayings came this advice:

> If you are a man of standing, you should found your household and love your wife at home as is fitting. Fill her belly;

A HUNTING SCENE.   A favorite pastime of the Egyptian upper classes was hunting waterfowl in the stands of papyrus that grew along the river's banks. This tomb painting shows a wealthy Egyptian with members of his family hunting geese with throwsticks.

clothe her back. Ointment is the prescription for her body. Make her heart glad as long as you live. She is a profitable field for her lord. You should not contend with her at law, and keep her far from gaining control. . . . Let her heart be soothed through what may accrue to you; it means keeping her long in your house.[8]

Women's property and inheritance remained in their hands, even in marriage. Although most careers and public offices were closed to women, some did operate businesses. Peasant women worked long hours in the fields and at numerous domestic tasks. Upper-class women could function as priestesses, and a few queens even became pharaohs in their own right. Most famous was Hatshepsut in the New Kingdom. She served as regent for her stepson Thutmosis III but assumed the throne for herself and remained in power until her death.

Hatshepsut's reign was a prosperous one, which is especially evident in her building activity. She is most famous for the temple dedicated to herself at Deir el Bahri on the west bank of the Nile at Thebes. As pharaoh, Hatshepsut sent out military expeditions, encouraged mining, fostered agriculture, and sent a trading expedition to lower Africa. Because pharaohs were almost always male, Hatshepsut's official statues show her clothed and bearded like a king. She was addressed as "His Majesty." That Hatshepsut was aware of her unusual position is evident from an inscription she had placed on one of her temples. It read: "Now my heart turns to and fro, in thinking what will the people say, they who shall see my monument in after years, and shall speak of what I have done."

Marriages were arranged by parents. The primary concerns were family and property, and clearly the chief purpose of marriage was to produce children, especially sons (see the box on p. 22). From the New Kingdom came this piece of wisdom: "Take to yourself a wife while you are [still] a youth, that she may produce a son for you."[9] Only sons could carry on the family name. Daughters were not slighted, however. Numerous tomb paintings show the close and affectionate relationship parents had with both sons and daughters. Although marriages were arranged, some of the surviving love poems from ancient Egypt indicate an element of romance in some marriages. Marriages could and did end in divorce, which was allowed, apparently with compensation for the wife. Adultery, however, was strictly prohibited, and punishments were severe, especially for women, who could have their noses cut off or be burned at the stake.

A Father's Advice

Upper-class Egyptians enjoyed compiling collections of wise sayings to provide guidance for leading an upright and successful life. This excerpt is taken from The Instruction of the Vizier Ptah-hotep *and dates from around 2450* B.C. *The vizier was the pharaoh's chief official. In this selection, Ptah-hotep advises his son on how to be a successful official.*

❋ The Instruction of the Vizier Ptah-hotep

Then he said to his son:

Let not your heart be puffed-up because of your knowledge; be not confident because you are a wise man. Take counsel with the ignorant as well as the wise. The full limits of skill cannot be attained, and there is no skilled man equipped to his full advantage. Good speech is more hidden than the emerald, but it may be found with maidservants at the grindstones. . . .

If you are a leader commanding the affairs of the multitude, seek out for yourself every beneficial deed, until it may be that your own affairs are without wrong. Justice is great, and its appropriateness is lasting; it has been disturbed since the time of him who made it, whereas there is punishment for him who passes over its laws. It is the right path before him who knows nothing. Wrongdoing has never brought its undertaking into port. It may be that it is fraud that gains riches, but the strength of justice is that it lasts. . . .

If you are a man of intimacy, whom one great man sends to another, be thoroughly reliable when he sends you. Carry out the errand for him as he has spoken. Do not be reserved about what is said to you, and beware of any act of forgetfulness. Grasp hold of truth, and do not exceed it. Mere gratification is by no means to be repeated. Struggle against making words worse, thus making one great man hostile to another through vulgar speech. . . .

If you are a man of standing and found a household and produce a son who is pleasing to god, if he is correct and inclines toward your ways and listens to your instruction, while his manners in your house are fitting, and if he takes care of your property as it should be, seek out for him every useful action. He is your son, . . . you should not cut your heart off from him.

But a man's seed often creates enmity. If he goes astray and transgresses your plans and does not carry out your instruction, so that his manners in your household are wretched, and he rebels against all that you say, while his mouth runs on in the most wretched talk, quite apart from his experience, while he possesses nothing, you should cast him off: he is not your son at all. He was not really born to you. Thus you enslave him entirely according to his own speech. He is one whom god has condemned in the very womb. . . .

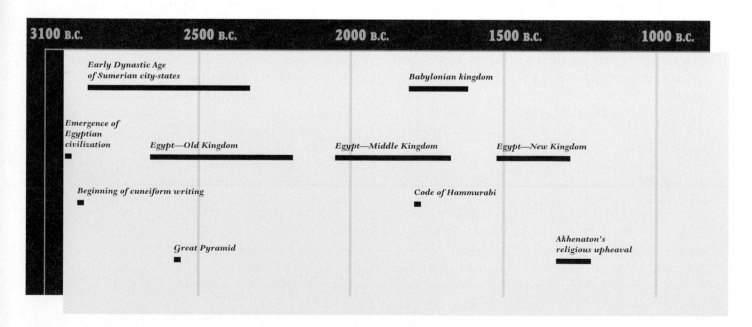

Conclusion

The foundation stones for the building of Western civilization were laid by the Mesopotamians and Egyptians. They developed cities and struggled with the problems of organized states. They developed writing to keep records and created literature. They constructed monumental architecture to please their gods, symbolize their power, and preserve their culture for all time. They developed new political, military, social, and religious structures to deal with the basic problems of human existence and organization. These first literate civilizations left detailed records that allow us to view how they grappled with three of the fundamental problems that humans have pondered: the nature of human relationships, the nature of the universe, and the role of divine forces in the cosmos. Although later peoples in Western civilization would provide different answers from those of the Mesopotamians and Egyptians, it was they who first posed the questions, gave answers, and wrote them down. Human memory begins with these two civilizations.

By the middle of the second millennium B.C., the creative impulse of the Mesopotamian and Egyptian civilizations was beginning to wane. The invasion of the Sea Peoples around 1200 B.C. ushered in a whole new pattern of petty states and new kingdoms that would lead to the largest empires the ancient Near East had seen.

Notes

1. Quoted in Amélie. Kuhrt, *The Ancient Near East, c. 3000–330 B.C.* (London, 1995), Vol. 1, p. 68.
2. Quoted in Thorkild Jacobsen, "Mesopotamia," in Henri Frankfort et al., *Before Philosophy* (Baltimore, 1949), p. 139.
3. James B. Pritchard, *Ancient Near Eastern Texts*, 3d ed. (Princeton, N.J., 1969), p. 372.
4. Quoted in Milton Covensky, *The Ancient Near Eastern Tradition* (New York, 1966), p. 51.
5. Quoted in B. G. Trigger, B. J. Kemp, D. O'Connor, and A. B. Lloyd, *Ancient Egypt: A Social History* (Cambridge, 1983), p. 74.
6. Pritchard, *Ancient Near Eastern Texts*, p. 34.
7. Ibid., p. 36.
8. Ibid., p. 413.
9. Ibid., p. 420.

Suggestions for Further Reading

For a beautifully illustrated introduction to the ancient world, see *Past Worlds: The Times Atlas of Archaeology* (Maplewood, N.J., 1988), written by an international group of scholars. A detailed history of the ancient world with chapters written by different specialists is available in the twelve volumes of *The Cambridge Ancient History*, now in its third edition. Less detailed but sound surveys can be found in C. G. Starr, *A History of the Ancient World*, 4th ed. (New York, 1991), and L. De Blois and R. J. van der Spek, *An Introduction to the Ancient World*, trans. S. Mellor (London, 1997). The following works are of considerable value in examining the prehistory of humankind: M. N. Cohen, *The Food Crisis in Prehistory: Overpopulation and the Origins of Agriculture* (New Haven, Conn., 1977); R. Leakey, *The Making of Mankind* (London, 1981); P. Mellars and C. Stringer, *The Human Revolution* (Edinburgh, 1989); D. O. Henry, *From Foraging to Agriculture* (Philadelphia, 1989); and C. Redman, *The Rise of Civilization* (San Francisco, 1978). For a specialized study of the role of women in early human society, see F. Dahlberg, ed., *Woman the Gatherer* (New Haven, Conn., 1981).

A fascinating introduction to the world of ancient Near Eastern studies can be found in W. D. Jones, *Venus and Sothis: How the Ancient Near East Was Rediscovered* (Chicago, 1982). A very competent general survey primarily of the political history of Mesopotamia and Egypt is W. W. Hallo and W. K. Simpson, *The Ancient Near East: A History* (New York, 1971). Also valuable are A. Kuhrt, *The Ancient Near East, c. 3000–330 B.C.* (London, 1996); A. B. Knapp, *The History and Culture of Ancient Western Asia and Egypt* (Chicago, 1987); W. von Soden, *The Ancient Orient: An Introduction to the Study of the Ancient Near East* (Grand Rapids, Mich., 1994); and H. J. Nissen, *The Early History of the Ancient Near East, 9000–2000 B.C.* (Chicago, 1988). H. W. F. Saggs, *Babylonians* (Norman, Okla., 1995), provides an overview of the peoples of ancient Mesopotamia. On the economic and social history of the ancient Near East, see D. C. Snell, *Life in the Ancient Near East* (New Haven, Conn., 1997). The fundamental collection of translated documents from the ancient Near East is J. B. Pritchard, *Ancient Near Eastern Texts*, 3d ed. with supplement (Princeton, N.J., 1969). For a good translation of *The Epic of Gilgamesh*, see the edition by N. K. Sandars (London, 1972).

General works on ancient Mesopotamia include J. N. Postgate, *Early Mesopotamia: Society and Economy at the Dawn of History* (London, 1992); S. Lloyd, *The Archaeology of Mesopotamia*, rev. ed. (London, 1984); and G. Roux, *Ancient Iraq* (Harmondsworth, England, 1966). A beautifully illustrated survey can be found in M. Roaf, *Cultural Atlas of Mesopotamia and the Ancient Near East* (New York, 1996). The world of the Sumerians has been well described in S. N. Kramer, *The Sumerians* (Chicago, 1963) and *History Begins at Sumer* (New York, 1959). See also the recent summary of the historical and archaeological evidence by H. Crawford, *Sumer and the Sumerians* (Cambridge, 1991). The fundamental work on the spiritual perspective of ancient Mesopotamia is T. Jacobsen, *The Treasures of Darkness: A History of Mesopotamian Religion* (New Haven, Conn., 1976). On art, see P. Amiet, *Art of the Ancient Near East* (New York, 1980).

For a good introduction to ancient Egypt, see the beautifully illustrated works by J. Baines and J. Málek, *The Cultural Atlas of the World: Ancient Egypt* (Alexandria, Va., 1991); and D. P. Silverman, ed., *Ancient Egypt* (New York, 1997). Other general surveys include C. Hobson, *The World of the Pharaohs* (New York, 1987); N. Grimal, *A History of Ancient Egypt*, trans. I. Shaw (Oxford, 1992); and N. Grant, *The Egyptians* (New York, 1996). For an interesting introduction to Egyptian history, see B. J. Kemp, *Ancient Egypt* (London, 1989). A new approach is attempted in B. G. Trigger, B. J. Kemp, D. O'Connor, and A. B. Lloyd, *Ancient Egypt: A Social History* (Cambridge, 1983). On Akhenaton and his religious changes, see D. Redford, *Akhenaten: The Heretic King* (Princeton, N.J., 1984). Egyptian religion is covered in H. Frankfort, *Ancient Egyptian Religion* (New York, 1948), a brief but superb study, and E. Hornung,

Conceptions of God in Ancient Egypt: The One and the Many (Ithaca, N.Y., 1982). On culture in general, see J. A. Wilson, *The Culture of Ancient Egypt* (Chicago, 1956). The leading authority on the pyramids is I. E. S. Edwards, *The Pyramids of Egypt,* rev. ed. (Harmondsworth, England, 1993). On art, see H. Schäfer, *The Principles of Egyptian Art* (Oxford, 1974). An important new study on women is G. Robins, *Women in Ancient Egypt* (Cambridge, Mass., 1993). Daily life in ancient Egypt can be examined in E. Strouhal, *Life of the Ancient Egyptians* (Norman, Okla., 1992), and T. G. H. James, *Pharaoh's People: Scenes from Life in Imperial Egypt* (London, 1984).

 For additional reading, go to InfoTrac College Edition, your online research library at http://web1.infotrac-college.com

Enter the search term *antiquities* using the Subject Guide.

Enter the search term *Mesopotamia* using Key Terms.

Enter the search terms *archaeology research* using the Subject Guide.

Enter the search terms *Egypt history* using the Subject Guide.

The Ancient Near East: Peoples and Empires

CHAPTER OUTLINE

- On the Fringes of Civilization
- The Hebrews: "The Children of Israel"
- The Assyrian Empire
- The Persian Empire
- Conclusion

FOCUS QUESTIONS

- In what ways was the Jewish faith unique in the ancient Near East, and how did it evolve over time?
- What effect did the other peoples of the ancient Near East have on the history of Israel and the development of the Jewish faith?
- What methods and institutions did the Assyrians and Persians use to amass and maintain their respective empires?
- What were the chief teachings of Zoroastrianism, and what role did it play in the Persian Empire?

AROUND 970 B.C., *Solomon came to the throne of Israel, a small state in western Asia. He was lacking in military prowess but excelled in many other ways. Through trade and a series of foreign alliances, he created a strong, flourishing state. But he was especially famed for his skill as a judge. When two women came before him, each claiming that the same infant was her natural child, Solomon ordered his servant to cut the child in half and give half to each woman. The first woman objected: "Please, my lord, give her the living baby! Don't kill him!" The second woman replied, "Neither I nor you shall have him. Cut him in two!" Then Solomon rendered his judgment: "Give the living baby to the first woman. Do not kill him; she is his mother." According to the biblical account, "when all Israel heard the verdict the king had given, they held the king in awe, because they saw that he had wisdom from God to administer justice." After Solomon's death, Israel's power began to crumble. But how* had such a small nation been able to survive for as long as it did in a Near East dominated by mighty empires?

The weakening of Egypt around 1200 B.C. left no dominant powers in the Near East, allowing a patchwork of petty kingdoms and city-states to emerge, especially in the area of Syria and Palestine. One of these small states, the Hebrew nation known as Israel, has played a role in Western civilization completely disproportionate to its size. The Hebrews played a minor part in the politics of the ancient Near East, but their spiritual heritage—in the form of Judeo-Christian values—is one of the basic pillars of Western civilization.

The small states did not last, however. Ever since the first city-states had arisen in the Near East around 3000 B.C., there had been an ongoing movement toward the creation of larger territorial states with more sophisticated systems of control. This process reached a high point in the first millennium B.C. with the appearance of vast empires. Between 1000 and 500 B.C., the Assyrians, the Chaldeans, and the Persians all forged empires that encompassed large areas of the ancient Near East. Each had impressive and grandiose capital cities that emphasized the power and wealth of its rulers. Each brought peace and order for a time by employing new administrative techniques. Each eventually fell to other conquerors. In the long run, these large empires had less impact on Western civilization than the Hebrew people. In human history, the power of ideas is often more significant than the power of empires.

◆ On the Fringes of Civilization

Our story of the beginnings of Western civilization has been dominated so far by Mesopotamia and Egypt. But significant developments were also taking place on the fringes of these civilizations. Farming had spread into the Balkan peninsula of Europe by 6500 B.C., and by 4000 B.C., it was well established in southern France, central Europe, and the coastal regions of the Mediterranean. Although migrating farmers from the Near East may have brought some farming techniques into Europe, historians now believe that the Neolithic peoples of Europe domesticated animals and began to farm largely on their own.

One outstanding feature of late Neolithic Europe was the building of megalithic structures. *Megalith* is

Greek for "large stone." Radiocarbon dating, a technique that allows scientists to determine the age of objects, shows that the first megalithic structures were built around 4000 B.C., more than a thousand years before the great pyramids were built in Egypt. Between 3200 and 1500 B.C., standing stones that were placed in circles or lined up in rows were erected throughout the British Isles and northwestern France. Other megalithic constructions have been found as far north as Scandinavia and as far south as the islands of Corsica, Sardinia, and Malta. Some archaeologists have demonstrated that the stone circles were used as observatories to detect not only such simple astronomical phenomena as the midwinter and midsummer sunrises but also such sophisticated observations as the major and minor standstills of the moon.

By far the most famous of these megalithic constructions is Stonehenge in England. Stonehenge consists of a series of concentric rings of standing stones. Its construction sometime between 2100 and 1900 B.C.

STONEHENGE. The Bronze Age in northwestern Europe is known for its megaliths, or large standing stones. Between 3200 and 1500 B.C., standing stones that were placed in circles or lined up in rows were erected throughout the British Isles and northwestern France. By far, the most famous of these megalithic constructions is Stonehenge in England.

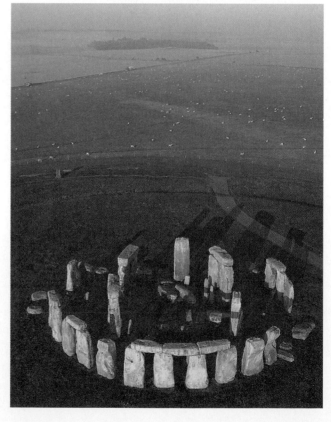

was no small accomplishment. The eighty bluestones used at Stonehenge, for example, weigh 4 tons each and were transported to the site from their original source 135 miles away. Like other megalithic structures, Stonehenge indicates a remarkable awareness of astronomy on the part of its builders, as well as an impressive coordination of workers.

❀ *The Impact of the Indo-Europeans*

For many historians, both the details of construction and the purpose of the megalithic structures of Europe remain a mystery. Also puzzling is the role of Indo-European people. The name *Indo-European* refers to people who used a language derived from a single parent tongue. Indo-European languages include Greek, Latin, Persian, Sanskrit, and the Germanic languages (see Table 2.1). It has been suggested that the original Indo-European-speaking peoples were based somewhere in the steppe region north of the Black Sea or in southwestern Asia, in modern Iran or Afghanistan. Although there had been earlier migrations, around 2000 B.C. these people began major nomadic movements into Europe (including present-day Italy and Greece), India, and western Asia. One group of Indo-Europeans who moved into Asia Minor and Anatolia (modern Turkey) around 1750 B.C. coalesced with the native peoples to form the Hittite kingdom with its capital at Hattusha (Bogazköy in modern Turkey).

Between 1600 and 1200 B.C., the Hittites assembled their own empire in western Asia and even

Table 2.1　Some Indo-European Languages

SUBFAMILY	LANGUAGES
Indo-Iranian	*Sanskrit;* Persian
Balto-Slavic	Russian, Serbo-Croatian, Czech, Polish, Lithuanian
Hellenic	Greek
Italic	*Latin,* romance languages (French, Italian, Spanish, Portuguese, Romanian)
Celtic	Irish, Gaelic
Germanic	Swedish, Danish, Norwegian, German, Dutch, English

Note: Languages in italic type are no longer spoken.

threatened the power of the Egyptians. The Hittites were the first of the Indo-European peoples to make use of iron, enabling them to construct weapons that were stronger and cheaper to make because of the widespread availability of iron ore. But around 1200 B.C., new waves of invading Indo-European peoples known only as the Sea Peoples destroyed the Hittite empire. The destruction of the Hittite kingdom and the weakening of Egypt around 1200 B.C. left a power vacuum in western Asia, allowing a patchwork of petty kingdoms and city-states to emerge, especially in the area at the eastern end of the Mediterranean Sea. The Hebrews were one of these peoples.

◆ The Hebrews: "The Children of Israel"

The Hebrews were a Semitic-speaking people who had a tradition concerning their origins and history that was eventually written down as part of the Hebrew Bible, known to Christians as the Old Testament. Describing them as nomads organized in clans, the Hebrews' tradition states that they were descendants of the patriarch Abraham who had migrated from Mesopotamia to Palestine, where they became identified as the "Children of Israel." Again according to tradition, a drought in Palestine caused many Hebrews to migrate to Egypt, where they lived peacefully until they were enslaved by pharaohs who used them as laborers on building projects. These Hebrews remained in bondage until Moses led them eastward out of Egypt in the Exodus, which some historians have argued would have occurred in the first half of the thirteenth century B.C. According to the biblical account, the Hebrews then wandered for many years in the desert until they entered Palestine. Organized in twelve tribes, they became embroiled in conflict with the Philistines, a people who had settled in the coastal area of Palestine but were beginning to move into the inland areas.

Many scholars today doubt that the early books of the Hebrew Bible reflect the true history of the early Israelites. They argue that the early books of the Bible, written centuries after the events described, preserve only what the Israelites came to believe about themselves and that recent archaeological evidence often contradicts the details of the biblical account. Some of these scholars have even argued that the Israelites were not nomadic invaders but indigenous peoples in the Palestinian hill country.

What is generally agreed, however, is that between 1200 and 1000 B.C., the Israelites emerged as a distinct group of people, possibly organized in tribes or a league of tribes, who established a united kingdom known as Israel.

�֍ *The United Kingdom*

The first king of the Israelites was Saul (c. 1020–1000 B.C.), who initially achieved some success in the ongoing struggle with the Philistines. But after his death in a disastrous battle with this enemy, a brief period of anarchy ensued until one of Saul's lieutenants, David (c. 1000–970 B.C.), reunited the Israelites, defeated the Philistines, and established control over all of Palestine (see Map 2.1). According to the biblical account, some of his conquests led to harsh treatment for the conquered people:

MAP 2.1 Palestine in the First Millennium B.C.

"David also defeated the Moabites. He made them lie down on the ground and measured them off with a length of cord. Every two lengths of them were put to death, and the third length was allowed to live. So the Moabites became subject to David and brought tribute." Among David's conquests was the city of Jerusalem, which he made into the capital of a united kingdom. David centralized Israel's political organization and accelerated the integration of the Israelites into a settled community based on farming and urban life.

David's son Solomon (c. 970–930 B.C.) did even more to strengthen royal power. He expanded the political and military establishments and was especially active in extending the trading activities of the Israelites. Solomon is best known for his building projects, of which the most famous was the Temple in the city of Jerusalem. The Israelites viewed the Temple as the symbolic center of their religion, and hence of the kingdom of Israel itself. The Temple now housed the Ark of the Covenant, a holy chest containing the sacred relics of the Hebrew religion and, symbolically, the throne of the invisible God of Israel. Under Solomon, ancient Israel was at the height of its power, but his efforts to extend royal power throughout his kingdom led to dissatisfaction among some of his subjects.

✖ *The Divided Kingdom*

After Solomon's death, tensions within Israel between the northern and southern tribes led to the establishment of two separate kingdoms—the kingdom of Israel, composed of the ten northern tribes, with its capital eventually at Samaria, and the southern kingdom of Judah, consisting of two tribes, with its capital at Jerusalem. By the end of the ninth century B.C., the independence of the kingdom of Israel was increasingly threatened by the rising power of the Assyrians. In 722 B.C., the Assyrians destroyed Samaria, overran the kingdom of Israel, and deported many Hebrews to other parts of the Assyrian empire. These dispersed Hebrews (the "ten lost tribes") merged with neighboring peoples and gradually lost their identity.

The southern kingdom of Judah was also forced to pay tribute to Assyria but managed to retain its independence as Assyrian power declined. A new enemy, however, appeared on the horizon. The Chaldeans brought the final destruction of Assyria, conquered the kingdom of Judah, and completely destroyed Jerusalem in 586 B.C. Many people from Judah were deported to Babylonia; the memory of their exile is still evoked in the stirring words of Psalm 137:

> By the rivers of Babylon, we sat and wept when we remembered Zion. . . .
>
> How can we sing the songs of the Lord while in a foreign land?
>
> If I forget you, O Jerusalem, may my right hand forget its skill.
>
> May my tongue cling to the roof of my mouth if I do not remember you,
>
> if I do not consider Jerusalem my highest joy.[1]

But the Babylonian captivity of the people of Judah did not last. A new set of conquerors, the Persians, destroyed the Chaldean kingdom but allowed the people of Judah to return to Jerusalem and rebuild their city and temple. The revived kingdom of Judah remained under Persian control until the conquests of Alexander the Great in the fourth century B.C. The people of Judah survived, eventually becoming known as the Jews and giving their name to Judaism, the religion of Yahweh, the Jewish God.

✺ The Spiritual Dimensions of Israel

The spiritual perspective of the Israelites evolved over time. Early Israelites probably worshiped many gods, including nature spirits dwelling in trees and rocks. For some Israelites, Yahweh was the chief god of Israel, but

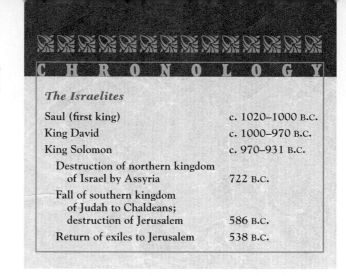

CHRONOLOGY	
The Israelites	
Saul (first king)	c. 1020–1000 B.C.
King David	c. 1000–970 B.C.
King Solomon	c. 970–931 B.C.
Destruction of northern kingdom of Israel by Assyria	722 B.C.
Fall of southern kingdom of Judah to Chaldeans; destruction of Jerusalem	586 B.C.
Return of exiles to Jerusalem	538 B.C.

many, including kings of Israel and Judah, worshiped other gods as well. It was among the Babylonian exiles that Yahweh—the God of Israel—came to be seen as the only God. After the return of these exiles to Judah, their point of view eventually became dominant, and pure monotheism, or the belief that there is only one God for all peoples, came to be the major tenet of Judaism.

⚜ "I AM THE LORD YOUR GOD": RULER OF THE WORLD

According to the Jewish conception, there is but one God, whom the Jews called Yahweh. God is the creator of the world and everything in it. Indeed, Yahweh means "he causes to be." To the Jews, the gods of all other peoples were idols. The Jewish God ruled the world; he was subject to nothing. All peoples were his servants, whether they knew it or not. This God was also transcendent. He had created nature but was not in nature. The stars, moon, rivers, wind, and other natural phenomena were not divinities or suffused with divinity, as other peoples of the ancient Near East believed, but they were God's handiwork. All of God's creations could be admired for their awesome beauty but not worshiped as gods.

This omnipotent creator of the universe was not removed from the life he had created, however, but was a just and good God who expected goodness from his people. If they did not obey his will, they would be punished. But he was also a God of mercy and love: "The Lord is gracious and compassionate, slow to anger and rich in love. The Lord is good to all; he has compassion on all he has made."[2] Despite the powerful dimensions of God as creator and sustainer of the universe, the Jewish message also emphasized that

THE KING OF ISRAEL PAYS TRIBUTE TO THE KING OF ASSYRIA. By the end of the ninth century B.C., the kingdom of Israel had been forced to pay tribute to the Assyrian Empire. The Assyrians overran the kingdom in 722 B.C. and destroyed the capital city of Samaria. In this scene from a black obelisk, Jehu, king of Israel, is shown paying tribute to the king of Assyria.

The Covenant and the Law: The Book of Exodus

During the Exodus from Egypt, the Hebrews are said to have made a covenant with Yahweh. They agreed to obey their God and follow his law. In return, Yahweh promised to take special care of his chosen people. This selection from the Book of Exodus describes the making of the covenant and God's commandments to the Hebrews.

❊ *Exodus 19: 1–8*

In the third month after the Israelites left Egypt—on the very day—they came to the Desert of Sinai. After they set out from Rephidim, they entered the desert of Sinai, and Israel camped there in the desert in front of the mountain. Then Moses went up to God, and the Lord, called to him from the mountain, and said, "This is what you are to say to the house of Jacob and what you are to tell the people of Israel: 'You yourselves have seen what I did to Egypt, and how I carried you on eagles's wings and brought you to myself. Now if you obey me fully and keep my covenant, then out of all nations you will be my treasured possession. Although the whole earth is mine, you will be for me a kingdom of priests and a holy nation.' These are the words you are to speak to the Israelites." So Moses went back and summoned the elders of the people and set before them all the words the Lord had commanded him to speak. The people all responded together, "We will do everything the Lord has said." So Moses brought their answer back to the Lord.

❊ *Exodus 20: 1–17*

And God spoke all these words, "I am the Lord your God, who brought you out of Egypt, out of the land of slavery. You shall have no other gods before me. You shall not make for yourself an idol in the form of anything in heaven above or on the earth beneath or in the waters below. You shall not bow down to them or worship them; for I, the Lord your God, am a jealous God, punishing the children for the sin of the fathers to the third and fourth generation of those who hate, but showing love to a thousand generations of those who love me and keep my commandments. You shall not misuse the name of the Lord your God, for the Lord will not hold anyone guiltless who misuse his name. Remember the Sabbath day by keeping it holy. Six days you shall labor and do all your work, but the seventh day is a Sabbath to the Lord your God. On it you shall not do any work, neither you, nor your son or daughter, nor your manservant or maidservant, nor your animals, nor the alien within your gates. For in six days the Lord made the heavens and the earth, the sea, and all that is in them, but he rested on the seventh day. Therefore the Lord blessed the Sabbath day and made it holy. Honor your father and your mother, so that you may live long in the land the Lord your God is giving you. You shall not murder. You shall not commit adultery. You shall not steal. You shall not give false testimony against your neighbor. You shall not covet your neighbor's house. You shall not covet your neighbor's wife, or his manservant or maidservant, his ox or donkey, or anything that belongs to your neighbor.

---

each person could have a personal relationship with this powerful being. As the psalmist sang: "My help comes from the Lord, the Maker of heaven and earth. He will not let your foot slip—he who watches over you will not slumber."[3]

❧ "YOU ONLY HAVE I CHOSEN": COVENANT, LAW, AND PROPHETS

Three aspects of the Hebrew religious tradition had special significance: the covenant, law, and the prophets. The Israelites believed that during the Exo-

dus from Egypt, when Moses supposedly led his people out of bondage into the "promised land," a special event occurred that determined the Jewish experience for all time. According to tradition, God entered into a covenant or contract with the tribes of Israel who believed that Yahweh had spoken to them through Moses (see the box above). The Israelites promised to obey Yahweh and follow his law. In return, Yahweh promised to take special care of his chosen people, "a peculiar treasure unto me above all people."

This covenant between Yahweh and his chosen people could be fulfilled, however, only by obedience to the law of God. Law became a crucial element of the Jewish world and had a number of different dimensions. In some instances, it set forth specific requirements, such as payments for offenses. Most important, since the major characteristic of God was his goodness, ethical concerns stood at the center of the law. Sometimes these took the form of specific standards of moral behavior: "You shall not murder. You shall not commit adultery. You shall not steal."[4] But these concerns were also expressed in decrees that regulated the economic, social, and political life of the community since God's laws of morality applied to all areas of life. These laws made no class distinctions and emphasized the protection of the poor, widows, orphans, and slaves.

The Israelites believed that certain religious leaders or "holy men," called prophets, were sent by God to serve as his voice to his people. In the ninth century B.C., the prophets were particularly vociferous about the tendency of the Israelites to accept other gods, chiefly the fertility and earth gods of other peoples in Palestine. They warned of the terrible retribution that Yahweh would exact from the Hebrews if they did not keep the covenant to remain faithful to him alone and just in their dealings with one another.

The golden age of prophecy began in the mideighth century B.C. and continued during the time when the people of Israel and Judah were threatened by Assyrian and Chaldean conquerors. These "men of God" went through the land warning the Israelites that they had failed to keep God's commandments and would be punished for breaking the covenant: "I will punish you for all your iniquities." Amos prophesied the fall of the northern kingdom of Israel to Assyria; twenty years later, Isaiah said the kingdom of Judah too would fall (see the box on p. 32).

Out of the words of the prophets came new concepts that enriched the Jewish tradition and ultimately Western civilization, including a notion of universalism and a yearning for social justice. Although the Jews' religious practices gave them a sense of separateness from other peoples, the prophets transcended this by embracing a concern for all humanity. All nations would someday come to the God of Israel: "all the earth shall worship you." A universal community of all people under God would someday be established by Israel's effort. This vision encompassed the elimination of war and the establishment of peace for all the nations of the world. In the words of the prophet Isaiah: "He will judge between the nations and will settle disputes for many people. They will beat their

THE HEBREW BIBLE. The Hebrew Bible was the main source of information about the spiritual conceptions of the Israelites. Shown here is a twelfth-century Hebrew manuscript of the Torah, the first five books of the Hebrew Bible.

swords into plowshares and their spears into pruning hooks. Nation will not take up sword against nation, nor will they train for war anymore."[5]

The prophets also cried out against social injustice. They condemned the rich for causing the poor to suffer, denounced luxuries as worthless, and threatened Israel with prophecies of dire punishments for these sins. God's command was to live justly, share with one's neighbors, care for the poor and the unfortunate, and act with compassion. When God's command was not followed, the social fabric of the community was threatened. These proclamations by Israel's prophets became a source for Western ideals of social justice, even if they have never been very perfectly realized.

Although the prophets eventually developed a sense of universalism, the demands of the Jewish

The Hebrew Prophets: Micah, Isaiah, and Amos

The Hebrew prophets warned the Israelites that they must obey God's commandments or face being punished for breaking their covenant with God. These selections from the prophets Micah, Isaiah, and Amos make clear that God's punishment would fall upon the Israelites for their sins. Even the Assyrians, as Isaiah indicated, would be used as God's instrument to punish them.

✹ *Micah 6: 9–16*

Listen! The Lord is calling to the city—and to fear your name is wisdom—"Heed the rod and the One who appointed it. Am I still to forget, O wicked house, your ill-gotten treasures. . . ? Shall I acquit a man with dishonest scales, with a bag of false weights? Her rich men are violent; her people are liars and their tongues speak deceitfully. Therefore, I have begun to destroy you, to ruin you because of your sins. You will eat but not be satisfied; your stomach will still be empty. You will store up but save nothing, because what you save I will give to the sword. You will plant but not harvest; you will press olives but not use the oil on yourselves, you will crush grapes but not drink the wine. . . . Therefore I will give you over to ruin and your people to derision; you will bear the scorn of the nations."

✹ *Isaiah 10: 1–6*

Woe to those who make unjust laws, to those who issue oppressive decrees, to deprive the poor of their rights and withhold justice from the oppressed of my people, making their prey and robbing the fatherless. What will you do on the day of reckoning, when disaster comes from afar? To whom will you run for help? Where will you leave your riches? Nothing will remain but to cringe among the captives or fall among the slain. Yet for all this, his anger is not turned away, his hand is still upraised. "Woe to the Assyrian, the rod of my anger, in whose hand is the club of my wrath! I send him against a godless nation, I dispatch him against a people who anger me, to seize loot and snatch plunder, and to trample them down like mud in the streets."

✹ *Amos 3: 1–2*

Hear this word the Lord has spoken against you, O people of Israel—against the whole family I brought up out of Egypt: "You only have I chosen of all the families of the earth; therefore, I will punish you for all your sins."

---

religion—the obligation to obey their God—encouraged a separation between the Jews and their non-Jewish neighbors. Unlike most other peoples of the Near East, Jews could not simply be amalgamated into a community by accepting the gods of their conquerors and their neighbors. To remain faithful to the demands of their God, they might even have to refuse loyalty to political leaders.

✹ *The Neighbors of the Israelites*

The Israelites were not the only people who settled in Palestine. The Philistines, who invaded from the sea, established five towns on the coastal plain of the region. They settled down as farmers and eventually entered into conflict with the Israelites. Although the Philistines were newcomers to the area, the Phoenicians had resided there for some time but now found themselves with a new independence. A Semitic-speaking people, the Phoenicians resided along the Mediterranean coast on a narrow band of land 120 miles long. They had rebuilt their major cities after destruction by the Sea Peoples. Their newfound political independence helped the Phoenicians expand the trade that was already the foundation of their prosperity. In fact, the Phoenician city of Byblos had been the principal distribution center for Egyptian papyrus outside Egypt (the Greek word for book, *biblos*, is derived from the name Byblos).

The chief cities of Phoenicia—Byblos, Tyre, and Sidon—were ports on the eastern Mediterranean, but they also served as distribution centers for the lands to the east in Mesopotamia. The Phoenicians themselves produced a number of goods for foreign markets, including purple dye, glass, wine, and lumber from the famous cedars of Lebanon. In addition, the Phoenicians improved their ships and became the great international sea traders of the ancient Near East. They charted new routes, not only in the Mediterranean but also in the Atlantic Ocean, where they reached Britain and sailed south along the west coast of Africa. The Phoenicians established a number of colonies in the western Mediterranean, including settlements in southern Spain, Sicily, and Sardinia. Carthage, the Phoenicians' most famous colony, was located on the North African coast.

Culturally, the Phoenicians are best known as transmitters. Instead of using pictographs or signs to represent whole words and syllables as the Mesopotamians and Egyptians did, the Phoenicians simplified their writing by using twenty-two different signs to represent the sounds of their speech. These twenty-two characters or letters could be used to spell out all the words in the Phoenician language. Although the Phoenicians were not the only people to invent an alphabet, theirs would have special significance because it was eventually passed on to the Greeks. The Phoenicians achieved much while independent, but they ultimately fell subject to the Assyrians, Chaldeans, and Persians.

◆ The Assyrian Empire

The existence of independent states in Palestine was possible only because of the power vacuum existing in the ancient Near East after the destruction of the Hittite kingdom and the weakening of the Egyptian empire. But this condition did not last; new empires soon arose and came to dominate vast stretches of the ancient Near East. The first of these empires emerged in Assyria, an area whose location on the upper Tigris River brought it into both cultural and political contact with southern Mesopotamia.

Although part of Mesopotamia, Assyria, with its hills and adequate, if not ample, rainfall, had a different terrain and climate. The Assyrians were a Semitic-speaking people who exploited the use of iron weapons to establish an empire by 700 B.C. that included Mesopotamia, parts of the Iranian plateau, sections of Asia Minor, Syria, Palestine, and Egypt down to Thebes (see Map 2.2). Ashurbanipal (669–626 B.C.) was one of the strongest Assyrian rulers, but it was already becoming apparent during his

MAP 2.2   **The Assyrian and Neo-Babylonian Empires.**

reign that the Assyrian Empire was greatly overextended. Internal strife intensified as powerful Assyrian nobles gained control of vast territories and waged their own private military campaigns. Moreover, subject peoples, such as the Babylonians, greatly resented Assyrian rule and rebelled against it. Soon after Ashurbanipal's reign, the Assyrian Empire began to disintegrate rapidly. The capital city of Nineveh fell to a coalition of Chaldeans and Medes in 612 B.C., and in 605 B.C., the rest of the empire was finally divided between the coalition powers.

At its height, the Assyrian Empire was ruled by kings whose power was considered absolute. Under their leadership, the Assyrian Empire became well organized. By eliminating governorships held by nobles on a hereditary basis and instituting a new hierarchy of local officials directly responsible to the king, the Assyrian kings gained greater control over the resources of the empire. The Assyrians also developed an efficient system of communication to administer their empire more effectively. A network of posting stages was established throughout the empire that used relays of horses (mules or donkeys in mountainous terrain) to carry messages. The system was so effective that a provincial governor anywhere in the empire (except Egypt) could send a question and receive an answer from the king in his palace within a week.

The ability of the Assyrians to conquer and maintain an empire was due to a combination of factors. Over many years of practice, the Assyrians developed effective military leaders and fighters. They were able to enlist and deploy troops numbering in the hundreds of thousands, although most campaigns were not conducted on such a large scale. In 845 B.C., an Assyrian army of 120,000 men crossed the Euphrates on a campaign. Size alone was not decisive, however. The Assyrian army was extremely well organized and disciplined. It included a standing army of infantrymen as its core, accompanied by cavalrymen and horse-drawn war chariots that were used as mobile platforms for shooting arrows. Moreover, the Assyrians had the advantage of having the first large armies equipped with iron weapons. The Hittites had been the first to develop iron metallurgy, but iron came to be used extensively only after new methods for hardening it became common after 1000 B.C.

Another factor in the army's success was its ability to use different kinds of military tactics (see the box on p. 35). The Assyrian army was capable of waging guerrilla warfare in the mountains and set battles on open ground as well as laying siege to cities. The Assyrians were especially renowned for their siege warfare. They would hammer a city's walls with heavy, wheeled siege towers and armored battering rams,

KING ASHURBANIPAL'S LION HUNT. This relief, sculptured on alabaster as a decoration for the northern palace in Nineveh, depicts King Ashurbanipal engaged in a lion hunt. The relief sculpture, one of the best-known forms of Assyrian art, ironically reached its high point under Ashurbanipal just as the Assyrian Empire began to disintegrate.

The Assyrian Military Machine

The Assyrians won a reputation for having a mighty military machine. They were able to use a variety of military tactics and were successful whether they were employing guerrilla warfare, fighting set battles, or laying siege to cities. In these three selections, Assyrian kings describe their military conquests.

✳ King Sennacherib (704–681 B.C.) Describes a Battle with the Elamites in 691

At the command of the god Ashur, the great Lord, I rushed upon the enemy like the approach of a hurricane. . . . I put them to rout and turned them back. I transfixed the troops of the enemy with javelins and arrows. . . . I cut their throats like sheep. . . . My prancing steeds, trained to harness, plunged into their welling blood as into a river; the wheels of my battle chariot were bespattered with blood and filth. I filled the plain with the corpses of their warriors like herbage. . . . As to the sheikhs of the Chaldeans, panic from my onslaught overwhelmed them like a demon. They abandoned their tents and fled for their lives, crushing the corpses of their troop as they went. . . . In their terror they passed scalding urine and voided their excrement into their chariots.

✳ King Sennacherib Describes His Siege of Jerusalem (701 B.C.)

As to Hezekiah, the Jew, he did not submit to my yoke, I laid siege to forty-six of his strong cities, walled forts and to the countless small villages in their vicinity, and conquered them by means of well-stamped earth-ramps, and battering-rams brought thus near to the walls combined with the attack by foot soldiers, using mines, breeches as well as sapper work. I drove out of them 200,150 people, young and old, male and female, horses, mules, donkeys, camels, big and small cattle beyond counting, and considered them booty. Himself I made a prisoner in Jerusalem, his royal residence, like a bird in a cage. I surrounded him with earthwork in order to molest those who were leaving his city's gate.

✳ King Ashurbanipal (669–626 B.C.) Describes His Treatment of Conquered Babylon

I tore out the tongues of those whose slanderous mouths had uttered blasphemies against my god Ashur and had plotted against me, his god-fearing prince; I defeated them completely. The others, I smashed alive with the very same statues of protective deities with which they had smashed my own grandfather Sennacherib—now finally as a belated burial sacrifice for his soul. I fed their corpses, cut into small pieces, to dogs, pigs, . . . vultures, the birds of the sky and also the fish of the ocean. After I had performed this and thus made quiet again the hearts of the great gods, my lords, I removed the corpses of those whom the pestilence had felled, whose leftovers after the dogs and pigs had fed on them were obstructing the streets, filling the places of Babylon, and of those who had lost their lives through the terrible famine.

while sappers dug tunnels to undermine the walls' foundations and cause them to collapse. The besieging Assyrian armies learned to cut off supplies so effectively that if a city did not fall to them, the inhabitants could be starved into submission.

A final factor in the effectiveness of the Assyrian military machine was its ability to create a climate of terror as an instrument of warfare. The Assyrians became famous for their terror tactics, although some historians believe that their policies were no worse than those of other conquerors.

As a matter of regular policy, the Assyrians laid waste the land in which they were fighting, smashing dams, looting and destroying towns, setting crops on fire, and cutting down trees, particularly fruit trees. The Assyrians were especially known for committing atrocities on their captives. King Ashurnasirpal recorded this account of his treatment of prisoners:

> 3000 of their combat troops I felled with weapons. . . .
> Many of the captives taken from them I burned in a fire.
> Many I took alive; from some of these I cut off their hands

to the wrist, from others I cut off their noses, ears and fingers; I put out the eyes of many of the soldiers. . . . I burned their young men and women to death.[6]

After conquering another city, the same king wrote: "I fixed up a pile of corpses in front of the city's gate. I flayed the nobles, as many as had rebelled, and spread their skins out on the piles. . . . I flayed many within my land and spread their skins out on the walls."[7] (Obviously, not a king to play games with!) Note that this policy of extreme cruelty to prisoners was not used against all enemies but was reserved primarily for those who were already part of the empire and then rebelled against Assyrian rule.

※ *Assyrian Society and Culture*

Unlike the Hebrews, the Assyrians were not fearful of mixing with other peoples. In fact, the Assyrian policy of deporting many prisoners of newly conquered territories to Assyria created a polyglot society in which ethnic differences were not very important. It has been estimated that over a period of three centuries, between four and five million people were deported to Assyria, resulting in a population that was very racially and linguistically mixed. What gave identity to the Assyrians themselves was their language, although even that was akin to that of their southern neighbors in Babylonia, who also spoke a Semitic tongue. Religion was also a cohesive force. Assyria was literally "the land of Ashur," a reference to its chief god. The king, as the human representative of the god Ashur, provided a final unifying focus.

Agriculture formed the principal basis of Assyrian life. Assyria was a land of farming villages with relatively few significant cities, especially in comparison to southern Mesopotamia. Unlike the river valleys, where farming required the minute organization of large numbers of people to control irrigation, Assyrian farms received sufficient moisture from regular rainfall.

Trade was second to agriculture in economic importance. For internal trade, metals, such as gold, silver, copper, and bronze, were used as a medium of exchange. Various agricultural products also served as a form of payment or exchange. Because of their geographical location, the Assyrians served as middlemen and participated in an international trade in which they imported timber, wine, and precious metals and stones while exporting textiles produced in palaces, temples, and private villas.

Assyrian culture was a hybrid. The Assyrians assimilated much of Mesopotamian civilization and saw themselves as guardians of Sumerian and Babylonian culture. Ashurbanipal, for example, established a large library at Nineveh that included the available works of Mesopotamian history. Assyrian kings also tried to maintain old traditions when they rebuilt damaged temples by constructing the new buildings on the original foundations, not in new locations. Assyrian religion reflected this assimilation of other cultures as well. Although the Assyrians had their own national god, Ashur, as their chief deity, virtually all of their remaining gods and goddesses were Mesopotamian.

Among the best-known objects of Assyrian art are the relief sculptures found in the royal palaces in three of the Assyrian capital cities, Nimrud, Nineveh, and Khorsabad. These reliefs, which were begun in the ninth century and reached their high point in the reign of Ashurbanipal in the seventh century, depicted two different kinds of subject matter: ritual or ceremonial scenes, revolving around the person of the king, and scenes of hunting and war. The latter show realistic action scenes of the king and his warriors engaged in battle or hunting animals, especially lions. These pictures depict a strongly masculine world where discipline, brute force, and toughness are the enduring values, indeed, the very values of the Assyrian military monarchy.

◆ The Persian Empire

The Chaldeans, a Semitic-speaking people, had gained ascendancy in Babylonia by the seventh century and came to form the chief resistance to Assyrian control of Mesopotamia. After the collapse of the Assyrian Empire, the Chaldeans, under their king Nebuchadnezzar II (605–562 B.C.), regained for Babylonia a position as the leading power in the ancient Near East.

Nebuchadnezzar rebuilt Babylon as the center of his empire, giving it a reputation as one of the great cities of the ancient world. Babylon was surrounded by great walls, 8 miles in length, encircled by a moat filled by the Euphrates River. The city was adorned with temples and palaces; most famous of all were the Hanging Gardens, known as one of the Seven Wonders of the ancient world. These were supposedly built to satisfy Nebuchadnezzar's wife, a princess from the land of Media, who missed the mountains of her

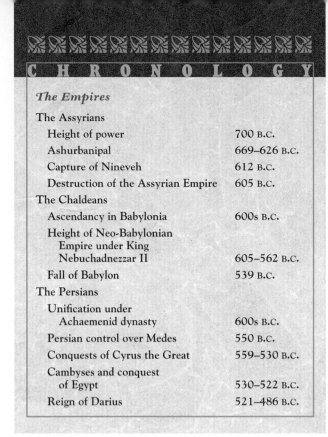

homeland. A series of terraces led to a plateau, an artificial mountain, at the top of which grew the lush gardens irrigated by water piped to the top. From a distance the gardens appeared to be suspended in air. But the splendor of the Neo-Babylonian Empire proved to be short-lived when Babylon fell to the Persians in 539 B.C.

The Persians were an Indo-European-speaking people who lived in southwestern Iran. Primarily nomadic, the Persians were organized in tribes or clans led by petty kings assisted by a group of warriors who formed a class of nobles. At the beginning of the seventh century, the Persians became unified under the Achaemenid dynasty, based in Persis in southern Iran. One of the dynasty's members, Cyrus (559–530 B.C.), created a powerful Persian state that rearranged the political map of the ancient Near East.

In 550 B.C., Cyrus established Persian control over Media, making it the first Persian satrapy or province. Three years later, Cyrus defeated the prosperous Lydian kingdom in western Asia Minor, and Lydia became another Persian satrapy. Cyrus's forces then went on to conquer the Greek city-states that had been established on the Ionian coast. Cyrus then turned eastward, subduing the eastern part of the Iranian plateau, Sogdiana, and even western India. His

eastern frontiers secured, Cyrus entered Mesopotamia in 539 and captured Babylon. His treatment of Babylonia showed remarkable restraint and wisdom. Babylonia was made into a Persian province under a Persian satrap, but many government officials were kept in their positions. Cyrus took the title "King of All, Great King, Mighty King, King of Babylon, King of the Land of Sumer and Akkad, King of the Four Rims (of the Earth), the Son of Cambyses the Great King, King of Anshan"[8] and insisted that he stood in the ancient, unbroken line of Babylonian kings. By appealing to the vanity of the Babylonians, he won their loyalty. Cyrus also issued an edict permitting the Jews, who had been brought to Babylon in the sixth century B.C., to return to Jerusalem with their sacred temple objects and to rebuild their temple as well.

To his contemporaries, Cyrus the Great was deserving of his epithet. The Greek historian Herodotus recounted that the Persians viewed him as a "father," a ruler who was "gentle, and procured them all manner of goods."[9] Certainly, Cyrus must have been an unusual ruler for his time, a man who demonstrated considerable wisdom and compassion in the conquest and organization of his empire. Cyrus attempted—successfully—to obtain the favor of the priesthoods in his conquered lands by restoring temples and permitting a wide degree of religious toleration. He won approval by using not only Persians, but also native peoples as government officials in their own states. Unlike the Assyrian rulers of an earlier empire, he had a reputation for mercy. Medes, Babylonians, Hebrews, all accepted him as their legitimate ruler. Indeed, the Hebrews regarded him as the anointed one of God: "I am the Lord who says of Cyrus, 'He is my shepherd and will accomplish all that I please'; he will say of Jerusalem, 'Let it be rebuilt'; and of the temple, 'Let its foundations be laid.' This is what the Lord says to his anointed, to Cyrus, whose right hand I take hold of to subdue nations before him."[10] Cyrus had a genuine respect for ancient civilizations—in building his palaces, he made use of Assyrian, Babylonian, Egyptian, and Lydian practices. Indeed, Cyrus had a sense that he was creating a "world empire" that include peoples who had ancient and venerable traditions and institutions.

Cyrus's successors extended the territory of the Persian Empire. His son Cambyses (530–522 B.C.) undertook a successful invasion of Egypt and made it into a satrapy with Memphis as its capital. Darius (521–486 B.C.) added a new Persian province in western India that extended to the Indus River and moved

MAP 2.3   The Persian Empire at the Time of Darius.

into Europe proper, conquering Thrace and making the Macedonian king a vassal (see Map 2.3). A revolt of the Ionian Greek cities in 499 B.C. resulted in temporary freedom for these communities in western Asia Minor. Aid from the Greek mainland, most notably from Athens, encouraged the Ionians to invade Lydia and burn Sardis, center of the Lydian satrap. This event led to Darius's involvement with the mainland Greeks. After reestablishing control of the Ionian Greek cities, Darius undertook an invasion of the Greek mainland, which culminated in the famous Athenian victory in the Battle of Marathon in 490 B.C. (see Chapter 3).

✳ *Governing the Empire*

By the reign of Darius, the Persians had created the largest empire the world had yet seen. It included not only all the old centers of power in the Near East, Egypt, Mesopotamia, and Assyria but also extended into Thrace and Asia Minor in the west and into India in the east. For administrative purposes, the empire had been divided into approximately twenty provinces called satrapies. Each province was ruled by a gover-

nor or satrap, literally a "protector of the Kingdom." Although Darius had not introduced the system of satrapies, he did see that it was organized more rationally. He created a sensible system for calculating the tribute that each satrapy owed to the central government and gave satraps specific civil and military duties. They collected tributes, were responsible for justice and security, raised military levies for the royal army, and normally commanded the military forces within their satrapies. In terms of real power, the satraps were miniature kings with courts imitative of the Great King's.

From the time of Darius on, satraps were men of Persian descent. The major satrapies were given to princes of the royal family, and their position became essentially hereditary. The minor satrapies were placed in the hands of Persian nobles. Their offices, too, tended to pass from father to son. The hereditary nature of the governors' offices made it necessary to provide some checks on their power. Consequently, royal officials at the satrapal courts acted as spies for the Great King.

An efficient system of communication was crucial to sustaining the Persian Empire. Well-maintained roads facilitated the rapid transit of military and government personnel. One in particular, the so-called Royal Road, stretched from Sardis, the center of Lydia in Asia Minor, to Susa, the chief capital of the Persian Empire. Like the Assyrians, the Persians established staging posts equipped with fresh horses for the king's messengers.

In this vast administrative system, the Persian king occupied an exalted position. Although not considered to be a god in the manner of an Egyptian pharaoh, he was nevertheless the elect one or regent of the Persian god Ahuramazda. All subjects were the king's servants, and he was the source of all justice, possessing the power of life and death over everyone. Persian kings were largely secluded and not easily accessible. They resided in a series of splendid palaces. Darius in particular was a palace builder on a grand scale. His description of the construction of a palace in the chief Persian capital of Susa demonstrated what a truly international empire Persia was:

> This is the . . . palace which at Susa I built. From afar its ornamentation was brought. . . . The cedar timber was brought from a mountain named Lebanon; the Assyrians brought it to Babylon, and from Babylon the Carians and Ionians brought it to Susa. Teakwood was brought from Gandara and from Carmania. The gold which was used here was brought from Sardis and from Bactria. The stone—lapis lazuli and carnelian—was brought from Sogdiana. . . . The silver and copper were brought from Egypt. The ornamentation with which the wall was adorned was brought from Ionia. The ivory was brought from Ethiopia, from India, and from Arachosia. The stone pillars were brought from . . . Elam. The artisans who dressed the stone were Ionians and Sardians. The goldsmiths who wrought the gold were Medes and Egyptians. . . . Those who worked the baked brick (with figures) were Babylonians. The men who adorned the wall were Medes and Egyptians. At Susa here a splendid work was ordered; very splendid did it turn out.[11]

DARIUS, THE GREAT KING.   Darius ruled the Persian Empire from 521 to 486 B.C. He is shown here on his throne in Persepolis, a new capital city that he built. In his right hand, Darius holds the royal staff. In his left hand, he grasps a lotus blossom with two buds, a symbol of royalty.

But Darius was unhappy with Susa. He did not really consider it his homeland, and it was oppressively hot in the summer months. He built another residence at Persepolis, a new capital located to the southeast of the old one at a higher elevation.

The policies of Darius also tended to widen the gap between the king and his subjects. As the Great King himself said of all his subjects: "what was said to them by me, night and day it was done."[12] Over a period of time, the Great Kings in their greed came to hoard immense quantities of gold and silver in the various treasuries located in the capital cities. Both their hoarding of wealth and their later overtaxation of their subjects are seen as crucial factors in the ultimate weakening of the Persian Empire (see the box on p. 40).

In its heyday, however, the empire stood supreme, and much of its power depended on the military. By the time of Darius, the Persian monarchs had created a standing army of professional soldiers. This army was truly international, composed of contingents from the various peoples who made up the empire. At its core was a cavalry force of 10,000 and an elite infantry force of 10,000 Medes and Persians

A Dinner with the Persian King

The Persian kings lived in luxury as a result of their conquests and ability to levy taxes from their conquered subjects. In this selection, we read a description of how a Persian king dined with his numerous guests.

✳ Athenaeus, The Deipnosophists, IV: 145–46

Heracleides of Cumae, author of the *Persian History*, writes in the second book of the work entitled *Equipment*: "All who attend upon the Persian kings when they dine first bathe themselves and then serve in white clothes, and spend nearly half the day on preparations for the dinner. Of those who are invited to eat with the king, some dine outdoors, in full sight of anyone who wishes to look on; others dine indoors in the king's company. Yet even these do not eat in his presence, for there are two rooms opposite each other, in one of which the king has his meal, in the other the invited guests. The king can see them through the curtain at the door, but they cannot see him. Sometimes, however, on the occasion of a public holiday, all dine in a single room with the king, in the great hall. And whenever the king commands a symposium [drinking-bout following the dinner] which he does often, he has about a dozen companions at the drinking. When they have finished dinner, that is the king by himself, the guests in the other room, these fellow-drinkers are summoned by one of the eunuchs; and

entering they drink with him, though even they do not have the same wine; moreover, they sit on the floor, while he reclines on a couch supported by feet of gold, and they depart after having drunk to excess. In most cases the king breakfasts and dines alone, but sometimes his wife and some of his sons dine with him. And throughout the dinner his concubines sing and play the lyre; one of them is the soloist, the others sing in chorus. And so, Heracleides continues, the 'king's dinner,' as it is called, will appear prodigal to one who merely hears about it, but when one examines it carefully it will be found to have been got up with economy and even with parsimony; and the same is true of the dinners among other Persians of high station. For one thousand animals are slaughtered daily for the king; these comprise horses, camels, oxen, asses, deer, and most of the small animals; many birds are also consumed, including Arabian ostriches—and the creature is large—geese, and cocks. And of all these only moderate portions are served to each of the king's guests, and each of them may carry home whatever he leaves untouched at the meal. But the greater part of these meats and other foods are taken into the courtyard for the body-guard and light-armed troopers maintained by the king; there they divide all the half-eaten remnants of meat and bread and share them in equal portions. . . ."

known as the Immortals because they were never allowed to fall below 10,000 in number. When one was killed, he was immediately replaced. The Persians made effective use of their cavalry, especially for operating behind enemy lines and breaking up lines of communication.

✳ Persian Religion

Of all the Persians' cultural contributions, the most original was their religion. The popular religion of the Iranians before the advent of Zoroastrianism in the sixth century B.C. focused on the worship of the powers of nature, such as the sun, moon, fire, and winds. Mithra was an especially popular god of light and war who came to be viewed as a sun god. The people wor-

shiped and sacrificed to these powers of nature with the aid of priests, known as Magi.

Zoroaster was a semilegendary figure who, according to Persian tradition, was born in 660 B.C. After a period of wandering and solitude, he experienced revelations that caused him to be revered as a prophet of the "true religion." It is difficult to know what Zoroaster's original teachings were since the sacred book of Zoroastrianism, the *Zend Avesta*, was not written down until the third century A.D. Scholars believe, however, that the earliest section of the *Zend Avesta*, known as the *Yasna*, consisting of seventeen hymns or *gathas*, contains the actual writings of Zoroaster. This enables us to piece together his message.

That spiritual message was grounded in a monotheistic framework. Although Ahuramazda was not a new god to the Iranians, to Zoroaster he was the only god and the religion he preached was the only perfect one. Ahuramazda (the "Wise Lord") was the supreme deity who brought all things into being:

> This I ask of You, O Ahuramazda; answer me well:
> Who at the Creation was the first father of Justice?—
> Who assigned their path to the sun and the stars?—
> Who decreed the waxing and waning of the moon, if it
>   was not You?— . . .
> Who has fixed the earth below, and the heaven above
>   with its clouds that it might not be moved?—
> Who has appointed the waters and the green things
>   upon the earth?—
> Who has harnessed to the wind and the clouds their
>   steeds?— . . .
> Thus do I strive to recognize in You, O Wise One,
> Together with the Holy Spirit, the Creator of all
>   things.[13]

According to Zoroaster, Ahuramazda also possessed abstract qualities or states that all humans should aspire to, such as Good Thought, Right, and Piety. Although Ahuramazda was supreme, he was not unopposed. Right is opposed by the Lie, Truth by Falsehood, Life by Death. At the beginning of the world, the good spirit of Ahuramazda was opposed by the evil spirit (in later Zoroastrianism, the evil spirit is identified with Ahriman). Although it appears that Zoroaster saw it as simply natural that where there is good, there will be evil, later followers had a tendency to make these abstractions concrete and overemphasize the reality of an evil spirit. Humans also played a role in this cosmic struggle between good and evil. Ahuramazda, the creator, gave all humans free will and the power to choose between right and wrong. The good person chooses the right way of Ahuramazda. Zoroaster taught that there would be an end to the struggle between good and evil. Ahuramazda would eventually triumph, and at the last judgment at the end of the world, the final separation of good and evil would occur. Zoroaster also provided for individual judgment as well. Each soul faced a final evaluation of its actions. If a person had performed good deeds, he or she would achieve paradise, the "House of Song" or the "Kingdom of Good Thought"; if evil deeds, then the soul would be thrown into an abyss, the "House of Worst Thought," where it would experience future ages of darkness, torment, and misery.

The spread of Zoroastrianism was due to its acceptance by the Great Kings of Persia. The inscriptions of Darius make clear that he believed Ahuramazda was the only god. Although Darius himself may

ARCHERS OF THE PERSIAN GUARD. One of the main pillars supporting the Persian Empire was the military. This frieze, composed of enameled brick, depicts members of the famous infantry force known as the Immortals, so called because their number was never allowed to drop below 10,000. Those killed would be replaced immediately. The men in the frieze carry the standard lance and bow and arrow of the infantry.

have been a monotheist, as the kings and Magi propagated Zoroaster's teachings on Ahuramazda, dramatic changes occurred. Zoroastrianism lost its monotheistic emphasis, and the old nature worship resurfaced. Persian religion returned to polytheism, with Ahuramazda becoming the chief of a number of gods of light. Mithra, the sun god, became a helper of Ahuramazda and later, in Roman times, the source of another religion. Persian kings were also very tolerant of other religions, and gods and goddesses of those religions tended to make their way into the Persian pantheon. Moreover, as frequently happens to the ideas of founders of religions, Zoroaster's teachings acquired concrete forms that he had never originally intended. The struggle between good and evil was taken beyond the abstractions of Zoroaster into a strong ethical dualism. The spirit of evil became an actual being who had to be warded off by the use of spells and incantations. Descriptions of the last judgment came to be filled with minute physical details. Some historians believe that Zoroastrianism, with its emphasis on good and evil, a final judgment, and individual judgment of souls, had an impact on Christianity, a religion that eventually surpassed it in significance.

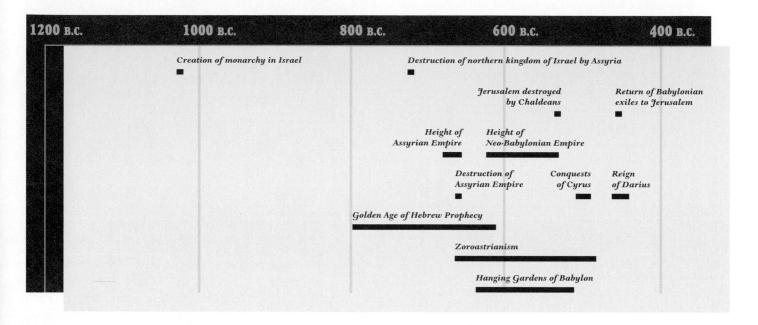

| 1200 B.C. | 1000 B.C. | 800 B.C. | 600 B.C. | 400 B.C. |

Creation of monarchy in Israel

Destruction of northern kingdom of Israel by Assyria

Jerusalem destroyed by Chaldeans

Return of Babylonian exiles to Jerusalem

Height of Assyrian Empire

Height of Neo-Babylonian Empire

Destruction of Assyrian Empire

Conquests of Cyrus

Reign of Darius

Golden Age of Hebrew Prophecy

Zoroastrianism

Hanging Gardens of Babylon

Conclusion

Around 1200 B.C., the decline of the Hittites and Egyptians had created a void that allowed a number of small states to emerge and flourish temporarily. All of them were eventually overshadowed by the rise of the great empires of the Assyrians, Chaldeans, and Persians. The Assyrian Empire was the first to unite almost all of the ancient Near East. Even larger, however, was the empire of the Great Kings of Persia. Although it owed much to the administrative organization created by the Assyrians, the Persian Empire had its own peculiar strengths. Persian rule was tolerant as well as efficient. Conquered peoples were allowed to keep their own religions, customs, and methods of doing business. The many years of peace that the Persian Empire brought to the Near East facilitated trade and the general well-being of its peoples. It is no wonder that many peoples expressed their gratitude for being subjects of the Great Kings of Persia.

The Hebrews were one of these peoples. They created no empire and were dominated by the Assyrians, Chaldeans, and Persians. Nevertheless, they left a spiritual legacy that influenced much of the later development of Western civilization. The evolution of Hebrew monotheism helped Judaism become one of the world's greatest religions; it influenced the development of both Christianity and Islam. When we speak of the Judeo-Christian heritage of Western civilization, we refer not only to the concept of monotheism but also to ideas of law, morality, and social justice that have become important parts of Western culture.

On the western fringes of the Persian Empire, another relatively small group of people, the Greeks, were evolving cultural and political ideals that would also have an important impact on Western civilization. It is to the Greeks that we must now turn.

Notes

1. Psalms 137: 1, 4–6.
2. Psalms 145: 8–9.
3. Psalms 121: 2–3.
4. Exodus 20: 13–15.
5. Isaiah 2: 4.
6. Quoted in H. W. F. Saggs, *The Might That Was Assyria* (London, 1984), p. 261.
7. Ibid., p. 262.
8. Quoted in J. M. Cook, *The Persian Empire* (New York, 1983), p. 32.
9. Herodotus, *The Persian Wars*, trans. George Rawlinson (New York, 1942), p. 257.
10. Isaiah, 44: 28; 45: 1.
11. Quoted in A. T. Olmstead, *History of the Persian Empire* (Chicago, 1948), p. 168.
12. Quoted in Cook, *The Persian Empire*, p. 76.
13. Yasna 44: 3–4, 7, as quoted in A. C. Bouquet, *Sacred Books of the World* (Harmondsworth, England, 1954), pp. 111–112.

Suggestions for Further Reading

On the Sea Peoples, see the standard work by N. K. Sandars, *The Sea Peoples: Warriors of the Ancient Mediterranean* (London, 1978). A good introductory survey on the Hittites can be found in O. R. Gurney, *The Hittites*, 2d ed. (Harmondsworth, England, 1981).

For an excellent general survey of the material covered in this chapter, see A. Kuhrt, *The Ancient Near East, c. 3000–330 B.C.*, Vol. 2 (London, 1995). An enormous amount of literature on ancient Israel exists. Two good studies on the archaeological aspects are A. Mazar, *Archaeology of the Land of the Bible* (New York, 1992), and A. Ben-Tor, ed., *The Archaeology of Ancient Israel* (New Haven, Conn., 1992). For historical narratives, see especially J. Bright, *A History of Israel*, 3d ed. (Philadelphia, 1981), a fundamental study; J. M. Miller and J. H. Hayes, *A History of Ancient Israel and Judah* (Philadelphia, 1986); the well-done survey by M. Grant, *The History of Ancient Israel* (New York, 1984); J. A. Soggin, *A History of Israel* (London, 1984); and H. Shanks, *Ancient Israel: A Short History from Abraham to the Roman Destruction of the Temple* (Englewood Cliffs, N.J., 1988). For a new perspective, see N. P. Lemche, *Ancient Israel: A New History of Israelite Society* (Sheffield, England, 1988). A brief summary of Hebrew history and thought can be found in J. H. Hexter, *The Judaeo-Christian Tradition* (New York, 1966).

For general studies on the religion of the Hebrews, see R. Albertz, *A History of Israelite Religion in the Old Testament Period* (Louisville, Ky., 1994), and W. J. Doorly, *The Religion of Israel* (New York, 1997). The role of the prophets is examined in J. Lindblom, *Prophecy in Ancient Israel* (Oxford, 1962), and R. B. Y. Scott, *The Relevance of the Prophets* (New York, 1968).

For a good account of the Phoenician domestic and overseas expansion, see D. Harden, *The Phoenicians*, rev. ed. (Harmondsworth, England, 1980). See also M. E. Aubet, *The Phoenicians and the West: Politics, Colonies and Trade* (Cambridge, 1993).

A detailed account of Assyrian political, economic, social, military, and cultural history is H. W. F. Saggs, *The Might That Was Assyria* (London, 1984). A. T. Olmstead, *History of Assyria* (Chicago, 1975), is a basic survey of the Assyrian Empire. Information from the Assyrians themselves can be found in A. Grayson, *Assyrian and Babylonian Chronicles* (New York, 1975). The Neo-Babylonian Empire can be examined in J. Oates, *Babylon* (London, 1979), and H. W. F. Saggs, *Babylonians* (Norman, Okla., 1995).

The classic work on the Persian Empire is A. T. Olmstead, *History of the Persian Empire* (Chicago, 1948), but J. M. Cook, *The Persian Empire* (New York, 1983), provides additional material and fresh interpretations. Also of value are J. Curtis, *Ancient Persia* (Cambridge, Mass., 1990); B. Dicks, *The Ancient Persians* (Newton Abbott, England, 1979); and R. Frye, *The Heritage of Persia* (Cleveland, Ohio, 1963). On the history of Zoroastrianism, see especially R. C. Zaehner, *The Dawn and Twilight of Zoroastrianism: Their Religious Beliefs and Practices* (London, 1979).

For additional reading, go to InfoTrac College Edition, your online research library at http://web1.infotrac-college.com

Enter the search terms *Ancient Israel* using Key Terms.

Enter the search term *Assyrian* using Key Terms.

Enter the search term *Babylonian* using Key Terms.

Enter the search term *Phoenician* using Key Terms.

Enter the search term *Persian* using Key Terms.

3

The Civilization of the Greeks

CHAPTER OUTLINE

- Early Greece
- The Greeks in a Dark Age (c. 1100–c. 750 B.C.)
- The World of the Greek City-States (c. 750–c. 500 B.C.)
- The High Point of Greek Civilization: Classical Greece
- Conclusion

FOCUS QUESTIONS

- How did the geography of Greece affect Greek history?
- What was the *polis*, or city-state, and how did the major city-states of Athens and Sparta differ?
- What effect did the two great conflicts of the fifth century—the Persian Wars and the Peloponnesian War—have on Greek civilization?
- Upon what ideals was classical Greek art based, and how were these ideals expressed?
- What questions did the Greek philosophers pose, and what answers did they suggest?

*I*N 431 B.C., *war erupted in Greece as two very different Greek city-states—Athens and Sparta—fought for domination of the Greek world. The people of Athens felt secure behind their walls and in the first winter of the war held a public funeral to honor those who had died in battle. On the day of the ceremony, the citizens of Athens joined in a procession, with the relatives of the dead wailing for their loved ones. As was the custom in Athens, one leading citizen was asked to address the crowd, and on this day it was Pericles who spoke to the people. He talked about the greatness of Athens and reminded the Athenians of the strength of their political system: "Our constitution," he said, "is called a democracy because power is in the hands not of a minority but of the whole people. When it is a question of settling private disputes, everyone is equal* *before the law. Just as our political life is free and open, so is our day-to-day life in our relations with each other. . . . Here each individual is interested not only in his own affairs but in the affairs of the state as well."*

In this famous Funeral Oration, Pericles gave voice to the ideal of democracy and the importance of the individual. It was the Greeks who created the intellectual foundations of our Western heritage. They asked some basic questions about human life that still dominate our own intellectual pursuits: What is the nature of the universe? What is the purpose of human existence? What is our relationship to divine forces? What constitutes a community? What constitutes a state? What is true education? What are the true sources of law? What is truth itself and how do we realize it? Not only did the Greeks provide answers to these questions, but they created a system of logical, analytical thought to examine them. This rational outlook has remained an important feature of Western civilization.

The story of ancient Greek civilization is a remarkable one that begins with the first arrival of the Greeks around 2000 B.C. By the eighth century B.C., the characteristic institution of ancient Greek life, the polis *or city-state, had emerged. Greek civilization flourished and reached its height in the classical era of the fifth century* B.C., *which has come to be closely identified with the achievements of Athenian democracy.*

◆ Early Greece

Geography played an important role in the evolution of Greek history. Compared to the landmasses of Mesopotamia and Egypt, Greece occupied a small area. It was a mountainous peninsula that encompassed only 45,000 square miles of territory, about the size of the state of Louisiana. The mountains and the sea played especially significant roles in the development of Greek history. Much of Greece consists of small plains and river valleys surrounded by mountain ranges 8,000 to 10,000 feet high. The mountainous terrain had the effect of isolating Greeks from one another. Consequently, Greek communities tended to follow their own separate paths and develop their own way of life. Over a period of time, these communities became attached to their independence and were only too willing to fight one another to gain advantage. No doubt the small size of these independent Greek com-

munities fostered participation in political affairs and unique cultural expressions, but the rivalry among these communities also led to the bitter warfare that ultimately devastated Greek society.

The sea also influenced the evolution of Greek society. Greece had a long seacoast, dotted by bays and inlets that provided numerous harbors. The Greeks also inhabited a number of islands to the west, south, and particularly the east of the Greek mainland. It is no accident that the Greeks became seafarers who sailed out into the Aegean and the Mediterranean Seas first to make contact with the outside world and later to establish colonies that would spread Greek civilization throughout the Mediterranean world.

Greek topography helped determine the major territories into which Greece was ultimately divided. South of the Gulf of Corinth was the Peloponnesus, virtually an island (see Map 3.1). Consisting mostly of hills, mountains, and small valleys, the Peloponnesus was the location of Sparta, as well as the site of Olympia, where famous athletic games were held. Northeast of the Peloponnesus was the Attic peninsula (or Attica), the home of Athens, hemmed in by mountains to the north and west and surrounded by the sea to the south and east. Northwest of Attica was Boeotia in central Greece with its chief city of Thebes. To the north of Boeotia was Thessaly, which contained the largest plains and became a great producer of grain and horses. To the north of Thessaly lay Macedonia, which was not of much importance in Greek history until 338 B.C. when the Macedonian king Philip II conquered the Greeks.

※ *Minoan Crete*

The earliest civilization in the Aegean region emerged on Crete. By 2800 B.C., a Bronze Age civilization that used metals, especially bronze, for the construction of weapons had been established on the large island about 100 miles southeast of the Peloponnesus. The civilization of Minoan Crete was first discovered by the English archaeologist Arthur Evans, who named it *Minoan* after Minos, a legendary king of Crete. Evans's excavations on Crete at the beginning of the twentieth century led to the discovery of an enormous palace complex at Knossus near modern Heracleion. The remains revealed a rich and prosperous culture with Knossus as the probable center of a far-ranging "sea empire," probably largely commercial. We know from archaeological remains that the people of Minoan Crete were accustomed to sea travel and had

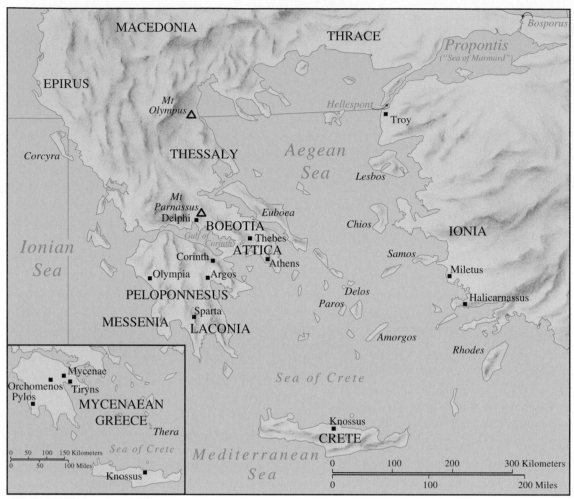

MAP 3.1 Classical Greece.

made contact with the more advanced civilization of Egypt.

The Minoan civilization reached its height between 2000 and 1450 B.C. The palace at Knossus, the royal seat of the kings, demonstrates the obvious prosperity and power of this civilization. It was an elaborate structure built around a central courtyard and included numerous private living rooms for the royal family and workshops for making decorated vases, small sculptures, and jewelry. Even bathrooms, with elaborate drains, formed part of the complex. The rooms were decorated with frescoes in bright colors showing sporting events and naturalistic scenes that have led some observers to conclude that the Cretans had a great love of nature. Storerooms in the palace held enormous jars of oil, wine, and grain, presumably paid as taxes to the king.

The centers of Minoan civilization on Crete suffered a sudden and catastrophic collapse around 1450 B.C. The cause of this destruction has been vigorously debated. Some historians believe that a tsunami triggered by a powerful volcanic eruption on the island of Thera was responsible for the devastation. Most historians, however, maintain that the destruction was the result of invasion and pillage by mainland Greeks known as the Mycenaeans.

✸ The First Greek State: The Mycenaeans

The term *Mycenaean* is derived from Mycenae, a remarkable fortified site first excavated by the amateur German archaeologist Heinrich Schliemann. Mycenae was one center in a Mycenaean Greek civilization that flourished between 1600 and 1100 B.C. The Mycenaean Greeks were part of the Indo-European family of peoples (see Chapter 2) who spread from their original location into southern and western Europe, India, and Iran. One group entered the territory of Greece from the north around 1900 B.C. and managed to gain control of the Greek mainland and develop a civilization.

THE MINOAN SPORT OF BULL LEAPING. Minoan bull games were held on festival days in the great palaces on the island of Crete. As seen in this fresco from the east wing of the palace at Knossus, women and men acrobats (the man in red) somersaulted over the back of the bull. Another person waited behind the bull to catch the leapers.

Mycenaean civilization, which reached its high point between 1400 and 1200 B.C., consisted of a number of powerful monarchies that resided in fortified palace complexes. Like Mycenae, they were built on hills and surrounded by gigantic stone walls. These various centers of power probably formed a loose confederacy of independent states, with Mycenae being the strongest. Next in importance to the kings in these states were the army commanders, priests, and the bureaucrats who kept careful records. The free citizenry included peasants, soldiers, and artisans, and the lowest rung of the social ladder consisted of serfs and slaves.

The Mycenaeans were, above all, a warrior people who prided themselves on their heroic deeds in battle. Some scholars believe that the Mycenaeans, led by Mycenae itself, spread outward militarily, conquering Crete and making it part of the Mycenaean world. The most famous of all their supposed military adventures has come down to us in the epic poetry of Homer (see "Homer" on pp. 48–49). Did the Mycenaean Greeks, led by Agamemnon, king of Mycenae, sack the city of Troy on the northwestern coast of Asia Minor around 1250 B.C.? Since the excavations of Heinrich Schliemann, begun in 1870, scholars have debated this question. Many believe that Homer's account does have a basis in fact.

By the late thirteenth century B.C., Mycenaean Greece was showing signs of serious trouble. Mycenae itself was torched around 1190 B.C., and other Mycenaean centers show similar patterns of destruction as new waves of Greek-speaking invaders moved into Greece from the north. By 1100 B.C., the Mycenaean culture was coming to an end, and the Greek world was entering a new period of considerable insecurity.

◆ The Greeks in a Dark Age (c. 1100–c. 750 B.C.)

After the collapse of Mycenaean civilization, Greece entered a difficult period in which the population declined and food production dropped. Because of the difficult conditions and our lack of knowledge about the period, historians call it a Dark Age. Not until 850 B.C. did farming revive. At the same time, some new developments were forming the basis for a revived Greece.

During the Dark Age, large numbers of Greeks left the mainland and migrated across the Aegean Sea to various islands and especially to the western shores of Asia Minor, a strip of territory that came to be called Ionia. Based on their dialect, the Greeks who

Homer's Ideal of Excellence

The Iliad *and the* Odyssey *were used as basic texts for the education of Greeks for hundreds of years in antiquity. This passage from the* Iliad, *describing a conversation between Hector, prince of Troy, and his wife, Andromache, illustrates the Greek ideal of gaining honor through combat. At the end of the passage, Homer also reveals what became the Greek attitude toward women: women are supposed to spin and weave and take care of their households and their children.*

❊ *Homer,* Iliad

Hector looked at his son and smiled, but said nothing. Andromache, bursting into tears, went up to him and put her hand in his. "Hector," she said, "you are possessed. This bravery of yours will be your end. You do not think of your little boy or your unhappy wife, whom you will make a widow soon. Some day the Achaeans [Greeks] are bound to kill you in a massed attack. And when I lose you I might as well be dead. . . . I have no father, no mother, now. . . . I had seven brothers too at home. In one day all of them went down to Hades' House. The great Achilles of the swift feet killed them all. . . ."

"So you, Hector, are father and mother and brother to me, as well as my beloved husband. Have pity on me now; stay here on the tower; and do not make your boy an orphan and your wife a widow. . . ."

"All that, my dear," said the great Hector of the glittering helmet, "is surely my concern. But if I hid myself like a coward and refused to fight, I could never face the Trojans and the Trojan ladies in their trailing gowns. Besides, it would go against the grain, for I have trained myself always, like a good soldier, to take my place in the front line and win glory for my father and myself. . . ."

As he finished, glorious Hector held out his arms to take his boy. But the child shrank back with a cry to the bosom of his girdled nurse, alarmed by his father's appearance. He was frightened by the bronze of the helmet and the horsehair plume that he saw nodding grimly down at him. His father and his lady mother had to laugh. But noble Hector quickly took his helmet off and put the dazzling thing on the ground. Then he kissed his son, dandled him in his arms, and prayed to Zeus and the other gods: "Zeus; and you other gods, grant that this boy of mine may be, like me, preeminent in Troy; as strong and brave as I; a mighty king of Ilium. May people say, when he comes back from battle, 'Here is a better man than his father.' Let him bring home the blood-stained armor of the enemy he has killed, and make his mother happy."

Hector handed the boy to his wife, who took him to her fragrant breast. She was smiling through her tears, and when her husband saw this he was moved. He stroked her with his hand and said: "My dear, I beg you not to be too much distressed. No one is going to send me down to Hades before my proper time. But Fate is a thing that no man born of woman, coward or hero, can escape. Go home now, and attend to your own work, the loom and the spindle, and see that the maidservants get on with theirs. War is men's business; and this war is the business of every man in Ilium, myself above all."

---

resided there were called Ionians. Two other major groups of Greeks settled in established parts of Greece. The Aeolian Greeks, located in northern and central Greece, colonized the large island of Lesbos and the adjacent territory of the mainland. The Dorians established themselves in southwestern Greece, especially in the Peloponnesus, as well as on some of the islands in the south Aegean Sea, including Crete.

Other important activities occurred in this Dark Age as well. Greece saw a revival of some trade and some economic activity besides agriculture. Iron came into use for the construction of weapons. And at some point in the eighth century B.C., the Greeks adopted the Phoenician alphabet to give themselves a new system of writing. Near the very end of this Dark Age appeared the work of Homer, who has come to be viewed as one of the great poets of all time.

❊ *Homer*

The *Iliad* and the *Odyssey*, the first great epic poems of early Greece, were based on stories that had been passed on from generation to generation. It is generally assumed that early in the eighth century B.C., Homer made use of these oral traditions to compose

---

the *Iliad*, his epic of the Trojan War. The war was caused by an act of Paris, a prince of Troy. By kidnapping Helen, wife of the king of the Greek state of Sparta, he outraged all the Greeks. Under the leadership of the Spartan king's brother, Agamemnon of Mycenae, the Greeks attacked Troy. Ten years later, the Greeks finally won and sacked the city.

But the *Iliad* is not so much the story of the war itself as it is the tale of the Greek hero Achilles and how the "wrath of Achilles" led to disaster. As is true of all great literature, the *Iliad* abounds in universal lessons. Underlying them all is the clear message, as one commentator has observed, that "men will still come and go like the generations of leaves in the forest; that he will still be weak, and the gods strong and incalculable; that the quality of a man matters more than his achievement; that violence and recklessness will still lead to disaster, and that this will fall on the innocent as well as on the guilty."[1]

The *Odyssey*, Homer's other masterpiece, is an epic romance that recounts the journeys of one of the Greek heroes, Odysseus, after the fall of Troy and his ultimate return to his wife. But there is a larger vision here as well: the testing of the heroic stature of Odysseus until, by both cunning and patience, he prevails. In the course of this testing, the underlying moral message is "that virtue is a better policy than vice."[2]

Although the *Iliad* and the *Odyssey* supposedly deal with the heroes of the Mycenaean age of the thirteenth century B.C., many scholars believe that they really describe the social conditions of the Dark Age. According to the Homeric view, Greece was a society based on agriculture in which a landed warrior-aristocracy controlled much wealth and exercised considerable power. Homer's world reflects the values of aristocratic heroes.

This, of course, explains the importance of Homer to later generations of Greeks. Homer did not so much record history as make it. The Greeks regarded the *Iliad* and the *Odyssey* as authentic history as recorded by one poet, Homer. These masterpieces gave the Greeks an ideal past with a cast of heroes and came to be used as standard texts for the education of generations of Greek males. As one Athenian stated, "My father was anxious to see me develop into a good man . . . and as a means to this end he compelled me to memorize all of Homer."[3] The values Homer taught were essentially the aristocratic values of courage and honor (see the box on p. 48). A hero strives for excellence, which the Greeks called *arete*. In the warrior-aristocratic world of Homer, *arete* is won in struggle or contest. Through his willingness to fight,

the hero protects his family and friends, preserves his own honor and that of his family, and earns his reputation. In the Homeric world, aristocratic women, too, were expected to pursue excellence. Penelope, for example, the wife of Odysseus, the hero of the *Odyssey*, remains faithful to her husband and displays great courage and intelligence in preserving their household during her husband's long absence. Upon his return, Odysseus praises her for her excellence: "Madame, there is not a man in the wide world who could find fault with you. For your fame has reached heaven itself, like that of some perfect king, ruling a populous and mighty state with the fear of god in his heart, and upholding the right."[4] Homer gave to the Greeks a model of heroism, honor, and nobility. But in time, as a new world of city-states emerged in Greece, new values of cooperation and community also transformed what the Greeks learned from Homer.

◆ The World of the Greek City-States (c. 750–c. 500 B.C.)

In the eighth century B.C., Greek civilization burst forth with new energies. Two major developments stand out in this era: the evolution of the *polis* as the central institution in Greek life and the Greeks' colonization of the Mediterranean and Black Seas.

✤ The Polis

The Greek *polis* (plural, *poleis*) developed slowly during the Dark Age and by the eighth century B.C. had emerged as a truly unique and fundamental institution in Greek society. In a physical sense, the *polis* encompassed a town or city or even a village and its surrounding countryside. But the town or city or village served as the focus or central point where the citizens of the *polis* could assemble for political, social, and religious activities. In some *poleis*, this central meeting point was a hill, like the Acropolis at Athens, which could serve as a place of refuge during an attack and later in some sites came to be the religious center on which temples and public monuments were erected. Below the acropolis would be an *agora*, an open place that served both as a place where citizens could assemble and as a market.

Poleis varied greatly in size, from a few square miles to a few hundred square miles. The larger ones were the product of consolidation. The territory of Attica, for example, had once had twelve *poleis* but eventually became a single *polis* (Athens) through a process of amalgamation. The population of Athens grew to over 300,000 by the fifth century B.C. Most *poleis* were much smaller, consisting of only a few hundred to several thousand people.

Although our word *politics* is derived from the Greek term *polis,* the *polis* itself was much more than just a political institution. It was, above all, a community of citizens in which all political, economic, social, cultural, and religious activities were focused. As a community, the *polis* consisted of citizens with political rights (adult males), citizens with no political rights (women and children), and noncitizens (slaves and resident aliens). All citizens of a *polis* possessed fundamental rights, but these rights were coupled with responsibilities. The Greek philosopher Aristotle argued that the citizen did not just belong to himself; "we must rather regard every citizen as belonging to the state." The unity of citizens was important and often meant that states would take an active role in directing the patterns of life. However, the loyalty that citizens had to their *poleis* also had a negative side. *Poleis* distrusted one another, and the division of Greece into fiercely patriotic sovereign units helped bring about its ruin.

As the *polis* developed, so did a new military system. In earlier times, wars in Greece had been fought by aristocratic cavalry soldiers—nobles on horseback. These aristocrats, who were large landowners, also dominated the political life of their *poleis.* But by the end of the eighth century and beginning of the seventh, a new military order came into being that was based on hoplites, heavily armed infantrymen who wore bronze or leather helmets, breastplates, and greaves (shin guards). Each carried a round shield, a short sword, and a thrusting spear about 9 feet long. Hoplites advanced into battle as a unit, forming a phalanx (a rectangular formation) in tight order, usually

THE HOPLITE FORCES. The Greek hoplites were infantrymen equipped with large round shields and long thrusting spears. In battle, they advanced in tight phalanx formation and were dangerous opponents as long as this formation remained unbroken. This vase painting of the seventh century B.C. shows two groups of hoplite warriors engaged in battle. The piper on the left is leading another line of soldiers preparing to enter the fray.

eight ranks deep. As long as the hoplites kept their order, were not outflanked, and did not break, they either secured victory or, at the very least, suffered no harm. The phalanx was easily routed, however, if it broke its order. The safety of the phalanx depended, above all, on the solidarity and discipline of its members. As one seventh-century B.C. poet noted, a good hoplite was "a short man firmly placed upon his legs, with a courageous heart, not to be uprooted from the spot where he plants his legs."[5]

The hoplite force had political as well as military repercussions. The aristocratic cavalry was now outdated. Since each hoplite provided his own armor, men of property, both aristocrats and small farmers, made up the new phalanx. Those who could become hoplites and fight for the state could also challenge aristocratic control.

❋ Colonization and the Rise of Tyrants

Between 750 and 550 B.C., large numbers of Greeks left their homeland to settle in distant lands. Poverty and land hunger created by the growing gulf between rich and poor, overpopulation, and the development of trade were all factors that led to the establishment of colonies. Some Greek colonies were simply trading posts or centers for the transshipment of goods to Greece. Most were larger settlements that included good agricultural land taken from the native populations found in those areas. Each colony was founded as a *polis* and was usually independent of the *metropolis* ("mother *polis*") that had established it.

In the western Mediterranean, new Greek settlements were established along the coastline of southern Italy, southern France, eastern Spain, and northern Africa west of Egypt. To the north, the Greeks set up colonies in Thrace, where they sought good farmland to grow grains. Greeks also settled along the shores of the Black Sea and secured the approaches to it with cities on the Hellespont and Bosporus, most noticeably Byzantium, site of the later Constantinople (Istanbul). By establishing these settlements, the Greeks spread their culture throughout the Mediterranean basin. Colonization also led to increased trade and industry. The Greeks on the mainland sent their pottery, wine, and olive oil to these areas; in return, they received grains and metals from the west and fish, timber, wheat, metals, and slaves from the Black Sea region. In many *poleis*, the expansion of trade and industry created a new group of rich men who desired political privileges commensurate with their wealth but found them impossible to gain because of the power of the ruling aristocrats.

The desires of these new groups opened the door to the rise of tyrants in the seventh and sixth centuries B.C. They were not necessarily oppressive or wicked as our word *tyrant* connotes. Greek tyrants were rulers who seized power by force and who were not subject to the law. Support for the tyrants came from the new rich who made their money in trade and industry as well as from poor peasants who were in debt to landholding aristocrats. Both groups were opposed to the domination of political power by aristocratic oligarchies.

Tyrants usually achieved power by a local coup d'état and maintained it by using mercenary soldiers. Once in power, they built new marketplaces, temples, and walls that not only glorified the city but also enhanced their own popularity. Tyrants also favored the interests of merchants and traders. Despite these achievements, however, tyranny fell out of favor by the end of the sixth century B.C. Its very nature as a system outside the law seemed contradictory to the ideal of law in a Greek community. Although tyranny did not last, it played a significant role in the evolution of Greek history by ending the rule of narrow aristocratic oligarchies. The end of tyranny opened the door to greater numbers of people in government. Although this trend culminated in the development of democracy in some communities, in other states expanded oligarchies of one kind or another managed to remain in power. Greek states exhibited considerable variety in their governmental structures; this can perhaps best be seen by examining the two most famous and most powerful Greek city-states, Sparta and Athens.

❋ Sparta

The Spartans originally occupied four small villages in the southwestern Peloponnesus, in an area known as Laconia, that eventually became unified into a single *polis*. This unification made Sparta a strong community in Laconia and enabled the Spartans to conquer the neighboring Laconians and subject them to serfdom. Known as helots (the name is derived from a Greek word for "capture"), these conquered Laconians were bound to the land and forced to work on farms and as household servants for the Spartans.

When the land in Laconia proved unable to maintain the growing number of Spartan citizens, the Spartans looked for land nearby and, beginning around 730 B.C., undertook the conquest of

The Lycurgan Reforms

To maintain control over the conquered Messenians, the Spartans instituted the reforms that created their military state. These reforms are associated with the name of the lawgiver Lycurgus, although historians are not sure of his historicity. In this account of Lycurgus, the ancient Greek historian Plutarch discusses the effect of these reforms on the treatment and education of boys.

✽ *Plutarch*, Lycurgus

Lycurgus was of another mind; he would not have masters brought out of the market for his young Spartans, . . . nor was it lawful, indeed, for the father himself to breed up the children after his own fancy; but as soon as they were seven years old they were to be enrolled in certain companies and classes, where they all lived under the same order and discipline, doing their exercises and taking their play together. Of these, he who showed the most conduct and courage was made captain; they had their eyes always upon him, obeyed his orders, and underwent patiently whatsoever punishment he inflicted; so that the whole course of their education was one continued exercise of a ready and perfect obedience. The old men, too, were spectators of their performances, and often raised quarrels and disputes among them, to have a good opportunity of finding out their different characters, and of seeing which would be valiant, which a coward, when they should come to more dangerous encounters. Reading and writing they gave them just enough to serve their turn; their chief care was to make them good subjects, and to teach them to endure pain and conquer in battle. To this end, as they grew in years, their discipline was proportionately increased; their heads were close-clipped, they were accustomed to go barefoot, and for the most part to play naked.

After they were twelve years old, they were no longer allowed to wear any undergarments, they had one coat to serve them a year; their bodies were hard and dry, with but little acquaintance of baths and unguents; these human indulgences they were allowed only on some few particular days in the year. They lodged together in little bands upon beds made of the rushes which grew by the banks of the river Eurotas, which they were to break off with their hands with a knife; if it were winter, they mingled some thistledown with their rushes, which it was thought had the property of giving warmth. By the time they were come to this age there was not any of the more hopeful boys who had not a lover to bear him company. The old men, too, had an eye upon them, coming often to the grounds to hear and see them contend either in wit or strength with one another, and this as seriously . . . as if they were their fathers, their tutors, or their magistrates; so that there scarcely was any time or place without some one present to put them in mind of their duty, and punish them if they had neglected it.

[Spartan boys were also encouraged to steal their food.] They stole, too, all other meat they could lay their hands on, looking out and watching all opportunities, when people were asleep or more careless than usual. If they were caught, they were not only punished with whipping, but hunger, too, being reduced to their ordinary allowance, which was but very slender, and so contrived on purpose, that they might set about to help themselves, and be forced to exercise their energy and address. This was the principal design of their hard fare.

---

neighboring Messenia despite its larger size and population. Messenia possessed a large, fertile plain ideal for growing grain. After its conquest, which was not completed until the seventh century B.C., the Messenians were reduced to serfdom and made to work for the Spartans. To ensure control over their conquered Laconian and Messenian helots, the Spartans made a conscious decision to create a military state.

By the early sixth century B.C., the Spartans had transformed their state into a military camp (see the box above). The lives of all Spartans were now rigidly organized. At birth, each child was examined by state officials who decided whether it was fit to live. Infants judged unfit were exposed to die. Boys were taken from their mothers at the age of seven and put under control of the state. They lived in military-like barracks, where they were subjected to harsh discipline to make them tough and given an education that stressed military training and obedience to authority. At twenty, Spartan males were enrolled in the army for regular military service. Although allowed to marry, they continued to live in the barracks and ate all their meals in public dining halls with their fellow soldiers. Meals were simple; the famous Spartan black broth consisted of a piece of pork boiled in blood, salt, and vinegar, causing a visitor who ate in a public mess to remark that he now understood why Spartans were not afraid to die. At thirty, Spartan males were allowed to vote in the assembly and live at home, but they stayed in the army until the age of sixty.

While their husbands remained in military barracks until age thirty, Spartan women lived at home. Because of this separation, Spartan women had greater freedom of movement and greater power in the household than was common for women elsewhere in Greece. They were encouraged to exercise and remain fit to bear and raise healthy children. Like the men, Spartan women engaged in athletic exercises in the nude. Many Spartan women upheld the strict Spartan values, expecting their husbands and sons to be brave in war. The story is told that as a Spartan mother was burying her son, an old woman came up to her and said, "You poor woman, what a misfortune." "No," replied the other, "because I bore him so that he might die for Sparta and that is what has happened, as I wished."[6] Another Spartan woman, as she was handing her son his shield, told him to come back carrying his shield or being carried on it.

The Spartan government was headed by two kings who led the Spartan army on its campaigns. A group of five men, known as the ephors, were elected each year and were responsible for the education of youth and the conduct of all citizens. A council of elders, composed of the two kings and twenty-eight citizens over the age of sixty, decided on the issues that would be presented to an assembly. This assembly of all male citizens did not debate but only voted on the issues put before it by the council of elders.

To make their new military state secure, the Spartans deliberately turned their backs on the outside world. Foreigners, who might bring in new ideas, were discouraged from visiting Sparta. Nor were Spartans, except for military reasons, encouraged to travel abroad where they might pick up new ideas that might prove dangerous to the stability of the state. Likewise, Spartan citizens were discouraged from studying philosophy, literature, or the arts—subjects that might encourage new thoughts. The art of war and ruling was the Spartan ideal. All other arts were frowned on.

In the sixth century, Sparta used its military might and the fear it inspired to gain greater control of the Peloponnesus by organizing an alliance of almost all the Peloponnesian states. Sparta's strength enabled it to dominate this Peloponnesian League and

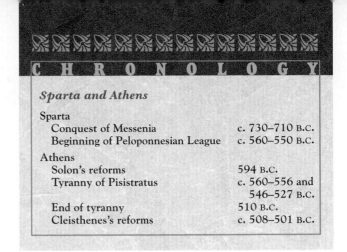

CHRONOLOGY

Sparta and Athens

Sparta	
Conquest of Messenia	c. 730–710 B.C.
Beginning of Peloponnesian League	c. 560–550 B.C.
Athens	
Solon's reforms	594 B.C.
Tyranny of Pisistratus	c. 560–556 and 546–527 B.C.
End of tyranny	510 B.C.
Cleisthenes's reforms	c. 508–501 B.C.

determine its policies. By 500 B.C., the Spartans had organized a powerful military state that maintained order and stability in the Peloponnesus. Raised from early childhood to believe that total loyalty to the Spartan state was the basic reason for existence, the Spartans viewed their strength as justification for their militaristic ideals and regimented society.

✳ Athens

By 700 B.C., Athens had established a unified *polis* on the peninsula of Attica. Although early Athens had been ruled by a monarchy, by the seventh century it had fallen under the control of its aristocrats. They possessed the best land and controlled political and religious life by means of a council of nobles, assisted by a board of nine archons. Although there was an assembly of full citizens, it possessed few powers.

Near the end of the seventh century B.C., Athens faced political turmoil because of serious economic problems. Many Athenian farmers found themselves sold into slavery when they were unable to repay the loans they had borrowed from their aristocratic neighbors, pledging themselves as collateral. Over and over, there were cries to cancel the debts and give land to the poor. Athens seemed on the verge of civil war.

The ruling Athenian aristocrats responded to this crisis by choosing Solon, a reform-minded aristocrat, as sole archon in 594 B.C. and giving him full power to make changes. Solon canceled all current land debts, outlawed new loans based on humans as collateral, and freed people who had fallen into slavery for debts. He refused, however, to carry out the redistribution of the land and hence failed to deal with the basic cause of the economic crisis.

Like his economic reforms, Solon's political measures were also a compromise. Though by no means eliminating the power of the aristocracy, they opened the door to the participation of new people, especially the nonaristocratic wealthy, in the government. But Solon's reforms, though popular, did not solve Athens' problems. Aristocratic factions continued to vie for power, and the poorer peasants resented Solon's failure to institute land redistribution. Internal strife finally led to the very institution Solon had hoped to avoid—tyranny. Pisistratus, an aristocrat, seized power in 560 B.C. Pursuing a foreign policy that aided Athenian trade, Pisistratus remained popular with the merchants. But the Athenians rebelled against his son and ended the tyranny in 510 B.C. Although the aristocrats attempted to reestablish an aristocratic oligarchy, Cleisthenes, another aristocratic reformer, opposed this plan and, with the backing of the Athenian people, gained the upper hand in 508 B.C. The reforms of Cleisthenes now established the basis for Athenian democracy.

Cleisthenes enrolled all citizens in ten new tribes, each of which contained inhabitants located in the country districts of Attica, the coastal areas, and Athens. The ten tribes thus contained a cross section of the population and reflected all of Attica, a move that diminished local interests and increased loyalty to the *polis*. Each of the ten tribes chose fifty members by lot each year for a new council of 500, which was responsible for the administration of both foreign and financial affairs and prepared the business that would be handled by the assembly. This assembly of all male citizens had final authority in the passing of laws after free and open debate; thus Cleisthenes's reforms strengthened the central role of the assembly of citizens in the Athenian political system.

The reforms of Cleisthenes created the foundations for Athenian democracy. More changes would come in the fifth century when the Athenians themselves would begin to use the word *democracy* to describe their system (from the Greek words *demos*, "people," and *kratia*, "power"). By 500 B.C., Athens was more united than it had been and was about to assume a more important role in Greek affairs.

◆ The High Point of Greek Civilization: Classical Greece

Classical Greece is the name given to the period of Greek history from around 500 B.C. to the conquest of Greece by the Macedonian king Philip II in 338 B.C.

It was a period of brilliant achievement, much of it associated with the flowering of democracy in Athens under the leadership of Pericles. Many of the lasting contributions of the Greeks occurred during this period. The age began with a mighty confrontation between the Greek states and the mammoth Persian Empire.

※ *The Challenge of Persia*

As Greek civilization grew and expanded throughout the Mediterranean, it was inevitable that it would come into contact with the Persian Empire to the east. The Ionian Greek cities in western Asia Minor had already fallen subject to the Persian Empire by the mid-sixth century B.C. An unsuccessful revolt by the Ionian cities in 499—assisted by the Athenian navy—led the Persian ruler Darius to seek revenge by attacking the mainland Greeks in 490. The Persians landed an army on the plain of Marathon, only 26 miles from Athens. There a mostly Athenian army, though clearly outnumbered, went on the attack and defeated the Persians decisively.

Xerxes, the new Persian monarch after the death of Darius in 486 B.C., vowed revenge and renewed the invasion of Greece. In preparation for the attack, some of the Greek states formed a defensive league under Spartan leadership, while the Athenians pursued a new military policy by developing a navy. By the time of the Persian invasion in 480 B.C., the Athenians had produced a fleet of about two hundred vessels.

Xerxes led a massive invasion force into Greece: close to 150,000 troops, almost seven hundred naval ships, and hundreds of supply ships to keep their large army fed. The Greeks decided to fight a delaying action at the pass of Thermopylae along the main road into central Greece, probably to give the Greek fleet of three hundred ships the chance to fight the Persian fleet. The Greeks knew that the Persian army was dependent on the fleet for supplies. A Greek force numbering close to nine thousand, under the leadership of the Spartan king Leonidas and his contingent of three hundred Spartans, held off the Persian army for two days. The Spartan troops were especially brave. When told that Persian arrows would darken the sky in battle, one Spartan warrior supposedly responded, "That is good news. We will fight in the shade!" Unfortunately for the Greeks, a traitor told the Persians how to use a mountain path to outflank the Greek force. King Leonidas and the three hundred Spartans fought to the last man.

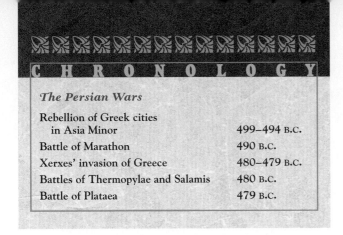

The Persian Wars

Rebellion of Greek cities in Asia Minor	499–494 B.C.
Battle of Marathon	490 B.C.
Xerxes' invasion of Greece	480–479 B.C.
Battles of Thermopylae and Salamis	480 B.C.
Battle of Plataea	479 B.C.

The Athenians, now threatened by the onslaught of the Persian forces, abandoned their city. While the Persians sacked and burned Athens, the Greek fleet remained offshore near the island of Salamis and challenged the Persian navy to fight. Although the Greeks were outnumbered, they managed to outmaneuver the Persian fleet and utterly defeated it. A few months later, early in 479 B.C., the Greeks formed the largest Greek army seen up to that time and decisively defeated the Persian army at Plataea, northwest of Attica. The Greeks had won the war and were now free to pursue their own destiny.

✻ The Growth of an Athenian Empire in the Age of Pericles

After the defeat of the Persians, Athens stepped in to provide new leadership against the Persians by forming a confederation called the Delian League. Organized in the winter of 478–477 B.C., the Delian League was dominated by the Athenians from the beginning. Its main headquarters was the island of Delos, but its chief officials, including the treasurers and commanders of the fleet, were Athenian. Under the leadership of the Athenians, the Delian League pursued the attack against the Persian Empire. Virtually all of the Greek states in the Aegean were liberated from Persian control. Arguing that the Persian threat was now over, some members of the Delian League wished to withdraw. But the Athenians forced them to remain in the league and to pay tribute. "No secession" became Athenian policy. The Delian League was rapidly becoming the nucleus of an Athenian Empire.

At home, Athenians favored the new imperial policy, especially after 461 B.C., when a political faction, led by a young aristocrat named Pericles, triumphed. Under Pericles, Athens embarked on a policy of expanding democracy at home while severing its ties with Sparta and expanding its new empire abroad. This period of Athenian and Greek history, which historians have subsequently labeled the Age of Pericles, witnessed the height of Athenian power and the culmination of its brilliance as a civilization.

In the Age of Pericles, the Athenians became deeply attached to their democratic system. The sovereignty of the people was embodied in the assembly, which consisted of all male citizens over eighteen years of age. In the 440s, that was probably a group of about 43,000. Not all attended, however, and the number present at the meetings, which were held every ten days on a hillside east of the Acropolis, seldom reached 6,000. The assembly passed all laws and made final decisions on war and foreign policy. Pericles expanded the Athenians' involvement in their democracy (see the box on p. 56) by making lower-class citizens eligible for public offices formerly closed to them and introducing state pay for officerholders, including those who served on large Athenian juries. Poor citizens could now afford to participate in public affairs.

A large body of city magistrates, usually chosen by lot without regard to class, handled routine administrative tasks. The overall directors of policy, a board of ten officials known as generals, were elected by public vote and were usually wealthy aristocrats, even though the people were free to select others. The generals could be reelected, enabling individual leaders to play an important political role. Pericles, for example, was elected to the generalship thirty times between 461 and 429 B.C. But all public officials were subject to scrutiny and could be deposed from office if they lost the people's confidence. The Athenians had also devised the practice of ostracism to protect themselves against overly ambitious politicians. Members of the assembly could write on a broken pottery fragment (*ostrakon*) the name of a person they most disliked or considered most harmful to the *polis*. A person who received a majority (if at least 6,000 votes were cast) was exiled for ten years.

The Athenian pursuit of democracy at home was coupled with increasing imperialism abroad. Citing the threat of the Persian fleet in the Aegean, the Athenians moved the treasury of the league from the island of Delos to Athens itself in 454 B.C. Members were, in effect, charged a fee (tribute) for the Athenian claim of protection. Pericles also used the money in the league treasury, without the approval of its members, to build new temples in Athens, an arrogant reminder that the Delian League had become the

Athenian Democracy: The Funeral Oration of Pericles

In his History of the Peloponnesian War, *the Greek historian Thucydides presented his reconstruction of the eulogy given by Pericles in the winter of 431–430 B.C. to honor the Athenians killed in the first campaigns of the Great Peloponnesian War. It is a magnificent, idealized description of the Athenian democracy at its height.*

✳ *Thucydides,* History of the Peloponnesian War

Our constitution is called a democracy because power is in the hands not of a minority but of the whole people. When it is a question of settling private disputes, everyone is equal before the law; when it is a question of putting one person before another in positions of public responsibility, what counts is not membership of a particular class, but the actual ability which the man possesses. No one, so long as he has it in him to be of service to the state, is kept in political obscurity because of poverty. And, just as our political life is free and open, so is our day-to-day life in our relations with each other. We do not get into a state with our next-door neighbor if he enjoys himself in his own way, nor do we give him the kind of black looks which, though they do no real harm, still do hurt people's feeling. We are free and tolerant in our private lives; but in public affairs we keep to the law. This is because it commands our deep respect.

We give our obedience to those whom we put in positions of authority, and we obey the laws themselves, especially those which are for the protection of the oppressed, and those unwritten laws which it is an acknowledged shame to break. . . . Here each individual is interested not only in his own affairs but in the affairs of the state as well: even those who are mostly occupied with their own business are extremely well-informed on general politics—this is a peculiarity of ours: we do not say that a man who takes no interest in politics is a man who minds his own business; we say that he has no business here at all. We Athenians, in our own persons, take our decisions on polity or submit them to proper discussions: for we do not think that there is an incompatibility between words and deeds; the worst thing is to rush into action before the consequences have been properly debated. . . . Taking everything together then, I declare that our city is an education to Greece, and I declare that in my opinion each single one of our citizens, in all the manifold aspects of life, is able to show himself the rightful lord and owner of his own person and do this, moreover, with exceptional grace and exceptional versatility. And to show that this is no empty boasting for the present occasion, but real tangible fact, you have only to consider the power which our city possesses and which has been won by those very qualities which I have mentioned.

Athenian Empire. But Athenian imperialism alarmed the other Greek states, and soon all Greece was confronted with a new war.

✳ *The Great Peloponnesian War and the Decline of the Greek States*

During the forty years after the defeat of the Persians, the Greek world divided into two major camps: Sparta and its supporters and the Athenian Empire. In his classic *History of the Peloponnesian War,* the great Greek historian Thucydides pointed out that the fundamental, long-range cause of the Peloponnesian War was the fear that Sparta and its allies had of the growing Athenian Empire. Then, too, Athens and Sparta

had built two very different kinds of societies, and neither state was able to tolerate the other's system. A series of disputes finally led to the outbreak of war in 431 B.C.

At the beginning of the war, both sides believed they had winning strategies. The Athenians planned to remain behind the protective walls of Athens while the overseas empire and the navy kept them supplied. Pericles knew perfectly well that the Spartans and their allies could beat the Athenians in pitched battles, which was the chief aim of the Spartan strategy. The Spartans and their allies surrounded Athens, hoping that the Athenians would send out their army to fight beyond the walls. But Pericles was convinced that Athens was secure behind its walls and retaliated by sending out naval excursions to ravage the seacoast of the Peloponnesus.

In the second year of the war, however, plague devastated the crowded city of Athens and wiped out possibly one-third of the Athenian population. Pericles himself died the following year (429 B.C.), a severe loss to Athens. Despite decimation by the plague, the Athenians fought on in a struggle that dragged on for another twenty-seven years. A crushing blow came in 405 B.C., when the Athenian fleet was destroyed at Aegospotami on the Hellespont. Athens was besieged and surrendered in 404. Its walls were torn down, the navy was disbanded, and the Athenian Empire was destroyed. The great war was finally over.

The Great Peloponnesian War weakened the major Greek states and dashed any possibility of cooperation among the Greek states. The next seventy years of Greek history are a sorry tale of efforts by Sparta, Athens, and Thebes, a new Greek power, to dominate Greek affairs. In continuing their petty wars, the Greeks remained oblivious to the growing power of Macedonia to their north and demonstrated convincingly that their genius was not in politics. Culture, however, was quite a different story.

✻ The Culture of Classical Greece

Classical Greece saw a period of remarkable intellectual and cultural growth throughout the Greek world. Historians agree, however, that Periclean Athens was the most important center of classical Greek culture.

✢ THE WRITING OF HISTORY

History as we know it, the systematic analysis of past events, was a Greek creation. Herodotus (c. 484–c. 425 B.C.), a Dorian Greek from Asia Minor, was the author of *The Persian Wars*, a work commonly regarded as the first real history in Western civilization. The Greek word *historia* (from which we derive our word *history*) means "research" or "investigation," and it is in the opening line of Herodotus' *History* that we find the first recorded use of the word:

> These are the researches [*historia*] of Herodotus of Halicarnassus, which he publishes, in the hope of thereby preserving from decay the remembrance of what men have done, and of preventing the great and wonderful actions of the Greeks and the Barbarians from losing their due meed of glory; and withal to put on record what were their ground of feud.[7]

The central theme of Herodotus' work is the conflict between the Greeks and the Persians, which he viewed as a struggle between Greek freedom and Persian despotism. Herodotus traveled widely for his information and was dependent for his sources on what we today would call oral history. Although he was a master storyteller and sometimes included considerable fanciful material, Herodotus was also capable of exhibiting a critical attitude toward the materials he used. Regardless of its weaknesses, Herodotus' *History* is an important source of information on the Persians and our chief source on the Persian Wars themselves.

Thucydides (c. 460–c. 400 B.C.) was, by far, the better historian; in fact, historians consider him the greatest historian of the ancient world. Thucydides was an Athenian and a participant in the Peloponnesian War. He had been elected a general, but a defeat in battle led the fickle Athenian assembly to send him into exile, which gave him the opportunity to write his *History of the Peloponnesian War*.

Unlike Herodotus, Thucydides was not concerned with divine forces or gods as causal factors in history. He saw war and politics in purely rational terms, as the activities of human beings. He examined the causes of the Peloponnesian War in a clear and objective fashion, placing much emphasis on the accuracy of his facts. As he stated:

> And with regard to my factual reporting of the events of the war I have made it a principle not to write down the first story that came my way, and not even to be guided by my own general impressions; either I was present myself at the events which I have described or else I heard of them from eye-witnesses whose reports I have checked with as much thoroughness as possible.[8]

Thucydides also provided remarkable insight into the human condition. He believed that human nature was a constant, but he was not so naive as to believe in an exact repetition of events. He noted that similar political situations did recur over the years and felt that the study of history was therefore of great value for understanding the present.

✢ GREEK DRAMA

Drama, as we know it, was created by the Greeks and was clearly intended to do more than entertain. It was used to educate citizens and was supported by the state for that reason. Plays were presented in outdoor theaters as part of a religious festival. The form of Greek plays remained rather stable. Three male actors who wore masks acted all the parts. A chorus (also male) spoke the important lines that explained what was going on. Action was very limited, because the emphasis was on the story and its meaning. Content was generally based on myths or legends that the audience already knew.

The first Greek dramas were tragedies, plays based on the suffering of a hero and usually ending in disaster. Aeschylus (525–456 B.C.) is the first tragedian whose plays are known to us. Although he wrote ninety tragedies, only seven have survived. As was customary in Greek tragedy, his plots were simple. The entire drama focused on a single tragic event and its meaning. Greek tragedies were supposed to be presented in a trilogy (a set of three plays) built around a common theme. The only complete trilogy we possess, called the *Oresteia*, was written by Aeschylus. The theme of this trilogy is derived from Homer. Agamemnon, the king of Mycenae, returns a hero from the defeat of Troy. His wife, Clytemnestra, avenges the sacrificial death of her daughter Iphigenia by murdering Agamemnon, who had been responsible for Iphigenia's death. In the second play of the trilogy, Agamemnon's son Orestes avenges his father by killing his mother. Orestes is now pursued by the Furies, who torment him for killing his mother. Evil acts breed evil acts and suffering is one's lot, suggests Aeschylus. But Orestes is put on trial and acquitted by Athena, the patron goddess of Athens. Personal vendetta has been eliminated and law has prevailed. Reason has triumphed over the forces of evil.

Another great Athenian playwright was Sophocles (c. 496–406 B.C.), whose most famous play was *Oedipus the King*. The oracle of Apollo foretells how a man (Oedipus) will kill his own father and marry his mother. Despite all attempts at prevention, the tragic events occur. Although it appears that Oedipus suffered the fate determined by the gods, Oedipus also accepts that he himself as a free man must bear responsibility for his actions: "It was Apollo, friends, Apollo, that brought this bitter bitterness, my sorrows to completion. But the hand that struck me was none but my own."[9]

The third outstanding Athenian tragedian, Euripides (c. 485–406 B.C.), tried to create more realistic characters. His plots also became more complex and reflected a greater interest in real-life situations. Perhaps the greatest of all his plays was *The Bacchae*, which dealt with the introduction of the hysterical rites associated with Dionysus, god of wine. Euripides is often seen as a skeptic who questioned tradi-

tional moral and religious values. Euripides was also critical of the traditional view that war was glorious. He portrayed war as brutal and barbaric and expressed deep compassion for the women and children who suffered from it.

Greek tragedies dealt with universal themes still relevant in our day. They probed such problems as the nature of good and evil, the conflict between spiritual values and the demands of the state or family, the rights of the individual, the nature of divine forces, and human nature. Over and over, the tragic lesson was repeated: humans were free and yet could operate only within limitations imposed by the gods. The real task was to cultivate the balance and moderation that led to awareness of one's true position. But the pride in human accomplishment and independence is real. As the chorus chants in Sophocles' *Antigone:* "Is there anything more wonderful on earth, our marvelous planet, than the miracle of man?"[10]

Greek comedy developed later than tragedy. The plays of Aristophanes (c. 450–c. 385 B.C.), who used both grotesque masks and obscene jokes to entertain the Athenian audience, are examples of Old Comedy, which was used to attack or savagely satirize both politicians and intellectuals. In *The Clouds*, for example, Aristophanes characterized the philosopher Socrates as the operator of a thought factory where people could learn deceitful ways to handle other people. Later plays gave up the element of personal attack and featured contemporary issues. Of special importance to Aristophanes was his opposition to the Peloponnesian War. *Lysistrata*, performed in 411 B.C., at a time when Athens was in serious danger of losing the war, had a comic but effective message against the war.

THE ARTS: THE CLASSICAL IDEAL

The arts of the Western world have been largely dominated by the artistic standards established by the Greeks of the classical period. Classical Greek art did not aim at experimentation for experiment's sake but was concerned with expressing eternally true ideals. The subject matter was the human being, presented as an object of great beauty. The classic style, based on the ideals of reason, moderation, balance, and harmony in all things, was meant to civilize the emotions.

In architecture, the most important structure was the temple dedicated to a god or goddess. Because Greek religious ceremonies were held at altars in the open air, temples were not used to enclose the faith-

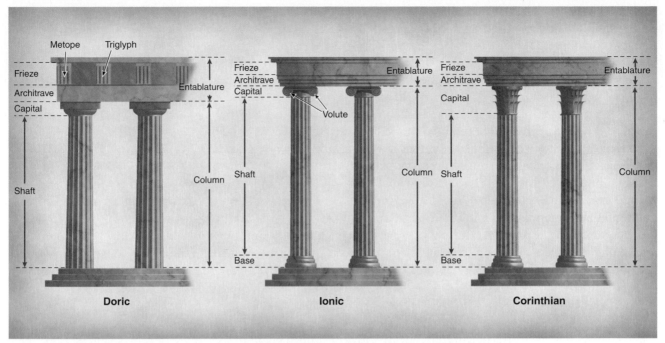

COLUMNS: THE DORIC, IONIC, AND CORINTHIAN ORDERS. The size and shape of columns were among the most important aspects of Greek temple architecture. The Doric order, with plain capitals and no base, developed first in the Dorian Peloponnesus and was rather simple in comparison to the slender Ionic column, which had an elaborate base and spiral-shaped capitals, and the Corinthian column, which featured leaf-shaped capitals.

ful, as modern churches are. At the center of Greek temples were walled rooms that housed the statues of deities and treasuries in which gifts to the gods and goddesses were safeguarded. These central rooms were surrounded by a screen of columns that make Greek temples open structures rather than closed ones. The columns were originally made of wood but changed to limestone in the seventh century and to marble in the fifth century B.C.

Some of the finest examples of Greek classical architecture were built in fifth-century Athens. The most famous building, regarded as the greatest example of the classical Greek temple, is the Parthenon, built between 447 and 432 B.C. The master builders Ictinus and Callicrates directed the construction of this temple consecrated to Athena, the patron goddess of Athens. The Parthenon typifies the principles of classical architecture: the search for calm, clarity, and freedom from superfluous detail. The individual parts of the temple were constructed in accordance with certain mathematical ratios also found in natural phenomena. The architects' concern with these laws of proportion is paralleled by the attempt of Greek philosophers to understand the general laws underlying nature.

THE PARTHENON. The arts in classical Greece were designed to express the eternal ideals of reason, moderation, balance, and harmony. In architecture, the most important structure was the temple, and the classical example of this kind of architecture is the Parthenon, built between 447 and 432 B.C. The Parthenon, located on the Acropolis, was dedicated to Athena, the patron goddess of the city, but it also served as a shining example of the power and wealth of the Athenian Empire.

Greek sculpture also developed a classic style that differed significantly from the artificial stiffness of earlier periods. Statues of the male nude, the favorite subject of Greek sculptors, now exhibited more relaxed attitudes; their faces were self-assured; their bodies were flexible and smooth-muscled. Although the figures possessed natural features that made them lifelike, Greek sculptors sought to achieve not realism but a standard of ideal beauty. Polyclitus, a fifth-century sculptor, authored a treatise (now lost) on a canon of proportions that he illustrated in a work known as the *Doryphoros*. His theory maintained that the use of ideal proportions, based on mathematical ratios found in nature, could produce an ideal human form, beautiful in its perfected and refined features. This search for ideal beauty was the dominant aspect of classical sculpture.

❧ THE GREEK LOVE OF WISDOM

Philosophy is a Greek word that literally means "love of wisdom." Early Greek philosophers were concerned with the development of critical or rational thought about the nature of the universe and the place of divine forces in it. The Sophists, however, were a group of philosophical teachers in fifth-century Athens who rejected such speculation as foolish; they argued that understanding the universe was beyond the reach of the human mind. It was more important for individuals to improve themselves, so the only worthwhile object of study was human behavior. The Sophists were wandering scholars who sold their services as professional teachers to the young men of Greece, especially those of Athens. The Sophists stressed the importance of rhetoric (the art of persuasive speaking) in winning debates and swaying an audience, a skill that was especially valuable in democratic Athens. To the Sophists, there was no absolute right or wrong—what was right for one individual might be wrong for another. True wisdom consisted of being able to perceive and pursue one's own good. Because of these ideas, many people viewed the Sophists as harmful to society and especially dangerous to the values of young people.

One of the critics of the Sophists was Socrates (469–399 B.C.). Because he left no writings, we know about him only from his pupils, especially his most famous one, Plato. By occupation, Socrates was a stonemason, but his true love was philosophy. He taught a number of pupils, but not for pay, because he believed that the goal of education was only to improve the individual. He made use of a teaching method that is still known by his name. The "Socratic method" utilizes a question-and-answer technique to lead pupils to see things for themselves by using their own reason. Socrates believed that all real knowledge is within each person; only critical examination was needed to call it forth. This was the real task of philosophy since "the unexamined life is not worth living."

Socrates' questioning of authority and public demonstration of others' lack of knowledge led him into trouble. Athens had had a tradition of free thought and inquiry, but its defeat in the Peloponnesian War had created an environment intolerant of open debate and soul-searching. Socrates was accused and convicted of corrupting the youth of Athens by his teaching. An Athenian jury sentenced him to death.

One of Socrates' disciples was Plato (c. 429–347 B.C.), considered by many the greatest philosopher of Western civilization. Unlike his master Socrates, who wrote nothing, Plato wrote a great deal. In his dialogues, he used Socrates as his chief philosophical debater. Plato's philosophical thought focused on the essence of reality and was centered in the concept of Ideas or ideal Forms. According to Plato, a higher world of eternal, unchanging Ideas or Forms has always existed. To know these Forms is to know truth. These ideal Forms constitute reality and can only be apprehended by a trained mind, which, of

DORYPHOROS. This statue, known as the *Doryphoros,* or spear-carrier, is by the fifth-century sculptor Polyclitus, who believed it illustrated the ideal proportions of the human figure. Classical Greek sculpture moved away from the stiffness of earlier statues but retained the young male nude as the favorite subject matter. The statues became more lifelike, with relaxed poses and flexible, smooth-muscled bodies. The aim of sculpture, however, was not simply realism but also the expression of ideal beauty.

course, is the goal of philosophy. The objects that we perceive with our senses are simply reflections of the ideal Forms. Hence they are shadows, while reality is found in the Forms themselves.

Plato's ideas of government were set out in his dialogue titled *The Republic*. Based on his experience in Athens, Plato had come to distrust the workings of democracy. It was obvious to him that individuals could not attain an ethical life unless they lived in a just and rational state. Plato's search for the just state led him to construct an ideal state in which the population was divided into three basic groups. At the top was an upper class, a ruling elite, the famous philosopher-kings: "Unless either philosophers become kings in their countries or those who are now called kings and rulers come to be sufficiently inspired with a genuine desire for wisdom; unless, that is to say, political power and philosophy meet together . . . there can be no rest from troubles . . . for states, nor yet, as I believe, for all mankind."[11] The second group consisted of citizens who showed courage, the warriors who protected the society. All the rest made up the masses, essentially people driven not by wisdom or courage but by desire. They would be the producers of society—the artisans, tradesmen, and farmers.

In Plato's ideal state, each group fulfilled its assigned role, creating a society that functioned harmoniously. The needs of the community, rather than the happiness of the individual, were Plato's concern, and he focused on the need for the guardians or rulers, above all, to be removed from any concerns for wealth or prestige so that they could strive for what was best for the community. To rid the guardians of these desires, Plato urged that they live together, forgoing both private property and family life. Plato believed that women, too, could be rulers; in this, he departed radically from the actual practices of the Greek states.

Plato established a school at Athens known as the Academy. One of his pupils, who studied there for twenty years, was Aristotle (384–322 B.C.), who later became a tutor to Alexander the Great. Aristotle differed significantly from his teacher in that he did not accept Plato's theory of ideal Forms. Like Plato, Aristotle believed in universal principles or forms, but he believed that form and matter were inseparable. By examining individual objects, we can perceive their form and arrive at universal principles, but they do not exist as a separate higher world of reality beyond material things; rather, they are a part of things themselves. Aristotle's interests, then, lay in analyzing and classifying things based on thorough research and investigation. His interests were wide ranging, and he wrote treatises on an enormous number of subjects: ethics, logic, politics, poetry, astronomy, geology, biology, and physics.

Like Plato, Aristotle wished for an effective form of government that would rationally direct human affairs. Unlike Plato, he did not seek an ideal state based on the embodiment of an ideal Form of justice; he tried to find the best form of government through a rational examination of existing governments. For his *Politics*, Aristotle examined the constitutions of 158 states and arrived at general categories for organizing governments. He identified three good forms of government: monarchy, aristocracy, and constitutional government. But based on his examination, he warned that monarchy can easily turn into tyranny, aristocracy into oligarchy, and constitutional government into radical democracy or anarchy. He favored constitutional government as the best form for most people.

Aristotle's philosophical and political ideas played an enormous role in the development of Western thought during the Middle Ages (see Chapter 10). So did his ideas on women. Aristotle believed that marriage was meant to provide mutual comfort between man and woman and contributed to the overall happiness of a community: "The community needs both male and female excellences or it can only be half-blessed."[12] Nevertheless, Aristotle maintained that women were biologically inferior to men: "A woman is, as it were, an infertile male. She is female in fact on account of a kind of inadequacy." Therefore, according to Aristotle, women must be subordinated to men, not only in the community but also in marriage: "The association between husband and wife is clearly an aristocracy. The man rules by virtue of merit, and in the sphere that is his by right; but he hands over to this wife such matters as are suitable for her."[13]

❖ Greek Religion

Greek religion was intricately connected to every aspect of daily life; it was both social and practical. Public festivals, which originated from religious practices, served specific functions: boys were prepared to be warriors, girls to be mothers. Since religion was related to every aspect of life, citizens had to have a proper attitude to the gods. Religion was a civic cult necessary for the well-being of the state. Temples dedicated to a god or goddess were the major buildings in Greek society.

Homer gave an account of the gods that provided Greek religion with a definite structure. Over a period of time, most Greeks came to accept a common religion based on twelve chief gods and goddesses who were thought to live on Mount Olympus, the highest mountain in Greece. Among the twelve were Zeus, the chief deity and father of the gods; Athena, goddess of wisdom and crafts; Apollo, god of the sun and poetry; Aphrodite, goddess of love; and Poseidon, brother of Zeus and god of the seas and earthquakes.

The twelve Olympian gods were common to all Greeks, who thus shared a basic polytheistic religion. Each *polis* usually singled out one of the twelve Olympians as a guardian deity of its community. Athena was the patron goddess of Athens, for example. But each *polis* also had its own local deities who remained important to the community as a whole, and each family had patron gods as well. Because it was desirable to have the gods look favorably on one's activities, ritual assumed enormous proportions in Greek religion. Prayers were often combined with gifts to the gods based on the principle "I give to you, the gods, so that you will give in return." Ritual also meant sacrifices of animals or food. Animals were burned on an altar in front of a temple or a small altar in front of a home.

Festivals also developed as a way to honor the gods and goddesses. Some of these (the Panhellenic celebrations) were important to all Greeks and were held at special locations, such as those dedicated to the worship of Zeus at Olympia or to Apollo at Delphi. Numerous events were held in honor of the gods at the great festivals, including athletic competitions to which all Greeks were invited. The first such games were held at the Olympic festival in 776 B.C. and then held every four years thereafter to honor Zeus. Initially, the Olympic contests consisted of foot races and wrestling, but later, boxing, javelin throwing, and various other contests were added.

The Greeks also had a great desire to know the will of the gods. To do so, they made use of the oracle, a sacred shrine dedicated to a god or goddess who revealed the future. The most famous was the oracle of Apollo at Delphi, located on the side of Mount Parnassus, overlooking the Gulf of Corinth. At Delphi, a priestess listened to questions while in a state of ecstasy that was believed to be induced by Apollo. Her responses were interpreted by the priests and given in verse form to the person asking questions. Representatives of states and individuals traveled to Delphi to consult the oracle of Apollo. States might inquire whether they should undertake a military expedition; individuals might raise such questions as "Heracleidas asks the god whether he will have offspring from the wife he has now." Responses were often enigmatic and at times even politically motivated. Croesus, the king of Lydia in Asia Minor, who was known for his vast wealth, sent messengers to the oracle at Delphi, ask-ing whether he should go to war with the Persians. The oracle replied that if Croesus attacked the Persians, a mighty empire would be destroyed. Overjoyed to hear these words, Croesus made war on the Persians but was crushed by the enemy forces. A mighty empire was indeed destroyed—his own.

❀ *Daily Life in Classical Athens*

The Greek city-state was, above all, a male community: only adult male citizens took part in public life. In Athens, this meant the exclusion of women, slaves, and foreign residents, or roughly 85 percent of the total population in Attica. Of the 150,000 citizens in Athens, about 43,000 were adult males who exercised political power. Resident foreigners, who numbered about 35,000, received the protection of the laws but were also subject to some of the responsibilities of citizens, namely, military service and the funding of festivals. The remaining social group, the slaves, numbered around 100,000.

Slavery was a common institution in the ancient world. Economic needs dictated the desirability of owning at least one slave, although the very poor in Athens did not own any. The really wealthy might own large numbers, but those who did usually employed them in industry. Most often, slaves in Athens performed domestic tasks, serving as cooks and maids, or worked in the fields. Few peasants could afford more than one or two. Other slaves worked as unskilled and skilled labor. Those slaves who worked in public construction were paid the same as citizens.

The Athenian economy was largely agricultural but highly diversified. Athenian farmers grew grains, vegetables, and fruit for local consumption; cultivated vines and olive trees for wine and olive oil, which were exportable products; and grazed sheep and goats for wool and milk products. Given the size of its population and the lack of abundant fertile land, Athens had to import between 50 and 80 percent of its grain, a staple in the Athenian diet. Trade was thus highly important to the Athenian economy. The building of the port at Piraeus and the Long Walls (a series of defensive walls $4^{1}/_{2}$ miles long connecting Athens and Piraeus) created the physical conditions that made Athens the leading trade center in the fifth-century Greek world.

Artisans were more important to the Athenian economy than their relatively small numbers might suggest. Athens was the chief producer of high-quality painted pottery in the fifth century. Other crafts had moved beyond the small workshop into the factory through the use of slave labor. The shield factory of

Lysias, for example, employed 120 slaves. Public works projects also provided jobs for Athenians. The building program of Pericles, financed from the Delian League treasury, made possible the hiring of both skilled and unskilled labor.

The Athenian lifestyle was basically simple. Athenian houses were furnished with necessities bought from artisans, such as beds, couches, tables, chests, pottery, stools, baskets, and cooking utensils. Wives and slaves made clothes and blankets at home. The Athenian diet was rather plain and relied on such basic foods as barley, wheat, millet, lentils, grapes, figs, olives, almonds, bread made at home, vegetables, eggs, fish, cheese, and chicken. Olive oil was widely used, not only for eating but also for lighting lamps and rubbing on the body after washing and exercise. Although country houses kept animals, they were used for reasons other than their flesh: oxen for plowing, sheep for wool, goats for milk and cheese.

The family was an important institution in ancient Athens. It was composed of husband, wife, and children (a nuclear family), although other dependent relatives and slaves were regarded as part of the family economic unit. The family's primary social function was to produce new citizens. Strict laws of the fifth century had stipulated that a citizen must be the offspring of a legally acknowledged marriage between two Athenian citizens whose parents were also citizens.

Women were citizens who could participate in most religious cults and festivals but were otherwise excluded from public life. They could not own property beyond personal items and always had a male guardian. The function of the Athenian woman as wife was very clear. Her foremost obligation was to bear children, especially male children who would preserve the family line. The marriage formula that Athenians used put it succinctly: "I give this woman for the procreation of legitimate children." A wife was also expected to take care of her family and her house, either doing the household work herself or supervising the slaves who did the actual work (see the box on p. 64).

Women were kept under strict control. Since they were married at fourteen or fifteen, they were taught about their responsibilities at an early age. Although many managed to learn to read and play musical instruments, they were often cut off from any formal education. And women were supposed to remain at home, out of sight, except when attending funerals or festivals. If they left the house, they were to be accompanied.

Male homosexuality was also a prominent feature of Athenian life. The Greek homosexual ideal

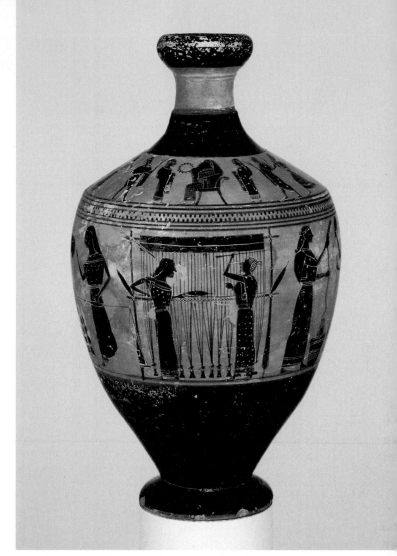

WOMEN IN THE LOOM ROOM. In Athens, women were citizens and could participate in religious ceremonies and festivals, but they had no rights and were barred from political activity. Women were to stay at home, caring for the children and the needs of the household. A principal activity of Greek women was the making of clothes. This vase shows two women working on a warp-weighted loom.

was a relationship between a mature man and a young male. It is most likely that this was an aristocratic ideal and not one practiced by the common people. Although the relationship was frequently physical, the Greeks also viewed it as educational. The older male (the "lover") won the love of his "beloved" by his value as a teacher and by the devotion he demonstrated in training his charge. In a sense, this love relationship was seen as a way of initiating young males into the male world of political and military dominance. The Greeks did not feel that the coexistence of homosexual and heterosexual predilections created any special problems for individuals or their society.

Household Management and the Role of the Athenian Wife

In fifth-century Athens, a woman's place was in the home. She had two major responsibilities: the bearing and raising of children and the management of the household. In his dialogue on estate management, Xenophon relates the instructions of an Attican gentleman to his new wife.

❋ *Xenophon,* Oeconomicus

[Ischomachus addresses his new wife] For it seems to me, dear, that the gods with great discernment have coupled together male and female, as they are called, chiefly in order that they may form a perfect partnership in mutual service. For, in the first place that the various species of living creatures may not fail, they are joined in wedlock for the production of children. Secondly, offspring to support them in old age is provided by this union, to human beings, at any rate. Thirdly, human beings live not in the open air, like beasts, but obviously need shelter. Nevertheless, those who mean to win stores to fill the covered place, have need of someone to work at the open-air occupations; since plowing, sowing, planting and grazing are all such open-air employments;

and these supply the needful food. . . . For he made the man's body and mind more capable of enduring cold and heat, and journeys and campaigns; and therefore imposed on him the outdoor tasks. To the woman, since he had made her body less capable of such endurance, I take it that God has assigned the indoor tasks. And knowing that he had created in the woman and had imposed on her the nourishment of the infants, he meted out to her a larger portion of affection for newborn babes than to the man. . . .

Your duty will be to remain indoors and send out those servants whose work is outside, and superintend those who are to work indoors, and to receive the incomings, and distribute so much of them as must be spent, and watch over so much as is to be kept in store, and take care that the sum laid by for a year be not spent in a month. And when wool is brought to you, you must see that cloaks are made for those that want them. You must see too that the dry corn is in good condition for making food. One of the duties that fall to you, however, will perhaps seem rather thankless: you will have to see that any servant who is ill is cared for.

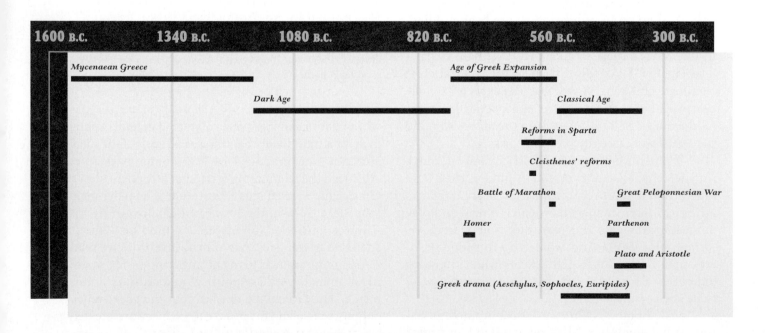

1600 B.C.	1340 B.C.	1080 B.C.	820 B.C.	560 B.C.	300 B.C.

Mycenaean Greece

Age of Greek Expansion

Dark Age

Classical Age

Reforms in Sparta

Cleisthenes' reforms

Battle of Marathon

Great Peloponnesian War

Homer

Parthenon

Plato and Aristotle

Greek drama (Aeschylus, Sophocles, Euripides)

Conclusion 🙰🙰🙰🙰🙰🙰🙰🙰🙰

The civilization of the ancient Greeks was the fountainhead of Western culture. Socrates, Plato, and Aristotle established the foundations of Western philosophy. Herodotus and Thucydides created the discipline of history. Our literary forms are largely derived from Greek poetry and drama. Greek notions of harmony, proportion, and beauty have remained the touchstones for all subsequent Western art. A rational method of inquiry, so important to modern science, was conceived in ancient Greece. Many political terms are of Greek origin, and so too are our concepts of the rights and duties of citizenship, especially as they were conceived in Athens, the first great democracy. Especially during their classical period, the Greeks raised and debated the fundamental questions about the purpose of human existence, the structure of human society, and the nature of the universe that have concerned Western thinkers ever since.

All of these achievements came from a group of small city-states in ancient Greece. And yet Greek civilization also contains an element of tragedy. For all of their brilliant accomplishments, the Greeks were unable to rise above the divisions and rivalries that caused them to fight each other and undermine their own civilization. Of course, their contributions to Western civilization have outlived their political struggles.

Notes 🙰🙰🙰🙰🙰🙰🙰🙰🙰🙰🙰🙰🙰

1. H. D. F. Kitto, *The Greeks* (Harmondsworth, England, 1951), p. 64.
2. Homer, *Odyssey*, trans. E. V. Rieu (Harmondsworth, England, 1946), p. 337.
3. Xenophon, *Symposium*, trans. O. J. Todd (Cambridge, Mass., 1968), III, 5.
4. Homer, *Odyssey*, pp. 290–291.
5. Quoted in Thomas R. Martin, *Ancient Greece* (New Haven, Conn., 1996), p. 62.
6. These words from Plutarch are quoted in E. Fantham, H. P. Foley, N. B. Kampen, S. B. Pomeroy, and H. A. Shapiro, *Women in the Classical World* (New York, 1994), p. 64.
7. Herodotus, *The Persian Wars*, trans. George Rawlinson (New York, 1942), p. 3.
8. Thucydides, *History of the Peloponnesian War*, trans. Rex Warner (Harmondsworth, England, 1954), p. 24.
9. Sophocles, *Oedipus the King*, trans. David Grene (Chicago, 1959), pp. 68–69.
10. Sophocles, *Antigone*, trans. Don Taylor (London, 1986), p. 146.
11. Plato, *The Republic*, trans. F. M. Cornford (New York, 1945), pp. 178–179.
12. Quotations from Aristotle are in Sue Blundell, *Women in Ancient Greece* (Cambridge, Mass., 1995), p. 106.
13. Ibid., p. 186.

Suggestions for Further Reading 🙰🙰🙰

A standard one-volume reference work for Greek history is J. B. Bury and R. Meiggs, *A History of Greece to the Death of Alexander the Great*, 4th ed. (New York, 1975). For a beautifully illustrated introduction, see F. Durando, *Ancient Greece: The Dawn of the Western World* (New York, 1997). Other good, general introductions to Greek history include *The Oxford History of the Classical World*, ed. J. Boardman, J. Griffin, and O. Murray (Oxford, 1986), pp. 19–314; R. Morkot, *The Penguin Historical Atlas of Ancient Greece* (Harmondsworth, England, 1996); T. R. Martin, *Ancient Greece* (New Haven, Conn., 1996); P. Cartledge, *The Cambridge Illustrated History of Ancient Greece* (Cambridge, 1998); and W. Donlan, S. B. Pomeroy, J. T. Roberts, and S. M. Burstein, *Ancient Greece: A Political, Social, and Cultural History* (New York, 1998). For a general survey of economic and social aspects, see M. M. Austin and P. Vidal-Naquet, *Economic and Social History of Ancient Greece: An Introduction* (Berkeley, 1978).

Early Greek history is examined in O. Murray, *Early Greece*, 2d ed. (Cambridge, Mass., 1993); M. I. Finley, *Early Greece: The Bronze and Archaic Ages*, 2d ed. (New York, 1982); and J. L. Fitton, *The Discovery of the Greek Bronze Age* (Cambridge, 1995). For good introductions to Homer, see J. Griffin, *Homer* (Oxford, 1980), and D. Page, *History and the Homeric Iliad* (Berkeley, 1959). On Homer and his world, see the modern classic by M. I. Finley, *The World of Odysseus*, 2d ed. (New York, 1979).

General works on Greek history from 750 to 500 B.C. include A. M. Snodgrass, *Archaic Greece* (London, 1980), and M. Grant, *The Rise of the Greeks* (London, 1987). Economic and social history of the period is covered in C. Starr, *The Economic and Social Growth of Early Greece, 800–500 B.C.* (Oxford, 1977). On colonization, see J. Boardman, *The Greeks Overseas*, rev. ed. (Baltimore, 1980). On tyranny, see J. F. McGlew, *Tyranny and Political Culture in Ancient Greece* (Ithaca, N.Y., 1993). The best histories of Sparta are W. Forrest, *A History of Sparta, 950–121 B.C.*, 2d ed. (London, 1980), and P. A. Cartledge, *Sparta and Laconia: A Regional History, 1300–362 B.C.* (London, 1979). On early Athens, see the still valuable A. Jones, *Athenian Democracy* (London, 1957), and R. Osborne, *Demos* (New York, 1985). The Persian Wars are examined in A. Burn, *Persia and the Greeks: The Defense of the West*, rev. ed. (Stanford, Calif., 1984).

A general history of classical Greece can be found in S. Hornblower, *The Greek World, 479–323 B.C.* (London, 1983), and J. K. Davies, *Democracy and Classical Greece*, 2d ed. (Cambridge, Mass., 1978). Economic aspects are examined in R. Hopper, *Trade and Industry in Classical Greece* (London, 1979). Valuable works on Athens include R. Garner, *Law and Society in Classical Athens* (New York, 1987); D. Stockton, *The Classical Athenian Democracy* (Oxford, 1990); and D. Kagan, *Pericles of Athens and the Birth of Democracy* (New York, 1991). On the development of the Athenian empire, see R. Meiggs, *The Athenian Empire* (Oxford, 1975), and M. F. McGregor, *The Athenians and Their Empire* (Vancouver, 1987). The best way to examine the Great Peloponnesian War is to read the work of Thucydides, *History of the Peloponnesian War*, trans. R. Warner (Harmondsworth, England, 1954). A detailed study has been done in the four books by D. Kagan, *Outbreak of the Peloponnesian War* (Ithaca, N.Y., 1969); *The Archidamian War* (Ithaca, N.Y., 1974); *The Peace of Nicias and the Sicilian Expedition* (Ithaca, N.Y., 1981); and *The Fall of the Athenian Empire* (Ithaca, N.Y., 1987).

For a comprehensive history of Greek art, see M. Robertson, *A History of Greek Art*, 2 vols. (Cambridge, 1975). A good, brief study is J. Boardman, *Greek Art* (London, 1985). On sculpture, see A. Stewart, *Greek Sculpture: An Exploration* (New Haven, Conn., 1990). A basic survey of architecture is H. W. Lawrence, *Greek Architecture*, rev. ed. (Harmondsworth, England, 1983). On Greek drama, see the general work by A. Dihle, *A History of Greek Literature* (London, 1994). For sound studies of Greek history writing, see J. A. S. Evans, *Herodotus* (Boston, 1982), and K. Dover, *Thucydides* (Oxford, 1973). On Greek philosophy, a detailed study is available in W. K. C. Guthrie, *A History of Greek Philosophy*, 6 vols. (Cambridge, 1962–1981). Individual works include J. Barnes, *Aristotle* (Oxford, 1982), and J. Findlay, *Plato and Platonism* (New York, 1978).

On Greek religion, see W. Burkert, *Greek Religion*, trans. J. Raffan (Cambridge, Mass., 1985), and H. W. Parke, *Greek Oracles* (London, 1967).

On the family and women, see S. B. Pomeroy, *Goddesses, Whores, Wives, and Slaves* (New York, 1975); E. Fantham, H. P. Foley, N. B. Kampen, S. B. Pomeroy, and H. A. Shapiro, *Women in the Classical World* (New York, 1994); S. Blundell, *Women in Ancient Greece* (Cambridge, Mass., 1995); and R. Just, *Women in Athenian Law and Life* (New York, 1989). For a good collection of documents on women, see M. R. Lefkowitz and M. B. Fant, *Women's Life in Greece and Rome: A Source Book in Translation* (Baltimore, 1982). On slavery, see Y. Garlan, *Slavery in Ancient Greece* (Ithaca, N.Y., 1988). On homosexuality, see K. J. Dover, *Greek Homosexuality* (London, 1978), and E. Cantarella, *Bisexuality in the Ancient World* (New Haven, Conn., 1992).

 For additional reading, go to InfoTrac College Edition, your online research library at http://web1.infotrac-college.com

Enter the search terms *Greece history* using Key Terms.

Enter the search terms *Greek mythology* using the Subject Guide.

Enter the search term *Homer* using the Subject Guide.

Enter the search terms *Peloponnesian War* using Key Terms.

FOCUS QUESTIONS

- How was Alexander able to amass his empire, and what might his rule have been like if he had lived?
- What role did cities play in the Hellenistic kingdoms?
- How did the political, economic, and social institutions of the Hellenistic world differ from those of the Greek classical age?
- What achievements in literature, art, and science occurred during the Hellenistic period?
- Which schools of philosophy and which religions were prominent during the Hellenistic period, and what does their popularity suggest about Hellenistic society?

*I*N 334 B.C., Alexander the Great led an army of Greeks and Macedonians into western Asia to launch his attack on the Persian Empire. Years of campaigning resulted in the complete defeat of the Persians, and in 327 Alexander and his troops pushed east into India. But two more years of fighting in an exotic and difficult terrain exhausted his troops, who rebelled and refused to go on. Reluctantly, Alexander turned back, leading his men across the arid lands of southern Persia. Conditions in the desert were appalling; the blazing sun and lack of water led to thousands of deaths. At one point, when a group of his soldiers found a little water, they scooped it up in a helmet and gave it to Alexander. Then, according to Arrian, an ancient Greek historian, Alexander, "with a word of thanks for the gift, took the helmet and, in full view of his troops, poured the water on the ground. So extraordinary was the effect of this action that the water wasted by Alexander was as good as a drink for every man in the army." Ever the great military leader, Alexander had found yet another way to inspire his troops.

Alexander the Great was the son of King Philip II of Macedonia, who in 338 B.C. had defeated the Greeks and established his control over the Greek peninsula. When Alexander became king after Philip's death, he led the Macedonians and Greeks on a spectacular conquest of the Persian Empire and opened the door to the spread of Greek culture throughout the ancient Near East. Greek settlers poured into the lands of the ancient Near East as bureaucrats, traders, soldiers, and scholars. Alexander's triumph gave rise to a new series of kingdoms that blended the achievements of the eastern world with the cultural outlook and attitudes of the Greeks. We use the term Hellenistic to designate this new order. The Hellenistic world was the world of Greeks and non-Greek easterners, and it resulted, in its own way, in a remarkable series of accomplishments that are sometimes underestimated. They form the story of this chapter.

◆ The Rise of Macedonia and the Conquests of Alexander

While the Greek city-states were continuing to fight each other, to their north a new and ultimately powerful kingdom was emerging in its own right. Its people, the Macedonians, were viewed as barbarians by their Greek neighbors to the south. The Macedonians were mostly rural folk and were organized in tribes, not city-states. Not until the end of the fifth century B.C. did Macedonia emerge as

BUST OF ALEXANDER THE GREAT. This bust of Alexander the Great is a Roman copy of the head of a statue, possibly by Lysippus. Although he aspired to be another Achilles, the tragic hero of Homer's *Iliad*, Alexander also sought more divine honors. He claimed to be descended from Heracles, a Greek hero worshiped as a god, and as pharaoh of Egypt he gained recognition as a living deity.

an important kingdom. When Philip II (359–336 B.C.) came to the throne, he built an efficient army and turned Macedonia into the chief power of the Greek world. He was soon drawn into the interstate conflicts of the Greeks.

The Greeks had mixed reactions to Philip's growing strength. Some viewed Philip as a savior who would rescue the Greeks from themselves by uniting them. Many Athenians, however, especially the orator Demosthenes, portrayed Philip as ruthless, deceitful, treacherous, and barbaric and called on the Athenians to undertake a struggle against him. In a speech to the Athenian assembly, Demosthenes exclaimed: "he [Philip] is not only no Greek, nor related to the Greeks, but not even a barbarian from any place that can be named with honor, but a pestilent knave from Macedonia, from where it was never yet possible to buy a decent slave."

Demosthenes' repeated calls for action, combined with Philip's rapid expansion, finally spurred Athens into action. Allied with a number of other Greek states, Athens fought the Macedonians at the Battle of Chaeronea, near Thebes, in 338 B.C. The Macedonian army crushed the Greeks, and Philip was now free to consolidate his control over the Greek peninsula. The independent Greek *polis*, long the basic political unit of the Greek world, came to an end as Philip formed an alliance of the Greek states that we call the Corinthian League because they met at Corinth. All members took an oath of loyalty: "I swear by Zeus, Earth, Sun, Poseidon, Athena, Ares, and all the gods and goddesses, I will abide by the peace, and I will not break the agreements with Philip the Macedonian, nor will I take up arms with hostile intent against any one of those who abide by the oaths either by land or by sea."[1]

Although Philip allowed the Greek city-states autonomy in domestic affairs, he retained the general direction of their foreign affairs. Many Greeks still objected to being subject to the less civilized master from the north, but Philip insisted that the Greek states end their bitter rivalries and cooperate with him in a war against Persia. Before Philip could undertake his invasion of Asia, however, he was assassinated, leaving the task to his son Alexander.

✺ Alexander the Great

Alexander was only twenty when he became king of Macedonia. The illustrious conqueror was in many ways prepared for kingship by his father, who had taken Alexander along on military campaigns and had given him control of the cavalry at the important Battle of Chaeronea. After his father's assassination, Alexander moved quickly to assert his authority, securing the Macedonian frontiers and smothering a rebellion in Greece. He then turned to his father's dream, the invasion of the Persian Empire.

THE CONQUESTS OF ALEXANDER

There is no doubt that Alexander was taking a chance in attacking the Persian Empire. Although weakened in some respects, it was still a strong state. Alexander's fleet was inferior to the Persian navy, and his finances were shaky at best. In the spring of 334 B.C., Alexander entered Asia Minor with an army of some 37,000 men. About half were Macedonians, the rest Greeks and other allies. The cavalry, which would play an important role as a striking force, numbered about 5,000. Architects, engineers, historians, and scientists accompanied the

army, a clear indication of Alexander's grand vision and positive expectations at the beginning of his campaign.

His first confrontation with the Persians, in a battle at the Granicus River in 334 B.C. (see Map 4.1), nearly cost him his life but resulted in a major victory. By spring 333, the entire western half of Asia Minor was in Alexander's hands, and the Ionian Greek cities of western Asia Minor had been "liberated" from the Persian oppressor. Meanwhile, the Persian king, Darius III, mobilized his forces to stop Alexander's army. Although the Persian troops outnumbered Alexander's, the Battle of Issus was fought on a narrow field that canceled the advantage of superior numbers and resulted in another Macedonian success. The Persian cause was certainly not helped when Darius made a spectacular exit from the battlefield before it was even clear who would be victorious. After his victory at Issus in 333 B.C., Alexander turned south, and by the winter of 332, Syria, Palestine, and Egypt were under his domination. He took the traditional title of pharaoh of Egypt and founded the first of a series of cities named after him (Alexandria) as the Greek administrative capital of Egypt. It became (and remains today) one of Egypt's and the Mediterranean world's most important cities.

MAP 4.1 The Conquests of Alexander the Great.

ALEXANDER AND DARIUS AT THE BATTLE OF ISSUS. This late Hellenistic mosaic from Pompeii depicts the battle between Alexander and Darius III, king of Persia, at Issus in 333 B.C. Alexander landed his forces in western Asia Minor in 334 B.C. to begin his Persian campaign and first met Darius at Issus, where the narrow field made the greater numbers of the Persians useless.

The next year, Alexander renewed his offensive, moving into the territory of the ancient Mesopotamian kingdoms and fighting a decisive battle with the Persians not far from Babylon. At Gaugamela, Alexander's men were clearly outnumbered by the Persian forces, which had established the battle site on a broad, open plain where their war chariots could maneuver to best advantage. Alexander was able to break through the center of the Persian line with his heavy cavalry, followed by the infantry. The battle turned into a rout, although Darius managed to escape.

After his victory, Alexander entered Babylon and then proceeded to the Persian capitals at Susa and Persepolis, where he acquired the Persian treasuries and took possession of vast quantities of gold and silver (see the box on p. 71). By 330, Alexander was again on the march, pursuing Darius. After Darius was killed by one of his own men, Alexander took the title and office of the Great King of the Persians. But he was not content to rest with the spoils of the Persian Empire. During the next three years, he moved east and northeast, as far as modern Pakistan. By summer 327 B.C., he had entered India. But two more years of fighting in an exotic and difficult terrain exhausted his troops, who mutinied and refused to go on. Reluctantly, Alexander surrendered to their demands and agreed to return, leading his troops through southern Persia across the Gedrosian Desert, where they suffered heavy losses from appalling desert conditions. Alexander and the remnant of his army went to Susa and then Babylon, where he planned still more campaigns. But in June 323 B.C., weakened from wounds, fever, and probably excessive alcohol, he died at the age of thirty-two.

THE LEGACY OF ALEXANDER

Alexander is one of the most puzzling great figures in history. Historians relying on the same sources give vastly different pictures of him. Some portray him as an idealistic visionary and others as a ruthless Machiavellian. No doubt he was a great military leader—a master of strategy and tactics, fighting in every kind of terrain and facing every kind of opponent. Alexander was a brave and even reckless fighter who was quite willing to lead his men into battle and risk his own life. His example inspired his troops to follow him into unknown lands and difficult situations. We know that he sought to imitate Achilles, the warrior-hero of Homer's *Iliad*, who was an ideal still important in Greek culture. Alexander kept a copy of the *Iliad*—and a dagger—under his pillow. He also claimed to be descended from Heracles, the Greek hero who came to be worshiped as a god. Alexander also aspired to divine honors; as pharaoh of Egypt, he became a living god according to Egyptian tradition and at one point even sent instructions to the Greek cities to "vote him a god."

Regardless of his ideals, motives, or views about himself, one fact stands out: Alexander truly created

The Destruction of the Persian Palace at Persepolis

After Alexander's decisive victory at Gaugamela, he advanced into Persia, where he captured the chief Persian cities. At Persepolis, he burned the Persian grand palace to the ground. The ancient historians Arrian and Diodorus of Sicily gave different explanations of this act: one argues that it was a deliberate act of revenge for the Persian invasion of Greece in the fifth century B.C., the other that the burning resulted from a wild drinking party. Modern historians do not agree on which version is more plausible. Arrian was a Greek-speaking Roman senator of the second century A.D.; Diodorus of Sicily lived in the first century B.C.

✳ *Arrian,* The Life of Alexander the Great

Thence he marched to Persepolis with such rapidity that the garrison had no time to plunder the city's treasure before his arrival. He also captured the treasure of Cyrus the First at Pasargadae. . . . He burnt the palace of the Persian kings, though this act was against the advice of Parmenio, who urged him to spare it for various reasons, chiefly because it was hardly wise to destroy what was now his own property, and because the Asians would, in his opinion, be less willing to support him if he seemed bent merely upon passing through their country as a conqueror rather than upon ruling it securely as a king. Alexander's answer was that he wished to punish the Persians for their invasion of Greece; his present act was retribution for the destruction of Athens, the burning of the temples, and all the other crimes they had committed against the Greeks.

✳ *Diodorus of Sicily,* Library of History

Alexander held games in honor of his victories. He performed costly sacrifices to the gods and enter-tained his friends bountifully. While they were feasting and the drinking was far advanced, as they began to be drunken a madness took possession of the minds of the intoxicated guests. At this point one of the women present, Thaïs by name and Attic by origin, said that for Alexander it would be the finest of all his feats in Asia if he joined them in a triumphal procession, set fire to the palaces, and permitted women's hands in a minute to extinguish the famed accomplishments of the Persians. This was said to men who were still young and giddy with wine, and so, as would be expected someone shouted out to form the procession and light torches, and urged all to take vengeance for the destruction of the Greek temples. Others took up the cry and said that this was a deed worthy of Alexander alone. When the king had caught fire at their words, all leaped up from their couches and passed the word along to form a victory procession in honor of Dionysus [god of wine and religious ecstasy].

Promptly many torches were gathered. Female musicians were present at the banquet, so the king led them all out for the procession to the sound of voices and flutes and pipes, Thaïs the courtesan leading the whole performance. She was the first, after the king, to hurl her blazing torch into the palace. As the others all did the same, immediately the entire palace area was consumed, so great was the conflagration. It was most remarkable that the impious act of Xerxes, king of the Persians, against the acropolis at Athens should have been repaid in kind after many years by one woman, a citizen of the land which had suffered it, and in sport.

---

a new age, the Hellenistic era. The word *Hellenistic* is derived from a Greek word meaning "to imitate Greeks." It is an appropriate way, then, to describe an age that saw the extension of the Greek language and ideas to the non-Greek world of the Near East. Alexander's destruction of the Persian monarchy had extended Greco-Macedonian rule over an enormous area. It created opportunities for Greek engineers, intellectuals, merchants, soldiers, and administrators. While the Greeks on the mainland might remain committed to the ideals of their city-states, those who followed Alexander and his successors participated in a new political unity based on the principle of monarchy. Alexander had transformed his army from a Macedonian force into an international one, owing loyalty only to himself. His successors used force to establish military monarchies that dominated the Hellenistic world after his death. Autocratic power, based on military strength and pretensions of divine rule, became a regular feature of those Hellenistic

A GAUL AND HIS WIFE: MONUMENT TO THE VICTORY OF A HELLENISTIC KING. After the death of Alexander, the empire he had created collapsed, and four Hellenistic kingdoms arose in its place. Warfare continued to be of importance to these kingdoms, because it was through warfare that they were created, maintained, and expanded. They did not just fight among themselves, however; they also faced foreign enemies, such as the Gauls, who first entered the Hellenistic world in 279 B.C. This statue of a Gaulish chieftain and his wife was part of a larger monument erected to commemorate the victory of Attalus I of Pergamum over the Gauls, a victory that gave Pergamum control over much of Asia Minor.

monarchies and was part of Alexander's political legacy to the Hellenistic world. His vision of empire no doubt inspired the Romans, who were, of course, the real heirs of Alexander's legacy.

But Alexander also left a cultural legacy. As a result of his conquests, Greek language, art, architecture, and literature spread throughout the Near East. The urban centers of the Hellenistic Age, many founded by Alexander and his successors, became springboards for the diffusion of Greek culture. Alexander had established a number of cities and military colonies named Alexandria to guard strategic points and supervise wide areas. Most of the settlers were Greek mercenaries. It has been estimated that in the course of his campaigns, Alexander summoned 60,000 to 65,000 additional mercenaries from Greece, at least 36,000 of whom took up residence in the garrisons and new cities. While the Greeks spread their culture in the East, they were also inevitably influenced by Eastern ways. Thus Alexander's legacy became one of the hallmarks of the Hellenistic world: the clash and fusion of different cultures.

◆ The World of the Hellenistic Kingdoms

The united empire that Alexander created by his conquests disintegrated soon after his death. All too soon, the most important Macedonian generals were engaged in a struggle for power. By 300 B.C., any hope of unity was dead, and eventually four Hellenistic kingdoms emerged as the successors to Alexander: Macedonia under the Antigonid dynasty, Syria and the lands to the east under the Seleucids, the Attalid kingdom of Pergamum in western Asia Minor, and

Egypt under the Ptolemies (see Map 4.2). All were eventually conquered by the Romans.

The Hellenistic monarchies created a semblance of stability for several centuries, even though Hellenistic kings refused to accept the new status quo and periodically engaged in wars to alter it. At the same time, an underlying strain always existed between the new Greco-Macedonian ruling class and the native populations. Together these factors generated a certain degree of tension that was never truly ended until the vibrant Roman state to the west stepped in and imposed a new order.

The Hellenistic kingdoms shared a common political system that represented a break with their Greek past. To the Greeks, monarchy was an institution for barbarians, associated in their minds with people like the Persians. Although they retained democratic forms of government in their cities, at the same time the Greeks of the Hellenistic world were forced to accept monarchy as a new fact of political life.

Although Alexander the Great had apparently planned to fuse Greeks and easterners—he used Persians as administrators and encouraged his soldiers to marry easterners, as he himself did—Hellenistic monarchs relied primarily on Greeks and Macedonians to form the new ruling class. It has been estimated that in the Seleucid kingdom, for example, only 2.5 percent of the people in authority were non-Greek, and most of them were commanders of local military units. Those who did advance to important administrative posts had learned Greek (all government business was transacted in Greek) and had become Hellenized in a cultural sense. The policy of excluding non-Greeks from leadership positions, it should be added, was not due to the incompetence of the natives but to the determination of the Greek ruling class to maintain its privileged position. It was the Greco-Macedonian ruling class that provided the only unity in the Hellenistic world.

✺ Hellenistic Cities

Cities played an especially important role in the Hellenistic kingdoms. Throughout his conquests, Alexander had founded a series of new cities and military settlements, and Hellenistic kings did likewise (see Map 4.2). The new population centers varied considerably in size and importance. Military settlements

MAP 4.2 The World of the Hellenistic Kingdoms.

were meant to maintain order and might consist of only a few hundred men who were strongly dependent on the king. But there were also new independent cities with thousands of inhabitants. Alexandria in Egypt was the largest city in the Mediterranean region by the first century B.C.

Hellenistic rulers encouraged this massive spread of Greek colonists to the Near East because of their intrinsic value to the new monarchies. Greeks (and Macedonians) provided not only a recruiting ground for the army but also a pool of civilian administrators and workers who would contribute to economic development. Even architects, engineers, dramatists, and actors were in demand in the new Greek cities. Many Greeks and Macedonians were quick to see the advantages of moving to the new urban centers and gladly sought their fortunes in the Near East. Greeks of all backgrounds joined the exodus, at least until around 250 B.C., when the outpouring began to slow significantly.

Within the Hellenistic cities, the culture was primarily Greek. The political institutions of the cities were modeled after those of the Greek *polis*. Greeks of the classical period would easily have recognized the councils, assemblies, and codes of law. The physical layout of the new cities was also modeled after those of the Greek homeland. Using the traditional rectilinear grid, cities were laid out with temples, altars, and stone theaters.

Many of the new urban centers were completely dominated by Greeks while the native populations remained cut off from all civic institutions. The Greeks commissioned purely Greek sculpture, read literature of the classical period, and had separate law courts for themselves. Complaints from resentful natives have been recorded. An Egyptian camel driver, for example, complained bitterly that he was not paid regularly because he did "not know how to behave like a Greek." Not only was it difficult for easterners to enter the ranks of the ruling class, but those who did so had to become thoroughly Hellenized. This often required alienation from one's own culture.

The Greeks' belief in their own cultural superiority provided an easy rationalization for their political dominance of the eastern cities. But Greek control of the new cities of the Near East was also necessary because the kings frequently used the cities as instruments of government, enabling them to rule considerable territory without an extensive bureaucracy. At the same time, for security reasons, the Greeks needed the support of the kings. After all, the Hellenistic cities were islands of Greek culture in a sea of non-

Greeks. The relationship between rulers and cities, therefore, was a symbiotic one that bore serious consequences for the cities.

In the political system, religious practices, and architecture of their new cities, the Greeks tried to recreate the *poleis* of their homeland. But it was no longer possible to do so. The new cities were not autonomous entities and soon found themselves dependent on the power of the Hellenistic monarchies. Although the kings did not rule the cities directly, they restricted freedom in other ways. Cities knew they could not conduct an independent foreign policy and did not try to do so. The kings also demanded tribute, which could be a heavy burden.

The Greek cities of the Hellenistic era were the chief agents for the spread of Hellenic culture in the Near East, as far, in fact, as modern Afghanistan and India. These Greek cities were also remarkably vibrant despite their subordination to the Hellenistic monarchies and persisted in being a focal point for the loyalty of their citizens.

❊ Economic and Social Trends in the Hellenistic World

Agriculture was still of primary importance to both the native populations and the new Greek cities of the Hellenistic world. The Greek cities continued their old agrarian patterns. A well-defined citizen body owned land and worked it with the assistance of slaves. But these farms were isolated units in a vast area of land ultimately owned by the king or assigned to large estate owners and worked by native peasants dwelling in villages. Overall, then, neither agricultural patterns nor methods of production underwent significant changes.

Few new products or manufacturing methods were introduced during the Hellenistic era, but the centers of manufacturing shifted significantly. Industry spread from Greece to the east—especially to Asia Minor, Rhodes, and Egypt. New textile centers were set up at Pergamum, while glass and silver crafts were developed in Syria. And busiest of all the cities in manufacturing was Alexandria in Egypt, center of the production of parchment, textiles, linens, oil, metalwork, and glass.

Commerce experienced considerable expansion in the Hellenistic era. Indeed, trading contacts linked much of the Hellenistic world together. The decline in the number of political barriers encouraged more commercial traffic. Although Hellenistic monarchs still fought wars, the conquests of Alexander and the policies of his successors made possible greater trade between east and west. An incredible variety of products were traded: gold and silver from Spain; salt from Asia Minor; timber from Macedonia; ebony, gems, ivory, and spices from India; frankincense (used on altars) from Arabia; slaves from Thrace, Syria, and Asia Minor; fine wines from Syria and western Asia Minor; olive oil from Athens; and numerous exquisite foodstuffs, such as the famous prunes of Damascus. The greatest trade, however, was in the basic staple of life—grain.

✎ NEW OPPORTUNITIES FOR WOMEN

One of the significant features of social life in the Hellenistic world was the emergence of new opportunities for women—at least, for upper-class women—especially in the economic area. Documents show increasing numbers of women involved in managing slaves, selling property, and making loans. Even then, legal contracts in which women were involved had to include their official male guardians, although in numerous instances these men no longer played an important function but were only listed to satisfy legal requirements. In Sparta, women were allowed to own land and manage their own economic affairs. Because many of their husbands were absent or had died in war, many Spartan women became noticeably wealthy; females owned 40 percent of Spartan land.

Spartan women, however, were an exception, especially on the Greek mainland. Women in Athens, for example, still remained highly restricted and supervised. Although a few philosophers welcomed female participation in men's affairs, many philosophers rejected equality between men and women and asserted that the traditional roles of wives and mothers were most satisfying for women. In her treatise "On Chastity," Phintys wrote that "serving as generals, public officials, and statesmen is appropriate for men," but "keeping house, remaining within, and taking care of husbands belongs to women."[2]

But the opinions of philosophers did not prevent upper-class women from making gains in areas other than the economic sphere (see the box on p. 76). New possibilities for females arose when women in some areas of the Hellenistic world were allowed to pursue education in the traditional fields of literature, music, and even athletics. Education, then, provided new opportunities for women: female poets appeared again in the third century B.C., and there are instances of women involved in both scholarly and artistic activities.

The creation of the Hellenistic monarchies, which represented a considerable departure from the world of the *polis*, also gave new scope to the role played by the monarchs' wives, the Hellenistic queens.

In Macedonia, a pattern of alliances between mothers and sons provided openings for women to take an active role in politics, especially in political intrigue. In Egypt, opportunities for royal women were even greater because the Ptolemaic rulers reverted to an Egyptian custom of kings marrying their own sisters. Of the first eight Ptolemaic rulers, four wed their sisters. Ptolemy II and his sister-wife Arsinoë II were both worshiped as gods in their lifetimes. Arsinoë played an energetic role in government and was involved in the expansion of the Egyptian navy. She was also the first Egyptian queen whose portrait appeared on coins with

PORTRAIT OF QUEEN ARSINOË II. **Arsinoë II, sister and wife of King Ptolemy II, played an active role in Egyptian political affairs. This statue from around 270–240 B.C. shows the queen in the traditional style of a pharaoh.**

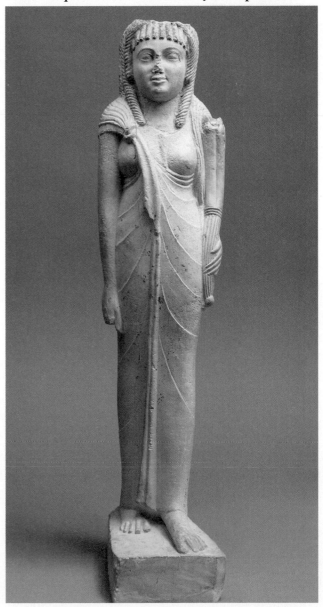

A New Autonomy for Women

There were noticeable gains for upper-class women in Hellenistic society. But even in the lives of ordinary women, a new assertiveness came to the fore despite the continuing domination of society by men. The first selection is taken from the letter of a wife to her husband, complaining about his failure to return home. In the second selection, a father complains that his daughter has abandoned him, contrary to the Egyptian law providing that children who have been properly raised should support their parents.

❈ *Letter from Isias to Hephaistion, 168 B.C.*

If you are well and other things are going right, it would accord with the prayer that I make continually to the gods. I myself and the child and all the household are in good health and think of you always. When I received your letter from Horos, in which you announce that you are in detention in the Serapeum at Memphis, for the news that you are well I straightway thanked the gods, but about your not coming home, when all the others who had been secluded there have come, I am ill-pleased, because after having piloted myself and your child through such bad times and been driven to every extremity owing to the price of wheat, I thought that now at least, with you at home, I should enjoy some respite, whereas you have not even thought of coming home nor given any regard to our circumstances, remembering how I was in want of everything while you were still here, not to mention this long lapse of time and these critical days, during which you have sent us nothing. As, moreover, Horos who delivered the letter has brought news of

your having been released from detention, I am thoroughly ill-pleased. Notwithstanding, as your mother also is annoyed, for her sake as well as for mine please return to the city, if nothing more pressing holds you back. You will do me a favor by taking care of your bodily health. Farewell.

❈ *Letter from Ktesikles to King Ptolemy, 220 B.C.*

I am wronged by Dionysios and by Nike my daughter. For though I raised her, my own daughter, and educated her and brought her to maturity, when I was stricken with bodily ill-health and was losing my eyesight, she was not minded to furnish me with any of the necessities of life. When I sought to obtain justice from her in Alexandria, she begged my pardon, and in the eighteenth year she swore me a written royal oath to give me each month twenty drachmas, which she was to earn by her own bodily labor. . . . But now corrupted by Dionysios, who is a comic actor, she does not do for me anything of what was in the written oath, despising my weakness and ill-health. I beg you, therefore, O King, not to allow me to be wronged by my daughter and by Dionysios the actor who corrupted her, but to order Diophanes the strategus [a provincial administrator] to summon them and hear us out; and if I am speaking the truth, let Diophanes deal with her corrupter as seems good to him and compel my daughter Nike to do justice to me. If this is done I shall no longer be wronged but by fleeing to you, O King, I shall obtain justice.

---

her husband. Hellenistic queens also showed an intense interest in culture. They wrote poems, collected art, and corresponded with intellectuals.

◆ Culture in the Hellenistic World

Although the Hellenistic kingdoms encompassed vast areas and many diverse peoples, the Greeks provided a sense of unity as a result of the diffusion of Greek culture throughout the Hellenistic world. The Hellenis-

tic era was a period of considerable cultural accomplishment in many areas—literature, art, science, and philosophy. Although these achievements occurred throughout the Hellenistic world, certain centers, especially the great Hellenistic cities of Alexandria and Pergamum, stood out. In both cities, cultural developments were encouraged by the rulers themselves. Rich Hellenistic kings had considerable resources with which to patronize culture.

The Ptolemies in Egypt made Alexandria an especially important cultural center. The library became the largest in ancient times, housing more than

500,000 scrolls. The museum (literally, "temple of the Muses") created a favorable environment for scholarly research. Alexandria became home to poets, writers, philosophers, and scientists—scholars of all kinds.

✳ New Directions in Literature and Art

The Hellenistic Age produced an enormous quantity of literature, most of which has not survived. Hellenistic monarchs, who held literary talent in high esteem, subsidized writers on a grand scale. The Ptolemaic rulers of Egypt were particularly lavish. The combination of their largess and the famous library drew a host of scholars and authors to Alexandria, including a circle of poets. Theocritus (c. 315–250 B.C.), originally a native of the island of Sicily, wrote "little poems" or idylls dealing with erotic subjects, lovers' complaints, and pastoral themes expressing his love of nature and its beauty.

In the Hellenistic era, Athens remained the theatrical center of the Greek world. As tragedy withered, writers invented New Comedy, which rejected political themes and sought only to entertain and amuse. The Athenian playwright Menander (c. 342–291 B.C.) was perhaps the best representative of New Comedy. Plots were simple: typically, a hero falls in love with a not-really-so-bad prostitute who turns out eventually to be the long-lost daughter of a rich neighbor. The hero marries her, and they live happily ever after.

The Hellenistic period saw a great outpouring of historical and biographical literature. The chief historian of the Hellenistic age was Polybius (c. 203–c. 120 B.C.), a Greek who lived for some years in Rome. He is regarded by many historians as second only to Thucydides among Greek historians. His major work consisted of forty books narrating the history of the "inhabited Mediterranean world" from 221 to 146 B.C. Only the first five books are extant, although long extracts from the rest of the books survive. His history focuses on the growth of Rome from a city-state to a vast empire. It is apparent that Polybius understood the significance of the Romans' achievement. He followed Thucydides in seeking rational motives for historical events. He also approached his sources critically and used firsthand accounts.

In addition to being patrons of literary talent, the Hellenistic monarchs were eager to spend their money to beautify and adorn the cities in their states. The founding of new cities and the rebuilding of old ones provided numerous opportunities for Greek architects and sculptors. The structures of the Greek homeland—gymnasia, baths, theaters, and, of course, temples—lined the streets of these cities. Most noticeable in these temples was the use of the more ornate Corinthian order, which became especially popular during the Hellenistic Age.

Sculptors were patronized by Hellenistic kings and rich citizens. Thousands of statues, many paid for by the people honored, were erected in towns and cities all over the Hellenistic world. Hellenistic sculptors traveled throughout this world, attracted by the material rewards offered by wealthy patrons. While maintaining the technical skill of the classical period, Hellenistic sculptors moved away from the idealism of fifth-century classicism to a more emotional and realistic art, seen in numerous statues of old women, drunks, and little children at play.

OLD MARKET WOMAN. Greek architects and sculptors were highly valued throughout the Hellenistic world, as kings undertook projects to beautify the cities of their kingdoms. The sculptors of this period no longer tried to capture ideal beauty in their sculpture, a quest that characterized Greek classicism, but moved toward a more emotional and realistic art. This statue of an old market woman is typical of this new trend in art.

✤ A Golden Age of Science

The Hellenistic era witnessed a more conscious separation of science from philosophy. In classical Greece, what we would call the physical and life sciences had been divisions of philosophical inquiry. Nevertheless, the Greeks, by the time of Aristotle, had already established an important principle of scientific investigation, empirical research, or systematic observation as the basis for generalization. In the Hellenistic Age, the sciences tended to be studied in their own right.

One of the traditional areas of Greek science was astronomy, and two Alexandrian scholars continued this exploration. Aristarchus of Samos (c. 310–230 B.C.) developed a heliocentric view of the universe, contending that the sun and the fixed stars remained stationary while the earth rotated around the sun in a circular orbit. This view was not widely accepted, and most scholars clung to the earlier geocentric view of the Greeks, which held that the earth was at the center of the universe. Another astronomer—Eratosthenes (c. 275–194 B.C.)—determined that the earth was round and calculated the earth's circumference at 24,675 miles, within 200 miles of the actual figure.

A third Alexandrian scholar was Euclid, who lived around 300 B.C. He established a school in Alexandria but is primarily known for his *Elements*. This was a systematic organization of the fundamental elements of geometry as they had already been worked out; it became the standard textbook of plane geometry and was used up to modern times.

By far the most famous of the scientists of the Hellenistic period, Archimedes (287–212 B.C.) came from the western Mediterranean region. Archimedes was especially important for his work on the geometry of spheres and cylinders, for establishing the value of the mathematical constant pi, and for creating the science of hydrostatics. Archimedes was also a practical inventor. He may have devised the so-called Archimedean screw used to pump water out of mines and to lift irrigation water as well as a compound pulley for transporting heavy weights. During the Roman siege of his native city of Syracuse, he constructed a number of devices to thwart the attackers. According to Plutarch's account, the Romans became so frightened "that if they did but see a little rope or a piece of wood from the wall, instantly crying out, that there it was again, Archimedes was about to let fly some engine at them, they turned their backs and fled."[3] Archimedes' accomplishments inspired a wealth of semilegendary stories. Supposedly, he discovered specific gravity by observing the water he displaced in his bath and became so excited by his realization that he jumped out of the water and ran home naked, shouting "Eureka!" ("I have found it!"). He is said to have emphasized the importance of levers by proclaiming to the king of Syracuse: "Give me a lever and a place to stand on, and I will move the earth." The king was so impressed that he encouraged Archimedes to lower his sights and build defensive weapons instead.

✤ Philosophy: New Schools of Thought

While Alexandria and Pergamum became the renowned cultural centers of the Hellenistic world, Athens remained the prime center for philosophy. After Alexander the Great, the home of Socrates, Plato, and Aristotle continued to attract the most illustrious philosophers from the Greek world, who chose to establish their schools there. New schools of philosophical thought (the Epicureans and Stoics) reinforced Athens' reputation as a philosophical center.

Epicurus (341–270 B.C.), the founder of Epicureanism, established a school in Athens near the end of the fourth century B.C. Epicurus' famous belief in a doctrine of pleasure began with his view of the world. Though he did not deny the existence of the gods, he did not believe they played any active role in the world. The universe ran on its own. This left human beings free to follow self-interest as a basic motivating force. Happiness was the goal of life, and the means to achieving it was the pursuit of pleasure, the only true good. But the pursuit of pleasure was not meant in a physical, hedonistic sense:

> When, therefore, we maintain that pleasure is the end, we do not mean the pleasures of profligates and those that consist in sensuality, as is supposed by some who are either ignorant or disagree with us or do not understand, but freedom from pain in the body and from trouble in the mind. For it is not continuous drinkings and revellings, nor the satisfaction of lusts, nor the enjoyment of fish and other luxuries of the wealthy table, which produce a pleasant life, but sober reasoning, searching out the motives for all choice and avoidance, and banishing mere opinions, to which are due the greatest disturbance of the spirit.[4]

Pleasure was not satisfying one's desire in an active, gluttonous fashion but rather freedom from emotional turmoil, freedom from worry, the freedom that came from a mind at rest. To achieve this passive pleasure, one had to free oneself from public activity: "We must release ourselves from the prison of affairs and politics." They were too strenuous to give peace of mind. But this was not a renunciation of all social life, for to

The Stoic Ideal of Harmony with God

The Stoic Cleanthes (331–232 B.C.) succeeded Zeno as head of this school of philosophy. One historian of Hellenistic civilization has called this work by Cleanthes the greatest religious hymn in Greek literature. Certainly, it demonstrates that Stoicism, unlike Epicureanism, did have an underlying spiritual foundation. This poem has been compared to the great psalms of the Hebrews.

✳ *Cleanthes,* Hymn to Zeus

Nothing occurs on the earth apart from you, O God,
nor in the heavenly regions nor on the sea,
except what bad men do in their folly;

but you know to make the odd even,
and to harmonize what is dissonant; to you the alien is akin.
And so you have wrought together into one all things that are good and bad,
So that there arises one eternal logos [rationale] of all things,
Which all bad mortals shun and ignore,
Unhappy wretches, ever seeking the possession of good things
They neither see nor hear the universal law of God,
By obeying which they might enjoy a happy life.

Epicurus, a life could only be complete when it was centered on the basic ideal of friendship: "Of all the things which wisdom acquires to produce the blessedness of the complete life, far the greatest is the possession of friendship."[5] Epicurus' own life in Athens was an embodiment of his teachings. He and his friends created their own private community where they could pursue their ideal of true happiness.

Epicureanism was eventually overshadowed by another school of thought known as Stoicism, which became the most popular philosophy of the Hellenistic world and later flourished in the Roman Empire as well. It was the product of a teacher named Zeno (335–263 B.C.), who came to Athens and began to teach in a public colonnade known as the Painted Portico (the *Stoa Poikile*—hence Stoicism). Like Epicureanism, Stoicism was concerned with how individuals find happiness. But Stoics took a radically different approach to the problem. To them, happiness, the supreme good, could be found only in virtue, which meant essentially living in harmony with the divine will. One achieved happiness by choosing to follow the divine will through the free exercise of one's own will. To the Stoics, the divine will was the same thing as the will of nature because nature was simply a manifestation or expression of the gods. "Living according to nature," therefore, meant following the divine will or the natural laws that the gods established to run the universe.

Virtuous living, then, was living in accordance with the laws of nature or submitting to the divine will (see the box above). This led to the acceptance of whatever one received in life since the divine will

for us was by its very nature good. By accepting divine law, people mastered themselves and gained inner peace. Life's problems could not disturb such individuals, and they could bear whatever life offered (hence our word *stoic*).

Unlike Epicureans, Stoics did not believe in the need to separate oneself from the world and politics. Public service was regarded as noble. The real Stoic was a good citizen and could even be a good government official. Because Stoics believed that a divine principle was present throughout the universe, each human being also contained a divine spark. This led to a belief in the oneness of humanity. The world constituted a single society of equal human beings. Although they were not equal in the outer world, because each contained the divine spark, all were free to follow the divine will (what was best for each individual). All persons then, even slaves, though unfree in body, were equal at the level of the soul.

Epicureanism and especially Stoicism appealed to large numbers of people in the Hellenistic world. Both of these philosophies focused primarily on the problem of human happiness. Their popularity would suggest a fundamental change in the character of the Greek lifestyle. In the classical Greek world, the happiness of individuals and the meaning of life were closely associated with the life of the *polis*. One found fulfillment within the community. In the Hellenistic kingdoms, although the *polis* continued to exist, the sense that one could find satisfaction and fulfillment through life in the *polis* had weakened. Not only did individuals seek new philosophies that offered personal happiness, but in the cosmopolitan world of the

---

Hellenistic states, with their mixtures of peoples, a new openness to thoughts of universality could also emerge. For some people, Stoicism embodied this larger sense of community. The appeal of new philosophies in the Hellenistic era can also be explained by the apparent decline in certain aspects of traditional religion, which we can see by examining the status of Hellenistic religion.

✹ Religion in the Hellenistic World

When the Greeks spread throughout the Hellenistic kingdoms, they took their gods with them. Although the construction of temples may have been less important than in classical times, there were still many demonstrations of a lively religious faith. But over a period of time, there was a noticeable decline in the vitality of the traditional Greek Olympian religion. Much of Greek religion had always revolved around ritual, but the civic cults based on the traditional gods no longer seemed sufficient to satisfy people's emotional needs.

The decline in traditional Greek religion left Greeks receptive to the numerous religious cults of the eastern world. The Greeks were always tolerant of other existing religious institutions. Hence in the Hellenistic cities of the Near East, the traditional civic cults of their own gods and foreign cults existed side by side. Alexandria had cults of the traditional Greek gods, Egyptian deities such as Isis and Horus, the Babylonian Astarte, and the Syrian Atargatis. The strongest appeal of eastern religions to Greeks, however, came from the mystery religions. What was the source of their attraction?

The normal forms of religious worship in Hellenistic communities had lost some of their appeal. The practices of traditional, ritualized Greek religion in the civic cults seemed increasingly meaningless. For many people, the search for personal meaning remained unfulfilled, and they sought alternatives. Among educated Greeks, the philosophies of Epicureanism and especially Stoicism offered help. Another source of solace came in the form of mystery religions.

Mystery cults, with their secret initiations and promises of individual salvation, were not new to the Greek world. But the Greeks of the Hellenistic era were also strongly influenced by eastern mystery cults, such as those of Egypt, which offered a distinct advantage over the Greek mystery religions. The latter had usually been connected to specific locations (such as Eleusis), which meant that a would-be initiate had to undertake a pil-

THE CULT OF ISIS. The cult of Isis was one of the most popular mystery religions in the Hellenistic world. This fresco from Herculaneum in Italy depicts a religious ceremony in front of the temple of Isis. At the top, a priest holds a golden vessel while below him another priest leads the worshipers with a staff. A third priest fans the flames at the altar.

grimage in order to participate in the rites. In contrast, the eastern mystery religions were readily available since temples to their gods and goddesses were located throughout the Greek cities of the east.

All of the mystery religions were based on the same fundamental premises. Individuals could pursue a path to salvation and achieve eternal life by being initiated into a union with a savior god or goddess who had died and risen again. The ritual of initiation, by which the seeker identified with the god or goddess, was, no doubt, a highly emotional experience.

The Egyptian cult of Isis was one of the most popular of the mystery religions. The cult of Isis was very ancient but became truly universal in Hellenistic times. Isis was the goddess of women, marriage, and children, as one of her hymns states: "I am she whom women call goddess. I ordained that women should be loved by men: I brought wife and husband together, and invented the marriage contract. I ordained that women should bear children. . . ."[6] Isis was also portrayed as the giver of civilization who had brought laws and letters to all humankind. The cult of Isis offered a precious commodity to its initiates—the promise of eternal life. In many ways, the mystery religions of the Hellenistic era helped pave the way for Christianity.

THE JEWS IN THE HELLENISTIC WORLD

In observing the similarities among their gods and goddesses, Greeks and easterners tended to assume they were the same beings with different names, giving rise to a process of syncretism. But a special position was occupied in the Hellenistic world by the Hebrews, whose monotheistic religion was exclusive and did not permit this kind of fusion of spiritual beings.

The Jewish province of Judaea was ruled by the Ptolemies until it fell under the control of the Seleucids by 200 B.C. In the reign of the Seleucid king Antiochus IV (175–163 B.C.), conflict erupted in Judaea. Hellenistic monarchs were generally tolerant of all religions, but problems with Rome prompted Antiochus to try to impose more cultural and religious unity throughout his kingdom. When he sent troops to Jerusalem and seized the Temple, he sparked a Jewish uprising led by Judas Maccabaeus (164 B.C.). The rebels succeeded in recapturing the Temple, a joyous event that has been celebrated every year since in the Jewish holiday of Hanukkah, the Festival of Lights. Although the conflict in Judaea continued, the Seleucids ultimately made concessions and allowed the Jews considerable freedom.

But large numbers of Jews no longer lived in Judaea. There was a large Jewish population in Egypt, particularly in Alexandria, as well as Jewish settlements throughout the cities of Asia Minor and Syria. In each city, Jews generally set up a synagogue and formed a private association for worship as other foreigners did. But some city authorities also allowed the Jews to form a political corporation that gave them greater rights than other resident aliens. Most important, they gained the privilege to live by their own laws and their own judicial system. The Jews were not really interested in citizenship in the cities in which they resided since full citizenship meant worship of the city's gods, anathema to Jews, who believed only in Yahweh.

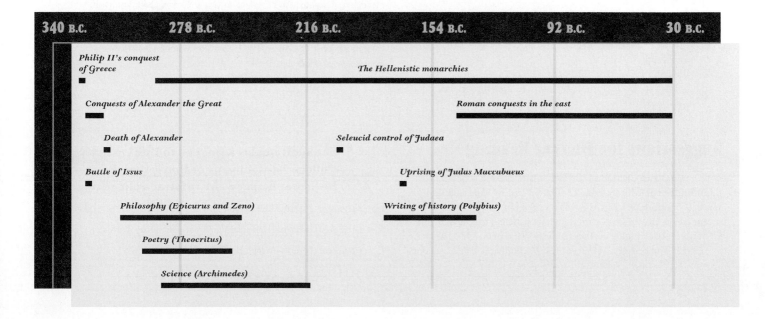

Conclusion

Although historians once viewed the Hellenistic era as a period of stagnation after the brilliant Greek civilization of the fifth century B.C., *our survey of the Hellenistic world has shown the inaccuracy of that position. The Hellenistic period was vibrant in its own way. New cities arose and flourished. New philosophical ideas captured the minds of many. Significant achievements occurred in art, literature, and science. Greek culture spread throughout the Near East and made an impact wherever it was carried. In some areas of the Hellenistic world, queens played an active role in political life, and many upper-class women found new avenues for expressing themselves.*

But serious problems remained. Hellenistic kings continued to engage in inconclusive wars. Much of the formal culture was the special preserve of the Greek conquerors, whose attitude of superiority kept them largely separated from the native masses of the Hellenistic kingdoms. Although the Hellenistic world achieved a degree of political stability, by the late third century B.C. *signs of decline were beginning to multiply. Some of the more farsighted perhaps realized the danger presented to the Hellenistic world by the growing power of Rome. The Romans would ultimately inherit Alexander's empire, and we must now turn to them and try to understand what made them such successful conquerors.*

Notes

1. Quoted in Sarah B. Pomeroy, Stanley M. Burstein, Walter Donlan, and Jennifer Tolbert Roberts, *Ancient Greece: A Political, Social, and Cultural History* (Oxford, 1999), p. 390.
2. Quoted in M. B. Fant and M. R. Lefkowitz, *Women's Life in Greece and Rome: A Source Book in Translation* (Baltimore, 1992), no. 208
3. Plutarch, *Life of Marcellus*, trans. John Dryden (New York, n.d.), p. 378.
4. *Epicurus: The Extant Remains*, trans. Cyril Bailey (Oxford, 1926), pp. 89–90.
5. Ibid., pp. 115, 101.
6. Quoted in W. W. Tarn, *Hellenistic Civilization* (London, 1930), p. 324.

Suggestions for Further Reading

For a general introduction to the Hellenistic era, see J. Boardman, J. Griffin, and O. Murray, eds., *The Oxford History of the Classical World* (Oxford, 1986), pp. 315–385. A brief but excellent guide to recent trends in scholarship on the Hellenistic era can be found in C. Starr, *Past and Future in Ancient History* (Lanham, Md., 1987), pp. 19–32. The best general survey is F. W. Walbank, *The Hellenistic World* (Cambridge, Mass., 1993). Other studies include C. B. Welles, *Alexander and the Hellenistic World* (Toronto, 1970); W. W. Tarn and G. T. Griffith, *Hellenistic Civilization*, 3d ed. (London, 1952); M. Grant, *From Alexander to Cleopatra: The Hellenistic World* (London, 1982); and P. Green, *Alexander to Actium: The Historic Evolution of the Hellenistic Age* (Berkeley, 1990).

For a good introduction to the early history of Macedonia, see E. N. Borza, *In the Shadow of Olympus: The Emergence of Macedon* (Princeton, N.J., 1990), and R. M. Errington, *A History of Macedonia* (Berkeley, 1990). Philip is covered well in G. L. Cawkwell, *Philip of Macedon* (London, 1978). There are considerable differences of opinion on Alexander the Great. Good biographies include R. L. Fox, *Alexander the Great* (London, 1973); J. R. Hamilton, *Alexander the Great* (London, 1973); N. G. L. Hammond, *Alexander the Great* (London, 1981); and P. Green, *Alexander of Macedon* (Berkeley, 1991).

Studies on the various Hellenistic monarchies include N. G. L. Hammond and F. W. Walbank, *A History of Macedonia*, vol. 3 (Oxford, 1988); N. Lewis, *Greeks in Ptolemaic Egypt* (Oxford, 1986); R. E. Allen, *The Attalid Kingdom* (Oxford, 1983); and S. Sherwin-White and A. Kuhrt, *From Samarkhand to Sardis: A New Approach to the Seleucid Empire* (London, 1993).

A good survey of Hellenistic cities can be found in A. H. M. Jones, *The Greek City from Alexander to Justinian* (Oxford, 1940). Alexandria is covered in P. M. Fraser, *Ptolemaic Alexandria* (Oxford, 1972). On economic and social trends, see M. I. Finley, *The Ancient Economy*, 2d ed. (London, 1985), and the classic and still indispensable M. I. Rostovtzeff, *Social and Economic History of the Hellenistic World*, 3 vols., 2d ed. (Oxford, 1953).

Hellenistic women are examined in two works by S. B. Pomeroy, *Goddesses, Whores, Wives, and Slaves* (New York, 1975), pp. 120–148, and *Women in Hellenistic Egypt* (New York, 1984).

For a general introduction to Hellenistic culture, see J. Onians, *Art and Thought in the Hellenistic Age* (London, 1979). On art, see J. J. Pollitt, *Art in the Hellenistic Age* (New York, 1986). The best general survey of Hellenistic philosophy is A. A. Long, *Hellenistic Philosophy: Stoics, Epicureans, Skeptics*, 2d ed. (London, 1986). A superb work on Hellenistic science is G. E. R. Lloyd, *Greek Science After Aristotle* (London, 1973).

On various facets of Hellenistic religion, see L. Martin, *Hellenistic Religions: An Introduction* (New York, 1987), and R. E. Witt, *Isis in the Graeco-Roman World* (London, 1971).

On the entry of Rome into the Hellenistic world, see the basic work by E. S. Gruen, *The Hellenistic World and the Coming of Rome*, 2 vols. (Berkeley, 1984).

 For additional reading, go to InfoTrac College Edition, your online research library at http://web1.infotrac-college.com

Enter the search terms *Greece history* using Key Terms.

Enter the search terms *Alexander the Great* using Key Terms.

Enter the search term *Archimedes* using Key Terms.

CHAPTER 5

The Roman Republic

CHAPTER OUTLINE

- The Emergence of Rome
- The Roman Republic (c. 509–264 B.C.)
- The Roman Conquest of the Mediterranean (264–133 B.C.)
- Society and Culture in the Roman World
- The Decline and Fall of the Roman Republic (133–31 B.C.)
- Conclusion

FOCUS QUESTIONS

- What influence did the Etruscans and Greeks have on early Roman history?
- What policies and institutions help explain the Romans' success in conquering first Italy and then the entire Mediterranean world?
- What were the characteristics of the Roman family, and how did the family change between the early and the late Republic?
- How did the acquisition of an empire affect Roman social and economic institutions, values and attitudes, and art and literature?
- What were the main problems Rome faced during the last century of the Republic, and how were they ultimately resolved?

*E*ARLY ROMAN HISTORY *is filled with legendary stories that tell of the heroes who made Rome great. One of the best known is the story of Horatius at the bridge. Threatened by attack from the neighboring Etruscans, Roman farmers abandoned their fields and moved into the city, where they would be protected by the walls. One weak point in the Roman defenses, however, was a wooden bridge over the Tiber River. Horatius was on guard at the bridge when a sudden assault by the Etruscans caused many Roman troops to throw down their weapons and flee. Horatius urged them to make a stand at the bridge to protect Rome; when they hesitated, as a last resort he told them to destroy the bridge behind him while he held the Etruscans back. Astonished at the sight of a single defender, the* confused Etruscans threw their spears at Horatius, who caught them on his shield and barred the way. By the time the Etruscans had regrouped and were about to overwhelm the lone defender, the Roman soldiers brought down the bridge. When Horatius heard the bridge crash into the river behind him, he dived fully armed into the water and swam safely to the other side through a hail of arrows. Rome had been saved by the courageous act of a Roman who knew his duty and was determined to carry it out. Courage, duty, determination—these qualities would also serve the many Romans who believed that it was their mission to rule nations and peoples.

In the first millennium B.C., a group of Latin-speaking people established a small community on the plain of Latium on the Italian peninsula. This community, called Rome, was merely one of the numerous communities founded by Latin-speaking peoples throughout Latium and the rest of Italy. Roman history is basically the story of the Romans' conquest of the plain of Latium, then Italy, and finally the entire Mediterranean world. Why were the Romans able to do this? Scholars do not really know all the answers. The Romans made the right decisions at the right time; in other words, they had political wisdom.

The Romans were also practical. Unlike the Greeks, who reserved their citizenship for small, select groups, the Romans often offered their citizenship to the peoples they conquered, thus laying the groundwork for a strong, integrated empire. The Romans also did not hesitate to borrow ideas and culture from the Greeks. Roman strength lay in government, law, and engineering. The Romans knew how to govern people, establish legal structures, and construct the roads that took them to the ends of the known world. Throughout their empire, they carried their law, their political institutions, their engineering skills, and their Latin language. And even after the Romans were gone, those same gifts continued to play an important role in the civilizations that came after them.

◆ The Emergence of Rome

Italy is a peninsula extending about 750 miles from north to south (see Map 5.1). It is not very wide, however, averaging about 120 miles across. The Apennine Mountains traverse the peninsula from north to south, forming a ridge down the middle that divides west from east. Nevertheless, Italy has some fairly large fertile plains ideal for farming. Most important were the Po valley in the north, probably the most fertile agricultural area; the plain of Latium, on which Rome was located; and Campania to the south of Latium. East of the Italian peninsula is the Adriatic Sea and to the west the Tyrrhenian Sea with the nearby large islands of Corsica and Sardinia. Sicily lies just west of the toe of the boot-shaped Italian peninsula.

Geography had an impact on Roman history. Although the Apennines bisected Italy, they were less rugged than the mountain ranges of Greece and did not divide the peninsula into many small isolated communities. Italy also possessed considerably more productive farmland than Greece, enabling it to support a large population. Rome's location was favorable from a geographical point of view. Located 18 miles inland on the Tiber River, Rome had access to the sea and yet was far enough inland to be safe from pirates. Built on the famous seven hills, it was easily defended. Situated where the Tiber could be readily forded, Rome became a natural crossing point for north-south traffic in western Italy. All in all, Rome had a good central location in Italy from which to expand.

Moreover, the Italian peninsula juts into the Mediterranean, making it an important crossroads between the western and eastern Mediterranean. Once Rome had unified Italy, involvement in Mediterranean affairs was natural. And after the Romans had conquered their Mediterranean empire, governing it was made considerably easier by Italy's central location.

✳ The Greeks and Etruscans

We know little about the Indo-European peoples who moved into Italy during the second half of the second millennium B.C. By the first millennium B.C., other peoples had also settled in Italy—the two most notable being the Greeks and the Etruscans. The Greeks arrived on the Italian peninsula in large numbers during the age of Greek colonization (750–550 B.C.; see Chapter 3). Initially, the Greeks settled in southern Italy and gradually migrated around the coast and up the peninsula as far as Brindisi. They also occupied the eastern two-thirds of Sicily. Ultimately, the Greeks had considerable influence on Rome. They cultivated the olive and the vine, passed on their alphabetic system of writing, and provided artistic and cultural models through their sculpture, architecture, and literature. Indeed, many historians view Roman culture as a con-

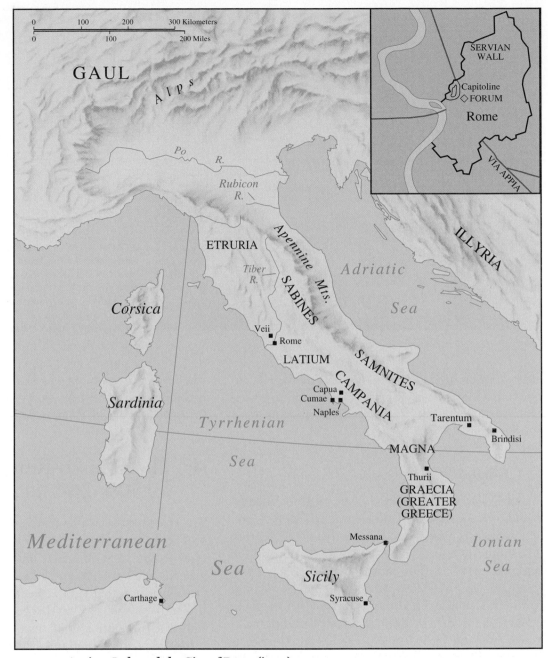

MAP 5.1   Ancient Italy and the City of Rome (inset).

tinuation of Greek culture. While Greek influence initially touched Rome indirectly through the Etruscans, the Roman conquest of southern Italy and Sicily brought them into direct contact with Greeks.

The initial development of Rome, however, was influenced most by a people known as the Etruscans, who had settled north of Rome in Etruria. The origins of the Etruscans are not clear, but after 650 B.C., they expanded in Italy and became the dominant cultural and economic force in a number of areas. To the north, they moved into north-central Italy, including the Po

valley. To the south, according to Roman tradition and archaeological evidence, they controlled Rome and possibly all of Latium. From Latium they moved south and came into direct conflict with Greek colonists in southern Italy. In the sixth century B.C., the Etruscans were at the height of their power. But by 480 B.C., Etruscan power had begun to decline, and by 400 B.C., the Etruscans were limited to Etruria itself. Later they were invaded by the Gauls and then conquered by the Romans. But by then the Etruscans had already made an impact. By transforming villages into towns and

ETRUSCAN MARRIED COUPLE. This sculpture, dating from 550 B.C., depicts a wealthy Etruscan married couple reclining on a couch. The Etruscans greatly influenced the early development of Rome and had an impact on Roman religion, sporting events, and military institutions.

cities, they brought urbanization to northern and central Italy (the Greeks brought urbanization to southern Italy). Rome was, of course, the Etruscans' most famous product.

✳ *Early Rome*

According to Roman legend, Rome was founded by twin brothers, Romulus and Remus, in 753 B.C., and archaeologists have found that by the eighth century B.C. there was a settlement consisting of huts on the tops of Rome's hills. The early Romans, basically a pastoral people, spoke Latin, which, like Greek, belongs to the Indo-European family of languages (see Table 2.1 in Chapter 2). The Roman historical tradition also maintained that early Rome (753–509 B.C.) had been under the control of seven kings and that two of the last three had been Etruscans. Some historians believe that the king list may have some historical accuracy. What is certain is that Rome did fall under the influence of the Etruscans for about one hundred years during the period of the kings.

By the beginning of the sixth century, under Etruscan influence, Rome began to change from a pastoral community to an actual city. The Etruscans were responsible for an outstanding building program. They constructed the first roadbed of the chief street through Rome—the Sacred Way—before 575 B.C. and oversaw the development of temples, markets, shops, streets, and houses. By 509 B.C., the date when the monarchy was supposedly overthrown and a republi-

can form of government was established, a new Rome had emerged, essentially as a result of the fusion of Etruscan and native Roman elements.

◆ The Roman Republic (c. 509–264 B.C.)

The transition from a monarchy to a republican government was not easy. Rome felt threatened by enemies from every direction and, in the process of meeting these threats, embarked on a course of military expansion that led to the conquest of the entire Italian peninsula. During this period of expansion in Italy, the Roman Republic developed political institutions that were, in many ways, determined by the social divisions that existed within the community.

✳ *The Roman State*

In politics and law, as in conquest, the Romans took a practical approach and fashioned political institutions in response to problems as they arose. Hence it is important to remember that the political institutions we will discuss evolved over a period of centuries.

⚘ POLITICAL INSTITUTIONS

The chief executive officers of the Roman Republic were the consuls and praetors. Two consuls, chosen annually, administered the government and led the

Roman army into battle. They possessed *imperium*, or "the right to command." In 366 B.C., a new office, that of the praetor, was created. The praetor also possessed *imperium* and could govern Rome when the consuls were away from the city and could also lead armies. The praetor's primary function, however, was the execution of justice. He was in charge of the civil law as it applied to Roman citizens. In 242 B.C., reflecting Rome's growth, another praetor was added to judge cases in which one or both people were noncitizens.

As Rome expanded into the Mediterranean, additional praetors were established to govern the newly conquered provinces (two in 227, two more in 197). But as the number of provinces continued to grow, the Romans devised a new system in which ex-consuls and ex-praetors who had served their one-year terms were given the title of proconsul and propraetor and sent out as provincial governors. This demonstrates once again the Romans' practical solution to an immediate problem. It was reasonable to assume that officials with governmental experience would make good provincial administrators, although this was not always true in practice due to the opportunities for financial corruption in the provinces.

The Roman state also had administrative officials with specialized duties. Quaestors were assigned to assist consuls and praetors in the administration of financial affairs. Aediles supervised the public games and watched over the grain supply of the city, a major problem for a rapidly growing urban community that relied on imported grain to feed its population.

The Roman senate held an especially important position in the Roman Republic. The senate or council of elders was a select group of about three hundred men who served for life. The senate was not a legislative body and could only advise the magistrates. This advice of the senate was not taken lightly, however, and by the third century B.C. it had virtually the force of law. No doubt the prestige of the senate's members furthered this development. But it also helped that the senate met continuously, while the chief magistrates changed annually and the popular assemblies operated slowly and met only periodically.

The Roman Republic possessed a number of popular assemblies. By far the most important was the centuriate assembly, essentially the Roman army functioning in its political role. Organized by classes based on wealth, it was structured in such a way that the wealthiest citizens always had a majority. The centuriate assembly elected the chief magistrates and passed laws. Another assembly, the council of the

LICTORS WITH *FASCES*. Pictured are lictors bearing the *fasces,* an ax surrounded by a bundle of rods tied with a red thong, an insignia borrowed from the Etruscan kings. The *fasces* was a symbol of the power to rule, and the consuls, the chief executives of the Roman Republic, were always preceded by twelve lictors bearing the *fasces.*

plebs, came into being in 471 B.C. as a result of the struggle of the orders.

The government of the Roman Republic, then, consisted of three major elements. Two consuls and later other elected officials served as magistrates and ran the state. An assembly of adult males (the centuriate assembly), controlled by the wealthiest citizens, elected these officials, while the senate, a small group of large landowners, advised them. The Roman state, then, was an aristocratic republic controlled by a relatively small group of privileged people.

❧ THE STRUGGLE OF THE ORDERS: SOCIAL DIVISIONS IN THE ROMAN REPUBLIC

The most noticeable element in the social organization of early Rome was the division between two groups—the patricians and the plebeians. The patrician class in Rome consisted of families who were descended from the original senators appointed during the period of the kings. Their initial prominence was probably due to their wealth as great landowners. Thus patricians constituted an aristocratic governing class. Only they could be consuls, other magistrates, and senators. Through their patronage of large numbers of dependent clients, they could control the centuriate assembly and many other facets of Roman life.

The plebeians constituted the considerably larger group of "independent, unprivileged, poorer, and vulnerable men" as well as large nonpatrician landowners, less wealthy landholders, craftspeople, merchants, and small farmers. Although they were citizens, they did not possess the same rights as the patricians. Both patricians and plebeians could vote, but only the patricians could be elected to governmental offices. Both had the right to make legal contracts and marriages, but intermarriage between patricians and plebeians was forbidden. At the beginning of the fifth century B.C., the plebeians began a struggle to seek both political and social equality with the patricians.

The first success of the plebeians came in 494 B.C., when they withdrew physically from the state. The patricians, who by themselves could not defend Rome, were forced to compromise. Two new officials known as tribunes of the plebs were instituted (later raised to five and then ten in number). These tribunes were given the power to protect plebeians against arrest by patrician magistrates. Moreover, after a new popular assembly for plebeians only, called the council of the plebs, was created in 471 B.C., the tribunes became responsible for convoking it and placing proposals before it. If adopted, these measures became *plebiscita* ("it is the opinion of the plebs"), but they were binding only on the plebeians, not the patricians. Nevertheless, the council of the plebs gave the plebeians considerable political leverage. After 445 B.C., when a law allowed patricians and plebeians to intermarry, the division between the two groups became less important. In the fourth century B.C., the consulship was opened to the plebeians. The climax of the struggle between the orders came in 287 B.C. with passage of a law that stipulated that all *plebiscita* passed by the council of the plebs had the force of law and were binding on the entire community, including patricians.

The struggle between the orders, then, had a significant impact on the development of the Roman constitution. Plebeians could hold the highest offices of state, they could intermarry with the patricians, and they could pass laws binding on the entire Roman community. Although the struggle had been long, the Romans had handled it by compromise, not violent revolution. Theoretically, by 287 B.C., all Roman citizens were equal under the law, and all could strive for political office. But in reality, as a result of the right of intermarriage, a select number of patrician and plebeian families formed a new senatorial aristocracy that came to dominate the political offices. The Roman Republic had not become a democracy.

✳ *The Roman Conquest of Italy*

At the beginning of the Republic, Rome was surrounded by enemies, including the Etruscans to the north and the Sabines, Volscians, and Aequi to the east and south. The Latin communities on the plain of Latium posed an even more immediate threat. If we are to believe Livy, one of the chief ancient sources for the history of the early Roman Republic, Rome was engaged in almost continuous warfare with the Volscians, Sabines, Aequi, and others for the next hundred years.

In his account of these years, Livy provided a detailed narrative of Roman efforts. Many of Livy's stories were legendary in character and indeed were modeled after events in Greek history. But Livy, writing in the first century B.C., used such stories to teach Romans the moral values and virtues that had made Rome great. These included tenacity, duty, courage, and especially discipline (see the box on p. 89). Indeed, Livy recounted stories of military leaders who executed their own sons for leaving their place in battle, a serious offense, since the success of the hoplite infantry depended on maintaining a precise order. These stories had little basis in fact, but like the story of George Washington and the cherry tree in American history, they provided mythical images to reinforce Roman patriotism.

By 340 B.C., Rome had crushed the Latin states in Latium. During the next fifty years, the Romans waged a fierce struggle with the Samnites, a hill people from the central Apennines, some of whom had settled in Campania, south of Rome. Rome was again victorious. The conquest of the Samnites gave Rome considerable control over a large part of Italy and also brought it into direct contact with the Greek communities of southern Italy. Soon after their conquest of the Samnites, the Romans were involved in hostilities with some of these Greek cities and by 267 B.C. had completed their conquest of southern Italy. After crushing the remaining Etruscan states to the north in 264 B.C., Rome had conquered all of Italy except the extreme north.

To rule Italy, the Romans devised the Roman confederation. Under this system, Rome allowed some peoples—especially the Latins—to have full Roman citizenship. Most of the remaining communities were made allies. They remained free to run their own local affairs but were required to provide

Cincinnatus Saves Rome: A Roman Morality Tale

There is perhaps no better account of how the virtues of duty and simplicity enabled good Roman citizens to prevail during the travails of the fifth century B.C. *than Livy's account of Cincinnatus. He was chosen dictator, supposedly in 457* B.C., *to defend Rome against the attacks of the Aequi. The position of dictator was a temporary expedient used only in emergencies; the consuls would resign, and a leader with unlimited power would be appointed for a limited period (usually six months). In this account, Cincinnatus did his duty, defeated the Aequi, and returned to his simple farm in just fifteen days.*

❊ *Livy,* **The Early History of Rome**

The city was thrown into a state of turmoil, and the general alarm was as great as if Rome herself were surrounded. Nautius was sent for, but it was quickly decided that he was not the man to inspire full confidence; the situation evidently called for a dictator, and, with no dissenting voice, Lucius Quinctius Cincinnatus was named for the post.

Now I would solicit the particular attention of those numerous people who imagine that money is everything in this world, and that rank and ability are inseparable from wealth: let them observe that Cincinnatus, the one man in whom Rome reposed all her hope of survival, was at that moment working a little three-acre farm . . . west of the Tiber, just opposite the spot where the shipyards are today. A mission from the city found him at work on his land—digging a ditch, maybe, or plowing. Greetings were exchanged, and he was asked—with a

prayer for divine blessing on himself and his country—to put on his toga and hear the Senate's instructions. This naturally surprised him, and, asking if all were well, he told his wife Racilia to run to their cottage and fetch his toga. The toga was brought, and wiping the grimy sweat from his hands and face he put it on; at once the envoys from the city saluted him, with congratulations, as Dictator, invited him to enter Rome, and informed him of the terrible danger of Municius's army. A state vessel was waiting for him on the river, and on the city bank he was welcomed by his three sons who had come to meet him, then by other kinsmen and friends, and finally by nearly the whole body of senators. Closely attended by all these people and preceded by his lictors he was then escorted to his residence through streets lined with great crowds of common folk who, be it said, were by no means so pleased to see the new Dictator, as they thought his power excessive and dreaded the way in which he was likely to use it.

[Cincinnatus proceeds to raise an army, march out, and defeat the Aequi.]

In Rome the Senate was convened by Quintus Fabius the City Prefect, and a decree was passed inviting Cincinnatus to enter in triumph with his troops. The chariot he rode in was preceded by the enemy commanders and the military standards, and followed by his army loaded with its spoils. . . . Cincinnatus finally resigned after holding office for fifteen days, having originally accepted it for a period of six months.

---

soldiers for Rome. Moreover, the Romans made it clear that loyal allies could improve their status and even aspire to becoming Roman citizens. Thus the Romans had found a way to give conquered peoples a stake in Rome's success.

The Romans' conquest of Italy can hardly be said to be the result of a direct policy of expansion. Much of it was opportunistic. The Romans did not hesitate to act when they felt that their security was threatened. And surrounded by potential enemies, Rome in a sense never felt secure. Yet once embarked on a course of expansion, the Romans pursued consistent policies that help explain their success. The Romans

excelled at making correct diplomatic decisions. Though firm and even cruel when necessary—rebellions were crushed without mercy—they were also shrewd in extending their citizenship and allowing autonomy in domestic affairs. In addition, the Romans were not only good soldiers but persistent ones. The loss of an army or a fleet did not cause them to quit but instead spurred them on to build new armies and new fleets. Finally, the Romans had a practical sense of strategy. As they conquered, they settled Romans and Latins in new communities outside Latium. By 264 B.C., the Romans had established colonies—fortified towns—at all strategic locations. By building roads to these settlements and connecting them, the Romans assured themselves of an impressive military and communications network that enabled them to rule effectively and efficiently. By insisting on military service from the allies in the Roman Confederation, Rome essentially mobilized the entire military manpower of all Italy for its wars.

◆ The Roman Conquest of the Mediterranean (264–133 B.C.)

After their conquest of the Italian peninsula, the Romans found themselves face to face with a formidable Mediterranean power—Carthage. Founded around 800 B.C. by Phoenicians from Tyre, Carthage in North Africa was located in a favorable position for commanding Mediterranean trade routes and had become an important commercial center (see Map 5.2). It had become politically and militarily strong as well. By the third century B.C., the Carthaginian

empire included the coast of northern Africa, southern Spain, Sardinia, Corsica, and western Sicily. With its monopoly of western Mediterranean trade, Carthage was the largest and richest state in the area. The presence of Carthaginians in Sicily made the Romans apprehensive about Carthaginian encroachment on the Italian coast. In 264 B.C., mutual suspicions drove the two powers into a lengthy struggle for control of the western Mediterranean.

❋ The Struggle with Carthage

The First Punic War (264–241 B.C.) (the Latin word for Phoenician was *punicus*) began when the Romans decided to intervene in a struggle between two Sicilian cities by sending an army to Sicily. The Carthaginians, who considered Sicily within their own sphere of influence, considered this just cause for war. In going to war, both sides determined on the conquest of Sicily. The Romans realized that the war would be long and drawn out if they could not supplement land operations with a navy and promptly developed a substantial naval fleet. The Carthagini-

MAP 5.2   Roman Conquests in the Mediterranean, 264–133 B.C.

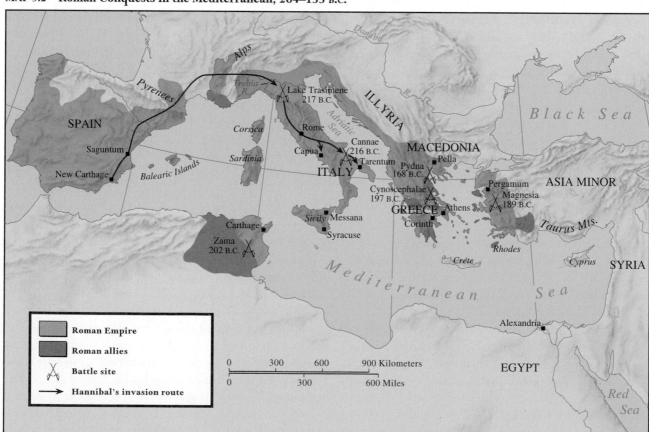

ans, for their part, had difficulty finding enough mercenaries to continue the fight. After a long struggle in which both sides lost battles in northern Africa and Sicily, a Roman fleet defeated the Carthaginian navy off Sicily, and the war quickly came to an end. In 241 B.C., Carthage gave up all rights to Sicily and had to pay an indemnity.

After the war, Carthage made an unexpected recovery and extended its domains in Spain to compensate for the territory lost to Rome. The Carthaginians proceeded to organize a formidable land army in the event of a second war with Rome, because they realized that defeating Rome on land was essential to victory. When the Romans encouraged one of Carthage's Spanish allies to revolt against Carthage, Hannibal, the greatest of the Carthaginian generals, struck back, beginning the Second Punic War (218–201 B.C.).

This time the Carthaginians decided to bring the war home to the Romans by fighting them in their own backyard. Hannibal went into Spain, moved east, and crossed the Alps with an army of 30,000 to 40,000 men and 6,000 horses and elephants. The Alps took a toll on the Carthaginian army; most of the elephants did not survive the trip. The remaining army, however, posed a real threat. At Cannae in 216 B.C., the Romans lost an army of almost 40,000 men. Rome seemed on the brink of disaster but refused to give up, raised yet another army, and gradually recovered. Although Hannibal remained free to roam in Italy, he had neither the men nor the equipment to lay siege to the major cities, including Rome itself. The Romans began to reconquer some of the Italian cities that had rebelled against Roman rule after Hannibal's successes.

More important, the Romans pursued a strategy that aimed at undermining the Carthaginian empire in Spain. By 206 B.C., the Romans had pushed the Carthaginians out of Spain.

The Romans then took the war directly to Carthage. Late in 204 B.C., a Roman army under Publius Cornelius Scipio, later known as Scipio Africanus, moved from Sicily into northern Africa and forced the Carthaginians to recall Hannibal from Italy. At the Battle of Zama in 202 B.C., the Romans decisively defeated Hannibal's forces, and the war was over. By terms of the peace treaty signed the following year, Carthage lost Spain, agreed to pay an indemnity, and promised not to go to war without Rome's permission. Spain, like Sicily, Corsica, and Sardinia earlier, was made into a Roman province. Rome had become the dominant power in the western Mediterranean.

But some Romans wanted even more. A number of prominent Romans, especially the conservative politician Cato, advocated the complete destruction of Carthage. Cato ended every speech he made to the senate with the words, "And I think Carthage must be destroyed." When the Carthaginians technically broke their peace treaty with Rome by going to war against one of Rome's North African allies who had been encroaching on Carthage's home territory, the Romans declared war. Roman forces undertook their third and last war with Carthage (149–146 B.C.). This time Carthage was no match for the Romans, who in 146 B.C. seized this opportunity to carry out the final destruction of Carthage. The territory was made a Roman province called Africa.

A ROMAN LEGIONARY. The Roman legionaries, with their legendary courage and tenacity, made possible the creation of the Roman Empire. This picture shows a bronze figure of a Roman legionary in full dress at the height of the empire in the second century A.D. The soldier's cuirass is constructed of overlapping metal bands.

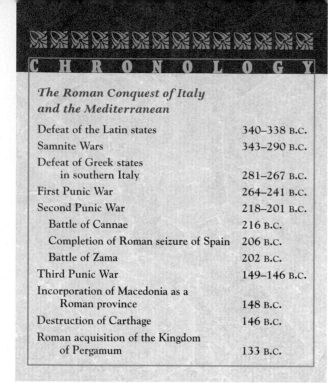

The Roman Conquest of Italy and the Mediterranean

Defeat of the Latin states	340–338 B.C.
Samnite Wars	343–290 B.C.
Defeat of Greek states in southern Italy	281–267 B.C.
First Punic War	264–241 B.C.
Second Punic War	218–201 B.C.
Battle of Cannae	216 B.C.
Completion of Roman seizure of Spain	206 B.C.
Battle of Zama	202 B.C.
Third Punic War	149–146 B.C.
Incorporation of Macedonia as a Roman province	148 B.C.
Destruction of Carthage	146 B.C.
Roman acquisition of the Kingdom of Pergamum	133 B.C.

❋ The Eastern Mediterranean

During the Punic Wars, Rome had become acutely aware of the Hellenistic states of the eastern Mediterranean when the king of Macedonia made an alliance with Hannibal after the Roman defeat at Cannae. But Rome was preoccupied with the Carthaginians, and it was not until after the defeat of Carthage that Rome became involved in the world of Hellenistic politics as an advocate of the freedom of the Greek states. This support of the Greeks brought the Romans into conflict with both Macedonia and the kingdom of the Seleucids. Roman military victories and diplomatic negotiations rearranged the territorial boundaries of the Hellenistic kingdoms and brought the Greek states their freedom in 196 B.C. For fifty years, the Romans tried to be a power broker in the affairs of the Greeks without direct control of their lands. When the effort failed, the Romans changed their policy.

Macedonia was made a Roman province in 148 B.C., and when some of the Greek states rose in revolt against Rome's restrictive policies, Rome acted decisively. The city of Corinth, leader of the revolt, was destroyed in 146 B.C. to teach the Greeks a lesson, and Greece was placed under the control of the Roman governor of Macedonia. Thirteen years later, in 133 B.C., the king of Pergamum deeded his kingdom to Rome, giving Rome its first province in Asia. Rome was now master of the Mediterranean Sea.

❋ The Nature of Roman Imperialism

Rome's empire was built in three stages: the conquest of Italy, the conflict with Carthage and expansion into the western Mediterranean, and the involvement with and domination of the Hellenistic kingdoms in the eastern Mediterranean. The Romans did not have a master plan for the creation of an empire; as it had been in Italy, much of their continued expansion was opportunistic, in response to perceived threats to their security. The more they expanded, the more threats to their security appeared on the horizon, involving them in yet more conflicts. Indeed, the Romans liked to portray themselves as declaring war only for defensive reasons or to protect allies. That is only part of the story, however. It is likely, as some historians have recently suggested, that at some point a group of Roman aristocratic leaders emerged who favored expansion both for the glory it offered and for the economic benefits it provided. Certainly, by the second century B.C., aristocratic senators perceived new opportunities for lucrative foreign commands, enormous spoils of war, and an abundant supply of slave labor for their growing landed estates. By that same time, the destruction of Corinth and Carthage indicate that Roman imperialism had become more arrogant and brutal as well. Rome's foreign success also had enormous repercussions for the internal development of the Roman Republic.

◆ Society and Culture in the Roman World

One of the most noticeable aspects of Roman culture and society is the impact of the Greeks. The Romans had experienced Greek influence early on through the Greek cities in southern Italy. By the end of the third century B.C., however, Greek civilization was playing an ever-increasing role in Roman culture. Greek ambassadors, merchants, and artists traveled to Rome and spread Greek thought and practices. After their conquest of the Hellenistic kingdoms, Roman military commanders shipped Greek manuscripts and artworks back to Rome. Multitudes of educated Greek slaves were used in Roman households. Virtually every area of Roman life, from literature and philosophy to religion and education, was affected by Greek models. Rich Romans hired Greek tutors and sent their sons to Athens to study. As the Roman poet Horace said, "Captive Greece took captive her rude conqueror."

Greek thought captivated the less sophisticated Roman mind, and the Romans became willing transmitters of Greek culture—not, however, without some resistance from Romans who had nothing but contempt for Greek politics and who feared the end of old Roman values. Even those who favored Greek culture blamed the Greeks for Rome's new vices, including luxury and homosexual practices.

�֍ Roman Religion

Every aspect of Roman society was permeated with religion. The official state religion focused on the worship of a pantheon of gods and goddesses, including Jupiter, Juno, Minerva, and Mars. As Rome developed and came into contact with other peoples and gods, the community simply adopted new deities. Hence the Greek Hermes became the Roman Mercury. By the end of the third century B.C., a rather complete amalgamation of Greek and Roman religion had occurred.

Roman religion focused on the worship of the gods for a very practical reason—human beings were thought to be totally dependent on them. Not morality but the exact performance of ritual was crucial to establishing a right relationship with the gods. What was true for individuals was also valid for the state: it also had to observe correct ritual in order to receive its reward. Accurate performance of ritual was performed by a college of priests or pontiffs, who thus bore responsibility for maintaining the right relationship between the state and the gods. If the rituals were performed correctly, then the Romans would obtain the "peace of the gods." No doubt the Roman success in creating an empire was a visible confirmation of divine favor. As Cicero, the first-century B.C. politician and writer, claimed, "We have overcome all the nations of the world, because we have realized that the world is directed and governed by the gods."[1]

Just as the state had an official cult, so did families. Because the family was regarded as a small state within the state, it had its own household cults, which included Janus, the spirit of the doorway, and Vesta, goddess of the hearth. Here, too, proper ritual was important, and it was the responsibility of the *paterfamilias* as head of the family to ensure that religious obligations were properly fulfilled.

Religious festivals were an important part of Roman religious practice. There were two kinds: public festivals ordained and paid for by the state and private festivals celebrated by individuals and families.

TEMPLE OF PORTUNUS. The Romans considered the proper worship of the gods an important element of their success. Typical of Roman religious architecture was the small urban temple located in the midst of a crowded commercial center. Pictured here is a rectangular temple built in Rome in the late second or early first century B.C. and dedicated to Portunus, the god of harbors. The temple was located in the cattle market close to the Tiber River.

By the mid-second century B.C., six public festivals were celebrated annually, each lasting several days. The practice of holding games also grew out of religious festivals. The games were inaugurated in honor of Jupiter Optimus Maximus (best and greatest), the patron deity of Rome, but had become annual events by 366 B.C. In the late Republic, both the number of games and the number of days they lasted were increased. Originally, the games consisted of chariot racing in the Circus Maximus; later, animal hunts and theatrical performances were added. In the empire, gladiatorial contests would become the primary focus.

Slavery was a common institution throughout the ancient world, but no people possessed more slaves or relied so much on slave labor as the Romans eventually did. Before the third century B.C., a small Roman farmer might possess one or two slaves who would help farm his few acres and perform domestic chores. These slaves would most likely be from Italy and be regarded as part of the family household. Only the very rich would have large numbers of slaves.

The Roman conquest of the Mediterranean brought a drastic change in the use of slaves. Large numbers of foreign slaves were brought back to Italy. During the Republic, then, the chief source of slaves was from capture in war, followed by piracy. Of course, the children of slaves also became slaves. While some Roman generals brought back slaves to be sold to benefit the public treasury, ambitious generals of the first century B.C., such as Pompey and Caesar, made personal fortunes by treating slaves captured by their armies as private property.

Slaves were used in many ways in Roman society. The rich, of course, owned the most and the best. In the late Republic, it became a badge of prestige to be attended by many slaves. Greeks were in much demand as tutors, musicians, doctors, and artists. Roman businessmen would employ them as shop assistants or artisans. Slaves were also used as farm laborers; in fact, huge gangs of slaves living in pitiful conditions worked the large landed estates known as *latifundia*. Cato the Elder argued that it was cheaper to work slaves to death and then replace them than to treat them well. Many slaves of all nationalities were used as menial household workers, such as cooks, valets, waiters, cleaners, and gardeners. Roads, aqueducts, and other public facilities were constructed by contractors using slave labor. The total number of slaves is difficult to judge—estimates vary from 20 to 30 percent of the population.

It is also difficult to generalize about the treatment of Roman slaves. There are numerous instances of humane treatment by masters and situations where slaves even protected their owners from danger out of gratitude and esteem. But slaves were also subject to severe punishments, torture, abuse, and hard labor that drove some to run away or even revolt against their owners. The Republic had stringent laws against aiding a runaway slave. The murder of a master by a slave might mean the execution of all the other household slaves. Near the end of the second century B.C., large-scale slave revolts occurred in Sicily, where enormous gangs of slaves were subjected to horrible working conditions on large landed estates. Slaves were branded, beaten, inadequately fed, worked in chains, and housed at night in underground prisons. It took three years (from 135 to 132 B.C.) to crush a revolt of 70,000 slaves, and the great revolt on Sicily (104–101 B.C.) involved most of the island and took a Roman army of 17,000 men to suppress. The most famous revolt on

HOUSEHOLD SLAVES. It became a sign of status for upper-class Romans to have numerous specialist slaves at work in a household. This wall painting from central Italy depicts an elaborate dressing room where a female slave is arranging a girl's hair while the girl's mother and sister look on.

Cato the Elder on Women

During the Second Punic War, the Romans enacted the Oppian Law, which limited the amount of gold women could possess and restricted their dress and use of carriages. In 195 B.C., an attempt was made to repeal the law, and women demonstrated in the streets on behalf of the effort. According to the Roman historian Livy, the conservative Roman official Cato the Elder spoke against repeal and against the women favoring it. Although the words are probably not Cato's own, they do reflect a traditional male Roman attitude toward women.

✳ Livy, The History of Rome

"If each of us, citizens, had determined to assert his rights and dignity as a husband with respect to his own spouse, we should have less trouble with the sex as a whole; as it is, our liberty, destroyed at home by female violence, even here in the Forum is crushed and trodden underfoot, and because we have not kept them individually under control, we dread them collectively. . . . But from no class is there not the greatest danger if you permit them meetings and gatherings and secret consultations. . . .

"Our ancestors permitted no woman to conduct even personal business without a guardian to intervene in her behalf; they wished them to be under the control of fathers, brothers, husbands; we (Heaven help us!) allow them now even to interfere in public affairs, yes, and to visit the Forum and our informal and formal sessions. What else are they doing now on the streets and at the corners except urging the bill of the tribunes and voting for the repeal of the law? Give loose rein to their uncontrollable nature and to this untamed creature and expect that they will themselves set bounds to their license; unless you act, this is the least of the things enjoined upon women by custom or law and to which they submit with a feeling of injustice. It is complete liberty or rather, if we wish to speak the truth, complete license that they desire.

"If they win in this, what will they not attempt? Review all the laws with which your forefathers restrained their license and made them subject to their husbands; even with all these bonds you can scarcely control them. What of this? If you suffer them to seize these bonds one by one and wrench themselves free and finally to be placed on a parity with their husbands, do you think you will be able to endure them? The moment they begin to be your equals, they will be your superiors. . . .

"Now they publicly address other women's husbands, and, what is more serious, they beg for law and votes, and from various men they get what they ask. In matters affecting yourself, your property, your children, you, Sir, can be importuned; once the law has ceased to set a limit to your wife's expenditures you will never set it yourself. Do not think, citizens, that the situation which existed before the law was passed will ever return. . . ."

---

the Italian peninsula occurred in 73 B.C. Led by Spartacus, a slave who had been a Thracian gladiator, the revolt broke out in southern Italy and involved 70,000 slaves. Spartacus managed to defeat several Roman armies before he was finally trapped and killed in southern Italy in 71 B.C. Six thousand of his followers were crucified, the traditional form of execution for slaves.

✳ The Roman Family

At the heart of the Roman social structure stood the family, headed by the *paterfamilias*—the dominant male. The household also included the wife, sons with their wives and children, unmarried daughters, and slaves. A family was virtually a small state within the state, and the power of the *paterfamilias* was parallel to that of the state magistrates over the citizens. Like the Greeks, Roman males believed that the weakness of the female sex necessitated male guardians (see the box above). The *paterfamilias* exercised that authority; on his death, sons or nearest male relatives assumed the role of guardians. By the late Republic, however, although the rights of male guardians remained legally in effect, upper-class women found numerous ways to circumvent the power of their guardians.

Fathers arranged the marriages of daughters, although there are instances of mothers and daughters having influence on the choice. In the Republic, women married *cum manu,* "with legal control" passing from father to husband. By the mid-first century

B.C., the dominant practice had changed to *sine manu*, "without legal control," which meant that married daughters officially remained within the father's legal power. Since the fathers of most married women were dead, not being in the "legal control" of a husband made possible independent property rights that forceful women could translate into considerable power within the household and outside it. Traditionally, Roman marriages were intended to be for life, but divorce was introduced in the third century B.C. and became relatively easy to obtain since either party could initiate it and no one needed to prove the breakdown of the marriage. Divorce became especially prevalent in the first century B.C.—a period of political turmoil—when marriages were used to cement political alliances.

Some parents in upper-class families provided education for their daughters. Some girls had private tutors, and others may have gone to primary schools. But at the age when boys were entering secondary schools, girls were pushed into marriage. The legal minimum age was twelve, although fourteen was a more common age in practice. Although some Roman doctors warned that early pregnancies could be dangerous for young girls, early marriages persisted due to the desire to benefit from dowries as soon as possible and the reality of early mortality. A good example is Tullia, Cicero's beloved daughter. She was married at sixteen, widowed at twenty-two, remarried one year later, divorced at twenty-eight, remarried at twenty-nine, and divorced at thirty-three. She died at thirty-four, not unusual for females in Roman society.

❋ *The Evolution of Roman Law*

One of Rome's chief gifts to the Mediterranean world of its day and to succeeding generations was its development of law. The Twelve Tables of 450 B.C. were the first codification of Roman law (see the box on p. 97), and although inappropriate for later times, they were never officially abrogated and were still memorized by schoolboys in the first century B.C. Civil law derived from the Twelve Tables proved inadequate for later Roman needs, however, and gave way to corrections and additions by the praetors. On taking office, a praetor issued an edict listing his guidelines for dealing with different kinds of legal cases. The praetors were knowledgeable in law, but they also relied on Roman jurists—amateur legal experts—for advice in preparing their edicts. The interpretations of the jurists, often embodied in the edicts of the praetors, created a body of legal principles.

In 242 B.C., the Romans appointed a second praetor who was responsible for examining suits between a Roman and a non-Roman as well as between two non-Romans. The Romans found that although some of their rules of law could be used in these cases, special rules were often needed. These rules gave rise to a body of law known as the law of nations, defined by the Romans as "that part of the law which we apply both to ourselves and to foreigners." But the influence of Greek philosophy, primarily Stoicism, led Romans in the late Republic to develop the idea of the law of nature—or universal divine law derived from right reason. The Romans came to view their law of nations as derived from or identical to this law of nature, thus giving Roman jurists a philosophical justification for systematizing Roman law according to basic principles.

❋ *The Development of Literature and Art*

The Romans produced little literature before the third century B.C., and the Latin literature that emerged in that century was strongly influenced by Greek models. The demand for plays at public festivals eventually led to a growing number of native playwrights. One of the best known was Plautus (c. 254–184 B.C.), who used plots from Greek New Comedy (see Chapter 4) for his own plays. The actors wore Greek costumes and Greek masks and portrayed the same basic stock characters: lecherous old men, skillful slaves, prostitutes, young men in love. Plautus wrote for the masses and became a very popular playwright in Rome.

In the last century of the Republic, the Romans began to produce a new poetry, less dependent on epic themes and more inclined to personal expressions. Latin poets were now able to use various Greek forms to express their own feelings about people, social and political life, and love. The finest example of this can be seen in the work of Catullus (c. 87–54 B.C.), Rome's "best lyric poet" and one of the greatest in world literature.

Catullus became a master at adapting and refining Greek forms of poetry to express his emotions. He wrote a variety of poems on, among other things, political figures, social customs, the use of language, the death of his brother, and the travails of love. Catullus became infatuated with Clodia, the promiscuous sister of a tribune and wife of a provincial

The Twelve Tables

In 451 B.C., plebeian pressure led to the creation of a special commission of ten men who were responsible for codifying Rome's laws and making them public. In so doing, the plebeians hoped that they could restrict the arbitrary power of the patrician magistrates, who alone had access to the laws. The Twelve Tables represent the first formal codification of Roman laws and customs. The laws dealt with litigation procedures, debt, family relations, property, and other matters of public and sacred law. The code was inscribed on bronze plaques, which were eventually destroyed. These selections are taken from reconstructions of the code preserved in later writings.

Selections from the Twelve Tables

❊ Table III: Execution; Law of Debt

When a debt has been acknowledged, or judgment about the matter has been pronounced in court, thirty days must be the legitimate time of grace. After that, the debtor may be arrested by laying on of hands. Bring him into court. If he does not satisfy the judgment, or no one in court offers himself as surety in his behalf, the creditor may take the defaulter with him. He may bind him either in stocks or in fetters. . . .

Unless they make a settlement, debtors shall be held in bond for sixty days. During that time they shall be brought before the praetor's court in the meeting place on three successive market days, and the amount for which they are judged liable shall be announced; on the third market day they shall suffer capital punishment or be delivered up for sale abroad, across the Tiber.

❊ Table IV: Rights of Head of Family

Quickly kill . . . a dreadfully deformed child.

If a father three times surrenders a son for sale, the son shall be free from the father.

A child born ten months after the father's death will not be admitted into legal inheritance.

❊ Table V: Guardianship; Succession

Females shall remain in guardianship even when they have attained their majority.

A spendthrift is forbidden to exercise administration over his own goods. . . . A person who, being insane or a spendthrift, is prohibited from administering his own goods shall be under trusteeship of agnates [nearest male relatives].

❊ Table VII: Rights Concerning Land

Branches of a tree may be lopped off all round to a height of more than 15 feet. . . . Should a tree on a neighbor's farm be bent crooked by a wind and lean over your farm, action may be taken for removal of that tree.

It is permitted to gather up fruit falling down on another man's farm.

❊ Table VIII: Torts or Delicts

If any person has sung or composed against another person a song such as was causing slander or insult to another, he shall be clubbed to death.

If a person has maimed another's limb, let there be retaliation in kind unless he makes agreement for settlement with him.

Any person who destroys by burning any building or heap of corn deposited alongside a house shall be bound, scourged, and put to death by burning at the stake, provided that he has committed the said misdeed with malice aforethought, but if he shall have committed it by accident, that is, by negligence, it is ordained that he repair the damage.

❊ Table IX: Public Law

The penalty shall be capital punishment for a judge or arbiter legally appointed who has been found guilty of receiving a bribe for giving a decision.

❊ Table XI: Supplementary Laws

Intermarriage shall not take place between plebeians and patricians.

governor, and addressed a number of poems to her (he called her Lesbia), describing his passionate love and hatred for her (Clodia had many other lovers besides Catullus):

> You used to say that you wished to know only Catullus,
>   Lesbia, and wouldn't take even Jove before me!
> I didn't regard you just as my mistress then: I cherished
>   you as a father does his sons or his daughters'
>   husbands.
> Now that I know you, I burn for you even more
>   fiercely, though I regard you as almost utterly
>   worthless.
> How can that be, you ask? It's because such cruelty
>   forces lust to assume the shrunken place of affection.[2]

The ability of Catullus to express in simple fashion his intense feelings and curiosity about himself and his world had a noticeable impact on later Latin poets.

The development of Roman prose was greatly aided by the practice of oratory. Romans had great respect for oratory since the ability to persuade people in public debate meant success in politics. Oratory was brought to perfection in a literary fashion by Cicero (106–43 B.C.), the best exemplar of the literary and intellectual interests of the senatorial elite of the late Republic and, indeed, the greatest prose writer of that period. For Cicero, oratory was not simply skillful speaking. An orator was a statesman, a man who achieved his highest goal by pursuing an active life in public affairs.

Later, when the turmoil of the late Republic forced him into semiretirement politically, Cicero became more interested in the writing of philosophical treatises. He was not an original thinker but served a most valuable purpose for Roman society by popularizing and making understandable the works of Greek philosophers. In his philosophical works, Cicero, more than anyone else, transmitted the classical intellectual heritage to the Western world. Cicero's original contributions came in the field of politics. His works *On the Laws* and *On the Republic* provided fresh insights into political thought. His emphasis on the need to pursue an active life to benefit and improve humankind would greatly influence the later Italian Renaissance.

The Romans were also dependent on the Greeks for artistic inspiration. During the third and second centuries B.C., they adopted many features of the Hellenistic style of art. The Romans developed a taste for Greek statues, which they placed not only in public buildings but also in their homes. Once demand outstripped the supply of original works, reproductions of Greek statues became fashionable. The Romans' own portrait sculpture was characterized by an intense realism that included even unpleasant physical details. Wall paintings and frescoes in the houses of the rich realistically depicted landscapes, portraits, and scenes from mythological stories.

The Romans excelled in architecture, a highly practical art. Although they continued to employ Greek styles and made use of colonnades, rectangular structures, and post-and-lintel construction, the Romans were also innovative. They made considerable use of curvilinear forms: the arch, vault, and dome. The Romans were also the first people in antiquity to use concrete on an enormous scale. By combining concrete and curvilinear forms, they were able to construct massive buildings—public baths and amphitheaters, the most famous of which was the Coliseum in Rome, capable of seating 50,000 spectators. These large buildings were made possible by Roman engineering skills. These same skills were put to use in constructing roads (the Romans built a network of 50,000 miles of roads throughout their empire), aqueducts (in Rome, almost a dozen aqueducts kept a population of one million supplied with water), and bridges.

✿ Values and Attitudes

The Romans were by nature a conservative people. They were very concerned about maintaining the *mos maiorum*, the customs or traditions of their ancestors. They emphasized parental authority and, above all, their obligations to the state. The highest virtue was *pietas*—the dutiful execution of one's obligations to one's fellow citizens, to the gods, and to the state.

By the second century B.C., however, the assembling of an empire had begun to weaken the old values. The Romans began to focus more on affluence, status, and material possessions. Emphasis shifted toward individualism and away from collective well-being, the old public spirit that had served Rome so well. Observers worried about the decline of the old values blamed it on different causes. Some felt that after the destruction of Carthage, the Romans no longer had any strong enemies to challenge them. Others believed that the Romans had simply been overwhelmed by the affluence afforded by the new empire. And some blamed everything on the Greeks for importing ideas and practices baneful to the Romans. Of course, there were also many Romans who, though desirous of maintaining traditional values, were also well aware that the acquisition of an empire had created a new world with new demands and values.

◆ The Decline and Fall of the Roman Republic (133–31 B.C.)

By the mid-second century B.C., Roman domination of the Mediterranean Sea was well established. Yet the process of building an empire had weakened and threatened the internal stability of Rome. This internal instability characterizes the period of Roman history from 133 until 31 B.C., when the armies of Octavian defeated Mark Antony and stood supreme over the Roman world. By that time, the constitution of the Roman Republic was in shambles.

By the second century B.C., the senate had become the effective governing body of the Roman state. It comprised some three hundred men, drawn primarily from the landed aristocracy; they remained senators for life and held the chief magistracies of the Republic. During the wars of the third and second centuries, the senate came to exercise enormous power. It directed the wars and took control of both foreign and domestic policy, including financial affairs.

Moreover, the magistracies and senate were increasingly controlled by a relatively select circle of wealthy and powerful families—both patrician and plebeian—called the *nobiles* ("nobles"). In the hundred years from 233 to 133 B.C., 80 percent of the consuls came from twenty-six families; moreover, 50 percent came from only ten families. Hence the *nobiles* constituted a governing oligarchy that managed, through its landed wealth, system of patronage, and intimidation, to maintain its hold over the magistracies and senate and thus guide the destiny of Rome while running the state in its own interests.

By the end of the second century B.C., two types of aristocratic leaders, called the *optimates* ("the best men") and the *populares* ("favoring the people"), became prominent. *Optimates* and *populares* were terms of political rhetoric that were used by individuals within the aristocracy against fellow aristocratic rivals to distinguish one set of tactics from another. The *optimates* controlled the senate and wished to maintain their oligarchical privileges, while the *populares* were usually other ambitious aristocrats who used the people's assemblies as instruments to break the domination of the *optimates*. The conflicts between these two types of aristocratic leaders and their supporters engulfed the first century B.C. in political turmoil.

Of course, the aristocrats formed only a tiny minority of the Roman people. The backbone of the Roman state and army had traditionally been the small farmers. But economic changes that began in the period of the Punic Wars increasingly undermined the position of that group. Their lands had been severely damaged during the Second Punic War when Hannibal invaded Italy. Moreover, in order to win the wars, Rome had to increase the term of military service from two to six years. When they returned home, many farmers found their farms so deteriorated that they chose to sell out instead of remaining on the land. By this time, capitalistic agriculture was also increasing rapidly. Landed aristocrats had been able to develop large estates (the *latifundia*) by taking over state-owned land and by buying out small peasant owners. These large estates relied on slave and tenant labor and frequently concentrated on cash crops, such as grapes for wine, olives, and sheep for wool, which small farmers could not afford to do. Thus the rise of the *latifundia* contributed to the decline in the number of small citizen farmers. Because the latter group traditionally provided the foundation of the Roman army, the number of men available for military service declined. Moreover, many of these small farmers drifted to the cities, especially Rome, forming a large class of day laborers who possessed no property. This new urban proletariat was a highly unstable mass with the potential for much trouble in depressed times.

In 133 B.C., Tiberius Gracchus, himself a member of the aristocracy and a new tribune, came to believe that the underlying cause of Rome's problems was the decline of the small farmer. Consequently, Tiberius bypassed the senate, where he knew his rivals would oppose his proposal, and had the council of the plebs pass a land-reform bill that authorized the government to reclaim public land held by large landowners and to distribute it to landless Romans. Many senators, themselves large landowners whose estates included large tracts of public land, were furious, and a group of senators took the law into their own hands and assassinated Tiberius.

The efforts of Tiberius Gracchus were continued by his brother Gaius, elected tribune for both 123 and 122 B.C. Gaius, too, pushed for the distribution of land to displaced farmers. But he broadened his reform program with measures that would benefit the equestrian order, a rising group of wealthy people who wanted a share in the political power held by the ruling aristocracy. Many senators, hostile to Gaius' reforms and fearful of his growing popularity, instigated mob action that resulted in the death of the reformer and many of his friends in 121 B.C. The attempts of the Gracchus brothers to bring reforms had opened the door to more instability and further violence.

✷ A New Role for the Roman Army: Marius and Sulla

In the closing years of the second century B.C., a series of military disasters gave rise to a fresh outburst of popular anger against the old leaders of the senate. Military defeats in northern Africa under a senate-appointed general encouraged Marius—a "new man" from the equestrian order—to run for the consulship on a "win the war" campaign slogan. Marius won and became a consul for 107 B.C. Marius then took command of the army in Africa and brought the war to a successful conclusion. He was then called on to defeat the Celts, who threatened an invasion of Italy. Marius was made consul for five years, from 104 to 100 B.C., raised a new army, and decisively defeated the Celts, leaving him in a position of personal ascendancy in Rome.

In raising a new army, Marius initiated military reforms that proved to have drastic consequences. The Roman army had traditionally been a conscript army of small landholders. Marius recruited volunteers from both the urban and rural proletariat who possessed no property. These volunteers swore an oath of loyalty to the general, not the senate, and thus inaugurated a professional-type army that might no longer be subject to the state. Moreover, to recruit these men, a general would promise them land, so that generals had to play politics in order to get legislation passed that would provide the land for their veterans. Marius left a powerful legacy. He had created a new system of military recruitment that placed much power in the hands of the individual generals.

Lucius Cornelius Sulla was the next general to take advantage of the new military system. The senate had placed him in charge of a war in Asia Minor, but when the council of the plebs tried to transfer command of this war to Marius, a civil war ensued. Sulla won and seized Rome itself in 82 B.C. He forced the senate to grant him the title of dictator to "reconstitute the Republic." After conducting a reign of terror to wipe out all opposition, Sulla revised the constitution to restore power to the senate and elim-

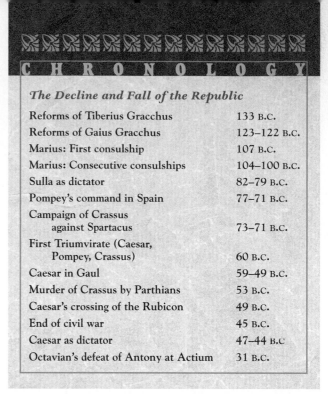

CHRONOLOGY

The Decline and Fall of the Republic

Reforms of Tiberius Gracchus	133 B.C.
Reforms of Gaius Gracchus	123–122 B.C.
Marius: First consulship	107 B.C.
Marius: Consecutive consulships	104–100 B.C.
Sulla as dictator	82–79 B.C.
Pompey's command in Spain	77–71 B.C.
Campaign of Crassus against Spartacus	73–71 B.C.
First Triumvirate (Caesar, Pompey, Crassus)	60 B.C.
Caesar in Gaul	59–49 B.C.
Murder of Crassus by Parthians	53 B.C.
Caesar's crossing of the Rubicon	49 B.C.
End of civil war	45 B.C.
Caesar as dictator	47–44 B.C
Octavian's defeat of Antony at Actium	31 B.C.

inated most of the powers of the popular assemblies and the tribunes of the plebs. In 79 B.C., believing that he had created a firm foundation for the traditional Republic governed by a powerful senate, he retired. But his real legacy was quite different from what he had intended. His example of using an army to seize power would prove most attractive to ambitious men.

✷ The Collapse of the Republic

For the next fifty years, Roman history would be characterized by two important features: the jostling for power by a number of powerful individuals and the civil wars generated by their conflicts. Three powerful individuals came to hold enormous military and political power—Crassus, Pompey, and Julius Caesar. Crassus, who was known as the richest man in Rome, had successfully put down the major slave rebellion led by Spartacus. Pompey had returned from a successful military command in Spain in 71 B.C. and had been hailed as a military hero. Julius Caesar had been a spokesman for the *populares* from the beginning of his political career and had a military command in Spain. In 60 B.C., Caesar joined with Crassus and Pompey to form a coalition that historians call the First Triumvirate.

Though others had made political deals before, the combined wealth and power of these three men was enormous, enabling them to dominate the political scene and achieve their basic aims: Pompey received lands for his veterans and a command in Spain, Crassus was given a command in Syria, and Caesar was granted a special military command in Gaul (modern France). When Crassus was killed in battle in 53 B.C., his death left two powerful men with armies in direct competition. Caesar had used his time in Gaul wisely. He had conquered all of Gaul and gained fame, wealth, and military experience as well as an army of seasoned veterans who were loyal to him. When leading senators fastened on Pompey as the less harmful to their cause and voted for Caesar to lay down his command and return as a private citizen to Rome, Caesar refused. He chose to keep his army and moved into Italy by illegally crossing the Rubicon, the river that formed the southern boundary of his province. ("Crossing the Rubicon" is a phrase used today to mean being unable to turn back.) Caesar marched on Rome, starting a civil war between his forces and those of Pompey and his allies. The defeat of Pompey's forces left Caesar in complete control of the Roman government.

Caesar had officially been made dictator in 47 B.C., and three years later, he was made dictator for life.

He continued to hold elections for offices but saw to it that his supporters chose the people he recommended. Upon becoming Rome's ruler, he quickly instituted a number of ambitious reforms. He increased the senate to nine hundred members by filling it with many of his supporters and granted citizenship to a number of people in the provinces who had helped him. By establishing colonies of Roman citizens in North Africa, Gaul, and Spain, he initiated a process of Romanization in those areas. He tried to reorganize the administrative structures of cities in Italy in order to create some sense of rational order in their government.

Caesar was a generous victor and pardoned many of the republican leaders who had opposed him, allowing them to return to Rome. He also reformed the calendar by introducing the Egyptian solar year of 365 days (with changes in 1582, it became the basis of our current calendar). He planned much more in the way of building projects and military adventures in the east, but in 44 B.C., a group of leading senators who resented his domination assassinated him in the belief that they had struck a blow for republican liberty (see the box on p. 102). In truth, they had set the stage for

CAESAR.   Conqueror of Gaul and member of the First Triumvirate, Julius Caesar is perhaps the best-known figure of the late Republic. Caesar became dictator of Rome in 47 B.C. and after his victories in the civil war was made dictator for life. Some members of the senate who resented his power assassinated him in 44 B.C. Pictured is a marble copy of a bust of Caesar.

The Assassination of Julius Caesar

When it quickly became apparent that Julius Caesar had no intention of restoring the Republic as they conceived it, about sixty senators, many of them his friends or pardoned enemies, formed a conspiracy to assassinate the dictator. It was led by Gaius Cassius and Marcus Brutus, who naively imagined that this act would restore the traditional Republic. The conspirators set the Ides of March (March 15), 44 B.C., as the date for the assassination. Although warned about a plot against his life, Caesar chose to disregard it. This account of his death is taken from his biography by the Greek writer Plutarch.

❋ Plutarch, Life of Caesar

Fate, however, is to all appearance more unavoidable than unexpected. For many strange prodigies and apparitions are said to have been observed shortly before this event. . . . One finds it also related by many that a soothsayer bade him [Caesar] prepare for some great danger on the Ides of March. When this day was come, Caesar, as he went to the senate, met this soothsayer, and said to him mockingly, "The Ides of March are come," who answered him calmly, "Yes, they are come, but they are not past. . . ."

All these things might happen by chance. But the place which was destined for the scene of this murder, in which the senate met that day, was the same in which Pompey's statue stood, and was one of the edifices which Pompey had raised and dedicated with his theater to the use of the public, plainly showing that there was something of a supernatural influence which guided the action and ordered it to that particular place. Cassius, just before the act, is said to have looked toward Pompey's statue, and silently implored his assistance. . . . When Caesar entered, the senate stood up to show their respect to him, and of Brutus' confederates, some came about his chair and stood behind it, others met him, pretending to add their petitions to those of Tillius Cimber, in behalf of his brother, who was in exile; and they followed him with their joint applications till he came to his seat. When he sat down, he refused to comply with their requests, and upon their urging him further began to reproach them severely for their demand, when Tillius, laying hold of his robe with both his hands, pulled it down from his neck, which was the signal for the assault. Casca gave him the first cut in the neck, which was not mortal nor dangerous, as coming from one who at the beginning of such a bold action was probably very much disturbed; Caesar immediately turned about, and laid his hand upon the dagger and kept hold of it. And both of them at the same time cried out, he that received the blow, in Latin, "Vile Casca, what does this mean?" and he that gave it, in Greek to his brother, "Brother, help!" Upon this first onset, those who were not privy to the design were astonished, and their horror and amazement at what they saw were so great that they dared not fly nor assist Caesar, nor so much as speak a word. But those who came prepared for the business enclosed him on every side, with their naked daggers in their hands. Which way soever he turned he met with blows, and saw their swords leveled at his face and eyes, and was encompassed like a wild beast in the toils on every side. For it had been agreed they should each of them make a thrust at him, and flesh themselves with his blood: for which reason Brutus also gave him one stab in the groin. Some say that he fought and resisted all the rest, shifting his body to avoid the blows, and calling out for help, but that when he saw Brutus' sword drawn, he covered his face with his robe and submitted, letting himself fall, whether it were by chance or that he was pushed in that direction by his murderers, at the foot of the pedestal on which Pompey's statue stood, and which was thus wetted with his blood. So that Pompey himself seemed to have presided, as it were, over the revenge done upon his adversary, who lay here at his feet, and breathed out his soul through his multitude of wounds, for they say he received three-and-twenty. And the conspirators themselves were many of them wounded by each other while they all leveled their blows at the same person.

another civil war that delivered the death blow to the Republic.

Within a few years after Caesar's death, two men had divided the Roman world between them—Octavian, Caesar's heir and grandnephew, taking the west, and Antony, Caesar's ally and assistant, the east. But the empire of the Romans, large as it was, was still too small for two masters, and Octavian and Antony eventually came into conflict. Antony allied himself with the Egyptian queen Cleopatra VII, with whom, like Caesar before him, he fell deeply in love. Octavian began a propaganda campaign, accusing Antony of catering to Cleopatra and giving away Roman territory to this "whore of the east." Finally, at the Battle of Actium in Greece in 31 B.C., Octavian's forces smashed the army and navy of Antony and Cleopatra. Both fled to Egypt where, according to the account of the Roman historian Florus, they committed suicide a year later:

> Antony was the first to commit suicide, by the sword. Cleopatra threw herself at Octavian's feet, and tried her best to attract his gaze: in vain, for his self-control was impervious to her beauty. It was not her life she was after, for that had already been granted, but a portion of her kingdom. When she realized this was hopeless and that she had been earmarked to feature in Octavian's triumph in Rome, she took advantage of her guard's carelessness to get herself into the mausoleum, as the royal tomb is called. Once there, she put on the royal robes which she was accustomed to wear, and lay down in a richly perfumed coffin beside her Antony. Then she applied poisonous snakes to her veins and slipped into death as though into a sleep.[3]

Octavian, at the age of thirty-two, stood supreme over the Roman world (see Map 5.3). The civil wars were ended. And so was the Republic.

MAP 5.3 Roman Dominions in the Late Republic, 31 B.C.

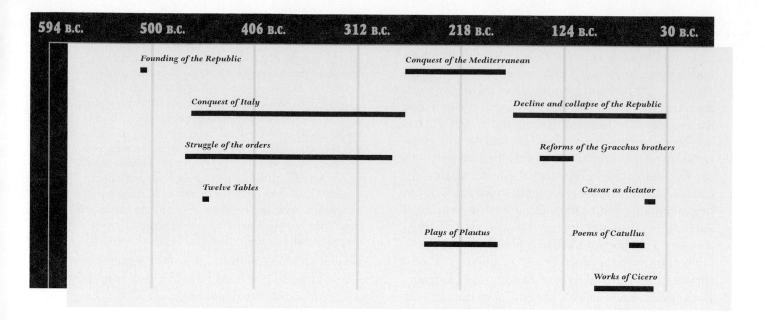

| 594 B.C. | 500 B.C. | 406 B.C. | 312 B.C. | 218 B.C. | 124 B.C. | 30 B.C. |

Founding of the Republic

Conquest of the Mediterranean

Conquest of Italy

Decline and collapse of the Republic

Struggle of the orders

Reforms of the Gracchus brothers

Twelve Tables

Caesar as dictator

Plays of Plautus

Poems of Catullus

Works of Cicero

Conclusion

In the eighth and seventh centuries B.C., *the pastoral community of Rome emerged as an actual city. Between 509 and 264* B.C., *the expansion of this city led to the union of almost all of Italy under Rome's control. Even more dramatically, between 264 and 133* B.C., *Rome expanded to the west and east and became master of the Mediterranean Sea.*

After 133 B.C., *however, Rome's republican institutions proved inadequate for the task of ruling an empire. In the breakdown that ensued, ambitious individuals saw opportunities for power unparalleled in Roman history and succumbed to the temptations. After a series of bloody civil wars, peace was finally achieved when Octavian defeated Antony and Cleopatra. Octavian's real task was at hand: to create a new system of government that seemed to preserve the Republic while establishing the basis for a new order that would rule the empire in an orderly fashion. Octavian proved equal to the task of establishing a Roman imperial state.*

Notes

1. Quoted in Chester Starr, *Past and Future in Ancient History* (Lanham, Md., 1987), pp. 38–39.
2. *The Poems of Catullus*, trans. Charles Martin (Baltimore, 1990), p. 109.
3. Florus, *Epitome of Roman History*, trans. E. S. Forster (Cambridge, Mass., 1961), IV, ii, 149–151.

Suggestions for Further Reading

For a general account of the Roman Republic, see J. Boardman, J. Griffin, and O. Murray, eds., *The Oxford History of the Roman World* (Oxford, 1991). A brief but excellent guide to recent trends in

scholarship on the Roman Republic can be found in C. Starr, *Past and Future in Ancient History* (Lanham, Md., 1987), pp. 33–45. A standard one-volume reference is M. Cary and H. H. Scullard, *A History of Rome down to the Reign of Constantine*, 3d ed. (New York, 1975). Good surveys of Roman history include M. H. Crawford, *The Roman Republic*, 2d ed. (Cambridge, Mass., 1993); H. H. Scullard, *History of the Roman World, 753–146* B.C., 4th ed. (London, 1978), and *From the Gracchi to Nero*, 4th ed. (London, 1976); M. Le Glay, J. L. Voisin, and Y. Le Bohec, *A History of Rome*, trans. A. Nevill (Oxford, 1996); and A. Kamm, *The Romans* (London, 1995). For a beautifully illustrated survey, see J. F. Drinkwater and A. Drummond, *The World of the Romans* (New York, 1993). The history of early Rome is well covered in M. Pallottino, *A History of Earliest Italy* (London, 1991), and T. J. Cornell, *The Beginnings of Rome: Italy and Rome from the Bronze Age to the Punic Wars (c. 1000–264* B.C.*)* (London, 1995). A good work on the Etruscans is M. Pallottino, *The Etruscans*, rev. ed. (Bloomington, Ind., 1975).

Aspects of the Roman political structure can be studied in A. N. Sherwin-White, *The Roman Citizenship*, 2d ed. (Oxford, 1973), and R. E. Mitchell, *Patricians and Plebeians: The Origin of the Roman State* (Ithaca, N.Y., 1990). On Roman military practices, see F. Adcock, *The Roman Art of War Under the Republic*, rev. ed. (Cambridge, Mass., 1963). Changes in Rome's economic life can be examined in K. Hopkins, *Conquerors and Slaves* (Cambridge, 1978). On the Roman social structure, see G. Alfoeldy, *The Social History of Rome* (London, 1985).

A general account of Rome's expansion in the Mediterranean world is provided by R. M. Errington, *The Dawn of Empire: Rome's Rise to World Power* (Ithaca, N.Y., 1971). On the conquest of Italy, see J. M. David, *The Roman Conquest of Italy*, trans. A. Nevill (Oxford, 1996). The best work on Carthage is B. H. Warmington, *Carthage*, rev. ed. (London, 1969). On Rome's struggle with Carthage, see N. Bagnall, *The Punic Wars* (London, 1990). On Roman expansion in the eastern Mediterranean, see A. N. Sherwin-White, *Roman Foreign Policy in the Greek East* (London, 1984).

Roman religion can be examined in J. Liebeschuetz, *Continuity and Change in Roman Religion* (Oxford, 1979), and H. H. Scullard, *Festivals and Ceremonies of the Roman Republic* (Ithaca,

N.Y., 1981). For a general study of daily life in Rome, see F. Dupont, *Daily Life in Ancient Rome* (Oxford, 1994). On the Roman family, see S. Dixon, *The Roman Family* (Baltimore, 1992). Roman women are examined in J. Balsdon, *Roman Women*, rev. ed. (London, 1974); S. Pomeroy, *Goddesses, Whores, Wives, and Slaves: Women in Classical Antiquity* (New York, 1976), pp. 149–189; R. Baumann, *Women and Politics in Ancient Rome* (New York, 1995); and S. Dixon, *The Roman Mother* (Norman, Okla., 1988). On various aspects of Roman law, see H. F. Jolowicz and B. Nicholas, *Historical Introduction to Roman Law* (Cambridge, 1972). On slavery and its consequences, see K. R. Bradley, *Slavery and Rebellion in the Roman World, 140* B.C.–*70* B.C. (Bloomington, Ind., 1989). For a brief and readable survey of Latin literature, see R. M. Ogilvie, *Roman Literature and Society* (Harmondsworth, England, 1980). On Roman art and architecture, see R. Ling, *Roman Painting* (New York, 1991); D. E. Kleiner, *Roman Sculpture* (New Haven, Conn., 1992); and M. Wheeler, *Roman Art and Architecture* (London, 1964).

An excellent account of basic problems in the history of the late Republic can be found in M. Beard and M. H. Crawford, *Rome in the Late Republic* (London, 1985). The classic work on the fall of the Republic is R. Syme, *The Roman Revolution* (Oxford, 1960). A more recent work is D. Shotter, *The Fall of the Roman Republic* (London, 1994). Numerous biographies provide many details on the politics of the period. Especially worthwhile are D. Stockton, *The Gracchi* (Oxford, 1979); C. Meier, *Caesar* (London, 1995); R. Seager, *Pompey: A Political Biography* (Berkeley, 1980); A. Ward, *Marcus Crassus and the Late Roman Republic* (Columbia, Mo., 1977); and D. Stockton, *Cicero: A Political Biography* (London, 1971).

For additional reading, go to InfoTrac College Edition, your online research library at http://web1.infotrac-college.com

Enter the search terms *Rome history* using Key Terms.

Enter the search terms *Roman republic* using Key Terms.

Enter the search terms *Roman mythology* using the Subject Guide.

Enter the search terms *Roman law* using the Subject Guide.

6

The Roman Empire

FOCUS QUESTIONS

- In his efforts to solve the problems Rome had faced during the late Republic, what changes did Augustus make in Rome's political, military, and social institutions?
- What were the chief features of the Roman Empire at its height during the second century?
- What problems did the Roman Empire face during the third century?
- What reforms did Diocletian and Constantine institute, and were they successful in solving the Empire's problems?
- What characteristics of Christianity enabled it to grow and ultimately to triumph?

WITH THE VICTORIES OF OCTAVIAN, *peace finally settled on the Roman world. Although occasional civil conflict still arose, the new imperial state constructed by Octavian experienced a period of remarkable stability for the next two hundred years. The Romans imposed their peace on the largest empire established in antiquity. Indeed, Rome's writers proclaimed that "by heaven's will my Rome shall be capital of the world."[1] To the Romans, their divine mission was clearly to rule nations and peoples. Hadrian, an emperor during the second century A.D., was but one of many Roman rulers who believed in Rome's mission. He was a strong* and intelligent ruler who took his responsibilities quite seriously. Between 121 and 132, he visited all of the provinces in the empire. According to his Roman biographer, Aelius Spartianus, "Hardly any emperor ever traveled with such speed over so much territory." When he arrived in a province, Hadrian dealt firsthand with any problems and bestowed many favors on the local population. He also worked to establish the boundaries of the provinces and provide for their defense. New fortifications, such as the 80-mile-long Hadrian's Wall across northern Britain, were built to defend the borders. Hadrian insisted on rigid discipline for frontier armies and demanded that the soldiers be kept in training, "just as if war were imminent." He also tried to lead by personal example; according to his biographer, he spent time with the troops and "cheerfully ate out of doors such camp food as bacon, cheese, and vinegar." Moreover, he "would walk as much as twenty miles fully armed."

By the third century A.D., however, Rome's ability to rule nations and people began to weaken as the empire began to experience renewed civil war, economic chaos, and invasions. Although order was reestablished by the beginning of the fourth century, Rome's decline was halted only temporarily. In the meantime, the growth of Christianity, one of the remarkable success stories of Western civilization, led to the emergence of a vibrant and powerful institution that picked up the pieces left by Rome's collapse and provided the core for a new medieval civilization.

◆ The Age of Augustus (31 B.C.–A.D. 14)

In 27 B.C., Octavian proclaimed the "restoration of the Republic." He understood that only traditional republican forms would satisfy the senatorial aristocracy. At the same time, Octavian was aware that the Republic could not be fully restored and managed to arrive at a compromise that worked at least during his lifetime. In 27 B.C., the senate awarded him the title of Augustus—"the revered one." He preferred the title *princeps,* meaning "chief citizen" or "first among equals." The system of rule that Augustus established is sometimes called the principate, conveying the idea of a constitutional monarch as coruler with the senate. But while Augustus worked to maintain this appearance, in reality power was heavily weighted in favor of the *princeps.*

 ## *The New Order*

In the new constitutional order that Augustus created, the basic governmental structure consisted of the *princeps* (Augustus) and an aristocratic senate. Augustus retained the senate as the chief deliberative body of the Roman state. Its decrees, screened in advance by the *princeps,* now had the effect of law. The title of princeps carried no power in itself, but Augustus held the office of consul each year until 23 B.C., when he

AUGUSTUS. Octavian, Caesar's adopted son, emerged victorious from the civil conflict that rocked the Republic after Caesar's assassination. Augustus operated through a number of legal formalities to ensure that control of the Roman state rested firmly in his hands. This marble statue from Prima Porta depicts the *princeps* Augustus.

The Achievements of Augustus

This excerpt is taken from a text written by Augustus and inscribed on a bronze tablet at Rome. Copies of the text were displayed in stone in many provincial capitals. Called "the most famous ancient inscription," the Res Gestae of Augustus summarizes his accomplishments in three major areas: his offices, his private expenditures on behalf of the state, and his exploits in war and peace. While factual in approach, it is a highly subjective account.

✻ *Augustus,* Res Gestae

Below is a copy of the accomplishments of the deified Augustus by which he brought the whole world under the empire of the Roman people, and of the moneys expended by him on the state and the Roman people, as inscribed on two bronze pillars set up in Rome.

1. At the age of nineteen, on my own initiative and at my own expense, I raised an army by means of which I liberated the Republic, which was oppressed by the tyranny of a faction [Mark Antony and his supporters]. . . .

2. Those who assassinated my father [Julius Caesar, his adoptive father] I drove into exile, avenging their crime by due process of law; and afterwards when they waged war against the state, I conquered them twice on the battlefield.

3. I waged many wars throughout the whole world by land and by sea, both civil and foreign, and when victorious I spared all citizens who sought pardon. . . .

5. The dictatorship offered to me . . . by the people and the senate, both in my absence and in my presence, I refused to accept. . . .

17. Four times I came to the assistance of the treasury with my own money, transferring to those in charge of the treasury 150,000,000 sesterces. And in the consulship of Marcus Lepidus and Lucius Arruntius I transferred out of my own patrimony 170,000,000 sesterces to the soldiers' bonus fund, which was established on my advice for the purpose of providing bonuses for soldiers who had completed twenty or more years of service. . . .

22. I gave a gladiatorial show three times in my own name, and five times in the names of my sons or grandsons; at these shows about 10,000 fought. . . .

25. I brought peace to the sea by suppressing the pirates. In that war I turned over to their masters for punishment nearly 30,000 slaves who had run away from their owners and taken up arms against the state. . . .

26. I extended the frontiers of all the provinces of the Roman people on whose boundaries were peoples not subject to our empire. . . .

27. I added Egypt to the empire of the Roman people. . . .

28. I established colonies of soldiers in Africa, Sicily, Macedonia, in both Spanish provinces, in Achaea, Asia, Syria, Narbonese Gaul, and Pisidia. Italy, moreover, has twenty-eight colonies established by me, which in my lifetime have grown to be famous and populous. . . .

35. When I held my thirteenth consulship, the senate, the equestrian order, and the entire Roman people gave me the title of "father of the country." . . . At the time I wrote this document I was in my seventy-sixth year.

assumed the power of a tribune, which enabled him to propose laws and veto any item of public business. By observing proper legal forms for his power, Augustus proved highly popular. As the Roman historian Tacitus commented, "Indeed, he attracted everybody's goodwill by the enjoyable gift of peace. . . . Opposition did not exist."[2] No doubt the ending of the civil wars had greatly bolstered Augustus's popularity (see the box above). At the same time, his continuing control of the army, while making possible the Roman peace, was a crucial source of his power.

Augustus was especially eager to stabilize the military and administrative structures of the Roman Empire. The peace of the empire depended on the army, and so did the security of the *princeps*. While primarily responsible for guarding the frontiers of the empire, the army was also used to maintain domestic order within the provinces. Augustus maintained a standing army of twenty-eight legions, or about 150,000 men. Roman legionaries were recruited only from the citizenry and, under Augustus, largely from Italy. Augustus also maintained a large contingent of auxiliary forces—around 130,000—enlisted from the subject peoples. Augustus was also responsible for establishing the praetorian guard. Although nominally a military reserve, these "nine cohorts of elite troops," roughly nine thousand men, had the important task of guarding the person of the *princeps*. Eventually the praetorian guard would play a weighty role in making and deposing emperors.

The role of the *princeps* as military commander gave rise to a title by which this ruler eventually came to be known. When victorious, a military commander was acclaimed by his troops as *imperator*. Augustus was so acclaimed on a number of occasions. *Imperator* is our word *emperor*. Although this title was applied to Augustus and his successors, Augustus himself preferred to use the title of *princeps*.

Augustus inaugurated a new system for governing the provinces. Under the Republic, the senate had appointed the provincial governors. Now certain provinces were allotted to the *princeps*, who assigned deputies known as legates to govern them. These legates were from the senatorial class and held office as long as the emperor chose. The senate continued to designate the governors of the remaining provinces, but the authority of Augustus enabled him to overrule the senatorial governors and establish a uniform imperial policy.

Augustus also stabilized the frontiers of the Roman Empire. He conquered the central and maritime Alps and then expanded Roman control of the Balkan peninsula up to the Danube River. His attempt to conquer Germany failed when three Roman legions under Varus were massacred in A.D. 9 in the Teutoburg Forest by a coalition of German tribes. The defeat severely dampened Augustus' enthusiasm for continued expansion in central Europe. Thereafter, the Romans were content to use the Rhine as the frontier between the Roman province of Gaul and the German tribes to the east. In fact, Augustus' difficulties had convinced him that "the empire should not be extended beyond its present frontiers."[3] His defeats in Germany taught Augustus that Rome's power was not unlimited. They also left him devastated; for months he beat his head against a door, shouting "Varus, give me back my legions."

❀ *Augustan Society*

Roman society in the Early Empire was characterized by a system of social stratification, inherited from the Republic, in which Roman citizens were divided into three basic classes: the senatorial, equestrian, and lower classes. Augustus had accepted the senatorial order as a ruling class for the empire. Senators filled the chief magistracies of the Roman government, held the most important military posts, and governed the provinces. One needed to possess property worth 1,000,000 sesterces (an unskilled laborer in Rome received 3 sesterces a day; a Roman legionary, 900 sesterces a year in pay) to belong to the senatorial order. The equestrian order was open to all Roman citizens of good standing who possessed property valued at 400,000 sesterces. They, too, could now hold military and governmental offices, but the positions open to them were less important than those of the senators.

Citizens not of the senatorial or equestrian order belonged to the lower classes, who made up the overwhelming majority of the free citizens. The diminution of the power of the Roman assemblies ended whatever political power they may have possessed earlier in the Republic. Many of these people were provided with free grain and public spectacles to keep them from creating disturbances. Nevertheless, by gaining wealth and serving as lower officers in the Roman legions, it was sometimes possible for them to advance to the equestrian order.

Augustus' belief that Roman morals had been corrupted during the late Republic led him to initiate social legislation to arrest the decline. He thought that increased luxury had undermined traditional Roman frugality and simplicity and caused a decline in morals, evidenced by easy divorce, a falling birthrate among the upper classes, and lax behavior manifested in hedonistic parties and the love affairs of prominent Romans with fashionable women and elegant boys.

Through his new social legislation, Augustus hoped to restore respectability to the upper classes and reverse the declining birthrate as well. Expenditures for feasts were limited, and other laws made adultery a criminal offense. In fact, Augustus' own daughter Julia was exiled for adultery. Augustus also revised the tax laws to penalize bachelors, widowers, and married persons who had fewer than three children.

The Augustan Age was a lengthy one. Augustus died in A.D. 14 after dominating the Roman world for forty-five years. He had created a new order while placating the old by restoring and maintaining traditional values, a fitting combination for a leader whose favorite maxim was "make haste slowly." By the time of his death, his new order was so well established that few agitated for an alternative. Indeed, as the Roman historian Tacitus pointed out, "Actium had been won before the younger men were born. Even most of the older generation had come into a world of civil wars. Practically no one had ever seen truly Republican government. . . . Political equality was a thing of the past; all eyes watched for imperial commands."[4] The Republic was now only a memory and, given its last century of warfare, an unpleasant one at that. The new order was here to stay.

◆ The Early Empire (14–180)

There was no serious opposition to Augustus' choice of his stepson Tiberius as his successor. By designating a family member as *princeps*, Augustus established the Julio-Claudian dynasty; the next four successors of Augustus were related either to his own family or that of his wife, Livia.

Several major tendencies emerged during the reigns of the Julio-Claudians (14–68). In general, more and more of the responsibilities that Augustus had given to the senate tended to be taken over by the emperors, who also instituted an imperial bureaucracy, staffed by talented freedmen, to run the government on a daily basis. As the Julio-Claudian successors of Augustus acted more openly as real rulers rather than "first citizens of the state," the opportunity for arbitrary and corrupt acts also increased. Nero (54–68) freely eliminated people he wanted out of the way, including his own mother, whom he had murdered. Without troops, the senators proved unable to oppose these excesses. However, Nero's extravagances did provoke a revolt of the Roman legions. Abandoned by the guards, Nero chose to commit suicide by stabbing himself in the throat after uttering his final words, "What an artist the world is losing in me." A new civil war erupted in 69, known as the year of the four emperors. The signifi-cance of the year 69 was summed up precisely by Tacitus when he stated that "a well-hidden secret of the principate had been revealed: it was possible, it seemed, for an emperor to be chosen outside Rome."[5]

❈ The Five "Good Emperors" (96–180)

At the beginning of the second century, however, a series of five so-called good emperors created a period of peace and prosperity that lasted for almost a hundred years. These rulers treated the ruling classes with respect, cooperated with the senate, ended arbitrary executions, maintained peace throughout the empire, and supported domestic policies generally beneficial to the empire. Though absolute monarchs, they were known for their tolerance and diplomacy. By adopting capable men as their successors, the first four good emperors reduced the chances of succession problems.

Under the five good emperors, the powers of the emperor continued to be extended at the expense of the senate. Increasingly, imperial officials appointed and directed by the emperor took over the running of the government. The good emperors also extended the scope of imperial administration to areas previously untouched by the imperial government. Trajan (98–117) established a program that provided state funds to assist poor parents in raising and educating their children.

The good emperors were widely praised by their subjects for their extensive building programs. Trajan and Hadrian (117–138) were especially active in constructing public works— aqueducts, bridges, roads, and harbor facilities—throughout the provinces and in Rome. Trajan built a new forum in Rome to provide a setting for his celebrated victory column. Hadrian's Pantheon, a temple of "all the gods," is one of the grandest ancient buildings surviving in Rome.

THE EMPEROR HADRIAN. **The rule of the five good emperors brought a period of peace and prosperity to the Early Empire. All five treated the ruling classes with respect and implemented beneficial domestic policies. Hadrian was the third of the five good emperors.**

✳ *The Roman Empire at Its Height: Frontiers and Provinces*

Although Trajan broke with Augustus' policy of defensive imperialism by extending Roman rule into Dacia (modern Romania), Mesopotamia, and the Sinai peninsula, his conquests represent the high-water mark of Roman expansion (see Map 6.1). His successors recognized that the empire was overextended and pursued a policy of retrenchment. Hadrian withdrew Roman forces from much of Mesopotamia. Although he retained Dacia and Arabia, he went on the defensive in his frontier policy by reinforcing the fortifications along a line connecting the Rhine and Danube Rivers and by building a defensive wall 80 miles long across northern Britain to keep the Scots out of Roman Britain. By the end of the second century, the vulnerability of the empire had become apparent. Frontiers were stabilized, and the Roman forces were established in permanent bases behind the frontiers. But when one frontier was attacked, troops had to be drawn from other frontiers, leaving them vulnerable to attack. The empire lacked a real strategic reserve, and in the next century its weakness would be ever more apparent.

At its height in the second century, the Roman Empire was one of the greatest states the world had seen. It covered about 3.5 million square miles and had a population, like that of Han China, that has been estimated at more than 50 million. While the emperors and the imperial administration provided a degree of unity, considerable leeway was given to local customs, and the privileges of Roman citizenship were extended to many people throughout the empire. In 212, the emperor Caracalla completed the process by giving Roman citizenship to every free inhabitant of the empire. Latin was the language of the western part of the empire, while Greek was used in the east. Although Roman culture spread to all parts of the empire, there were limits to Romanization because

MAP 6.I   The Roman Empire from I4 to II7 (Augustus to Trajan).

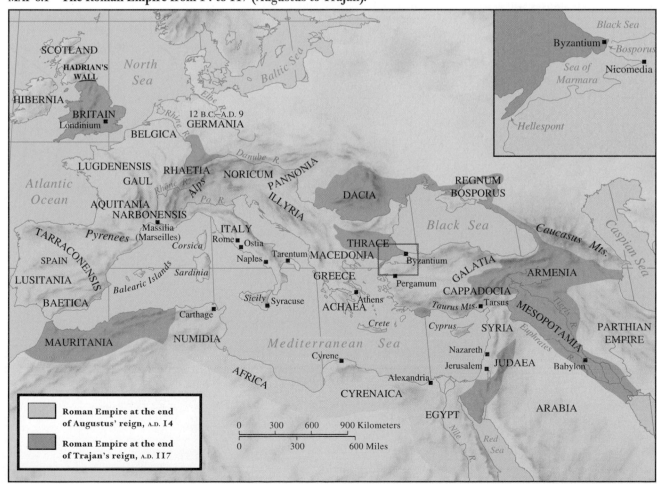

local languages persisted and many of the empire's residents spoke neither Latin nor Greek.

The administration and cultural life of the Roman Empire depended greatly on cities and towns. A provincial governor's staff was not large, so local city officials were expected to act as Roman agents in carrying out many government functions, especially those related to taxes. Most towns and cities were not large by modern standards. The largest was Rome, but there were also some large cities in the east: Alexandria in Egypt numbered over 300,000 inhabitants, Ephesus in Asia Minor had 200,000, Antioch in Syria around 150,000. In the west, cities were usually small, with only a few thousand inhabitants. Cities were important in the spread of Roman culture, law, and the Latin language. They were also uniform in physical appearance with similar temples, markets, amphitheaters, and other public buildings.

Magistrates and town councillors chosen from the ranks of the wealthy upper classes directed municipal administration. These municipal offices were unsalaried but were nevertheless desired by wealthy citizens because they received prestige and power at the local level as well as Roman citizenship. Roman municipal policy effectively tied the upper classes to Roman rule and ensured that these classes would retain control over the rest of the population.

The process of Romanization in the provinces was reflected in significant changes in the governing classes of the empire. In the course of the first century, there was a noticeable decline in the number of senators from Italian families. Increasingly, the Roman senate was being recruited from wealthy provincial equestrian families. The provinces also provided many of the legionaries for the Roman army and, beginning with Trajan, supplied many of the emperors.

❋ Prosperity in the Early Empire

The Early Empire was a period of considerable prosperity. Internal peace resulted in unprecedented levels of trade (see Map 6.2). Merchants from all over the

MAP 6.2   **Trade Routes and Products in the Roman Empire, c. 200.**

empire came to the chief Italian ports of Puteoli on the Bay of Naples and Ostia at the mouth of the Tiber. Trade extended beyond the Roman boundaries and included even silk goods from China. The importation of large quantities of grain to feed the people of Rome and an incredible quantity of luxury items for the wealthy upper classes in the west led to a steady drain of gold and silver coins from Italy and the west to the eastern part of the empire.

Increased trade helped stimulate manufacturing. The cities of the east still produced the items made in Hellenistic times. The first two centuries of the empire also witnessed the high point of industrial development in Italy. Some industries became concentrated in certain areas, such as bronze work in Capua and pottery in Arretium in Etruria. Other industries, such as brickmaking, were pursued in rural areas on large landed estates. Much production remained small scale and was done by individual craftsmen, usually freedmen or slaves. In the course of the first century, Italian centers of industry began to experience increasing competition from the provinces.

Despite the extensive trade and commerce, agriculture remained the chief occupation of most people and the underlying basis of Roman prosperity. While the large landed estates called *latifundia* still dominated agriculture, especially in southern and central Italy, small peasant farms persisted, particularly in Etruria and the Po valley. Although large estates concentrating on sheep and cattle raising used slaves, the lands of some *latifundia* were worked by free tenant farmers who paid rent in labor, produce, or sometimes cash.

In considering the prosperity of the Roman world, it is important to remember the enormous gulf between rich and poor (see the box on p. 114). The development of towns and cities, so important to the creation of any civilization, is based in large degree on the agricultural surpluses of the countryside. In ancient times, the margin of surplus produced by each farmer was relatively small. Therefore, the upper classes and urban populations had to be supported by the labor of a large number of agricultural producers who never found it easy to produce much more than for themselves. In lean years, when there were no surpluses, the townspeople often took what they wanted, leaving little for the peasants.

◆ Roman Culture and Society in the Early Empire

The high point of Latin literature was reached in the time of Augustus. The literary accomplishments of the Augustan Age were such that the period has been called the golden age of Latin literature.

❊ The Golden Age of Latin Literature

The most distinguished poet of the Augustan Age was Virgil (70–19 B.C.). The son of a small landholder in northern Italy, he welcomed the rule of Augustus and wrote his greatest work in the emperor's honor. Virgil's masterpiece was the *Aeneid*, an epic poem clearly meant to rival the work of Homer. The connection between Troy and Rome is made explicitly. Aeneas, the son of Anchises of Troy, survives the destruction

THE SHIPPING OF GRAIN. Trade was an important ingredient in the prosperity of the Early Empire. This tomb painting from Ostia, the port of Rome at the mouth of the Tiber River, shows workers loading grain onto the *Isis Giminiana,* a small merchant ship, for shipment upriver to Rome. The captain of the ship stands by the rudder. Next to him is Abascantus, the ship's owner.

Menu from a Roman Banquet

Wealthy Roman homes contained a formal dining room, scene of the dinner parties that were the chief feature of Roman social life. The banquet usually consisted of three courses: appetizers, main course, and dessert. As this menu from a cookbook by Apicius illustrates, each course included an enormous variety of exotic foods. Banquets *lasted an entire evening and were accompanied by entertainment provided by acrobats, musicians, dancers, and even poets. Naturally, the diet of lower-class Romans was considerably simpler, consisting of the traditional staples of bread, olives, and grapes. Poorer Romans ate little meat.*

A Sample Banquet Menu

❋ **Appetizers** ❋

Jellyfish and eggs
Sow's udders stuffed with salted sea urchins
Patina of brains cooked with milk and eggs
Boiled tree fungi with peppered fish-fat sauce
Sea urchins with spices, honey, oil and egg sauce

Roast parrot
Dormice stuffed with pork and pine kernels
Ham boiled with figs and bay leaves, rubbed with
honey, baked in pastry crust
Flamingo boiled with dates

❋ **Main Course** ❋

Fallow deer roasted with onion sauce and rue
Jericho dates, raisins, oil, and honey
Boiled ostrich with sweet sauce
Turtle dove boiled in its feathers

❋ **Dessert** ❋

Fricassee of roses with pastry
Stoned dates stuffed with nuts and pine kernels,
fried in honey
Hot African sweet-wine cakes with honey

---

of Troy and eventually settles in Latium; hence Roman civilization is linked to Greek history. The character of Aeneas is portrayed as the ideal Roman—his virtues are duty, piety, and faithfulness. Virgil's overall purpose was to show that Aeneas had fulfilled his mission to establish the Romans in Italy and thereby start Rome on its divine mission to rule the world.

> Let others fashion from bronze more lifelike, breathing
>   images—
> For so they shall—and evoke living faces from marble;
> Others excel as orators, others track with their
>   instruments
> The planets circling in heaven and predict when stars
>   will appear.
> But, Romans, never forget that government is your
>   medium!
> Be this your art:—to practise men in the habit of
>   peace,
> Generosity to the conquered, and firmness against
>   aggressors.[6]

As Virgil expressed it, ruling was Rome's gift.

Another prominent Augustan poet was Horace (65–8 B.C.), a friend of Virgil's. Horace was a very sophisticated writer whose overriding concern was to point out to his contemporaries the "follies and vices of his age." In the *Satires*, a medley of poems on a variety of subjects, Horace is revealed as a detached observer of human weaknesses. He directed his attacks against movements, not living people, and took on such subjects as sexual immorality, greed, and job dissatisfaction ("How does it happen, Maecenas, that no man alone is content with his lot?").[7] Horace mostly laughs at the weaknesses of humankind and calls for forbearance: "Supposing my friend has got liquored and wetted my couch, . . . is he for such a lapse to be deemed less dear as a friend, or because when hungry he snatched up before me a chicken from my side of the dish?"[8]

Ovid (43 B.C.–A.D. 18) was the last of the great poets of the golden age. He belonged to a youthful, privileged social group in Rome that liked to ridicule old Roman values. In keeping with the spirit of this group, Ovid wrote a frivolous series of love poems known as the *Amores*. Intended to entertain and shock, they achieved their goal. Another of Ovid's works was *The Art of Love*. This was essentially a take-off on didactic poems. Whereas authors of earlier didactic poems had written guides to farming, hunting, or some such subject, Ovid's work was a handbook on the seduction of women (see the box on p. 115).

The most famous Latin prose work of the golden age was written by the historian Livy (59 B.C.–A.D. 17). Livy's masterpiece was the *History of Rome* from the

Ovid and the Art of Love

Ovid has been called the last great poet of the Augustan golden age of literature. One of his most famous works was The Art of Love, *a guidebook for the seduction of women. Unfortunately for Ovid, the work appeared at a time when Augustus was anxious to improve the morals of the Roman upper class. Augustus considered the poem offensive, and Ovid soon found himself in exile.*

❋ *Ovid,* **The Art of Love**

Now I'll teach you how to captivate and hold the woman of your choice. This is the most important part of all my lessons. Lovers of every land, lend an attentive ear to my discourse; let goodwill warm your hearts, for I am going to fulfill the promises I made you.

First of all, be quite sure that there isn't a woman who cannot be won, and make up your mind that you will win her. Only you must prepare the ground. Sooner would the birds cease their song in the springtime, or the grasshopper be silent in the summer. . . . than a woman resist the tender wooing of a youthful lover. . . .

Now the first thing you have to do is to get on good terms with the fair one's maid. She can make things easy for you. Find out whether she is fully in her mistress's confidence, and if she knows all about her secret dissipations. Leave no stone unturned to win her over. Once you have her on your side, the rest is easy. . . .

In the first place, it's best to send her a letter, just to pave the way. In it you should tell her how you dote on her; pay her beauty compliments and say all the nice things lovers always say. . . . Even the gods are moved by the voice of entreaty. And promise, promise, promise. Promises will cost you nothing. Everyone's a millionaire where promises are concerned. . . .

If she refuses your letter and sends it back unread, don't give up; hope for the best and try again. . . .

Don't let your hair stick up in tufts on your head; see that your hair and your beard are decently trimmed. See also that your nails are clean and nicely filed; don't have any hair growing out of your nostrils; take care that your breath is sweet, and don't go about reeking like a billy-goat. All other toilet refinements leave to the women or to perverts. . . .

When you find yourself at a feast where the wine is flowing freely, and where a woman shares the same couch with you, pray to that god whose mysteries are celebrated during the night, that the wine may not overcloud your brain. 'Tis then you may easily hold converse with your mistress in hidden words whereof she will easily divine the meaning. . . .

By subtle flatteries you may be able to steal into her heart, even as the river insensibly overflows the banks which fringe it. Never cease to sing the praises of her face, her hair, her taper fingers and her dainty foot. . . .

Tears too, are a mighty useful resource in the matter of love. They would melt a diamond. Make a point, therefore, of letting your mistress see your face all wet with tears. Howbeit, if you can't manage to squeeze out any tears—and they won't always flow just when you want them to—put your finger in your eyes.

---

foundation of the city to 9 B.C. Only 35 of the original 142 books have survived, although we do possess brief summaries of the whole work from other authors. Livy perceived history in terms of moral lessons. He stated in the preface that

> the study of history is the best medicine for a sick mind; for in history you have a record of the infinite variety of human experience plainly set out for all to see; and in that record you can find for yourself and your country both examples and warnings: fine things to take as models, base things, rotten through and through, to avoid.[9]

For Livy, human character was the determining factor in history.

Livy's history celebrated Rome's greatness. He built scene upon scene that not only revealed the character of the chief figures but also demonstrated the virtues that had made Rome great. Of course, he had serious weaknesses as a historian. He was not always concerned about the factual accuracy of his stories. But he was an excellent storyteller, and his work remained the standard history of Rome for centuries.

The Silver Age of Latin Literature

In the history of Latin literature, the century and a half after Augustus is often labeled the "silver age" to indicate that the literary efforts of the period, though good, were not equal to the high standards of the Augustan golden age. The popularity of rhetorical training encouraged the use of clever literary expressions at the expense of original content. A good example of this trend can be found in the works of Seneca.

Educated in Rome, Seneca (c. 4 B.C.–A.D. 65) became strongly attached to the philosophy of Stoicism. In letters written to a young friend, he expressed the basic tenets of Stoicism: living according to nature, accepting events dispassionately as part of the divine plan, and universal love for all humanity. Thus "the first thing philosophy promises us is the feeling of fellowship, of belonging to mankind and being members of a community. . . . Philosophy calls for simple living, not for doing penance, and the simple way of life need not be a crude one."[10] Viewed in retrospect, Seneca displays some glaring inconsistencies. While preaching the virtues of simplicity, he amassed a fortune and was ruthless at times in protecting it. His letters show humanity, benevolence, and fortitude, but his sentiments are often undermined by an attempt to be clever with words.

The greatest historian of the silver age was Tacitus (c. 56–120). His main works included the *Annals* and *Histories*, which presented a narrative account of Roman history from the reign of Tiberius through the assassination of Domitian (14–96). Tacitus believed that history had a moral purpose: "It seems to me a historian's foremost duty to ensure that merit is recorded, and to confront evil deeds and words with the fear of posterity's denunciations."[11] As a member of the senatorial class, Tacitus was disgusted with the abuses of power perpetrated by the emperors and was determined that the "evil deeds" of wicked men would not be forgotten. Many historians believe he went too far in projecting the evils of his own day into his account of the past. His work *Germania* is especially important as a source of information about the early Germans. But it too is colored by Tacitus' attempt to show the Germans as noble savages in comparison with the decadent Romans.

Roman Law

The Early Empire experienced great progress in the study and codification of the law. The second and early third centuries A.D. witnessed the "classical age of Roman law," a period in which a number of great jurists classified and compiled basic legal principles that have proved extremely valuable to the Western world. Most jurists emphasized the emperor as the source of law: "What has pleased the emperor has the force of law."

In the "classical age of Roman law," the identification of the law of nations with natural law led to a concept of natural rights. According to the jurist Ulpian (d. 228), natural rights implied that all men are born equal and should therefore be equal before the law. In practice, however, such a principle was not applied, particularly in the third and later centuries. The Romans did, however, establish standards of justice, applicable to all people, that included principles that we would immediately recognize. A person was regarded as innocent until proven otherwise. People accused of wrongdoing were allowed to defend themselves before a judge. A judge, in turn, was expected to weigh evidence carefully before arriving at a decision. These principles lived on in Western civilization long after the fall of the Roman Empire.

The Upper-Class Roman Family

By the second century A.D., significant changes were occurring in the Roman family. The foundations of the authority of the *paterfamilias* over his family, which had already begun to weaken in the late Republic, were further undermined. The *paterfamilias* no longer had absolute authority over his children; he could no longer sell his children into slavery or have them put to death. Moreover, the husband's absolute authority over his wife also disappeared, a process that had begun in the late Republic. In the Early Empire, the idea of male guardianship continued to weaken significantly, and by the late second century, guardianships had become a formality.

Upper-class Roman women in the Early Empire had considerable freedom and independence. They had acquired the right to own, inherit, and dispose of property. Upper-class women could attend races, the theater, and events in the amphitheater, although in the latter two places they were forced to sit in separate female sections. Moreover, ladies of rank were still accompanied by maids and companions when they went out. Some women operated businesses, such as shipping firms. Women could still not participate in politics, but the Early Empire saw a number of important women who influenced politics through their husbands, including

Livia, the wife of Augustus; Agrippina, the mother of Nero; and Plotina, the wife of Trajan.

�֍ Imperial Rome

At the center of the colossal Roman Empire was the ancient city of Rome (see Map 6.3). Truly a capital city, Rome had the largest population of any city in the empire. It is estimated that its population was close to one million by the time of Augustus. For anyone with ambitions, Rome was the place to be. A magnet to many people, Rome was extremely cosmopolitan. Nationalities from all over the empire resided there, with entire sections inhabited by specific groups, such as Greeks and Syrians.

Rome was no doubt an overcrowded and noisy city. Because of the congestion, cart and wagon traffic was banned from the streets during the day. The noise from the resulting vehicular movement at night often made sleep difficult. Evening pedestrian travel was dangerous. Although Augustus had organized a police force, lone travelers could be assaulted, robbed, or soaked by filth thrown out of the upper-story windows of Rome's massive apartment buildings.

An enormous gulf existed between rich and poor in the city of Rome. While the rich had comfortable villas, the poor lived in apartment blocks called *insulae,* which might be six stories high. Constructed of concrete, they were often poorly built and prone to collapse. The use of wooden beams in the floors and movable stoves, torches, candles, and lamps within the rooms for heat and light made the danger of fire a constant companion. Once started, fires were extremely difficult to put out. The famous conflagration of 64, which Nero was unjustly accused of starting, devastated a good part of the city. Besides the hazards of collapse and fire, living conditions were also poor. High rents forced entire families into one room. The absence of plumbing, central heating, and open fireplaces made life so uncomfortable that poorer Romans spent most of their time outdoors in the streets.

Fortunately for these people, Rome boasted public buildings unequaled anywhere in the empire. Its temples, forums, markets, baths, theaters, triumphal arches, governmental buildings, and amphitheaters gave parts of the city an appearance of grandeur and magnificence.

Though the center of a great empire, Rome was also a great parasite. Beginning with Augustus, the emperors accepted responsibility for providing food for the urban populace, with about 200,000 people receiving free grain. Even with the free grain, conditions were grim for the poor. Early in the second century, a Roman doctor noted that rickets was common among children in the city.

In addition to food, entertainment was also provided on a grand scale for the inhabitants of Rome. The

MAP 6.3 Imperial Rome.

poet Juvenal said of the Roman masses: "But nowadays, with no vote to sell, their motto is 'Couldn't care less.' Time was when their plebiscite elected generals, heads of state, commanders of legions: but now they've pulled in their horns, there's only two things that concern them: Bread and Circuses."[12] Public spectacles were provided by the emperor and other state officials as part of the great festivals—most of them religious in origin—celebrated by the state. More than one hundred days a year were given over to these public holidays. The festivals included three major types of entertainment. At the Circus Maximus, horse and chariot races attracted hundreds of thousands, while dramatic and other performances were held in theaters. But the most famous of all the public spectacles were the gladiatorial shows.

❋ The Gladiatorial Shows

The gladiatorial shows were an integral part of Roman society. They took place in amphitheaters, the first permanent one of which had been constructed at Rome in 29 B.C. Perhaps the most famous was the Flavian amphitheater, called the Colosseum, constructed at Rome to seat 50,000 spectators. Amphitheaters were also constructed throughout the empire. They varied greatly in size, with capacities ranging from a few thousand to tens of thousands. In most cities and towns, amphitheaters came to be the biggest buildings, rivaled only by the circuses for races and the public baths. Where a society invests its money gives one an idea of its priorities. Since the amphitheater was the primary location for the gladiatorial games, it is fair to say that public slaughter was an important part of Roman culture.

Gladiatorial games were held from dawn to dusk. Contests to the death between trained fighters formed the central focus of these games. Most gladiators were slaves or condemned criminals and were trained for combat in special gladiatorial schools.

Gladiatorial games included other forms of entertainment as well. Criminals of all ages and both sexes were sent into the arena without weapons to face certain death from wild animals who would tear them to pieces. Numerous kinds of animal contests were also staged: wild beasts against each other, such as bears against buffaloes; staged hunts with men shooting safely from behind iron bars; and gladiators in the arena with bulls, tigers, and lions. Reportedly, five thousand beasts were killed in one day of games when the Emperor Titus inaugurated the Colosseum in A.D. 80. Enormous resources were invested in the capture and shipment of wild animals for slaughter, and whole species were hunted to extinction in parts of the empire.

These bloodthirsty spectacles were wildly popular with the Roman people. The Roman historian Tacitus said, "Few indeed are to be found who talk of any other subjects in their homes, and whenever we enter a classroom, what else is the conversation of the

THE GLADIATORIAL GAMES. Although some gladiators were free men enticed by the possibility of rewards, most were condemned criminals, slaves, or prisoners of war who were trained in special schools. A great gladiator could win his freedom through the games. This mosaic from the fourth century A.D. depicts different aspects of gladiatorial fighting and clearly shows the bloody nature of the gladiatorial games

youths."[13] But the gladiatorial games served a purpose beyond mere entertainment. Like the other forms of public entertainment, they fulfilled both a political and social need by diverting thoughts of the idle masses from political unrest. It was said of the Emperor Trajan that he understood that although the distribution of grain and money satisfied the individual, spectacles were necessary for the "contentment of the masses."

◆ The Decline of the Roman Empire

In the course of the third century, the Roman Empire came near to collapse. After a series of civil wars, Septimius Severus (193–211), who was born in North Africa and spoke Latin with an accent, used his legions to seize power. Septimius Severus' deathbed admonition to his sons "to pay the soldiers and ignore everyone else" set the tone for the new dynasty he established. The Severan rulers (193–235) began to create a military monarchy. The army was expanded, soldiers' pay was increased, and military officers were appointed to important government positions.

Military monarchy was followed by military anarchy. For a period of almost fifty years, from 235 to 284, the Roman Empire was mired in the chaos of continual civil war as contenders for the imperial throne found that bribing soldiers was the primary way to become emperor. In these five decades, there were twenty-two emperors, only two of whom did not meet a violent end. At the same time, the empire was beset by a series of invasions, no doubt exacerbated by the civil wars. In the east, the Sassanid Persians made inroads into Roman territory. A fitting symbol of Rome's decline was the capture of the Roman emperor Valerian (253–260) by the Persians and his death in captivity, an event previously unheard of in Roman history. Germanic tribes also poured into the empire. The Goths overran the Balkans and moved into Greece and Asia Minor. The Franks advanced into Gaul and Spain. It was not until the reign of Aurelian (270–275) that most of the boundaries were restored.

Invasions, civil wars, and plague came close to causing an economic collapse of the Roman Empire in the third century. The population declined drastically, possibly by as much as one-third. There was a noticeable decline in trade and small industry. The labor shortage created by plague affected both military recruiting and the economy. Farm production deteri-

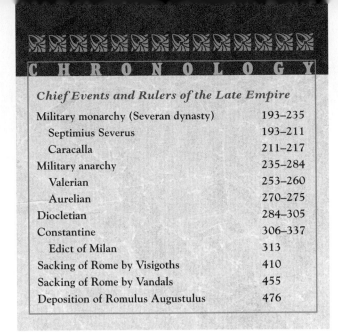

orated significantly. Fields were ravaged by Germanic tribes, but even more often by the defending Roman armies. Many farmers complained that Roman commanders and their soldiers were confiscating produce and livestock. Provincial governors seemed powerless to stop these depredations, and some even joined in the extortion. The monetary system began to show signs of collapse as a result of debased coinage and the beginnings of serious inflation.

Armies were needed more than ever, but financial strains made it difficult to enlist and pay the necessary soldiers. Whereas in the second century the Roman army had been recruited from among the inhabitants of frontier provinces, by the mid-third century the state had to rely on hiring Germans to fight under Roman commanders. These soldiers had no understanding of Roman traditions and no real attachment to either the empire or the emperors.

❈ The Reforms of Diocletian and Constantine

At the end of the third and beginning of the fourth centuries, the Roman Empire gained a new lease on life through the efforts of two strong emperors, Diocletian and Constantine, who restored order and stability. The Roman Empire was virtually transformed into a new state: the so-called Late Empire, which included a new governmental structure, a rigid economic and social system, and a new state religion—Christianity.

Believing that the empire had grown too large for a single ruler, Diocletian (284–305) divided it into four administrative units (see Map 6.4), each with its own prefect. Despite the appearance of four-man rule, however, Diocletian's military seniority enabled him to claim a higher status and hold the ultimate authority. Constantine (306–337) continued and even expanded the autocratic policies of Diocletian. Both rulers greatly strengthened and enlarged the administrative bureaucracies of the Roman Empire. Henceforth, civil and military bureaucracies were sharply separated. Each contained a hierarchy of officials who exercised control at the various levels. The emperor presided over both hierarchies of officials and served as the only link between them. New titles of nobility—such as *illustres* ("illustrious ones") and *illustrissimi* ("the most illustrious ones")—were instituted to dignify the holders of positions in the civil and military bureaucracies.

Additional military reforms were also inaugurated. The army was enlarged to 500,000 men, including barbarian units. Mobile units were established that could be quickly moved to support frontier troops where the borders were threatened. Although larger, the army was less competent, being made up of recruits from Germany and the Balkans with less training than the traditional legions.

Constantine was especially interested in building programs despite the strain they placed on the budget. His biggest project was the construction of a new capital city in the east on the site of the Greek city of Byzantium on the shores of the Bosporus. Eventually renamed Constantinople (modern Istanbul), it was developed for defensive reasons: it had an excellent strategic location. Calling it his "New Rome," Constantine endowed the city with a forum, large palaces, and a vast amphitheater.

The political and military reforms of Diocletian and Constantine greatly enlarged two institutions—the army and civil service—that drained most of the public funds. Though more revenues were needed to

MAP 6.4   Divisions of the Restored Roman Empire, c. 300.

THE EMPEROR CONSTANTINE. Constantine played an important role in restoring order and stability to the Roman Empire at the beginning of the fourth century. This marble head of Constantine, which is 8½ feet high, was part of an enormous seated statue of the emperor in Rome. Constantine used these awe-inspiring statues throughout the empire to build support for imperial policies.

pay for the army and bureaucracy, the population was not growing, so the tax base could not be expanded. Diocletian and Constantine devised new economic and social policies to deal with these financial burdens, but like their political policies, they were all based on coercion and loss of individual freedom. To fight inflation, Diocletian resorted to issuing a price edict in 301 that established maximum wages and prices for the entire empire, but despite severe penalties, it was unenforceable and failed to work.

Coercion also came to form the underlying basis for numerous occupations in the Late Roman Empire. To ensure the tax base and keep the empire going despite the shortage of labor, the emperors issued edicts that forced people to remain in their designated vocations. Hence basic jobs, such as bakers and shippers, became hereditary. Free tenant farmers continued to decline and soon found themselves bound to the land by large landowners who took advantage of depressed agricultural conditions to enlarge their landed estates.

In general, the economic and social policies of Diocletian and Constantine were based on an unprecedented degree of control and coercion. Though temporarily successful, such authoritarian policies in the long run stifled the very vitality the Late Empire needed to revive its sagging fortunes.

◆ The Transformation of the Roman World: The Development of Christianity

The rise of Christianity marks a fundamental break with the dominant values of the Greco-Roman world. Christian views of God, human beings, and the world were quite different from those of the Greeks and Romans. Nevertheless, to understand the rise of Christianity, we must first examine both the religious environment of the Roman world and the Jewish background from which Christianity emerged.

❊ The Religious World of the Roman Empire

Augustus had taken a number of steps to revive the Roman state religion, which had declined during the turmoil of the late Republic. The official state religion focused on the worship of a pantheon of gods and goddesses. Observance of proper ritual by state priests theoretically established the proper relationship between Romans and the gods and guaranteed security, peace, and prosperity. The polytheistic Romans were extremely tolerant of other religions. The Romans allowed the worship of native gods and goddesses throughout their provinces and even adopted some of the local gods. In addition, the imperial cult of Rome and Augustus was developed to bolster support for the emperors. After Augustus, deceased emperors deified by the Roman senate were included in the official imperial cult.

The desire for a more emotional spiritual experience led many people to the mystery religions of the Hellenistic east, which flooded into the western Roman world during the Early Empire. The mystery religions offered secret teachings that promised their followers advantages unavailable through Roman religion: an entry into a higher world of reality and the promise of a future life superior to the present one. They also featured elaborate rituals with deep emotional appeal. By participating in their ceremonies and performing their rites, an adherent could achieve communion with spiritual beings and undergo purification that opened the door to life after death.

Although many mystery cults competed for the attention of the Roman world, perhaps the most important was Mithraism. Mithras was the chief agent of Ahuramazda, the supreme god of light in Persian Zoroastrianism (see Chapter 2). In the Roman world, Mithras came to be identified with the sun god and was known by his Roman title of the Unconquered Sun. Mithraism had spread rapidly in Rome and the western provinces by the second century A.D. and was especially favored by soldiers, who viewed Mithras as their patron deity. Mithraists paid homage to the sun on the first day of the week (Sunday), commemorated the sun's birthday around December 25, and celebrated ceremonial meals. All of these practices had parallels in Christianity.

� The Jewish Background

In Hellenistic times, the Jewish people had been granted considerable independence by their Seleucid rulers (see Chapter 4). Roman involvement with the Jews began in 63 B.C., and by A.D. 6, Judaea (which embraced the lands of the old Hebrew kingdom of Judah) had been made a province and placed under the direction of a Roman procurator. But unrest continued, augmented by divisions among the Jews themselves. The Sadducees favored a rigid adherence to Hebrew law, rejected the possibility of personal immortality, and favored cooperation with the Romans. The Pharisees followed a strict adherence to Jewish ritual and, although they wanted Judaea to be free from Roman control, they did not advocate violent means to achieve this goal. The Essenes were a Jewish sect that lived in a religious community near the Dead Sea. As revealed in the Dead Sea Scrolls, a collection of documents first discovered in 1947, the Essenes, like many other Jews, awaited a Messiah who would save Israel from oppression, usher in the kingdom of God, and establish a true paradise on earth. A fourth group, the Zealots, were militant extremists who advocated the violent overthrow of Roman rule. A Jewish revolt in A.D. 66 was crushed by the Romans four years later. The Jewish temple in Jerusalem was destroyed, and Roman power once more stood supreme in Judaea.

� The Rise of Christianity

In the midst of the confusion and conflict in Judaea, Jesus of Nazareth (c. 6 B.C.–A.D. 29) began his public preaching. Jesus grew up in Galilee, an important center of the militant Zealots. Jesus' message was basically simple. He reassured his fellow Jews that he did not plan to undermine their traditional religion: "Do not think that I have come to abolish the Law or the Prophets; I have not come to abolish them but to fulfill them."[14] According to Jesus, what was important was not strict adherence to the letter of the law and attention to rules and prohibitions but the transformation of the inner person: "So in everything, do to others what you would have them do to you, for this sums up the Law and the Prophets."[15] God's command was a simple one—to love God and one another: "Love the Lord your God with all your heart and with all your soul and with all your mind and with all your strength. The second is this: Love your neighbor as yourself."[16] In the Sermon on the Mount (see the box on p. 123), Jesus presented the ethical concepts—humility, charity, and brotherly love—that would form the basis for the value system of medieval Western civilization. As we have seen, these were not the values of classical Greco-Roman civilization.

Although some people welcomed Jesus as the Messiah who would save Israel from oppression and establish God's kingdom on earth, Jesus spoke of a heavenly kingdom, not an earthly one: "My kingdom is not of this world."[17] Consequently, he disappointed the radicals. At the same time, conservative religious leaders believed Jesus was another false Messiah who was undermining respect for traditional Jewish religion. To the Roman authorities of Palestine and their local allies, the Nazarene was a potential revolutionary who might transform Jewish expectations of a messianic kingdom into a revolt against Rome. Therefore, Jesus found himself denounced on many sides and was given over to the Roman authorities. The procurator Pontius Pilate ordered his crucifixion. But that did not solve the problem. A few loyal followers of Jesus spread the story that Jesus had overcome death, had been resurrected, and had then ascended into heaven. The belief in Jesus' resurrection became an important tenet of Christian doctrine. Jesus was now hailed as the "anointed one" (*Christos* in Greek), the Messiah who would return and usher in the kingdom of God on earth.

Christianity began, then, as a religious movement within Judaism and was viewed that way by Roman authorities for many decades. Although tradition holds that one of Jesus' disciples, Peter, founded the Christian church at Rome, the most important figure in early Christianity after Jesus was Paul of Tarsus (c. 5–c. 67). Paul reached out to non-Jews and transformed Christianity from a Jewish sect into a broader religious movement.

Called the "second founder of Christianity," Paul was a Jewish Roman citizen who had been strongly influenced by Hellenistic Greek culture. He believed that the message of Jesus should be preached not only to Jews but to Gentiles (non-Jews) as well. Paul was responsible for founding Christian communities throughout Asia Minor and along the shores of the Aegean.

Christian Ideals: The Sermon on the Mount

Christianity was simply one of many religions competing for attention in the Roman Empire during the first and second centuries. The rise of Christianity marked a fundamental break with the value system of the upper-class elites who dominated the world of classical antiquity. As these excerpts from the Sermon on the Mount in the Gospel of Matthew illustrate, Christians emphasized humility, charity, brotherly love, and a belief in the inner being and a spiritual kingdom superior to this material world. These values and principles were not those of classical Greco-Roman civilization as exemplified in the words and deeds of its leaders.

✻ *The Gospel According to Matthew*

Now when he saw the crowds, he went up on a mountainside and sat down. His disciples came to him, and he began to teach them saying:

> *Blessed are the poor in spirit: for theirs is the kingdom of heaven.*
> *Blessed are those who mourn: for they will be comforted.*
> *Blessed are the meek: for they will inherit the earth.*
> *Blessed are those who hunger and thirst for righteousness: for they will be filled.*
> *Blessed are the merciful: for they will be shown mercy.*
> *Blessed are the pure in heart: for they will see God.*
> *Blessed are the peacemakers: for they will be called sons of God.*
> *Blessed are those who are persecuted because of righteousness for theirs is the kingdom of heaven. . . .*

You have heard that it was said, "Eye for eye, and tooth for tooth." But I tell you, Do not resist an evil person. If someone strikes you on the right cheek, turn to him the other also. . . .

You have heard that it was said, "Love your neighbor, and hate your enemy." But I tell you, Love your enemies and pray for those who persecute you. . . .

Do not store up for yourselves treasures on earth, where moth and rust destroy, and where thieves break in and steal. But store up for yourselves treasures in heaven, where moth and rust do not destroy, and where thieves do not break in and steal. For where your treasure is, there you heart will be also. . . .

No one can serve two masters. Either he will hate the one and love the other, or he will be devoted to the one and despise the other. You cannot serve both God and Money.

Therefore I tell you, do not worry about your life, what you will eat or drink; or about your body, what you will wear. Is not life more important than food, and the body more important than clothes? Look at the birds of the air; they do not sow or reap to store away in barns, and yet your heavenly Father feeds them. Are you not much more valuable than they? . . . So do not worry, saying, What shall we eat? or What shall we drink? or What shall we wear? For the pagans run after all these things, and your heavenly Father knows that you need them. But seek first his kingdom and his righteousness, and all these things will be given to you as well.

It was Paul who provided a universal foundation for the spread of Jesus' ideas. He taught that Jesus was, in effect, a savior-God, the son of God, who had come to earth to save all humans who were basically sinners as a result of Adam's original sin of disobedience against God. By his death, Jesus had atoned for the sins of all humans and made it possible for all men and women to experience a new beginning with the potential for individual salvation. By accepting Jesus Christ as their Savior, they too could be saved.

At first, Christianity spread slowly. Although the teachings of early Christianity were mostly disseminated by the preaching of convinced Christians, written materials also appeared. Paul had written a series of letters, or epistles, outlining Christian beliefs for different Christian communities. Some of Jesus' disciples may also have preserved some of the sayings of the master in writing and would have passed on personal memories that became the basis of the written gospels—the "good news" concerning Jesus—which attempted to provide a record of Jesus' life and teachings and formed the core of the New Testament. Although Jerusalem was the first center of Christianity, its destruction by the Romans in A.D. 70 left individual Christian churches with considerable independence. By 100, Christian churches had been established in most of the major cities of the east and in some places in the western part of the empire.

Many early Christians came from the ranks of Hellenized Jews and the Greek-speaking populations of the east. But in the second and third centuries, an increasing number of followers came from Latin-speaking people. A Latin translation of the Greek New Testament that appeared soon after 200 aided this process.

Although some of the fundamental values of Christianity differed markedly from those of the Greco-Roman world, the Romans initially did not pay much attention to the Christians, whom they regarded at first as simply another sect of Judaism. The structure of the Roman Empire itself aided the growth of Christianity. Christian missionaries, including some of Jesus' original twelve disciples, or apostles, used Roman roads to travel throughout the empire spreading their "good news."

As time passed, however, the Roman attitude toward Christianity began to change. The Romans were tolerant of other religions except when they threatened public order or public morals. Many Romans came to view Christians as harmful to the order of the Roman state. Because Christians held their meetings in secret and seemed to be connected to Christian groups in other areas, the government could view them as potentially dangerous to the state.

Some Romans felt that Christians were overly exclusive and hence harmful to the community and public order. The Christians did not recognize other gods and therefore abstained from public festivals honoring these divinities. Finally, Christians refused to participate in the worship of the state gods and imperial cult. Since the Romans regarded these as important to the state, the Christians' refusal undermined the security of the state and hence constituted an act of treason, punishable by death. But to the Christians, who believed there was only one real God, the worship of state gods and the emperors was idolatry and would endanger their own salvation.

Roman persecution of Christians in the first and second centuries was never systematic, only sporadic and local. Persecution began during the reign of Nero. After the fire that destroyed much of Rome, the emperor used the Christians as scapegoats, accusing them of arson and hatred of the human race and subjecting them to cruel deaths in Rome. In the second century, Christians were largely ignored as harmless. By the end of the reigns of the five good emperors, Christians still represented a small minority, but one of considerable strength.

✸ The Growth of Christianity

The sporadic persecution of Christians by the Romans in the first and second centuries had done nothing to stop the growth of Christianity. It had, in fact, served to strengthen Christianity as an institution in the second and third centuries by causing it to shed the loose structure of the first century and move toward a more centralized organization of its various church communities. Crucial to this change was the emerging role of the bishops, who began to assume more control over church communities. The Christian church was creating a well-defined hierarchical structure in which the bishops and clergy were salaried officers separate from the laity or regular church members.

Christianity grew slowly in the first century, took root in the second, and had spread widely by the third. Why was Christianity able to attract so many followers? First of all, the Christian message had much to offer the Roman world. The promise of salvation, made possible by Jesus' death and resurrection, had immense appeal in a world full of suffering and injus-

JESUS AND HIS APOSTLES. Pictured is a fourth-century fresco from a Roman catacomb depicting Jesus and his apostles. Catacombs were underground cemeteries where early Christians buried their dead. Christian tradition holds that in times of imperial repression, Christians withdrew to the catacombs to pray and even hide.

tice. Christianity seemed to imbue life with a meaning and purpose beyond the simple material things of everyday reality. Second, Christianity was not entirely unfamiliar. It could be viewed as simply another eastern mystery religion, offering immortality as the result of the sacrificial death of a savior-God. At the same time, it offered advantages that the other mystery religions lacked. Jesus had been a human figure, not a mythological one, such as Mithras. Moreover, Christianity had universal appeal. Unlike Mithraism, it was not restricted to men. Furthermore, it did not require a painful or expensive initiation rite as other mystery religions did. Initiation was accomplished simply by baptism—a purification by water—by which one entered into a personal relationship with Jesus. In addition, Christianity gave new meaning to life and offered what the Roman state religions could not—a personal relationship with God and a link to higher worlds.

Finally, Christianity fulfilled the human need to belong. Christians formed communities bound to one another in which people could express their love by helping each other and offering assistance to the poor, the sick, widows, and orphans. Christianity satisfied the need to belong in a way that the huge, impersonal, and remote Roman Empire could never do.

Christianity proved attractive to all classes. The promise of eternal life was for all—rich, poor, aristocrats, slaves, men, and women. As Paul stated in his Epistle to the Colossians: "And [you] have put on the new self, which is being renewed in knowledge in the image of its Creator. Here there is no Greek nor Jew, circumcised or uncircumcised, barbarian, Scythian, slave or free, but Christ is all, and is in all."[18] Although it did not call for revolution or social upheaval, Christianity emphasized a sense of spiritual equality for all people.

Many women, in fact, found that Christianity offered them new roles and new forms of companionship with other women. Christian women fostered the new religion in their own homes and preached their convictions to other people in their towns and villages. Many also died for their faith, and their deaths gave rise to a literature known as the Apocryphal Gospels, in which women were honored for creating new role models as virgins and widows, dedicated to their faith, who defied husbands, fathers, and their traditional gender roles to pursue their new lives.

As the Christian church became more organized, some emperors in the third century responded with more systematic persecutions, but their schemes failed to work. The last great persecution was by Diocle-

tian at the beginning of the fourth century. But even he had to admit what had become apparent in the course of the third century—Christianity had become too strong to be eradicated by force.

In the fourth century, Christianity flourished after Constantine became the first Christian emperor. According to the traditional story, before a crucial battle, he saw a vision of a Christian cross with the writing, "In this sign you will conquer." Having won the battle, the story goes, Constantine was convinced of the power of the Christian God. Although he was not baptized until the end of his life, in 313 he issued the famous Edict of Milan officially tolerating the existence of Christianity. Under Theodosius "the Great" (378–395), it was made the official religion of the Roman Empire. Christianity had triumphed.

◆ The Fall of the Western Roman Empire

The restored empire of Diocletian and Constantine limped along for more than a century. After Constantine, the empire continued to divide into western and eastern parts, a division that was made complete in 395, when the western and eastern parts of the empire became two independent states.

The west came under increasing pressure from invading barbarian forces. The major breakthrough into the Roman Empire came in the second half of the fourth century. Ferocious warriors from Asia, known as Huns, moved into eastern Europe and put pressure on the Germanic Visigoths, who in turn moved south and west, crossed the Danube into Roman territory, and settled down as Roman allies. But the Visigoths soon revolted, and the Roman attempt to stop them at Adrianople in 378 led to a crushing defeat.

Increasing numbers of barbarians now crossed the frontiers. In 410, the Visigoths under Alaric sacked Rome. Vandals poured into southern Spain and Africa, Visigoths into Spain and Gaul. The Vandals crossed into Italy from North Africa and sacked Rome in 455. Twenty-one years later, the western emperor Romulus Augustulus (475–476) was deposed, and a series of German kingdoms replaced the Roman Empire in the west while an Eastern Roman Empire continued with its center at Constantinople.

The end of the Roman Empire has given rise to numerous theories that purport to explain the "decline and fall of the Roman Empire." These include the following: Christianity's emphasis on a spiritual kingdom undermined Roman military virtues and patriotism;

traditional Roman values declined as non-Italians gained prominence in the empire; lead poisoning through leaden water pipes and cups caused a mental decline; plague killed one-tenth of the population; Rome failed to advance technologically because of slavery; and Rome was unable to achieve a workable political system. There may be an element of truth in each of these theories, but each of them has also been challenged. History is an intricate web of relationships, causes, and effects. No single explanation will ever suffice to explain historical events. One thing is clear: the Roman army in the west was simply not able to fend off the hordes of people invading Italy and Gaul. In contrast, the eastern Roman Empire, which would survive for another thousand years, remained largely free of invasion.

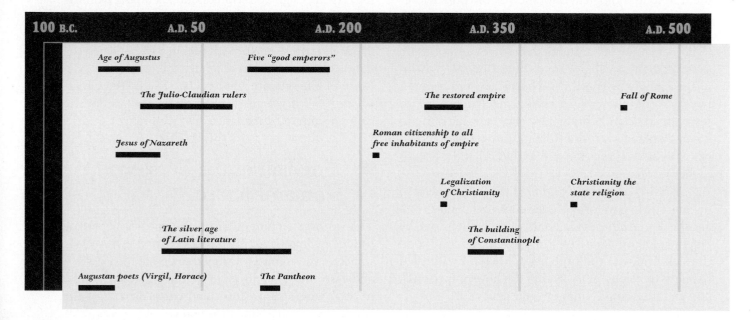

100 B.C.　　　　A.D. 50　　　　A.D. 200　　　　A.D. 350　　　　A.D. 500

Age of Augustus

Five "good emperors"

The Julio-Claudian rulers

The restored empire

Fall of Rome

Jesus of Nazareth

Roman citizenship to all free inhabitants of empire

Legalization of Christianity

Christianity the state religion

The silver age of Latin literature

The building of Constantinople

Augustan poets (Virgil, Horace)

The Pantheon

Conclusion

After a century of internal upheaval, Augustus established a new order that began the Roman Empire, which experienced a lengthy period of peace and prosperity between 14 and 180. During this Pax Romana, trade flourished and the provinces were governed efficiently. In the course of the third century, however, the Roman Empire came near to collapse due to invasions, civil wars, and economic decline. Although the emperors Diocletian and Constantine brought new life to the so-called Late Empire, their efforts merely shored up the empire temporarily. In the course of the fifth century, the empire divided into western and eastern parts, and in 476, the Roman Empire in the west came to an end with the ouster of Emperor Romulus Augustulus.

The Roman Empire was the largest empire in antiquity. Using their practical skills, the Romans made achievements in language, law, engineering, and government that were bequeathed to the future. The Romance languages of today (French, Italian, Spanish, Portuguese, and Romanian) are based on Latin. Western practices of impartial justice and trial by jury owe much to Roman law. As great builders, the Romans left monuments to their skills throughout Europe, some of which, such as aqueducts and roads, are still in use today. Aspects of Roman administrative practices survived in the Western world for centuries. The Romans also preserved the intellectual heritage of the ancient world.

While we are justified in praising the empire, it is also important to remember its other side: the enormous gulf between rich and poor, the dependence on enslaved or otherwise subject human beings, the bloodthirsty spectacles in the amphitheaters, and the use of institutionalized terror to maintain the order for which the empire is so often praised. In its last two hundred years, as Christianity spread, a slow transformation of the Roman world took place. The Germanic invasions greatly accelerated this process, and while many aspects of the Roman world would continue, a new civilization was emerging that would carry on yet another stage in the development of Western civilization.

Notes

1. Livy, *The Early History of Rome*, trans. Aubrey de Sélincourt (Harmondsworth, England, 1960), p. 35.
2. Tacitus, *The Annals of Imperial Rome*, trans. Michael Grant (Harmondsworth, England, 1956), p. 30.
3. Ibid., p. 37.
4. Ibid., p. 31.

5. Tacitus, *The Histories,* trans. Kenneth Wellesley (Harmondsworth, England, 1964), p. 23.

6. Virgil, *The Aeneid,* trans. C. Day Lewis (Garden City, N.Y., 1952), p. 154.

7. Horace, *Satires,* in *The Complete Works of Horace,* trans. Lord Dunsany and Michael Oakley (London, 1961), 1.1, p. 139.

8. Ibid., 1.3, p. 151.

9. Livy, *The Early History of Rome,* p. 18.

10. Seneca, *Letters from a Stoic,* trans. Robin Campbell (Harmondsworth, England, 1969), Letter 5.

11. Tacitus, *The Annals of Imperial Rome,* p. 147.

12. Juvenal, *The Sixteen Satires,* trans. Peter Green (Harmondsworth, England, 1967), Satire 10, p. 207.

13. Tacitus, *A Dialogue on Oratory,* in *The Complete Works of Tacitus,* trans. Alfred Church and William Brodribb (New York, 1942), 29, p. 758.

14. Matthew 5: 17.

15. Matthew 7: 12.

16. Mark 12: 30–31.

17. John 18: 36.

18. Colossians 3: 10–11.

Suggestions for Further Reading

For a general account of the Roman Empire, see J. Boardman, J. Griffin, and O. Murray, eds., *The Oxford History of the Roman World* (Oxford, 1991). A brief and reliable guide to recent trends in scholarship on the Roman Empire can be found in C. Starr, *Past and Future in Ancient History* (Lanham, Md., 1987), pp. 45–57. Good surveys of the Early Empire include P. Garnsey and R. P. Saller, *The Roman Empire: Economy, Society and Culture* (London, 1987); C. Wells, *The Roman Empire,* 2d ed. (London, 1992); J. Wacher, *The Roman Empire* (London, 1987); and F. Millar, *Roman Empire and Its Neighbors,* 2d ed. (London, 1981).

Studies of Roman emperors of the first and second centuries include D. Shotter, *Augustus Caesar* (London, 1991); M. Griffin, *Nero: The End of a Dynasty* (London, 1984); and M. Hammond, *The Antonine Monarchy* (Rome, 1959). For brief biographies of all the Roman emperors, see M. Grant, *The Roman Emperors* (New York, 1985). A fundamental work on Roman government and the role of the emperor is F. Millar, *The Emperor in the Roman World* (London, 1977).

There are many specialized studies on various aspects of the administrative, economic, and social conditions in the Early Empire. On the growth of cities in Italy and the spread of Roman citizenship outside Italy, see A. N. Sherwin White, *The Roman Citizenship,* 2d ed. (Oxford, 1973). For a detailed examination of economic matters, see M. I Rostovtzeff, *Social and Economic History of the Roman Empire,* 2d ed., 2 vols. (Oxford, 1957), and R. Duncan-Jones, *The Economy of the Roman Empire* (New York, 1982).

The Roman army is examined in G. Webster, *The Imperial Army of the First and Second Centuries* A.D., 2d ed. (London, 1979); L. Keppie, *The Making of the Roman Army* (London, 1984); and J. B. Campbell, *The Emperor and the Roman Army* (Oxford, 1984). On the provinces and Roman foreign policy, see E. M. Luttwak, *The Grand Strategy of the Roman Empire from the First Century* A.D. *to the*

Third (Baltimore, 1976), and B. Isaac, *The Limits of Empire: The Roman Empire in the East* (Oxford, 1990).

A good survey of Roman literature can be found in R. M. Ogilvie, *Roman Literature and Society* (Harmondsworth, England, 1980). More specialized studies include R. O. Lyne, *The Latin Love Poets from Catullus to Horace* (Oxford, 1980), and K. Galinsky, *Augustan Culture* (Princeton, N.J., 1996).

Various aspects of Roman society are covered in J. P. V. D. Balsdon, *Life and Leisure in Ancient Rome* (London, 1969). See also the essay by P. Veyne "The Roman Empire," in P. Veyne, ed., *A History of Private Life,* vol. 1 (Cambridge, Mass., 1987). Also useful on urban life is O. F. Robinson, *Ancient Rome: City Planning and Administration* (New York, 1992). Studies on Roman women include J. P. V. D. Balsdon, *Roman Women: Their History and Habits* (London, 1969), and S. B. Pomeroy, *Goddesses, Whores, Wives, and Slaves: Women in Classical Antiquity* (New York, 1975), pp. 149–226. On Roman law, see J. Crook, *Law and Life of Rome* (London, 1967). On the gladiators, see T. Wiedemann, *Emperors and Gladiators* (New York, 1992).

For a general introduction to early Christianity, see J. Court and K. Court, *The New Testament World* (Cambridge, 1990). Useful works on early Christianity include W. A. Meeks, *The First Urban Christians* (New Haven, Conn., 1983); W. H. C. Frend, *The Rise of Christianity* (Philadelphia, 1984); and R. MacMullen, *Christianizing the Roman Empire* (New Haven, Conn., 1984). On Christian women, see D. M. Scholer, ed., *Women in Early Christianity* (New York, 1993), and R. Kraemer, *Her Share of the Blessings: Women's Religion Among the Pagans, Jews and Christians in the Graeco-Roman World* (Oxford, 1995).

The classic work on the "decline and fall" of the Roman Empire is E. Gibbon, *The Decline and Fall of the Roman Empire,* J. B. Bury ed. (London, 1909–1914). Also valuable are A. Cameron, *The Later Roman Empire* (Cambridge, Mass., 1993), and R. MacMullen, *Corruption and the Decline of Rome* (New Haven, Conn., 1988). On the fourth century, see M. Grant, *Constantine the Great: The Man and His Times* (New York, 1993), and S. Williams, *Diocletian and the Roman Recovery* (London, 1985). On economic and social history, including the bureaucracy, see A. H. M. Jones, *The Later Roman Empire* (Oxford, 1964). Recent studies analyzing the aristocratic circles, the barbarian invasions, and the military problem include E. A. Thompson, *Romans and Barbarians* (Madison, 1982); A. Ferrill, *The Fall of the Roman Empire: The Military Explanation* (London, 1986); and J. M. O'Flynn, *Generalissimos of the Western Roman Empire* (Edmonton, Canada, 1983).

 For additional reading, go to InfoTrac College Edition, your online research library at http://web1.infotrac-college.com

Enter the search terms *Roman empire* using Key Terms.

Enter the search terms *Roman mythology* using the Subject Guide.

Enter the search terms *Roman law* using the Subject Guide.

Enter the search term *Constantine* using the Subject Guide.

The Passing of the Roman World and the Emergence of Medieval Civilization

CHAPTER OUTLINE

- The Transformation of the Roman World: The Role of the Germanic Peoples
- The Role and Development of the Christian Church
- The Byzantine Empire
- The Rise of Islam
- Conclusion

FOCUS QUESTIONS

- What were the main features of Germanic law and society, and how did they differ from those of the Romans?
- How and why did the organization of the Christian church change during the fourth and fifth centuries?
- What were the chief characteristics of Benedictine monasticism, and what role did monks play in both the conversion of Europe to Christianity and the intellectual life of the Germanic kingdom?
- How did the Byzantine Empire that had emerged by the eighth century differ from the empire of Justinian and from the Germanic kingdoms in the west?
- What was the basic message of Islam, and why was it able to expand so successfully?

*T*HE PERIOD THAT SAW THE DISINTEGRATION *of the western part of the Roman Empire also witnessed the emergence of medieval European civilization. Scholars know that major historical transitions are never tidy; chaos is often the ground out of which new civilizations are born. The early medieval civilization that arose out of the dissolution of the Western Roman Empire was formed by the coalescence of three major elements: the Germanic peoples who moved into the western empire and established new kingdoms, the continuing attraction of the Greco-Roman cultural legacy, and the Christian church. Christianity was* *the most distinctive and powerful component of the new medieval civilization. The church assimilated the classical tradition and through its clergy, especially the monks, brought Christianized civilization to the Germanic tribes.*

The conversion to Christianity of the pagan leaders of German tribes was sometimes dramatic, at least as it is reported by the sixth-century historian Gregory of Tours. Clovis, leader of the Franks, married Clotilde, daughter of the king of the Burgundians. She was a Christian, but Clovis refused her pleas to become a Christian, telling her, "Your god can do nothing." But during a battle with the Alemanni, when Clovis' army was close to utter destruction, "He saw the danger; his heart was stirred; and he raised his eyes to heaven, saying, 'Jesus Christ, I beseech the glory of your aid. If you shall grant me victory over these enemies, I will believe in you and be baptized in your name.'" When he had uttered these words, the Alemanni began to flee. Clovis soon became a Christian.

During the time when the Germanic kingdoms were establishing their roots in the west, the eastern part of the old Roman Empire, increasingly Greek in culture, continued to survive as the Byzantine Empire. While serving as a buffer between Europe and the peoples to the east, the Byzantine or Eastern Roman Empire also preserved the intellectual and legal accomplishments of Greek and Roman antiquity. At the same time, a new world of Islam emerged in the east; it occupied large parts of the old Roman Empire, preserved much of Greek culture, and created its own flourishing civilization. This chapter, then, largely concerns the heirs of Rome and the new world they created.

◆ The Transformation of the Roman World: The Role of the Germanic Peoples

The Germanic peoples were an important element of the new medieval civilization. Around 500 B.C., the Germans began to migrate from their northern Scandinavian homeland south into what are now the Baltic states and Germany and east into the fertile lands of the Ukraine. Although the Romans had established a series of political frontiers in the western empire, Romans and Germans often came into contact across those boundaries. For some time, the Romans had hired Germanic tribes to fight other Germanic tribes that threatened Rome's security or enlisted groups of Germans to fight for Rome.

In the late fourth century A.D., the Germanic tribes came under new pressures when the Huns, a fierce tribe of nomads from Asia, moved into the Black Sea region and forced Germanic groups westward. One of the largest groups, the Visigoths, crossed the Danube in 378, crushed a Roman army, and settled along the Danube within the Roman Empire, as allies. But the Visigoths were soon on the move. Under their king Alaric, they moved into Italy and sacked Rome in 410. Then, at the urging of the emperor, they moved into Spain and southern Gaul as Roman allies (see Map 7.1).

The Roman experience with the Visigoths established a precedent. The emperors in the first half of the fifth century made alliances with whole groups of Germanic peoples, who settled peacefully in the western part of the empire. The Burgundians settled themselves in much of eastern Gaul, just south of another German tribe called the Alemanni. Only the Vandals consistently remained hostile to the Romans. They sacked parts of Gaul and crossed the Pyrenees into Spain. Defeated by incoming Visigoths, the Vandals crossed the Straits of Gibraltar and conquered the province of Africa. In 455, the Vandals even attacked Rome, sacking it more ferociously than the Visigoths had in 410.

Increasingly, German military leaders dominated the imperial courts of the western empire. One such leader finally ended the charade of Roman imperial rule. Odoacer deposed the Roman emperor, Romulus Augustulus, in 476 and began to rule on his own. Meanwhile, the Ostrogoths, another branch of the Goths, under their king Theodoric (493–526), marched into Italy, killed Odoacer, and established control of Italy in 493.

✻ The New Kingdoms

By 500, the Western Roman Empire was being replaced politically by a series of kingdoms ruled by German kings (see Map 7.2). The pattern of settlement and the fusion of the Romans and Germans took different forms in the various barbarian kingdoms.

⚕ THE OSTROGOTHIC KINGDOM OF ITALY

More than any other Germanic state, the Ostrogothic kingdom of Italy managed to maintain the Roman tradition of government. The Ostrogothic king,

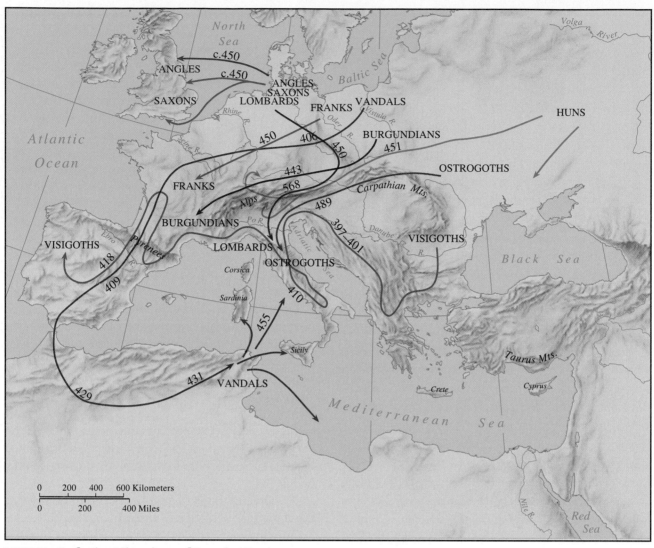

MAP 7.1   Barbarian Migration and Invasion Routes.

Theodoric, had received a Roman education while a hostage in Constantinople. After taking control of Italy, he was eager to create a synthesis of Ostrogothic and Roman practices. In addition to maintaining the entire structure of imperial Roman government, he established separate systems of rule for the Ostrogoths and Romans. The Italian population lived under Roman law administered by Roman officials. The Ostrogoths were governed by their own customs and their own officials.

After Theodoric's death in 526, it quickly became apparent that much of his success had been due to the force of his own personality. His successors soon found themselves face to face with opposition from the imperial forces of the Byzantine or Eastern Roman Empire. Under Emperor Justinian (527–565) (see "The Byzantine Empire" later in this chapter), Byzantine armies reconquered Italy between 535 and 554, devastating much of the peninsula and in the process destroying Rome as one of the great urban centers of the Mediterranean world. The Byzantine reconquest proved ephemeral, however. Another German tribe, the Lombards, invaded in 568 and conquered much of northern and central Italy. Unlike the Ostrogoths, the Lombards were harsh rulers who cared little for Roman structures and traditions.

THE VISIGOTHIC KINGDOM OF SPAIN

The Visigothic kingdom in Spain demonstrated a number of parallels to the Ostrogothic kingdom of Italy. Both favored coexistence between the Roman and German populations; both featured a warrior caste dominating a larger native population; and both con-

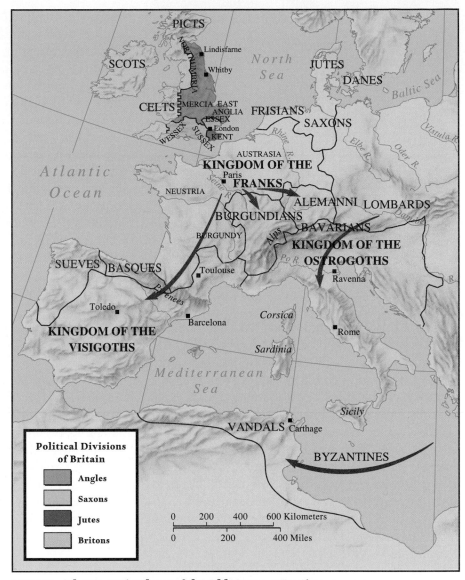

MAP 7.2   The New Kingdoms of the Old Western Empire.

tinued to maintain much of the Roman structure of government while largely excluding Romans from power. There were also noticeable differences, however. Laws preventing intermarriage were dropped, and the Visigothic and Hispano-Roman peoples began to blend. A new body of law common to both peoples also developed.

The Visigothic kingdom possessed one fatal weakness. With no established procedure for choosing new rulers, powerful Visigoths fought constantly to lay claim to the kingship. Church officials tried to help develop a sense of order, as this decree illustrates: "No one of us shall dare to seize the kingdom; no one shall arouse sedition among the citizenry; no one shall think of killing the king. . . ." Church edicts failed to stop

the feuds, however, and assassinations remained a way of life in Visigothic Spain. In 711, Muslim invaders destroyed the Visigothic kingdom itself (see "The Rise of Islam" later in this chapter).

THE FRANKISH KINGDOM

Only one of the German states on the European continent proved long-lasting—the kingdom of the Franks. The establishment of a Frankish kingdom was the work of Clovis (c. 482–511), a member of the Merovingian dynasty who became a Catholic Christian around 500. He was not the first German king to convert to Christianity, but the others had joined the Arian sect of Christianity (see later section

"Organization and Religious Disputes"). The Christian church in Rome, which had become known as the Roman Catholic church, regarded the Arians as heretics, or people who believed in teachings different from the official church doctrine. Clovis found that his conversion to Catholic Christianity gained him the support of the Roman Catholic church, which was only too eager to obtain the friendship of a major Germanic ruler who was a Catholic Christian.

By 510, Clovis had established a powerful new Frankish kingdom stretching from the Pyrenees in the west to German lands in the east (modern-day France and western Germany). After the death of Clovis, however, his sons divided the newly created kingdom, as was the Frankish custom. During the sixth and seventh centuries, the once-united Frankish kingdom came to be partitioned into three major areas: Neustria in northern Gaul; Austrasia, consisting of the ancient Frankish lands on both sides of the Rhine; and the former kingdom of Burgundy.

During this time, the Frankish kingdom witnessed a process of fusion between Gallo-Roman and Frankish cultures and peoples, a process accompanied by a significant decline in Roman standards of civilization and commercial activity. The Franks were warriors and did little to encourage either urban life or trade. By 750, Frankish Gaul was basically an agricultural society in which the old Roman villa system of the late empire had continued unimpeded. Institutionally, however, Germanic concepts of kingship and customary law replaced the Roman governmental structure.

ANGLO-SAXON ENGLAND

The barbarian pressures on the Western Roman Empire had forced the emperors to withdraw the Roman armies and abandon Britain by the beginning of the fifth century. This opened the door to the Angles and Saxons, Germanic tribes from Denmark and northern Germany. Although these same peoples had made plundering raids for the past century, the withdrawal of the Roman armies enabled them to make settlements instead. They met with resistance

BAPTISM OF CLOVIS. The conversion of Clovis to Catholic Christianity was an important factor in gaining papal support for his Frankish kingdom. In this illustration from a medieval manuscript, bishops and nobles look on while Clovis is baptized. One of the nobles holds a crown while a dove, symbol of the Holy Spirit (the third person of the Trinity—Father, Son, and Holy Spirit), descends from heaven bringing sacred oil for the ceremony.

from the Celtic Britons, however, who still controlled the western regions of Cornwall, Wales, and Cumberland at the beginning of the seventh century. The German invaders eventually succeeded in carving out small kingdoms throughout the island, Kent in southeast England being one of them.

✳ *The Society of the Germanic Peoples*

As Germans and Romans intermarried and began to create a new society, some of the social customs of the Germanic people began to play an important role. The crucial social bond among the Germanic peoples was the family, especially the extended or patriarchal family of husbands, wives, children, brothers, sisters, cousins, and grandparents. In addition to working the land together and passing it down to succeeding generations, the extended family provided protection, which was sorely needed in the violent atmosphere of Merovingian times.

The German conception of family affected the way Germanic law treated the problem of crime and punishment. In the Roman system, as in our own, a crime such as murder was considered an offense against society or the state and was handled by a court that heard evidence and arrived at a decision. Germanic law tended to be personal. An injury by one person against another could mean a blood feud in which the family of the injured party took revenge on the kin of the wrongdoer. Feuds could lead to savage acts of revenge, such as hacking off hands or feet, gouging out eyes, or slicing off ears and noses. Because this system could easily get out of control, an alternative system arose that made use of a fine called *wergeld,* which was paid by a wrongdoer to the family of the person he had injured or killed. *Wergeld,* which means "man money," was the value of a person in monetary terms. That value varied considerably according to social status. An offense against a nobleman, for example, cost considerably more than one against a freeman or a slave.

Under German customary law, compurgation and the ordeal were the two most commonly used procedures for determining whether an accused person was guilty and should have to pay *wergeld.* Compurgation was the swearing of an oath by the accused person, backed up by a group of "oath helpers," numbering twelve or twenty-five, who would also swear that the accused person should be believed. The ordeal functioned in a variety of ways, all of which were based on the principle of divine intervention; divine forces (whether pagan or Christian) would not allow an innocent person to be harmed (see the box on p. 134).

✳ THE FRANKISH FAMILY AND MARRIAGE

For the Franks, like other Germanic peoples, the extended family was at the center of social organization. The Frankish family structure was quite simple. Males were dominant and made all the important decisions. A woman obeyed her father until she married and then fell under the legal domination of her husband. A widow, however, could hold property without a male guardian. In Frankish law, the *wergeld* of a wife of childbearing age—of value because she could bear children—was considerably higher than that of a man. The Salic Law stated: "If any one killed a free woman after she had begun bearing children, he shall be sentenced to 24,000 denars. . . . After she can have no more children, he who kills her shall be sentenced to 8,000 denars. . . ."[1]

Because marriage affected the extended family group, fathers or uncles could arrange marriages for the good of the family without considering their children's wishes. Most important was the engagement ceremony in which a prospective son-in-law made a payment symbolizing the purchase of paternal authority over the bride. The essential feature of the marriage itself involved placing the married couple in bed to achieve their physical union. In first marriages, it was considered important that the wife be a virgin, which ensured that any children would be the husband's. A virgin symbolized the ability of the bloodline to continue. Accordingly, adultery was viewed as pollution of the woman and her offspring, hence poisoning the future. Adulterous wives were severely punished (an adulterous woman could be strangled or even burned alive); adulterous husbands were not. Divorce was relatively simple and was initiated primarily by the husband. Divorced wives simply returned to their families.

For most women in the new Germanic kingdoms, their legal status reflected the material conditions of their lives. Archaeological evidence suggests that most women had life expectancies of only thirty to forty years, and 10 to 15 percent of women died in their childbearing years, no doubt due to complications associated with childbirth. For most women, life consisted of domestic labor: providing food and clothing for the household, caring for the children, and assisting with numerous farming chores. Of all women's labors, the most important was childbearing, because it was indispensable to perpetuating the family and its possessions.

Germanic Customary Law: The Ordeal

In Germanic customary law, the ordeal came to be a means by which accused persons might clear themselves. Although the ordeal took different forms, all involved a physical trial of some sort, such as holding a red-hot iron. It was believed that God would protect the innocent and allow them to come through the ordeal unharmed. This sixth-century account by Gregory of Tours describes an ordeal by hot water.

✻ *Gregory of Tours, An Ordeal of Hot Water (c. 580)*

An Arian presbyter disputing with a deacon of our religion made venomous assertions against the Son of God and the Holy Ghost, as is the habit of that sect [the Arians]. But when the deacon had discoursed a long time concerning the reasonableness of our faith and the heretic, blinded by the fog of unbelief, continued to reject the truth, . . . the former said: "Why weary ourselves with long discussions? Let acts approve the truth; let a kettle be heated over the fire and someone's ring be thrown into the boiling water. Let him who shall take it from the heated liquid be approved as a follower of the truth, and afterward let the other party be converted to the knowledge of the truth. And do you also understand, O heretic, that this our party will fulfill the conditions with the aid of the Holy Ghost; you shall confess that there is no discordance, no dissimilarity in the Holy Trinity." The heretic consented to the proposition and they separated after appointing the next morning for the trial. But the fervor of faith in which the deacon had first made this suggestion began to cool through the instigation of the enemy. Rising with the dawn he bathed his arm in oil and smeared it with oint-

ment. But nevertheless he made the round of the sacred places and called in prayer on the Lord. . . . About the third hour they met in the market place. The people came together to see the show. A fire was lighted, the kettle was placed upon it, and when it grew very hot the ring was thrown into the boiling water. The deacon invited the heretic to take it out of the water first. But he promptly refused, saying, "You who did propose this trial are the one to take it out." The deacon all of a tremble bared his arm. And when the heretic presbyter saw it besmeared with ointment he cried out: "With magic arts you have thought to protect yourself, that you have made use of these salves, but what you have done will not avail." While they were thus quarreling there came up a deacon from Ravenna named Iacinthus and inquired what the trouble was about. When he learned the truth he drew his arm out from under his robe at once and plunged his right hand into the kettle. Now the ring that had been thrown in was a little thing and very light so that it was thrown about by the water as chaff would be blown about by the wind; and searching for it a long time he found it after about an hour. Meanwhile the flame beneath the kettle blazed up mightily so that the greater heat might make it difficult for the ring to be followed by the hand; but the deacon extracted it at length and suffered no harm, protesting rather that at the bottom the kettle was cold while at the top it was just pleasantly warm. When the heretic beheld this he was greatly confused and audaciously thrust his hand into the kettle saying, "My faith will aid me." As soon as his hand had been thrust in all the flesh was boiled off the bones clear up to the elbow. And so the dispute ended.

◆ The Role and Development of the Christian Church

By the end of the fourth century, Christianity had become the predominant religion of the Roman Empire. As the official Roman state disintegrated, the Christian church played an increasingly important role in the emergence and growth of the new European civilization.

✻ *Organization and Religious Disputes*

By the fourth century, the Christian church had developed a system of government. The Christian community in each city was headed by a bishop, whose area of jurisdiction was known as a bishopric or diocese. The bishoprics of each Roman province were clustered together under the direction of an archbishop. The bishops of four great cities, Rome, Jerusalem, Alexandria, and Antioch, held positions of special power in church affairs because the churches in these cities all asserted that they had been founded by the original apostles sent out by Jesus.

One reason the church needed a more formal organization was the problem of heresy. As Christianity developed and spread, contradictory interpretations of important doctrines emerged. Heresy came to be viewed as a teaching different from the official catholic or universal beliefs of the church. In a world where people were concerned about salvation, the question of whether Jesus' nature was divine or human took on great significance. These doctrinal differences also became political issues, creating political factions that actually warred with one another. It is highly unlikely that ordinary people understood what these debates meant.

One of the major heresies of the fourth century was Arianism, which was a product of the followers of Arius, a priest from Alexandria in Egypt. Arius believed that Jesus Christ had been human and thus not truly God. Arius was opposed by Athanasius, a bishop of Alexandria, who argued that Jesus was human but also truly God. Emperor Constantine, disturbed by the controversy, called the first ecumenical council of the church, a meeting composed of representatives from the entire Christian community. The Council of Nicaea, held in 325, condemned Arianism and stated that Jesus was of "the same substance" as God: "We believe in one God the Father All-sovereign, maker of all things visible and invisible; And in one Lord Jesus Christ, the Son of God, begotten of the Father, only-begotten, that is, of the substance of the Father, God of God, Light of Light, true God of true God, begotten not made, of one substance with the Father. . . ."[2] The Council of Nicaea did not end the controversy, however; not only did Arianism persist in some parts of the Roman Empire for many years, but many of the Germanic Goths who established states in the west converted to Arian Christianity. As a result of these fourth-century theological controversies, the Roman emperor came to play an increasingly important role in church affairs. At the same time, such divisions also created a need for leadership within the church.

✳ The Power of the Pope

One of the far-reaching developments in the history of the Christian church was the emergence of one bishop—that of Rome—as the recognized leader of the western Christian church. According to church tradition, Jesus had given the keys to the kingdom of heaven to Peter, who was considered the chief apostle and the first bishop of Rome. Subsequent bishops of Rome were considered Peter's successors and came to be known as popes (from the Latin word *papa*, meaning "father") of the Catholic church.

Although western Christians came to accept the bishop of Rome as head of the church in the fourth and fifth centuries, there was certainly no unanimity on the extent of the powers the pope possessed as a result of this position. Nevertheless, the emergence in the sixth century of a strong pope, Gregory I, known as Gregory the Great, set the papacy and the Roman Catholic church, as the Christian church of the west came to be called, on an energetic path that enabled the church in the seventh and eighth centuries to play an increasingly prominent role in civilizing the Germans and aiding the emergence of a distinctly new European civilization.

As pope, Gregory I (590–604) took charge of Rome and its surrounding area and made it into an

POPE GREGORY I. Pope Gregory the Great became one of the most important popes of the Early Middle Ages. This tenth-century ivory book cover shows Gregory working at his desk. On his right shoulder is a dove, symbol of the Holy Spirit, which is providing divine inspiration. The lower scene shows a monastic scriptorium, or writing room, with three monks busy at their work.

The Life of Saint Anthony

In the third and early fourth centuries, the lives of martyrs had provided important models for early Christianity. But in the course of the fourth century, monks or desert fathers, who attempted to achieve spiritual perfection through asceticism, the denial of earthly life, and the struggle with demons, became the new spiritual ideal for Christians. Consequently, spiritual biographies of early monks became a significant new form of Christian literature. Especially noteworthy was The Life of Saint Anthony *by Saint Athanasius, the defender of Catholic orthodoxy against the Arians. His work had been translated into Latin before 386. This excerpt describes how Anthony fought off the temptations of Satan.*

❊ *Athanasius,* **The Life of Saint Anthony**

Now when the Enemy [Satan] saw that his craftiness in this matter was without profit, and that the more he brought temptation into Saint Anthony, the more strenuous the saint was in protecting himself against him with the armor of righteousness, he attacked him by means of the vigor of early manhood which is bound up in the nature of our humanity. With the goadings of passion he sued to trouble him by night, and in the daytime also he would vex him and pain him with the same to such an extent that even those who saw him knew from his appearance that he was waging war against the Adversary. But the more the Evil One brought unto him filthy and maddening thoughts, the more Saint Anthony took refuge in prayer and in abundant supplication, and amid them all he remained wholly chaste. And the Evil One was working upon him every shameful deed according to his wont, and at length he even appeared unto Saint Anthony in the form of a woman; and other things which resembled this he performed with ease, for such things are a subject for boasting to him.

But the blessed Anthony knelt down upon his knees on the ground, and prayed before Him who said, "Before you criest unto Me, I will answer you," and said, "O my Lord, this I entreat you. Let not Your love be blotted out from my mind, and behold, I am, by your grace, innocent before You." And again the Enemy multiplied in him the thoughts of lust, until Saint Anthony became as one who was being burned up, not through the Evil One, but through his own lusts; but he girded himself about with the threat of the thought of the Judgment, and of the torture of Gehenna, and of the worm which does not die. And while meditating on the thoughts which could be directed against the Evil One, he prayed for thoughts which would be hostile to him. Thus, to the reproach and shame of the Enemy, these things could not be performed; for he who imagined that he could be God was made a mock of by a young man, and he who boasted over flesh and blood was vanquished by a man who was clothed with flesh. . . .

---

administrative unit that eventually came to be known as the Papal States. Gregory also pursued a policy of extending papal authority over the Christian church in the west. He intervened in ecclesiastical conflicts throughout Italy and corresponded with the Frankish rulers, urging them to reform the church in Gaul. He successfully initiated the efforts of missionaries to convert England to Christianity and was especially active in converting the pagan peoples of Germanic Europe. His primary instrument was the monastic movement.

❊ *The Monks and Their Missions*

A monk (Latin *monachus,* meaning "someone who lives alone") was a person who sought to live a life divorced from the world, cut off from ordinary human society, in order to pursue an ideal of godliness or total dedication to the will of God. Christian monasticism, which developed first in Egypt, was initially based on the model of the solitary hermit who forsakes all civilized society to pursue spirituality. Saint Anthony (c. 250–350) was a prosperous peasant in Egypt who decided to follow Jesus' injunction in the Gospel of St. Mark: "Go your way, sell whatsoever you have, and give to the poor, and you shall have treasure in heaven: and come, take up the cross, and follow me." Anthony gave away his 300 acres of land to the poor and went into the desert to pursue his ideal of holiness (see the box above). Others did likewise, often to extremes. Saint Simeon the Stylite lived for three decades in a basket atop a pillar over 60 feet high. These spiritual gymnastics established a new ideal for Christianity. Whereas the early Christian model had been the martyr who died for the faith and achieved eternal life in the process, the new ideal was the monk who died to the world and achieved spiritual life through denial, asceticism, and mystical experience of God.

These early monks, however, soon found themselves unable to live in solitude. Their feats of holiness attracted followers on a wide scale, and as the monastic ideal spread throughout the east, a new form of monasticism based on the practice of communal life soon became the dominant form. Monastic communities came to be seen as the ideal Christian society that could provide a moral example to the wider society around them.

✂ BENEDICTINE MONASTICISM

Saint Benedict of Nursia (c. 480–c. 543), who founded a monastic house for which he wrote a set of rules sometime between 520 and 530, established the fundamental form of monastic life in the western Christian church. The Benedictine rule came to be used by other monastic groups and was crucial to the growth of monasticism in the western Christian world.

Benedict's rule favored an ideal of moderation. In chapter 40 of the rule, on the amount a monk should drink, this sense of moderation becomes apparent:

> "Every man has his proper gift from God, one after this manner, another after that." And therefore it is with some misgiving that we determine the amount of food for someone else. Still, having regard for the weakness of some brothers, we believe that a hemina of wine [a quarter liter] per day will suffice for all. Let those, however, to whom God gives the gift of abstinence, know that they shall have their proper reward. But if either the circumstances of the place, the work, or the heat of summer necessitates more, let it lie in the discretion of the abbot to grant it. But let him take care in all things lest satiety or drunkenness supervene.[3]

At the same time, moderation did not preclude a disciplined existence based on the ideals of poverty, chastity, and obedience.

Benedict's rule divided each day into a series of activities with primary emphasis on prayer and manual labor. Physical work of some kind was required of all monks for several hours a day because idleness was "the enemy of the soul." At the very heart of community practice was prayer, the proper "Work of God." While this included private meditation and reading, all monks gathered together seven times during the day for common prayer and chanting of psalms. A

LIFE OF SAINT BENEDICT.   This illustration with its six scenes is from an eleventh-century manuscript of Pope Gregory the Great's *Life of Saint Benedict*, written in 593 or 594. *Top left*, Benedict writes his rule; *top right*, the death of Benedict; *middle left*, his burial; *middle right and bottom left*, scenes of miracles attributed to Saint Benedict's intercession; *bottom right*, Gregory finishes his *Life of Saint Benedict*.

Benedictine life was a communal one; monks ate, worked, slept, and worshiped together.

Each Benedictine monastery was strictly ruled by an abbot, or "father" of the monastery, who held complete authority over them; unquestioning obedience to the will of the abbot was expected of each monk. Each Benedictine monastery owned lands that enabled it to be a self-sustaining community, isolated from and independent of the world surrounding it. Within the monastery, however, monks were to fulfill their vow of poverty: "Let all things be common to all, as it is written, lest anyone should say that anything is his own or arrogate it to himself."[4] By the eighth century, Benedictine monasticism had spread throughout the west.

Although the original monks were men, women soon followed suit in withdrawing from the world to dedicate themselves to God. The first monastic rule for western women was produced by Caesarius of Arles for his sister in the fifth century. It strongly emphasized a rigid cloistering of these nuns to preserve them from dangers.

→ Monasticism played an indispensible role in early medieval civilization. Monks became the new heroes of Christian civilization. Their dedication to God became the highest ideal of Christian life. Monks copied Latin works and passed on the legacy of the ancient world to Western civilization in its European stage. Moreover, the monks played an increasingly significant role in spreading Christianity to the entire European world.

❧ MONKS AS MISSIONARIES

The British Isles, in particular, became an important center of Christian culture and missionary fervor. After their conversion, the Celts of Ireland and Anglo-Saxons of England created new centers of Christian learning and in turn themselves became enthusiastic missionaries.

By the sixth century, Irish monasticism was a flourishing institution with its own unique characteristics. Unlike Benedictine monasticism, it was strongly ascetic. Monks performed strenuous fasts, prayed and meditated frequently under extreme privations, and confessed their sins on a regular basis to their superiors. In fact, Irish monasticism gave rise to the use of penitentials or manuals that provided a guide for examining one's life to see what sins, or offenses against the will of God, one had committed (see the box on p. 139). A great love of learning also characterized Irish monasticism. The Irish eagerly absorbed both Latin and Greek culture and fostered education as a major part of their monastic life.

Their emphasis on asceticism led many Irish monks to go into voluntary exile. This "exile for the love of God" was not into isolation, however, but into missionary activity. Irish monks became fervid missionaries. Saint Columba (521–597) left Ireland in 565 as a "pilgrim for Christ" and founded a highly influential monastic community off the coast of Scotland on the island of Iona. From there Irish missionaries went to northern England to begin the process of converting the Angles and Saxons. Meanwhile, other Irish monks traveled to the European continent. New monasteries founded by the Irish became centers of learning wherever they were located.

At the same time the Irish monks were busy bringing their version of Christianity to the Anglo-Saxons of Britain, Pope Gregory the Great had also set into motion his own effort to convert England to Roman Christianity. His most important agent was Augustine, a monk from Rome, who arrived in England in 597. England at that time had a number of Germanic kingdoms. Augustine went first to Kent, where he converted King Ethelbert; most of the king's subjects then followed suit. Pope Gregory's conversion techniques emphasized persuasion rather than force and, as seen in this excerpt from one of his letters, he was willing to assimilate old pagan practices in order to coax the pagans into the new faith:

> We wish you [Abbot Mellitus] to inform him [Augustine] that we have been giving careful thought to the affairs of the English, and have come to the conclusion that the temples of the idols among that people should on no account be destroyed. The idols are to be destroyed, but the temples themselves are to be aspersed with holy water, altars set up in them, and relics deposited there. For if these temples are well-built, they must be purified from the worship of demons and dedicated to the service of the true God.[5]

Freed of their pagan past, temples had become churches, as one Christian commentator noted with joy: "The dwelling place of demons has become a house of God. The saving light has come to shine, where shadows covered all. Where sacrifices once took place and idols stood, angelic choirs now dance. Where God was angered once, now God is made content."[6] Likewise, old pagan feasts were given new names and incorporated into the Christian calendar. No doubt Gregory was aware that early Christians had done the same. The Christian feast of Christmas, for example, was held on December 25, the day of the pagan celebration of the winter solstice.

As Roman Christianity spread northward in Britain, it encountered Irish Christianity moving southward. Roman Christianity prevailed, although the English church, despite its newfound unity and loyalty to Rome, retained some Irish features. Most important was the concentration on monastic culture with special emphasis on learning and missionary work. By 700, the English church had become the best trained and most learned in western Europe.

Following the Irish example, English monks spread to the European continent to carry on the work of con-

Irish Monasticism and the Penitential

Irish monasticism became well known for its ascetic practices. Much emphasis was placed on careful examination of conscience to determine if one had committed a sin against God. To facilitate this examination, penitentials were developed that listed possible sins with appropriate penances. Penance usually meant fasting a number of days each week on bread and water. Although these penitentials were eventually used throughout Christendom, they were especially important in Irish Christianity. This excerpt from the Penitential of Cummean, an Irish abbot, was written about 650 and demonstrates a distinctive feature of the penitentials, an acute preoccupation with sexual sins.

❊ *The Penitential of Cummean*

A bishop who commits fornication shall be degraded and shall do penance for twelve years.

A presbyter or a deacon who commits natural fornication, having previously taken the vow of a monk, shall do penance for seven years. He shall ask pardon every hour; he shall perform a special fast during every week except in the days between Easter and Pentecost.

He who defiles his mother shall do penance for three years, with perpetual pilgrimage.

So shall those who commit sodomy do penance every seven years.

He who merely desires in his mind to commit fornication, but is not able, shall do penance for one year, especially in the three forty-day periods.

He who is willingly polluted during sleep shall arise and sing nine psalms in order, kneeling. On the following day, he shall live on bread and water.

A cleric who commits fornication once shall do penance for one year on bread and water; if he begets a son he shall do penance for seven years as an exile; so also a virgin.

He who loves any woman, but is unaware of any evil beyond a few conversations, shall do penance for forty days.

He who is in a state of matrimony ought to be continent during the three forty-day periods and on Saturday and on Sunday, night and day, and in the two appointed week days [Wednesday and Friday], and after conception, and during the entire menstrual period.

After a birth he shall abstain, if it is a son, for thirty-three [days]; if a daughter, for sixty-six [days].

Boys talking alone and transgressing the regulations of the elders [in the monastery], shall be corrected by three special fasts.

Children who imitate acts of fornication, twenty days; if frequently, forty.

But boys of twenty years who practice masturbation together and confess [shall do penance] twenty or forty days before they take communion.

---

version (see Map 7.3). Most important was Boniface (c. 680–755), who undertook the conversion of pagan Germans in Frisia, Bavaria, and Saxony. By 740, Saint Boniface, the "Apostle of the Germans," had become the most famous churchman in Europe. Fourteen years later, he was killed while trying to convert the pagan Frisians. Boniface was a brilliant example of the numerous Irish and English monks whose tireless efforts made Europe the bastion of the Roman Catholic faith.

❧ WOMEN AND MONASTICISM

Women, too, played an important role in the monastic missionary movement and the conversion of the Germanic kingdoms. So-called double monasteries in which both monks and nuns lived in separate houses but attended church services together were found in both the English and Frankish kingdoms. The monks and nuns followed a common rule under a common head. Frequently, this leader was an abbess rather than an abbot. Many of these abbesses belonged to royal houses, especially in Anglo-Saxon England. In the kingdom of Northumbria, for example, Saint Hilda founded the monastery of Whitby in 657. As abbess, she was responsible for giving learning an important role in the life of the monastery; five future bishops were educated under her tutelage. For female intellectuals, monasteries offered opportunities for learning not found elsewhere in the society of their day.

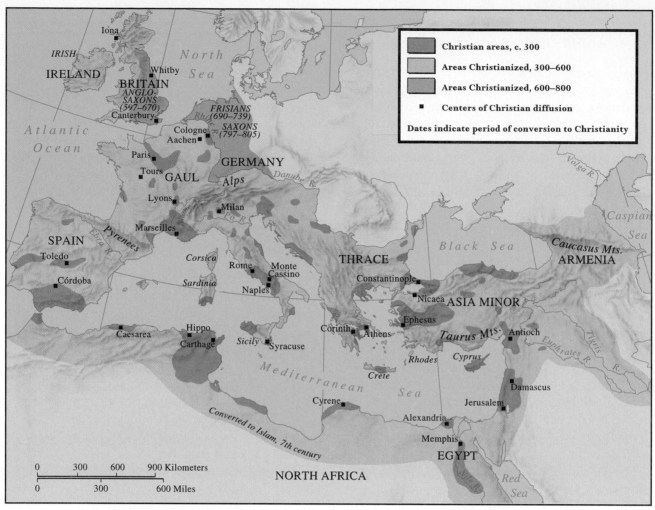

MAP 7.3 The Spread of Christianity, 400–750.

Nuns of the seventh and eighth centuries also played an important role in the spread of Christianity. The great English missionary Boniface relied on nuns in England for books and money. He also asked the abbess of Wimborne to send groups of nuns to establish convents in newly converted German lands. A nun named Leoba established the first convent in Germany at Bischofsheim.

It is difficult to assess what Christianity meant to the converted pagans, especially the peasants on whom the Irish and English monks had expended their greatest efforts. As Pope Gregory had recommended, Christian beliefs and values were usually superimposed on older pagan customs. Though effective in producing quick conversions, it is an open question how much people actually understood of Christian teachings. Popular belief tended to focus on God as a judge who needed to be appeased to avert disasters in daily

life and gain salvation. Except for the promise of salvation, this image of God was not all that different from Roman religious practices.

❋ Christianity and Intellectual Life

Many early Christians expressed considerable hostility toward the pagan culture of the classical world. Tertullian (c. 160–c. 225), a Christian writer from Carthage, had proclaimed: "What has Jerusalem to do with Athens, the Church with the Academy, the Christian with the heretic? . . . After Jesus Christ we have no need of speculation, after the Gospel no need of research."[7] To many early Christians, the Bible contained all the knowledge anyone needed. Others, however, thought it was not possible to separate Christian thought from classical traditions and education and encouraged Christianity to absorb the classical heritage. As it spread in the eastern Roman world, Christianity adopted Greek as its language; the New Testament was written in Greek. Christians also turned to Greek thought for help in expressing complicated theological concepts. In many ways, then, Christianity served to preserve Greco-Roman culture.

The work of Augustine (354–430) provides one of the best examples of how Christianity absorbed pagan culture in the service of Christianity. Born in North Africa, he was reared by his mother, an ardent Christian. Augustine eventually became a professor of rhetoric at Milan in 384. After experiencing a profound and moving religious experience, he gave up his teaching position and went back to North Africa, where he became bishop of Hippo from 396 until his death in 430.

Augustine's most famous work, *The City of God*, was a profound expression of a Christian philosophy of government and history. In it, he theorized on the ideal relations between two kinds of societies existing throughout time—the City of God and the City of the World. Those who loved God would be loyal to the City of God, whose ultimate location was the kingdom of heaven. Earthly society would always be uncertain because of human beings' fallen nature and inclination to sin. And yet the City of the World was still necessary, for it was the duty of rulers to curb the depraved instincts of sinful humans and maintain the peace necessary for Christians to live in the world. Hence Augustine posited that secular government and authority were necessary for the pursuit of the true Christian life on earth; in doing so, he provided a justification for secular political authority that would play an important role in medieval thought.

Another important intellectual of the early church was Jerome (345–420), who pursued literary studies in Rome and became a master of Latin prose. Jerome had mixed feelings about his love for classical studies, however, and like Augustine, he experienced a spiritual conversion after which he tried to dedicate himself more fully to Jesus. Ultimately, Jerome found a compromise by purifying the literature of the pagan world and then using it to further the Christian faith. Jerome was a great scholar, and his extensive knowledge of both Hebrew and Greek enabled him to translate the Old and New Testaments into Latin. In the process, he created the so-called Latin Vulgate, or common text, of the Scriptures that became the standard edition for the Catholic church in the Middle Ages.

Although the Christian church came to accept classical culture, it was not easy to do so in the world of the new German kingdoms. Nevertheless, some Christian scholars managed to keep learning alive. Most prominent was Cassiodorus (c. 490–c. 585), who came from an aristocratic Roman family and served as an official of the Ostrogothic king Theodoric. The conflicts that erupted after the death of Theodoric led Cassiodorus to withdraw from public life and retire to his landed estates in southern Italy, where he wrote his final work, *Divine and Human Readings*. This was a compendium of the literature of both Christian and pagan antiquity. Cassiodorus accepted the advice of earlier Christian intellectuals to make use of classical works while treasuring the Scriptures above all else.

Cassiodorus continued the tradition of late antiquity of classifying knowledge according to certain subjects. In assembling his compendium of authors, he followed the works of late ancient authors in placing all secular knowledge into the categories of the seven liberal arts, which were divided into two major groups: the *trivium*, consisting of grammar, rhetoric, and dialectic or logic; and the *quadrivium*, consisting of the mathematical subjects of arithmetic, geometry, astronomy, and music. The seven liberal arts would become the cornerstone of education until the seventeenth century.

◆ The Byzantine Empire

In the fourth century, a noticeable separation between the western and eastern parts of the Roman Empire began to develop. In the course of the fifth century, the Germanic tribes moved into the western part of the empire and established their states while the Roman Empire in the east, centered on Constantinople, continued to exist.

❋ *The Reign of Justinian (527–565)*

When he became emperor of the Eastern Roman Empire, Justinian was determined to reestablish the Roman Empire in the entire Mediterranean world. His army, commanded by Belisarius, probably the best general of the late Roman world, sailed to North Africa and quickly destroyed the Vandals in two major battles. From North Africa, Belisarius led his forces onto the Italian peninsula and defeated the Ostrogoths. By 552, Justinian appeared to have achieved his goals. He had restored the Roman Empire in the Mediterranean. His empire included Italy, part of Spain, North Africa,

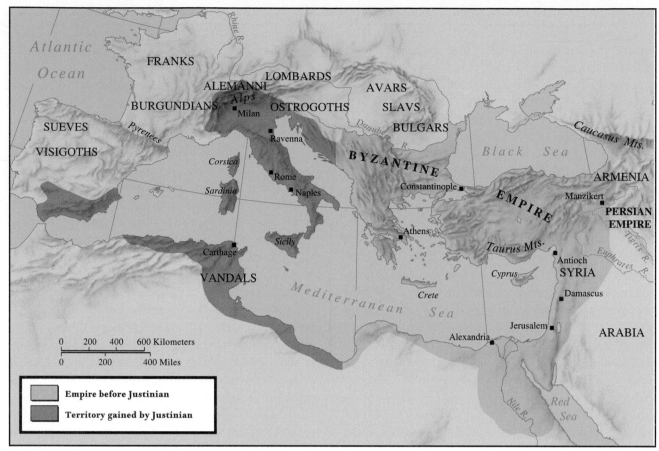

MAP 7.4 The Byzantine Empire in the Time of Justinian.

Asia Minor, Palestine, and Syria (see Map 7.4). But the reconquest of the western empire proved fleeting. Only three years after Justinian's death, the Lombards conquered much of Italy. Although the eastern empire maintained the fiction of Italy as a province, its forces were limited to southern and central Italy, Sicily, and some coastal areas.

Justinian's most important contribution was his codification of Roman law. The eastern empire had inherited a vast quantity of legal materials connected to the development of Roman law, which Justinian wished to simplify. The result was the *Corpus Iuris Civilis (Body of Civil Law)*, a codification of Roman law that remained the basis of imperial law in the Eastern Roman Empire until its end in 1453. More important, however, because it was written in Latin (it was in fact the last product of eastern Roman culture to be written in Latin, which was soon replaced by Greek), it was also eventually used in the west and ultimately became the basis of the legal system of all of continental Europe.

LIFE IN CONSTANTINOPLE: THE EMPEROR'S BUILDING PROGRAM

After riots destroyed much of Constantinople in 532, Emperor Justinian rebuilt the city and gave it the appearance it would keep for almost a thousand years. With a population estimated in the hundreds of thousands, Constantinople was the largest city in Europe during the Middle Ages. It viewed itself as center of an empire and a special Christian city.

Until the twelfth century, Constantinople was Europe's greatest commercial center, the chief marketplace where western and eastern products were exchanged. Highly desired in Europe were the products of the east: silk from China, spices from southeast Asia and India, jewelry and ivory from India (the latter used by artisans for church items), wheat and furs from southern Russia, and flax and honey from the Balkans. Many of these eastern goods were then shipped to the Mediterranean area and northern Europe. Moreover, imported raw materials were used

THE EMPEROR JUSTINIAN SURROUNDED BY HIS COURT. The church of San Vitale at Ravenna contains some of the finest examples of sixth-century Byzantine mosaics. This mosaic depicts the Byzantine emperor Justinian and his court dressed in their elaborate court robes.

in Constantinople for local industries. During Justinian's reign, two Christian monks smuggled silkworms from China to begin a Byzantine silk industry. The state controlled the production of silk cloth, and the workshops themselves were housed in Constantinople's royal palace complex. European demand for silk cloth made it the city's most lucrative product.

Much of Constantinople's appearance in the Middle Ages was due to Justinian's program of rebuilding in the sixth century. The city was dominated by an immense palace complex, hundreds of churches, and a huge arena known as the Hippodrome. No residential district was particularly fashionable; palaces, tenements, and slums ranged alongside one another. Justinian added many new buildings. His public works projects included roads, bridges, walls, public baths, law courts, and colossal underground reservoirs to hold the city's water supply. He also built hospitals, schools, monasteries, and churches. Churches were his special passion, and in Constantinople alone he built or rebuilt thirty-four of them. His greatest achievement was the famous Hagia Sophia—the Church of the Holy Wisdom, completed in 537. The center of Hagia Sophia consisted of four large piers crowned by an

enormous dome, which seemed to be floating in space. In part this impression was created by ringing the base of the dome with forty-two windows, which allowed an incredible play of light within the cathedral. Light served to remind the worshipers of God. As invisible light illuminates darkness, so too was it believed that invisible spirit illuminates the world.

The Hippodrome was a huge amphitheater, constructed of brick covered by marble, holding between 40,000 and 60,000 spectators. Although gladiator fights were held there, the main events were the chariot races; twenty-four would usually be presented in one day. The citizens of Constantinople were passionate fans of chariot racing. Successful charioteers were acclaimed as heroes and honored with public statues.

✳ From East Roman to Byzantine Empire

Justinian's accomplishments had been spectacular, but when he died he left the Eastern Roman Empire with serious problems: too much territory to protect far from Constantinople, an empty treasury, a decline in population after a plague, and renewed threats to its

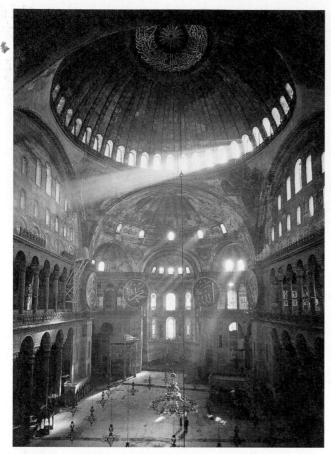

INTERIOR VIEW OF HAGIA SOPHIA. The Church of the Holy Wisdom was constructed during Justinian's reign by Anthemius of Tralles and Isidore of Milan. The pulpits and the great plaques bearing inscriptions from the Qur'an were introduced when the Turks converted this church into a mosque in the fifteenth century.

frontiers. In the first half of the seventh century, the empire faced attacks from the Persians to the east and the Slavs to the north.

The most serious challenge to the Eastern Roman Empire came from the rise of Islam, which unified the Arab tribes and created a powerful new force that swept through the east (see the next section, "The Rise of Islam"). The defeat of an eastern Roman army at Yarmuk in 636 meant the loss of the provinces of Syria and Palestine. The Arabs also moved into the old Persian Empire and conquered it. Arabs and eastern Roman forces now faced each other along a frontier in southern Asia Minor.

Problems arose along the northern frontier as well, especially in the Balkans, where an Asiatic people known as the Bulgars had arrived earlier in the sixth century. In 679, the Bulgars defeated the eastern

Roman forces and took possession of the lower Danube valley, creating a strong Bulgarian kingdom.

By the beginning of the eighth century, the Eastern Roman Empire was greatly diminished in size. Consisting only of the eastern Balkans and Asia Minor, it was no longer an eastern Mediterranean state. The external challenges had important internal repercussions as well. By the eighth century, the Eastern Roman Empire had been transformed into what historians call the Byzantine Empire, a civilization with its own unique character that would last until 1453 (Constantinople was built on the site of an older city named Byzantium—hence the term *Byzantine*).

The Byzantine Empire was both a Greek and Christian state. Increasingly, Latin fell into disuse as Greek became both the common and the official language of the Byzantine Empire. The Byzantine Empire was also built on a faith in Jesus that was shared by almost all of its citizens. An enormous amount of artistic talent was poured into the construction of churches, church ceremonies, and church decoration. Spiritual principles deeply permeated Byzantine art.

The emperor occupied a crucial position in the Byzantine state. Portrayed as chosen by God, the emperor was crowned in sacred ceremonies, and his subjects were expected to prostrate themselves in his presence. His power was considered absolute and was limited in practice only by deposition or assassination. Because the emperor appointed the head of the church (known as the patriarch), he also exercised control over both church and state. The Byzantines believed that God had commanded their state to preserve the true Christian faith. Emperor, clergy, and state officials were all bound together in service to this ideal. It can be said that spiritual values truly held the Byzantine state together.

By 750, it was apparent that two of Rome's heirs, the Germanic kingdoms and the Byzantine Empire, were moving in different directions. Nevertheless, Byzantine influence on the medieval western world was significant. The images of a Roman imperial state that continued to haunt the west had a living reality in the Byzantine state. The legal system of the west owed much to Justinian's codification of Roman law. In addition, the Byzantine Empire served in part as a buffer state, protecting the west for a long time from incursions from the east. Although the Byzantine Empire would continue to influence the west until its demise in 1453, it went its own unique way. One of its bitterest enemies was the new power of Islam,

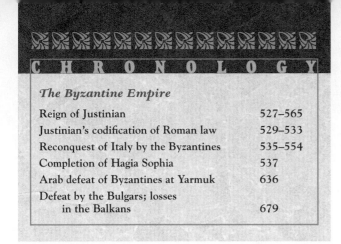

which erupted out of Arabia in the name of the holy man Muhammad. This third heir of Rome soon controlled large areas of the old Roman Mediterranean area.

◆ The Rise of Islam

Like the Hebrews and the Assyrians, the Arabs were a Semitic-speaking people of the Near East with a long history. In Roman times, the Arabian peninsula was dominated by Bedouins, tribes of nomads who moved constantly to find water and food for themselves and their animals. Although some Arabs prospered from trading activities, especially in the north, most Arabs were poor Bedouins, whose tribes were known for their independence, their warlike qualities, and their dislike of urban-dwelling Arabs.

Although these early Arabs were polytheistic, there was a supreme God named Allah (*Allah* is the Arabic name for God) that ruled over the other gods. Allah was symbolized by a sacred stone, and each tribe had its own stone. All tribes, however, worshiped a massive black meteorite—the Black Stone, which had been placed in a central shrine called the *Ka'ba* in the city of Mecca.

In the fifth and sixth centuries A.D., the Arabian peninsula took on new importance. As a result of political disorder in Mesopotamia and Egypt, the usual trade routes in the region began to change. A new trade route—from the Mediterranean through Mecca to Yemen and then by ship across the Indian Ocean—became more popular and communities in that part of the Arabian peninsula, such as Mecca, began to prosper from this caravan trade. As a result, tensions arose between the Bedouins in the desert and the increasingly wealthy merchant classes in the towns. Into this intense world stepped Muhammad.

Born in Mecca to a merchant family, Muhammad (c. 570–632) was orphaned at the age of five. Muhammad grew up to become a caravan manager and eventually married a rich widow who was also his employer. In his middle years, he began to experience visions that he believed were inspired by Allah. Muhammad believed that while Allah had already revealed himself in part through Moses and Jesus—and thus through the Hebrew and Christian traditions—the final revelations were now being given to him. Out of his revelations, which were eventually written down, came the Qur'an (or Koran), which contained the guidelines by which followers of Allah were to live. Muhammad's teachings formed the basis for the religion known as Islam, which means "submission to the will of Allah." Allah was the all-powerful being who had created the universe and everything in it. Humans must subject themselves to Allah if they wished to achieve everlasting life. Those who became his followers were called Muslims, meaning those who practiced Islam.

After receiving the revelations, Muhammad set out to convince the people of Mecca of the truth of his revelations. At first, many thought he was insane, and others feared that his attacks on the corrupt society around him would upset the established social and political order. Discouraged by the failure of the Meccans to accept his message, in 622 Muhammad and some of his closest supporters left the city and moved north to the rival city of Yathrib, later renamed Medina ("city of the Prophet"). The year of the journey to Medina, known in history as the *Hegira*, became year one in the official calendar of Islam.

Muhammad, who had been invited to the town by a number of prominent residents, soon began to win support from people in Medina as well as from members of Bedouin tribes in the surrounding countryside. From these groups, he formed the first Muslim community. Muslims saw no separation between political and religious authority; submission to the will of Allah meant submission to his Prophet, Muhammad. Muhammad soon became both a religious and political leader. His political and military skills enabled him to put together a reliable military force, with which he returned to Mecca in 630, conquering the city and converting the townspeople to the new faith. From Mecca, Muhammad's ideas spread quickly across the Arabian peninsula and within a relatively short time had resulted in both the religious and political union of Arab society.

At the heart of Islam was the Qur'an, with the basic message that there is no God but Allah and

The Qur'an and the Spread of the Muslim Faith

The Qur'an is the sacred book of the Muslims, comparable to the Bible in Christianity. In this selection from Chapter 47, titled "Muhammad, Revealed at Medina," it is apparent that Islam encourages the spreading of the faith. Believers who died for Allah were promised a garden of paradise quite unlike the arid desert homeland of the Arab warriors.

❋ The Qur'an, Chapter 47, "Muhammad, Revealed at Medina"

Allah will bring to nothing the deeds of those who disbelieve and debar others from His path. As for the faithful who do good works and believe in what is revealed to Muhammad—which is the truth from their Lord—He will forgive them their sins and ennoble their state.

This, because the unbelievers follow falsehood, while the faithful follow the truth from their Lord. Thus Allah coins their sayings for mankind.

When you meet the unbelievers in the battlefield strike off their heads and, when you have laid them low, bind your captives firmly. Then grant them their freedom or take ransom from them, until War shall lay down her armor. . . .

As for those who are slain in the cause of Allah, he will not allow their works to perish. He will vouchsafe them guidance and ennoble their state; He will admit them to the Paradise He has made known to them.

Believers, if you help Allah, Allah will help you and make you strong. But the unbelievers shall be consigned to perdition. He will bring their deeds to nothing. Because they have opposed His revelations, he will frustrate their works.

Have they never journeyed through the land and seen what was the end of those who have gone before them? Allah destroyed them utterly. A similar fate awaits the unbelievers, because Allah is the protector of the faithful; because the unbelievers have no protector.

Allah will admit those who embrace the true faith and do good works to gardens watered by running streams. The unbelievers take their full of pleasure and eat as the beasts eat: but Hell shall be their home. . . .

This is the Paradise which the righteous have been promised. There shall flow in it rivers of unpolluted water, and rivers of milk forever fresh; rivers of delectable wine and rivers of clearest honey. They shall eat therein of every fruit and receive forgiveness from their Lord. Is this like the lot of those who shall abide in Hell for ever and drink scalding water which will tear their bowels? . . .

Know that there is no god but Allah. Implore Him to forgive your sins and to forgive the true believers, men and women. Allah knows your busy haunts and resting-places.

Muhammad is his Prophet (see the box above). Essentially, the Qur'an contains Muhammad's revelations of a heavenly book written down by secretaries. Consisting of 114 chapters, the Qur'an is the sacred book of Islam, which recorded the beliefs of the Muslims and served as their code of ethics and law.

Islam was a direct and simple faith, emphasizing the need to obey the will of Allah. This meant following a basic ethical code consisting of the "five pillars" of Islam: belief in Allah and Muhammad as his Prophet; standard prayer five times a day and public prayer on Friday at midday to worship Allah; observance of the holy month of Ramadan (the ninth month in the Muslim calendar) with fasting from dawn to sunset; making a pilgrimage (known as the *hajj*), if possible, to Mecca in one's lifetime; and giving alms to the poor and unfortunate. The faithful who observed the law were guaranteed a place in an eternal paradise.

Islam was not just a set of religious beliefs but a way of life as well. After the death of Muhammad, Muslim scholars drew up a law code, called the *Shari'a*, to provide believers with a set of prescriptions to regulate their daily lives. Much of the *Shari'a* was drawn from the Qur'an. Believers were subject to strict guidelines for their behavior. In addition to the "five pillars," Muslims were forbidden to gamble, to eat pork, to drink alcoholic beverages, and to engage in dishonest behavior. Sexual practices were also strictly regulated. Marriages were to be arranged by parents, and contact

MUSLIMS CELEBRATING THE END OF RAMADAN. Ramadan is the holy month of Islam during which all Muslims must fast from dawn to sunset. Observance of this holy month is regarded as one of the "five pillars" of the faith. Muhammad instituted the fast during his stay at Medina. It was designed to replace the single Jewish Day of Atonement. This Persian miniature depicts Muslims on horseback celebrating the end of Ramadan.

between unmarried men and women was discouraged. In accordance with Bedouin custom, males were permitted to have more than one wife, but Muhammad attempted to limit the practice by restricting the number of wives to four.

✳ The Expansion of Islam

The death of Muhammad in 632 presented his followers with a dilemma. Although Muhammad had not claimed to be divine, Muslims saw no separation between religious and political authority. Submission to the will of Allah was the same thing as submission to his Prophet, Muhammad. But Muhammad had never named a successor, and although he had several daughters, he left no sons. In a male-oriented society, who would lead the community of the faithful? Shortly after Muhammad's death, some of his closest followers selected Abu Bakr, a wealthy merchant who was Muhammad's father-in-law, as caliph, or temporal leader, of the Islamic community.

Muhammad and the early caliphs who succeeded him took up the Arabic tribal custom of making raids against one's enemies. The Qur'an called this activity "striving in the way of Lord," or a *jihad*. Although misleadingly called a holy war, the *jihad* grew out of the Arabic tradition of tribal raids, which were permitted as a way to channel the warlike energies of the Bedouin tribes. Such aggression was not carried out to

convert others, since conversion to Islam was purely voluntary. Those who did not convert were required only to submit to Muslim rule and pay taxes.

The Byzantines and the Persians were the first to feel the strength of the newly united Arabs. At Yarmuk in 636, the Muslims defeated the Byzantine army, and by 640 they had taken possession of the province of Syria (see Map 7.5). To the east, the Arabs went on to conquer the Persian Empire by 650. In the meantime, by 642, Egypt and other areas of northern Africa had been added to the new Muslim empire. Led by a series of brilliant generals, the Arabs had put together a large and highly motivated army whose valor was enhanced by the belief that Muslim warriors were guaranteed a place in paradise if they died in battle.

Early caliphs, ruling from Medina, organized their newly conquered territories into taxpaying provinces. By the mid-seventh century, problems arose again over the succession to the Prophet until Ali, Muhammad's son-in-law, was assassinated and the general Muawiya, the governor of Syria and one of Ali's chief rivals, became caliph in 661. He was known for one outstanding virtue: he used force only when necessary. As he said, "I never use my sword when my whip will do, nor my whip when my tongue will do."[8] Muawiya moved quickly to make the caliphate hereditary in his own family, thus establishing the Umayyad dynasty. As one of its first actions, the Umayyad dynasty moved the capital of the Muslim empire from

The Rise of Islam

Birth of Muhammad	c. 570
Muhammad's flight from Mecca (Hegira)	622
Death of Muhammad	632
Defeat of Byzantines at Yarmuk	636
Seizure of Byzantine provinces of Syria and Egypt	640–642
Defeat of Persians	650
Invasion of Spain	710

a Muslim state with its center at Córdoba. In 732, a Muslim army, making a foray into southern France, was defeated at the Battle of Tours. Muslim expansion in Europe came to a halt.

Meanwhile, in 717, another Muslim force had launched a naval attack on Constantinople with the hope of destroying the Byzantine Empire. In the spring of 718, the Byzantines destroyed the Muslim fleet and saved the Byzantine Empire and indirectly Christian Europe, because the fall of Constantinople would no doubt have opened the door to Muslim invasion of eastern Europe. The Byzantine Empire and Islam now established an uneasy frontier in southern Asia Minor.

The Arab advance had finally come to an end, but not before the southern and eastern Mediterranean parts of the old Roman Empire had been conquered. Islam had truly become heir to much of the old Roman Empire. The Umayyad dynasty at Damascus now ruled an enormous empire. While expansion had conveyed untold wealth and new ethnic groups into the fold of Islam, it also brought contact with Byzantine and Persian civilization. As a result, the new Arab empire would be influenced by Greek culture as well as the older civilizations of the ancient Near East.

Medina to Damascus in Syria. This internal dissension over the caliphate created a split in Islam between the Shi'ites, or those who accepted only the descendants of Ali, Muhammad's son-in-law, as the true rulers, and the Sunnites, who claimed that the descendants of the Umayyads were the true caliphs. This seventh-century split in Islam has lasted until the present day.

The internal dissension, however, did not stop the expansion of Islam. After sweeping across North Africa, the Muslims crossed the Strait of Gibraltar and moved into Spain around 710. The Visigothic kingdom collapsed, and by 725, most of Spain had become

MAP 7.5   The Expansion of Islam.

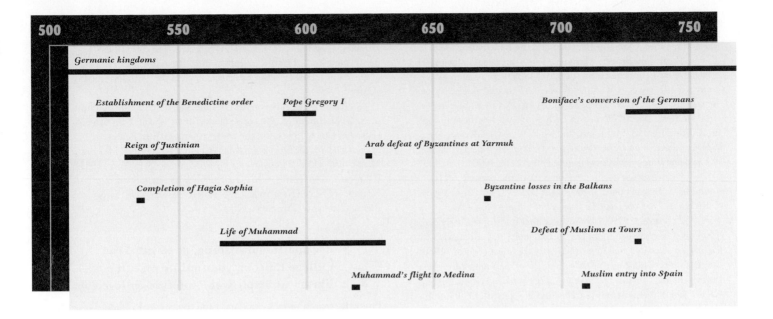

500 550 600 650 700 750

Germanic kingdoms

Establishment of the Benedictine order

Pope Gregory I

Boniface's conversion of the Germans

Reign of Justinian

Arab defeat of Byzantines at Yarmuk

Completion of Hagia Sophia

Byzantine losses in the Balkans

Life of Muhammad

Defeat of Muslims at Tours

Muhammad's flight to Medina

Muslim entry into Spain

Conclusion

The period from 400 to 750 was both chaotic and creative. Three new entities fell heir to Roman civilization: the German kingdoms, the Byzantine Empire, and the world of Islam. In the west, Roman elements combined with German and Celtic influences; in the east, Greek and eastern elements of late antiquity were of more consequence. Although the Germanic kingdoms of the west and the Byzantine civilization of the east came to share a common bond in Christianity, the faith proved incapable of keeping them in harmony politically, and the two civilizations continued to move apart. But Christianity remained a dominant influence in both civilizations, and in the west it was especially important as a civilizing agent that brought pagan peoples into a new European civilization that was slowly being born. The rise of Islam, Rome's third heir, resulted in the loss of the southern and eastern Mediterranean worlds of the old Roman Empire to a religious power that was neither Roman nor Christian. The new Islamic empire forced Europe back on itself, and slowly there emerged a new culture that became the heart of what we know as Western civilization.

Notes

1. Ernest F. Henderson, *Select Historical Documents of the Middle Ages* (London, 1892), p. 181.
2. "The Creed of Nicaea," in Henry Bettenson, ed., *Documents of the Christian Church* (London, 1963), p. 35.
3. Norman F. Cantor, ed., *The Medieval World: 300–1300* (New York, 1963), p. 104.
4. Ibid., p. 103.
5. Bede, *A History of the English Church and People*, trans. Leo Sherley-Price (Harmondsworth, England, 1968), pp. 86–87.
6. Quoted in Peter Brown, *The Rise of Western Christendom: Triumph and Adversity*, A.D. 200–1000 (Oxford, 1997), p. 98.
7. Tertullian, "The Prescriptions Against the Heretics," in *The Library of Christian Classics*, vol. 5, *Early Latin Theology*, ed. and trans. S. L. Greenslade (Philadelphia, 1956), p. 36.
8. Quoted in Arthur Goldschmidt Jr., *A Concise History of the Middle East*, 4th ed. (Boulder, Colo., 1991), p. 56.

Suggestions for Further Reading

Good general histories of the entire medieval period can be found in S. Painter and B. Tierney, *Western Europe in the Middle Ages, 300–1475* (New York, 1983); E. Peters, *Europe and the Middle Ages*, 2d ed. (Englewood Cliffs, N.J., 1989); D. Nicholas, *The Evolution of the Medieval World: Society, Government, and Thought in Europe, 312–1500* (London, 1993); and G. Holmes, ed., *The Oxford Illustrated History of Medieval Europe* (Oxford, 1988). For a good general survey of the social history of the Middle Ages, see C. B. Bouchard, *Life and Society in the West: Antiquity and the Middle Ages* (San Diego, 1988). An excellent reference work on medieval history is J. R. Strayer, ed., *Dictionary of the Middle Ages*, 13 vols. (New York, 1982–1989).

Brief histories of the period covered in this chapter include R. Collins, *Early Medieval Europe, 300–1000* (New York, 1991); M. Grant, *Dawn of the Middle Ages* (New York, 1981), which contains a lively text and excellent illustrations; and J. M. Wallace-Hadrill, *The Barbarian West*, rev. ed. (Oxford, 1985).

For surveys on the German tribes and their migrations, see L. Musset, *The German Invasions* (University Park, Pa., 1975); T. S. Burns, *A History of the Ostrogoths* (Bloomington, Ind., 1984); P. Heather, *Goths and Romans* (Oxford, 1991); E. James, *The Franks* (Oxford, 1988); and especially H. Wolfram, *The Goths*, trans. T. J. Dunlop (Berkeley, 1988). Also valuable is P. Geary, *Before France and Germany* (Oxford, 1988).

For a superb introduction to early Christianity, see P. Brown, *The Rise of Western Christendom* (Oxford, 1997). On Augustine and Jerome, see P. Brown, *Augustine of Hippo* (Berkeley, 1969), and

J. N. D. Kelly, *Saint Jerome* (London, 1975). For a good account of early monasticism, see C. H. Lawrence, *Medieval Monasticism*, 2d ed. (London, 1989). On Saint Benedict and the Benedictine ideal, see L. von Matt, *Saint Benedict* (London, 1961), and O. Chadwick, *The Making of the Benedictine Ideal* (London, 1981). For women in monastic life, see S. F. Wemple, *Women in Frankish Society: Marriage and the Cloister, 500–900* (Philadelphia, 1981). On women in general, see L. M. Bitel, "Women in Early Medieval Northern Europe," in R. Bridenthal, S. M. Stuard, and M. E. Weisner, eds., *Becoming Visible*, 3d ed. (New York, 1998), and D. Herlihy, *Opera Muliebria; Women and Work in Medieval Europe* (New York, 1990).

A brief survey of the development of the papacy can be found in G. Barraclough, *The Medieval Papacy* (New York, 1968). J. Richards, *The Popes and the Papacy in the Early Middle Ages, 476–752* (Boston, 1979), is a more detailed study of the early papacy. On Pope Gregory the Great, see the biography by J. Richards, *Consul of God: The Life and Times of Gregory the Great* (Boston, 1980). On Irish monasticism, see L. M. Bitel, *Isle of the Saints: Monastic Settlement and Christian Community in Early Ireland* (Ithaca, N.Y., 1990). On Christianity and intellectual life, see J. J. O'Donnell, *Cassiodorus* (Berkeley, 1979).

Brief but good introductions to Byzantine history can be found in H. W. Haussig, *A History of Byzantine Civilization* (New York, 1971), and C. Mango, *Byzantium: The Empire of New Rome* (London, 1980). For a comprehensive survey of the Byzantine Empire, see W. Treadgold, *A History of the Byzantine State and Society* (Stanford, Calif., 1997). On Justinian, see J. Moorhead, *Justinian,* (London, 1995), and J. A. S. Evans, *The Age of Justinian* (New York, 1996). The role of the Christian church is discussed in J. Hussey, *The Orthodox Church in the Byzantine Empire* (Oxford, 1986).

A good brief survey of the Islamic Middle East can be found in A. Goldschmidt Jr., *A Concise History of the Middle East*, 5th ed. (Boulder, Colo., 1995). On the rise of Islam, see F. E. Peters, *Muhammad and the Origins of Islam* (Albany, N.Y., 1994); M. Lings, *Muhammad: His Life Based on the Earliest Sources* (New York, 1983); P. Crone and M. Hinds, *God's Caliph: Religious Authority in the First Centuries of Islam* (New York, 1986); and F. Donner, *The Early Islamic Conquests* (Princeton, N.J., 1980).

 For additional reading, go to InfoTrac College Edition, your online research library at http://web1.infotrac-college.com

Enter the search term *Byzantium* using the Subject Guide.

Enter the search terms *early Christianity* using Key Terms.

Enter the search term *Augustine* using Key Terms.

Enter the search terms *Middle Ages* using the Subject Guide.

CHAPTER

8

European Civilization in the Early Middle Ages, 750–1000

CHAPTER OUTLINE

- The World of the Carolingians
- The Disintegration of the Carolingian Empire
- The Emerging World of Lords and Vassals
- The Zenith of Byzantine Civilization
- The Slavic Peoples of Central and Eastern Europe
- The World of Islam
- Conclusion

FOCUS QUESTIONS

- What was the significance of Charlemagne's coronation as emperor?
- How did both the intellectual life and daily life in the Carolingian Empire represent a fusion of Gallo-Roman, Germanic, and Christian practices?
- What was fief-holding, and why did it develop?
- What was manorialism, and how was it related to fief-holding?
- How did conditions in the Byzantine Empire and the Islamic world in the eighth and ninth centuries differ from the situation in western Europe?

I N 800, *Charlemagne, the king of the Franks, journeyed to Rome to help Pope Leo III, who was barely clinging to power in the face of rebellious Romans. On Christmas Day, Charlemagne and his family, attended by Romans, Franks, and even visitors from the Byzantine Empire, crowded into St. Peter's Basilica to hear Mass. Quite unexpectedly, according to a Frankish writer, "as the king rose from praying before the tomb of the blessed apostle Peter, Pope Leo placed a golden crown on his head." In keeping with ancient tradition, the people in the church shouted, "Long life and victory to Charles Augustus, crowned by God the great and pacific Emperor of the Romans." Seemingly, the Roman Empire in the West had* been reborn, and Charles had become the first western emperor since 476. But this "Roman emperor" was actually a German king, and he had been crowned by the head of the Western Christian church. In truth, the coronation of Charlemagne was a sign not of the rebirth of the Roman Empire but of the emergence of a new European civilization.

By the year of Charlemagne's coronation, the contours of this new European civilization were beginning to emerge in western Europe. Increasingly, Europe would become the focus and center of Western civilization. Building on a fusion of Germanic, classical, and Christian elements, the medieval European world first became visible in the Carolingian Empire of Charlemagne. The agrarian foundations of the eighth and ninth centuries proved inadequate to maintain a large monarchical system, however, and a new political and military order based on the decentralization of political power subsequently evolved to become an integral part of the political world of the Middle Ages.

European civilization began on a shaky and uncertain foundation, however. In the ninth century, Vikings, Magyars, and Muslims posed threats that could easily have stifled the new society. But a vibrant civilization can absorb such challenges, and European civilization did just that. The Vikings and Magyars were assimilated, and recovery slowly began. By 1000, European civilization was ready to embark on a period of dazzling vitality and expansion.

◆ The World of the Carolingians

By the eighth century, the Merovingian dynasty was losing its control of the Frankish lands. Charles Martel, the Carolingian mayor of the palace of Austrasia, became the virtual ruler of these territories. When Charles died in 741, Pepin, his son, deposed the Merovingians and assumed the kingship of the Frankish state, an action approved by the pope. In imitation of an Old Testament practice, Pepin (751–768) was crowned and formally anointed by a representative of the pope with holy oil. The anointing not only symbolized that the king had been entrusted with a sacred office but also provided yet another example of the fusion between Germanic institutions and Christian practices in the Early Middle Ages.

✳ Charlemagne and the Carolingian Empire (768–814)

Pepin was succeeded on the throne of the Frankish kingdom by his son, a dynamic and powerful ruler known to history as Charles the Great, or Charlemagne (*Carolus magnus* in Latin—hence our word *Carolingian*). Charlemagne was a determined and decisive man, highly intelligent and inquisitive. A fierce warrior, he was also a wise patron of learning and a resolute statesman (see the box on p. 153). He greatly expanded the territory of the Carolingian Empire during his lengthy rule.

✍ EXPANSION OF THE CAROLINGIAN EMPIRE

In the tradition of the Germanic kings, Charlemagne was a determined warrior who undertook fifty-four military campaigns. Even though the Frankish army was relatively small—only eight thousand men gathered each spring for campaigning—supplying it and transporting it to distant areas could still present serious problems. The Frankish army consisted mostly of infantry, with some cavalry armed with swords and spears.

Charlemagne's campaigns took him to many parts of Europe. In 773, Charlemagne led his army into Italy, crushed the Lombards, and took control of the Lombard state. Although his son was crowned king of Italy, Charlemagne was its real ruler. Four years after his invasion of Italy, Charlemagne moved his forces into northern Spain. This campaign proved disappointing: not only did the Basques harass his army as it crossed the Pyrenees on the way home, but they also ambushed and annihilated his rear guard.

Charlemagne was considerably more successful with his eastern campaigns into Germany, especially against the Saxons located between the Elbe River and the North Sea. As Einhard, Charlemagne's biographer, recounted it:

> No war ever undertaken by the Frank nation was carried on with such persistence and bitterness, or cost so much labor, because the Saxons, like almost all the tribes of Germany, were a fierce people, given to the worship of devils, and hostile to our religion, and did not consider it dishonorable to transgress and violate all law, human and divine.[1]

Charlemagne's insistence that the Saxons convert to Christianity simply fueled their resistance. Not until 804, after eighteen campaigns, was Saxony finally pacified and added to the Carolingian domain.

The Achievements of Charlemagne

Einhard, the biographer of Charlemagne, was born in the valley of the Main River in Germany about 775. Raised and educated in the monastery of Fulda, an important center of learning, he arrived at the court of Charlemagne in 791 or 792. Although he did not achieve high office under Charlemagne, he served as private secretary to Louis the Pious, Charlemagne's son and successor. Einhard's Life of Charlemagne was modeled on Suetonius' Lives of the Caesars, especially his biography of Augustus. Einhard's work, written between 817 and 830, was the "first medieval biography of a lay figure." In this selection, he discusses some of Charlemagne's accomplishments.

❋ Einhard, **Life of Charlemagne**

Such are the wars, most skillfully planned and successfully fought, which this most powerful king waged during the forty-seven years of his reign. He so largely increased the Frank kingdom, which was already great and strong when he received it at his father's hands, that more than double its former territory was added to it. . . . He subdued all the wild and barbarous tribes dwelling in Germany between the Rhine and the Vistula, the Ocean and the Danube, all of which speak very much the same language, but differ widely from one another in customs and dress. . . .

He added to the glory of his reign by gaining the good will of several kings and nations. . . . The Emperors of Constantinople [the Byzantine emperors] sought friendship and alliance with Charles by several embassies; and even when the Greeks [the Byzantines] suspected him of designing to take the empire from them, because of his assumption of the title Emperor, they made a close alliance with him, that he might have no cause of offense. In fact, the power of the Franks was always viewed with a jealous eye, whence the Greek proverb, "Have the Frank for your friend, but not for your neighbor."

This King, who showed himself so great in extending his empire and subduing foreign nations, and was constantly occupied with plans to that end, undertook also very many works calculated to adorn and benefit his kingdom, and brought several of them to completion. Among these, the most deserving of mention are the basilica of the Holy Mother of God at Aix-la-Chapelle, built in the most admirable manner, and a bridge over the Rhine River at Mainz, half a mile long, the breadth of the river at this point. . . . Above all, sacred buildings were the object of his care throughout his whole kingdom; and whenever he found them falling to ruin from age, he commanded the priests and fathers who had charge of them to repair them, and made sure by commissioners that his instructions were obeyed. . . . Thus did Charles defend and increase as well as beautify his kingdom. . . .

He cherished with the greatest fervor and devotion the principles of the Christian religion, which had been instilled into him from infancy. Hence it was that he built the beautiful church at Aix-la-Chapelle, which he adorned with gold and silver and lamps, and with rails and doors of solid brass. He had the columns and marbles for this structure brought from Rome and Ravenna, for he could not find such as were suitable elsewhere. He was a constant worshiper at this church as long as his health permitted, going morning and evening, even after nightfall, besides attending mass. . . .

He was very forward in caring for the poor, so much so that he not only made a point of giving in his own country and his own kingdom, but when he discovered that there were Christians living in poverty in Syria, Egypt, and Africa, at Jerusalem, Alexandria, and Carthage, he had compassion on their wants, and used to send money over the seas to them. . . . He sent great and countless gifts to the popes, and throughout his whole reign the wish that he had nearest at heart was to reestablish the ancient authority of the city of Rome under his care and by his influence, and to defend and protect the Church of St. Peter, and to beautify and enrich it out of his own store above all other churches.

In southeastern Germany, Charlemagne invaded the land of the Bavarians in 787 and brought them into his empire by the following year, an expansion that then brought him into contact with the southern Slavs and the Avars. The latter disappeared from history after their utter devastation at the hands of Charlemagne's army. Now at its height, Charlemagne's empire covered much of western and central Europe; not until the time of Napoleon in the nineteenth century would an empire its size be seen again in Europe.

GOVERNING THE EMPIRE

Charlemagne continued the efforts of his father in organizing the Carolingian kingdom. Because there was no system of public taxation, Charlemagne was highly dependent on the royal estates for the resources he needed to govern his empire. Food and goods derived from these lands provided support for the king, his household staff, and officials. To keep the nobles in his service, Charlemagne granted part of the royal lands as lifetime holdings to nobles who assisted him.

Besides the household staff, the administration of the empire was accomplished by counts, who were the king's chief representatives in local areas, although in dangerous border districts officials known as margraves (literally, "counts of the border district") were used. Counts were members of the nobility who had already existed under the Merovingians. They had come to control public services in their own lands and thus acted as judges, military leaders, and agents of the king. Gradually, as the rule of the Merovingian kings weakened, many counts had simply attached the royal lands and services performed on behalf of the king to their own family possessions.

In an effort to gain greater control over his kingdom, Charlemagne attempted to limit the power of the counts. They were required to serve outside their own family lands and were moved about periodically rather than being permitted to remain in a county for life. By making the offices appointive, Charlemagne tried to prevent the counts' children from automatically inheriting their offices. Moreover, as another check on the counts, Charlemagne instituted the *missi dominici* ("messengers of the lord king"), a lay lord and a church official who were sent out to local districts to ensure that the counts were executing the king's wishes. The counts also had assistants, but these were members of their households, not part of a bureaucratic office.

The last point is an important reminder that we should not think of Carolingian government in the

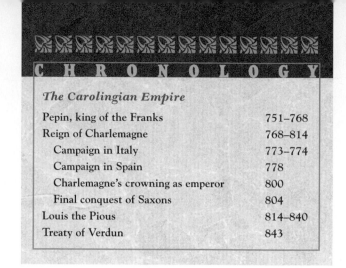

modern sense of government offices run by officials committed to an impersonal ideal of state service. The Carolingian system was glaringly inefficient. Great distances had to be covered on horseback, making it impossible for Charlemagne and his household staff to exercise much supervision over local affairs. What held the system together was personal loyalty to a king who was strong enough to ensure loyalty by force when necessary.

Charlemagne also realized that the Catholic church could provide valuable assistance in governing his kingdom. By the end of the seventh century, the system of ecclesiastical government within the Christian church that had been created in the Late Roman Empire had largely disintegrated. Many church offices were not filled or were held by grossly unqualified relatives of the royal family. Both Pepin and his son Charlemagne took up the cause of church reform by creating new bishoprics and archbishoprics, restoring old ones, and seeing to it that the clergy accepted the orders of their superiors and executed their duties.

CHARLEMAGNE AS EMPEROR

As Charlemagne's power grew, so did his prestige as the most powerful Christian ruler; one monk even wrote of his empire as the "kingdom of Europe." In 800, Charlemagne acquired a new title—emperor of the Romans—largely as a result of the ever-closer relationship between the papacy and the Frankish monarchs.

Already during the reign of Pepin, a growing alliance emerged between the kingdom of the Franks and the papacy. The popes welcomed this support, and in the course of the second half of the eighth century, they increasingly severed their ties with the Byzantine Empire and drew closer to the Frankish kingdom. Charlemagne encouraged this development.

In 799, after a rebellion against his authority, Pope Leo III (795–816) managed to escape from Rome and flee to safety at Charlemagne's court. Charlemagne offered assistance, and when he went to Rome in November 800 to settle affairs, he was received by the pope like an emperor. On Christmas Day in 800, Pope Leo placed a crown on Charlemagne's head and declared him emperor of the Romans.

The significance of this imperial coronation has been much debated. Charlemagne's biographer Einhard claimed that Charlemagne "at first had such an aversion that he declared that he would not have set foot in the Church the day that it was conferred, although it was a great feastday, if he could have foreseen the design of the Pope."[2] But Charlemagne also perceived the usefulness of the imperial title; after all, he was now on a level of equality with the Byzantine emperor, a status he did not reject. Moreover, the papacy now had a defender of great stature, although later popes in the Middle Ages would become involved in fierce struggles with emperors over who possessed the higher power.

In any case, Charlemagne's coronation as Roman emperor certainly demonstrated the strength, even after three hundred years, of the concept of an enduring Roman Empire. More important, it symbolized the fusion of the Roman, Christian, and Germanic elements that constituted the foundation of European civilization. A Germanic king had been crowned emperor of the Romans by the spiritual leader of Western Christendom. A new civilization had emerged.

✺ The Carolingian Intellectual Renewal

Charlemagne had a strong desire to revive learning in his kingdom, an attitude that stemmed from his own intellectual curiosity as well as the need to provide educated clergy for the church and literate officials for the government. His efforts led to a revival of learning and culture that some historians have labeled the Carolingian Renaissance, or "rebirth" of learning.

For the most part, the revival of classical studies and the efforts to preserve Latin culture took place in the monasteries, many of which had been established by the Irish and English missionaries of the seventh and eighth centuries. By the ninth century, the "work" required of Benedictine monks was the copying of manuscripts. Monasteries established *scriptoria*, or writing rooms, where monks copied not only the

THE CORONATION OF CHARLEMAGNE.
After a rebellion in 799 forced Pope
Leo III to seek refuge at Charlemagne's
court, Charlemagne went to Rome to
settle the affair. There, on Christmas
Day 800, he was crowned emperor
of the Romans by the pope. This
manuscript illustration shows Leo III
placing a crown on Charlemagne's head.

TRAVELERS ARRIVING AT AN INN. Inns provided refuge for the many pilgrims, merchants, and others who traveled Europe's dangerous roads in the Middle Ages. In this illustration, a group of merchants has stopped at an inn, which like most medieval inns provided basic necessities but not individual beds. Medieval people generally slept in the nude.

works of early Christianity, such as the Bible, but also the works of Latin classical authors. The production of manuscripts in Carolingian monastic *scriptoria* was a crucial factor in the preservation of the ancient legacy. About eight thousand manuscripts survive from Carolingian times. Virtually 90 percent of the ancient Roman works that we have today exist because they were copied by Carolingian monks.

✳ *Life in the Carolingian World*

In daily life as well as intellectual life, the newly emerging European world of the Carolingian era witnessed an amalgamation of Roman, Germanic, and Christian practices. These last in particular seem to have exercised an ever-increasing influence.

✻ THE FAMILY AND MARRIAGE

By Carolingian times, the Catholic church had begun to make a significant impact on Frankish family life and marital and sexual attitudes. Marriages in Frankish society were arranged by fathers or uncles to meet the needs of the extended family. Although wives were expected to be faithful to their husbands, Frankish aristocrats often kept concubines, either slave girls or free women from their estates. Even the "most Christian king" Charlemagne kept a number of concubines.

To limit such sexual license, the church increasingly emphasized its role in marriage and attempted to Christianize it. Although marriage was a civil arrangement, priests tried to add their blessings and strengthen the concept of a special marriage ceremony. Moreover, the church tried to serve as the caretaker of marriage by stipulating that a girl over fifteen must give her consent to her guardian's choice of a husband or her marriage was not valid in the eyes of the church. To stabilize marriages, the church also began to emphasize monogamy and permanence. A Frankish church council in 789 stipulated that marriage was "indissoluble" and condemned the practice of concubinage and easy divorce, and during the reign of Emperor Louis the Pious (814–840), the church finally established the right to prohibit divorce. Now a man who married was expected to remain with his wife "even though she were sterile, deformed, old, dirty, drunken, a frequenter of bad company, lascivious, vain, greedy, unfaithful, quarrelsome, abusive . . . , for when that man was free, he freely engaged himself."[3]

The acceptance and spread of the Catholic church's views on the indissolubility of marriage encouraged the development of the nuclear family at the expense of the extended family. Although the kin was still an influential social and political force, the conjugal unit came to be seen as the basic unit of society. The new practice of young couples establishing their own households brought a dynamic element to European society. It also had a significant impact on women (see the box on p. 157). In the extended family, the eldest woman controlled all the other female members; in the nuclear family, the wife was still dominated by her husband, but at least she now had control of her own household and children.

✻ CHRISTIANITY AND SEXUALITY

The early church fathers had stressed that celibacy and complete abstinence from sexual activity constituted an ideal state superior to marriage. Subsequently, the early church gradually developed a case for clerical celibacy, although it proved impossible to enforce in the Early Middle Ages. The early fathers had also emphasized, however, that not all people had the self-discipline to remain celibate. It was thus permissible

Advice from a Carolingian Mother

The wife of a Carolingian aristocrat bore numerous responsibilities. She was entrusted with the management of the household and even the administration of extensive landed estates while her husband was absent in the royal service or on a military campaign. A wife was also expected to bear larger numbers of children and to supervise their upbringing. This selection by Dhouda, wife of Bernard, marquis of Septimania (in southern France), is taken from a manual she wrote to instruct her son on his duties to his new lord, King Charles the Bald (840–877).

⁜ *Dhouda,* Handbook for William

Direction on your comportment toward your lord.

You have Charles as your lord; you have him as lord because, as I believe, God and your father, Bernard, have chosen him for you to serve at the beginning of your career, in the flower of your youth. Remember that he comes from a great and noble lineage on both sides of his family. Serve him not only so that you please him in obvious ways, but also as one clearheaded in matters of both body and soul. Be steadfastly and completely loyal to him in all things. . . .

This is why, my son, I urge you to keep this loyalty as long as you live, in your body and in your mind. For the advancement that it brings you will be of great value both to you and to those who in turn serve you. May the madness of treachery never, not once, make you offer an angry insult. May it never give rise in your heart to the idea of being disloyal to your lord. There is harsh and shameful talk about men who act in this fashion. I do not think that such will befall you or those who fight alongside you because such an attitude has never shown itself among your ancestors. It has not been seen among them, it is not seen now, and it will not be seen in the future.

Be truthful to your lord, my son William, child of their lineage. Be vigilant, energetic, and offer him ready assistance as I have said here. In every matter of importance to royal power take care to show yourself a man of good judgment—in your own thoughts and in public—to the extent that God gives you strength. Read the sayings and the lives of the holy Fathers who have gone before us. You will there discover how you may serve your lord and be faithful to him in all things. When you understand this, devote yourself to the faithful execution of your lord's commands. Look around as well and observe those who fight for him loyally and constantly. Learn from them how you may serve him. Then, informed by their example, with the help and support of God, you will easily reach the celestial goal I have mentioned above. And may your heavenly Lord God be generous and benevolent toward you. May he keep you safe, be your kind leader and your protector. May he deign to assist you in all your actions and be your constant defender.

---

to marry, as Paul had indicated in his first epistle to the Corinthians:

> It is good for a man not to touch a woman. Nevertheless, to avoid fornication, let every man have his own wife, and let every woman have her own husband. . . . I say therefore to the unmarried and widows, it is good for them if they abide even as I. But if they cannot contain, let them marry: for it is better to marry than to burn.[4]

The church thus viewed marriage as the lesser of two evils; it was a concession to human weakness and fulfilled the need for companionship, sex, and children. In the church of the Early Middle Ages, it was generally agreed that marriage gave the right to indulge in sexual intercourse. Sex, then, was permissible within marriage, but only so long as it was used for the sole purpose of procreation, not for pleasure.

Because the church developed the tradition that sexual relations between man and wife were only legitimate if done for purposes of procreation, it condemned all forms of contraception. The church also strongly condemned abortion, although its prohibition failed to stop the practice. Various herbal potions were available to prohibit conception or cause abortion. The Catholic church accepted only one way to limit children: periodic or total abstinence from intercourse.

The Catholic church's condemnation of sexual activity outside marriage also included homosexuality. Neither Roman religion nor Roman law had recognized any real difference between homosexual and heterosexual eroticism, and the Roman Empire had taken no legal measures against the practice of homosexuality between adults. Later, in the Byzantine Empire, the Emperor Justinian in 538 condemned homosexuality, emphasizing that such practices brought down the wrath of God ("we have provoked Him to anger") and endangered the welfare of the state. Justinian recommended that the guilty parties be punished by castration. Although the church in the Early Middle Ages similarly condemned homosexuality, it also pursued a flexible policy in its treatment of homosexuals. In the Early Middle Ages, homosexuals were treated less harshly than married couples who practiced contraception.

DIET AND HEALTH

For both rich and poor, the fundamental staple of the Carolingian diet was bread. The aristocratic classes, as well as the monks, consumed it in large quantities. Ovens at the monastery of Saint Gall were able to bake a thousand loaves of bread. Sometimes a gruel made of barley and oats was substituted for bread in the peasant diet.

The upper classes in Carolingian society enjoyed a much more varied diet than the peasants. Pork was the primary meat. Domestic pigs, allowed to run wild in the forests to find their own food, were collected and slaughtered in the fall, then smoked and salted to be eaten during the winter months. Because Carolingian aristocrats were especially fond of roasted meat, hunting wild game became one of their favorite activities. They ate little beef and mutton, however, because cattle were kept as dairy cows and oxen to draw plows, and sheep were raised for wool.

Dairy products became prevalent in the Carolingian diet. Milk, which spoiled rapidly, was made into cheese and butter. Chickens were raised for their eggs. Vegetables also formed a crucial part of the diet of both the rich and the poor. These included legumes, such as beans, peas, and lentils, and roots, such as garlic, onions, and carrots.

Both gluttony and drunkenness were vices shared by many people in Carolingian society. Monastic rations were greatly enlarged in the eighth century to include a daily allotment of 3.7 pounds of bread (nuns were only permitted 3 pounds), 1.5 quarts of wine or ale, 2 to 3 ounces of cheese, and 8 ounces of vegetables (4 for nuns). These rations totaled 6,000 calories a day, and since only heavy and fatty foods—bread, milk, and cheese—were considered nourishing,

we begin to understand why some Carolingians were known for their potbellies. Malnutrition, however, remained a widespread problem for common people in this period.

Everyone in Carolingian society, including abbots and monks, drank heavily and often to excess. Taverns became a regular feature of life and were found everywhere: in marketplaces, pilgrimage centers, and on royal, episcopal, and monastic estates. Drinking contests were not unusual; one penitential stated: "Does drunken bravado encourage you to attempt to out-drink your friends? If so, thirty days' fast."

The aristocrats and monks favored wine above all other beverages, and much care was lavished on its production, especially by monasteries. Ale was especially popular in the northern and eastern parts of the Carolingian world. Water was also drunk as a beverage, but much care had to be taken to obtain pure sources from wells or clear streams. Monasteries were particularly active in going to the sources of water and building conduits to bring it to the cloister or kitchen fountains.

Medical practice in Carolingian times stressed the use of medicinal herbs and bleeding. Although the latter was practiced regularly, moderation was frequently recommended. Some advised carefulness as well: "Who dares to undertake a bleeding should see to it that his hand does not tremble." Physicians were also available when people faced serious illnesses. Many were clerics, and monasteries trained their own. Monasteries kept medical manuscripts copied from ancient works and grew herbs to provide stocks of medicinal plants. Carolingian medical manuscripts contained descriptions of illnesses, recipes for medical potions, and even gynecological advice, although monks in particular expended little effort on female medical needs. Some manuals even included instructions for operations, especially for soldiers injured in battle.

Physicians of the Early Middle Ages supplemented their medicines and natural practices with appeals for otherworldly help. Magical rites and influences were carried over from pagan times; Germanic tribes had used magical medicine for centuries. Physicians recommended that patients wear amulets and charms around their bodies to ward off diseases:

Procure a little bit of the dung of a wolf, preferably some which contains small bits of bone, and pack it in a tube which the patient may easily wear as an amulet.

For epilepsy take a nail of a wrecked ship, make it into a bracelet and set therein the bone of a stag's heart taken from its body while alive; put it on the left arm; you will be astonished at the result.[5]

But as pagans were converted to Christianity, miraculous healing through the intervention of God, Jesus, or the saints soon replaced pagan practices. Medieval chronicles abound with accounts of people healed by touching a saint's body.

◆ The Disintegration of the Carolingian Empire

The Carolingian Empire began to disintegrate soon after Charlemagne's death. Charlemagne was survived by his son Louis the Pious (814–840), who was unable to control either the Frankish aristocracy or his own four sons, who fought continually. In 843, after their father's death, the three surviving brothers signed the Treaty of Verdun. This agreement divided the Carolingian Empire among them into three major sections (see Map 8.1): Charles the Bald (843–877) obtained the west Frankish lands, which formed the core of the eventual kingdom of France; Louis the German (843–876) took the eastern lands, which became Germany; and Lothair (840–855) received the title of emperor and a "Middle Kingdom" extending from the North Sea to Italy, including the Netherlands, the Rhineland, and northern Italy. The territories of the Middle Kingdom became a source of incessant struggle between the other two Frankish rulers and their heirs. Indeed, France and Germany would fight over the territories of the Middle Kingdom for centuries.

Although this division of the Carolingian Empire was made for political reasons (dividing a kingdom among the male heirs was a traditional Frankish custom), two different cultures began to emerge. By the ninth century, inhabitants of the west Frankish area were speaking a Romance language derived from Latin that became French. Eastern Franks spoke a Germanic dialect. The later kingdoms of France and Germany did not yet exist, however. In the ninth century, the frequent struggles among the numerous heirs of the sons of Louis the Pious led to further disintegration of the Carolingian Empire. In the meantime, while powerful aristocrats acquired even more power

MAP 8.1   The Carolingian Empire.

in their own local territories at the expense of the squabbling Carolingian rulers, the process of disintegration was abetted by external attacks on different parts of the old Carolingian world.

✹ Invasions of the Ninth and Tenth Centuries

In the ninth and tenth centuries, western Europe was beset by a wave of invasions of several non-Christian peoples—one old enemy, the Muslims, and two new ones, the Magyars and Vikings (see Map 8.2). The Muslims began a new series of attacks in the Mediterranean in the ninth century. They raided the southern coasts of Europe, especially Italy; occupied Sicily; destroyed the Carolingian defenses in northern Spain; and conducted forays into southern France. The Magyars were a people from western Asia who moved into eastern and central Europe at the end of the ninth century. They established themselves on the plains of Hungary and from there made raids into western Europe. The Magyars were finally crushed at the Battle of Lechfeld in Germany in 955. At the end of the

tenth century, they were converted to Christianity and settled down to establish the kingdom of Hungary.

✤ THE VIKINGS

By far the most devastating and far-reaching attacks of the time came from the Northmen or Norsemen of Scandinavia, also known to us as the Vikings. The Vikings were a Germanic people who had settled in Scandinavia. Why they invaded other areas of Europe is uncertain. Perhaps overpopulation and the emergence of more effective monarchs in Denmark, Norway, and Sweden caused some of the freedom-loving Scandinavians to seek escape from the growing order. The Vikings' great love of adventure and their search for booty and new avenues of trade may also have been important factors.

Two features of Viking society help explain what the Vikings accomplished. First of all, they were warriors. Second, they were superb shipbuilders and sailors. Their ships were the best of the period. Long and narrow with beautifully carved arched prows, the Viking dragon ships carried about fifty men. Their

MAP 8.2   Invasions of the Ninth and Tenth Centuries.

shallow draft enabled them to sail up European rivers and attack places at some distance inland. Vikings sacked villages and towns, destroyed churches, and easily defeated small local armies. Viking attacks frightened people and led many a clergyman to plead with them to change their behavior and appease God's anger, as is revealed in this sermon in 1014 by an English archbishop:

> Things have not gone well now for a long time at home or abroad, but there has been devastation and persecution in every district again and again, and the English have been for a long time now completely defeated and too greatly disheartened through God's anger; and the pirates [Vikings] so strong with God's consent that often in battle one puts to flight ten, and sometimes less, sometimes more, all because of our sins. . . . We pay them continually and they humiliate us daily; they ravage and they burn, plunder, and rob and carry on board; and lo, what else is there in all these events except God's anger clear and visible over this people?[6]

Because there were different groups of Scandinavians, Viking expansion varied a great deal. Norwegian Vikings moved into Ireland and western England, while the Danes attacked eastern England, Frisia, and the Rhineland and navigated rivers to enter western Frankish lands. Swedish Vikings dominated the Baltic Sea and progressed into the Slavic areas to the east. Moving into northwestern Russia, they went down the rivers to Novgorod and Kiev and established fortified ports throughout these territories.

Early Viking raids had been carried out largely in the summer; by the mid-ninth century, however, the Northmen had begun to establish winter settlements in Europe from which they could make expeditions to conquer and settle new lands. By 850, groups of Norsemen had settled in Ireland, and the Danes occupied an area known as the Danelaw in northeast England by 878. Beginning in 911, the ruler of the western Frankish lands gave one band of Vikings land at the mouth of the Seine River, forming a section of France that ultimately became known as Normandy. This policy of settling the Vikings and converting them to Christianity was a deliberate one, since the new inhabitants served as protectors against additional Norseman attacks.

The Vikings were also daring explorers. After 860, they sailed westward in their long ships across the north Atlantic, reaching Iceland in 874. Erik the Red, a Viking exiled from Iceland, traveled even farther west and discovered Greenland in 985. A Viking site in North America was founded in Newfoundland.

VIKINGS ATTACKING ENGLAND. This illustration from an eleventh-century English manuscript depicts a group of armed Vikings invading England. Two ships have already reached the shore, and a few Vikings are shown walking down a long gangplank onto English soil.

By the tenth century, Viking expansion was drawing to a close, but not before Viking settlements had been made throughout many parts of Europe. Like the Magyars, the Vikings were also assimilated into European civilization. Once again, Christianity proved a decisive civilizing force in Western civilization in its European form. Europe and Christianity were becoming virtually synonymous.

The Viking raids and settlements also had important political repercussions. The inability of royal authorities to protect their peoples against these incursions caused local populations to turn instead to the local aristocrats who provided security for them. In the process, the landed aristocrats not only increased their strength and prestige but also assumed even more of the functions of local governments that had previously belonged to kings; over time these developments led to a new political and military order.

◆ The Emerging World of Lords and Vassals

The renewed invasions and the disintegration of the Carolingian world led to the emergence of a new type of relationship between free individuals. When governments ceased to be able to defend their subjects, it became important to find some powerful lord who could offer protection in exchange for service. The contract sworn between a lord and his subordinate (known as a vassal) is the basis of a form of social organization that later generations of historians called feudalism. But feudalism was never a system, and many historians today prefer to avoid using the term.

The practice of vassalage was derived from Germanic society, in which warriors swore an oath of loyalty to their leader. They fought for their chief, and he in turn took care of their needs. By the eighth century, an individual who served a lord in a military capacity was known as a vassal.

With the breakdown of governments, powerful nobles took control of large areas of land. They needed men to fight for them, so the practice arose of giving grants of land to vassals who in return would fight for their lord. The Frankish army had originally consisted of foot soldiers, dressed in coats of mail and armed with swords. But in the eighth century, when larger horses and the stirrup were introduced, a military change began to occur. Earlier, horsemen had been throwers of spears. Now they wore armored coats of mail (the larger horse could carry the weight) and wielded long lances that enabled them to act as battering rams (the stirrups kept them on their horses). For almost five hundred years, warfare in Europe was dominated by heavily armored cavalry, or knights, as they came to be called. The knights came to have the greatest social prestige and formed the backbone of the European aristocracy.

Of course, a horse, armor, and weapons were expensive to purchase and maintain, and learning to wield these instruments skillfully from a horse took much time and practice. Consequently, lords who wanted men to fight for them had to grant each vassal a piece of land that provided for the support of the vassal and his family. In return for the land, the vassal provided his lord with one major service, his fighting skills. Each needed the other. In the society of the Early Middle Ages, where there was little trade and wealth was based primarily on land, land became the most important gift a lord could give to a vassal in return for military service.

The relationship between lord and vassal was made official by a public ceremony. To become a vassal, a man performed an act of homage to his lord, as described in this passage from a medieval digest of law:

> The man should put his hands together as a sign of humility, and place them between the two hands of his lord as a token that he vows everything to him and promises faith to him; and the lord should receive him and promise to keep faith with him. Then the man should say: "Sir, I enter your homage and faith and become your man by mouth and hands [i.e., by taking the oath and placing his hands between those of the lord], and I swear and promise to keep faith and loyalty to you against all others, and to guard your rights with all my strength."[7]

As in the earlier Germanic band, loyalty to one's lord was the chief virtue.

By the ninth century, the land granted to a vassal in return for military service had come to be known as a fief. In time, many vassals who held such grants of land came to exercise rights of jurisdiction or political and legal authority within their fiefs. As the Carolingian world disintegrated politically under the impact of internal dissension and invasions, an increasing number of powerful lords arose. Instead of a single government, many people were now responsible for keeping order.

Fief-holding also became increasingly complicated with the development of subinfeudation. The vassals of a king, who were themselves great lords,

A KNIGHT'S EQUIPMENT, SHOWING SADDLE AND STIRRUPS. **In return for his fighting skills, a knight received a piece of land from his lord that provided for his economic support. Pictured here is a charging knight with his equipment. The introduction of the high saddle, stirrup, and larger horses allowed horsemen to wear heavier armor and to wield long lances, thereby increasing the importance of the cavalry.**

might also have vassals who would owe them military service in return for a grant of land from their estates. Those vassals, in turn, might likewise have vassals, who at this low level would be simple knights with barely enough land to provide their equipment. The lord-vassal relationship, then, bound together both greater and lesser landowners. At all levels, the lord-vassal relationship was always an honorable relationship between free men and did not imply any sense of servitude. Since kings could no longer provide security in the midst of the breakdown created by the invasions of the ninth century, the practice of subinfeudation became ever more widespread. With their rights of jurisdiction, fiefs gave lords virtual possession of the rights of government.

The new practice of lordship was basically a product of the Carolingian world, but it also spread to England, Germany, central Europe, and in some form to Italy. Fief-holding came to be characterized by a set of practices that determined the relationship between a lord and his vassal. The major obligation of a vassal to his lord was to perform military service, usually about forty days a year. A vassal was also required to appear at his lord's court when summoned to give advice to the lord. He might also be asked to sit in judgment in a legal case because the important vassals of a lord were peers and only they could judge each other. Finally, vassals were also responsible for aids, or financial payments to the lord on a number of occasions, including the knighting of the lord's eldest son, the marriage of his eldest daughter, and the ransom of the lord's person in the event he was captured.

In turn, a lord had responsibilities toward his vassals. His major obligation was to protect his vassal, either by defending him militarily or by taking his side in a court of law if necessary. The lord was also responsible for the maintenance of the vassal, usually by granting him a fief.

❊ *The Manorial System*

The landholding class of nobles and knights comprised a military elite whose ability to function as warriors depended on having the leisure time to pursue the arts of war. Landed estates, located on the fiefs given to a vassal by his lord and worked by a dependent peasant class, provided the economic sustenance that made this way of life possible. A manor or villa (see Map 8.3) was simply an agricultural estate operated by a lord and worked by peasants.

Manorialism grew out of the unsettled circumstances of the Early Middle Ages, when small farmers often needed protection or food in a time of bad harvests. Free peasants gave up their freedom to the lords of large landed estates in return for protection and use of the lord's land. Although a large class of free peasants continued to exist, increasing numbers of free peasants became serfs—peasants bound to the land and required to provide labor services, pay rents, and be subject to the lord's jurisdiction. By the ninth century, probably 60 percent of the population of western Europe had become serfs.

Labor services consisted of working the lord's demesne, the land retained by the lord, which might

MAP 8.3   A Manor.

PEASANTS IN THE MANORIAL SYSTEM. In the manorial system, peasants were required to provide labor services for their lord. This thirteenth-century illustration shows a group of English peasants harvesting grain. Overseeing them is a bailiff, or manager, who supervised the work of the peasants.

consist of one-third to one-half of the cultivated lands scattered throughout the manor. The rest would be used by the peasants for themselves. Building barns and digging ditches were also part of the labor services. Serfs usually worked about three days a week for their lord.

The serfs paid rents by giving the lord a share of every product they raised. Moreover, serfs paid the lord for the use of the manor's common pasturelands, streams, ponds, and surrounding woodlands. For example, if a serf fished in the pond or stream on a manor, he turned over part of the catch to his lord. Peasants were also obliged to pay a tithe (a tenth of their produce) to their local village church.

Lords possessed a variety of legal rights over their serfs as a result of their unfree status. Serfs were legally bound to the lord's lands and could not leave without his permission. Although free to marry, serfs could not marry anyone outside their manor without the lord's approval. Moreover, lords sometimes exercised public rights or political authority on their lands, which gave them the right to try peasants in their own court. In fact, the lord's manorial court provided the only law that most peasants knew. Peasants also had to pay the lord for certain services; for example, they might be required to bring their grain to the lord's mill and pay a fee to have it ground into flour. Thus the rights a lord possessed on his manor gave him virtual control over both the lives and property of his serfs.

In the Early Middle Ages, whether free or unfree, a vast majority of men and women, possibly 90 percent, worked the land. Although trade declined precipitously in this period, it never entirely disappeared. Overall, however, compared to the Byzantine Empire or Muslim caliphates, western Europe in the Early Middle Ages was an underdeveloped, predominantly agricultural society and could not begin to match the splendor of either of the other heirs of the Roman Empire.

◆ The Zenith of Byzantine Civilization

In the seventh and eighth centuries, the Byzantine Empire had lost much of its territory to Slavs, Bulgars, and Muslims. By 750, the empire consisted only of Asia Minor, some lands in the Balkans, and the southern coast of Italy. Although Byzantium was beset with internal dissension and invasions in the ninth century, it was able to deal with them and not only endured but even expanded, reaching its high point in the tenth century, which some historians have called the "golden age of Byzantine civilization."

During the reign of Michael III (842–867), the Byzantine Empire continued to be plagued by problems. The Bulgars mounted new attacks, and the Arabs continued to harass the empire. Moreover, a new church problem with political repercussions erupted over differences between the pope as leader of the western Christian church and the patriarch of Constantinople as leader of the eastern (or Orthodox) Christian church. Patriarch Photius condemned the pope as a heretic for accepting a revised form of the Nicene Creed stating that the Holy Spirit proceeded from the Father and the Son instead of "The Holy Spirit, who proceeds from the Father." A council of eastern bishops followed Photius' wishes and excommunicated the pope, creating the so-called Photian schism. Although the differences were later papered over, this controversy served to further the division between the eastern and western Christian churches.

The problems that arose during Michael's reign were effectively dealt with by the efforts of a new dynasty of Byzantine emperors, known as the Macedonians (867–1081). In general, this dynastic line managed to repel the external enemies, go over to the offensive, and reestablish domestic order. Supported by the church, the

A Western View of the Byzantine Empire

Bishop Liudprand of Cremona undertook diplomatic missions to Constantinople on behalf of two western kings, Berengar of Italy and Otto I of Germany. This selection is taken from his description of his mission to the Byzantine emperor Constantine VII in 949 as an envoy for Berengar, king of Italy from 950 until his overthrow by Otto I of Germany in 964. Liudprand had mixed feelings about Byzantium: admiration, yet also envy and hostility because of its superior wealth.

✵ *Liudprand of Cremona,* Antapodosis

Next to the imperial residence at Constantinople there is a palace of remarkable size and beauty which the Greeks called Magnavra . . . the name being equivalent to "fresh breeze." In order to receive some Spanish envoys, who had recently arrived, as well as myself . . . , Constantine gave orders that his palace should be got ready. . . .

Before the emperor's seat stood a tree, made of bronze gilded over, whose branches were filled with birds, also made of gilded bronze, which uttered different cries, each according to its varying species. The throne itself was so marvelously fashioned that at one moment it seemed a low structure, and at another it rose high into the air. It was of immense size and was guarded by lions, made either of bronze or of wood covered over with gold, who beat the ground with their tails and gave a dreadful roar with open mouth and quivering tongue. Leaning upon the shoulders of two eunuchs I was brought into the emperor's presence. At my approach the lions began to roar and the birds to cry out, each according to its kind; but I was neither terrified nor surprised, for I had previously made enquiry about all these things from people who

were well acquainted with them. So after I had three times made obeisance to the emperor with my face upon the ground, I lifted my head, and behold! The man whom just before I had seen sitting on a moderately elevated seat had now changed his raiment and was sitting on the level of the ceiling. How it was done I could not imagine, unless perhaps he was lifted up by some such sort of device as we use for raising the timbers of a wine press. On that occasion he did not address me personally . . . but by the intermediary of a secretary he inquired about Berengar's doings and asked after his health. I made a fitting reply and then, at a nod from the interpreter, left his presence and retired to my lodging.

It would give me some pleasure also to record here what I did then for Berengar. . . . The Spanish envoys . . . had brought handsome gifts from their masters to the emperor Constantine. I for my part had brought nothing from Berengar except a letter and that was full of lies. I was very greatly disturbed and shamed at this and began to consider anxiously what I had better do. In my doubt and perplexity it finally occurred to me that I might offer the gifts, which on my account I had brought for the emperor, as coming from Berengar, and trick out my humble present with fine words. I therefore presented him with nine excellent curaisses, seven excellent shields with gilded bosses, two silver gift cauldrons, some swords, spears and spits, and what was more precious to the emperor than anything, four carzimasia; that being the Greek name for young eunuchs who have had both their testicles and their penis removed. This operation is performed by traders at Verdun, who take the boys into Spain and make a huge profit.

---

emperors continued to think of the Byzantine Empire as a continuation of the Christian Roman Empire of late antiquity. Although for diplomatic reasons they occasionally recognized the imperial title of western emperors, such as Charlemagne, they still regarded them as little more than barbarian parvenus.

The Macedonian emperors could boast of a remarkable number of achievements in the late ninth and tenth centuries. They worked to strengthen the position of free farmers, who felt threatened by the attempts of landed aristocrats to expand their estates

at the expense of the farmers. The emperors were well aware that the free farmers made up the rank and file of the Byzantine cavalry and provided the military strength of the empire. The Macedonian emperors also fostered a burst of economic prosperity by expanding trade relations with western Europe, especially by selling silks and metalworks. Thanks to this prosperity, the city of Constantinople flourished. Foreign visitors continued to be astounded by its size, wealth, and physical surroundings. To western Europeans, it was the stuff of legends and fables (see the box above).

In the midst of this prosperity, Byzantine cultural influence expanded due to the active missionary efforts of eastern Byzantine Christians. Eastern Orthodox Christianity was spread to eastern European peoples, such as the Bulgars and Serbs. Perhaps the greatest missionary success occurred when the prince of Kiev in Russia converted to Christianity in 987 (see the next section).

Under the Macedonian rulers, Byzantium enjoyed a strong civil service, talented emperors, and military advances. In the tenth century, these competent emperors combined with a number of talented generals to mobilize the empire's military resources and take the offensive. The Bulgars were defeated, and both the eastern and western parts of Bulgaria were annexed to the empire. The Byzantines went on to add the islands of Crete and Cyprus to the empire and defeat the Muslim forces in Syria, expanding the empire to the upper Euphrates. By the end of the reign of Basil II (976–1025), the Byzantine Empire was the largest it had been since the beginning of the seventh century.

◆ The Slavic Peoples of Central and Eastern Europe

North of Byzantium and east of the Carolingian Empire lay a spacious plain through which a number of Asiatic nomads, such as the Huns, Bulgars, Avars, and Magyars, had pushed their way westward, terrorizing and plundering the settled peasant communities. Eastern Europe was ravaged by these successive waves of invaders who found it relatively easy to create large empires that, in turn, were overthrown by the next invaders. Over a period of time, the invaders themselves were largely assimilated with the native Slavic peoples of the area.

The Slavic peoples were originally a single people in central Europe who, through mass migrations and nomadic invaders, were gradually divided into three major groups: the western, southern, and eastern Slavs (see Map 8.4). In the region east of the eastern Frankish or Germanic kingdom emerged the Polish and Bohemian kingdoms of the western Slavs. The Germans assumed responsibility for the conversion of these Slavic peoples since some German emperors considered it their duty to spread Christianity to the barbarians. Of course, it also gave them the opportunity to extend their political authority as well. German missionaries had converted the Czechs in Bohemia by the end of the ninth century, and a bishopric eventually occupied by a Czech bishop was established at Prague in the tenth century. The Slavs

CHRONOLOGY

Byzantium, the Slavs, and the Islamic World

The Byzantine Empire	
Michael III	842–867
Macedonian dynasty	867–1081
Basil II	976–1025
The Slavic peoples of central and eastern Europe	
Establishment of Novgorod	c. 862
Cyril and Methodius' conversion of Moravian Slavs	863
Founding of Principality of Kiev	c. 873–913
Reign of Prince Mieszko; conversion of Slavs in Poland to Christianity	c. 960–992
Vladimir's conversion to Christianity	987
Saint Stephen, king of Hungary	997–1038
The world of Islam	
Overthrow of Umayyad dynasty by Abbasids	750
Creation of emirate of al-Andalus	756
Harun-al-Rashed	786–809
Establishment of Fatimid caliphate in Egypt	973

in Poland were not converted until the reign of Prince Mieszko (c. 960–992). In 1000, an independent Polish archbishopric was set up at Gniezno by the pope. The non-Slavic kingdom of Hungary, which emerged after the Magyars settled down after their defeat at Lechfeld in 955, was also converted to Christianity by German missionaries. Saint Stephen, king of Hungary from 997 to 1038, facilitated the acceptance of Christianity by his people. The Poles, Czechs, and Hungarians all accepted Catholic or western Christianity and became closely tied to the Roman Catholic church and its Latin culture.

The southern and eastern Slavic populations largely took a different path because of their proximity to the Byzantine Empire. The Slavic peoples of Moravia were converted to the Eastern Orthodox Christianity of the Byzantine Empire by two Byzantine missionary brothers, Cyril and Methodius, who began their activities in 863. They created a Slavonic (Cyrillic) alphabet, translated the Bible into Slavonic, and created Slavonic church services. While the southern Slavic peoples accepted Christianity, a split eventually developed between the Croats, who accepted the Roman church, and the Serbs, who remained loyal to eastern Christianity.

Although the Bulgars were originally an Asiatic people who conquered much of the Balkan peninsula,

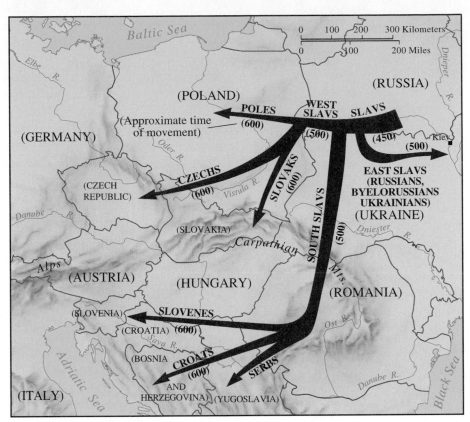

MAP 8.4 The World of the Slavs.

they were eventually absorbed by the larger native south Slavic population. Together, by the ninth century, they formed a largely Slavic Bulgarian kingdom. Although the conversion to Christianity of this state was complicated by the rivalry between the Roman Catholic and Eastern Orthodox churches, the Bulgarians eventually accepted the latter. By the end of the ninth century, they embraced the Slavonic church services earlier developed by Cyril and Methodius. The acceptance of Eastern Orthodoxy by the southern Slavic peoples, the Serbs and Bulgarians, meant that their cultural life was also linked to the Byzantine state.

The eastern Slavic peoples, from whom the modern Russians, White Russians (Byelorussians), and Ukrainians are descended, had settled in the territory of present-day Ukraine and European Russia. There, beginning in the late eighth century, they began to encounter Viking invaders. Swedish Vikings, known to the eastern Slavs as Varangians, moved down the extensive network of rivers into the lands of the eastern Slavs in search of booty and new trade routes. After establishing trading links with the Byzantine state, the Varangians built trading settlements, became involved in the civil wars among the Slavic peoples, and eventually came to dominate the native peoples, just as their fellow Vikings were doing in parts of west-

ern Europe. According to the traditional version of the story, the semilegendary Rurik secured his ruling dynasty in the Slavic settlement of Novgorod in 862. Rurik and his fellow Vikings were called "the Rus," from which the name Russia is derived; eventually, that name became attached to the state they founded (see the box on p. 168). Although much about Rurik is unclear, it is certain that his follower Oleg (c. 873–913) took up residence in Kiev and created the Rus state or union of east Slavic territories known as the principality of Kiev. Oleg's successors extended their control over the eastern Slavs and expanded the territory of Kiev until it encompassed the lands between the Baltic and Black Seas and the Danube and Volga Rivers. By marrying Slavic wives, the Viking ruling class was gradually assimilated into the Slavic population, a process confirmed by their assumption of Slavic names.

The growth of the principality of Kiev attracted religious missionaries, especially from the Byzantine Empire. One Rus ruler, Vladimir (c. 980–1015), married the Byzantine emperor's sister and officially accepted Christianity for himself and his people in 987. His primary motive was probably not a spiritual one. By all accounts, Vladimir was a cruel and vicious man who believed an established church would be

A Muslim's Description of the Rus

Despite the difficulties that travel presented, some contact among the various cultures did occur through trade, diplomacy, and the conquest and migration of peoples. This document is a description of the Swedish Rus who eventually merged with the native Slavic peoples to form the principality of Kiev, commonly regarded as the first Russian state. This account was written by Ibn Fadlan, a Muslim diplomat sent from Baghdad in 921 to a settlement on the Volga River. His comments on the filthiness of the Rus reflect the Muslim preoccupation with cleanliness.

❋ *Ibn Fadlan, Description of the Rus*

I saw the Rus folk when they arrived on their trading-mission and settled at the river Atul (Volga). Never had I seen people of more perfect physique. They are tall as date-palms, and reddish in color. They wear neither coat not kaftan, but each man carried a cape which covers one half of his body, leaving one hand free. No one is ever parted from his axe, sword, and knife. Their swords are Frankish in design, broad, flat, and fluted. Each man has a number of trees, figures, and the like from the fingernails to the neck. Each woman carried on her bosom a container made of iron, silver, copper or gold—its size and substance depending on her man's wealth. . . .

They [the Rus] are the filthiest of God's creatures. They do not wash after discharging their natural functions, neither do they wash their hands after meals. They are as lousy as donkeys. They arrive from their distant river, and there they build big houses on its shores. Ten or twenty of them may live together in one house, and each of them has a couch of his own where he sits and diverts himself with the pretty slave girls whom he had brought along for sale. He will make love with one of them while a comrade looks on; sometimes they indulge in a communal orgy, and, if a customer should turn up to buy a girl, the Rus man will not let her go till he has finished with her.

They wash their hands and faces every day in incredibly filthy water. Every morning the girl brings her master a large bowl of water in which he washes his hands and face and hair, then blows his nose into it and spits into it. When he has finished the girl takes the bowl to his neighbor—who repeats the performance. Thus the bowl goes the rounds of the entire household. . . .

If one of the Rus folk falls sick they put him in a tent by himself and leave bread and water for him. They do not visit him, however, or speak to him, especially if he is a serf. Should he recover he rejoins the others; if he dies they burn him. But if he happens to be a serf they leave him for the dogs and vultures to devour. If they catch a robber they hang him to a tree until he is torn to threads by wind and weather. . . .

---

helpful in the development of an organized state. From the end of the tenth century on, Byzantine Christianity became the model for Russian religious life, just as Byzantine imperial ideals came to influence the outward forms of Russian political life.

◆ The World of Islam

The Umayyad dynasty of caliphs had established Damascus as the center of an Islamic empire created by Arab expansion in the seventh and eighth centuries. But Umayyad rule created resentment, and the Umayyads also helped bring about their own end by their corrupt behavior. One caliph, for example, supposedly swam in a pool of wine and drank enough of it to lower the wine level considerably. Finally, in 750, Abu al-Abbas, a descendant of the uncle of Muhammad, brought an end to the Umayyad dynasty and established the Abbasid dynasty, which lasted until 1258.

The Abbasid rulers brought much change to the world of Islam. They tried to break down the distinctions between Arab and non-Arab Muslims. All Muslims, regardless of their ethnic background, could now hold both civil and military offices. This helped open Islamic life to the influences of the civilizations they had conquered. Many Arabs now began to intermarry with the peoples they had conquered.

In 762, the Abbasids built a new capital city, Baghdad, on the Tigris River far to the east of Damascus. The new capital was well placed. It took advantage of river traffic to the Persian Gulf and was located on the caravan route from the Mediterranean to Central Asia. The move eastward allowed Persian influence to come to the fore, encouraging a new cultural orientation. Under the Abbasids, judges, merchants, and government officials, rather than warriors, were viewed as the ideal citizens.

The new Abbasid dynasty experienced a period of splendid rule well into the ninth century. Best known of the caliphs of the time was Harun al-Rashed (786–809), whose reign is often described as the golden age of the Abbasid caliphate. His son al-Ma'mun (813–833) was a great patron of learning. He founded an astronomical observatory and created a foundation for translating classical Greek works. This was also a period of growing economic prosperity. The Arabs had conquered many of the richest provinces of the old Roman Empire, and they now controlled the trade routes to the east. Baghdad became the center of an enormous trade empire that extended into Europe, Asia, and Africa, greatly adding to the wealth of the Islamic world.

Despite the prosperity, all was not quite well in the empire of the Abbasids. There was much fighting over the succession to the caliphate. When Harun al-Rashed died, his two sons fought to succeed him in a struggle that almost destroyed the city of Baghdad. As the tenth-century Muslim historian al-Mas'udi wrote: "Mansions were destroyed, most remarkable monuments obliterated; prices soared. . . . Brother turned his sword against brother, son against father, as some fought for Amin, others for Ma'mun. Houses and palaces fuelled the flames; property was put to the sack."[8]

Vast wealth also gave rise to financial corruption. By awarding important positions to court favorites, the Abbasid caliphs began to undermine the foundations of their own power and become figureheads. Rulers of the provinces of the empire broke away from the control of the caliphs and established their own independent dynasties. Even earlier, in the eighth century, Spain had already established its own caliphate when Abd-al-Rahman of the Umayyad dynasty had fled there. In 756, he seized control of southern Spain and then expanded his power into the center of the peninsula. He took the title of emir, or commander, and set up the emirate of al-Andalus with its center at Córdoba. Under Abd-al-Rahman's successors, a unique society developed in which all religions were tolerated. The court also supported writers and artists, creating a brilliant and flourishing culture.

The breakup of the Islamic empire accelerated in the tenth century. A caliphate of the Fatimid family was established in Egypt in 973, and an independent dynasty also operated in North Africa. Despite the political disunity of the Islamic world, however, there was an underlying Islamic civilization based on two common bonds, the Qur'an and the spread of the Arabic language.

✴ *Islamic Civilization*

From the beginning of their empire, Muslim Arabs had demonstrated a willingness to absorb the culture of their conquered territories. The Arabs were truly heirs to the remaining Greco-Roman culture of the Roman Empire. Just as readily, they assimilated Byzantine and Persian culture. In the eighth and ninth centuries, numerous Greek, Syrian, and Persian scientific and philosophical works were translated into Arabic. As the chief language in the southern Mediterranean and the Near East and the required language of Muslims, Arabic became a truly international tongue.

The Muslims created a brilliant urban culture at a time when western Europe was predominantly a rural world of petty villages. This can be seen in such new cities as Baghdad and Cairo, but also in Córdoba, the capital of the Umayyad caliphate in Spain. With a population of possibly 100,000, Córdoba was Europe's largest city after Constantinople. Its library was also the largest in Europe.

MOSQUE AT CÓRDOBA. **The first Great Mosque of Córdoba was built by Abd-al-Rahman, founder of the Umayyad dynasty of Spain, in the eighth century. The mosque was later enlarged in the tenth century. Shown here is the interior of the sanctuary, with its two levels of arches. Although the Umayyad caliphs of Damascus were overthrown and replaced by the Abbasid dynasty in the eighth century, the independent Umayyad dynasty in Spain lasted until the eleventh century.**

During the first few centuries of the Arab empire, it was the Islamic world that saved and spread the scientific and philosophical works of ancient civilizations. At a time when the ancient Greek philosophers were largely unknown in Europe, key works by Plato and Aristotle were translated into Arabic. They were put in a library called the "House of Wisdom" in Baghdad, where they were read and studied by Muslim scholars. Texts on mathematics were brought from India. This process was aided by the use of paper. The making of paper was introduced from China in the eighth century, and by the end of the century, paper factories had been established in Baghdad. Booksellers and libraries soon followed. European universities later benefited from this scholarship when these works were translated from Arabic into Latin.

Although Islamic scholars are rightly praised for preserving much of classical knowledge for the West, they also made considerable advances of their own. Nowhere is this more evident than in their contributions to mathematics and the natural sciences. The list of Muslim achievements in mathematics and astronomy alone is impressive. They adopted and passed on the numerical system of India, including the use of the zero. In Europe, it became known as the "Arabic" system. A ninth-century Iranian mathematician created the mathematical discipline of algebra. In astronomy, Muslims set up an observatory at Baghdad to study the position of the stars. They were aware that the earth was round and named many stars. They also perfected the astrolabe, an instrument used by sailors to determine their location by observing the positions of heavenly bodies. It was the astrolabe that made it possible for Europeans to sail to the Americas.

Muslims scholars also made many new discoveries in chemistry and developed medicine as a field of scientific study. Especially well known was Ibn Sina (Avicenna to the West, 980–1037) who authored a medical encyclopedia that, among other things, stressed the contagious nature of certain diseases and showed how they could be spread by contaminated water supplies. After its translation into Latin, Avicenna's work became a basic medical textbook for medieval European university students. Avicenna was but one of many Arabic scholars whose work was translated into Latin and helped the development of intellectual life in Europe in the twelfth and thirteenth centuries.

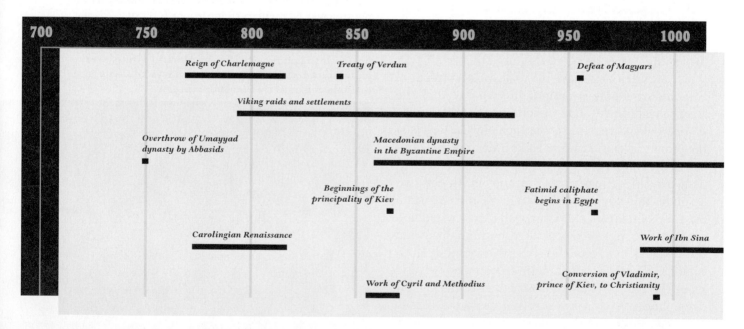

Conclusion ⌘ ⌘ ⌘ ⌘ ⌘ ⌘ ⌘ ⌘ ⌘ ⌘ ⌘

After the turmoil of the disintegration of the Roman Empire and the establishment of the Germanic states, a new European civilization began to emerge slowly in the Early Middle Ages. The coronation of Charlemagne, descendent of a Germanic tribe converted to Christianity, as Roman emperor in 800 symbolized the fusion of the three chief components of the new European civilization: the German tribes, the classical tradition, and Christianity. In the long run, the creation of a western empire fostered the idea of a distinct European identity and marked the shift of power from the south to the north. Italy and the Mediterranean had been the center of the Roman Empire. The lands north of the Alps now became the political center of Europe.

With the disintegration of the Carolingian Empire, new forms of political institutions began to develop in Europe. These were characterized by a decentralization of political power, in which lords exercised legal, administrative, and military power. The practice of feudalism transferred public power into many private hands and seemed to provide the security sorely lacking in a time of weak central government and new invasions by Muslims, Magyars, and Vikings. While Europe struggled, the Byzantine and Islamic worlds continued to prosper and flourish, the brilliance of their urban cultures standing in marked contrast to the underdeveloped rural world of Europe. By 1000, however, that rural world had not only recovered but was beginning to expand in ways undreamed of by previous generations. Europe stood poised for a giant leap.

Notes

1. Einhard, *The Life of Charlemagne*, trans. Samuel Turner (Ann Arbor, Mich., 1960), p. 30.
2. Ibid., p. 57.
3. Quoted in Pierre Riché, *Daily Life in the World of Charlemagne*, trans. Jo Ann McNamara (Philadelphia, 1978), p. 56.
4. 1 Corinthians 7: 1–2, 8–9.
5. Quoted in Brian Inglis, *A History of Medicine* (New York, 1965), p. 51.
6. Quoted in Simon Keynes, "The Vikings in England, c. 790–1016," in Peter Sawyer, ed., *The Oxford Illustrated History of the Vikings* (Oxford, 1997), p. 81.
7. Quoted in Oliver Thatcher and Edgar McNeal, eds., *A Source Book for Medieval History* (New York, 1905), p. 363.
8. al-Mas'udi, *The Meadows of Gold: The Abbasids*, ed. Paul Lunde and Caroline Stone (London, 1989), p. 151.

Suggestions for Further Reading

Surveys of Carolingian Europe include P. Riché, *The Carolingians: A Family Who Forged Europe* (Philadelphia, 1993); J. Boussard, *The Civilization of Charlemagne*, trans. F. Partridge (New York, 1971); and R. McKitterick, *The Frankish Kingdoms Under the Carolingians, 751–987* (London, 1983). On Charlemagne, see H. R. Loyn and J. Percival, *The Reign of Charlemagne* (New York, 1976); the popular biography by R. Winston, *Charlemagne: From the Hammer to the Cross* (Indianapolis, 1954); and L. Halphen, *Charlemagne and the Carolingian Empire* (New York, 1977). On Carolingian culture, see R. McKitterick, *Carolingian Culture: Emulation and Innovation* (New York, 1994), and the collection of essays titled *The Frankish Kings and Culture in the Early Middle Ages* (Brookfield, Vt., 1995).

Various aspects of social life in the Carolingian world are examined in P. Riché, *Daily Life in the World of Charlemagne*, trans. J. A. McNamara (Philadelphia, 1978); M. Rouche, "The Early Middle Ages in the West," in P. Veyne, ed., *A History of Private Life*

(Cambridge, Mass., 1987), vol. 1, pp. 411–549; C. C. Bouchard, *Life and Society in the West: Antiquity and the Middle Ages* (San Diego, 1988), ch. 5; S. F. Wemple, *Women in Frankish Society: Marriage and the Cloister* (Philadelphia, 1981); and S. Rubin, *Medieval English Medicine* (New York, 1974). On the attitudes toward sexuality in the early Christian church, see the important works by P. Brown, *The Body and Society* (New York, 1988), and E. Pagels, *Adam, Eve, and the Serpent* (New York, 1988).

A good introduction to the problems of the late ninth and tenth centuries can be found in G. Barraclough, *The Crucible of Europe* (Berkeley, 1976). The Vikings are examined in P. Sawyer, *Kings and Vikings* (London, 1982); F. D. Logan, *The Vikings in History*, 2d ed. (London, 1991); G. Jones, *A History of the Vikings*, rev. ed. (Oxford, 1984); and P. Sawyer, ed., *The Oxford Illustrated History of the Vikings* (New York, 1997).

Two important introductory works on fief-holding are J. R. Strayer, *Feudalism* (Princeton, N.J., 1985), and the classic work by M. Bloch, *Feudal Society*, trans. L. A. Manyon (London, 1961). For an important revisionist view, see S. Reynolds, *Fiefs and Vassals* (Oxford, 1994).

For the economic history of the Early Middle Ages, see G. Duby, *The Early Growth of the European Economy: Warriors and Peasants from the Seventh to the Twelfth Century* (Ithaca, N.Y., 1974). An important work on medieval agriculture is G. Duby, *Rural Economy and Country Life in the Medieval West*, trans. C. Postan (London, 1968). On the manorial court, see Z. Razi and R. Smith, eds., *Medieval Society and the Manor Court* (New York, 1996).

Byzantine civilization in this period is examined in R. Jenkins, *Byzantium: The Imperial Centuries, 610–1071* (New York, 1969), and W. Treadgold, *The Byzantine Revival, 780–842* (Stanford, Calif., 1988). D. Obolensky, *The Byzantine Commonwealth* (New York, 1971), examines the impact of the Byzantine Empire on its neighbors. On the Slavic peoples of central and eastern Europe, see F. Dvornik, *The Making of Central and Eastern Europe* (London, 1949) and *The Slavs in European History and Civilization* (New Brunswick, N.J., 1962); A. P. Vlasto, *The Entry of the Slavs into Christendom* (Cambridge, 1970); and Z. Vana, *The World of the Ancient Slavs* (London, 1983). The world of Islam in this period is discussed in H. Kennedy, *The Prophet and the Age of the Caliphates: The Islamic Near East from the Sixth to the Eleventh Century* (London, 1986); J. Lassner, *The Shaping of Abbasid Rule* (Princeton, N.J., 1980); and O. Grabar, *The Formation of Islamic Art* (New Haven, Conn., 1971).

 For additional reading, go to InfoTrac College Edition, your online research library at http://web1.infotrac-college.com

Enter the search term *Carolingian* using Key Terms.

Enter the search term *Charlemagne* using Key Terms.

Enter the search terms *Vikings not Minnesota* using Key Terms.

Enter the search term *feudalism* and also the search term *feudal* using the Subject Guide.

The Recovery and Growth of European Society in the High Middle Ages

CHAPTER OUTLINE

- Land and People in the High Middle Ages
- The Recovery and Reform of the Catholic Church
- Christianity and Medieval Civilization
- The Crusades
- Conclusion

FOCUS QUESTIONS

- What roles did peasants and aristocrats play in the civilization of the High Middle Ages?
- What was at issue in the Investiture Controversy, and what effect did the controversy have on the church and on Germany?
- What were the characteristics of the papal monarchy and the new religious orders of the High Middle Ages, and what role did women play in the religious life of the period?
- What was the church's attitude toward heretics and Jews during the High Middle Ages?
- What were the reasons for the crusades, and what did they accomplish?

*T*HE NEW EUROPEAN CIVILIZATION *that had emerged in the ninth and tenth centuries began to come into its own in the eleventh and twelfth centuries as Europeans established new patterns that reached their zenith in the thirteenth century. The High Middle Ages (1000–1300) was a period of recovery and growth for Western civilization, characterized by a greater sense of security and a burst of energy and enthusiasm as Europe recovered from the invasions and internal dissension of the Early Middle Ages. New agricultural practices that increased the food supply helped spur a commercial and urban revival and a burst of population growth that brought dynamism to the once static society.*

The recovery of the Catholic church produced a reform movement that led to exalted claims of papal authority and subsequent conflict with state authorities. At the same time, vigorous papal leadership combined with new dimensions of religious life to make the Catholic church a forceful presence in every area of life. The role of the church in the new European civilization was quite evident in the career of a man named Samson, who became head of the great English abbey of Bury St. Edmonds in 1182. According to Jocelyn of Brakeland, a monk who assisted him, Abbot Samson was a devout man who wore "undergarments of horsehair and a horsehair shirt." He loved virtue and "abhorred liars, drunkards and talkative folk." His primary concern was the spiritual well-being of his monastery, but he spent much of his time working on problems in the world beyond the abbey walls. Since the monastery had fallen into debt under his predecessors, Abbot Samson toiled tirelessly to recoup the abbey's fortunes by carefully supervising its manors. But his actions were not always tolerant or beneficial. He was instrumental in driving the Jews from the town of Bury and was not above improving the abbey's possessions at the expense of his neighbors: "He built up the bank of the fish-pond at Babwell so high, for the service of a new mill, that by the keeping back the water there is not a man, rich or poor, but has lost his garden and his orchards." The abbot's worldly cares weighed heavily on him, but he had little choice if his abbey were to flourish and fulfill its spiritual and secular functions. Nevertheless, he did have regrets; "if he could have returned to the circumstances he had enjoyed before he became a monk," Jocelyn revealed, "he would never have become a monk or an abbot."

◆ Land and People in the High Middle Ages

In the Early Middle Ages, Europe was a sparsely populated expanse dotted with villages of farmers and warriors and covered with forests, which provided both building and heating materials and game. Although the weather began to improve around 700 after a centuries-long period of wetter and colder conditions, natural disasters were still a threat. Drought or too much rain could mean bad harvests, famine, and dietary deficiencies that made people particularly susceptible to a wide range of diseases. Life expectancy remained low.

The High Middle Ages, from 1000 to 1300, witnessed an improvement in climate as a small rise in

temperature made for longer and better growing seasons. At the same time, Europe experienced a dramatic increase in population: the European population virtually doubled between 1000 and 1300, from 38.5 to 73.5 million people (see Table 9.1). This rise in population was physically evident in the growth of agricultural villages, towns, cities, and the increase in arable land.

Why this dramatic rise in population? For one thing, conditions in Europe were more settled and peaceful after the invasions of the Early Middle Ages had stopped. Agricultural production also rose dramatically after 1000. Were it not for this increase in food supplies, the expansion in population could never have been sustained.

✳ The New Agriculture

During the High Middle Ages, significant changes occurred in the way Europeans farmed. Although the improvement in climate produced better growing conditions, another factor in increasing the output of food was the expansion of cultivated or arable land, done chiefly by clearing forested areas for cultivation. Land-hungry peasants cut down trees and drained swamps. By the thirteenth century, the total acreage used for

Table 9.1   Population Estimates (in millions), 1000 and 1340

AREA	1000	1340
Mediterranean		
Greece and Balkans	5	6
Italy	5	10
Iberia	7	9
Total	17	25
Western and Central Europe		
France and Low Countries	6	19
British Isles	2	5
Germany and Scandinavia	4	11.5
Total	12	35.5
Eastern Europe		
Russia	6	8
Poland	2	3
Hungary	1.5	2
Total	9.5	13
Total	38.5	73.5

Source: J. C. Russell, *The Control of Late Ancient and Medieval Population* (Philadelphia: The American Philosophical Society, 1985) p. 36. These are estimates; some figures, especially those for eastern Europe, could be radically revised by new research.

farming in Europe was greater than at any time before or since.

Technological changes also furthered the development of agriculture. Many depended on the use of iron, which was mined in various areas of Europe. Iron was in demand to make swords and armor as well as scythes, axheads, and hoes for use on farms and saws, hammers, and nails for building purposes. Iron was crucial in making the *carruca*, a heavy, wheeled plow strong enough to turn over the heavy clay soil north of the Alps and allow for drainage.

Because of the *carruca*'s weight, six or eight oxen were needed to pull it, but oxen were slow. Two new inventions for the horse made it possible to plow faster. A new horse collar, which appeared in the tenth cen-

THE HEAVY, WHEELED PLOW. The heavy, wheeled plow was an important invention that enabled peasants to turn over the heavy clay soil of northern Europe. This sixteenth-century illumination shows the heavy, wheeled plow pulled by draft horses with collars.

tury, distributed the weight around the shoulders and chest, rather than along the throat, and could be used to hitch up a series of horses, enabling them to pull the heavy new plow faster and cultivate more land. And horseshoes, iron pads nailed to the horses' hooves, gave them better traction in the rocky, clayey soil.

The use of the heavy, wheeled plow also led to cooperative agricultural villages. Because iron was expensive, the plow had to be purchased by the entire community. Similarly, an individual family could not afford a team of animals, so villagers shared their beasts. Moreover, the plow's size and weight made it hard to maneuver, so land was cultivated in long strips to minimize the amount of turning that would have to be done.

People in the High Middle Ages learned to harness the power of water and wind to do jobs formerly done by human or animal muscle. Mills, located along streams and powered by the rushing water, were used to grind grains and produce flour. Dams were built to increase the force of the water. Europeans also developed windmills to capture the power of the wind. These two types of mills were the most important inventions for the harnessing of power until the steam engine in the eighteenth century, and their spread had revolutionary consequences for producing more food.

The shift from a two-field to a three-field system also contributed to the increase in agricultural production. In the Early Middle Ages, it was common to plant one field while allowing another of equal size to lie fallow to regain its fertility. Now estates were divided into three parts. One field was planted in the fall with winter grains, such as rye and wheat, while spring grains, such as oats and barley, and vegetables, such as peas, beans, or lentils, were planted in the second field. The third was allowed to lie fallow. By rotating the fields, only one-third, rather than one-half, of the land lay fallow at any time. The rotation of crops also prevented the soil from being exhausted so quickly, and more crops could now be grown.

By the thirteenth century, the growing demand for agricultural produce in the towns and cities led to higher food prices. This encouraged lords to try to grow more food for profit. One way to do this was to lease their demesne land to their serfs. Labor services were then transformed into money payments or fixed rents, thereby converting many unfree serfs into free peasants. Although many peasants still remained economically dependent on their lords, they were no longer legally tied to the land. Lords, in turn, became collectors of rents, rather than operators of manors with both political and legal privileges. The political and legal powers formally exercised by lords were increasingly reclaimed by the monarchical states.

❋ Daily Life of the Peasantry

Peasant activities were largely determined by the seasons of the year. Each season brought a new round of tasks appropriate for the time, although some periods were considerably more hectic than others, especially harvest time in August and September. A new cycle began in October, when the peasants prepared the ground for planting winter crops. In February and March, the land was plowed for spring crops—oats, barley, peas, beans, and lentils. Early summer was a comparatively relaxed time, although there was still weeding and sheepshearing to be done. In every season, serfs worked not only their own land but also the lord's demesne. They also tended the small gardens attached to their dwellings where they grew the vegetables that made up much of their diet.

Religious feast days, Sunday Mass, baptisms, marriages, and funerals all brought peasants into contact with the village church, a crucial part of manorial life. In the village church, the peasant was baptized as an infant, confirmed in his or her faith, sometimes married, and given the sacrament of Holy Communion as well as the last rites of the church before death. The village priest taught the peasants the basic elements of Christianity so that they would gain the Christian's ultimate goal, salvation.

The lifestyle of the peasants was very simple. Their cottages consisted of wood frames with walls made of laths or sticks; the spaces between the laths were stuffed with straw and rubble and then plastered over with clay. Roofs were thatched. The houses of poorer peasants consisted of a single room, but others had at least two rooms—a main room for cooking, eating, and other activities and another room for sleeping. There was little privacy in a medieval peasant household.

Peasant women occupied both an important and a difficult position in manorial society. They were expected to carry and bear their children and at the same time fulfill their obligation to labor in the fields. Their ability to manage the household might determine whether a peasant family would starve or survive in difficult times.

Though simple, a peasant's daily diet was nutritious when food was available. The basic staple of the peasant diet, and the medieval diet in general, was bread. After the women made dough for the bread, the loaves were baked in community ovens, which were owned by the lord of the manor. Peasant bread generally contained not only wheat and rye but also barley, millet, and oats, giving it a dark appearance and a heavy, hard texture. Bread was supplemented by vegetables from the household gardens, cheese from cow's or goat's milk, nuts and berries from woodlands, and fruits such as apples, pears, and cherries. Chickens provided eggs and sometimes meat.

Grains were important not only for bread but also for making ale. In northern Europe, ale was the most common drink of the poor. If records are accurate, enormous quantities of it were consumed. A monastery in the twelfth century records a daily allotment to the monks of three gallons a day, far above the weekend consumption of many present-day college students. Peasants in the field undoubtedly consumed even more. This high consumption of alcohol might explain the large number of accidental deaths recorded in medieval court records.

❋ The Aristocracy of the High Middle Ages

In the High Middle Ages, European society was dominated by a group of men whose chief preoccupation was warfare, the lords and vassals of medieval society. The lords were the kings, dukes, counts, barons, and viscounts (and even bishops and archbishops) who held extensive lands and considerable political power. They formed an aristocracy or nobility that held real political, economic, and social power. Nobles relied for military help on knights, mounted warriors who fought for them in return for weapons and daily sustenance. As warriors united by the institution of knighthood, lords and knights came to form a common group, albeit a group with social divisions based on extremes of wealth and landholdings.

Medieval theory maintained that the warlike qualities of the nobility were justified by their role as defenders of society, and the growth of the European nobility in the High Middle Ages was made visible by an increasing number of castles scattered across the landscape. Although castle architecture varied considerably, castles did possess two common features: they were permanent residences for the noble family, its retainers, and servants, and they were defensible fortifications. For defensive purposes, castles were surrounded by open areas and large stone walls. At the heart of the castle was the keep, a large, multistoried building that housed kitchens, stables, storerooms; a

CASTLE AND ARISTOCRATS. This illustration from the *Très Riches Heures* of Jean, duke of Berry, depicts the Chateau of Dourdan, France, and its surrounding lands. In the foreground, elaborately dressed aristocratic men and women are seen amusing themselves.

great hall for visitors, dining, and administrative business; and numerous rooms for sleeping and living. The growing wealth of the High Middle Ages made it possible for the European nobility to build more elaborate castles with thicker walls and more elaborately decorated interiors. As castles became more sturdily built, they proved to be more easily defended and harder to seize by force.

❧ THE WAY OF THE WARRIOR

At the age of seven or eight, the sons of the nobility were sent either to a clerical school to pursue a religious career or to another nobleman's castle, where they prepared for the life of a noble. Their chief lessons were military; they learned how to joust, hunt, ride, and handle weapons properly. After his apprenticeship in knighthood, at about the age of twenty-one, a young man formally entered the adult world in a ceremony of "knighting." A sponsor girded a sword on the young candidate and struck him on the cheek or neck with an open hand (or later touched him three times on the shoulder with the blade of a sword), possibly signifying the passing of the sponsor's military valor to the new knight.

In the eleventh and twelfth centuries, under the influence of the church, an ideal of civilized behavior called chivalry gradually evolved among the nobility. Chivalry represented a code of ethics that knights were supposed to uphold. In addition to defending the church and the defenseless, knights were expected to treat captives as honored guests instead of putting them in dungeons. Chivalry also implied that knights should fight only for glory, but this account of a group of English knights by a medieval writer reveals another motive for battle: "The whole city was plundered to the last farthing, and then they proceeded to rob all the churches throughout the city, . . . and seizing gold and silver, cloth of all colors, gold rings, goblets, and precious stones . . . they all returned to their own lords rich men."[1] Apparently, not all chivalric ideals were taken seriously.

After his formal initiation into the world of warriors, a young man returned home to find himself once again subject to his parents' authority. Young men were discouraged from marrying until their fathers died, at which time they could marry and become lords of the castle. Trained to be warriors but with no adult responsibilities, young knights had little to do but fight. As the church stepped up efforts to curb socially destructive fighting in the twelfth century, tournaments began to be organized. Initially, tournaments consisted of the melee, in which warriors on horseback fought with blunted weapons in free-for-all combat. By late in the century, the melee was preceded by the joust, or individual combat between two knights. Gradually, the joust became the main part of the tournament. Knights saw tournaments as an excellent way to train for war. As one knight explained: "A knight cannot distinguish himself in [war] if he has not trained for it in tourneys. He must have seen his blood flow, heard his teeth crack under fist blows, felt his opponent's weight bear down upon him as he lay on the ground and, after

THE TOURNAMENT.   The tournament arose as a socially acceptable alternative to the private warfare that plagued the nobility. This illustration from *The Book of Tourneys* by **King René of Anjou** shows knights lined up for a mock battle. At the top, red-robed judges and female supporters, seated in boxes, look on.

being twenty times unhorsed, have risen twenty times to fight."[2]

⚜ ARISTOCRATIC WOMEN

Although women could legally hold property, most women remained under the control of men—their fathers until they married (usually at the age of fifteen or sixteen) and their husbands after they married. Nevertheless, aristocratic women had numerous opportunities for playing important roles. Because the lord was often away at war, on a Crusade (described later in this chapter), or at court, the lady of the castle had to manage the estate, a considerable responsibility in view of the fact that households, even of lesser aristocrats, could include large numbers of officials and servants. The lady of the castle was also responsible on a regular basis for overseeing the food supply and maintaining all other supplies for the smooth operation of the household.

Although women were expected to be subservient to their husbands (see the box on p. 178), there were many strong women who advised and sometimes even dominated their husbands. Perhaps the most famous was Eleanor of Aquitaine (c. 1122–1204), heiress to the duchy of Aquitaine in southwestern France. Married to King Louis VII of France (1137–1180), Eleanor accompanied her husband on a crusade, but her alleged affair with her uncle during the crusade led Louis to have their marriage annulled. Eleanor then married Henry, duke of Normandy and count of Anjou, who became King Henry II of England (1154–1189). She took an active role in politics, even assisting her sons in rebelling against Henry in 1173

Women in Medieval Thought

Whether a nun or the wife of an aristocrat, townsman, or peasant, a woman in the Middle Ages was considered inferior to a man and by nature subject to a man's authority. Although there are a number of examples of strong women who ignored such attitudes, church teachings also reinforced these notions. The first selection from Gratian, the twelfth-century jurist who wrote the first systematic work on canon law, supports this view. The second selection was written by a wealthy fifty-year-old merchant in Paris who wanted to instruct his fifteen-year-old bride on how to be a good wife.

❋ *Gratian,* **Decretum**

Women should be subject to their men. The natural order for mankind is that women should serve men and children their parents, for it is just that the lesser serve the greater.

The image of God is in man and it is one. Women were drawn from man, who has God's jurisdiction as if he were God's vicar, because he has the image of one God. Therefore woman is not made in God's image.

Woman's authority is nil; let her in all things be subject to the rule of man. . . . And neither can she teach, nor be a witness, nor give a guarantee, nor sit in judgment.

Adam was beguiled by Eve, not she by him. It is right that he whom woman led into wrongdoing should have her under his direction, so that he may not fail a second time through female-levity.

❋ *A Merchant of Paris, On Marriage*

I entreat you to keep his linen clean, for this is up to you. Because the care of outside affairs is men's work, a husband must look after these things, and go and come, run here and there in rain, wind, snow, and hail—sometimes wet, sometimes dry, sometimes sweating, other times shivering, badly fed, badly housed, badly shod, badly bedded—and nothing harms him because he is cheered by the anticipation of the care his wife will take of him on his return—of the pleasures, joys, and comforts she will provide, or have provided for him in her presence: to have his shoes off before a good fire, to have his feet washed, to have clean shoes and hose, to be well fed, provided with good drink, well served, well honored, well bedded in white sheets and white nightcaps, well covered with good furs, and comforted with other joys and amusements, intimacies, affections, and secrets about which I am silent. And on the next day fresh linen and garments. . . .

Also keep peace with him. Remember the country proverb that says there are three things that drive a good man from his home: a house with a bad roof, a smoking chimney, and a quarrelsome woman. I beg you, in order to preserve your husband's love and good will, be loving, amiable, and sweet with him. . . . Thus protect and shield your husband from all troubles, give him all the comfort you can think of, wait on him, and have him waited on in your home. . . . If you do what is said here, he will always have his affection and his heart turned toward you and your service, and he will forsake all other homes, all other women, all other help, and all other households.

---

and 1174. Imprisoned for her activities, after Henry's death she again assumed an active political life, providing both military and political support for her sons.

◆ The Recovery and Reform of the Catholic Church

In the Early Middle Ages, the Catholic church had played a leading role in converting and civilizing first the Germanic invaders and later the Vikings and Magyars. Although highly successful, this effort brought challenges that undermined the spiritual life of the church itself.

❋ *The Problems of Decline*

Since the fifth century, the popes of the Catholic church had reigned supreme over the affairs of the church. They had also come to exercise control over the territories in central Italy that came to be known as the Papal States; this kept popes involved in political matters, often at the expense of their spiritual obligations. At the same time, the church became increasingly entangled in the evolving lord-vassal relationships. High officials of the church, such as bishops and abbots, came to hold their offices as fiefs from nobles. As vassals, they were obliged to carry out the usual duties, including military service. Of course, lords assumed the right to choose their vassals, even when those vassals included bishops and abbots. Because lords often selected their vassals from other noble families for political reasons, these bishops and abbots were often worldly figures who cared little about their spiritual responsibilities.

The monastic ideal had also suffered during the Early Middle Ages. Benedictine monasteries had sometimes been exemplary centers of Christian living and learning, but the invasions of Vikings, Magyars, and Muslims wreaked havoc with many monastic establishments. Discipline declined, and with it the monastic reputation for learning and holiness. At the same time, a growing number of monasteries fell under the control of local lords, as did much of the church. A number of people believed that the time for reform had come.

❁ *The Cluniac Reform Movement*

Reform of the Catholic church began in Burgundy in eastern France in 910 when Duke William of Aquitaine founded the abbey of Cluny. The monastery began with a renewed dedication to the highest spiritual ideals of the Benedictine rule and was fortunate in possessing a series of abbots in the tenth century who maintained these ideals. Cluny was deliberately kept independent from secular control. As Duke William stipulated in his original charter: "It has pleased us also to insert in this document that, from this day, those same monks there congregated shall be subject neither to our yoke, nor to that of our relatives, nor to the sway of the royal might, nor to that of any earthly power."[3]

The Cluniac reform movement sparked an enthusiastic response, first in France and eventually in all of western and central Europe. New monasteries were founded on Cluniac ideals, and existing monasteries rededicated themselves by adopting the Cluniac program. The movement also began to reach beyond monasticism and into the papacy itself, which was in dire need of help.

❁ *Reform of the Papacy*

By the eleventh century, church leaders realized the need to free the church from the interference of lords in the appointment of church officials. This issue of lay investiture, the practice by which secular rulers both chose and invested their nominees to church offices with the symbols of their office, was dramatically taken up by the greatest of the reform popes of the eleventh century, Gregory VII (1073–1085).

Elected pope in 1073, Gregory was convinced that he had been chosen by God to reform the church. In pursuit of those aims, Gregory claimed that he, as pope, was God's "vicar on earth" and that the pope's authority extended over all Christians, including rulers. Gregory sought the elimination of lay investiture. Only then could the church regain its freedom, by which Gregory meant the right to appoint its own clergy and run its own affairs. If rulers did not accept these "divine" commands, they could be deposed by the pope in his capacity as the vicar of Christ.

Gregory VII soon found himself in conflict with King Henry IV (1056–1106) of Germany over these claims. For many years, German kings had appointed high-ranking clerics, especially bishops, as their vassals in order to use them as administrators. Without them, the king could not hope to maintain his own power vis-à-vis the powerful German nobles. In 1075, Pope Gregory issued a decree forbidding important clerics from receiving their investiture from lay leaders: "We decree that no one of the clergy shall receive the investiture with a bishopric or abbey or church from the hand of an emperor or king or of any lay person."[4] Henry had no intention of obeying a decree that challenged the very heart of his administration.

The struggle between Henry IV and Gregory VII, which is known as the Investiture Controversy, was one of the great conflicts between church and state in the High Middle Ages. It dragged on until 1122, when a new German king and a new pope achieved a compromise in the Concordat of Worms. Under this agreement, a bishop in Germany was first elected by church officials. After election, the nominee paid homage to the king as his lord, who in turn invested him with the symbols of temporal office. A representative of the pope then invested the new bishop with the symbols of his spiritual office.

◆ Christianity and Medieval Civilization

Christianity was an integral part of the fabric of medieval European society and the consciousness of Europe. Papal directives affected the actions of kings and princes alike, while Christian teaching and practices touched the economic, social, intellectual, cultural, and daily lives of all Europeans.

❁ Growth of the Papal Monarchy

The popes of the twelfth century did not abandon the reform ideals of Gregory VII, but they were less dogmatic and more inclined to consolidate their power and build a strong administrative system. By the twelfth century, the Catholic church possessed a clearly organized hierarchical structure. The pope and papal curia (staffed by high church officials known as cardinals, the pope's major advisers and administrators) were at the center of the administrative structure. Below them were the bishops, since all of Christendom was divided into dioceses under their direction. Archbishops were in principle more powerful than the bishops, but at this time they were unable to exercise any real control over the internal affairs of the bishops' dioceses.

In the thirteenth century, the Catholic church reached the height of its political, intellectual, and secular power. The papal monarchy extended its sway over both ecclesiastical and temporal affairs, as was especially evident during the papacy of Pope Innocent III (1198–1216). At the beginning of his pontificate, in a letter to a priest, Innocent made a clear statement of his views on papal supremacy:

> As God, the creator of the universe, set two great lights in the firmament of heaven, the greater light to rule the day, and the lesser light to rule the night so He set two great dignities in the firmament of the universal church, . . . the greater to rule the day, that is, souls, and the lesser to rule the night, that is, bodies. These dignities are the papal authority and the royal power. And just as the moon gets her light from the sun, and is inferior to the sun . . . so the royal power gets the splendor of its dignity from the papal authority.[5]

Innocent's actions were those of a man who believed that he, as pope, was the supreme judge of European affairs. He forced King Philip Augustus of France to take back his wife and queen after Philip had tried to have the marriage annulled. The pope intervened in German affairs and established his candidate as emperor. He compelled King John of England to accept the papal choice for the position of archbishop of Canterbury. To achieve his political ends, Innocent did not hesitate to use the spiritual weapons at his command, especially the interdict, which forbade priests to dispense the sacraments of the church in the hope that

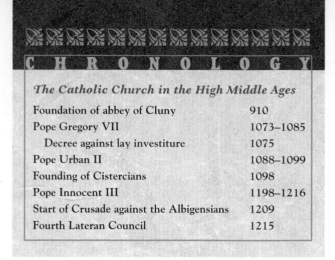

the people, deprived of the comforts of religion, would exert pressure against their ruler. Pope Innocent's interdict was so effective that it caused Philip to restore his wife to her rightful place as queen of France.

❁ New Religious Orders and Spiritual Ideals

In the second half of the eleventh century and the first half of the twelfth century, a wave of religious enthusiasm seized Europe, leading to a spectacular growth in the number of monasteries and the emergence of new monastic orders. Most important was the Cistercian order, founded in 1098 by a group of monks dissatisfied with the lack of strict discipline at their Benedictine monastery. Cistercian monasticism spread rapidly from southern France into the rest of Europe.

The Cistercians were strict. They ate a simple diet and possessed only a single robe each. All decorations were eliminated from their churches and monastic buildings. More time for prayer and manual labor was provided by shortening the number of hours spent at religious services. The Cistercians played a major role in developing a new, activist spiritual model for twelfth-century Europe. A Benedictine monk often spent hours in prayer to honor God. The Cistercian ideal had a different emphasis: "Arise, soldier of Christ, arise! Get up off the ground and return to the battle from which you have fled! Fight more boldly after your flight, and triumph in glory!"[6] These were the words of Saint Bernard of Clairvaux (1090–1153), who more than any other person embodied the new spiritual ideal of Cistercian monasticism (see the box on p. 181).

Women were also active participants in the spiritual movements of the age. The number of women

A Miracle of Saint Bernard

Saint Bernard of Clairvaux has been called the most widely respected holy man of the twelfth century. He was an outstanding preacher, wholly dedicated to the service of God. His reputation reportedly influenced many young men to join the Cistercian order. He also inspired a myriad of stories dealing with his miracles.

❋ A Miracle of Saint Bernard

A certain monk, departing from his monastery . . . threw off his habit, and returned to the world at the persuasion of the Devil. And he took a certain parish living; for he was a priest. Because sin is punished with sin, the deserter from his Order lapsed into the vice of lechery. He took a concubine to live with him, as in fact is done by many, and by her he had children.

But as God is merciful and does not wish anyone to perish, it happened that many years after, the blessed abbot [Saint Bernard] was passing through the village in which this same monk was living, and went to stay at his house. The renegade monk recognized him, and received him very reverently, and waited on him devoutly . . . but as yet the abbot did not recognize him.

On the morrow, the holy man said Matins and prepared to be off. But as he could not speak to the priest, since he had got up and gone to the church for Matins, he said to the priest's son "Go, give this message to your master." Now the boy had been born dumb. He obeyed the command and feeling in himself the power of him who had given it, he ran to his father and uttered the words of the Holy Father clearly and exactly. His father, on hearing his son's voice for the first time, wept for joy, and made him repeat the same words . . . and he asked what the abbot had done to him. "He did nothing to me," said the boy, "except to say 'Go and say this to your father.'"

At so evident a miracle the priest repented, and hastened after the holy man and fell at his feet saying "My Lord and Father, I was your monk so-and-so, and at such-and-such a time I ran away from your monastery. I ask your Paternity to allow me to return with you to the monastery, for in your coming God has visited my heart." The saint replied unto him, "Wait for me here, and I will come back quickly when I have done my business, and I will take you with me." But the priest, fearing death (which he had not done before), answered, "Lord, I am afraid of dying before then." But the saint replied, "Know this for certain, that if you die in this condition, and in this resolve, you will find yourself a monk before God."

The saint [eventually] returned and heard that the priest had recently died and been buried. He ordered the tomb to be opened. And when they asked him what he wanted to do, he said, "I want to see if he is lying as a monk or a clerk in his tomb." "As a clerk," they said; "we buried him in his secular habit." But when they had dug up the earth, they found that he was not in the clothes in which they had buried him; but he appeared in all points, tonsure and habit, as a monk. And they all praised God.

---

joining religious houses increased perceptibly with the spread of the new orders of the twelfth century. In the High Middle Ages, most nuns were from the ranks of the landed aristocracy. Convents were convenient for families unable or unwilling to find husbands for their daughters and for aristocratic women who did not wish to marry. Female intellectuals found them a haven for their activities. Most of the learned women of the Middle Ages, especially in Germany, were nuns. One of the most distinguished was Hildegard of Bingen (1098–1179), who became abbess of a convent at Disibodenberg in western Germany.

Hildegard shared in the religious enthusiasm of the twelfth century. Soon after becoming abbess, she began to write an account of the mystical visions she had experienced for years. "A great flash of light from heaven pierced my brain and . . . in that instant my mind was imbued with the meaning of the sacred books,"[7] she wrote in a description typical of the world's mystical literature. Eventually she produced three books based on her visions. Hildegard gained considerable renown as a mystic and prophet, and popes, emperors, kings, dukes, and bishops eagerly sought her advice.

A GROUP OF NUNS. Although still viewed by the medieval church as inferior to men, women were as susceptible to the spiritual fervor of the twelfth century as men, and female monasticism grew accordingly. This miniature shows a group of Flemish nuns listening to the preaching of an abbot, Gilles li Muisis. The nun at the far left wearing a white robe is a novice.

In the thirteenth century, two new religious orders emerged that had a profound impact on the lives of ordinary people. The friars were particularly active in the cities, where, by their example, they strove to provide a more personal religious experience. Like their founder, Saint Francis of Assisi (1182–1226), the Franciscan friars lived among the people, preaching repentance and aiding the poor. Their calls for a return to the simplicity and poverty of the early church, reinforced by their own example, were especially effective and made them very popular.

The Dominicans arose out of the desire of a Spanish priest, Dominic de Guzmán (1170–1221), to defend church teachings from heresy. The spiritual revival of the High Middle Ages had also led to the emergence of heretical movements, which became especially widespread in southern France. Unlike Francis, Dominic was an intellectual who was appalled by the growth of heresy within the church. He believed that a new religious order of men who lived lives of poverty but were learned and capable of preaching effectively would best be able to attack heresy.

✳ *Popular Religion in the High Middle Ages*

We have witnessed the actions of popes, bishops, and monks. But what of ordinary clergy and laypeople? What were their religious hopes and fears? What were their spiritual aspirations?

The sacraments of the Catholic church ensured that the church was an integral part of people's lives, from birth to death. There were (and still are) seven sacraments, administered only by the clergy. Sacraments, such as baptism and the Eucharist (the Lord's Supper), were viewed as outward symbols of an inward grace (grace was God's freely given gift that enabled humans to be saved) and were considered imperative for a Christian's salvation. Therefore, the clergy were seen to have a key role in the attainment of salvation.

Other church practices were also important to ordinary people. Saints, it was believed, were men and women who, through their holiness, had achieved a special position in heaven, enabling them to act as intercessors before God. The saints' ability to protect poor souls enabled them to take on great importance at the popular level. Jesus' apostles were recognized throughout Europe as saints, but there were also numerous local saints who had special significance. New cults developed rapidly, particularly in the intense religious atmosphere of the eleventh and twelfth centuries. The English introduced Saint Nicholas, the patron saint of children, who remains instantly recognizable today through his identification with Santa Claus.

Of all the saints, the Virgin Mary occupied the foremost position in the High Middle Ages. Mary was viewed as the most important mediator with her son Jesus, the judge of all sinners. Moreover, from the eleventh century on, a fascination with Mary as Jesus' human mother became more evident. A sign of Mary's importance was the growing number of churches all over Europe that were dedicated to her in the twelfth and thirteenth centuries.

Emphasis on the role of the saints was closely tied to the use of relics, which also increased noticeably in the High Middle Ages. Relics were usually the bones of saints or objects intimately connected to saints that were considered worthy of veneration by the faithful. A twelfth-century English monk began his description of the abbey's relics by saying, "There is kept there a thing more precious than gold, . . . the right arm of St. Oswald. . . . This we have seen with our own eyes and have kissed, and have handled with our own hands. . . . There are kept here also part of his ribs and of the soil on which he fell."[8] The monk went on to list additional relics possessed by the abbey, which purported to include two pieces of Jesus' swaddling clothes, pieces of Jesus' manger, and part of the five loaves of bread with which Jesus fed five thousand people. Because the holiness of the saint was considered to be inherent in his relics, these objects were believed to be capable of healing people or producing other miracles.

✸ Voices of Protest and Intolerance

The desire for more personal and deeper religious experience, which characterized the spiritual revival of the High Middle Ages, also led people in directions hostile to the institutional church. From the twelfth century on, heresy, or the holding of religious doctrines different from the orthodox teachings of the church, became a serious problem for the Catholic church. The best-known heresy of the twelfth and thirteenth centuries was Catharism. The Cathars (from the Greek word for "pure") were also called Albigensians, after the city of Albi, one of their strongholds in southern France. They believed in a dualist system in which good and evil were separate and distinct. The things of the spirit were good because they were created by God, the source of light; the things of the world were evil because they were created by Satan, the prince of darkness. Humans, too, were enmeshed in dualism. Their souls, which were good, were trapped in material bodies, which were evil. According to the Cathars, the Catholic church, itself a materialistic institution, had nothing to do with God and was essentially evil. There was no need to follow its teachings or recognize its authority. The Cathar

movement gained valuable support from important nobles in southern France and northern Italy.

The spread of heresy in southern France alarmed the church authorities. Pope Innocent III appealed to the nobles of northern France for a Crusade (a military campaign in defense of Christianity) against the heretics. The Crusade against the Albigensians, which began in the summer of 1209 and lasted for almost two decades, was a bloody fight. Thousands of heretics (and innocents) were slaughtered, including entire populations of some towns. In Béziers, for example, seven thousand men, women, and children were massacred when they took refuge in the local church.

Southern France was devastated, but Catharism remained, which caused the Catholic church to devise a regular method for discovering and dealing with heretics. This led to the emergence of the Holy Office, as the papal Inquisition was called, a formal court whose job it was to ferret out and try heretics. Anyone accused of heresy who refused to confess was still considered guilty and was turned over to the secular authorities for execution. To the Christians of the thirteenth century, who believed that there was only one path to salvation, heresy was a crime against God and against humanity, and force was justified to save souls from damnation. The fanaticism and fear unleashed

EXPULSION OF ALBIGENSIAN HERETICS. In 1209, Pope Innocent III authorized a Crusade against the heretical Albigensians. In this medieval illustration, French knights are shown expelling Albigensian heretics from the town of Carcassonne near Albi, an Albigensian stronghold in southern France.

in the struggle against heretics were also used against others, especially the Jews.

PERSECUTION OF THE JEWS

The Jews were the only religious minority in medieval Europe that was allowed to practice a non-Christian religion. But the religious enthusiasm of the High Middle Ages produced an outburst of intolerance against the supposed enemies of Christianity. After crusades were launched against the Muslims starting in 1096, European Christians took up the search for enemies at home, persecuting Jews in France and the Rhineland. Jews in Speyer, Worms, Mainz, and Cologne were all set upon by bands of Christian crusaders.

In the thirteenth century, in the supercharged atmosphere of fear created by the struggle with the heretics, Jews were persecuted more and more (see the box on p. 185). Friars urged action against these "murderers of Christ," contending that the Jews, having turned Jesus over to the Roman authorities, were responsible for his death, and organized the public burning of Jewish books. The Fourth Lateran Council in 1215 decreed that Jews must wear distinguishing marks, such as ribbons, yellow badges, and special veils and cloaks, to differentiate themselves from Christians. The same council encouraged the development of Jewish ghettos, neighborhoods built behind walled enclosures to isolate Jews from Christians. The persecution and demonization of Jews stimulated a tradition of anti-Semitism that proved to be one of Christian Europe's most insidious contributions to the Western heritage.

European kings, who had portrayed themselves as protectors of the Jews, had so fleeced the Jewish communities of their money by the end of the thirteenth century that they no longer had reason to resist the mob fury. Edward I expelled all Jews from England in 1290. The French followed suit in 1306. As this policy spread into central Europe, most northern European Jews were driven into Poland.

INTOLERANCE AND HOMOSEXUALITY

The climate of intolerance that characterized thirteenth-century attitudes toward Muslims, heretics, and Jews was also evident toward another minority group, homosexuals. Although the church had condemned homosexuality in the Early Middle Ages, it had not been overly concerned with homosexual behavior, an attitude also prevalent in the secular world. By the thirteenth century, these tolerant attitudes had altered drastically. Some historians connect this change to the century's climate of fear and intolerance against any minority group that deviated from the standards of the majority. A favorite approach of the critics was to identify homosexuals with other detested groups. Homosexuality was portrayed as a regular practice of Muslims and such notorious heretics as the Albigensians. Between 1250 and 1300, what had been tolerated in most of Europe became a criminal act deserving of death.

The legislation against homosexuality commonly referred to it as a "sin against nature." This is precisely the argument developed by Thomas Aquinas (see Chapter 10), who formed Catholic opinion on the subject for centuries to come. In his *Summa Theologica*, Aquinas argued that because the purpose of sex was procreation, it could only legitimately take place in ways that did not exclude this possibility. Hence homosexuality (like all other sexual practices that could not result in pregnancy) was "contrary to nature" and a deviation from the natural order established by God. This argument and laws prohibiting homosexual activity on pain of death remained the norm in Europe until the twentieth century.

◆ The Crusades

Another manifestation of the religious enthusiasm that seized Europe in the High Middle Ages was a series of Crusades mounted against the Muslims. These campaigns gave the revived papacy of the High Middle Ages yet another opportunity to demonstrate its influence over European society. The Crusades were a curious mix of God and warfare, two of the chief concerns of the Middle Ages.

Background to the Crusades

Although European civilization developed in relative isolation, it had never entirely lost contact with the lands and empires of the east. At the end of the eleventh century, that contact increased, in part because developments in the Islamic and Byzantine worlds prompted the first major attempt of the new European civilization to expand beyond Europe proper.

THE ISLAMIC EMPIRE

By the mid-tenth century, the Islamic empire led by the Abbasid caliphate in Baghdad was in the process of disintegration. A Shi'ite dynasty known as the

Treatment of the Jews

The developement of new religious sensibilities in the High Middle Ages also had a negative side—the turning of Christians against their supposed enemies. Although the Crusades provide the most obvious example, Christians also turned on the "murderers of Christ," the Jews. As a result, Jews suffered increased persecution. These three documents show different sides of the picture. The first is Canon 68 of the decrees of the Fourth Lateran Council called by Pope Innocent III in 1215. The decree specifies the need for special dress, one of the ways Christians tried to separate Jews from their community. The second excerpt is a chronicler's account of the most absurd charge levied against the Jews—that they were guilty of the ritual murder of Christian children to obtain Christian blood for the Passover service. This charge led to the murder of many Jews. The third document, taken from a list of regulations issued by the city of Avignon, France, illustrates the contempt Christian society held for the Jews.

❀ Canon 68

In some provinces a difference in dress distinguishes the Jews or Saracens from the Christians, but in certain others such a confusion has grown up that they cannot be distinguished by any difference. Thus it happens at times that through error Christians have relations with the women of Jews or Saracens, and Jews or Saracens with Christian women. Therefore, that they may not, under pretext of error of this sort, excuse themselves in the future for the excesses of such prohibited intercourse, we decree that such Jews and Saracens of both sexes in every Christian province and at all times shall be marked off in the eyes of the public from other peoples through the character of their dress. . . .

Moreover, during the last three days before Easter and especially on Good Friday, they shall not go forth in public at all, for the reason that some of them on these very days, as we hear, do not blush to go forth better dressed and are not afraid to mock the Christians who maintain the memory of the most holy Passion by wearing signs of mourning.

❀ The Jews and Ritual Murder of Christian Children

[. . . The eight-year-old-boy] Harold, who is buried in the Church of St. Peter the Apostle, at Gloucester . . . is said to have been carried away secretly by Jews, in the opinion of many, on Feb. 21, and by them hidden till March 16. On that night, on the sixth of the preceding feast, the Jews of all England coming together as if to circumcise a certain boy, pretend deceitfully that they are about to celebrate the feast [Passover] appointed by law in such case, and deceiving the citizens of Gloucester with the fraud, they tortured the lad placed before them with immense tortures. It is true no Christian was present, or saw or heard the deed, nor have we found that anything was betrayed by any Jew. But a little while after when the whole convent of monks of Gloucester and almost all the citizens of that city, and innumerable persons coming to the spectacle, saw the wounds of the dead body, scars of fire, the thorns fixed on his head, and liquid wax poured into the eyes and face, and touched it with the diligent examination of their hands, those tortures were believed or guessed to have been inflicted on him in that manner. It was clear that they had made him a glorious martyr to Christ, being slain without sin, and having bound his feet with his own girdle, threw him into the river Severn.

❀ The Regulations of Avignon, 1243

Likewise, we declare that Jews or whores shall not dare to touch with their hands either bread or fruit put out for sale, and that if they should do this they must buy what they have touched.

Fatimids managed to conquer Egypt and establish the new city of Cairo as their capital. In establishing a Shi'ite caliphate, they became rivals to the Sunni caliphate of Baghdad, creating a division in the Islamic world. Nevertheless, the Fatimid dynasty prospered and surpassed the Abbasid caliphate as the dynamic center of the Islamic world. The Fatimids created a strong army by using nonnative peoples as mercenaries. One of these peoples, the Seljuk Turks, soon posed a threat to the Fatimids themselves.

The Seljuk Turks were a nomadic people from Central Asia who had been converted to Islam and flourished as military mercenaries for the Abbasid caliphate. Moving gradually into Persia and Armenia, they grew in number until by the eleventh century they were able to take over the eastern provinces of the Abbasid empire. In 1055, a Turkish leader captured Baghdad and assumed command of the Abbasid empire with the title of sultan ("holder of power"). By the last quarter of the eleventh century, the Seljuk Turks were exerting military pressure on Egypt and the Byzantine Empire. When the Byzantine emperor foolishly challenged the Turks, the latter routed the Byzantine army at Manzikert in 1071. In dire straits, the Byzantines turned to the west for help, setting in motion the papal pleas that led to the Crusades. To understand the complexities of the situation, however, we need to look first at the Byzantine Empire.

THE BYZANTINE EMPIRE

The Macedonian dynasty of the tenth and eleventh centuries had restored much of the power of the Byzantine Empire; its incompetent successors, however, reversed most of the gains. After the Macedonian dynasty was extinguished in 1056, the empire was beset by internal struggles for power between ambitious military leaders and aristocratic families who attempted to buy the support of the great landowners of Anatolia by allowing them greater control over their peasants.

The growing division between the Catholic church of the west and the Eastern Orthodox church of the Byzantine Empire also weakened the Byzantine state. The Eastern Orthodox church was unwilling to accept the pope's claim that he was the sole head of the church. This issue reached a climax when Pope Leo IX and the Patriarch Michael Cerularius, head of the Byzantine church, formally excommunicated each other in 1054, initiating a schism between the two great branches of Christianity that has not been completely healed to this day.

The Byzantine Empire faced external threats to its security as well. The greatest challenge came from the Seljuk Turks who had moved into Asia Minor, the heartland of the empire and its main source of food and manpower. After the disastrous defeat of Byzantine forces in 1071, the Turks advanced into Anatolia, where many peasants, already disgusted by their exploitation at the hands of Byzantine landowners, readily accepted Turkish control.

A new dynasty, however, soon breathed new life into the Byzantine Empire. The Comneni, under Alexius I Comnenus (1081–1118), were victorious on the Greek Adriatic coast against the Normans, defeated the Pechenegs in the Balkans, and stopped the Turks in Anatolia. Lacking the resources to undertake additional campaigns against the Turks, Emperor Alexius I turned to the west for military assistance. It was the positive response of the west to the emperor's request that led to the Crusades.

The Early Crusades

The Crusades were conceived as a holy war against the infidel or unbeliever. The immediate impetus for the Crusades came when the Byzantine emperor Alexius I asked Pope Urban II (1088–1099) for help against the Seljuk Turks. The pope saw a golden opportunity to provide papal leadership for a great cause: to rally the warriors of Europe for the liberation of Jerusalem and the Holy Land from the Muslim infidel. At the Council of Clermont in southern France near the end of 1095, Urban challenged Christians to take up their weapons against the infidel and join in a holy war to recover the Holy Land (see the box on p. 187). The pope promised remission of sins: "All who die by the way, whether by land or by sea, or in battle against the pagans, shall have immediate remission of sins. This I grant them through the power of God with which I am invested."[9]

The warriors of western Europe, particularly France, formed the first crusading armies. The knights who made up this first serious crusading host were motivated by religious fervor, but there were other attractions as well. Some sought adventure and welcomed a legitimate opportunity to pursue their favorite pastime—fighting. Others saw an opportunity to gain territory, riches, status, possibly a title, and even salvation—had the pope not offered a full remission of sins for those who participated in these "armed pilgrimages"? From the perspective of the pope and European monarchs, the Crusades offered a way to rid Europe of contentious young nobles who disturbed the peace and wasted lives and energy fighting each other. Then, too, merchants in many Italian cities sought new trading opportunities in Muslim lands.

Three organized crusading bands of noble warriors, most of them French, made their way to the east. This first crusading army probably numbered several thousand cavalry and as many as ten thousand foot soldiers. After the capture of Antioch in 1098, much of the crusading host proceeded down the coast of Palestine, evading the garrisoned coastal cities, and reached

Pope Urban II Proclaims a Crusade

Toward the end of the eleventh century, the Byzantine emperor Alexius I sent Pope Urban II a request for aid against the Seljuk Turks. At the Council of Clermont, Urban II appealed to a large crowd to take up weapons and recover Palestine from the Muslims. This description of Urban's appeal is taken from an account by Fulcher of Chartres.

✸ Pope Urban II

Pope Urban II . . . addressed [the French] in a very persuasive speech, as follows: "O race of the Franks, O people who live beyond the mountain [that is, reckoned from Rome], O people loved and chosen of God, as is clear from your many deeds, distinguished over all nations by the situation of your land, your catholic faith, and your regard for the holy church, we have a special message and exhortation for you. For we wish you to know what a grave matter has brought us to your country. The sad news has come from Jerusalem and Constantinople that the people of Persia, an accursed and foreign race [the Seljuk Turks], enemies of God, . . . have invaded the lands of those Christians and devastated them with the sword, rapine, and fire. Some of the Christians they have carried away as slaves, others they have put to death. The churches they have either destroyed or turned into mosques. They desecrate and overthrow the altars. They circumcise the Christians and pour the blood from the circumcision on the altars or in the baptismal fonts. Some they kill in a horrible way by cutting open the abdomen, taking out a part of the entrails and tying them to a stake; they then beat them and compel them to walk until all their entrails are drawn out and they fall to the ground. Some they use as targets for their arrows. They compel some to stretch out their necks and then they try to see whether they can cut off their heads with one strike of the sword. It is better to say nothing of their horrible treatment of the women. They have taken from the Greek empire a tract of land so large that it takes more than two months to walk through it. Whose duty is to avenge this and recover that land, if not yours? For to you more than to any other nations the Lord has given the military spirit, courage, agile bodies, and the bravery to strike down those who resist you. Let your minds be stirred to bravery by the deeds of your forefathers, and by the efficiency and greatness of Karl the Great [Charlemagne], . . . and of the other kings who have destroyed Turkish kingdoms, and established Christianity in their lands. You should be moved especially by the holy grave of our Lord and Savior which is now held by unclean peoples, and by the holy places which are treated with dishonor and irreverently befouled with their uncleanness. . . ."

"O bravest of knights, descendants of unconquered ancestors, do not be weaker than they, but remember their courage. . . . Set out on the road to the holy sepulchre, take the land from that wicked people, and make it your own. . . . Jerusalem is the best of all lands, more fruitful than all others. . . . This land our Savior made illustrious by his birth, beautiful with his life, and sacred with his suffering. . . . This royal city is now held captive by her enemies, and made pagan by those who know not God. She asks and longs to be liberated and does not cease to beg you to come to her aid. . . . Set out on this journey and you will obtain the remission of your sins and be sure of the incorruptible glory of the kingdom of heaven."

When Pope Urban had said this and much more of the same sort, all who were present were moved to cry out with one accord, "It is the will of God, it is the will of God." When the pope heard this he raised his eyes to heaven and gave thanks to God, and commanding silence with a gesture of his hand, he said: "My dear brethren, today there is fulfilled in you that which the Lord says in the Gospel, 'Where two or three are gathered together in my name, there am I in the midst.' For unless the Lord God had been in your minds you would not all have said the same thing. . . . So I say unto you, God, who put those words into your hearts, has caused you to utter them. Therefore let these words be your battle cry, because God caused you to speak them. Whenever you meet the enemy in battle, you shall all cry out, 'It is the will of God, it is the will of God. . . .' Whoever therefore shall determine to make this journey and shall make a vow to God and shall offer himself as a living sacrifice, holy, acceptable to God, shall wear a cross on his brow or on his breast. And when he returns after having fulfilled his vow he shall wear the cross on his back."

MAP 9.I   **The Crusades.**

Jerusalem in June 1099 (see Map 9.1). After a five-week siege, the Holy City was taken amid a horrible massacre of the inhabitants, men, women, and children.

After further conquest of Palestinian lands, the crusaders ignored the wishes of the Byzantine emperor (who foolishly believed the crusaders were working on his behalf) and organized four crusader states (Edessa, Antioch, Tripoli, and Jerusalem). Because the crusader states were surrounded by Muslim enemies, they grew increasingly dependent on the Italian commercial

EXECUTING MUSLIMS AT ACRE. The Third Crusade was organized in response to the capture of the kingdom of Jerusalem by the Sunni Muslims under the leadership of Saladin. Though Saladin forbade the massacre of Christians, his Christian foes were more harsh. Here Richard the Lionhearted (at right, wearing crown) watches the execution of 2,700 Muslims at Acre.

cities for supplies from Europe. Some Italian cities, such as Genoa, Pisa, and above all, Venice, became rich and powerful in the process.

But it was not easy for the crusader states to maintain themselves in the east. Already by the 1120s, the Muslims had begun to strike back. In 1144, Edessa became the first of the four Latin states to be recaptured. Its fall led to renewed calls for another Crusade, especially from the monastic firebrand Saint Bernard of Clairvaux, who exclaimed: "Now, on account of our sins, the sacrilegious enemies of the cross have begun to show their faces. . . . What are you doing, you servants of the cross? Will you throw to the dogs that which is most holy? Will you cast pearls before swine?"[10] Bernard aimed his message at knights and even managed to enlist two powerful rulers, King Louis VII of France and Emperor Conrad III of Germany. Their Second Crusade, however, proved a total failure.

The Third Crusade was a reaction to the fall of the Holy City of Jerusalem in 1187 to the Muslim forces under Saladin. Now all of Christendom was ablaze with calls for a new Crusade in the east. Three major monarchs agreed to lead new crusading forces in person: Emperor Frederick Barbarossa of Germany (1152–1190), Richard I the Lionhearted of England (1189–1199), and Philip II Augustus, king of France (1180–1223). Some of the crusaders finally arrived in the east by 1189 only to encounter problems. Frederick Barbarossa drowned while swimming in a local river, and his army quickly fell apart. The English and

French arrived by sea and met with success against the coastal cities, where they had the support of their fleets, but when they moved inland, they failed miserably. Eventually, after Philip went home, Richard negotiated a settlement whereby Saladin agreed to allow Christian pilgrims free access to Jerusalem.

✲ The Crusades of the Thirteenth Century

After the death of Saladin in 1193, Pope Innocent III initiated a Fourth Crusade. On its way to the east, the crusading army became involved in a dispute over the succession to the Byzantine throne. The Venetian leaders of the Fourth Crusade saw an opportunity to neutralize their greatest commercial competitor: the Byzantine Empire. Diverted to Constantinople, the crusaders sacked that great capital city in 1204 and declared the new Latin Empire of Constantinople. Not until 1261 did a Byzantine army recapture Constantinople. The Byzantine Empire had been saved, but it was no longer a great Mediterranean power. The restored empire now comprised only the city of Constantinople and its surrounding territory as well as some lands in Asia Minor. Though reduced in size, the empire limped along for another 190 years until its weakened condition finally enabled the Ottoman Turks to conquer it in 1453.

Despite the failures, the crusading ideal was not yet completely lost. In Germany in 1212, a youth known as

Nicholas of Cologne announced that God had inspired him to lead a "Children's Crusade" to the Holy Land. Thousands of young people joined Nicholas and made their way down the Rhine and across the Alps to Italy, where the pope told them to go home. Most tried to do so. At about the same time, a group of about twenty thousand French children, also inspired by the desire to free the Holy Land from the Muslims, made their way to Marseilles, where two shipowners agreed to transport them to the Holy Land. Seven ships packed with hymn-singing youths soon left the port. Two of the ships perished in a storm near Sardinia; the other five sailed to North Africa, where the children were sold into slavery. Four more Crusades of adult warriors over the next half century were no more successful.

✳ Effects of the Crusades

All in all, the Crusades had little impact on the Islamic world; after all, the crusaders failed to accomplish their primary goal of holding the Holy Land for the Christian west. Whether the Crusades had much effect on European civilization is widely debated. The crusaders made little long-term impact on the east, where the only visible remnants of their conquests were their castles. There may have been some broadening of perspective that comes from the exchange between two cultures, but the interaction of Christian Europe with the Muslim world was actually both more intense and more meaningful in Spain and Sicily than in the Holy Land.

Did the Crusades help stabilize European society by removing large numbers of young warriors who would have fought each other in Europe? Some historians think so and believe that western monarchs established their

control more easily as a result. There is no doubt that the Italian seaports, especially Genoa, Pisa, and Venice, benefited economically from the Crusades, but even without them, Italian merchants would have pursued new trade contacts with the eastern world.

The Crusades did have unfortunate side effects that would afflict European society for generations. The first widespread attacks on the Jews occurred during the Crusades. Some Christians argued that to undertake holy wars against infidel Muslims while the "murderers of Christ" ran free at home was unthinkable. The massacre of Jews became a regular feature of medieval European life.

CHRONOLOGY

The Crusades

Pope Urban II's call for a Crusade at Clermont	1095
First Crusade	1096–1099
Fall of Edessa	1144
Second Crusade	1147–1149
Saladin's conquest of Jerusalem	1187
Third Crusade	1189–1192
Fourth Crusade—sack of Constantinople	1204
Latin Empire of Constantinople	1204–1261
Children's Crusade	1212
Fifth Crusade	1219–1221
Sixth Crusade	1228
Seventh Crusade	1248–1254
Eighth Crusade	1270
Surrender of Acre and end of Christian presence in the Holy Land	1291

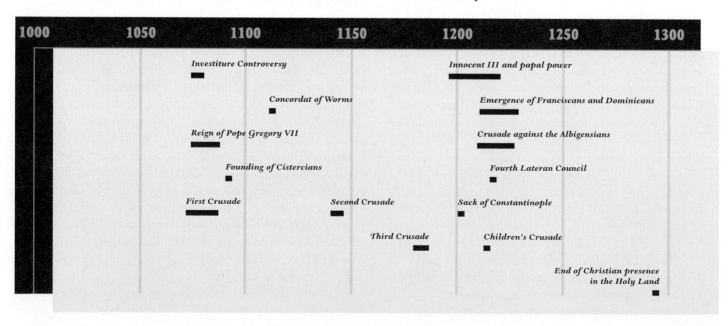

1000 1050 1100 1150 1200 1250 1300

Investiture Controversy

Innocent III and papal power

Concordat of Worms

Emergence of Franciscans and Dominicans

Reign of Pope Gregory VII

Crusade against the Albigensians

Founding of Cistercians

Fourth Lateran Council

First Crusade

Second Crusade

Sack of Constantinople

Third Crusade

Children's Crusade

End of Christian presence
in the Holy Land

Conclusion

The new European civilization that had emerged in the Early Middle Ages began to flourish in the High Middle Ages. Climatic improvements that produced better growing conditions, an expansion of cultivated land, and technological and agricultural changes combined to enable Europe's food supply to increase significantly after 1000. This increase helped sustain a dramatic rise in population that was reflected in the expansion of towns and cities.

The Catholic church shared in the challenge of new growth by reforming itself and striking out on a path toward greater papal power within the church and extending that control to European society. The High Middle Ages witnessed a spiritual renewal that bolstered papal leadership, the development of centralized administrative machinery that buttressed papal authority, and new dimensions to the religious life of the clergy and laity. At the same time, this spiritual renewal also gave rise to crusading "holy warriors" who killed for God.

The religious enthusiasm of the twelfth century continued well into the thirteenth as new orders of friars gave witness to spiritual growth and passion, but underneath the calm exterior lay seeds of discontent and change. Dissent from church teaching and practices grew, leading to a climate of fear and intolerance as the church responded with inquisitorial procedures to enforce conformity to its teachings. At the same time, papal claims of supremacy over secular authorities were increasingly challenged by the rising power of a new breed of monarchical authorities, who, because of the growth of cities, the revival of trade, and the emergence of a money economy, were now able to hire soldiers and officials to carry out their wishes. It is to this new world of cities and kingdoms that we must now turn.

Notes

1. Quoted in Joseph and Frances Gies, *Life in a Medieval Castle* (New York, 1974), p. 175.
2. Quoted in Robert Delort, *Life in the Middle Ages*, trans. Robert Allen (New York, 1972), p. 218.
3. Ernest F. Henderson, ed., *Select Historical Documents of the Middle Ages* (London, 1892), p. 332.
4. Ibid., p. 365.
5. Oliver J. Thatcher and Edgar H. McNeal, eds., *A Source Book for Medieval History* (New York, 1905), p. 208.
6. Quoted in R. H. C. Davis, *A History of Medieval Europe from Constantine to Saint Louis*, 2d ed. (New York, 1988), p. 252.
7. Hildegard of Bingen, *The Book of Divine Works* (Santa Fe, 1987), 1:1.
8. Quoted in Rosalind and Christopher Brooke, *Popular Religion in the Middle Ages* (London, 1984), p. 19.
9. Oliver J. Thatcher and Edgar H. McNeal, *Source Book for Medieval History*, p. 517.
10. Quoted in Hans E. Mayer, *The Crusades*, trans. John Gillingham (New York, 1972), pp. 99–100.

Suggestions for Further Reading

For a good introduction to this period, see C. N. L. Brooke, *Europe in the Central Middle Ages, 962–1154*, rev. ed. (New York, 1988); M. Barber, *The Two Cities: Medieval Europe 1050–1320* (London, 1992); and R. Bartlett, *The Making of Europe: Conquest, Colonization, and Cultural Change, 950–1350* (Princeton, N.J., 1993). On economic conditions, see N. J. G. Pounds, *An Economic History of Medieval Europe* (New York, 1974). On peasant life, see R. Fossier, *Peasant Life in the Medieval West* (New York, 1988). Technological changes are discussed in J. Gimpel, *The Medieval Machine* (Harmondsworth, England, 1976), and J. Langdon, *Horses, Oxen, and Technological Innovation* (New York, 1986).

Works on the function and activities of the nobility in the High Middle Ages include S. Reynolds, *Kingdoms and Communities in Western Europe, 900–1300* (Oxford, 1984); R. W. Barber, *The Knight and Chivalry* (Rochester, N.Y., 1995); and G. Duby, *The Chivalrous Society* (Berkeley, 1977). Various aspects of the social history of the nobility can be found in G. Duby, *The Knight, the Lady, and the Priest* (London, 1984), on noble marriages; R. Barber and J. Barker, *Tournaments: Jousts, Chivalry, and Pageants in the Middle Ages* (New York, 1989), on tournaments; N. J. G. Pounds, *The Medieval Castle in England and Wales: A Social and Political History* (New York, 1990); and C. B. Bouchard, *Life and Society in the West: Antiquity and the Middle Ages* (San Diego, 1988), ch. 6. Also enjoyable is the popular study by J. Gies and F. Gies, *Life in a Medieval Castle* (New York, 1974). On women, see S. M. Stuard, ed., *Women in Medieval Society* (Philadelphia, 1976).

For a good survey of religion in medieval Europe, see B. Hamilton, *Religion in the Medieval West* (London, 1986). On Europe during the time of the Investiture Controversy, see U. R. Blumenthal, *The Investiture Controversy* (Philadelphia, 1988). For a general survey of church life, see R. W. Southern, *Western Society and the Church in the Middle Ages*, rev. ed. (New York, 1990).

On the papacy in the High Middle Ages, see the general surveys by C. Morris, *The Papal Monarchy* (Oxford, 1989), and I. S. Robinson, *The Papacy* (Cambridge, 1990). The papacy of Innocent III is covered in J. E. Sayers, *Innocent III, Leader of Europe, 1198–1216* (New York, 1994).

Good works on monasticism include B. Bolton, *The Medieval Reformation* (London, 1983); C. H. Lawrence, *Medieval Monasticism* (London, 1984), a good general account; and H. Leyser, *Hermits and the New Monasticism* (London, 1984). On the Cistercians, see L. J. Lekai, *The Cistercians* (Kent, Ohio, 1977). S. Flanagan, *Hildegard of Bingen*, 2d ed. (London, 1998), is a good account of the twelfth-century mystic. For a good introduction to popular religion in the eleventh and twelfth centuries, see R. Brooke and C. N. L. Brooke, *Popular Religion in the Middle Ages* (London, 1984). The image of women in the secular and religious realms is discussed in P. S. Gold, *The Lady and the Virgin: Image, Attitude, and Experience in Twelfth-Century France* (Chicago, 1985).

On dissent and heresy, see M. Lambert, *Medieval Heresy* (New York, 1977), and J. Strayer, *The Albigensian Crusades*, 2d ed. (New York, 1992). On the Inquisition, see B. Hamilton, *The Medieval Inquisition* (New York, 1981). The persecution of Jews in the thirteenth century can be examined in J. Marcus, *The Jew in the Medieval World* (New York, 1972), and J. Cohen, *The Friars and the Jews* (Oxford, 1985). The basic study on intolerance and homosexuality is J. Boswell, *Christianity, Social Tolerance, and Homosexuality* (Chicago, 1980).

Two good general surveys of the Crusades are H. E. Mayer, *The Crusades*, 2d ed. (New York, 1988), and J. Riley-Smith, *The*

Crusades: A Short History (New Haven, Conn., 1987). Other works of value are J. Riley-Smith, ed., *The Oxford Illustrated History of the Crusades* (New York, 1995), and R. C. Smail, *Crusading Warfare, 1097–1193*, 2d ed. (New York, 1995). For works on the Byzantine and Islamic Empires, see the bibliography at the end of Chapter 8 and also M. Angold, *The Byzantine Empire, 1025–1204* (London, 1984). An excellent and beautifully illustrated collection of first-hand accounts can be found in E. Hallam, ed., *Chronicles of the Crusades* (New York, 1989). The disastrous Fourth Crusade is examined in J. Godfrey, *1204: The Unholy Crusade* (Oxford, 1980). On the later Crusades, see N. Housley, *The Later Crusades, 1274–1580* (New York, 1992).

 For additional reading, go to InfoTrac College Edition, your online research library at http://web1.infotrac-college.com

Enter the search term *peasantry* using the Subject Guide.

Enter the search terms *Saint Francis* using Key Terms.

Enter the search term *Crusades* using the Subject Guide.

CHAPTER OUTLINE

- The New World of Trade and Cities
- The Intellectual and Artistic World of the High Middle Ages
- The Emergence and Growth of European Kingdoms, 1000–1300
- Conclusion

FOCUS QUESTIONS

- What developments contributed to the revival of trade during the High Middle Ages, and what areas were the primary beneficiaries of the revival?
- What were the major features of medieval cities?
- What were the major intellectual and cultal achievements of European civilization in the High Middle Ages?
- What steps did the rulers of England and France take during the High Middle Ages to reverse the decentralizing tendencies of fief-holding?
- Why were the Holy Roman Emperors less successful than the rulers of England and France at laying the foundations for a centralized state during the High Middle Ages?

*B*Y THE FIFTH CENTURY A.D., *the towns and cities that had been such an integral part of the Roman world began to decline, and the Europe of the Early Middle Ages became predominantly agricultural. Beginning in the late tenth and early eleventh centuries, however, a renewal of commercial life led to a revival of cities. Old Roman sites came back to life while new towns arose at major crossroads or natural harbors favorable to trading activities. Townspeople themselves were often great enthusiasts for their new way of life. In the twelfth century, William Fitz-Stephen spoke of London as one of the noble cities of the world: "It is happy in the healthiness of its air, in the Christian religion, in the strength of its defenses, the nature of its site, the honor of its citizens, the modesty of its women; pleasant in sports; fruitful of noble men." To*

Fitz-Stephen, London offered a myriad of opportunities and pleasures at fairs and markets. Then, too, there are the happy inhabitants of the city—where else has one "ever met such a wonderful show of people this side or the other side of the sea?" Sporting events and leisure activities are available in every season of the year: "In Easter holidays they fight battles on water." In summer, "the youths are exercised in leaping, dancing, shooting, wrestling, casting the stone; the maidens dance as long as they can well see." In winter, "when the great fen, or moor, which waters the walls of the city on the north side, is frozen, many young men play upon the ice; some, striding as wide as they may, do slide swiftly." To Fitz-Stephen, in London, "every convenience for human pleasure is known to be at hand." One would hardly know from his cheerful description that medieval cities faced overcrowded conditions, terrible smells from rotten sanitation, and the constant challenge of epidemics and fires.

By the twelfth and thirteenth centuries, both the urban centers and the urban population of Europe were experiencing a dramatic expansion. New forms of cultural expression also arose in this new urban world. Although European society in the High Middle Ages remained overwhelmingly agricultural, the growth of trade and cities, along with the development of a money economy and new commercial practices and institutions, constituted a veritable commercial revolution that affected most of Europe, including its political structures. Although lords and vassals seemed forever mired in endless petty conflicts, cities and a money economy helped some medieval kings exert a centralizing authority and inaugurate the process of developing new kinds of monarchical states. By the thirteenth century, European monarchs were solidifying their governmental institutions in pursuit of greater power.

◆ The New World of Trade and Cities

Medieval Europe was an overwhelmingly agrarian society, with most people living in small villages. In the eleventh and twelfth centuries, however, new elements were introduced that began to transform the economic foundation of Western civilization: a revival of trade, considerable expansion in the circulation of money, a restoration of specialized craftspeople and artisans, and the growth and development of towns. These changes were made possible by the new agricultural practices and subsequent increase in food production, which freed some European families from the need to produce their own food. Merchants and artisans could now buy their necessities.

✳ The Revival of Trade

The revival of commercial activity was a gradual process. During the chaotic conditions of the Early Middle Ages, large-scale trade had declined in western Europe except for Byzantine contacts with Italy and the Jewish traders who moved back and forth between the Muslim and Christian worlds. By the end of the tenth century, however, people with both the skills and the products for commercial activity were emerging in Europe. Cities in Italy assumed a leading role in the revival of trade (see Map 10.1). By the end of the eighth century, for example, Venice, on the northeastern coast, had emerged as a town with close trading ties to the Byzantine Empire. It developed a mercantile fleet and by the end of the tenth century had become the chief western trading center for Byzantine and Islamic commerce.

While the northern Italian cities were busy trading in the Mediterranean, the towns of Flanders were doing likewise in northern Europe. Flanders, the area along the coast of present-day Belgium and northern France, was known for the production of a much desired, high-quality woolen cloth. The location of Flanders made it a logical entrepot for the traders of northern Europe. Merchants from England, Scandinavia, France, and Germany converged there to trade their wares for woolen cloth. Flanders prospered in the eleventh and twelfth centuries, and such Flemish towns as Bruges and Ghent became centers for the trade and manufacture of woolen cloth.

By the twelfth century, it was almost inevitable that a regular exchange of goods would develop between Flanders and Italy. To encourage this trade, the counts of Champagne in northern France devised a series of six fairs held annually in the chief towns of their territory. Northern merchants brought the furs, woolen cloth, tin, hemp, and honey of northern Europe to the fairs of Champagne and exchanged them for the cloth and swords of northern Italy and the silks, sugar, and spices of the East.

As trade increased, both gold and silver came to be in demand at fairs and trading markets of all kinds. Slowly, a money economy began to emerge. New trading companies as well as banking firms were set

MAP I0.I Medieval Trade Routes.

up to manage the exchange and sale of goods. All of these new practices were part of the rise of commercial capitalism, an economic system in which people invested in trade and goods in order to make profits.

✳ *The Growth of Cities*

The revival of trade led to a revival of cities. Merchants needed places where they could live and build warehouses to store their goods. Towns had greatly declined in the Early Middle Ages, especially in Europe north of the Alps. Old Roman cities continued to exist but had dwindled in size and population. With the revival of trade, merchants began to settle in these old cities, followed by craft workers or artisans, people who had developed skills on manors or elsewhere and now perceived the opportunity to ply their trade producing objects that could be sold by the merchants. In the course of the eleventh and twelfth centuries, the old Roman cities came alive with new populations and growth.

Beginning in the late tenth century, many new cities or towns were also founded, particularly in northern Europe. Usually, a group of merchants established a settlement near some fortified stronghold, such as a castle or monastery. The original meaning of the English *borough* or *burgh* and the German *Burg* as a fortress or walled enclosure is still evident in the name of many cities, such as Edinburgh and Nuremberg. Castles were particularly favored because they were usually located along major routes of transportation or at the intersection of two important trade routes; the lords of the castle also offered protection. As the settlement prospered and expanded outward, new walls were built to protect it.

Most towns were closely tied to their surrounding territories because they were dependent on the countryside for their food supplies. In addition, they were often part of the territory belonging to a lord and were subject to his jurisdiction. Although lords wanted to treat towns and townspeople as they would their vassals and serfs, cities had totally different needs and a different perspective. Townspeople needed mobility to trade. Consequently, the merchants and artisans of these boroughs and burghs, who came to be called burghers or bourgeoisie, constituted a revolutionary group who needed their own unique laws to meet their requirements. Since the townspeople were profiting from the growth of trade and sale of their products, they were willing to pay for the right to make their own laws and govern themselves. In many instances, lords and kings saw the potential for vast new sources of revenues and were willing to grant (or sell) to the townspeople the liberties they were beginning to demand.

By 1100, burghers were obtaining charters of liberties from their territorial lords that granted them the privileges they wanted, including the right to bequeath goods and sell property, freedom from any military obligation to the lord, written urban law that guaranteed them their freedom, and the right to become a free person after residing a year and a day in the town. The last provision made it possible for a runaway serf who could avoid capture to become a free person in a city. Almost all new urban communities gained these elementary liberties, but only some towns obtained the right to govern themselves by choosing their own officials and administering their own courts of law.

Over time, medieval cities developed their own governments for running the affairs of the community. Citizens (only males who had been born in the city or who had lived there for some time) elected members of a city council that ran the affairs of the city and also served as judges and magistrates. The electoral process was carefully engineered to ensure that only members of the wealthiest and most powerful families, who came to be called the patricians, were elected.

City governments kept close watch over the activities of their community. To care for the welfare of the community, a government might regulate air and water pollution; provide water barrels and delegate responsibility to people in every section of the town to fight fires, which were an ever-present danger; construct warehouses to stockpile grain in the event of food emergencies; and set the standards of weights and measures used in the various local industries. Urban crime was not a major problem in the towns of the High Middle Ages because the relatively small size of communities made it difficult for criminals to operate openly. Nevertheless, medieval urban governments did organize town guards to patrol the streets by night and the city walls by day. People caught committing criminal acts were quickly tried for their offenses. Serious offenses, such as murder, were punished by execution, usually by hanging. Lesser crimes were punished by fines, flogging, or branding.

Medieval cities remained relatively small in comparison to either ancient or modern cities. A large trading city would number about five thousand inhabitants. By 1300, London was the largest city in England, with almost forty thousand people. On the Continent north of the Alps, only a few great urban centers of commerce, such as Bruges and Ghent, had a population close to that. Italian cities tended to be larger, with Venice, Florence, Genoa, Milan, and Naples numbering almost one hundred thousand inhabitants each. Even the largest European city, however, seemed insignificant alongside the Byzantine capital of Constantinople or the Arab cities of Damascus, Baghdad, and Cairo. For a long time to come, Europe remained predominantly rural, but in the long run, the rise of towns and the growth of trade laid the foundations for the eventual transformation of Europe from a rural agricultural society to an urban industrial one.

❋ Life in the Medieval City

Medieval towns were surrounded by stone walls that were expensive to build, so the space within was precious and tightly filled. This gave medieval cities their characteristic appearance of narrow, winding streets with houses crowded against each other and the second and third stories of the dwellings built out over the streets. Because dwellings were constructed mostly of wood before the fourteenth century and candles and wood fires were used for light and heat, the danger of fire was great. Medieval cities burned rapidly once a fire started.

Most of the people who lived in cities were merchants involved in trade and artisans engaged in manufacturing of some kind. Generally, merchants and artisans had their own sections within a city. The merchant area included warehouses, inns, and taverns. Artisan sections were usually divided along craft lines; each craft had its own street where its activity was pursued.

The Medieval City

Environmental pollution was not new to the twentieth century. Medieval cities and towns had their own problems with filthy living conditions. This excerpt is taken from an order sent by the king of England to the town of Boutham. It demands rectification of the town's pitiful physical conditions. There is little evidence to indicate that the king's order changed the situation significantly.

❊ *The King's Command to Boutham*

To the bailiffs of the abbot of St. Mary's, York, at Boutham. Whereas it is sufficiently evident that the pavement of the said town of Boutham is so very greatly broke up that all and singular passing and going through that town sustain immoderate damages and grievances, and in addition the air is so corrupted and infected by the pigsties situated in the king's highways and in the lanes of that town and by the swine feeding and frequently wandering about in the streets and lanes and by dung and dunghills and many other foul things placed in the streets and lanes, that great repugnance overtakes the king's ministers staying in that town and also others there dwelling and passing through, the advantage of more wholesome air is impeded; the state of men is grievously injured, and other unbearable inconveniences and many other injuries are known to proceed from such corruption, to the nuisance of the king's ministers aforesaid and of others there dwelling and passing through, and to the peril of their lives. . . . The king, being unwilling longer to tolerate such great and unbearable defects there, orders the bailiffs to cause the pavement to be suitably repaired within their liberty before All Saints next, and to cause the pigsties, aforesaid streets and lanes to be cleansed from all dung and dunghills, and to cause proclamation to be made throughout their bailiwick forbidding any one, under pain of grievous forfeiture, to cause or permit their swine to feed or wander outside his house in the king's streets or the lanes aforesaid.

SHOPS IN A MEDIEVAL TOWN. **Most urban residents were merchants involved in trade and artisans who manufactured a wide variety of products. Master craftsmen had their workshops in the ground-level rooms of their houses. In this illustration, two well-dressed burghers are touring the shopping districts of a French town. Tailors, furriers, a barber, and a grocer (from left to right) are visible at work in their shops.**

The physical environment of medieval cities was not pleasant. They were often dirty and rife with smells from animal and human waste deposited in backyard privies or on the streets (see the box above). Air pollution was also a fact of life, not only from the ubiquitous wood fires, but also from the use of a cheaper fuel, coal, used industrially by lime burners, brewers, and dyers, as well as poor people who could not afford to purchase wood. Cities were also unable to stop water pollution, especially from the tanning and animal-slaughtering industries. Butchers dumped blood and all remaining waste products from their butchered animals into the river, while tanners threw in tannic acids, dried blood, fat, hair, and the other waste products of their operations.

Because of the pollution, cities were not inclined to use the rivers for drinking water but relied instead on wells. Some communities repaired the system of aqueducts left over from Roman times and some even constructed new ones. Private and public baths also existed in medieval towns. Paris, for example, had thirty-two public baths for men and women. City laws did not allow lepers and people with "bad reputations" to use them, but such measures did not prevent the public baths from being known for permissiveness due to public nudity. One contemporary commented on what occurred in public bathhouses: "Shameful things. Men make a point of staying all night in the public baths and women at the break of day come in and through 'ignorance' find themselves in the men's rooms."[1] Authorities came under increasing pressure to close the baths down, and the great plague of the fourteenth century sealed their fate.

There were considerably more men than women in medieval cities. Women, in addition to supervising the household, purchasing food and preparing meals, raising the children, and managing the family finances, were also often expected to help their husbands in their trades. Some women also developed their own trades to earn extra money. Margery Kempe, for example, although the daughter of a major and the wife of a wealthy merchant, pursued the trade of brewing ale. When some master craftsmen died, their widows carried on their trades. Some women in medieval towns were thus able to lead lives of considerable independence.

❊ *Industry in Medieval Cities*

The revival of trade enabled cities and towns to become important centers for manufacturing a wide range of products, such as cloth, metalwork, shoes, and leather goods. A host of crafts were carried on in houses along the narrow streets of the medieval cities. From the twelfth century on, artisans began to organize themselves into guilds, which came to play a leading role in the economic life of the cities.

By the thirteenth century, virtually every group of craft workers, including tanners, carpenters, and bakers, had their own guild, and specialized groups of merchants, such as dealers in silk, spices, wool, or banking, had their separate guilds as well. Craft guilds directed almost every aspect of the production process. They set standards for the articles produced, specified the actual methods of production to be used, and fixed the price at which the finished goods could be sold. Guilds also determined the number of men who could enter a specific trade and the procedure they must follow to do so.

A person who wanted to learn a trade first became an apprentice to a master craftsman, usually at around the age of ten. After five to seven years of service, in which they learned their craft, apprentices became journeymen (or journeywomen, although most were male), who then worked for wages for other masters. Journeymen aspired to become masters as well. To do so, they were expected to produce a "masterpiece," a finished piece in their craft that allowed the master craftsmen of the guild to judge whether the journeymen were qualified to become masters and join the guild.

◆ The Intellectual and Artistic World of the High Middle Ages

The High Middle Ages was a time of tremendous intellectual and artistic vitality. The period witnessed the growth of educational institutions, a rebirth of interest in ancient culture, a quickening of theological thought, the development of a vernacular literature, and a burst of activity in architecture. While monks continued to play an important role in intellectual activity, the secular clergy, cities, and courts, whether of kings, princes, or high church officials, began to exert a newfound influence. Especially significant were the new cultural expressions that emerged in towns and cities.

❊ *The Rise of Universities*

The university as we know it—with faculty, students, and degrees—was a product of the High Middle Ages. The word *university* is derived from the Latin word *universitas*, meaning a corporation or guild, and referred to either a guild of teachers or a guild of students. Medieval universities were educational guilds or corporations that produced educated and trained individuals.

The first European university appeared in Bologna, Italy, and coincided with the revival of interest in Roman law, especially the rediscovery of Justinian's *Body of Civil Law*. In the twelfth century, Irnerius (1088–1125), a great teacher of Roman law in Bologna, attracted students from all over Europe. Most of them were laymen, usually older individuals who served as administrators to kings and princes and were eager to learn more about law so they could apply it in their jobs. To protect themselves, students at Bologna formed a guild or *universitas*, which was recognized by Emperor Frederick Barbarossa and given a charter in 1158. Although the faculty also organized

MAP 10.2   **Main Intellectual Centers of Medieval Europe. Education in the Early Middle Ages rested primarily with the clergy, especially the monks. Although monastic schools were the centers of learning from the ninth century to the early eleventh, they were surpassed in the course of the eleventh century by the cathedral schools organized by the secular (nonmonastic) clergy. In the twelfth and thirteenth centuries, the universities surpassed both monastic and cathedral schools as intellectual centers.**

itself as a group, the *universitas* of students at Bologna was far more influential. It obtained a promise of freedom for students from local authorities, regulated the price of books and lodging, and determined the curriculum, fees, and standards for their masters. Teachers were fined if they missed a class or began their lectures late.

The first university in northern Europe was the University of Paris. The University of Oxford in England, organized on the Paris model, first appeared in 1208. A migration of scholars from Oxford in 1209 led to the establishment of Cambridge University. In the Late Middle Ages, kings, popes, and princes vied to found new universities. By the end of the Middle Ages, there were eighty universities in Europe, most of them located in England, France, Italy, and Germany (see Map 10.2).

A student's initial studies at a medieval university centered around the traditional liberal arts curriculum, which consisted of grammar, rhetoric, logic, arithmetic, geometry, astronomy, and music. All classes were conducted in Latin, which provided a common means of communication for students, regardless of their country of origin. Basically, medieval university instruction was done by a lecture method. The word *lecture* is derived from the Latin verb meaning "to read." Before the development of the printing press in the fifteenth century, books were expensive, and few students could afford them, so masters read from a text (such as a collection of law if the subject were law) and then added their commentaries. No exams were given after a series of lectures, but when a student applied for a degree, he (women did not attend universities in the Middle

UNIVERSITY CLASSROOM. This illustration shows a university classroom in fourteenth-century Germany. As was customary in medieval classrooms, the master is reading from a text. The students obviously vary considerably in age and in the amount of attention they are willing to give the lecturer.

Ages) was given a comprehensive oral examination by a committee of teachers. These exams were taken after a four- or six-year period of study. The first degree a student could earn was the *artium baccalaureus,* or bachelor of arts; later he might receive an *artium magister,* or master of arts. All degrees were technically licenses to teach, although most students receiving them did not become teachers.

After completing the liberal arts curriculum, a student could go on to study law, medicine, or theology, which was the most highly regarded subject of the medieval curriculum. The study of law, medicine, or theology could take a decade or more. A student who passed his final oral examinations was granted a doctoral degree, which officially allowed him to teach his subject. Students who received degrees from medieval universities could pursue other careers besides teaching that proved to be much more lucrative. A law degree was deemed essential for those who wished to serve as advisers to kings and princes. The growing administrative bureaucracies of popes and kings also demanded a supply of clerks with a university education who could keep records and draw up official documents. Medieval universities provided the teachers, administrators, lawyers, and doctors for medieval society.

Medieval universities shared in the violent atmosphere of the age. Records from courts of law reveal numerous instances of disturbances in European universities. One German professor was finally dismissed for stabbing one too many of his colleagues in faculty meetings. A student in Bologna was attacked in the classroom by another student armed with a sword. Oxford regulations attempted to dampen the violence by forbidding students to bring weapons to class. Not uncommonly, town and gown struggles ("gown" refers to the academic robe worn by teachers and students) escalated into bloody riots between townspeople and students (see the box on p. 201).

❈ *A Revival of Classical Antiquity*

Another aspect of the intellectual revival of the High Middle Ages was a resurgence of interest in the works of classical antiquity—the works of the Greeks and Romans. In the twelfth century, western Europe was introduced to a large number of Greek scientific and philosophical works, including those of Galen and Hippocrates on medicine, Ptolemy on astronomy, and Euclid on mathematics. Above all, the West now had available the complete works of Aristotle. During the second half of the twelfth century, all of Aristotle's scientific works were translated into Latin. This great influx of Aristotle's works had an overwhelming impact on the West. He came to be viewed as the "master of those who know," the

University Students and Violence at Oxford

Medieval universities shared in the violent atmosphere of their age. Town-and-gown quarrels often resulted in bloody conflicts, especially during the universities' formative period. This selection is taken from an anonymous description of a student riot at Oxford at the end of the thirteenth century.

❈ A Student Riot at Oxford

They [the townsmen] seized and imprisoned all scholars on whom they could lay hands, invaded their inns [halls of residence], made havoc of their goods and trampled their books under foot. In the face of such provocation the Proctors [university officials] sent their assistants about the town, forbidding the students to leave their inns. But all commands and exhortations were in vain. By nine o'clock next morning, bands of scholars were parading the streets in martial array. If the Proctors failed to restrain them, the mayor was equally powerless to restrain his townsmen. The great bell of St. Martin's rang out an alarm; oxhorns were sounded in the streets; messengers were sent into the country to collect rustic allies. The clerks [students and teachers], who numbered three thousand in all, began their attack simultaneously in various quarters. They broke open warehouses in the Spicery, the Cutlery and elsewhere. Armed with bow and arrows, swords and bucklers, slings and stones, they fell upon their opponents. Three they slew, and wounded fifty or more. One band . . . took up a position in High Street between the Churches of St. Mary and All Saints', and attacked the house of a certain Edward Hales. This Hales was a longstanding enemy of the clerks. There were no half measures with him. He seized his crossbow, and from an upper chamber sent an unerring shaft into the eye of the pugnacious rector. The death of their valiant leader caused the clerks to lose heart. They fled, closely pursued by the townsmen and country-folk. Some were struck down in the streets, and others who had taken refuge in the churches were dragged out and driven mercilessly to prison, lashed with thongs and goaded with iron spikes.

Complaints of murder, violence and robbery were lodged straightway with the King by both parties. The townsmen claimed three thousand pounds' damage. The commissioners, however, appointed to decide the matter, condemned them to pay two hundred marks, removed the bailiffs, and banished twelve of the most turbulent citizens from Oxford.

man who seemed to have understood every field of knowledge.

The recovery of Greek scientific and philosophical works was not a simple process, however. Little knowledge of Greek had survived in Europe. It was through the Muslim world that the West recovered the works of Aristotle and other Greeks. The translation of Greek works into Arabic was one aspect of the brilliant Muslim civilization; in the twelfth century, these writings were translated from Arabic into Latin, making them available to the West.

The Islamic world had more to contribute intellectually to the West than translations, however. Scientific work in the ninth and tenth centuries had enabled it to forge far ahead of the Western world, and in the twelfth and thirteenth centuries, Arabic works on physics, mathematics, medicine, and optics became available to the West in Latin translations. In addition, when Aristotle's works were brought into the West in the second half of the twelfth century, they were accompanied by commentaries written by outstanding Arabic and Jewish philosophers. One example was Ibn-Rushd, also known as Averroës (1126–1198), who lived in Córdoba and composed a systematic commentary on virtually all of Aristotle's surviving works.

❈ The Development of Scholasticism

The importance of Christianity in medieval society probably made it certain that theology would play a central role in the European intellectual world. Theology, the formal study of religion, was "queen of the sciences" in the new universities. Beginning in the eleventh century, the effort to apply reason or logical analysis to the church's basic doctrines had a significant impact on the study of theology. The word *scholasticism* is used to refer to the philosophical and theological system of the medieval schools. A primary preoccupation of scholasticism was the attempt to reconcile faith and reason—to demonstrate that what was accepted on faith was in harmony with what could be learned by reason.

Scholasticism had its beginnings in the theological world of the eleventh and twelfth centuries but reached its high point in the thirteenth century. The overriding task of scholasticism in the thirteenth century was to harmonize Christian revelation with the work of Aristotle. The great influx of Aristotle's works into the West in the High Middle Ages threw many theologians into consternation. Aristotle was so highly regarded that he was called simply "the Philosopher," yet he had arrived at his conclusions by rational thought—not revelation—and some of his doctrines, such as the mortality of the individual soul, contradicted the teachings of the church. The most famous attempt to reconcile Aristotle and the doctrines of Christianity was that of Saint Thomas Aquinas.

Thomas Aquinas (1225–1274) studied theology at Cologne and Paris and taught at both Naples and Paris, and it was at the latter that he finished his famous *Summa Theologica* (*A Summa of Theology*—a summa was a compendium that attempted to bring together all the knowledge on a given subject). Aquinas' masterpiece was organized according to the dialectical method of the scholastics. Aquinas first posed a question, cited sources that offered opposing opinions on the question, and then resolved them by arriving at his own conclusions. In this fashion, Aquinas raised and discussed some six hundred articles or issues.

Aquinas' reputation derives from his masterful attempt to reconcile faith and reason. He took it for granted that there were truths derived by reason and truths derived by faith. He was certain, however, that the two truths could not be in conflict:

> The light of faith that is freely infused into us does not destroy the light of natural knowledge [reason] implanted in us naturally. For although the natural light of the human mind is insufficient to show us these things made manifest by faith, it is nevertheless impossible that these things which the divine principle gives us by faith are contrary to these implanted in us by nature [reason]. Indeed, were that the case, one or the other would have to be false, and, since both are given to us by God, God would have to be the author of untruth, which is impossible. . . . It is impossible that those things which are of philosophy can be contrary to those things which are of faith.[2]

The natural mind, unaided by faith, could arrive at truths concerning the physical universe. Without the help of God's grace, however, unaided reason alone could not grasp spiritual truths, such as the Trinity (the belief that God, Jesus, and the Holy Spirit are three manifestations of the same unique Deity) or the Incarnation (the belief that Jesus in his lifetime was God in human form).

✾ *Literature in the High Middle Ages*

Latin was the universal language of medieval civilization. Used in the church and schools, it enabled learned people to communicate anywhere in Europe. But in the twelfth century, much new literature was being written in the vernacular (the local language, such as Spanish, French, English, or German). A new market for vernacular literature appeared in the twelfth century when educated laypeople at court and in the new urban society sought fresh avenues of entertainment.

Perhaps the most popular vernacular literature of the twelfth century was troubadour poetry, which was chiefly the product of nobles and knights. This poetry focused on the love of a knight for a lady, generally a married noble lady, who inspires him to become a braver knight and a better poet. A good example is found in the laments of the crusading noble Jaufré Rudel, who cherished a dream lady from afar whom he said he would always love but feared he would never meet:

> Most sad, most joyous shall I go away,
> Let me have seen her for a single day,
>   My love afar,
> I shall not see her, for her land and mine
> Are sundered, and the ways are hard to find,
> So many ways, and I shall lose my way,
>   So wills it God.[3]

First appearing in southern France, troubadour poetry soon spread to northern France, Italy, and Germany.

Another type of vernacular literature was the *chanson de geste*, or heroic epic. The earliest and finest example is *The Song of Roland*, which appeared around 1100 and was written in a dialect of French, a language derived from Latin (see the box on p. 203). The *chansons de geste* were written for a male-dominated society. The chief events described in these poems are battles and political contests. Their world is one of combat in which knights fight courageously for their kings and lords. Women play little or no role in this literary genre.

The Song of Roland

The Song of Roland *is one of the best examples of the medieval chanson de geste or heroic epic. Inspired by a historical event, it recounts the ambush of the rear guard of Charlemagne's Frankish army in the Pyrenees. Written three hundred years after the event it supposedly describes, however, it reveals more about the eleventh century than about the age of Charlemagne The Basques who ambushed Charlemagne's army have been transformed into Muslims; the Frankish soldiers, into French knights. This selection describes the death of Roland, Charlemagne's nephew, who was the commander of the decimated rear guard.*

❊ The Song of Roland

Now Roland feels that he is at death's door;
Out of his ears the brain is running forth.
Now for his peers he prays God call them all,
And for himself St. Gabriel's aid implores;
Then in each hand he takes, lest shame befall,
His Olifant [horn] and Durendal his sword.
Far as a quarrel flies from a cross-bow drawn,
Toward land of Spain he goes, to a wide lawn,
And climbs a mound where grows a fair tree tall,
And marble stones beneath it stand by four.

Face downward there on the green grass he falls,
And swoons away, for he is at death's door. . . .
Now Roland feels death press upon him hard;
It's creeping down from his head to his heart.
Under a pine-tree he hastens him apart,
There stretches him face down on the green grass,
And lays beneath him his sword and Olifant.
He's turned his head to where the Paynims [Muslims]
    are,
And this he does for the French and for Charles,
Since fain is he that they should say, brave heart,
That he has died a conqueror at the last.
He beats his breast full many a time and fast,
Gives, with his glove, his sins into God's charge.
Now Roland feels his time is at an end;
On the steep hill-side, toward Spain he's turned his
    head,
And with one hand he beats upon his breast;
Saying: "Mea culpa; Thy mercy, Lord, I beg
For all the sins, both the great and the less,
That e'er I did since first I drew my breath
Unto this day when I'm struck down by death."
His right-hand glove he unto God extends;
Angels from Heaven now to his side descend.

❊ Romanesque Architecture: "A White Mantle of Churches"

The eleventh and twelfth centuries witnessed an explosion of building, both private and public. The construction of castles and churches absorbed most of the surplus resources of medieval society and at the same time reflected its basic preoccupations, God and warfare. The churches were by far the most conspicuous of the public buildings. A chronicler of the eleventh century commented:

> As the year 1000 approached, people all over the world, but especially in Italy and France, began to rebuild their churches. Although most of them were well built and in little need of alterations, Christian nations were rivalling each other to have the most beautiful edifices. One might say the world was shaking herself, throwing off her old garments, and robing herself with a white mantle of churches. Then nearly all the cathedrals, the monasteries dedicated to different saints, and even the small village chapels were reconstructed more beautifully by the faithful.[4]

Hundreds of new cathedrals, abbeys, and pilgrimage churches, as well as thousands of parish churches in rural villages, were built in the eleventh and twelfth centuries. This building spree reflected a revived religious culture and the increased wealth of the period produced by agriculture, trade, and the growth of cities.

The cathedrals of the eleventh and twelfth centuries were built in the Romanesque style, a truly international style. The construction of churches required the services of a cadre of professional master builders whose employment throughout Europe guaranteed international unity in basic features.

Romanesque churches were normally built in the basilica shape used in the construction of churches

BARREL VAULTING. The eleventh and twelfth centuries witnessed an explosion of church construction. Using the basilica shape, master builders replaced flat wooden roofs with long, round stone vaults known as barrel vaults. As this illustration of a Romanesque church in Vienne, France, indicates, the barrel vault limited the size of the church and left little room for windows.

INTERIOR OF A GOTHIC CATHEDRAL. The use of ribbed vaults and pointed arches gave the Gothic cathedral a feeling of upward movement. Moreover, thanks to flying buttresses on the outside, the cathedral could have thin walls with stained glass windows that filled the interior with light. The flying buttress was a heavy pier of stone built outside the wall to bear the weight of the vaulted ceiling.

in the Late Roman Empire. Basilicas were simply rectangular buildings with flat wooden roofs. Elaborating on this basic plan, Romanesque builders made a significant innovation by replacing the flat wooden roof with a long, round stone vault called a barrel vault or a cross vault where two barrel vaults intersected (a vault is simply a curved roof made of masonry). The barrel vault was used when a transept was added to create a church plan in the shape of a cross. Although barrel and cross vaults were technically difficult to construct, they were considered aesthetically pleasing and technically proficient. They also had fine acoustics.

Because stone roofs were extremely heavy, Romanesque churches required massive pillars and walls to hold them up. This left little space for windows, making Romanesque churches quite dark inside. The massive walls and pillars gave Romanesque churches a sense of solidity and a look reminiscent of a fortress.

❋ The Gothic Cathedral

Begun in the twelfth century and brought to perfection in the thirteenth, the Gothic cathedral remains one of the great artistic triumphs of the High Middle Ages. Soaring skyward, as if to reach heaven, it was a fitting symbol for medieval people's preoccupation with God.

Two fundamental innovations of the twelfth century made Gothic cathedrals possible. The combination of ribbed vaults and pointed arches replaced the barrel vault of Romanesque churches and enabled builders to make Gothic churches higher than their Romanesque counterparts. The use of pointed arches and ribbed vaults created an impression of upward movement, a sense of weightless upward thrust that implied the energy of God. Another technical innovation, the flying buttress, basically a heavy arched pier of stone built onto the outside of the walls, made it possible to distribute the weight of the church's vaulted ceilings outward and down and thus reduce the thickness of the heavy walls used in Romanesque churches to hold the weight of the massive barrel vaults. The thinner walls of Gothic cathedrals could consequently be filled with magnificent stained-glass windows, which created a play of light inside that varied with the sun at different times of the day. The preoccupation with colored light in Gothic cathedrals was inspired by the belief that natural light was a symbol of the divine light of God.

The first fully Gothic church was the abbey church of St. Denis near Paris, inspired by its famous abbot Suger and built between 1140 and 1150. A product of northern France, the Gothic style had spread by the mid-thirteenth century to England, Spain, Germany, and virtually all the rest of Europe. The most brilliant Gothic cathedrals were still to be found in France—in Paris (Notre Dame), Reims, Amiens, and Chartres.

A Gothic cathdral was the work of an entire community. All classes of society contributed to its construction. Money was raised from wealthy towns-people, who had profited from the new trade and industries, as well as from kings and nobles. Master masons, who were both architects and engineers, designed the cathedrals. They drew up the plans and supervised the work of construction. Stonemasons and other craftspeople were paid a daily wage and provided the skilled labor to build the cathedrals. A Gothic cathedral symbolized the chief preoccupation of a medieval Christian community, its dedication to a spiritual ideal. As we have observed before, the largest buildings of an era reflect the values of its society. The Gothic cathedral, with its towers soaring toward heaven, gave witness to an age when a spiritual impulse still underlay most of existence.

THE GOTHIC CATHEDRAL. The Gothic cathedral was one of the greatest artistic and architectural triumphs of the High Middle Ages. Shown here is the cathedral of Notre Dame in Paris. Begun in 1163, it was not completed until the beginning of the fourteenth century.

◆ The Emergence and Growth of European Kingdoms, 1000–1300

The domination of society by the nobility reached its apex in the High Middle Ages. During the same period, however, kings began the process of extending their power in more effective ways. Out of these growing monarchies would eventually come the European states that dominated much of later European history.

Kings possessed some sources of power that other lords did not. Usually, kings had greater opportunities to increase their lands through war and marriage alliances and then could use their new acquisitions to reward their followers and bind powerful nobles to them. In the High Middle Ages, kings found ways to strengthen governmental institutions and consequently to extend their powers. The growth of cities, the revival of commerce, and the emergence of a money economy enabled monarchs to hire soldiers and officials and to rely less on their vassals.

❊ *England in the High Middle Ages*

In 1066, an army of heavily armed knights under William of Normandy landed on the coast of England and soundly defeated King Harold and the Anglo-Saxon foot soldiers at the Battle of Hastings on October 14. William (1066–1087) was crowned king of England at Christmastime in London and began the process of combining Anglo-Saxon and Norman institutions. Many of the Norman knights were given parcels of land that they held as fiefs from the new English king. William made all nobles swear an oath of loyalty to him and insisted that all people owed loyalty to the king rather than to their lords. Gradually, fusion between the victorious Normans and the defeated Anglo-Saxons created a new England. Although the Norman ruling class spoke French, the intermarriage of the Norman-French with Anglo-Saxon nobility gradually blended Anglo-Saxon and French into a new English language. The Normans also took over existing Anglo-Saxon institutions, such as the office of sheriff. William took a census and more fully developed the system of taxation and royal courts begun by the Anglo-Saxon kings of the tenth and eleventh centuries. All in all, William of Normandy created a strong, centralized monarchy.

The Norman conquest of England had other repercussions as well. Because the new king of England was still the duke of Normandy, he was both a king (of England) and at the same time a vassal to a king (of France), but a vassal who was now far more powerful than his lord. This connection with France kept England heavily involved in continental affairs throughout the High Middle Ages.

In the twelfth century, the power of the English monarchy was greatly enlarged during the reign of Henry II (1154–1189), the founder of the Plantagenet dynasty. The new king was particularly successful in strengthening the power of the royal courts. Henry expanded the number of criminal cases tried in the king's court and also devised ways of taking property cases from local courts to the royal courts. Henry's goals were clear: expanding the jurisdiction of royal courts extended the king's power and, of course, brought revenues into his coffers. Moreover, because the royal courts were now found throughout England, a body of common law (law that was common to the whole kingdom) began to replace the local law codes, which differed from place to place.

Henry was less successful at imposing royal control over the church. The king claimed the right to punish clergymen in church courts, but Thomas à Becket, archbishop of Canterbury and therefore the highest-ranking English cleric, claimed that only church courts could try clerics. Attempts at compromise failed, and the angry king publicly expressed the desire to be rid of Becket: "Who will free me of this priest?" he screamed. Four knights took the challenge, went to Canterbury, and murdered the archbishop in the cathedral. Met with public outrage, Henry was forced to allow the right of appeal from English church courts to the papal court.

Many English nobles came to resent the ongoing growth of the king's power and rose in rebellion during the reign of Henry's son, King John (1199–1216). At Runnymeade in 1215, John was forced to seal Magna Carta (the Great Charter). Magna Carta was, above all, a feudal document (see the box on p. 207). Feudal custom had always recognized that the relationship between king and vassals was based on mutual rights and obligations. Magna Carta gave written recognition to that fact and was used in subsequent years to strengthen the idea that the monarch's power was limited, not absolute.

During the reign of Edward I (1272–1307), an institution of great importance in the development of representative government—the English Parliament—emerged. Originally the word *parliament* was applied to meetings of the king's Great Council in which the greater barons and chief prelates of the church met with the king's judges and principal advisers to deal with judicial affairs. But out of a need for money, Edward in 1295 invited two knights from every county and two residents ("burgesses") from each town to meet with the Great Council to consent to new taxes. This was the first Parliament.

The English Parliament, then, came to be composed of two knights from every county and two burgesses from every town as well as the barons and ecclesiastical lords. Eventually, barons and church lords formed the House of Lords; knights and burgesses, the House of Commons. The Parliaments of Edward I granted taxes, discussed politics, passed laws, and handled judicial business. By the end of the thirteenth century, the law of the realm was being determined not by the king alone but by the king in consultation with representatives of various groups that constituted the community.

✳ The Growth of the French Kingdom

In 843, the Carolingian Empire had been divided into three major sections. The west Frankish lands formed the core of the eventual kingdom of France. In 987, after the death of the last Carolingian king, the west Frankish nobles chose Hugh Capet as the new king, thus establishing the Capetian dynasty of French kings. Although they carried the title of kings, the Capetians had little real power. They controlled as the royal domain (the lands of the king) only the lands around Paris known as the Île-de-France. As kings of France, the Capetians were formally the overlords of the great lords of France, such as the dukes of Normandy, Brittany, Burgundy, and Aquitaine (see Map 10.3). In reality, however, many of the dukes were considerably more powerful than the Capetian kings. It would take the Capetian dynasty hundreds of years to create a truly centralized monarchical authority in France.

The reign of King Philip II Augustus (1180–1223) was an important turning point. Philip II waged war against the Plantagenet rulers of England, who also ruled the French territories of Normandy,

Magna Carta

After the dismal failure of King John to reconquer Normandy from the French king, some of the English barons rebelled against their king. At Runnymeade in 1215, King John agreed to seal Magna Carta, the Great Charter of liberties regulating the relationship between the king and his vassals. What made Magna Carta an important historical document was its more general clauses defining rights and liberties. These were later interpreted in broader terms to make them applicable to all the English people.

�֎ Magna Carta

John, by the Grace of God, king of England, lord of Ireland, duke of Normandy and Aquitaine, count of Anjou, to the archbishops, bishops, abbots, earls, barons, justiciars, foresters, sheriffs, reeves, servants, and all bailiffs and his faithful people greeting.

1. In the first place we have granted to God, and by this our present charter confirmed, for us and our heirs forever, that the English church shall be free, and shall hold its rights entire and its liberties uninjured. . . .We have granted moreover to all free men of our kingdom for us and our heirs forever all the liberties written below, to be had and holden by themselves and their heirs from us and our heirs.

2. If any of our earls or barons, or others holding from us in chief by military service shall have died, and when he had died his heir shall be of full age and owe relief, he shall have his inheritance by the ancient relief; that is to say, the heir or heirs of an earl for the whole barony of an earl a hundred pounds; the heir or heirs of a baron for a whole barony a hundred pounds; the heir or heirs of a knight, for a whole knight's fee, a hundred shillings at most; and who owes less let him give less according to the ancient custom of fiefs.

3. If moreover the heir of any one of such shall be under age, and shall be in wardship, when he comes of age he shall have his inheritance without relief and without a fine. . . .

12. No scutage or aid shall be imposed in our kingdom except by the common council of our kingdom, except for the ransoming of our body, for the making of our oldest son a knight, and for once marrying our oldest daughter, and for these purposes it shall be only a reasonable aid. . . .

13. And the city of London shall have all its ancient liberties and free customs, as well by land as by water. Moreover, we will and grant that all other cities and boroughs and villages and ports shall have all their liberties and free customs.

14. And for holding a common council of the kingdom concerning the assessment of an aid otherwise than in the three cases mentioned above, or concerning the assessment of a scutage we shall cause to be summoned the archbishops, bishops, abbots, earls, and greater barons by our letters under seal; and besides we shall cause to be summoned generally, by our sheriffs and bailiffs all those who hold from us in chief, for a certain day, that is at the end of forty days at least, and for a certain place; and in all the letters of that summons, we will express the cause of the summons, and when the summons has thus been given the business shall proceed on the appointed day, on the advice of those who shall be present, even if not all of those who were summoned have come. . . .

39. No free man shall be taken or imprisoned or dispossessed, or outlawed, or banished, or in any way destroyed, nor will we go upon him, nor send upon him, except by the legal judgment of his peers or by the law of the land. . . .

60. Moreover, all those customs and franchises mentioned above which we have conceded in our kingdom, and which are to be fulfilled, as far as pertains to us, in respect to our men; all men of our kingdom as well as clergy as laymen, shall observe as far as pertains to them, in respect to their men.

MAP I0.3   **England and France in the High Middle Ages:** *(left)* **England and Its French holdings;** *(right)* **Growth of the French State.**

Maine, Anjou, and Aquitaine, and was successful in gaining control of most of these territories. Through these conquests, Philip quadrupled the income of the French monarchy and greatly enlarged its power. To administer justice and collect royal revenues in his new territories, Philip appointed new royal officials, thus inaugurating a French royal bureaucracy.

Capetian rulers after Philip II continued to add lands to the royal domain. Although Philip had used military force, other kings used both purchase and marriage to achieve the same end. Much of the thirteenth century was dominated by Louis IX (1226–1270), whom many consider the greatest of the medieval French kings. A deeply religious man, he was later canonized as a saint by the church, an unusual action regardless of the century. Louis was known for his attempts to bring justice to his people and ensure their rights. Sharing in the religious sentiments of

his age, Louis played a major role in two of the later Crusades, but both were failures, and he met his death during an invasion of North Africa.

One of Louis's successors, Philip IV the Fair (1285–1314), was particularly effective in strengthening the French monarchy. The machinery of government became even more specialized. French kings going back to the early Capetians had possessed a household staff for running their affairs. Over time, however, this household staff was enlarged and divided into three groups to form three major branches of royal administration: a council for advice, a chamber of accounts for finances, and a *parlement* or royal court. By the beginning of the fourteenth century, the Capetians had established firm foundations for a royal bureaucracy.

Philip IV also brought a French parliament into being by summoning representatives of the three

LOUIS IX DEPARTING FOR TUNIS. The pious French king Louis IX organized the last two major Crusades of the thirteenth century. Both failed miserably. This illustration shows a robust Louis IX setting out for Tunis in 1270. In truth, the king was so weak that he had to be carried to the ship.

estates, or classes—the clergy (first estate), the nobles (second estate), and the townspeople (third estate)—to meet with him. They did so in 1302, inaugurating the Estates-General, the first French parliament, although it had little real power. By the end of the thirteenth century, France was the largest, wealthiest, and best-governed monarchical state in Europe.

✸ Christian Reconquest: The Spanish Kingdoms

Much of Spain had been part of the Islamic world since the eighth century. Muslim Spain had flourished in the Early Middle Ages. Córdoba became a major urban center with a population exceeding 300,000 people. Agriculture prospered, and Spain became known as well for excellent leather, wool, silk, and paper. Beginning in the tenth century, however, the most noticeable feature of Spanish history was the beginning of a Christian reconquest that lasted until the final expulsion of the Muslims at the end of the fifteenth century.

By the beginning of the eleventh century, a number of small Christian kingdoms in northern Spain took the offensive against the Muslims. By the end of the twelfth century, the northern half of Spain had been consolidated into the Christian kingdoms of Castile, Navarre, Aragon, and Portugal, which had first emerged as a separate kingdom in 1139 (see Map 10.4). The southern half of Spain remained under the control of the Muslims. But in the thirteenth century, Aragon, Castile, and Portugal made significant conquests of Muslim territory. Castile subdued most of Andalusia in the south, down to the Atlantic and Mediterranean; at the same time, Aragon conquered Valencia. The Muslims remained ensconced only in the kingdom of Granada in the southeast of the Iberian peninsula, which remained an independent Muslim state.

The Spanish kingdoms followed no consistent policy in the treatment of the conquered Muslim

MAP 10.4   Christian Reconquests in the Western Mediterranean.

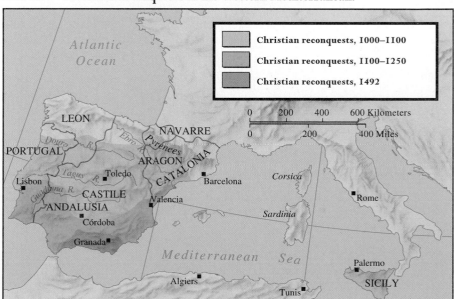

population. Muslim farmers continued to work the land but were forced to pay very high rents in Aragon. In Castile, King Alfonso X (1252–1284), who called himself the "King of Three Religions," encouraged the continued development of a cosmopolitan culture shared by Christians, Jews, and Muslims.

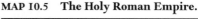 *The Lands of the Holy Roman Empire: Germany and Italy*

In the tenth century, the powerful dukes of the Saxons became kings of the lands of the eastern Frankish kingdom (or Germany, as it came to be known). The best known of the Saxon kings of Germany was Otto I (936–973), who intervened in Italian politics and for his efforts was crowned emperor of the Romans by the pope in 962, reviving a title that had not been used since the time of Charlemagne. Otto's creation of a new "Roman Empire" in the hands of the eastern Franks (or Germans, as they came to be called) added a tremendous burden to the kings of Germany, who now took on the onerous task of ruling Italy as well.

In the eleventh century, German kings created a strong monarchy and a powerful empire by leading armies into Italy. To strengthen their power, German kings had come to rely on their ability to control the church and select bishops and abbots, whom they could then use as royal administrators. But the struggle between church and state during the reign of Henry IV (1056–1106) weakened the king's ability to use church officials in this way (see Chapter 9). The German kings also tried to bolster their power by using their position as emperors to exploit the resources of Italy. But this tended to backfire; many a German king lost armies in Italy in pursuit of a dream of empire, and no German dynasty demonstrates this better than the Hohenstaufens.

Both Frederick I (1152–1190) and Frederick II (1212–1250), the two most famous members of the Hohenstaufen dynasty, tried to create a new kind of empire. Previous German kings had focused on building a strong German kingdom, to which Italy might be added as an appendage (see Map 10.5). Frederick I, known as Barbarossa (Redbeard) to the Italians, however, planned to get his chief revenues from Italy

MAP 10.5 The Holy Roman Empire.

as the center of a "holy empire," as he called it (hence the name Holy Roman Empire). But his attempt to conquer northern Italy ran into severe difficulties. The pope opposed him, fearful that the emperor wanted to include Rome and the Papal States as part of his realm. The cities of northern Italy, which had become used to their freedom, were also not willing to be Frederick's subjects. An alliance of these northern Italian cities, with the support of the papacy, defeated the forces of Emperor Frederick at Legnano in 1176.

Frederick II was the most brilliant of the Hohenstaufen rulers. King of Sicily in 1198, king of Germany in 1212, and crowned emperor in 1220, Frederick II was a truly remarkable man who awed his contemporaries. Frederick had been raised in Sicily, with its diverse peoples, languages, and religions, and his court brought together a brilliant array of lawyers, poets, artists, and scientists. His main goal was to establish a strong centralized state in Italy dominated by his kingdom in Sicily. Frederick's major task was to gain control of northern Italy. In reaching to extend his power in Italy, he became involved in a deadly struggle with the popes, who realized that a single ruler of northern and southern Italy meant the end of papal secular power in central Italy. The northern Italian cities were also unwilling to give up their freedom. Frederick waged a bitter struggle in northern Italy, winning many battles but ultimately losing the war.

Frederick's preoccupation with the creation of an empire in Italy left Germany in confusion and chaos until 1273, when the major German princes, serving as electors, chose an insignificant German noble, Rudolf of Habsburg, as the new German king. In choosing a weak king, the princes were ensuring that the German monarchy would remain impotent and incapable of reestablishing a centralized monarchical state. The failure of the Hohenstaufens had led to a situation where his exalted majesty, the German king and Holy Roman Emperor, had no real power over either Germany or Italy. Unlike France, England, and even Spain, neither Germany nor Italy created a unified national monarchy in the Middle Ages. Both became geographical designations for loose confederations of hundreds of petty states under the vague direction of king or emperor. In fact, neither Germany nor Italy would become united until the nineteenth century.

Following the death of Frederick II, Italy fell into considerable political confusion. While the papacy remained in control of much of central Italy, the defeat of imperial power left the cities and towns of northern Italy independent of any other authority. Gradually, the larger ones began to emerge as strong city-states. Florence assumed the leadership of Tuscany, and Milan, under the guidance of the Visconti family, took control of the Lombard region. With its great commercial wealth, the republic of Venice dominated the northeastern part of the peninsula.

❋ New Kingdoms in Eastern Europe

In eastern Europe, Hungary, which had been a Christian state since 1000, remained relatively stable throughout the High Middle Ages, but the history of Poland and Russia was far more turbulent. In the thirteenth century, eastern Europe was beset by two groups of invaders, the Teutonic Knights from the west and the Mongols from the east.

In the eleventh century, a Polish kingdom existed as a separate state, but with no natural frontiers (see Map 10.6). Consequently, German settlers encroached on its territory on a regular basis, leading to considerable intermarriage between Slavs

MAP 10.6 Eastern Europe.

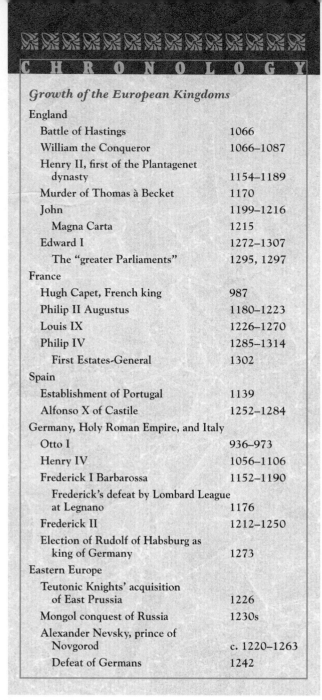

Central and eastern Europe had periodically been subject to invasions from fierce Asiatic nomads, including the Huns, Avars, Bulgars, and Magyars. In the thirteenth century, the Mongols exploded upon the scene, causing far more disruption than earlier invaders. Beginning in the 1230s, the Mongols moved into Europe. They conquered Russia, advanced into Poland and Hungary, and destroyed a force of Poles and Teutonic Knights in Silesia in 1241. Europe then seemingly got lucky when the Mongol hordes turned back because of internal fighting; western and southern Europe escaped the wrath of the Mongols. Over the long run, the Mongols left little of any real importance, although their occupation of Russia certainly had some affect on that land.

THE DEVELOPMENT OF RUSSIA

The Kiev Rus state, which had become formally Christian in 987, prospered considerably afterward, reaching its high point in the first half of the eleventh century. Kievan society was dominated by a noble class of landowners known as the boyars. Kievan merchants maintained regular trade with Scandinavia to the north and the Islamic and Byzantine worlds to the south. But destructive civil wars and new invasions by Asiatic nomads caused the principality of Kiev to collapse, and the sack of Kiev by north Russian princes in 1169 brought an inglorious end to the first Russian state.

The fundamental civilizing and unifying force of early Russia was the Christian church. The Russian church imitated the liturgy and organization of the Byzantine Empire, whose Eastern Orthodox priests had converted the Kievan Rus to Christianity at the end of the tenth century. The Russian church became known for its rigid religious orthodoxy. Although Christianity provided a common bond between Russian and European civilization, Russia's religious development guaranteed an even closer affinity between Russian and Byzantine civilization.

In the thirteenth century, the Mongols conquered Russia and cut it off even more from western Europe. The Mongols were not numerous enough to settle the vast Russian lands but were content to rule directly an area along the lower Volga and north of the Caspian and Black Seas to Kiev and rule indirectly elsewhere. In the latter territories, Russian princes were required to pay tribute to the Mongol overlords.

One Russian prince soon emerged as more powerful than the others. Alexander Nevsky

and Germans. During the thirteenth century, relations between the Germans and the Slavs of eastern Europe worsened due to the aggression of the Teutonic Knights. The Teutonic Knights had been founded near the end of the twelfth century to protect the Christian Holy Land. In the early thirteenth century, however, these Christian knights found greater opportunity to the east of Germany, where they attacked the pagan Slavs. East Prussia was given to the military order in 1226, and by the end of the thirteenth century, Prussia had become German and Christian as the pagan Slavs were forced to convert.

(c. 1220–1263), prince of Novgorod, defeated a German invading army in northwestern Russia in 1242. His cooperation with the Mongols won him their favor. The khan, leader of the western part of the Mongol empire, rewarded Alexander Nevsky with the title of grand-prince, enabling his descendants to become the princes of Moscow and eventually leaders of all Russia.

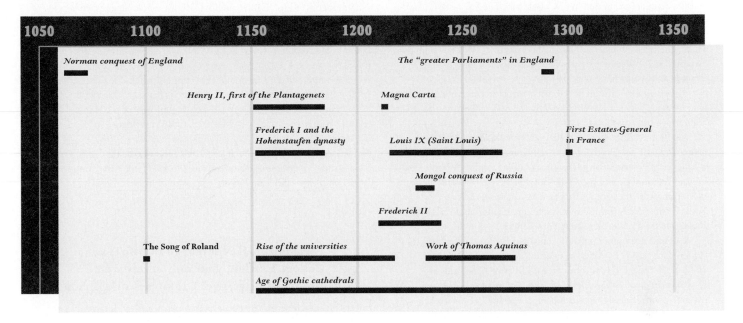

| 1050 | 1100 | 1150 | 1200 | 1250 | 1300 | 1350 |

Norman conquest of England

The "greater Parliaments" in England

Henry II, first of the Plantagenets

Magna Carta

Frederick I and the Hohenstaufen dynasty

Louis IX (Saint Louis)

First Estates-General in France

Mongol conquest of Russia

Frederick II

The Song of Roland

Rise of the universities

Work of Thomas Aquinas

Age of Gothic cathedrals

Conclusion

The period from 1000 to 1300 was a dynamic one in the development of Western civilization. It witnessed economic, social, and political changes that some historians believe set European civilization on a path that lasted until the Industrial Revolution of the late eighteenth century. The revival of trade, the expansion of towns and cities, and the development of a money economy did not mean the end of Europe's predominantly rural society, but they did open the door to new ways to make a living and new opportunities for people to expand and enrich their lives. Eventually, they laid the foundations for the development of a predominantly urban industrial society.

The High Middles Ages also gave birth to a cultural revival that led to a rediscovery of important aspects of the classical heritage, new centers of learning in the universities, the use of reason to systematize the study of theology, the development of a vernacular literature that appealed both to knights and townspeople, and a dramatic increase in the number and size of churches.

The nobles continued to dominate the medieval world politically, economically, and socially. But quietly and surely, within this world of castles and private power, kings gradually began to extend their public powers. By the thirteenth century, monarchs were developing the machinery of government that would enable them to challenge the exalted claims of papal power and become the centers of political authority in Europe.

The actions of these medieval monarchs paved the way for the European kingdoms and nations that have dominated the European political scene ever since.

Notes

1. Quoted in Jean Gimpel, *The Medieval Machine* (Harmondsworth, England, 1977), p. 92.
2. Quoted in John Mundy, *Europe in the High Middle Ages, 1150–1309* (New York, 1973), pp. 474–475.
3. Quoted in Helen Waddell, *The Wandering Scholars* (New York, 1961), p. 222.
4. Quoted in John W. Baldwin, *The Scholastic Culture of the Middle Ages, 1000–1300* (Lexington, Mass., 1971), p. 15.

Suggestions for Further Reading

On the revival of trade, see R. S. Lopez, *The Commercial Revolution of the Middle Ages, 950–1350* (Englewood Cliffs, N.J., 1971). Urban history is covered in D. Nicholas, *The Growth of the Medieval City: From Late Antiquity to the Early Fourteenth Century* (New York, 1997), and the classic work of H. Pirenne, *Medieval Cities* (Princeton, N.J., 1969). For a good collection of essays on urban culture, see B. A. Hanawalt and K. I. Reyerson, eds., *City and Spectacle in Medieval Europe* (Minneapolis, 1994). There is an extensive section on medieval cities in P. M. Hohenberg and L. H. Lees, *The Making of Urban Europe, 1000–1950* (Cambridge, Mass., 1985). A popular, readable study is J. Gies and F. Gies, *Life in a Medieval City* (New York, 1969). On women in the cities, see B. A. Hanawalt, ed., *Women and Work in Preindustrial Europe* (Bloomington, Ind., 1986).

The development of universities is covered in S. Ferruolo, *The Origin of the University* (Stanford, Calif., 1985); A. B. Cobban, *The Medieval Universities* (London, 1975); and the brief work by C. H. Haskins, *The Rise of Universities* (Ithaca, N.Y., 1957). Various aspects of the intellectual and literary developments of the High Middle Ages are examined in J. W. Baldwin, *The Scholastic Culture of the Middle Ages, 1000–1300* (Lexington, Mass., 1971); C. Morris, *The Discovery of the Individual, 1060–1200* (London, 1972); and H. Waddell, *The Wandering Scholars* (London, 1934). On Thomas Aquinas, see J. Weisheipl, *Friar Thomas d'Aquino: His Life, His Thought and Work* (New York, 1974).

For a good introduction to the art and architecture of the Middle Ages, see A. Shaver-Crandell, *The Middle Ages*, in the Cambridge Introduction to Art Series (Cambridge, 1982). A good introduction to Romanesque style is A. Petzold, *Romanesque Art* (New York, 1995). On the Gothic movement, see M. Camille, *Gothic Art: Glorious Visions* (New York, 1996), and C. Wilson, *The Gothic Cathedral* (London, 1990). Good books on the construction of Gothic cathedrals are J. Gimpel, *The Cathedral Builders* (New York, 1961), and A. Erlande-Brandenburg, *Cathedrals and Castles: Building in the Middle Ages* (New York, 1995).

There are numerous works on the different medieval states. On England, see F. Barlow, *The Feudal Kingdom of England, 1042–1216*, 3d ed. (New York, 1972); R. Frame, *The Political Development of the British Isles, 1100–1400* (Oxford, 1990); and M. T. Clanchy, *England and Its Rulers, 1066–1272* (New York, 1983). On France, see J. Dunbabin, *France in the Making, 843–1180* (Oxford, 1985), and E. M. Hallam, *Capetian France, 987–1328* (London, 1980), a well-done general account. On Spain, see G. Jackson, *The Making of Medieval Spain* (London, 1972); B. F. Reilly, *The Medieval Spains* (Cambridge, 1993); J. F. Powers, *A Society Organized for War* (Berkeley, 1988); and H. Dillard, *Daughters of the*

Reconquest (Cambridge, 1984). On Germany, see A. Haverkamp, *Medieval Germany* (Oxford, 1988); B. Arnold, *German Knighthood, 1050–1300* (Oxford, 1985); H. Fuhrmann, *Germany in the High Middle Ages, c. 1050–1250* (Cambridge, 1986), an excellent account; and B. Arnold, *Princes and Territories in Medieval Germany* (Cambridge, 1991). On Italy, see D. J. Herlihy, *Cities and Society in Medieval Italy* (London, 1980); J. K. Hyde, *Society and Politics in Medieval Italy* (London, 1973); and G. Tabacco, *The Struggle for Power in Medieval Italy* (New York, 1989). On eastern Europe and the Slavs, see N. Davies, *God's Playground: A History of Poland*, vol. 1 (Oxford, 1981); J. Fennell, *The Crisis of Medieval Russia, 1200–1304* (New York, 1983); and the books listed in Chapter 8.

For specialized studies in the political history of the thirteenth century, see J. C. Holt, *Magna Carta* (Cambridge, 1965); D. Abulafia, *Frederick II: A Medieval Emperor* (London, 1987); M. W. Labarge, *St. Louis: The Life of Louis IX of France* (London, 1968); and C. J. Halperin, *Russia and the Golden Horde: The Mongol Impact on Medieval Russian History* (Bloomington, Ind., 1987).

 For additional reading, go to InfoTrac College Edition, your online research library at http://web1.infotrac-college.com

Enter the search terms *Medieval Germany* using Key Terms.

Enter the search terms *Medieval England* using Key Terms.

Enter the search terms *Cities and Towns, Medieval* using the Subject Guide.

Enter the search terms *Middle Ages* using the Subject Guide.

The Late Middle Ages: Crisis and Disintegration in the Fourteenth Century

CHAPTER OUTLINE

- A Time of Troubles: Black Death and Social Crisis
- War and Political Instability
- The Decline of the Church
- Culture and Society in an Age of Adversity
- Conclusion

FOCUS QUESTIONS

- What was the Black Death, and what was its impact on European society?
- What major problems did European states face in the fourteenth century?
- How and why did the authority and prestige of the papacy decline in the fourteenth century?
- What were the major developments in art and literature in the fourteenth century?
- How did the adversities of the fourteenth century affect urban life?

THE HIGH MIDDLE AGES *of the eleventh, twelfth, and thirteenth centuries had been a period of great innovation, as evidenced by significant economic, social, political, religious, intellectual, and cultural changes. Yet by the end of the thirteenth century, certain tensions had begun to creep into European society. In the course of the next century, these tensions became a torrent of troubles. At mid-century, one of the most destructive natural disasters in history erupted—the Black Death. One contemporary observer named Henry Knighton, a canon of Saint Mary-of-the-Meadow Abbey in Leicester, England, was simply overwhelmed by the magnitude of the catastrophe. Knighton began his account of the great plague with these words: "In this year [1348] and in the following one there was a general mortality of people throughout the whole world." Few were left untouched; the plague struck even isolated monasteries: "At Montpellier,*

there remained out of a hundred and forty friars only seven." Knighton was also stunned by the economic and social consequences of the Black Death. Prices dropped: "And the price of everything was cheap, because of the fear of death; there were very few who took any care for their wealth, or for anything else." Meanwhile laborers were scarce, so their wages increased: "In the following autumn, one could not hire a reaper at a lower wage than eight pence with food, or a mower at less than twelve pence with food. Because of this, much grain rotted in the fields for lack of harvesting." So many people died that some towns were deserted and some villages disappeared altogether: "Many small villages and hamlets were completely deserted; there was not one house left in them, but all those who had lived in them were dead." Some people thought the end of the world was at hand.

Plague was not the only disaster in the fourteenth century, however. Signs of disintegration were everywhere: famine, economic depression, war, social upheaval, a rise in crime and violence, and a decline in the power of the universal Catholic church. Periods of disintegration, however, are often fertile grounds for change and new developments. Out of the dissolution of medieval civilization came a rebirth of culture that many historians have labeled the Renaissance.

◆ A Time of Troubles: Black Death and Social Crisis

Well into the thirteenth century, Europe had experienced good harvests and an expanding population. By the end of the thirteenth century, however, a period of disastrous changes had begun.

For one thing, there were noticeable changes in weather patterns as Europe entered a "little ice age." Shortened growing seasons and disastrous weather conditions, including heavy storms and constant rain, led to widespread famine and hunger. The great famine of 1315–1317 in northern Europe began an all-too-familiar pattern, as is evident in this scene described by a contemporary chronicler:

> We saw a larger number of both sexes, not only from nearby places but from as much as five leagues away, barefooted and maybe even, except for women, in a completely nude state, together with their priests coming in procession at the Church of the Holy Martyrs, their bones bulging

out, devoutly carrying bodies of saints and other relics to be adorned hoping to get relief.[1]

Some historians have pointed out that famine could have led to chronic malnutrition, which in turn contributed to increased infant mortality, lower birthrates, and higher susceptibility to disease because malnourished people are less able to resist infection. This, they argue, helps explain the virulence of the great plague known as the Black Death.

✳ *The Black Death*

The Black Death of the mid-fourteenth century was the most devastating natural disaster in European history, ravaging Europe's population and causing economic, social, political, and cultural upheaval. Contemporary chroniclers lamented how parents abandoned their children; one related the words: "Oh father, why have you abandoned me? . . . Mother, where have you gone?"[2] People were horrified by an evil force they could not understand and by the subsequent breakdown of all normal human relations.

The Black Death was all the more horrible because it was the first major epidemic disease to strike Europe since the seventh century, an absence that helps explain medieval Europe's remarkable population growth. This great plague originated in Central Asia. It was spread, it is believed, both by the Mongols as they expanded across Asia and by ecological changes that caused Central Asian rodents to move westward.

Bubonic plague, which was the most common and most important form of plague in the diffusion of the Black Death, was spread by black rats infested with fleas who were host to the deadly bacterium *Yersinia pestis*. Symptoms of bubonic plague include high fever, aching joints, swelling of the lymph nodes, and dark blotches caused by bleeding beneath the skin. Bubonic plague was actually the least toxic form of plague but nevertheless killed 50 to 60 percent of its victims. In pneumonic plague, the bacterial infection spread to the lungs, resulting in severe coughing, bloody sputum, and the relatively easy spread of the bacillus from human to human by coughing. Fortunately, because it was more deadly, this form of the plague occurred less frequently than bubonic plague.

The plague reached Europe in October 1347 when Genoese merchants brought it from Caffa, on the Black Sea, to the island of Sicily off the coast of

MAP 11.1   Spread of the Black Death.

southern Italy. It quickly spread to southern Italy and southern France and Spain by the end of 1347 (see Map 11.1). Usually, the diffusion of the Black Death followed commercial trade routes. In 1348, the plague spread through France and the Low Countries and into Germany. By the end of that year, it had moved to England, ravaging it in 1349. By the end of 1349, the plague had reached Scandinavia. Eastern Europe and Russia were affected by 1351, although mortality rates were never as high in eastern Europe as they were in western and central Europe.

Mortality figures for the Black Death were incredibly high. Italy was especially hard hit. Its crowded cities suffered losses of 50 to 60 percent (see the box on p. 219). In northern France, farming villages suffered mortality rates of 30 percent, and cities such as Rouen experienced losses as high as 40 percent. In England and Germany, entire villages disappeared. In Germany, of approximately 170,000 inhabited locations, only 130,000 were left by the end of the fourteenth century.

It has been estimated that the European population declined by 25 to 50 percent between 1347 and 1351. If we accept the recent scholarly assessment of a European population of 75 million in the early fourteenth century, this means a death toll of 19 to 38 million people in four years. And the plague did not end in 1351. There were major outbreaks again in 1361–1362 and 1369 and then regular recurrences during the remainder of the fourteenth century and all of the fifteenth century. The European population did not start to recover until the end of the fifteenth century; not until the mid-sixteenth century did Europe return to thirteenth-century population levels.

MASS BURIAL OF PLAGUE VICTIMS. The Black Death spread to northern Europe by the end of 1348. Shown here is a mass burial of victims of the plague in Tournai, located in modern Belgium. As is evident in the illustration, at this stage of the plague, there was still time to make coffins for the victims' burial. Later, as the plague intensified, the dead were thrown into open pits.

LIFE AND DEATH: REACTIONS TO THE PLAGUE

The attempt of contemporaries to explain the Black Death and mitigate its harshness led to extreme sorts of behavior. To many, the plague had either been sent by God as a punishment for humans' sins or been caused by the evil one, the devil. Some resorted to extreme asceticism to cleanse themselves of sin and gain God's forgiveness. Such was the flagellant movement, which became popular in 1348, especially in Germany. Groups of flagellants, both men and women, wandered from town to town, flogging each other with whips to win the forgiveness of a God whom they felt had sent the plague to punish humans for their sinful ways. One contemporary chronicler described a flagellant procession:

> The penitents went about, coming first out of Germany. They were men who did public penance and scourged themselves with whips of hard knotted leather with little iron spikes. Some made themselves bleed very badly between the shoulder blades and some foolish women had cloths ready to catch the blood and smear it on their eyes, saying it was miraculous blood. While they were doing penance, they sang very mournful songs about the nativity and the passion of Our Lord. The object of this penance was to put a stop to the mortality, for in that time . . . at least a third of all the people in the world died.[3]

The flagellants attracted attention and created mass hysteria wherever they went. The Catholic church, however, became alarmed when flagellant groups began to kill Jews and attack the clergy who opposed them. Pope Clement VI condemned the flagellants in October 1349 and urged the public authorities to crush them. By the end of 1350, most of the flagellant movements had been destroyed.

An outbreak of virulent anti-Semitism also accompanied the Black Death. Jews were accused of causing the plague by poisoning town wells. Although Jews were persecuted in Spain, the worst pogroms against this helpless minority were carried out in Germany; more than sixty major Jewish communities in Germany had been exterminated by 1351. Many Jews fled eastward to Russia and especially to Poland, where the king offered them protection. Eastern Europe became home to large Jewish communities.

The prevalence of death because of the plague and its recurrences affected people in profound ways. Some survivors apparently came to treat life as something cheap and passing. Violence and violent death appeared to be more common after the plague than before. Postplague Europe also demonstrated a morbid preoccupation with death. In their sermons, priests reminded parishioners that each night's sleep might be their last. Tombstones were decorated with macabre scenes of naked corpses in various stages of decomposition with snakes entwined in their bones and their innards filled with worms.

Economic Dislocation and Social Upheaval

The population collapse of the fourteenth century had dire economic and social consequences. Economic dislocation was accompanied by social upheaval. Both peasants and noble landlords were affected by the demographic crisis of the fourteenth century. Most noticeably, Europe experienced a serious labor shortage, which caused a dramatic rise in the price of labor. At Cuxham manor in England, for example, a farm

The Black Death

The Black Death was the most terrifying natural calamity of the Middle Ages. It has been estimated that 25 to 50 percent of the population died as the plague spread throughout Europe between 1347 and 1351. This contemporary description of the great plague in Florence is taken from the preface to the Decameron *by the fourteenth-century Italian writer Giovanni Boccaccio.*

❋ *Giovanni Boccaccio,* **Decameron**

In the year of Our Lord 1348 the deadly plague broke out in the great city of Florence, most beautiful of Italian cities. Whether through the operation of the heavenly bodies or because of our own iniquities which the just wrath of God sought to correct, the plague had arisen in the East some years before, causing the death of countless human beings. It spread without stop from one place to another, until, unfortunately, it swept over the West. Neither knowledge nor human foresight availed against it, though the city was cleansed of much filth by chosen officers in charge and sick persons were forbidden to enter it, while advice was broadcast for the preservation of health. Nor did humble supplications serve. Not once but many times they were ordained in the form of processions and other ways for the propitiation of God by the faithful, but, in spite of everything, toward the spring of the year the plague began to show its ravages. . . .

It did not manifest itself as in the East, where if a man bled at the nose he had certain warning of inevitable death. At the onset of the disease both men and women were afflicted by a sort of swelling in the groin or under the armpits which sometimes attained the size of a common apple or egg. Some of these swellings were larger and some smaller, and were commonly called boils. From these two starting points the boils began in a little while to spread and appear generally all over the body. Afterwards, the manifestation of the disease changed into black or livid spots on the arms, thighs, and the whole person. In many these blotches were large and far apart, in others small and closely clustered. Like the boils, which had been and continued to be a certain indication of coming death, these blotches had the same meaning for everyone on whom they appeared.

Neither the advice of physicians nor the virtue of any medicine seemed to help or avail in the cure of these diseases. Indeed, . . . not only did few recover, but on the contrary almost everyone died within three days of the appearance of the signs—some sooner, some later. . . . The virulence of the plague was all the greater in that it was communicated by the sick to the well by contact, not unlike fire when dry or fatty things are brought near it. But the evil was still worse. Not only did conversation and familiarity with the diseased spread the malady and even cause death, but the mere touch of the clothes or any other object the sick had touched or used, seemed to spread the pestilence. . . .

More wretched still were the circumstances of the common people and, for a great part, of the middle class, for, confined to their homes either by hope of safety or by poverty, and restricted to their own sections, they fell sick daily by thousands. There, devoid of help or care, they died almost without redemption. A great many breathed their last in the public streets, day and night; a large number perished in their homes, and it was only by the stench of their decaying bodies that they proclaimed their death to their neighbors. Everywhere the city was teeming with corpses. . . .

So many bodies were brought to the churches every day that the consecrated ground did not suffice to hold them, particularly according to the ancient custom of giving each corpse its individual place. Huge trenches were dug in the crowded churchyards and the new dead were piled in them, layer upon layer, like merchandise in the hold of a ship. A little earth covered the corpses of each row, and the procedure continued until the trench was filled to the top.

laborer who had received two shillings a week in 1347 was paid seven in 1349 and almost eleven by 1350. At the same time, the decline in population depressed the demand for agricultural produce, resulting in falling prices for output. Because landlords were having to pay more for labor at the same time that their income from rents was declining, they began to experience considerable adversity and lower standards of living. In England, aristocratic incomes dropped more than 20 percent between 1347 and 1353.

Landed aristocrats responded to adversity by seeking to lower the wage rate. The English Parliament passed the Statute of Laborers (1351), which attempted to limit wages to preplague levels and forbid the mobility of peasants as well. Although such laws proved largely unworkable, they did keep wages from rising as high as they might have in a free market. Overall, the position of noble landlords continued to deteriorate during the late fourteenth and early fifteenth centuries. At the same time, the position of peasants improved, though not uniformly throughout Europe.

The decline in the number of peasants after the Black Death accelerated the process of converting labor services to rents, freeing peasants from the obligations of servile tenure and weakening the system of manorialism. But there were limits to how much the peasants could advance. They faced the same economic hurdles as the lords while the latter also attempted to impose wage restrictions and reinstate old forms of labor service. New governmental taxes also hurt. Peasant complaints became widespread and soon gave rise to rural revolts.

❧ PEASANT REVOLTS

In 1358, a peasant revolt, known as the *Jacquerie*, broke out in northern France. The destruction of normal order by the Black Death and the subsequent economic dislocation were important factors in causing the revolt, but the ravages created by the Hundred Years' War (see "War and Political Instability" later in this chapter) also affected the French peasantry. Both the French and English forces followed a deliberate policy of laying waste to peasants' lands while bands of mercenaries lived off the land by taking peasants' produce as well.

Peasant anger was also exacerbated by growing class tensions. Landed nobles were eager to hold on to their privileged positions and felt increasingly threatened in the new postplague world of higher wages and lower prices. Many aristocrats looked on peasants with utter contempt. One French aristocrat said, "Should peasants eat meat? Rather should they chew grass on the heath with the horned cattle and go naked on all fours." The peasants reciprocated this contempt for their so-called social superiors.

The outburst of peasant anger led to savage confrontations. Castles were burned and nobles murdered. Such atrocities did not go unanswered, however. The *Jacquerie* failed when the privileged classes closed ranks, savagely massacred the rebels, and ended the revolt.

The English Peasants' Revolt of 1381 was the most prominent of all. It was a product not of desperation but of rising expectations. After the Black Death, the condition of the English peasants had improved as they enjoyed greater freedom and higher wages or lower rents. Aristocratic landlords had fought back with legislation to depress wages and an attempt

PEASANT REBELLION. The fourteenth century witnessed a number of revolts of the peasantry against noble landowners. Although the revolts were initially successful, they were soon crushed. This illustration shows nobles massacring the rebels in the French *Jacquerie*.

to reimpose old feudal dues. The most immediate cause of the revolt, however, was the monarchy's attempt to raise revenues by imposing a poll tax or a flat charge on each adult member of the population. Peasants in eastern England, the wealthiest part of the country, refused to pay the tax and expelled the collectors forcibly from their villages.

This action produced a widespread rebellion of both peasants and townspeople led by a well-to-do peasant called Wat Tyler and a preacher named John Ball. The latter preached an effective message against the noble class, as recounted by the chronicler Froissart:

> Good people, things cannot go right in England and never will, until goods are held in common and there are no more peasants and gentlefolk, but we are all one and the same. In what way are those whom we call lords greater masters than ourselves? How have they deserved it? Why do they hold us in bondage? If we all spring from a single father and mother, Adam and Eve, how can they claim or prove that they are lords more than us, except by making us produce and grow the wealth which they spend.[4]

The movement developed a famous jingle based on Ball's preaching: "When Adam delved and Eve span, who was then a gentleman?"

The revolt was initially successful as the rebels burned down the manor houses of aristocrats, lawyers, and government officials and murdered several important officials, including the archbishop of Canterbury. After the peasants marched on London, the young King Richard II (1377–1399) promised to accept the rebels' demands if they returned to their homes. They accepted the king's word and dispersed, but the king reneged and, with the assistance of the aristocrats, arrested hundreds of the rebels. The poll tax was eliminated, however.

✸ REVOLTS IN THE CITIES

Revolts also erupted in the cities. Commercial and industrial activity suffered almost immediately from the Black Death. An oversupply of goods and an enormous drop in demand led to a decline in trade after 1350. Some industries suffered greatly. Florence's woolen industry, one of the giants, produced 70,000 to 80,000 pieces of cloth in 1338; in 1378, it was yielding only 24,000 pieces. Bourgeois merchants and manufacturers responded to a decline in trade and production by attempts to restrict competition and resist the demands of the lower classes.

In urban areas, where capitalist industrialists paid low wages and managed to prevent workers from forming organizations to help themselves, industrial revolts broke out throughout Europe. Ghent experienced one in 1381, Rouen in 1382. Most famous was the revolt of the *ciompi* in Florence in 1378. The *ciompi* were wool workers in Florence's most prominent industry. In the 1370s, the woolen industry was depressed, and wool workers saw their real wages decline when the coinage in which they were paid was debased. Their revolt won them some concessions from the municipal government, including the right to form guilds and be represented in the government. But their newly won rights were short-lived. A counterrevolution by government authorities brought an end to *ciompi* participation in the government by 1382.

Although the peasant and urban revolts sometimes resulted in short-term gains for the participants, the uprisings were relatively easily crushed and their gains quickly lost. Accustomed to ruling, the established classes easily combined and quashed dissent. Nevertheless, the rural and urban revolts of the fourteenth century ushered in an age of social conflict that characterized much of later European history.

◆ War and Political Instability

Famine, plague, economic turmoil, social upheaval, and violence were not the only problems of the fourteenth century. War and political instability must also be added to the list. And of all the struggles of the period, the most famous and the most violent was the Hundred Years' War.

✸ *The Hundred Years' War*

In the thirteenth century, the English king still held one small possession in France, known as the duchy of Gascony. As duke of Gascony, the English king pledged loyalty as a vassal to the French king. But when King Philip VI of France seized Gascony in 1337, the duke of Gascony—King Edward III of England—declared war on Philip. The attack on Gascony was a convenient excuse; Edward had already laid claim to the throne of France after the senior branch of the Capetian dynasty had become extinct in 1328 and a cousin of the Capetians, the duke of Valois, had become king as Philip VI.

The war began in a burst of knightly enthusiasm. Trained to be warriors, knights viewed the clash of battle as the ultimate opportunity to demonstrate their fighting abilities. But this struggle would change the nature of warfare, for as it dragged on, the outcomes of battles were increasingly determined not by knights but by peasant foot soldiers. The French army of 1337, with its heavily armed noble cavalry, resembled its twelfth- and thirteenth-century forebears. Considering themselves the fighting elite, the noble cavalry looked with contempt on foot soldiers and crossbowmen because they were peasants or other social inferiors. The English army, however, had evolved differently and had included peasants as paid foot soldiers. Armed with pikes, many of these foot soldiers had also adopted the longbow, invented by the Welsh. The longbow had greater striking power, longer range, and more rapid speed of fire than the crossbow. Although the English also used heavily armed cavalry, they relied even more on large numbers of foot soldiers.

Edward III's early campaigns in France were indecisive and achieved little. In 1346, Edward was forced to fight at Crécy, just south of Flanders. The larger French army followed no battle plan but simply

JOAN OF ARC. Pictured here in a suit of armor, Joan of Arc is holding aloft a banner that shows Jesus and two angels. This portrait dates from the late fifteenth century; there are no portraits of Joan made from life.

attacked the English lines in a disorderly fashion. The arrows of the English archers decimated the French cavalry. As the chronicler Froissart described it, "The English continued to shoot into the thickest part of the crowd, wasting none of their arrows. They impaled or wounded horses and riders, who fell to the ground in great distress, unable to get up again without the help of several men."[5] It was a stunning victory for the English.

The Battle of Crécy was not decisive, however. The English simply did not possess the resources to subjugate all France, and hostilities continued intermittently for another fifty years until a twenty-year truce was negotiated in 1396, seemingly bringing an end to this protracted series of struggles between the French and English. However, the English king, Henry V (1413–1422), renewed the war in 1415. At the Battle of Agincourt (1415), the attempt of the heavy, armor-plated French knights to attack across a field turned to mud by heavy rain led to a disastrous French defeat and the death of fifteen hundred French nobles. Henry went on to reconquer Normandy and forge an alliance with the duke of Burgundy, making the English masters of northern France (see Map 11.2).

The seemingly hopeless French cause fell into the hands of Charles the dauphin (heir to the throne), who governed the southern two-thirds of French lands from Bourges. Charles was weak and timid and was unable to rally the French against the English, who in 1428 had turned south and were besieging the city of Orléans to gain access to the valley of the Loire. The French monarch was saved, quite unexpectedly, by a French peasant woman.

Joan of Arc was born in 1412 to well-to-do peasants in the village of Domrémy in Champagne. Deeply religious, Joan experienced visions and came to believe that her favorite saints had commanded her to free France and have the dauphin crowned king. In February 1429, Joan made her way to the dauphin's court, where her sincerity and simplicity persuaded Charles to allow her to accompany a French army to Orléans. Apparently inspired by the faith of the peasant girl, the French armies found new confidence in themselves and liberated Orléans, changing the course of the war. Within a few weeks, the entire Loire valley had been freed of the English. Joan had brought the war to a decisive turning point.

But she did not live to see the war concluded. Captured by the Burgundian allies of the English in 1430, Joan was turned over first to the English

C H R O N O L O G Y

The Hundred Years' War

Outbreak of hostilities	1337
Battle of Crécy	1346
Truce	1396
War renewed by Henry V (1413–1422)	1415
Battle of Agincourt	1415
French recovery under Joan of Arc	1429–1431
End of the war	1453

and then to the Inquisition on charges of witchcraft (see the box on p. 224). In the fifteenth century, spiritual visions were thought to be inspired either by God or the devil. Because Joan dressed in men's clothing, it was relatively easy to convince others that she was in league with the "prince of darkness." She was condemned to death as a heretic and burned at the stake in 1431. To the end, as the flames rose up around her, she declared "that her voices came from God and had not deceived her." Twenty-five years later, a new ecclesiastical court exonerated her of these charges, and five centuries later, in 1920, she was made

MAP 11.2   The Hundred Years' War.

The Trial of Joan of Arc

Feared by the English and Burgundians, Joan of Arc was put on trial on charges of witchcraft and heresy after her capture. She was condemned for heresy and burned at the stake on May 30, 1431. This excerpt is taken from the records of Joan's trial, which presented a dramatic confrontation between the judges, trained in the complexities of legal questioning, and a nineteen-year-old woman who relied only on the "voices" of saints who gave her advice. In this selection, Joan describes what these voices told her to do.

❋ The Trial of Joan of Arc

Afterward, she declared that at the age of thirteen she had a voice from God to help her and guide her. And the first time she was much afraid. And this voice came toward noon, in summer, in her father's garden. . . . She heard the voice on her right, in the direction of the church; and she seldom heard it without a light. This light came from the same side as the voice, and generally there was a great light. . . .

Asked what instruction this voice gave her for the salvation of her soul: she said it taught her to be good and to go to church often. . . . She said that the voice told her to come, and she could no longer stay where she was; and the voice told her again that she should raise the siege of the city of Orléans. She said moreover that the voice told her that she, Joan, should go to Robert de Baudricourt, in the town of Vaucouleurs of which he was captain, and he would provide an escort for her. And the said Joan answered that she was a poor maid, knowing nothing of riding or fighting. She said she went to an uncle of hers, and told him she wanted to stay with him for some time; and she stayed there about eight days. And she told her uncle she must go to the said town of Vaucouleurs, and so her uncle took her.

Then she said that when she reached Vaucouleurs she easily recognized Robert de Baudricourt, although she had never seen him before; and she knew him through her voice, for the voice had told her it was he. . . . The said Robert twice refused to hear her and repulsed her; the third time he listened to her and gave her an escort. And the voice had told her that it would be so.

---

a saint of the Roman Catholic church. Joan of Arc's accomplishments proved decisive. Although the war dragged on for another two decades, defeats of English armies in Normandy and Aquitaine led to French victory by 1453.

❋ Political Instability

The fourteenth century was a period of adversity for the internal political stability of European governments. Although government bureaucracies grew ever larger, at the same time the question of who should control the bureaucracies led to internal conflict and instability. Like the lord and serf relationship, the lord and vassal relationship based on land and military service was being replaced by a contract based on money. Especially after the Black Death, money payments called scutage were increasingly substituted for military service. Monarchs welcomed this development because they could now hire professional soldiers, who tended to be more reliable anyway. As lord and vassal relationships became less personal and less important, new relationships based on political advantage began to be formed, creating new avenues for political influence—and for corruption as well. Especially noticeable, as the landed aristocrats suffered declining rents and social uncertainties with the new relationships, was the formation of factions of nobles who looked for opportunities to advance their power and wealth at the expense of other noble factions and of their monarchs. Others went to the royal courts, offering to serve the kings.

The kings had their own problems, however. By the mid-fifteenth century, reigning monarchs in many European countries were not the direct descendants of those ruling in 1300. The founders of these new dynasties had to struggle for position as factions of nobles vied to gain material advantages for themselves. At the end of the fourteenth century and beginning of the fifteenth, there were two claimants to the throne of France, and two aristocratic factions fought for control of England; in Germany, three princes struggled to be recognized as emperor.

Fourteenth-century monarchs, whether of old or new dynasties, faced financial problems as well.

The shift to the use of mercenary soldiers left monarchs perennially short of cash. Traditional revenues, especially rents from property, increasingly proved insufficient to meet their needs. Monarchs attempted to generate new sources of revenues, especially through taxes, which often meant going through parliaments. This opened the door for parliamentary bodies to gain more power by asking for favors first. Although unsuccessful in most cases, the role of parliaments simply added another element of uncertainty and confusion to fourteenth-century politics. Turning now to a survey of western and central European states, we can see how these disruptive factors worked.

✳ *Western Europe: England and France*

In the fourteenth century, the lengthy reign of Edward III (1327–1377) was an important one for the evolution of English political institutions. Parliament increased in prominence and developed its basic structure and functions during Edward's reign. Due to his constant need for money to fight the Hundred Years' War, Edward came to rely on Parliament to levy new taxes. In return for regular grants, Edward made several concessions, including a commitment to levy no direct tax without Parliament's consent and to allow committees of Parliament to examine the government accounts to ensure that the money was being spent properly. By the end of Edward's reign, Parliament had become an important component of the English governmental system.

During this same period, Parliament began to assume the organizational structure it has retained to this day. The Great Council of barons became the House of Lords and evolved into a body composed of the chief bishops and abbots of the realm and aristocratic peers whose position in Parliament was hereditary. The representatives of the shires and boroughs, who were considered less important than the lay and ecclesiastical lords, held collective meetings to decide policy and soon came to be regarded as the House of Commons. Together, the House of Lords and the House of Commons constituted Parliament. Although the House of Commons did little beyond approving measures proposed by the Lords, during Edward's reign the Commons did begin the practice of drawing up petitions, which, if accepted by the Lords and king, became law.

After Edward III's death, England began to experience the internal instability of aristocratic factionalism that was racking other European countries. After Richard II was deposed in 1399 and soon killed, the leader of the revolt of the barons, Henry of Lancaster, was made king. Although Henry IV (1399–1413) proved to be a competent ruler, factions of nobles soon rose to take advantage of the new situation. England would soon be embroiled in a devastating series of civil wars known as the War of the Roses.

The Hundred Years' War left France prostrate. Depopulation, desolate farmlands, ruined commerce, and independent and unruly nobles made it difficult

RICHARD II. By aspiring to absolute power, Richard II caused a baronial revolt that led to his deposition as king of England. Richard commissioned this life-size portrait of himself in the early 1390s to be placed in Westminster Abbey. The artist's use of realistic details in the portrayal of the face ensured a genuine likeness of the king.

for the kings to assert their authority throughout the fourteenth century. The insanity of King Charles VI (1380–1422) especially opened the door to rival factions of French nobles aspiring to power and wealth. The dukes of Burgundy and Orléans competed to control Charles and the French monarchy. Their struggles created chaos for the French government and the French people. Many nobles supported the Orléanist faction; Paris and other towns favored the Burgundians. By the beginning of the fifteenth century, France seemed hopelessly mired in civil war. When the English renewed the Hundred Years' War in 1415, the Burgundians supported the English cause and the English monarch's claim to the throne of France.

❈ The German Monarchy

England and France had developed strong national monarchies in the High Middle Ages. By the end of the fourteenth century, they seemed in danger of disintegrating due to dynastic problems and the pressures generated by the Hundred Years' War. In contrast, the Holy Roman Empire, whose core consisted of the lands of Germany, had already begun to fall apart in the High Middle Ages. Northern Italy, which the German emperors had tried to include in their medieval empire, had been free from any real imperial control since the end of the Hohenstaufen dynasty in the thirteenth century. In Germany itself, the failure of the Hohenstaufens ended any chance of centralized monarchical authority, and Germany became a land of hundreds of virtually independent states. These varied in size and power and included princely states, such as the duchies of Bavaria and Saxony; free imperial city-states (self-governing cities directly under the control of the Holy Roman Emperor rather than a German territorial prince), such as Nuremberg; modest territories of petty imperial knights; and ecclesiastical states, such as the archbishopric of Cologne. In the ecclesiastical states, a high church official, such as a bishop, archbishop, or abbot, served in a dual capacity as an administrative official of the Catholic church and secular lord over the territories of the state. Although all of the rulers of these different states had some obligations to the German king and Holy Roman Emperor, more and more they acted independently.

Because of its unique pattern of development in the High Middle Ages, the German monarchy had become established on an elective rather than hered-itary basis. This principle of election was standardized in 1356 by the Golden Bull issued by Emperor Charles IV (1346–1378). This document stated that four lay princes and three ecclesiastical rulers would serve as electors with the legal power to elect the "king of the Romans and future emperor, to be ruler of the world and of the Christian people." "King of the Romans" was the official title of the German king; after his imperial coronation, he would also have the title of emperor.

In the fourteenth century, the electoral principle further ensured that kings of Germany were generally weak. Their ability to exercise effective power depended on the extent of their own family possessions. At the beginning of the fifteenth century, three emperors claimed the throne. Although the dispute was quickly settled, Germany entered the fifteenth century in a condition that verged on anarchy. Princes fought princes and leagues of cities. The emperors were virtually powerless to control any of them.

❈ The States of Italy

By the fourteenth century, Italy, too, had failed to develop a centralized monarchical state. Papal opposition to the rule of the Hohenstaufen emperors in the thirteenth century had virtually guaranteed that. Moreover, southern Italy was divided into the kingdom of Naples, ruled by the house of Anjou, and Sicily, whose kings came from the Spanish house of Aragon. The center of the peninsula remained under the rather shaky control of the papacy. Lack of centralized authority had enabled numerous city-states in northern and central Italy to remain independent of any political authority.

In the course of the fourteenth century, two general tendencies can be discerned in Italy: the replacement of republican governments by tyrants and the expansion of the larger city-states at the expense of the less powerful ones. Nearly all the cities of northern Italy began their existence as free communes with republican governments. But in the fourteenth century, intense internal strife led city-states to resort to temporary expedients, allowing rule by one man with dictatorial powers. Limited rule, however, soon became long-term despotism, as tyrants proved willing to use force to maintain power. Eventually, such tyrants tried to legitimize their power by purchasing titles from the emperor (still nominally ruler of northern Italy as Holy Roman Emperor). In this fashion, the

Visconti became the dukes of Milan and the d'Este the dukes of Ferrara.

The other change of great significance was the development of larger, regional entities as the larger states expanded at the expense of the smaller ones. By the end of the fourteenth century and the beginning of the fifteenth, three major states came to dominate northern Italy. In the fertile Po valley, where the chief trade routes from Italian coastal cities to the Alpine passes crossed, Milan was one of the richest city-states in Italy. Politically, it was also one of the most agitated until members of the Visconti family established themselves as hereditary dukes of Milan and extended their power over all of Lombardy. The republic of Florence dominated the region of Tuscany. In the course of the fourteenth century, a small but wealthy merchant oligarchy established control of the Florentine government, led the Florentines in a series of successful wars against their neighbors, and established Florence as a major territorial state in northern Italy. The other major northern Italian state was the maritime republic of Venice, which had grown rich from commercial activity throughout the eastern Mediterranean and into northern Europe. Venice remained an extremely stable political entity governed by a small oligarchy of merchant-aristocrats who had become extremely wealthy through their trading activities. Venice's commercial empire brought in enormous revenues and gave it the status of an international power. At the end of the fourteenth century, Venice embarked on the conquest of a territorial state in northern Italy to protect its food supply and its overland trade routes.

◆ The Decline of the Church

The papacy of the Roman Catholic church reached the height of its power in the thirteenth century. Theories of papal supremacy included a doctrine of "fullness of power" as the spiritual head of Christendom and claims to universal temporal authority over all secular rulers. But the growing secular monarchies of Europe presented a challenge to papal claims of temporal supremacy that led the papacy into a conflict with these territorial states that it was unable to win. Papal defeat in turn led to other crises that brought into question and undermined not only the pope's temporal authority over all Christendom but his spiritual authority as well.

✳ Boniface VIII and the Conflict with the State

The struggle between the papacy and the secular monarchies began during the pontificate of Pope Boniface VIII (1294–1303). One major issue appeared to be at stake between the pope and King Philip IV (1285–1314) of France. Looking for a source of new revenues, Philip expressed the right to tax the French clergy. Boniface VIII claimed that the clergy of any state could not pay taxes to their secular ruler without

POPE BONIFACE VIII. The conflict between church and state in the Middle Ages reached its height in the struggle between Pope Boniface VIII and King Philip IV of France. This fourteenth-century miniature depicts Boniface VIII presiding over a gathering of cardinals.

Boniface VIII's Defense of Papal Supremacy

One of the more remarkable documents of the fourteenth century was the exaggerated statement of papal supremacy issued by Pope Boniface VIII in 1302 in the heat of his conflict with the French king Philip IV. Ironically, this strongest statement ever made of papal supremacy was issued at a time when the rising power of the secular monarchies made it increasingly difficult for the premises to be accepted. Not long after issuing it, Boniface was taken prisoner by the French. Although freed by his fellow Italians, the humiliation of his defeat led to his death a short time later.

❖ *Pope Boniface VIII,* Unam Sanctam

We are compelled, our faith urging us, to believe and to hold—and we do firmly believe and simply confess—that there is one holy catholic and apostolic church, outside of which there is neither salvation nor remission of sins. . . . In this church there is one Lord, one faith and one baptism. . . . Therefore, of this one and only church there is one body and one head . . . Christ, namely, and the vicar of Christ, St. Peter, and the successor of Peter. For the Lord himself said to Peter, feed my sheep. . . .

We are told by the word of the gospel that in this His fold there are two swords—a spiritual, namely, and a temporal. . . . Both swords, the spiritual and the material, therefore, are in the power of the church; the one, indeed, to be wielded for the church, the other by the church; the one by the hand of the priest, the other by the hand of kings and knights, but at the will and sufferance of the priest. One sword, moreover, ought to be under the other, and the temporal authority to be subjected to the spiritual. . . .

Therefore if the earthly power err it shall be judged by the spiritual power; but if the lesser spiritual power err, by the greater. But if the greatest, it can be judged by God alone, not by man, the apostle bearing witness. A spiritual man judges all things, but he himself is judged by no one. This authority, moreover, even though it is given to man and exercised through man, is not human but rather divine, being given by divine lips to Peter and founded on a rock for him and his successors through Christ himself whom he has confessed; the Lord himself saying to Peter: "Whatsoever you shall bind, etc." Whoever, therefore, resists this power thus ordained by God, resists the ordination of God. . . .

Indeed, we declare, announce and define, that it is altogether necessary to salvation for every human creature to be subject to the Roman pontiff.

---

the pope's consent. Underlying this issue, however, was a basic conflict between the claims of the papacy to universal authority over both church and state, which necessitated complete control over the clergy, and the claims of the king that all subjects, including the clergy, were under the jurisdiction of the crown and subject to the king's authority on matters of taxation and justice. In short, the fundamental issue was the universal sovereignty of the papacy versus the royal sovereignty of the monarch.

Boniface VIII asserted his position in a series of papal bulls or letters, the most important of which was *Unam Sanctam,* issued in 1302. It was the strongest statement ever made by a pope on the supremacy of the spiritual authority over the temporal authority (see the box above). When it became apparent that the pope had decided to act on his principles by excommunicating Philip IV of France, the latter sent a small contingent of French forces to capture Boniface and bring him back to France for trial. The pope was captured in Anagni, although Italian nobles from the surrounding countryside soon rescued him. The shock of this experience, however, soon led to the pope's death. Philip's strong-arm tactics had produced a clear victory for the national monarchy over the papacy, since no later pope dared renew the extravagant claims of Boniface VIII. To ensure his position and avoid any future papal threat, Philip IV brought enough pressure on the college of cardinals to achieve the election of a Frenchman, Clement V (1305–1314), as pope. Using the excuse of turbulence in the city of Rome, the new pope took up residence in Avignon, on the east bank of the Rhone River. Although Avignon was located in the Holy Roman Empire and was not a French possession, it lay just across the river from the possessions of King Philip IV and was French in culture.

✤ The Papacy at Avignon (1305–1378)

The residency of the popes in Avignon for almost three-quarters of the fourteenth century led to a decline in papal prestige and growing antipapal sentiment. The city of Rome was the traditional capital of the universal church. The pope was the bishop of Rome, and his position was based on being the successor to the apostle Peter, the first bishop of Rome. It was unseemly that the head of the Catholic church should reside outside of Rome. In the 1330s, the popes began to construct a stately palace in Avignon, a clear indication that they intended to stay for some time.

Other factors also led to a decline in papal prestige during the Avignonese residency. Many contemporaries believed that the popes at Avignon were captives of the French monarchy. Although questionable, since Avignon did not belong to the French monarchy, it was easy to believe in view of Avignon's proximity to French lands. Moreover, during the seventy-three years of the Avignonese papacy, of the 134 new cardinals created by the popes, 113 of them were French. At the same time, the popes attempted to find new sources of revenue to compensate for their loss of revenue from the Papal States and began to impose new taxes on the clergy. Furthermore, the splendor in which the pope and cardinals were living in Avignon led to a highly vocal criticism of both clergy and papacy in the fourteenth century. Avignon had become a powerful symbol of abuses within the church, and many people began to call for the pope's return to Rome. One of the most prominent calls came from Catherine of Siena (c. 1347–1380), whose saintly demeanor and claims of visions from God led the city of Florence to send her on a mission to Pope Gregory XI (1370–1378) in Avignon. She told the pope, "Because God has given you authority and because you have accepted it, you ought to use your virtue and power; if you do not wish to use it, it might be better for you to resign what you have accepted; it would give more honor to God and health to your soul."[6]

✤ The Great Schism

Catherine of Siena's admonition seemed to be heeded in 1377, when at long last Pope Gregory XI, perceiving the disastrous decline in papal prestige, returned to Rome. He died soon afterward, however, in the spring of 1378. When the college of cardinals met in conclave to elect a new pope, the citizens of Rome, fearful that the French majority would choose another Frenchman who would return the papacy to Avignon, threatened that the cardinals would not leave Rome alive unless a Roman or an Italian were elected pope. Indeed, the guards of the conclave warned the cardinals that they "ran the risk of being torn in pieces" if they did not choose an Italian. Wisely, the terrified cardinals duly elected the Italian archbishop of Bari as Pope Urban VI (1378–1389). Five months later, a group of dissenting cardinals—the French ones—declared Urban's election null and void and chose one of their number, a Frenchman, who took the title of Clement VII and promptly returned to Avignon. Because Urban remained in Rome, there were now two popes, initiating what has been called the Great Schism of the church. Europe's loyalties became divided: France, Spain, Scotland, and southern Italy supported Clement, while England, Germany, Scandinavia, and most of Italy supported Urban. These divisions generally followed political lines. Because the French supported the Avignonese, so did their allies; their enemies, particularly England and its allies, supported the Roman pope. The need for political support caused both popes to subordinate their policies to the policies of these states.

The Great Schism badly damaged the faith of Christian believers. The pope was widely believed to be the leader of Christendom and, as Boniface VIII had pointed out, held the keys to the kingdom of heaven. Since both lines of popes denounced the other as the Antichrist, such a spectacle could not help but undermine the institution that had become the very foundation of the church. The Great Schism introduced uncertainty into the daily lives of ordinary Christians.

As dissatisfaction with the papacy grew, so also did the calls for a revolutionary approach to solving the church's institutional problems. Final authority in spiritual matters must reside not with the popes, reformers claimed, but with a general church council representing all members. The Great Schism led large numbers of serious churchmen to take up the theory of conciliarism in the belief that only a general council of the church could end the schism and bring reform to the church in its "head and members." In desperation, a group of cardinals from both lines of popes finally heeded these theoretical formulations and convened a general council. This Council of Pisa, which met in 1409, deposed the two popes and elected a new one. The council's action proved disastrous when the two deposed popes refused to step down. There were now three popes, and the church seemed more hopelessly divided than ever.

Leadership in convening a new council now passed to the Holy Roman Emperor, Sigismund. As a result of his efforts, a new ecumenical church council met at Constance from 1414 to 1418. It had three major objectives: to end the schism, to eradicate heresy, and to reform the church in "head and members." The ending of the schism proved to be the Council of Constance's easiest task. After the three competing popes either resigned or were deposed, a new conclave elected a Roman cardinal, a member of a prominent Roman family, as Pope Martin V (1417–1431). The council was much less successful in dealing with the problems of heresy and reform.

◆ Culture and Society in an Age of Adversity

In the midst of disaster, the fourteenth century proved creative in its own way. The rapid growth of vernacular literature and new inventions made an impact on European life at the same time that the effects of plague were felt in many areas of medieval towns and cities.

✳ The Development of Vernacular Literature

Although Latin remained the language of the church liturgy and the official documents of both church and state, the fourteenth century witnessed a surge in literature written in vernacular languages, especially in Italy. In the fourteenth and fifteenth centuries, the works of Dante, Chaucer, and Christine de Pizan helped make vernacular literature more popular. By the late fifteenth century, vernacular literary forms had become so celebrated that they could compete with and would eventually replace works in Latin.

Dante (1265–1321) came from an old Florentine noble family that had fallen on hard times. His masterpiece in the Italian vernacular was the *Divine Comedy*, written between 1313 and 1321. Cast in a typical medieval framework, the *Divine Comedy* is basically the story of the soul's progression to salvation, a fundamental medieval preoccupation. The lengthy poem was divided into three major sections corresponding to the realms of the afterworld: hell, purgatory, and heaven or paradise. In the "Inferno" (see the box on p. 231), Dante is led by his guide, the classical author Virgil, who is a symbol of human reason. But Virgil (or reason) can only lead the poet so far on his journey. At the end of "Purgatory," Beatrice (the true love of Dante's life), who represents revelation—which alone can explain the mysteries of heaven—becomes his guide into "Paradise." Here Beatrice presents Dante to Saint Bernard, a symbol of mystical contemplation. The saint turns Dante over to the Virgin Mary, since grace is necessary to achieve the final step of entering the presence of God, where one beholds "the love that moves the sun and the other stars."[7]

Geoffrey Chaucer (c. 1340–1400), brought a new level of sophistication to the English vernacular language in his famous work *The Canterbury Tales*. His beauty of expression and clear, forceful language were important in transforming his East Midland dialect into the chief ancestor of the modern English language. *The Canterbury Tales* is a collection of stories told by a group of twenty-nine pilgrims journeying from Southwark to the tomb of Saint Thomas at Canterbury. This format gave Chaucer the chance to portray an entire range of English society, both high and low born. Among others, he presented the Knight, the Squire, the Yeoman, the Prioress, the Monk, the Merchant, the Student, the Lawyer, the Carpenter, the Cook, the Doctor, the Plowman, and, of course, "A Good Wife was there from beside the city of Bath— a little deaf, which was a pity." The stories these pilgrims told to while away the time on the journey were just as varied as the storytellers themselves: knightly romances, fairy tales, saints' lives, sophisticated satires, and crude anecdotes.

One of the extraordinary vernacular writers of the age was Christine de Pizan (c. 1364–1430). Thanks to her father's position at the court of Charles V of France, she received a good education. Her husband died when she was only twenty-five (they had been married for ten years), leaving her with little

Dante's Vision of Hell

The Divine Comedy of Dante Alighieri is regarded as one of the greatest literary works of all time. Many consider it the supreme summary of medieval thought. It combines allegory with a remarkable amount of contemporary history. Indeed, forty-three of the seventy-nine people consigned to hell in the "Inferno" were Florentines. This excerpt is taken from canto 18 of the "Inferno," in which Dante and Virgil visit the eighth circle of hell, which is divided into ten trenches containing those who had committed malicious frauds upon their fellow human beings.

✳ Dante, "Inferno," Divine Comedy

We had already come to where the walk
crosses the second bank, from which it lifts
another arch, spanning from rock to rock.

Here we heard people whine in the next chasm,
and knock and thump themselves with open palms,
and blubber through their snouts as if in a spasm.

Steaming from that pit, a vapor rose
over the banks, crusting them with a slime
that sickened my eyes and hammered at my nose.

That chasm sinks so deep we could not sight
its bottom anywhere until we climbed
along the rock arch to its greatest height.

Once there, I peered down; and I saw long lines
of people in a river of excrement
that seemed the overflow of the world's latrines.

I saw among the felons of that pit
one wraith who might or might not have been tonsured—
one could not tell, he was so smeared with shit.

He bellowed: "You there, why do you stare at me
more than at all the others in this stew?"
And I to him: "Because if memory

serves me, I knew you when your hair was dry.
You are Alessio Interminelli da Lucca.
That's why I pick you from this filthy fry."

And he then, beating himself on his clown's head:
"Down to this have the flatteries I sold
the living sunk me here among the dead."

And my Guide prompted then: "Lean forward a bit
and look beyond him, there—do you see that one
scratching herself with dungy nails, the strumpet

who fidgets to her feet, then to a crouch?
It is the whore Thaïs who told her lover
when he sent to ask her, 'Do you thank me much?'

'Much? Nay, past all believing!' And with this
Let us turn from the sight of this abyss."

---

income and three small children and her mother to support. Christine took the unusual step of becoming a writer to earn her living. Her poems were soon in demand, and by 1400 she had achieved financial security.

Christine de Pizan is best known, however, for her French prose works written in defense of women. In *The Book of the City of Ladies*, written in 1404, she denounced the many male writers who had argued that women by their very nature were prone to evil, unable to learn, and easily swayed and consequently needed to be controlled by men. With the help of Reason, Righteousness, and Justice, who appear to her in a vision, Christine refutes these antifeminist attacks. Women, she argues, are not evil by nature and could learn as well as men if they were permitted to attend the same schools: "Should I also tell you whether a woman's nature is clever and quick enough to learn speculative sciences as well as to discover them, and likewise the manual arts. I assure you that women are equally well-suited and skilled to carry them out and to put them to sophisticated use once they have learned them."[8] She ends the book by encouraging women to defend themselves against the attacks of men, who are incapable of understanding them.

✳ Art and the Black Death

The fourteenth century produced an artistic outburst in new directions as well as a large body of morbid work influenced by the Black Death and the recurrence of the plague. The city of Florence witnessed the first dramatic break with medieval tradition in the work of Giotto (1266–1337), often considered a forerunner of Italian Renaissance painting. Although he worked throughout Italy, Giotto's most famous works were done in Padua and Florence. Coming out of the formal Byzantine school, Giotto transcended it with a new kind of realism, a desire to imitate nature that Renaissance artists later identified

GIOTTO, *PIETÀ*. The work of Giotto marked the first clear innovation in fourteenth-century painting, making him a forerunner of the Early Renaissance. In this fresco, which was part of an elaborate series in the Arena chapel in Padua begun in 1305, the solidity of Giotto's human figures gives them a three-dimensional sense.

as the basic component of classical art. Giotto's figures were solid and rounded and—placed realistically in relationship to each other and their background—provided a sense of three-dimensional depth. The expressive faces and physically realistic bodies gave his sacred figures human qualities with which spectators could identify.

The Black Death had a visible impact on art. For one thing, it wiped out entire guilds of artists. At the same time, survivors, including the newly rich who patronized artists, were no longer so optimistic. Some were more guilty about enjoying life and more concerned about gaining salvation. Postplague art began to concentrate on pain and death. A fairly large number of artistic works came to be based on the *ars moriendi*, the art of dying.

� Changes in Urban Life

One immediate by-product of the Black Death was a greater regulation of urban activities. Authorities tried to keep cities cleaner by enacting new ordinances against waste products in the streets. Viewed as unhealthy places, bathhouses were closed down, leading to a noticeable decline in cleanliness.

The effects of plague were also felt in other areas of medieval urban life. The basic unit of the late

medieval urban environment was the nuclear family of husband, wife, and children. Especially in wealthier families, there might also be servants, apprentices, and other relatives, including widowed mothers and the husband's illegitimate children.

Before the Black Death, late marriages were common for urban couples. It was not unusual for husbands to be in their late thirties or forties and wives in their early twenties. The expense of beginning a household probably necessitated the delay in marriage. But the situation changed dramatically after the plague, reflecting new economic opportunities for the survivors and a reluctance to postpone living in the presence of so much death. The economic difficulties of the fourteenth century also had a tendency to strengthen the development of gender roles and to set new limits on employment opportunities for women. Based on the authority of Aristotle, Thomas Aquinas and other thirteenth-century scholastic theologians had advanced the belief that according to the natural order, men were active and domineering while women were passive and submissive. As more and more lawyers, doctors, and priests, who had been trained in universities where these notions were taught, entered society, these ideas of man's and woman's different natures became widely acceptable. Increasingly, women were expected to forgo any active functions in society and remain subject to direction from males. A fourteenth-century Parisian provost commented on glass cutters that "no master's widow who keeps working at his craft after her husband's death may take on apprentices, for the men of the craft do not believe that a woman can master it well enough to teach a child to master it, for the craft is a very delicate one."[9] Although this statement suggests that some women were in fact running businesses, it also reveals that they were viewed as incapable of undertaking all of men's activities. Based on a pattern of gender, Europeans created a division of labor roles between men and women that continued until the Industrial Revolution of the eighteenth and nineteenth centuries.

✷ Inventions and New Patterns

Despite its problems, the fourteenth century witnessed a continuation of the technological innovations that had characterized the High Middle Ages. The most extraordinary of these inventions, and one that had a visible impact on European cities, was the clock. The mechanical clock was invented at the end of the thirteenth century but not perfected until the fourteenth.

The time-telling clock was actually a by-product of a larger astronomical clock. The best-designed one was constructed by Giovanni di Dondi in the mid-fourteenth century. Dondi's clock contained the signs of the zodiac but also struck on the hour. Because clocks were expensive, they were usually installed only in the towers of churches or municipal buildings. The first clock striking equal hours was in a church in Milan; in 1335, a chronicler described it as "a wonderful clock, with a very large clapper which strikes a bell twenty-four hours of the day and night and thus at the first hour of the night gives one sound, at the second two strikes . . . and so distinguishes one hour from another, which is of greatest use to men of every degree."[10]

Clocks introduced a wholly new conception of time into the lives of Europeans; they revolutionized how people thought about and used time. Throughout most of the Middle Ages, time was determined by natural rhythms (daybreak and nightfall) or church bells that were rung at more or less regular three-hour intervals, corresponding to the ecclesiastical offices of the church. Clocks made it possible to plan one's day and organize one's activities around the regular striking of bells. This brought a new regularity into the lives of workers and merchants, defining urban existence and enabling merchants and bankers to see the value of time in a new way.

Invented earlier by the Chinese, gunpowder also made its appearance in the West in the fourteenth century. The use of gunpowder eventually brought drastic changes to European warfare. Its primary use was in cannons, although early cannons were prone to blow up, making them as dangerous to the people firing them as to the enemy. Even as late as 1460, an attack on a castle using the "Lion," an enormous Flemish cannon, proved disastrous for the Scottish king James II when the "Lion" blew up, killing the king and a number of his retainers. Continued improvement in the construction of cannons, however, soon made them extremely valuable in reducing both castles and city walls.

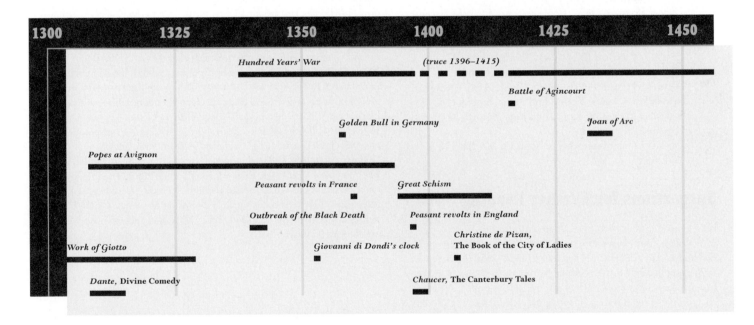

Conclusion

European civilization developed many of its fundamental features in the eleventh, twelfth, and thirteenth centuries. Territorial states, parliaments, capitalist trade and industry, banks, cities, and vernacular literatures were all products of that fertile period. During the same time, the Catholic church under the direction of the papacy reached its apogee. European society in the fourteenth century, however, was challenged by an overwhelming number of crises. Devastating plague, decline in trade and industry, bank failures, peasant revolts pitting lower classes against the upper classes, seemingly constant warfare, aristocratic factional conflict that undermined political stability, the absence of the popes from Rome, and even the spectacle of two popes condemning each other as the Antichrist all seemed to overpower Europeans in this "calamitous century." Not surprisingly, much of the art of the period depicted the Four Horsemen of the Apocalypse described in the New Testament book of Revelation: Death, Famine, Pestilence, and War. To some people, no doubt, the last days of the world seemed to be at hand.

The new European society, however, proved remarkably resilient. Periods of crisis usually give rise to new ideas and new practices. Intellectuals of the period saw themselves as standing on the threshold of a new age and a rebirth of the best features of classical civilization, an era widely referred to as the Renaissance.

Notes

1. Quoted in H. S. Lucas, "The Great European Famine of 1315, 1316, and 1317," *Speculum* 5 (1930): 359.
2. Quoted in David Herlihy, *The Black Death and the Transformation of the West*, ed. Samuel K. Cohn Jr. (Cambridge, Mass., 1997), p. 9.
3. Jean Froissart, *Chronicles*, ed. and trans. Geoffrey Brereton (Harmondsworth, England, 1968), p. 111.
4. Ibid., p. 212.
5. Ibid., p. 89.
6. Quoted in Robert Coogan, *Babylon on the Rhone: A Translation of Letters by Dante, Petrarch, and Catherine of Siena* (Washington, D.C., 1983), p. 115.
7. Dante Alighieri, *Divine Comedy*, trans. Dorothy Sayers (New York, 1962), "Paradise," canto 33, line 145.
8. Christine de Pizan, *The Book of the City of Ladies*, trans. E. Jeffrey Richards (New York, 1982), pp. 83–84.
9. Quoted in Susan Stuard, "Dominion of Gender: Women's Fortunes in the High Middle Ages," in Renate Bridenthal, Claudia Koonz, and Susan Stuard, eds., *Becoming Visible: Women in European History*, 2d ed. (Boston, 1987), p. 169.
10. Quoted in Jean Gimpel, *The Medieval Machine* (New York, 1976), p. 168.

Suggestions for Further Reading

For a general introduction to the fourteenth century, see D. P. Waley, *Later Medieval Europe*, 2d ed. (London, 1985); G. Holmes, *Europe: Hierarchy and Revolt, 1320–1450* (New York, 1975); and the well-written popular history by B. Tuchman, *A Distant Mirror* (New York, 1978).

On famine in the early fourteenth century, see W. C. Jordan, *The Great Famine: Northern Europe in the Early Fourteenth Century* (Princeton, N.J., 1996). On the Black Death, see P. Ziegler, *The Black Death* (New York, 1969); W. H. McNeill, *Plagues and People* (New York, 1976); and D. Herlihy, *The Black Death and the Transformation of the West*, ed. S. K. Cohn Jr. (Cambridge, Mass., 1997). There is a good collection of sources in R. Horrox, ed., *The Black Death* (New York, 1994). On the peasant and urban revolts of the fourteenth century, see M. Mollat and P. Wolff, *The Popular Revolutions of the Late Middle Ages* (Winchester, Mass., 1973).

Good accounts of the Hundred Years' War include A. Curry, *The Hundred Years' War* (New York, 1993), and R. H. Neillands, *The Hundred Years' War* (New York, 1990). On Joan of Arc, see M. Warner, *Joan of Arc: The Image of Female Heroism* (New York, 1981). On the political history of the period, see B. Guenée, *States and Rulers in Later Medieval Europe*, trans. J. Vale (Oxford, 1985). Works on individual countries include P. S. Lewis, *Later Medieval France: The Polity* (London, 1968); A. R. Myers, *England in the Late Middle Ages* (Harmondsworth, England, 1952); and F. R. H. Du Boulay, *Germany in the Later Middle Ages* (London, 1983). On the Italian political scene, see D. P. Waley, *The Italian City-Republics* (London, 1978), and J. Larner, *Italy in the Age of Dante and Petrarch, 1216–1380* (London, 1980).

A good general study of the church in the fourteenth century can be found in F. P. Oakley, *The Western Church in the Later Middle Ages* (Ithaca, N.Y., 1980). A good, readable biography is T. S. R. Boase, *Boniface VIII* (London, 1933). On the Avignonese papacy, see Y. Renouard, *The Avignon Papacy, 1305–1403* (London, 1970).

A classic work on the life and thought of the Later Middle Ages is J. Huizinga, *The Autumn of the Middle Ages*, trans. R. J. Payton and U. Mammitzsch (Chicago, 1996). On the impact of the plague on culture, see the brilliant study by M. Meiss, *Painting in Florence and Siena After the Black Death* (New York, 1964). On Dante, see J. Freccero, *Dante and the Poetics of Conversion* (Cambridge, Mass., 1986). On Chaucer, see G. Kane, *Chaucer* (New York, 1984). The best work on Christine de Pizan is by C. C. Willard, *Christine de Pizan: Her Life and Works* (New York, 1984).

A wealth of material on everyday life is provided in the second volume of *A History of Private Life* edited by G. Duby, *Revelations of the Medieval World* (Cambridge, Mass., 1988). On women in the Late Middle Ages, see S. Shahar, *The Fourth Estate: A History of Women in the Middle Ages*, trans. C. Galai (London, 1983), and D. Herlihy, *Women, Family, and Society: Historical Essays, 1978–1991* (Providence, R.I., 1995). For late medieval townspeople, see J. F. C. Harrison, *The Common People of Great Britain* (Bloomington, Ind., 1985). Poor people are discussed in M. Mollat, *The Poor in the Middle Ages* (New Haven, Conn., 1986). The importance of inventions is discussed in J. Gimpel, *The Medieval Machine* (New York, 1976). Another valuable discussion of medieval technology can be found in J. Le Goff, *Time, Work, and Culture in the Middle Ages* (Chicago, 1980).

For additional reading, go to InfoTrac College Edition, your online research library at http://web1.infotrac-college.com

Enter the search terms *Middle Ages* using the Subject Guide.

Enter the search terms *Black Death* using Key Terms.

Enter the search terms *Edward III* using Key Terms.

Enter the search terms *Hundred Years War* using Key Terms.

CHAPTER

12

Recovery and Rebirth: The Age of the Renaissance

CHAPTER OUTLINE

- Meaning and Characteristics of the Italian Renaissance
- The Making of Renaissance Society
- The Italian States in the Renaissance
- The Intellectual Renaissance in Italy
- The Artistic Renaissance
- The European State in the Renaissance
- The Church in the Renaissance
- Conclusion

FOCUS QUESTIONS

- What characteristics distinguish the Renaissance from the Middle Ages?
- How did Machiavelli's works reflect the political realities of Renaissance Italy?
- What was humanism, and what effect did it have on philosophy, education, and attitudes toward politics?
- What were the chief characteristics of Renaissance art, and how did it differ in Italy and northern Europe?
- Why do historians sometimes refer to the monarchies of the late fifteenth century as "new monarchies" or "Renaissance states"?

*W*ERE THE FOURTEENTH AND FIFTEENTH *centuries a continuation of the Middle Ages or the beginning of a new era? Both positions contain a modicum of truth. Although the disintegrative patterns of the fourteenth century continued into the fifteenth, at the same time there were elements of recovery that made the fifteenth century a period of significant political, economic, artistic, and intellectual change. The humanists or intellectuals of the age considered their period (from the mid-fourteenth to the mid-sixteenth century) an age of rebirth, believing that they had restored arts and letters to new glory* after they had been "neglected" or "dead" for centuries. The humanists also saw their age as one of great individuals who dominated the landscape of their time. Michelangelo, the great Italian artist of the early sixteenth century, and Pope Julius II, the "warrior pope," were two such titans. The artist's temperament and the pope's temper led to many lengthy and often loud quarrels between the two. Among other commissions, the pope had hired Michelangelo to paint the ceiling of the Sistine Chapel in Rome, a daunting task for a man long accustomed to being a sculptor. Michelangelo undertook the project but refused for a long time to allow anyone, including the pope, to see his work. Julius grew anxious, pestering Michelangelo on a regular basis about when the ceiling would be finished. Exasperated by the pope's requests, Michelangelo once replied, according to Giorgio Vasari, his contemporary biographer, that the ceiling would be completed "when it satisfies me as an artist." The pope responded, "And we want you to satisfy us and finish it soon," and then threatened that if Michelangelo did not "finish the ceiling quickly [the pope] would have him thrown down from the scaffolding." Fearing the pope's anger, Michelangelo "lost no time in doing all that was wanted" and quickly completed the ceiling, one of the great masterpieces in the history of Western art.

The humanists' view of their age as a rebirth of the classical civilization of the Greeks and Romans ultimately led historians to use the term Renaissance to identify this age. Although recent historians have emphasized the many elements of continuity between the Middle Ages and the Renaissance, the latter age was also distinguished by its own unique characteristics.

◆ Meaning and Characteristics of the Italian Renaissance

The word renaissance means "rebirth." A number of people who lived in Italy between 1350 and 1550 believed that they were witnessing a rebirth of antiquity or Greco-Roman civilization, marking a new age. To them, the thousand or so years between the end of the Roman Empire and their own era was a middle period (hence the "Middle Ages"), characterized by darkness because of its lack of classical culture. Historians of the nineteenth century later used similar terminology to describe this period in Italy. The Swiss historian and art critic Jacob Burckhardt created the modern concept of the Renaissance in his celebrated work Civilization of the Renaissance in Italy, published in 1860. He portrayed Italy in the fourteenth and fifteenth centuries as the birthplace of the modern world and saw the revival of antiquity, the "perfecting of the individual," and secularism ("worldliness of the Italians") as its distinguishing features. Burckhardt exaggerated the individuality and secularism of the Renaissance and failed to recognize the depths of its religious sentiment; nevertheless, he established the framework for all modern interpretations of the Renaissance. Although contemporary scholars do not believe that the Renaissance represents a sudden or dramatic cultural break with the Middle Ages (as Burckhardt argued)—there was, after all, much continuity between the two periods in economic, political, and social life—the Renaissance can still be viewed as a distinct period of European history that manifested itself first in Italy and then spread to the rest of Europe. What, then, are the characteristics of the Italian Renaissance?

Renaissance Italy was largely an urban society. The city-states, especially those of northern Italy, became the centers of Italian political, economic, and social life. Within this new urban society, a secular spirit emerged as increasing wealth created new possibilities for the enjoyment of worldly things (see the box on p. 237).

Above all, the Renaissance was an age of recovery from the "calamitous fourteenth century." Italy and Europe began a slow process of recuperation from the effects of the Black Death, political disorder, and economic recession. Recovery was accompanied by a rebirth of the culture of classical antiquity. Increasingly aware of their own historical past, Italian intellectuals became intensely interested in the Greco-Roman culture of the ancient Mediterranean world. This new revival of classical antiquity (the Middle Ages had in fact preserved much of ancient Latin culture) affected activities as diverse as politics and art and led to new attempts to reconcile the pagan philosophy of antiquity with Christian thought, as well as new ways of viewing human beings.

A revived emphasis on individual ability became characteristic of the Italian Renaissance. As the fifteenth-century Florentine architect Leon Battista Alberti expressed it, "Men can do all things if they will."[1] A high regard for human dignity and worth and a realization of individual potentiality created a new social ideal of the well-rounded personality or uni-

A Renaissance Banquet

As in Greek and Roman society, the Renaissance banquet was an occasion for good food, interesting conversation, music, and dancing. In Renaissance society, it was also a symbol of status and an opportunity to impress people with the power and wealth of one's family. Banquets were held to celebrate public and religious festivals, official visits, anniversaries, and weddings. The following menu lists the foods served at a grand banquet given by Pope Pius V in the sixteenth century.

A Sixteenth-Century Banquet

❋ First Course: ❋
Cold Delicacies from the Sideboard

Pieces of marzipan and marzipan balls
Neapolitan spice cakes
Malaga wine and Pisan biscuits
Fresh grapes
Prosciutto cooked in wine, served with capers
and grape pulp
Salted pork tongues cooked in wine, sliced
Spit-roasted songbirds, cold, with their
tongues sliced over them
Sweet mustard

❋ Second Course: ❋
Hot Foods from the Kitchen, Roasts

Fried veal sweetbreads and liver
Spit-roasted skylarks with lemon sauce
Spit-roasted quails with sliced eggplants
Stuffed spit-roasted pigeons with capers
sprinkled over them
Spit-roasted rabbits, with sauce and
crushed pine nuts
Partridges larded and spit-roasted,
served with lemon
Heavily seasoned poultry with lemon slices
Slices of veal, spit-roasted, with a sauce made
from the juices
Leg of goat, spit-roasted with a sauce made
from the juices
Soup of almond paste, with the flesh of three
pigeons to each serving

❋ Third Course: ❋
Hot Foods from the Kitchen,
Boiled Meats and Stews

Stuffed fat geese, boiled Lombard style and covered
with sliced almonds
Stuffed breast of veal, boiled, garnished with flowers
Very young calf, boiled, garnished with parsley
Almonds in garlic sauce
Turkish-style rice with milk, sprinkled with
cinnamon
Stewed pigeons with mortadella sausage and
whole onions
Cabbage soup with sausages
Poultry pie, two chickens to each pie
Fricasseed breast of goat dressed with fried onions
Pies filled with custard cream
Boiled calves' feet with cheese and egg

❋ Fourth Course: ❋
Delicacies from the Sideboard

Bean tarts
Quince pastries
Pear tarts, the pears wrapped in marzipan
Parmesan cheese and Riviera cheese
Fresh almonds on vine leaves
Chestnuts roasted over the coals and served
with salt and pepper
Milk curds
Ring-shaped cakes
Wafers made from ground corn

---

versal person (l'uomo universale) who was capable of achievements in many areas of life.

These general features of the Italian Renaissance were not characteristic of all Italians but were primarily the preserve of the wealthy upper classes, who constituted a small percentage of the total population.

The achievements of the Italian Renaissance were the product of an elite, rather than a mass, movement. Nevertheless, indirectly it did have some impact on ordinary people, especially in the cities where so many of the intellectual and artistic accomplishments of the period were most apparent.

◆ The Making of Renaissance Society

After the severe economic reversals and social upheavals of the second half of the fourteenth century, the European economy gradually recovered during the fifteenth century as manufacturing and trade increased in volume.

✾ Economic Recovery

By the fourteenth century, Italian merchants were carrying on a flourishing commerce throughout the Mediterranean and had also expanded their lines of trade north along the Atlantic seaboard. The great galleys of the Venetian Flanders Fleet maintained a direct sea route from Venice to England and the Netherlands, where Italian merchants came into contact with the increasingly powerful Hanseatic League of merchants. Hard hit by the plague, the Italians lost their commercial preeminence while the Hanseatic League continued to prosper.

As early as the thirteenth century, a number of north German coastal towns had formed a commercial and military league known as the Hansa or Hanseatic League. By 1500, more than eighty cities belonged to the League, which established settlements and commercial bases in northern Europe and England. For almost two hundred years, the Hansa had a monopoly on northern European trade in timber, fish, grain, metals, honey, and wines. Its southern outlet in Flanders, the city of Bruges, became the economic crossroads of Europe in the fourteenth century because it served as the meeting place between Hanseatic merchants and the Flanders Fleet of Venice. In the fifteenth century, however, as Bruges harbor began to silt up, the city slowly began to decline. So did the Hanseatic League as it proved increasingly unable to compete with the developing larger territorial states.

Overall, trade recovered dramatically from the economic contraction of the fourteenth century. The Italians and especially the Venetians continued to maintain a wealthy commercial empire. Not until the sixteenth century, when overseas discoveries gave new importance to the states facing the Atlantic, did the petty Italian city-states begin to suffer from the competitive advantages of the ever-growing and more powerful national territorial states.

The economic depression of the fourteenth century also affected patterns of manufacturing. The woolen industries of Flanders and the northern Italian cities had been particularly devastated. By the beginning of the fifteenth century, however, the Florentine woolen industry began to experience a recovery. At the same time, the Italian cities began to develop and expand luxury industries, including lace and silk, glassware, and handworked items in metal and precious stones.

Other new industries, especially printing, mining, and metallurgy, began to rival the textile industry in importance in the fifteenth century. New machinery and techniques for digging deeper mines and for separating metals from ore and purifying them were developed. When rulers began to transfer their titles to underground mineral rights to financiers as collateral for loans, these entrepreneurs quickly developed large mining operations to produce copper, iron, and silver. Especially valuable were the rich mineral deposits in central Europe, Hungary, the Tyrol, Bohemia, and Saxony. Expanding iron production and new skills in metalworking in turn contributed to the development of firearms that were more effective than the crude weapons of the fourteenth century.

The city of Florence regained its preeminence in banking in the fifteenth century, primarily due to the Medici family. In its best days (in the fifteenth century), the House of Medici was the greatest banking house in Europe, with branches in Venice, Milan, Rome, Avignon, Bruges, London, and Lyons. Moreover, the family had controlling interests in industrial enterprises for wool, silk, and the mining of alum, which was used to dye textiles. Despite its great success in the early and middle part of the fifteenth century, the Medici bank suffered a rather sudden decline at the end of the century due to poor leadership and a series of bad loans, especially uncollectible loans to rulers. In 1494, when the French expelled the Medici from Florence and confiscated their property, the Medicean financial edifice collapsed.

✾ Social Changes in the Renaissance

The Renaissance inherited its social structure from the Middle Ages. Society remained fundamentally divided into three estates: the first estate, the clergy, whose preeminence was grounded in the belief that people should be guided to spiritual ends; the second estate, the nobility, whose privileges were based on the principle that the nobles provided security and justice for society; and the third estate, the peasants and inhabitants of the towns and cities. This social order experienced certain adaptations in the Renaissance, which we can see by examining the second and third estates (the clergy will be examined in Chapter 13).

✷ THE NOBILITY

Throughout much of Europe, the landholding nobles faced declining real incomes during the greater part of the fourteenth and fifteenth centuries. But many members of the old nobility survived, and new blood infused its ranks. A reconstruction of the aristocracy was well under way by 1500. As a result of this reconstruction, the nobles, old and new, who constituted between 2 and 3 percent of the population in most countries, managed to dominate society as they had done in the Middle Ages, serving as military officers and holding important political posts as well as advising the king.

By 1500, the noble or aristocrat was expected to evince certain ideals. These ideals were best expressed in *The Book of the Courtier* by the Italian Baldassare Castiglione (1478–1529). First published in 1528, Castiglione's work soon became popular throughout Europe, and it remained a fundamental handbook for European aristocrats well into the twentieth century.

In *The Book of the Courtier*, Castiglione described the three basic attributes of the perfect courtier. First, nobles should possess fundamental native endowments, such as impeccable character, grace, talents, and noble birth. The perfect courtier must also cultivate certain achievements. Primarily, he should participate in military and bodily exercises because the principal profession of a courtier was arms. But unlike the medieval knight who had only been required to have military skill, the Renaissance courtier was also expected to have a classical education and adorn his life with the arts by playing a musical instrument, drawing, and painting. In Castiglione's hands, the Renaissance ideal of the well-developed personality became a social ideal of the aristocracy. Finally, the aristocrat was expected to follow a certain standard of conduct. Nobles were expected to make good impressions; while being modest, they should not hide their accomplishments but show them with grace.

What was the purpose of these courtly standards? Castiglione said:

> I think that the aim of the perfect Courtier, which we have not spoken of up to now, is so to win for himself, by means of the accomplishments ascribed to him by these gentlemen, the favor and mind of the prince whom he serves that he may be able to tell him, and always will tell him, the truth about everything he needs to know, without fear or risk of displeasing him; and that when he sees the mind

of his prince inclined to a wrong action, he may dare to oppose him . . . so as to dissuade him of every evil intent and bring him to the path of virtue.[2]

The aim of the perfect noble, then, was to serve his prince in an effective and honest way. Nobles would adhere to these principles for hundreds of years while they continued to dominate European life socially and politically.

✷ PEASANTS AND TOWNSPEOPLE

Peasants made up the overwhelming mass of the third estate, and except in the highly urbanized areas of northern Italy and Flanders, they continued to constitute as much as 85 to 90 percent of the total European population. The most noticeable trend produced by the economic crisis of the fourteenth century was the decline of the manorial system and the continuing elimination of serfdom. The contraction of the peasantry after the Black Death simply accelerated the process of converting servile labor dues into rents paid in money. By the end of the fifteenth century, primarily in western Europe, serfdom was declining, and more and more peasants were becoming legally free.

The remainder of the third estate centered around the inhabitants of towns and cities, originally the merchants and artisans who formed the bourgeoisie. The Renaissance town or city of the fifteenth century actually possessed a multitude of townspeople widely separated socially and economically.

At the top of urban society were the patricians, whose wealth from capitalistic enterprises in trade, industry, and banking enabled them to dominate their urban communities economically, socially, and politically. Below them were the petty burghers, the shopkeepers, artisans, guildmasters, and guildsmen who were largely concerned with providing goods and services for local consumption. Below these two groups were the propertyless workers earning pitiful wages and the unemployed, living squalid and miserable lives; these people constituted as much as 30 to 40 percent of the urban population. Everywhere in Europe in the late fourteenth and fifteenth centuries, urban poverty had increased dramatically. One rich merchant of Florence wrote:

> Those that are lazy and indolent in a way that does harm to the city, and who can offer no just reason for their condition, should either be forced to work or expelled from the Commune. The city would thus rid itself of that most harmful part of the poorest class. . . . If the lowest order of society earn enough food to keep them going from day to day, then they have enough.[3]

Marriage Negotiations

Marriages were so important in maintaining families in Renaissance Italy that much energy was put into arranging them. Parents made the choices for their children, most often for considerations that had little to do with the modern notion of love. This selection is taken from the letters of a Florentine matron of the illustrious Strozzi family to her son Filippo in Naples. The family's considerations were complicated by the fact that the son was in exile.

✳ *Alessandra Strozzi to Her Son Filippo in Naples*

[April 20, 1464] . . . Concerning the matter of a wife [for Filippo}, it appears to me that if Francesco di Messer Tanagli wishes to give his daughter, that it would be a fine marriage. . . . Now I will speak with Marco [Parenti, Alessandra's son-in-law], to see if there are other prospects that would be better, and if there are none, then we will learn if he wishes to give her [in marriage]. . . . Francesco Tanagli has a good reputation, and he has held office, not the highest, but still he has been in office. You may ask: "Why should he give her to someone in exile?" There are three reasons. First, there aren't many young men of good family who have both virtue and property. Secondly, she has only a small dowry, 1,000 florins, which is the dowry of an artisan [although not a small sum, either—senior officials in the government bureaucracy earned 300 florins a year]. . . . Third, I believe that he will give her away, because he has a large family and he will need help to settle them. . . .

[July 26, 1465] . . . Francesco is a good friend of Marco and he trusts him. On S. Jacopo's day, he spoke to him discreetly and persuasively, saying that for several months he had heard that we were interested in the girl and . . . that when we had made up our minds, she will come to us willingly. [He said that] you were a worthy man, and that his family had always made good marriages, but that he had only a small dowry to give her, and so he would prefer to send her outside of Florence to someone of worth, rather than to give her to someone here, from among those who were available, with little money. . . . We have information that she is affable and competent. She is responsible for a large family (there are twelve children, six boys and six girls), and the mother is always pregnant and isn't very competent. . . .

[August 31, 1465] . . . I have recently received some very favorable information [about the Tanagli girl] from two individuals. . . . They are in agreement that whoever gets her will be content. . . . Concerning her beauty, they told me what I had already seen, that she is attractive and well-proportioned. Her face is long, but I couldn't look directly into her face, since she appeared to be aware that I was examining her . . . and so she turned away from me like the wind. . . . She reads quite well . . . and she can dance and sing. . . .

So yesterday I sent for Marco and told him what I had learned. And we talked about the matter for a while, and decided that he should say something to the father and give him a little hope, but not so much that we couldn't withdraw, and find out from him the amount of the dowry. . . . May God help us to choose what will contribute to our tranquility and to the consolation of us all.

[September 13, 1465] . . . Marco came to me and said that he had met with Francesco Tanagli, who had spoken very coldly, so that I understand that he had changed his mind. . . .

[Filippo Strozzi eventually married Fiametta di Donato Adimari in 1466.]

But even this large group was not at the bottom of the social scale; beneath it stood a significantly large group of slaves, especially in the cities of Italy.

✳ *Family and Marriage in Renaissance Italy*

The family bond was a source of great security in the urban world of Renaissance Italy. To maintain the family, careful attention was given to marriages that were arranged by parents, often to strengthen business or family ties. Details were worked out well in advance, sometimes when children were only two or three, and reinforced by a legally binding marriage contract (see the box above). The important aspect of the contract was the size of the dowry, a sum of money presented by the wife's family to the husband upon marriage. The dowry could involve large sums of money and was expected of all families.

WEDDING BANQUET. Parents arranged marriages in Renaissance Italy to strengthen business or family ties. A legally binding marriage contract was considered a necessary part of the marital arrangements. So was a wedding feast. This painting by Botticelli shows the wedding banquet in Florence that celebrated the marriage of Nastagio degli Onesti and the daughter of Paulo Traversaro.

The father-husband was the center of the Italian family. He gave it his name, was responsible for it in all legal matters, managed all finances (his wife had no share in his wealth), and made the crucial decisions in his children's lives. A father's authority over his children was absolute until he died or formally freed his children. In Renaissance Italy, children did not become adults on reaching a certain age; adulthood came only when the father went before a judge and formally emancipated them. The age of emancipation varied from early teens to late twenties.

The wife managed the household, a position that gave women a certain degree of autonomy in their daily lives. Most wives, however, also knew that their primary function was to bear children. Upper-class wives were frequently pregnant; Alessandra Strozzi of Florence, for example, who had been married at the age of sixteen, bore eight children in ten years. Poor women did not conceive at the same rate since they nursed their own babies. Wealthy women gave their infants out to wet nurses, which enabled them to become pregnant more quickly after the birth of a child.

For women in the Renaissance, childbirth was a fearful occasion. Not only was it painful, but it could be deadly; possibly as many as 10 percent of mothers died in childbirth. In his memoirs, the Florence merchant Gregorio Dati recalled that three of his four wives died in childbirth. His third wife, after bearing eleven children in fifteen years, "died in childbirth after lengthy suffering, which she bore with remarkable strength and patience."[4] Nor did the tragedies end with childbirth. Surviving mothers often faced the death of their children. In Florence in the fifteenth century, for example, almost 50 percent of the children born to merchant families died before the age of twenty. Given these mortality rates, many upper-class families sought to have as many children as possible in order to ensure a surviving male heir to the family fortune. This concern is evident in the Florentine humanist Leon Battista Alberti's treatise *On the Family*, when one of the characters remarks, "How many families do we see today in decadence and ruin! . . . Of all these families not only the magnificence and greatness but the very men, not only the men but the very names are shrunk away and gone. Their memory . . . is wiped out and obliterated."[5]

◆ The Italian States in the Renaissance

By the fifteenth century, five major powers dominated the Italian peninsula—the duchy of Milan, Venice, Florence, the Papal States, and the kingdom of Naples (see Map 12.1). Northern Italy was divided between the duchy of Milan and Venice. After the death of the last Visconti ruler of Milan in 1447, Francesco Sforza, one of the leading *condottieri* (a *condottiere* was a leader of a mercenary band) of the time, turned on his Milanese employers, conquered the city, and became its new duke. Both the Visconti and Sforza rulers worked to create a highly centralized territorial state. They were especially successful in devising systems of taxation that generated enormous revenues for the government. The maritime republic of Venice remained an extremely stable political entity governed by a small oligarchy of merchant-aristocrats. Its commercial empire brought in enormous revenues and gave it the status of an international power.

The republic of Florence dominated the region of Tuscany. In 1434, Cosimo de' Medici (1434–1464) took control of the ruling oligarchy. Although the wealthy Medici family maintained republican forms of government for appearance's sake, it ran the government from behind the scenes. Through their lavish patronage and careful courting of political allies, Cosimo and later his grandson Lorenzo the Magnificent (1469–1492) were successful in dominating the city at a time when Florence was the center of the cultural Renaissance.

The Papal States lay in central Italy. Nominally under the control of the popes, papal residence in Avignon and the Great Schism had enabled individual cities and territories, such as Urbino and Ferrara, to become independent of papal authority. The popes of the fifteenth century directed much of their energy toward reestablishing their control over the Papal States. The kingdom of Naples, which encompassed most of Southern Italy and usually the island of Sicily, remained a backward monarchy that shared little in the cultural glories of the Renaissance.

A number of independent city-states under the control of powerful ruling families also became bril-

MAP 12.1 Renaissance Italy.

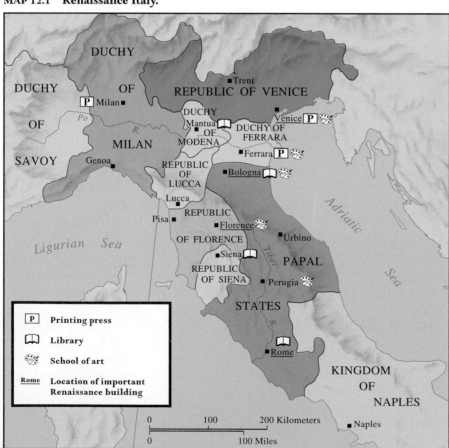

liant centers of Renaissance culture in the fifteenth century. Perhaps most famous was Urbino, ruled by the Montefeltro dynasty. Federigo da Montefeltro, who ruled Urbino from 1444 to 1482, received a classical education. He had also learned the skills of fighting, since the Montefeltro family compensated for the poverty of Urbino by hiring themselves out as *condottieri*. Federigo was not only a good ruler but also a rather unusual *condottiere* by fifteenth-century standards. Although not a brilliant general, he was reliable and honest. He did not break his promises, even when urged to do so by a papal legate. At the same time, Duke Federigo was one of the greatest patrons of Renaissance culture. Under his direction, Urbino became a well-known cultural and intellectual center.

A noticeable feature of these smaller Italian courts was the important role played by women. The most famous of the Italian ruling women was Isabella d'Este (1474–1539), daughter of the duke of Ferrara, who married Francesco Gonzaga, marquis of Mantua. Their court was another important center of art and learning in the Renaissance. Educated at the brilliant court of Ferrara, Isabella was known for her intelligence and political wisdom. Called the "first lady of the world," she attracted artists and intellectuals to the Mantuan court and was responsible for amassing one of the finest libraries in all of Italy. Her numerous letters to friends, family, princes, and artists all over Europe disclose her political acumen as well as a good sense of humor. Both before and after the death of her husband Francesco, she effectively ruled Mantua and won a reputation as a clever negotiator.

The growth of powerful monarchical states led to trouble for the Italians and brought an end to the independence of the Italian states. Attracted by the riches of Italy, the French king Charles VIII (1483–1498) led an army of thirty thousand men into Italy in 1494 and occupied the kingdom of Naples. Other Italian states turned for help to the Spanish, who gladly complied. For the next thirty years, the French and Spanish competed to dominate Italy, which was merely a pawn for the two great powers, a convenient arena for fighting battles. The terrible sack of Rome in 1527 by the armies of the Spanish king Charles I brought a temporary end to the Italian wars. Hereafter, the Spaniards dominated Italy; the Renaissance in Italy was at an end.

✾ Machiavelli and the New Statecraft

No one gave better expression to the Renaissance preoccupation with political power than Niccolò Machiavelli (1469–1527). Although he ably served as a diplomat for Florence, he was eventually forced into exile. Embittered by this and compelled by the great love of his life—politics—he wrote *The Prince*, one of the most influential works on political power in the Western world.

Machiavelli's major concerns in *The Prince* were the acquisition, maintenance, and expansion of political power as the means to restore and maintain order in his time. In the Middle Ages, many political theorists stressed the ethical side of a prince's activity—how a ruler ought to behave based on Christian moral principles. Machiavelli bluntly contradicted this approach:

> My hope is to write a book that will be useful, at least to those who read it intelligently, and so I thought it sensible to go straight to a discussion of how things are in real life and not waste time with a discussion of an imaginary world . . . for the gap between how people actually behave and how they ought to behave is so great that anyone who ignores everyday reality in order to live up to an ideal will soon discover he had been taught how to destroy himself, not how to preserve himself.[6]

Machiavelli considered his approach far more realistic than that of his medieval forebears.

NICCOLÒ MACHIAVELLI. In *The Prince*, Machiavelli gave concrete expression to the Renaissance preoccupation with political power. This slender volume remains one of the most famous Western treatises on politics. Machiavelli is seen here in a portrait by Santi di Tito.

Machiavelli: "Is it Better to be Loved than Feared?"

In 1513, Niccolò Machiavelli wrote a short treatise on political power that, justly or unjustly, has given him a reputation as a political opportunist. In this passage from Chapter 17 of The Prince, *Machiavelli analyzes whether it is better for a ruler to be loved than feared.*

❋ *Machiavelli,* The Prince

This leads us to a question that is in dispute: Is it better to be loved than feared, or vice versa? My reply is one ought to be both loved and feared; but, since it is difficult to accomplish both at the same time, I maintain it is much safer to be feared than loved, if you have to do without one of the two. For of men one can, in general, say this: They are ungrateful, fickle, deceptive and deceiving, avoiders of danger, eager to gain. As long as you serve their interests, they are devoted to you. They promise you their blood, their possessions, their lives, and their children, as I said before, so long as you seem to have no need of them. But as soon as you need help, they turn against you. Any ruler who relies simply on their promises and makes no other preparations, will be destroyed. For you will find that those whose support you buy, who do not rally to you because they admire your strength of character and nobility of soul, these are people you pay for, but they are never yours, and in the end you cannot get the ben-efit of your investment. Men are less nervous of offending someone who makes himself lovable, than someone who makes himself frightening. For love attaches men by ties of obligation, which, since men are wicked, they break whenever their interests are at stake. But fear restrains men because they are afraid of punishment, and this fear never leaves them. Still, a ruler should make himself feared in such a way that, if he does not inspire love, at least he does not provoke hatred. For it is perfectly possible to be feared and not hated. You will only be hated if you seize the property or the women of your subjects and citizens. Whenever you have to kill someone, make sure that you have a suitable excuse and an obvious reason; but, above all else, keep your hands off other people's property; for men are quicker to forget the death of their father than the loss of their inheritance. Moreover, there are always reasons why you might want to seize people's property; and he who begins to live by plundering others will always find an excuse for seizing other people's possessions; but there are fewer reasons for killing people, and one killing need not lead to another.

When a ruler is at the head of his army and has a vast number of soldiers under his command, then it is absolutely essential to be prepared to be thought cruel; for it is impossible to keep an army united and ready for action without acquiring a reputation for cruelty.

From Machiavelli's point of view, a prince's attitude toward power must be based on an understanding of human nature, which he perceived as basically self-centered. He said, "Of men one can, in general, say this: They are ungrateful, fickle, deceptive and deceiving, avoiders of danger, eager to gain." Political activity, therefore, could not be restricted by moral considerations. The prince acts on behalf of the state and for the sake of the state must be willing to let his conscience sleep. As Machiavelli put it:

> You need to understand this: A ruler, and particularly a ruler who is new to power, cannot conform to all those rules that men who are thought good are expected to respect, for he is often obliged, in order to hold on to power, to break his word, to be uncharitable, inhumane, and irreligious. So he must be mentally prepared to act as circumstances and changes in fortune require. As I have said, he should do what is right if he can; but he must be prepared to do wrong if necessary.[7]

In Cesare Borgia, the son of Pope Alexander VI, who used ruthless measures to achieve his goal of carving out a new state in central Italy, Machiavelli found a good example of the new Italian ruler. As he said, "So anyone who decides that the policy to follow when one has newly acquired power is to destroy one's enemies, to secure some allies, to win wars, whether by force or by fraud, to make oneself both loved and feared by one's subjects, . . . cannot hope to find, in the recent past, a better model to imitate than Cesare Borgia."[8] Machiavelli was among the first to abandon morality as the basis for the analysis of political activity (see the box above).

◆ The Intellectual Renaissance in Italy

Individualism and secularism—two characteristics of the Italian Renaissance—were most noticeable in the intellectual and artistic realms. Italian culture had matured by the fourteenth century. For the next two centuries, Italy was the cultural leader of Europe. This new Italian culture was primarily the product of a relatively wealthy, urban lay society. The most important literary movement associated with the Renaissance is humanism.

❊ *Italian Renaissance Humanism*

Renaissance humanism was an intellectual movement based on the study of the classical literary works of Greece and Rome. Humanists studied the liberal arts—grammar, rhetoric, poetry, moral philosophy or ethics, and history—all based on the writings of ancient Greek and Roman authors. These are the subjects we call the humanities.

Petrarch (1304–1374), often called the father of Italian Renaissance humanism, did more than any other individual in the fourteenth century to foster development of the movement. Petrarch sought to find forgotten Latin manuscripts and set in motion a search of monastic libraries throughout Europe. In his preoccupation with the classics and their secular content, Petrarch doubted at times whether he was sufficiently attentive to spiritual ideals. His qualms, however, did not prevent him from inaugurating the humanist emphasis on the use of pure classical Latin, making it fashionable for humanists to use Cicero as a model for prose and Virgil for poetry. Petrarch

said, "Christ is my God; Cicero is the prince of the language."

In Florence, the humanist movement took a new direction at the beginning of the fifteenth century when it became closely tied to Florentine civic spirit and pride, giving rise to what one modern scholar has labeled "civic humanism." Fourteenth-century humanists such as Petrarch had described the intellectual life as one of solitude. They rejected family and a life of action in the community. In the busy civic world of Florence, however, intellectuals began to take a new view of their role as intellectuals. The classical Roman statesman and intellectual Cicero became their model. Leonardo Bruni (1370–1444), a humanist, Florentine patriot, and chancellor of the city, wrote a biography of Cicero titled the *New Cicero*, in which he waxed enthusiastic about the fusion of political action and literary creation in Cicero's life. From Bruni's time on, Cicero served as the inspiration for the Renaissance ideal that it was the duty of an intellectual to live an active life for one's state. An individual only "grows to maturity—both intellectually and morally—through participation" in the life of the state. Civic humanism reflected the values of the urban society of the Italian Renaissance. Humanists came to believe that their study of the humanities should be put to the service of the state. It is no accident that humanists served the state as chancellors, councilors, and advisers.

Also evident in the humanism of the first half of the fifteenth century was a growing interest in classical Greek civilization. Bruni was one of the first Italian humanists to gain a thorough knowledge of Greek. He became an enthusiastic pupil of the Byzantine scholar Manuel Chrysoloras, who taught in Florence from 1396 to 1400. Humanists eagerly perused the works of Plato as well as Greek poets, dramatists, historians, and orators, such as Thucydides, Euripides, and Sophocles, all of whom had been neglected by the scholastics of the High Middle Ages.

❧ HUMANISM AND PHILOSOPHY

In the second half of the fifteenth century, a dramatic upsurge of interest in the works of Plato occurred. Cosimo de' Medici, the de facto ruler of Florence, encouraged this development by commissioning a translation of Plato's dialogues by Marsilio Ficino (1433–1499), who dedicated his life to the translation of Plato and the exposition of the Platonic philosophy known as Neoplatonism.

In two major works, Ficino undertook the synthesis of Christianity and Platonism into a single system. His Neoplatonism was based on two primary ideas, the Neoplatonic hierarchy of substances and a theory of spiritual love. The former postulated a hierarchy of substances, or great chain of being, from the lowest form of physical matter (plants) to the purest spirit (God), in which humans occupied a central or middle position. They were the link between the material world (through the body) and the spiritual world (through the soul), and their highest duty was to ascend toward that union with God that was the true end of human existence. Ficino's theory of spiritual or Platonic love maintained that just as all people are bound together in their common humanity by love, so too are all parts of the universe held together by bonds of sympathetic love.

Renaissance Hermeticism was another product of the Florentine intellectual environment of the late fifteenth century. At the request of Cosimo de' Medici, Ficino translated into Latin a Greek work titled the *Corpus Hermeticum*. The Hermetic manuscripts contained two kinds of writings. One type stressed the occult sciences, with emphasis on astrology, alchemy, and magic. The other focused on theological and philosophical beliefs and speculations. For Renaissance intellectuals, the Hermetic revival offered a new view of humankind. They believed that humans had been created as divine beings endowed with divine creative power but had freely chosen to enter the material world (nature). Humans could recover their divinity, however, through a regenerative experience or purification of the soul. Thus regenerated, they became true sages or magi, as the Renaissance called them, who had knowledge of God and of truth. In regaining their original divinity, they reacquired an intimate knowledge of nature and the ability to employ the powers of nature for beneficial purposes.

In Italy, the most prominent magi in the late fifteenth century were Ficino and his friend and pupil, Giovanni Pico della Mirandola (1463–1494). Pico produced one of the most famous writings of the Renaissance, *Oration on the Dignity of Man*. Pico combed diligently through the writings of many philosophers of different backgrounds for the common "nuggets of universal truth" that he believed were all part of God's revelation to humanity. In the *Oration* (see the box on p. 247), Pico offered a ringing statement of unlimited human potential: "To him it is granted to have whatever he chooses, to be whatever he wills."[9] Like Ficino, Pico took an avid interest in

Hermetic philosophy, accepting it as the "science of the Divine," which "embraces the deepest contemplation of the most secret things, and at last the knowledge of all nature."[10]

❋ Education in the Renaissance

The humanist movement had a profound affect on education. Renaissance humanists believed that human beings could be dramatically changed by education, and as a result, they wrote treatises on education and opened schools based on their ideas. At the core of humanist schools were the "liberal studies." Humanists believed that the "liberal studies" (what we call the liberal arts) were the key to true freedom, enabling inidividuals to reach their full potential. According to one humanist, "We call those studies liberal which are worthy of a free man; those studies by which we attain and practice virtue and wisdom; that education which calls forth, trains, and develops those highest gifts of body and mind which ennoble men."[11] The liberal studies included history, moral philosophy, eloquence (rhetoric), letters (grammar and logic), poetry, mathematics, astronomy, and music. The purpose of a liberal education was thus to produce individuals who followed a path of virtue and wisdom and possessed the rhetorical skills by which they could persuade others to do the same. Following the Greek precept of a sound mind in a sound body, humanist educators also stressed physical education. Pupils were taught the skills of javelin throwing, archery, and dancing and encouraged to run, wrestle, hunt, and swim.

The purpose of these humanist schools was to educate an elite, the ruling classes of their communities. Largely absent from such schools were females. The few female students who did attend humanist schools studied the classics and were encouraged to know some history and to ride, dance, sing, play the lute, and appreciate poetry. But they were told not to learn mathematics and rhetoric. Religion and morals were thought to hold first place in the education of Christian ladies and help prepare them for their roles as mothers and wives.

Humanist education was thought to be a practical preparation for life. Its aim was the creation not of a great scholar but of a complete citizen. As one humanist said, "Not everyone is obliged to excel in philosophy, medicine, or the law, nor are all equally favored by nature; but all are destined to live in society and to practice virtue."[12] Humanist schools

Pico della Mirandola and the Dignity of Man

Giovanni Pico della Mirandola was one of the foremost intellects of the Italian Renaissance. Pico boasted that he had studied all schools of philosophy, which he tried to demonstrate by drawing up nine hundred theses for public disputation at the age of twenty-four. As a preface to his theses, he wrote his famous oration, On the Dignity of Man, *in which he proclaimed the unlimited potentiality of human beings.*

❉ *Pico della Mirandola,* **Oration on the Dignity of Man**

At last the best of artisans [God] ordained that that creature to whom He had been able to give nothing proper to himself should have joint possession of whatever had been peculiar to each of the different kinds of being. He therefore took man as a creature of indeterminate nature, and assigning him a place in the middle of the world, addressed him thus: "Neither a fixed abode nor a form that is yours alone nor any function peculiar to yourself have we given you, Adam, to the end that according to your longing and according to your judgment you may have and possess what abode, what form, and what functions you yourself desire. The nature of all other beings is limited and constrained within the bounds of laws prescribed by Us. You, constrained by no limits, in accordance with your own free will, in whose hand We have placed you, shall ordain for yourself the limits of your nature. We have set you at the world's center that you may from there more easily observe whatever is in the world. We have made you neither of heaven nor of earth, neither mortal nor immortal, so that with freedom of choice and with honor, as though the maker and molder of yourself, you may fashion yourself in whatever shape you shall prefer. You shall have the power to degenerate into the lower forms of life, which are brutish. You shall have the power, out of your soul's judgment, to be reborn into the higher forms, which are divine."

O supreme generosity of God the Father, O highest and most marvelous felicity of man! To him it is granted to have whatever he chooses, to be whatever he wills. Beasts as soon as they are born bring with them from their mother's womb all they will ever possess. Spiritual beings, either from the beginning or soon thereafter, become what they are to be for ever and ever. On man when he came into life the Father conferred the seeds of all kinds and the germs of every way of life. Whatever seeds each man cultivates will grow to maturity and bear to him their own fruit. If they be vegetative, he will be like a plant. If sensitive, he will become brutish. If rational, he will grow into a heavenly being. If intellectual, he will be an angel and the son of God.

---

provided the model for the basic education of the European ruling classes until the twentieth century.

❉ *The Impact of Printing*

The Renaissance period witnessed the development of printing, one of the most important technological innovations of Western civilization. The art of printing had an immediate impact on European intellectual life and thought. Printing from hand-carved wooden blocks had been done in the West since the twelfth century and in China even before that. What was new to Europe in the fifteenth century was repeatable printing with movable metal type. The development of printing from movable type was a gradual process that culminated between 1445 and 1450; Johannes Gutenberg of Mainz played an important role in bringing the process to completion. Gutenberg's Bible, completed in 1455 or 1456, was the first true book in the West produced with movable type.

The new printing capability spread rapidly throughout Europe in the second half of the fifteenth century. Printing presses were established throughout the Holy Roman Empire in the 1460s and within ten years had spread to Italy, France, the Low Countries, Spain, and eastern Europe. Especially well known as a printing center was Venice, home by 1500 to almost one hundred printers who had produced almost two million volumes.

By 1500, there were more than a thousand printers in Europe who had published almost forty thousand titles (between eight and ten million copies).

Probably 50 percent of these books were religious—Bibles, books of devotion, and sermons. Next in importance were the Latin and Greek classics, medieval grammars, legal handbooks, works on philosophy, and an ever-growing number of popular romances.

Printing became one of the largest industries in Europe, and its effects were soon felt in many areas of European life. The printing of books encouraged the development of scholarly research and the desire to attain knowledge. Moreover, printing facilitated cooperation among scholars and helped produce standardized and definitive texts. Printing also stimulated the development of an ever-expanding lay reading public, a development that had an enormous impact on European society. Indeed, the new religious ideas of the Reformation would never have spread as rapidly as they did in the sixteenth century without the printing press.

◆ The Artistic Renaissance

Leonardo da Vinci, one of the great Italian Renaissance artists, once explained: "The painter will produce pictures of small merit if he takes for his standard the pictures of others, but if he will study from natural objects he will bear good fruit. . . . Those who take for their standard any one but nature . . . weary themselves in vain."[13] Renaissance artists considered the imitation of nature to be their primary goal. Their search for naturalism became an end in itself: to persuade onlookers of the reality of the object or event they were portraying. At the same time, the new artistic standards reflected a new attitude of mind as well, one in which human beings became the focus of attention, the "center and measure of all things," as one artist proclaimed.

The frescoes by Masaccio (1401–1428) in the Brancacci chapel in Florence have long been regarded as the first masterpieces of Early Renaissance art. In his use of monumental figures, the demonstration of a more realistic relationship between figures and landscape, and the visual representation of the laws of perspective, a new realistic style of painting was born. Onlookers became aware of a world of reality that appeared to be a continuation of their own world.

This new or Renaissance style was absorbed and modified by other Florentine painters in the fifteenth century. Especially important was the development of an experimental trend that took two directions. One emphasized the mathematical side of painting, the working out of the laws of perspective and the organization of outdoor space and light by geometry and perspective.

MASACCIO, *TRIBUTE MONEY*. With the frescoes of Masaccio, regarded by many as the first great works of Early Renaissance art, a new realistic style of painting was born. *Tribute Money* was one of a series of frescoes that Masaccio painted in the Brancacci chapel in the church of Santa Maria del Carmine in Florence. In illustrating a story from the Bible, Masaccio used a rational system of perspective to create a realistic relationship between the figures and their background.

The other aspect of the experimental trend involved the investigation of movement and anatomical structure. Indeed, the realistic portrayal of the human nude became one of the foremost preoccupations of Italian Renaissance art. The fifteenth century, then, was a period of experimentation and technical mastery.

The revolutionary achievements of Florentine painters in the fifteenth century were matched by equally stunning advances in sculpture and architecture. Donato di Donatello (1386–1466) spent time in Rome, studying and copying the statues of antiquity. His subsequent work in Florence reveals how well he had mastered the essence of what he saw. Among his numerous works was a statue of David, which is the first known "life-size free-standing bronze nude in European art since antiquity." Like Donatello's other statues, *David* radiated a simplicity and strength that reflected the dignity of humanity.

Filippo Brunelleschi (1377–1446) was a friend of Donatello's who accompanied him to Rome. Brunelleschi drew much inspiration from the architectural monuments of Roman antiquity, and when he returned to Florence, the Medici commissioned him to design the church of San Lorenzo. Inspired by Roman models, Brunelleschi created a church interior very different from that of the great medieval cathedrals. San Lorenzo's classical columns, rounded arches, and coffered ceiling created

FILIPPO BRUNELLESCHI, INTERIOR OF SAN LORENZO. Cosimo de' Medici contributed massive amounts of money to the rebuilding of the church of San Lorenzo. As seen in this view of the nave and choir of the church, Brunelleschi's architectural designs were based on the basilica plan borrowed by early Christians from pagan Rome. San Lorenzo's simplicity, evident in its rows of slender Corinthian columns, created a human-centered space.

DONATELLO, *DAVID*. Donatello's *David* first stood in the courtyard of the Medici Palace. On its base was an inscription praising Florentine heroism and virtue, leading art historians to assume that the statue was meant to commemorate the victory of Florence over Milan in 1428.

an environment that did not overwhelm the worshiper, materially or psychologically, as Gothic cathedrals did; instead, it comforted in that it was a space created to fit human, not divine, measurements.

By the end of the fifteenth century, Italian painters, sculptors, and architects had created a new artistic environment. Many artists had mastered the new techniques for a scientific observation of the world around them and were now ready to move into individualistic forms of creative expression. This final stage of Renaissance art, which flourished between 1480 and 1520, is called the High Renaissance. The High Renaissance was marked by the increasing importance of Rome as a new cultural center.

The High Renaissance was dominated by the work of three artistic giants, Leonardo da Vinci (1452–1519), Raphael (1483–1520), and Michelangelo (1475–1564). Leonardo represents a transitional figure in the shift to High Renaissance principles. He carried on the fifteenth-century experimental tradition by studying everything and even dissecting human bodies in order to see how nature worked. But Leonardo stressed the need to advance beyond such realism and initiated the High Renaissance's preoccupation with the idealization of

LEONARDO DA VINCI, *THE LAST SUPPER.* Leonardo da Vinci was the impetus behind the High Renaissance concern for the idealization of nature, moving from a realistic portrayal of the human figure to an idealized form. Evident in Leonardo's *Last Supper* is his effort to depict a person's character and inner nature by the use of gesture and movement. Unfortunately, Leonardo used an experimental technique in this fresco, which soon led to its physical deterioration.

nature, or the attempt to generalize from realistic portrayal to an ideal form. Leonardo's *Last Supper,* painted in Milan, is a brilliant summary of fifteenth-century trends in its organization of space and use of perspective to depict subjects three dimensionally. But it is also more. The figure of Philip is idealized, and there are profound psychological dimensions to the work. Jesus' words—"One of you shall betray me"—are experienced directly as each of the apostles reveals his personality and his relationship to the Savior. Through gestures and movement, Leonardo hoped to reveal a person's inner life.

Raphael blossomed as a painter at an early age; at twenty-five, he was already regarded as one of Italy's best painters. Raphael was acclaimed for his numerous madonnas (portraits of the Virgin Mary), in which he attempted to achieve an ideal of beauty far surpassing human standards. He is well known for his frescoes in the Vatican Palace; his *School of Athens* reveals a world of balance, harmony, and order—the underlying principles of the art of classical Greece and Rome.

Michelangelo, an accomplished painter, sculptor, and architect, was another giant of the High Renaissance. Fiercely driven by his desire to create, he worked with great passion and energy on a remarkable number of projects. Michelangelo was influenced by Neoplatonism, especially evident in his figures on the ceiling of the Sistine Chapel. These muscular figures reveal an ideal type of human being with perfect proportions. In good Neoplatonic fashion, their beauty is meant to be a reflection of divine beauty; the more beautiful the body, the more God-like the figure.

✸ *The Northern Artistic Renaissance*

In trying to provide an exact portrayal of their world, the artists of the north (especially the Low Countries) and Italy took different approaches. In Italy, the human form became the primary vehicle of expression as Italian artists sought to master the technical skills that allowed them to portray humans in realistic settings. The large wall spaces of Italian churches had given rise to the art of fresco painting, but in the north, the prevalence of Gothic cathedrals with their stained glass windows resulted in more emphasis on illuminated manuscripts and wooden panel painting for altarpieces. The space available in these works was limited, and great care was required to depict each object, leading northern painters to become masters at rendering details.

RAPHAEL, *SCHOOL OF ATHENS*. Raphael arrived in Rome in 1508 and began to paint a series of frescoes commissioned by Pope Julius II for the papal apartments at the Vatican. In the *School of Athens,* painted about 1510–1511, Raphael created an imaginary gathering of ancient philosophers. In the center stand Plato and Aristotle. At the left is Pythagoras, showing his system of proportions on a slate. At the right is Ptolemy, holding a celestial globe.

MICHELANGELO, *CREATION OF ADAM*. In 1508, Pope Julius II recalled Michelangelo to Rome and commissioned him to decorate the ceiling of the Sistine Chapel. This colossal project was not completed until 1512. Michelangelo attempted to tell the story of the Fall of Man by depicting nine scenes from the biblical Book of Genesis. In this scene, the well-proportioned figure of Adam, meant by Michelangelo to be a reflection of divine beauty, awaits the divine spark.

The most influential northern school of art in the fifteenth century was centered in Flanders. Jan van Eyck (c. 1380–1441) was among the first to use oil paint, a medium that enabled the artist to use a varied range of colors and make changes to create fine details. In the famous *Giovanni Arnolfini and His Bride*, van Eyck's attention to detail is staggering in the precise portraits, a glittering chandelier, and a mirror reflecting the objects in the room. Although each detail was rendered as observed, it is evident that van Eyck's comprehension of perspective was still uncertain. His work is truly indicative of northern Renaissance painters, who, in their effort to imitate nature, did so not by mastery of the laws of perspective and proportion but by empirical observation of visual reality and the accurate portrayal of details. Moreover, northern painters placed great emphasis on the emo-

tional intensity of religious feeling and created great works of devotional art, especially in their altarpieces. By the end of the fifteenth century, however, artists from the north began to study in Italy and were visually influenced by what artists were doing there.

One northern artist of this later period who was greatly influenced by the Italians was Albrecht Dürer (1471–1528) from Nuremberg. Dürer made two trips to Italy and absorbed most of what the Italians could teach, as is evident in his mastery of the laws of perspective and Renaissance theories of proportion. He wrote detailed treatises on both subjects. At the same time, as in his famous *Adoration of the Magi*, Dürer did not reject the use of minute details characteristic of northern artists. He did try, however, to integrate those details more harmoniously into his works and, like the Italian artists of the High Renaissance, tried to achieve

JAN VAN EYCK, *GIOVANNI ARNOLFINI AND HIS BRIDE*. Northern painters took great care in depicting each object and became masters at rendering details. This emphasis on a realistic portrayal is clearly evident in this oil painting, said to be a portrait of Giovanni Arnolfini, an Italian merchant who had settled in Bruges, and his wife, Giovanna Cenami.

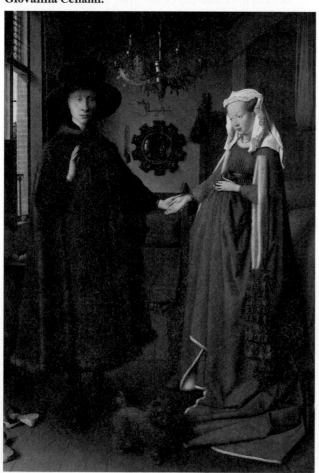

ALBRECHT DÜRER, *ADORATION OF THE MAGI*. By the end of the fifteenth century, northern artists began studying in Italy and adopting many of the techniques used by Italian painters. As is evident in this painting, which was the central panel for an altarpiece done for Frederick the Wise in 1504, Albrecht Dürer masterfully incorporated the laws of perspective and the ideals of proportion into his works. At the same time, he did not abandon the preoccupation with detail typical of northern artists.

a standard of ideal beauty by a careful examination of the human form.

◆ The European State in the Renaissance

In the first half of the fifteenth century, European states continued the disintegrative patterns of the previous century. In the second half of the century, however, recovery set in, and attempts were made to reestablish the centralized power of monarchical governments. To characterize the results, some historians have used the label "Renaissance states"; others have spoken of the "new monarchies," especially those of France, England, and Spain at the end of the fifteenth century. Whereas monarchs succeeded to varying degrees at extending their political authority in western Europe, rulers in central and eastern Europe were often weak and unable to impose their authority.

❉ The Renaissance State in Western Europe

Although the Hundred Years' War had made it difficult for French kings to assert their authority, the war had also developed a strong degree of French national feeling toward a common enemy that the kings could use to reestablish monarchical power. The process of developing a French territorial state was greatly advanced by King Louis XI (1461–1483), known as the Spider because of his wily and devious ways. Louis strengthened the use of the *taille*—an annual direct tax usually on land or property—as a permanent tax imposed by royal authority, giving him a sound, regular source of income. Louis repressed the French nobility and brought the provinces of Anjou, Maine, Bar, and Provence under royal control. Many historians believe that Louis created a base for the later development of a strong French monarchy.

The Hundred Years' War also strongly affected the other protagonist in that conflict, England. The cost of the war in its final years and the losses in manpower strained the English economy. Moreover, the end of the war brought even greater domestic turmoil to England when the War of the Roses broke out in the 1450s. This civil war pitted the ducal house of Lancaster, whose symbol was a red rose, against the ducal house of York, whose symbol was a white rose. Many aristocratic families of England were drawn into the conflict. Finally, in 1485, Henry Tudor, duke of Richmond, defeated the last Yorkist king, Richard III (1483–1485), at Bosworth Field and established a new dynasty.

As the first Tudor king, Henry VII (1485–1509) worked to reduce internal dissension and establish a strong monarchical government. Henry ended the private wars of the nobility by abolishing their armies. The new king was particularly successful in obtaining sufficient income from the traditional financial resources of the English monarch, such as the crown lands, judicial fees and fines, and customs duties. By using diplomacy to avoid wars, which are always expensive, the king avoided having to call Parliament on any regular basis to grant him funds. By not overburdening the landed gentry and middle class with taxes, Henry won their favor, and they provided much support for his monarchy. Henry's policies enabled him to leave England with a stable and prosperous government and an enhanced status for the monarchy itself.

Spain, too, experienced the growth of a strong national monarchy by the end of the fifteenth century. During the Middle Ages, several independent Christian kingdoms had emerged in the course of the long reconquest of the Iberian peninsula from the Muslims (see Map 12.2). Aragon and Castile were the strongest Spanish kingdoms; in the west was the independent monarchy of Portugal; in the north, the small kingdom of Navarre; and in the south, the Muslim kingdom of Granada.

A major step toward the unification of Spain was taken with the marriage of Isabella of Castile (1474–1504) and Ferdinand of Aragon (1479–1516) in 1469. This marriage was a dynastic union of two rulers, not a political union. Both kingdoms maintained their own parliaments (Cortes), courts, laws, coinage, speech, customs, and political organs. Nevertheless, the two rulers worked to strengthen royal control of government, especially in Castile. The royal council, which was supposed to supervise local administration and oversee the implementation of government policies, was stripped of aristocrats and filled primarily with middle-class lawyers. Trained in the principles of Roman law, these officials operated on the belief that the monarchy embodied the power of the state.

Ferdinand and Isabella reorganized the military forces of Spain, seeking to replace the undisciplined feudal levies they had inherited with a more professional royal army. The development of a strong infantry force as the heart of the new Spanish army made it the best in Europe by the sixteenth century,

MAP 12.2   Europe in the Renaissance.

and Spain emerged as an important power in European affairs.

Recognizing the importance of controlling the Catholic church, Ferdinand and Isabella secured from the pope the right to select the most important church officials in Spain, virtually making the clergy an instrument of royal power. Ferdinand and Isabella also pursued a policy of strict religious uniformity. Spain possessed two large religious minorities, the Jews and Muslims, both of whom had been largely tolerated in medieval Spain. Increased persecution in the fourteenth century, however, led the majority of Spanish Jews to convert to Christianity. But complaints about the sincerity of these Jewish converts prompted Ferdinand and Isabella to ask the pope to introduce the Inquisition into Spain in 1478. Under royal control, the Inquisition worked with cruel efficiency to guarantee the orthodoxy of the converts but had no authority over practicing Jews. Consequently, in 1492,

flush with the success of the conquest of Muslim Granada, Ferdinand and Isabella took the drastic step of expelling all professed Jews from Spain. It is estimated that 150,000 out of possibly 200,000 Jews fled. Muslims, too, were then "encouraged" to convert to Christianity, and in 1502, Isabella issued a decree expelling all professed Muslims from her kingdom. To a very large degree, the "most Catholic" monarchs had achieved their goal of absolute religious orthodoxy as a basic ingredient of the Spanish state. To be Spanish was to be Catholic, a policy of uniformity enforced by the Inquisition.

❀ Central Europe: The Holy Roman Empire

After 1438, the position of Holy Roman Emperor was in the hands of the Habsburg dynasty. Having gradually acquired a number of possessions along the

Danube, known collectively as Austria, the house of Habsburg had become one of the wealthiest land-holders in the empire and by the mid-fifteenth century began to play an important role in European affairs. Much of the Habsburg success in the fifteenth century was due not to military victories but to a well-executed policy of dynastic marriages.

Much was expected of the flamboyant Maximilian I (1493–1519) when he became emperor. Through the Reichstag, the imperial diet or parliament, Maximilian attempted to centralize the administration by creating new institutions common to the entire empire. Opposition from the German princes doomed these efforts, however. Maximilian's only real success lay in his marriage alliances, which led to a grandson, Charles, inheriting the traditional lands of the Habsburg, Burgundian, and Spanish monarchical lines at the beginning of the sixteenth century, making him the leading monarch of his age (see Chapter 13).

❉ The Struggle for Strong Monarchy in Eastern Europe

In eastern Europe, rulers struggled to achieve the centralization of their territorial states but faced serious obstacles. Although the population was mostly Slavic, there were islands of other ethnic groups that caused difficulties. Religious differences also troubled the area, as Roman Catholics, Greek Orthodox Christians, and pagans confronted each other.

Much of Polish history revolved around a bitter struggle between the crown and the landed nobility until the end of the fifteenth century, when the preoccupation of the Polish monarchy with problems in Bohemia and Hungary as well as war with the Russians and Turks enabled the aristocrats to reestablish their power. Through their control of the *Sejm* or national diet, the magnates reduced the peasantry to serfdom by 1511 and established the right to elect their kings. The Polish kings proved unable to establish a strong royal authority.

Since the conversion of Hungary to Roman Catholicism by German missionaries, its history had been closely tied to that of central and western Europe. The church became a large and prosperous institution. Wealthy bishops, along with great territorial lords, became powerful, independent political figures. For a brief while, Hungary developed into an important European state, the dominant power in eastern Europe. King Matthias Corvinus (1458–1490) broke the power of the wealthy lords and created a well-

CHRONOLOGY

The European State in the Renaissance

France	
Louis XI the Spider	1461–1483
England	
War of the Roses	1450s–1485
Richard III	1483–1485
Henry VII	1485–1509
Spain	
Isabella of Castile	1474–1504
Ferdinand of Aragon	1479–1516
Marriage of Ferdinand and Isabella	1469
Introduction of Inquisition	1478
Expulsion of the Jews	1492
Expulsion of the Muslims	1502
Holy Roman Empire	
Maximilian I	1493–1519
Eastern Europe	
Hungary: Matthias Corvinus	1458–1490
Russia: Ivan III	1462–1505
Fall of Constantinople and Byzantine Empire	1453

organized central administration. After his death, Hungary returned to weak rule, however, and the work of Corvinus was largely undone.

Since the thirteenth century, Russia had been under the domination of the Mongols. Gradually, the princes of Moscow rose to prominence by using their close relationship to the Mongol khans to increase their wealth and expand their possessions. In the reign of the great prince Ivan III (1462–1505), a new Russian state was born. Ivan III annexed other Russian principalities and took advantage of dissension among the Mongols to throw off their yoke by 1480.

❉ The Ottoman Turks and the End of the Byzantine Empire

Eastern Europe was increasingly threatened by the steadily advancing Ottoman Turks. The Byzantine Empire had served as a buffer between the Muslim Middle East and the Latin West for centuries, but it was severely weakened by the sack of Constantinople in 1204 and its occupation by the West. Although the Paleologus dynasty (1260–1453) had tried to reestablish Byzantine power in the Balkans, the threat from the Turks finally doomed the long-lasting empire.

Beginning in northeastern Asia Minor in the thirteenth century, the Ottoman Turks spread rapidly, seizing the lands of the Seljuk Turks and the Byzantine Empire. In 1345, they bypassed Constantinople and moved into the Balkans, which they conquered by the end of the century. Finally, in 1453, the great city of Constantinople fell to the Turks after a siege of several months. After consolidating their power, the Turks prepared to exert renewed pressure on the West, both in the Mediterranean and up the Danube valley toward Vienna. By the end of the fifteenth century, they were threatening Hungary, Austria, Bohemia, and Poland.

◆ The Church in the Renaissance

As a result of the efforts of the Council of Constance, the Great Schism of the Catholic church had finally been brought to an end in 1417. The ending of the schism proved to be the council's easiest task; it was much less successful in dealing with the problems of heresy and reform.

✵ *The Problems of Heresy and Reform*

The crisis in the Catholic church led to renewed calls for reform. A group of Czech reformers led by the chancellor of the university at Prague, John Hus (1374–1415), urged the elimination of the worldliness and corruption of the clergy and attacked the excessive power of the papacy within the Catholic church. Hus' objections fell on receptive ears. Criticism of the Catholic church was already widespread because the church was one of the largest landowners in Bohemia. Moreover, many clergymen were German, and the native Czechs' strong resentment of the Germans who dominated Bohemia also won attention for Hus' movement.

The Council of Constance attempted to deal with the growing problem of heresy by summoning Hus to the council. Granted safe conduct by Emperor Sigismund, Hus went in the hope of a free hearing of his ideas. Instead he was arrested, condemned as a heretic, and burned at the stake in 1415. This action turned the unrest in Bohemia into revolutionary upheaval, and the resulting Hussite wars racked the Holy Roman Empire until a truce was arranged in 1436.

The reform of the church was even less successful than the attempt to eradicate heresy. The Council of Constance passed two reform decrees. One stated that a general council of the church received its authority from God; hence every Christian, including the pope, was subject to its authority. The other decree provided for the regular holding of general councils to ensure that church reform would continue. Decrees alone, however, proved insufficient to reform the church. Councils could issue decrees, but popes had to execute them, and popes would not cooperate with councils that diminished their absolute authority. Beginning already in 1417, successive popes worked steadfastly for the next thirty years to defeat the conciliar movement.

By the mid-fifteenth century, the popes had reasserted their supremacy over the Catholic church. No longer, however, did they have any possibility of asserting supremacy over temporal governments as the medieval papacy had. Although the papal monarchy had been maintained, it had lost much moral prestige. In the fifteenth century, the Renaissance papacy contributed to an even further decline in the moral leadership of the popes.

✵ *The Renaissance Papacy*

The Renaissance papacy refers to the line of popes from the end of the Great Schism (1417) to the beginnings of the Reformation in the early sixteenth century. The primary concern of the papacy is governing the Catholic church as its spiritual leader. But as heads of the church, popes had temporal preoccupations as well, and the story of the Renaissance papacy is really an account of how the latter came to overshadow the popes' spiritual functions.

The manner in which Renaissance popes pursued their interests in the Papal States and Italian politics, especially their use of intrigue and even bloodshed, seemed shocking. Of all the Renaissance popes, Julius II (1503–1513) was most involved in war and politics. The fiery "warrior-pope" personally led armies against his enemies, much to the disgust of pious Christians who viewed the pope as a spiritual leader. As one intellectual wrote at the beginning of the sixteenth century: "How, O bishop standing in the room of the Apostles [the pope], dare you teach the people the things that pertain to war?"

To further their territorial aims in the Papal States, the popes needed loyal servants. Because they were not hereditary monarchs, popes could not build dynasties over several generations and came to rely on the practice of nepotism to promote their families' interests. Pope Sixtus IV (1471–1484), for example, made five of his nephews (the word *nepotism* is in fact derived from the Greek *nepos*, meaning "nephew") cardinals and gave them an abundance of church offices to build up their finances. The infamous Borgia pope, Alexander VI (1492–1503), known for his debauchery and sensuality, raised one son, one nephew, and the brother of one mistress to the cardinalate. Alexander scandalized the church by encouraging his son Cesare to carve a state out of the territories of the Papal States in central Italy.

The Renaissance popes were great patrons of Renaissance culture, and their efforts made Rome a cultural leader at the beginning of the sixteenth century. For the warrior-pope Julius II, the patronage of Renaissance culture was mostly a matter of policy as he endeavored to add to the splendor of his pontificate by tearing down the old basilica of Saint Peter and beginning construction of what was to be the greatest building in Christendom, Saint Peter's basilica. Julius' successor, Leo X (1513–1521), was also a patron of Renaissance culture, not as a matter of policy but as a deeply involved participant. A member of the Medici family, he was made a cardinal at the age of thirteen and acquired a refined taste in art, manners, and social life among the Florentine elite. He became pope at the age of thirty-seven, supposedly remarking to the Venetian ambassador, "Let us enjoy the papacy, since God has given it to us." Raphael was commissioned to do paintings, and the construction of St. Peter's was accelerated as Rome became the literary and artistic center of the Renaissance.

A RENAISSANCE POPE: SIXTUS IV. The Renaissance popes allowed secular concerns to overshadow their spiritual duties. They became concerned with territorial expansion, finances, and Renaissance culture. Pope Sixtus IV had the Sistine Chapel built and later had it decorated by some of the leading artists of his day. This fresco by Melozzo da Forlì shows the pope on his throne receiving the humanist Platina (kneeling), who was keeper of the Vatican Library.

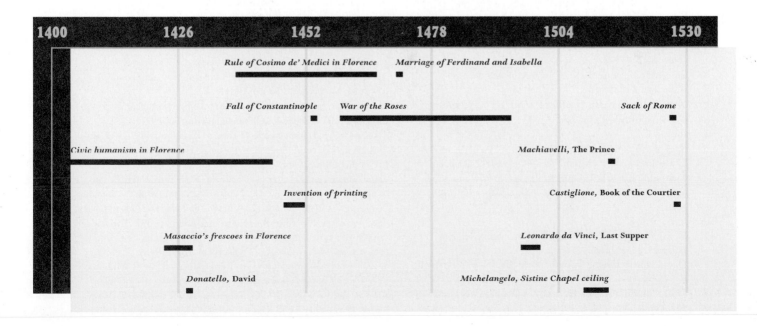

1400	1426	1452	1478	1504	1530

Rule of Cosimo de' Medici in Florence   *Marriage of Ferdinand and Isabella*

Fall of Constantinople   *War of the Roses*   *Sack of Rome*

Civic humanism in Florence   *Machiavelli,* **The Prince**

Invention of printing   *Castiglione,* **Book of the Courtier**

Masaccio's frescoes in Florence   *Leonardo da Vinci,* **Last Supper**

Donatello, **David**   *Michelangelo,* **Sistine Chapel ceiling**

Conclusion

The Renaissance was a period of transition that witnessed a continuation of the economic, political, and social trends that had begun in the High Middle Ages. It was also a movement in which intellectuals and artists proclaimed a new vision of humankind and raised fundamental questions about the value and importance of the individual. Of course, intellectuals and artists wrote and painted for the upper classes, and the brilliant intellectual, cultural, and artistic accomplishments of the Renaissance were really products of and for the elite. The ideas of the Renaissance did not have a broad base among the masses of the people. As Lorenzo the Magnificent, ruler of Florence, once commented, "Only men of noble birth can obtain perfection. The poor, who work with their hands and have no time to cultivate their minds, are incapable of it."

The Renaissance did, however, raise new questions about medieval traditions. In advocating a return to the early sources of Christianity and criticizing current religious practices, the humanists raised fundamental issues about the Catholic church, which was still an influential institution. In the sixteenth century, the intellectual revolution of the fifteenth century gave way to a religious renaissance that touched the lives of people, including the masses, in new and profound ways. After the Reformation, Europe would never again be the unified Christian commonwealth it once believed it was.

Notes

1. Quoted in Jacob Burckhardt, *The Civilization of the Renaissance in Italy*, trans. S. G. C. Middlemore (London, 1960), p. 81.
2. Baldassare Castiglione, *The Book of the Courtier*, trans. Charles S. Singleton (Garden City, N.Y., 1959), pp. 288–289.
3. Quoted in De Lamar Jensen, *Renaissance Europe* (Lexington, Mass., 1981), p. 94.
4. Gene Brucker, ed., *Two Memoirs of Renaissance Florence* (New York, 1967), p. 132.
5. Quoted in Margaret L. King, *Women of the Renaissance* (Chicago, 1991), p. 3.
6. Niccolò Machiavelli, *The Prince*, trans. David Wootton (Indianapolis, 1995), p. 48.
7. Ibid., p. 55.
8. Ibid., p. 27.
9. Giovanni Pico della Mirandola, *Oration on the Dignity of Man*, in E. Cassirer, P. O. Kristeller, and J. H. Randall Jr., eds., *The Renaissance Philosophy of Man* (Chicago, 1948), p. 225.
10. Ibid., pp. 247–249.
11. W. H. Woodward, *Vittorino da Feltre and Other Humanist Educators* (Cambridge, 1897), p. 102.
12. Quoted in Iris Origo, *The Light of the Past* (New York, 1959), p. 136.
13. Quoted in Elizabeth G. Holt, ed., *A Documentary History of Art* (Garden City, N.Y., 1959), vol. 1, p. 286.

Suggestions for Further Reading

The classic study of the Italian Renaissance is J. Burckhardt, *The Civilization of the Renaissance in Italy*, trans. S. G. C. Middlemore (London, 1960), first published in 1860. General works on the Renaissance in Europe include D. L. Jensen, *Renaissance Europe* (Lexington, Mass., 1981); P. Burke, *The European Renaissance: Centres and Peripheries* (Oxford, 1998); E. Breisach, *Renaissance Europe, 1300–1517* (New York, 1973); J. Hale, *The Civilization of Europe in the Renaissance* (New York, 1994); and the classic work by M. P. Gilmore, *The World of Humanism, 1453–1517* (New York, 1962). Although many of its interpretations are outdated, W. Ferguson's *Europe in Transition, 1300–1520* (Boston, 1962), contains a wealth of information. The brief study by P. Burke, *The Renaissance*, 2d ed. (New York, 1997), is a good summary of recent literature on the Renaissance. For beautifully illustrated introductions to the Renaissance, see G. Holmes, *Renaissance* (New York, 1996), and M. Aston, ed., *The Panorama of the Renaissance* (New York, 1996).

Brief but basic works on Renaissance economic matters are H. A. Miskimin, *The Economy of Early Renaissance Europe, 1300–1460* (New York, 1975) and *The Economy of Later Renaissance Europe, 1460–1600* (New York, 1978). For a new interpretation of economic matters, see L. Jardine, *Worldly Goods* (New York, 1996). Numerous facets of social life in the Renaissance are examined in J. R. Hale, *Renaissance Europe: The Individual and Society* (London, 1971); B. Pullan, *Rich and Poor in Renaissance Venice* (Cambridge, Mass., 1971); and G. Ruggiero, *The Boundaries of Eros: Sex Crime and Sexuality in Renaissance Venice* (Oxford, 1985). On family and marriage, see C. Klapisch-Zuber, *Women, Family, and Ritual in Renaissance Italy* (Chicago, 1985), and the well-told story by G. Brucker, *Giovanni and Lusanna: Love and Marriage in Renaissance Florence* (Berkeley, Calif., 1986). On women, see M. L. King, *Women of the Renaissance* (Chicago, 1991), and N. Z. Davis and A. Farge, eds., *A History of Women: Renaissance and Enlightenment Paradoxes* (Cambridge, Mass., 1993).

The best overall study of the Italian city-states is L. Martines, *Power and Imagination: City-States in Renaissance Italy* (New York, 1979), although D. Hay and J. Law, *Italy in the Age of the Renaissance* (London, 1989), is also a good survey. There is an enormous literature on Renaissance Florence. The best introduction is G. A. Brucker, *Renaissance Florence*, rev. ed. (Berkeley, Calif., 1983). A popular biography of Isabella d'Este is G. Marek, *The Bed and the Throne* (New York, 1976). On the *condottieri*, see M. Mallett, *Mercenaries and Their Masters: Warfare in Renaissance Italy* (Totowa, N.J., 1974). Machiavelli's life can be examined in Q. Skinner, *Machiavelli* (Oxford, 1981).

Brief introductions to Renaissance humanism can be found in D. R. Kelley, *Renaissance Humanism* (Boston, 1991); C. G. Nauert Jr., *Humanism and the Culture of Renaissance Europe* (Cambridge, 1995); and F. B. Artz, *Renaissance Humanism, 1300–1550* (Oberlin, Ohio, 1966). The fundamental work on fifteenth-century civic humanism is H. Baron, *The Crisis of the Early Italian Renaissance*, 2d ed. (Princeton, N.J., 1966). The classic work on humanist education is W. H. Woodward, *Vittorino da Feltre and Other Humanist Educators* (New York, 1963), first published in 1897. The impact of printing is exhaustively examined in E. Eisenstein, *The Printing Press as an Agent of Change*, 2 vols. (New York, 1978).

For brief introductions to Renaissance art, see R. M. Letts, *The Cambridge Introduction to Art: The Renaissance* (Cambridge, 1981), and B. Cole and A. Gealt, *Art of the Western World* (New York, 1989), chaps. 6–8. Good surveys of Renaissance art include F.

Hartt, *History of Italian Renaissance Art*, 4th ed. (Englewood Cliffs, N.J., 1994); S. Elliott, *Italian Renaissance Painting*, 2d ed. (London, 1993); R. Turner, *Renaissance Florence: The Invention of a New Art* (New York, 1997); and L. Murray, *The High Renaissance* (New York, 1967). For studies of individual artists, see J. H. Beck, *Raphael* (New York, 1994); M. Kemp, *Leonardo da Vinci: The Marvellous Works of Nature and of Man* (London, 1981); and A. Hughes, *Michelangelo* (London, 1997).

For a general work on the political development of Europe in the Renaissance, see J. H. Shennan, *The Origins of the Modern European State, 1450–1725* (London, 1974). On France, see D. Potter, *A History of France, 1460–1560* (London, 1995). Early Renaissance England is examined in J. R. Lander, *Crown and Nobility, 1450–1509* (London, 1976). On the first Tudor king, see S. B. Chrimes, *Henry VII* (Berkeley, Calif., 1972). Good coverage of Renaissance Spain can be found in J. N. Hillgarth, *The Spanish Kingdoms, 1250–1516*, vol. 2, *Castilian Hegemony, 1410–1516* (New York, 1978). Good works on eastern Europe include P. W. Knoll, *The Rise of the Polish Monarchy* (Chicago, 1972), and C. A. Macartney, *Hungary: A Short History* (Edinburgh, 1962). On the Ottomans and their expansion, see H. Inalcik, *The Ottoman Empire: The*

Classical Age, 1300–1600 (London, 1973), and the classic work by S. Runciman, *The Fall of Constantinople, 1453* (Cambridge, 1965).

On problems of heresy and reform, see C. Crowder, *Unity, Heresy and Reform, 1378–1460* (London, 1977). Aspects of the Renaissance papacy can be examined in E. Lee, *Sixtus IV and Men of Letters* (Rome, 1978), and M. Mallett, *The Borgias* (New York, 1969). On Rome, see especially P. Partner, *Renaissance Rome, 1500–1559: A Portrait of a Society* (Berkeley, Calif., 1976).

For additional reading, go to InfoTrac College Edition, your online research library at http://web1.infotrac-college.com

Enter the search term *Renaissance* using the Subject Guide.

Enter the search term *Machiavelli* using Key Terms.

Enter the search term *humanism* using the Subject Guide.

Enter the search terms *Leonardo da Vinci* using Key Terms.

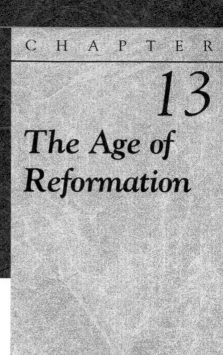

CHAPTER

13

The Age of Reformation

CHAPTER OUTLINE

- Prelude to Reformation
- Martin Luther and the Reformation in Germany
- The Spread of the Protestant Reformation
- The Social Impact of the Protestant Reformation
- The Catholic Reformation
- Conclusion

FOCUS QUESTIONS

- Who were the Christian humanists, and how did they differ from the Protestant reformers?
- What were Martin Luther's main disagreements with the Roman Catholic church, and why did the movement he began spread so quickly across Europe?
- What were the main tenets of Lutheranism, Zwinglianism, Calvinism, and Anabaptism, and how did they differ from each other and from Catholicism?
- What impact did the Protestant Reformation have on the society of the sixteenth century?
- What measures did the Roman Catholic church take to reform itself and to combat Protestantism in the sixteeth century?

O N APRIL 18, 1520, *a lowly monk stood before the emperor and princes of Germany in the city of Worms. He had been called before this august gathering to answer charges of heresy, charges that could threaten his very life. The monk was confronted with a pile of his books and asked if he wished to defend them all or reject a part. Courageously, Martin Luther defended them all and asked to be shown where any part was in error on the basis of "Scripture and plain reason." The emperor was outraged by Luther's response and made his own position clear the next day: "Not only I, but you of this noble German nation, would be forever disgraced if by our negligence not only heresy but the very suspicion of heresy were to survive. After having heard yesterday the obstinate defense of Luther, I regret that I have so long delayed in proceeding against him and his false teaching. I will have no more to do with him." Luther's appearance at Worms set the stage for a serious challenge to the authority of the Catholic church. This was by no means the first crisis in the church's fifteen-hundred-year history, but its consequences were more far reaching than anyone at Worms in 1520 could have imagined.*

Throughout the Middle Ages, the Catholic church continued to assert its primacy of position. It had overcome defiance of its temporal authority by emperors while challenges to its doctrines had been crushed by the Inquisition and combated by new religious orders that carried its message of salvation to all the towns and villages of medieval Europe. The growth of the papacy had paralleled the growth of the church, but by the end of the Middle Ages, challenges to papal authority from the rising power of monarchical states had resulted in a loss of papal temporal authority. An even greater threat to papal authority and church unity arose in the sixteenth century when the unity of Christendom was shattered by the Reformation.

The movement begun by Martin Luther when he made his dramatic stand quickly spread across Europe, a clear indication of dissatisfaction with Catholic practices. Within a short time, new religious practices, doctrines, and organizations, including Zwinglianism, Calvinism, Anabaptism, and Anglicanism, were attracting adherents all over Europe. Seemingly helpless to stop the new Protestant churches, the Catholic church too underwent a religious renaissance and managed by the mid-sixteenth century to revive its fortunes. Historians who speak of the Reformation as the beginning of the modern world exaggerate its importance, but there is no doubt that the splintering of Christendom ushered in new ways of thinking and prepared the ground for modern avenues of growth.

◆ Prelude to Reformation

Martin Luther's reform movement was not the first in sixteenth-century Europe. During the second half of the fifteenth century, the new classical learning that was part of Italian Renaissance humanism spread to northern Europe and spawned a movement called Christian or Northern Renaissance humanism, whose major goal was the reform of Christendom.

❈ Christian or Northern Renaissance Humanism

The most important characteristic of northern Renaissance humanism was its reform program. With their belief in the ability of human beings to reason and improve themselves, the northern humanists thought that through education in the sources of classical, and especially Christian, antiquity, they could instill a true inner piety or an inward religious feeling that would bring about a reform of the church and society. For this reason, Christian humanists supported schools, brought out new editions of the classics, and prepared new editions of the Bible and writings of such church fathers as Augustine, Ambrose, and Jerome. In the preface to his edition of the Greek New Testament, the famous humanist Erasmus wrote:

> Indeed, I disagree very much with those who are unwilling that Holy Scripture, translated into the vulgar tongue, be read by the uneducated, as if Christ taught such intricate doctrines that they could scarcely be understood by very few theologians, or as if the strength of the Christian religion consisted in men's ignorance of it. . . . I would that even the lowliest women read the Gospels and the Pauline Epistles. And I would that they were translated into all languages so that they could be read and understood not only by Scots and Irish but also by Turks and Saracens. . . . Would that, as a result, the farmer sing some portion of them at the plow, the weaver hum some parts of them to the movement of his shuttle, the traveler lighten the weariness of the journey with stories of this kind![1]

This belief in the power of education would remain an important characteristic of European civilization. Like later intellectuals, Christian humanists believed that to change society, they must first change the human beings who compose it.

The most influential of all the Christian humanists was the Dutch-born scholar Desiderius Erasmus (1466–1536). After withdrawing from a monastery, he wandered to France, England, Italy, Germany, and Switzerland, conversing everywhere in the classical Latin that might be called his mother tongue. The *Handbook of the Christian Knight*, published in 1503, reflected his preoccupation with religion. He called his conception of religion "the philosophy of Christ," by which he meant that Christianity should be a guiding philosophy for the direction of daily life rather than the system of dogmatic beliefs and practices that the medieval church seemed to stress. In other words, he emphasized inner piety and deemphasized the external forms of religion (such as the sacraments, pilgrimages, fasts, veneration of saints, and relics). To return to the simplicity of the early church, people needed to understand the original meaning of the Scriptures and early church fathers. Because Erasmus thought that the standard Latin edition of the Bible, known as the Vulgate, contained errors, he edited the Greek text of the New Testament from the earliest available manuscripts and published it, along with a new Latin translation, in 1516.

To Erasmus, the reform of the church meant spreading an understanding of the philosophy of Jesus, providing enlightened education in the sources of early Christianity, and making commonsense criticism of the abuses in the church. This critical approach is especially evident in *The Praise of Folly,* written in 1511, in which Erasmus was able to engage in a humorous yet effective criticism of the most corrupt practices of his own society. He was especially harsh on the abuses within the ranks of the clergy:

> Many of [the monks] work so hard at protocol and at traditional fastidiousness that they think one heaven hardly a suitable reward for their labors; never recalling, however, that the time will come when Christ will demand a reckoning of that which he had prescribed, namely charity, and that he will hold their deeds of little account. One monk will then exhibit his belly filled with every kind of fish; another will profess a knowledge of over a hundred hymns. Still another will reveal a countless number of fasts that he has made, and will account for his large belly by explaining that his fasts have always been broken by a single large meal.[2]

Erasmus' program did not achieve the reform of the church that he so desired. His moderation and his emphasis on education were quickly overwhelmed by the passions of the Reformation. Undoubtedly, though, his work helped prepare the way for the Reformation; as contemporaries proclaimed, "Erasmus laid the egg that Luther hatched." Yet Erasmus eventually disapproved of Luther and the Protestant reformers. He had no intention of destroying the unity of the medieval Christian church; instead, his whole program was based on reform within the church.

❋ Church and Religion on the Eve of the Reformation

Corruption in the Catholic church was another factor that encouraged people to want reform. No doubt the failure of the Renaissance popes to provide spir-

ERASMUS. Desiderius Erasmus was the most influential of the northern Renaissance humanists. He sought to restore Christianity to the early simplicity found in the teachings of Jesus. This portrait of Erasmus was painted in 1523 by Hans Holbein the Younger, who had formed a friendship with the great humanist while they were both in Basel.

itual leadership had affected the spiritual life of all Christendom. The papal court's preoccupation with finances had an especially strong impact on the clergy. So did the economic changes of the fourteenth and fifteenth centuries. The highest positions among the clergy were increasingly held by either nobles or wealthy members of the bourgeoisie. Moreover, to increase their revenues, high church officials (such as bishops, archbishops, and cardinals) took over more than one church office. This pluralism (the holding of multiple church offices) begat absenteeism: church officeholders ignored their duties and hired underlings who often had even less interest in the job. Complaints about the ignorance and ineptness of parish priests became widespread in the fifteenth century.

While the leaders of the church were failing to meet their responsibilities, ordinary people were clamoring for meaningful religious expression and certainty of salvation. As a result, the salvation process became almost mechanical. As more and more people sought salvation through the veneration of relics, collections of such objects grew. Frederick the Wise, elector of Saxony and Luther's prince, had amassed over five thousand relics to which were attached indulgences (remissions of the penalties for sin) that could reduce one's time in purgatory by 1,443 years. Other people sought salvation in the popular mystical movement known as the Modern Devotion. The Modern Devotion downplayed religious dogma and stressed the need to follow the teachings of Jesus. Thomas à Kempis, author of *The Imitation of Christ,* wrote that "truly, at the day of judgment we shall not be examined by what we have read, but what we have done; not how well we have spoken, but how religiously we have lived."

➔ What is striking about the revival of religious piety in the fifteenth century—whether expressed through such external forces such as the veneration of relics and the buying of indulgences or through the mystical path—was its adherence to the orthodox beliefs and practices of the Catholic church. The agitation for certainty of salvation and spiritual peace was done within the framework of the "holy mother Church." But as the devout experienced the clergy's inability to live up to their expectations, disillusionment grew. The intensification of religious feeling, especially in the second half of the fifteenth century, resonated little among the worldly-wise clergy, and this divergence may explain the tremendous and immediate impact of Luther's ideas.

◆ Martin Luther and the Reformation in Germany

The Protestant Reformation began with a typical medieval question: What must I do to be saved? Martin Luther, a deeply religious man, found an answer that did not fit within the traditional teachings of the late medieval church. Ultimately, he split with that church, destroying the religious unity of western Christendom. That other people were concerned with the same question is evident in the rapid spread of the Reformation. But religion was so entangled in the social, economic, and political forces of the period that Protestant reformers' hope of transforming the church quickly proved illusory.

Martin Luther was born in Germany on November 10, 1483. His father wanted him to become a lawyer, so Luther enrolled at the University of Erfurt. In 1505, after becoming a master in the liberal arts, the young man began to study law. But Luther was not content, not in small part due to his long-standing religious inclinations. That summer, while returning to Erfurt after a brief visit home, he was caught in a ferocious thunderstorm and vowed that if he survived unscathed, he would become a monk. He then entered the monastic order of the Augustinian Hermits in Erfurt, much to his father's disgust. In the monastery, Luther focused on his major concern, the assurance of salvation. The traditional beliefs and practices of the church seemed unable to relieve his obsession with this question. Luther threw himself into his monastic routine with a vengeance:

> I was indeed a good monk and kept my order so strictly that I could say that if ever a monk could get to heaven through monastic discipline, I was that monk. . . . And yet my conscience would not give me certainty, but I always doubted and said, "You didn't do that right. You weren't contrite enough. You left that out of your confession." The more I tried to remedy an uncertain, weak and troubled conscience with human traditions, the more I daily found it more uncertain, weaker and more troubled.[3]

Despite his herculean efforts, Luther achieved no certainty of salvation.

To help overcome his difficulties, his superiors recommended that the intelligent yet disturbed monk study theology. He received his doctorate in 1512 and then became a professor in the theological faculty at the University of Wittenberg, lecturing on the Bible. Probably sometime between 1513 and 1516, through his study of the Bible, he arrived at an answer to his problem.

Catholic doctrine had emphasized that both faith and good works were required of a Christian to achieve personal salvation. In Luther's eyes, human beings, weak and powerless in the sight of an almighty God, could never do enough good works to merit salvation. Through his study of the Bible, especially his work on Paul's Epistle to the Romans, Luther rediscovered another way of viewing this problem. To Luther, humans are saved not through their good works but through faith in the promises of God, made possible by the sacrifice of Jesus on the cross. The doctrine of salvation or justification by grace through faith alone became the primary doctrine of the Protestant Reformation (justification is the act by which a

Luther and the Ninety-Five Theses

To most historians, the publication of Luther's Ninety-Five Theses marks the beginning of the Reformation. To Luther, they were simply a response to what he considered the blatant abuse of Johann Tetzel's selling of indulgences. Although written in Latin, the theses were soon translated into German and disseminated widely across Germany. They made an immense impression on Germans already dissatisfied with the ecclesiastical and financial policies of the papacy.

✻ Martin Luther, Selections from the Ninety-Five Theses

5. The Pope has neither the will nor the power to remit any penalties beyond those he has imposed either at his own discretion or by canon law.

20. Therefore the Pope, by his plenary remission of all penalties, does not mean "all" in the absolute sense, but only those imposed by himself.

21. Hence those preachers of Indulgences are wrong when they say that a man is absolved and saved from every penalty by the Pope's Indulgences.

27. It is mere human talk to preach that the soul flies out [of purgatory] immediately the money clinks in the collection-box.

28. It is certainly possible that when the money clinks in the collection-box greed and avarice can increase; but the intercession of the Church depends on the will of God alone.

50. Christians should be taught that, if the Pope knew the exactions of the preachers of Indul-

gences, he would rather have the basilica of St. Peter reduced to ashes than built with the skin, flesh and bones of his sheep.

81. This wanton preaching of pardons makes it difficult even for learned men to redeem respect due to the Pope from the slanders or at least the shrewd questionings of the laity.

82. For example: "Why does not the Pope empty purgatory for the sake of most holy love and the supreme need of souls? This would be the most righteous of reasons, if he can redeem innumerable souls for sordid money with which to build a basilica, the most trivial of reasons."

86. Again: "Since the Pope's wealth is larger than that of the crassest Crassi of our time, why does he not build this one basilica of St. Peter with his own money, rather than with that of the faithful poor?"

90. To suppress these most conscientious questionings of the laity by authority only, instead of refuting them by reason, is to expose the Church and the Pope to the ridicule of their enemies, and to make Christian people unhappy.

94. Christians should be exhorted to seek earnestly to follow Christ, their Head, through penalties, deaths, and hells.

95. And let them thus be more confident of entering heaven through many tribulations rather than through a false assurance of peace.

---

person is made deserving of salvation). Because Luther had arrived at this doctrine from his study of the Bible, the Bible became for Luther, as for all other Protestants, the chief guide to religious truth. Justification by faith and the Bible as the sole authority in religious affairs were the twin pillars of the Protestant Reformation.

Luther did not see himself as either an innovator or a heretic, but his involvement in the indulgence controversy propelled him into an open confrontation with church officials and forced him to see the theological implications of justification by faith alone.

Luther was greatly distressed by the widespread selling of indulgences, certain that people were guaranteeing their eternal damnation by relying on these pieces of paper to assure themselves of salvation. Johann Tetzel, a rambunctious Dominican, hawked the indulgences with the slogan "As soon as the coin in the coffer [money box] rings, the soul from purgatory springs."

Greatly angered, Luther issued a stunning indictment of the abuses in the sale of indulgences, known as the Ninety-Five Theses (see the box above). It is doubtful that Luther intended to break with the church over the issue of indulgences. If the pope had clarified the use of indulgences, as Luther wished, Luther would probably have been satisfied and the controversy would have ended. But the Renaissance pope Leo X did not take the issue seriously and is even reported to have said that Luther was simply "some drunken German who will amend his ways when he sobers up." A German translation of the Ninety-Five Theses was quickly printed in thousands of copies and received sympathetically in a Germany that had a long tradition of dissatisfaction with papal policies and power.

In three pamphlets published in 1520, Luther moved toward a more definite break with the Catholic church. The *Address to the Nobility of the German Nation* was a political tract written in German in which Luther called on the German princes to overthrow the papacy in Germany and establish a reformed German church. *The Babylonian Captivity of the Church* attacked the sacramental system as the means by which the pope and church had held the real meaning of the Gospel in captivity for a thousand years. He called for the reform of monasticism and for the clergy to marry. While virginity is good, Luther argued, marriage is better, and freedom of choice is best. *On the Freedom of a Christian Man* was a short treatise on the doctrine of salvation. It is faith alone, not good works, that justifies, frees, and brings salvation through Jesus. Being saved and freed by his faith in Jesus, however, does not free the Christian from doing good works. Rather he performs good works out of gratitude to God: "Good works do not make a good man, but a good man does good works."[4]

Unable to accept Luther's forcefully worded dissent from traditional Catholic teachings, the church excommunicated him in January 1521. He was also summoned to appear before the imperial diet or Reichstag of the Holy Roman Empire in Worms, convened by the newly elected Emperor Charles V (1519–1556). Expected to recant the heretical doctrines he had

WOODCUT: LUTHER VERSUS THE POPE. In the 1520s, after Luther's return to Wittenberg, his teachings began to spread rapidly, ending ultimately in a reform movement supported by state authorities. Pamphlets containing picturesque woodcuts were important in the spread of Luther's ideas. In the woodcut shown here, the crucified Jesus attends Luther's service on the left, while on the right the pope is at a table selling indulgences.

espoused, Luther refused and made the famous reply that became the battle cry of the Reformation:

> Since then Your Majesty and your lordships desire a simple reply, I will answer without horns and without teeth. Unless I am convicted by Scripture and plain reason—I do not accept the authority of popes and councils, for they have contradicted each other—my conscience is captive to the Word of God. I cannot and I will not recant anything, for to go against conscience is neither right nor safe. Here I stand, I cannot do otherwise. God help me. Amen.[5]

The young Emperor Charles was outraged at Luther's audacity and gave his opinion that "a single friar who goes counter to all Christianity for a thousand years must be wrong." By the Edict of Worms, Martin Luther was made an outlaw within the empire. His works were to be burned and Luther himself captured and delivered to the emperor.

✳ The Development of Lutheranism

Between 1521 and 1525, Luther's religious movement became a revolution. Lutheranism had much appeal and spread rapidly. The preaching of evangelical sermons, based on a return to the original message of the Bible, found favor throughout Germany. Also useful to the spread of the Reformation were pamphlets illustrated with vivid woodcuts portraying the pope as a hideous Antichrist and titled with catchy phrases such as "I Wonder Why There Is No Money in the Land" (which, of course, was an attack on papal greed).

Luther was able to gain the support of his prince, the elector of Saxony, as well as other German rulers among the more than three hundred states that made up the Holy Roman Empire. Lutheranism spread to both princely and ecclesiastical states in northern and central Germany as well as to two-thirds of the free imperial cities, especially those of southern Germany, where prosperous burghers, for both religious and secular reasons, became committed to Luther's cause. At its outset, the Reformation in Germany was largely an urban phenomenon.

A series of crises in the mid-1520s made it apparent, however, that spreading the word of God was not as easy as Luther had originally envisioned—the usual plight of most reformers. Luther experienced dissent within his own ranks in Wittenberg as well as defection from many Christian humanists who feared that Luther's movement threatened the unity of Christendom. The Peasants' War constituted Luther's greatest challenge, however. In June 1524, peasants in Germany rose in revolt against their lords and looked to Luther for support. But Luther, who knew how much his reformation of the church depended on the full support of the German princes and magistrates, supported the rulers. To Luther, the state and its rulers were ordained by God and given the authority to maintain the peace and order necessary for the spread of the Gospel. It was the duty of princes to suppress all revolt. By May 1525, the German princes had ruthlessly suppressed the peasant hordes. By this time, Luther found himself ever more dependent on state authorities for the growth and maintenance of his reformed church.

The Lutheran churches in Germany (and later in Scandinavia) quickly became territorial or state churches in which the state supervised and disciplined church members. As part of the development of these state-dominated churches, Luther also instituted new religious services to replace the Mass. These featured a worship service consisting of a German liturgy that focused on Bible reading, preaching the word of God, and song. Following his own denunciation of clerical celibacy, Luther married a former nun, Katherina von Bora, in 1525. His union provided a model of married and family life for the new Protestant minister.

✳ Germany and the Reformation: Religion and Politics

From its very beginning, the fate of Luther's movement was closely tied to political affairs. In 1519, Charles I, king of Spain and the grandson of the Emperor Maximilian, was elected Holy Roman Emperor as Charles V (1519–1556). Charles V ruled over an immense empire, consisting of Spain and its overseas possessions, the traditional Austrian Habsburg lands, Bohemia, Hungary, the Low Countries, and the Kingdom of Naples in southern Italy (see Map 13.1). The extent of his possessions was reflected in the languages he used: "I speak Spanish to God, Italian to women, French to men, and German to my horse." Politically, Charles wanted to maintain his dynasty's control over his enormous empire; religiously, he hoped to preserve the unity of the Catholic faith throughout his empire. Despite his strengths, Charles spent a lifetime in futile pursuit of his goals. Four major problems—the French, the papacy, the Turks, and Germany's internal situation—cost him both his dream and his health. At the same time, the emperor's problems gave Luther's movement time to organize before facing the concerted onslaught of the Catholic forces.

MAP I3.I **The Empire of Charles V.**

The chief political concern of Charles V was his rivalry with the Valois king of France, Francis I (1515–1547). Encircled by the possessions of the Habsburg empire, Francis became embroiled in conflict with Charles over disputed territories in southern France, the Netherlands, the Rhineland, northern Spain, and Italy. These conflicts, known as the Habsburg-Valois Wars, were fought intermittently over twenty-four years (1521–1544).

At the same time, Charles faced opposition from Pope Clement VII (1523–1534), who, guided by political considerations, joined the side of Francis I. The advance of the Ottoman Turks into the eastern part of Charles' empire forced the emperor to divert forces there as well. Under the competent Suleiman the Magnificent (1520–1566), the Ottoman Turks over-

ran most of Hungary, moved into Austria, and advanced as far as Vienna, where they were finally repulsed in 1529.

Finally, the internal political situation in the Holy Roman Empire was also not in Charles' favor. Germany was a land of several hundred territorial states—princely states, ecclesiastical principalities, and free imperial cities. Although all owed loyalty to the emperor, Germany's medieval development had enabled these states to become quite independent of imperial authority. They had no desire to have a strong emperor. By the time Charles V was able to bring military forces to Germany in 1546, Lutheranism had become well established and the Lutheran princes were well organized. Unable to impose his will on Germany, Charles was forced to

CHARLES V. **Charles V sought to create religious unity throughout his vast empire by keeping all his subjects within the bounds of the Catholic church. Due to his conflict with Francis I as well as his difficulties with the Turks, the papacy, and the German princes, Charles was never able to check the spread of Lutheranism. This is a portrait of Charles V by the Venetian painter Titian.**

negotiate a truce. An end to religious warfare in Germany came in 1555 with the Peace of Augsburg, which marked an important turning point in the history of the Reformation. The division of Christianity was formally acknowledged, with Lutheranism granted equal legal standing with Catholicism. Moreover, the peace settlement accepted the right of each German ruler to determine the religion of his subjects. Charles' hope for a united empire had been completely dashed, and the ideal of medieval Christian unity was irretrievably lost. The rapid proliferation of new Protestant groups served to underscore the new reality.

◆ The Spread of the Protestant Reformation

For both Catholics and Protestant reformers, Luther's heresy also raised the question of how to determine what constituted the correct interpretation of the Bible. The inability to agree on this issue led not only to theological confrontations but also to bloody warfare because each Christian group was unwilling to admit that it could be wrong.

❋ *The Zwinglian Reformation*

In the sixteenth century, the Swiss Confederation was a loose association of thirteen self-governing states called cantons. Theoretically part of the Holy Roman Empire, they had become virtually independent in 1499. The six forest cantons were democratic republics, while the seven urban cantons, which included Zürich, Bern, and Basel, were governed primarily by city councils controlled by narrow oligarchies of wealthy citizens.

Ulrich Zwingli (1484–1531) was ordained a priest in 1506 and accepted an appointment as a cathedral priest in the Great Minster of Zürich in 1518. Zwingli's preaching of the Gospel caused such unrest that the city council in 1523 held a public disputation or debate in the town hall. Zwingli's party was accorded the victory, and the council declared that "Mayor, Council and Great Council of Zürich, in order to do away with disturbance and discord, have upon due deliberation and consultation decided and resolved that Master Zwingli should continue as heretofore to proclaim the Gospel and the pure sacred Scriptures."[6] Over the next two years, evangelical reforms were promulgated in Zürich by a city council strongly influenced by Zwingli. Relics and images were abolished; all paintings and decorations were removed from the churches and replaced by whitewashed walls. The Mass was replaced by a new liturgy consisting of Scripture reading, prayer, and sermons. Monasticism, pilgrimages, the veneration of saints, clerical celibacy, and the pope's authority were all abolished as remnants of papal Christianity.

As his movement began to spread to other cities in Switzerland, Zwingli sought an alliance with Martin Luther and the German reformers. Although both the German and Swiss reformers realized the need for unity to defend against the opposition of Catholic authorities, they were unable to agree on the interpretation of the Lord's Supper (see the box on p. 269).

A Reformation Debate: The Marburg Colloquy

Debates played a crucial role in the Reformation period. They were a primary instrument in introducing the Reformation into innumerable cities as well as a means of resolving differences among the like-minded Protestant groups. This selection contains an excerpt from the vivacious and often brutal debate between Luther and Zwingli over the sacrament of the Lord's Supper, held at Marburg in 1529. The two protagonists failed to reach agreement.

✸ The Marburg Colloquy, 1529

THE HESSIAN CHANCELLOR FEIGE: My gracious prince and lord [Landgrave Philip of Hesse] has summoned you for the express and urgent purpose of settling the dispute over the sacrament of the Lord's Supper. . . . And let everyone on both sides present his arguments in a spirit of moderation, as becomes such matters. . . . Now then, Doctor Luther, you may proceed.

LUTHER: Noble prince, gracious lord! Undoubtedly the colloquy is well intentioned. . . . Although I have no intention of changing my mind, which is firmly made up, I will nevertheless present the grounds of my belief and show where the others are in error. . . . Your basic contentions are these: In the last analysis you wish to prove that a body cannot be in two places at once, and you produce arguments about the unlimited body which are based on natural reason. I do not question how Christ can be God and man and how the two natures can be joined. For God is more powerful than all our ideas, and we must submit to his word.

Prove that Christ's body is not there where the Scripture says, "This is my body!" Rational proofs I will not listen to. . . . God is beyond all mathematics and the words of God are to be revered and carried out in awe. It is God who commands, "Take, eat, this is my body." I request, therefore, valid scriptural proof to the contrary.

Luther writes on the table in chalk, "This is my body," and covers the words with a velvet cloth.

OECOLAMPADIUS [leader of the reform movement in Basel and a Zwinglian partisan]: The sixth chapter of John clarifies the other scriptural passages. Christ is not speaking there about a local presence. "The flesh is of no avail," he says [John 6:63]. It is not my intention to employ rational, or geometrical, arguments—neither am I denying the power of God—but as long as I have the complete faith I will speak from that. For Christ is risen; he sits at the right hand of God; and so he cannot be present in the bread. Our view is neither new nor sacrilegious, but is based on faith and Scripture. . . .

ZWINGLI: I insist that the words of the Lord's Supper must be figurative. This is ever apparent, and even required by the article of faith: "taken up into heaven, seated at the right hand of the Father." Otherwise, it would be absurd to look for him in the Lord's Supper at the same time that Christ is telling us that he is in heaven. One and the same body cannot possibly be in different places. . . . I stand by this passage in the sixth chapter of John, verse 63, and shall not be shaken from it. You'll have to sing another tune.

LUTHER: You're being obnoxious.

ZWINGLI: (*excitedly*) Don't you believe that Christ was attempting in John 6 to help those who did not understand?

LUTHER: You're trying to dominate things! You insist on passing judgment! Leave that to someone else! . . . It is your point that must be proved, not mine. But let us stop this sort of thing. It serves no purpose.

ZWINGLI: It certainly does! It is for you to prove that the passage in John 6 speaks of a physical repast.

LUTHER: You express yourself poorly and make about as much progress as a cane standing in a corner. You're going nowhere.

ZWINGLI: No, no, no! This is the passage that will break your neck!

LUTHER: Don't be so sure of yourself. Necks don't break this way. You're in Hesse, not Switzerland. . . .

In October 1531, war erupted between the Swiss Protestant and Catholic cantons. Zürich's army was routed, and Zwingli was found wounded on the battlefield. His enemies killed him, cut up his body, and burned the pieces, scattering the ashes. This Swiss civil war of 1531 provided an early indication of what religious passions would lead to in the sixteenth century. Unable to find peaceful ways to agree on the meaning of the Gospel, the disciples of Christianity resorted to violence and decision by force.

✸ The Radical Reformation: The Anabaptists

Although many reformers were ready to allow the state to play an important, if not dominant, role in church affairs, some people rejected this kind of magisterial reformation and favored a far more radical reform movement. Collectively called the Anabaptists, these radicals actually formed a large variety of different groups who nevertheless shared some common characteristics. Anabaptism was especially attractive to those peasants, weavers, miners, and artisans who had been adversely affected by the economic changes of the age.

Anabaptists everywhere shared some common ideas. To them, the true Christian church was a voluntary association of believers who had undergone spiritual rebirth and had then been baptized into the church. Anabaptists advocated adult rather than infant baptism. They also tried to return literally to the practices and spirit of early Christianity. Adhering to the accounts of early Christian communities in the New Testament, they followed a strict sort of democracy in which all believers were considered equal. Each church chose its own minister, who might be any member of the community because all Christians were considered priests (though women were often excluded). Those chosen as ministers had the duty to lead services, which were very simple and contained nothing not found in the early church. Anabaptists rejected theological speculation in favor of simple Christian living according to what they believed was the pure Word of God. The Lord's Supper was interpreted as a remembrance, a meal of fellowship celebrated in the evening in private houses according to Jesus' example. Finally, unlike the Catholics and other Protestants, most Anabaptists believed in the complete separation of church and state. Not only was government to be excluded from the realm of religion, but it was not even supposed to exercise political jurisdiction over real Christians. Anabaptists refused to hold political office or bear arms

AN ANABAPTIST EXECUTION IN THE NETHERLANDS. The Anabaptists were the radicals of the Reformation. They advocated adult baptism and believed that the true Christian should not actively participate in or be governed by the secular state. Due to their radical ideas, the Anabaptists were persecuted and put to death by Catholics and Protestants alike. This sixteenth-century woodcut depicts the execution of Anabaptist reformers.

because many took the commandment "Thou shall not kill" literally, although some Anabaptist groups did become quite violent. Their political beliefs as much as their religious beliefs caused the Anabaptists to be regarded as dangerous radicals who threatened the very fabric of sixteenth-century society. Indeed, the chief thing Protestants and Catholics could agree on was the need to persecute Anabaptists.

One early group of Anabaptists known as the Swiss Brethren arose in Zürich. Their ideas frightened Zwingli, and they were soon expelled from the city. As their teachings spread through southern Germany, the Austrian Habsburg lands, and Switzerland, Anabaptists suffered ruthless persecution, especially after the Peasants' War of 1524–1525, when the upper classes resorted to repression. Virtually stamped out in Germany, Anabaptist survivors emerged in Moravia, Poland, and the Netherlands.

Menno Simons (1496–1561) was the most responsible for rejuvenating Dutch Anabaptism. A popular leader, Menno dedicated his life to the spread of a peaceful, evangelical Anabaptism that stressed separation from the world in order to live a truly Jesus-like life. The Mennonites, as his followers were called, spread from the Netherlands into northwestern Germany and eventually into Poland and Lithuania as well as the New World. Both the Mennonites and the Amish, who are also descended from the Anabaptists, can be found in the United States and Canada today.

❋ The Reformation in England

The English Reformation was initiated by an act of state. King Henry VIII (1509–1547) wanted to divorce his first wife, Catherine of Aragon, who had failed to produce a male heir. Furthermore, Henry had fallen in love with Anne Boleyn, a lady-in-waiting to Queen Catherine. Anne's unwillingness to be only the king's mistress and the king's desire to have a legitimate male heir made their marriage imperative, but the king's first marriage stood in the way.

Normally, church authorities might have been willing to grant the king an annulment of his marriage, but Pope Clement VII was dependent on the Holy Roman Emperor, Charles V, who happened to be Queen Catherine's nephew. Impatient with the pope's inaction, Henry sought to obtain an annulment of his marriage in England's own ecclesiastical courts. As archbishop of Canterbury and head of the highest ecclesiastical court in England, Thomas Cranmer held official hearings on the king's case and ruled in May 1533 that the king's marriage to Catherine was "null and absolutely void." He then validated Henry's secret marriage to Anne, who had become pregnant. At the beginning of June, Anne was crowned queen. Three months later, a child was born. Much to the king's disappointment, the baby was a girl, the future Queen Elizabeth.

In 1534, at Henry's request, Parliament moved to finalize the Church of England's break with Rome. The Act of Supremacy of 1534 declared that the king was "taken, accepted, and reputed the only supreme head on earth of the Church of England," a position that gave him control of doctrine, clerical appointments, and discipline. Using his new powers, Henry dissolved the monasteries. About four hundred religious houses were closed in 1536. Their land and possessions were confiscated by the king and sold to nobles, gentry, and some merchants. The king received a great boost to his treasury and attracted a group of supporters who now had a stake in the new Tudor order.

Although Henry VIII had broken with the papacy, little changed in matters of doctrine, theology, and ceremony. Some of his supporters, such as Archbishop Thomas Cranmer, sought a religious reformation as well as an administrative one, but Henry was unyielding. When Henry died in 1547, he was succeeded by his son, the underage and sickly Edward VI (1547–1553). During Edward's reign, Archbishop Cranmer and others inclined toward Protestant doctrines were able to move the Church of England (or Anglican church) in more of a Protestant direction. New acts of Parliament instituted the right of the clergy to marry, the elimination of images, and the creation of a revised Protestant liturgy that was elaborated in a new prayer book known as the Book of Common Prayer. These rapid changes in doctrine and liturgy aroused much opposition and prepared the way for the reaction that occurred when Mary, Henry's first daughter by Catherine of Aragon, came to the throne.

There was no doubt that Mary (1553–1558) was a Catholic who intended to restore England to Roman Catholicism. But her restoration of Catholicism aroused much opposition. There was widespread antipathy to Mary's unfortunate marriage to Philip II, the son of Charles V and future king of Spain. Philip was strongly disliked in England, and Mary's foreign policy of alliance with Spain simply aroused further hostility. The burning of more than three hundred Protestant heretics aroused further ire against "bloody Mary." As a result of her policies, Mary managed to achieve the opposite of what she had intended: England was more Protestant by the end of her reign than it had been at the beginning.

✤ John Calvin and the Development of Calvinism

Of the second generation of Protestant reformers, one stands out as the premier systematic theologian and organizer of the Protestant movement—John Calvin (1509–1564). Calvin was educated in his native France, but after his conversion to Protestantism, he was forced to flee to the safety of Switzerland. In 1536, he published the first edition of the *Institutes of the Christian Religion*, a masterful synthesis of Protestant thought that immediately secured Calvin's reputation as one of the new leaders of Protestantism.

On most important doctrines, Calvin stood very close to Luther. He adhered to the doctrine of justi-

JOHN CALVIN. After a conversion experience, John Calvin abandoned his life as a humanist and became a reformer. In 1536, Calvin began working to reform the city of Geneva, where he remained until his death in 1564. This sixteenth-century portrait of Calvin pictures him near the end of his life.

fication by faith alone to explain how humans achieved salvation. But Calvin also placed much emphasis on the absolute sovereignty of God or the "power, grace, and glory of God." One of the ideas derived from his emphasis on the absolute sovereignty of God—predestination—gave a unique cast to Calvin's teachings. This "eternal decree," as Calvin called it, meant that God had predestined some people to be saved (the elect) and others to be damned (the reprobate). According to Calvin, "He has once for all determined, both whom he would admit to salvation, and whom he would condemn to destruction."[7] Although Calvin stressed that there could be no absolute certainty of salvation, some of his followers did not always make this distinction. The practical psychological effect of predestination was to give some later Calvinists an unshakable conviction that they were doing God's work on earth. Thus Calvinism became a dynamic and activist faith. It is no accident that Calvinism became the militant international form of Protestantism.

To Calvin, the church was a divine institution responsible for preaching the word of God and administering the sacraments. Calvin kept only two sacraments, baptism and the Lord's Supper. Calvin believed in the real presence of Jesus in the sacrament of the Lord's Supper, but only in a spiritual sense. Jesus' body is at the right hand of God and thus cannot be in the sacrament, but to the believer, Jesus is spiritually present in the Lord's Supper.

In 1536, Calvin began working to reform the city of Geneva. He created a church government that used both clergy and laymen in the service of the church. The Consistory, a special body for enforcing moral discipline, was set up as a court to oversee the moral life and doctrinal purity of Genevans. The Consistory had the right to punish people who deviated from the church's teachings and moral principles. Indeed, citizens in Geneva were punished for such varied "crimes" as dancing, singing obscene songs, drunkenness, swearing, and playing cards.

Calvin's success in Geneva enabled the city to become a vibrant center of Protestantism. John Knox, the Calvinist reformer of Scotland, called Geneva "the most perfect school of Christ on earth." Following Calvin's lead, missionaries trained in Geneva were sent to all parts of Europe. Calvinism became established in France, the Netherlands, Scotland, and central and eastern Europe. By the mid-sixteenth century, Calvinism had replaced Lutheranism as the militant international form of Protestantism, and Calvin's Geneva stood as the fortress of the Reformation.

A Protestant Woman

In the initial zeal of the Protestant Reformation, women were frequently allowed to play unusual roles. Katherine Zell of Germany (c. 1497–1562) first preached beside her husband in 1527. After the death of her two children, she devoted the rest of her life to helping her husband and their Anabaptist faith. This selection is taken from one of her letters to a young Lutheran minister who had criticized her activities.

❋ Katherine Zell to Ludwig Rabus of Memmingen

I, Katherine Zell, wife of the late lamented Mathew Zell, who served in Strasbourg, where I was born and reared and still live, wish you peace and enhancement in God's grace. . . .

From my earliest years I turned to the Lord, who taught and guided me, and I have at all times, in accordance with my understanding and His grace, embraced the interests of His church and earnestly sought Jesus. Even in youth this brought me the regard and affection of clergymen and others much concerned with the church, which is why the pious Mathew Zell wanted me as a companion in marriage; and I, in turn, to serve the glory of Christ, gave devotion and help to my husband, both in his ministry and in keeping his house. . . . Ever since I was ten years old I have been a student and a sort of church mother, much given to attending sermons. I have loved and frequented the company of learned men, and I conversed much with them, not about dancing, masquerades, and worldly pleasures but about the kingdom of God. . . .

Consider the poor Anabaptists, who are so furiously and ferociously persecuted. Must the authorities everywhere be incited against them, as the hunter drives his dog against wild animals? Against those who acknowledge Christ the Lord in very much the same way we do and over which we broke with the papacy? Just because they cannot agree with us on lesser things, is this any reason to persecute them and in them Christ, in whom they fervently believe and have often professed in misery, in prison, and under the torments of fire and water?

Governments may punish criminals, but they should not force and govern belief, which is a matter for the heart and conscience not for temporal authorities. . . . When the authorities pursue one, they soon bring forth tears, and towns and villages are emptied.

◆ The Social Impact of the Protestant Reformation

Because Christianity was such an integral part of European life, it was inevitable that the Reformation would have an impact on the family and popular religious practices.

❋ The Family

For centuries, Catholicism had praised the family and sanctified its existence by making marriage a sacrament. But the Catholic church's high regard for abstinence from sex as the surest way to holiness made the celibate state of the clergy preferable to marriage. Nevertheless, because not all men could remain chaste, marriage offered the best means to control sexual intercourse and give it a purpose, the procreation of children. To some extent, this attitude persisted among the Protestant reformers; Luther, for example, argued that sex in marriage allowed one to "make use of this sex in order to avoid sin," and Calvin advised that every man should "abstain from marriage only so long as he is fit to observe celibacy." If "his power to tame lust fails him," then he must marry.

But the Reformation did bring some change to the conception of the family. Both Catholic and Protestant clergy preached sermons advocating a more positive side to family relationships. The Protestants were especially important in developing this new view of the family. Because Protestantism had eliminated any idea of special holiness for celibacy, abolishing both monasticism and a celibate clergy, the family could be placed at the center of human life, and a new stress on "mutual love between man and wife" could be extolled. But were doctrine and reality the same? For more radical religious groups, at times they were (see the box above). One Anabaptist wrote to his wife before his execution: "My faithful helper, my loyal friend. I praise God that he gave you to me, you who have sustained me in all my trial."[8] But more often reality reflected the traditional roles of husband as the ruler and wife as the obedient servant whose chief duty was to please her husband. Luther stated it clearly:

> The rule remains with the husband, and the wife is compelled to obey him by God's command. He rules the home and the state, wages war, defends his possessions, tills the soil, builds, plants, etc. The woman on the other hand is like a nail driven into the wall . . . so the wife should stay at home and look after the affairs of the household, as one who has been deprived of the ability of administering those affairs that are outside and that concern the state. She does not go beyond her most personal duties.[9]

But obedience to her husband was not a woman's only role; her other important duty was to bear children. To Calvin and Luther, this function of women was part of the divine plan. God punishes women for the sins of Eve by the burdens of procreation and feeding and nurturing their children, but "it is a gladsome punishment if you consider the hope of eternal life and the honor of motherhood which had been left to her."[10] Although the Protestant reformers sanctified this role of woman as mother and wife, viewing it as a holy vocation, Protestantism also left few alternatives for women. Because monasticism had been destroyed, that career avenue was no longer available; for most Protestant women, family life was their only destiny. At the same time, by emphasizing the father as "ruler" and hence the center of household religion, Protestantism even removed the woman from her traditional role as controller of religion in the home. Overall, the Protestant Reformation did not noticeably transform women's subordinate place in society.

✳ *Religious Practices and Popular Culture*

The attacks of Protestant reformers on the Catholic church led to radical changes in religious practices. The Protestant Reformation abolished or severely curtailed such customary practices as indulgences, the veneration of relics and saints, pilgrimages, monasticism, and clerical celibacy. The elimination of saints put an end to the numerous celebrations of religious holy days and changed a community's sense of time. Thus in Protestant communities, religious ceremonies and imagery, such as processions and statues, tended to be replaced with individual private prayer, family worship, and collective prayer and worship at the same time each week on Sunday.

In addition to abolishing saints' days and religious carnivals, some Protestant reformers even tried to eliminate customary forms of entertainment. English Puritans (as English Calvinists were known), for example, attempted to ban drinking in taverns, dramatic performances, and dancing. Dutch Calvinists denounced the tradition of giving small presents to children on the feast of Saint Nicholas in December. Many of these Protestant attacks on popular culture were unsuccessful, however. The importance of taverns in English social life made it impossible to eradicate them, and celebrations at Christmastime persisted in the Dutch Netherlands.

◆ The Catholic Reformation

By the mid-sixteenth century, Lutheranism had become established in Germany and Scandinavia, and Calvinism in parts of Switzerland, France, the Netherlands, and eastern Europe (see Map 13.2). In England, the split from Rome had resulted in the creation of a national church. The situation in Europe did not look particularly favorable for the Roman Catholic church. But even at the beginning of the sixteenth century, constructive, positive forces were at work for reform within the Catholic church, and by the mid-sixteenth century, these efforts were being directed by a revived and reformed papacy, giving the Catholic church new strength. We call the story of the revival of Roman Catholicism the Catholic Reformation, although some historians prefer to use the term Counter-Reformation, especially for those elements of the Catholic Reformation that were directly aimed at stopping the spread of the Protestant Reformation. Historians focus on three chief pillars of the Catholic Reformation: the development of the Jesuits, the creation of a reformed and revived papacy, and the Council of Trent.

✳ *The Society of Jesus*

The Society of Jesus, known as the Jesuits, was founded by a Spanish nobleman, Ignatius of Loyola (1491–1556), whose injuries in battle cut short his military career. Loyola experienced a spiritual torment similar to Luther's but, unlike Luther, resolved his problems not by a new doctrine but by a decision to submit to the will of the church. Unable to be a real soldier, he vowed to be a soldier of God. Over a period of twelve years, Loyola prepared for his life work by prayer, pilgrimages, going to school, and working out

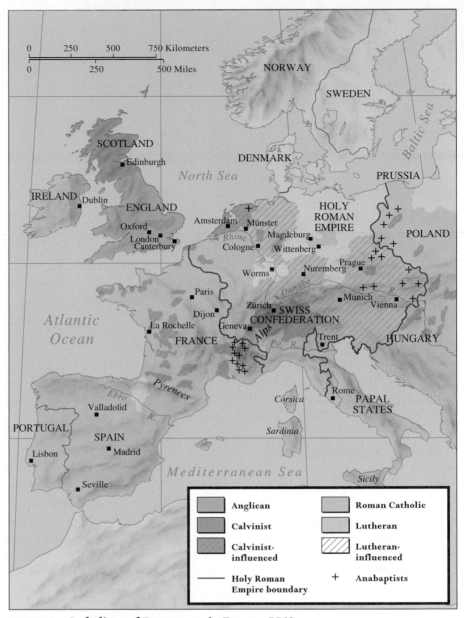

MAP 13.2 Catholics and Protestants in Europe, 1560.

a spiritual program in his brief but powerful book, *The Spiritual Exercises*. This was a training manual for spiritual development emphasizing exercises by which the human will could be strengthened and made to follow the will of God as manifested through his instrument, the Catholic church (see the box on p. 277).

Loyola gathered together a small group of individuals who were recognized as a religious order by a papal bull in 1540. The new order was grounded on the principles of absolute obedience to the papacy, a strict hierarchical order for the society, the use of education to achieve its goals, and a dedication to engage in "conflict for God." The Jesuit organization came to resem-

ble the structure of a military command. Executive leadership was put in the hands of a general, who nominated all important positions in the order and was to be revered as the absolute head of the order. Loyola served as the first general of the order until his death in 1556. A special vow of absolute obedience to the pope made the Jesuits an important instrument for papal policy.

The Jesuits pursued three major activities. They established highly disciplined schools, believing that the thorough education of young people was crucial to combat the advance of Protestantism. Another prominent Jesuit activity was the propagation of the Catholic faith among non-Christians. Jesuit activity

IGNATIUS LOYOLA. The Jesuits became the most important new religious order of the Catholic Reformation. Shown here in a sixteenth-century painting by an unknown artist is Ignatius Loyola, founder of the Society of Jesus. Loyola is seen kneeling before Pope Paul III, who officially recognized the Jesuits in 1540.

in China, especially that of the Italian Matteo Ricci, led to a number of conversions to Catholicism. Finally, the Jesuits were determined to carry the Catholic banner and fight Protestantism. Jesuit missionaries proved singularly successful in restoring Catholicism to parts of Germany and eastern Europe.

❋ A Revived Papacy

A reformed papacy was another important factor in the development of the Catholic Reformation. The involvement of the Renaissance papacy in dubious finances and Italian political and military affairs had given rise to numerous sources of corruption. It took the jolt of the Protestant Reformation to bring about serious reform. The pontificate of Pope Paul III (1534–1549) proved to be a turning point. Raised in the lap of Renaissance luxury, Paul III continued Renaissance papal practices by appointing his nephews as cardinals, involving himself in politics, and patronizing arts and letters on a lavish scale. Nevertheless, he perceived the need for change and expressed it decisively. Advocates of reform, such as Gasparo Contarini and Gian Pietro Caraffa, were made cardinals. In 1535, Paul took the audacious step of appointing a commission to study the church's condition. The Reform Commission's report in 1537 blamed the church's problems on the corrupt policies of popes and cardinals. It was also Paul III who formally recognized the Jesuits and began the Council of Trent.

A decisive turning point in the direction of the Catholic Reformation and the nature of papal reform came in the 1540s, when the Catholic moderates, such as Cardinal Contarini, who favored concessions to Protestants in the hope of restoring Christian unity, were overshadowed by hardliners who regarded all compromise with Protestant innovations as heresy. It soon became apparent that the conservative reformers were in the ascendancy when Cardinal Caraffa, one of the hardliners, was able to get Paul III to establish a Roman Inquisition or Holy Office in 1542 to ferret out doctrinal errors. There was to be no compromise with Protestantism.

When Cardinal Caraffa was chosen pope as Paul IV (1555–1559), he so increased the power of the Inquisition that even liberal cardinals were silenced. This "first true pope of the Catholic Counter-Reformation," as he has been called, also created the Index of Forbidden Books, a list of books that Catholics were not allowed to read. It included all the works of Protestant theologians as well as authors considered "unwholesome." Any hope of restoring Christian unity by compromise was fading fast. The activities of the Council of Trent, the third major pillar of the Catholic Reformation, made compromise virtually impossible.

❋ The Council of Trent

In March 1545, a group of cardinals, archbishops, bishops, abbots, and theologians met in the city of Trent on the border between Germany and Italy and initiated the Council of Trent, which met intermittently from 1545 to 1563 in three major sessions. Moderate Catholic reformers hoped that compromises would be

Loyola and Obedience to "Our Holy Mother, the Hierarchical Church"

In his Spiritual Exercises, *Ignatius Loyola developed a systematic program for "the conquest of self and the regulation of one's life" for service to the hierarchical Catholic church. Ignatius' supreme goal was the commitment of the Christian to active service in the Church of Christ (the Catholic church). In the final section of the* Spiritual Exercises, *Loyola explained the nature of that commitment in a series of "rules for thinking with the church."*

✸ Ignatius Loyola, "Rules for Thinking with the Church"

The following rules should be observed to foster the true attitude of mind we ought to have in the Church militant.

1. We must put aside all judgment of our own, and keep the mind ever ready and prompt to obey in all things the true Spouse of Jesus Christ, our holy Mother, the hierarchical Church.
2. We should praise sacramental confession, the yearly reception of the Most Blessed Sacrament [the Lord's Supper], and praise more highly monthly reception, and still more weekly Communion. . . .
3. We ought to praise the frequent hearing of Mass, the singing of hymns, psalmody, and long prayers whether in the church or outside. . . .
4. We must praise highly religious life, virginity, and continency; and matrimony ought not be praised as much as any of these. . . .
6. We should show our esteem for the relics of the saints by venerating them and praying to the saints. We should praise visits to the Sta-

tion Churches, pilgrimages, indulgences, jubilees, the lighting of candles in churches. . . .

8. We ought to praise not only the building and adornment of churches, but also images and veneration of them according to the subject they represent.
9. Finally, we must praise all the commandments of the Church, and be on the alert to find reasons to defend them, and by no means in order to criticize them.
10. We should be more ready to approve and praise the orders, recommendations, and way of acting of our superiors than to find fault with them. Though some of the orders, etc., may not have been praiseworthy, yet to speak against them, either when preaching in public or in speaking before the people, would rather be the cause of murmuring and scandal than of profit. As a consequence, the people would become angry with their superiors, whether secular or spiritual. But while it does harm in the absence of our superiors to speak evil of them before the people, it may be profitable to discuss their bad conduct with those who can apply a remedy.
13. If we wish to proceed securely in all things, we must hold fast to the following principle: What seems to me white, I will believe black if the hierarchical Church so defines. For I must be convinced that in Christ our Lord, the bridegroom, and in His spouse the Church, only one Spirit holds sway, which governs and rules for the salvation of souls.

---

made in formulating doctrinal definitions that would encourage Protestants to return to the church. Conservatives, however, favored an uncompromising restatement of Catholic doctrines in strict opposition to Protestant positions. The latter group won, although not without a struggle.

The final doctrinal decrees of the Council of Trent reaffirmed traditional Catholic teachings in opposition to Protestant beliefs. Scripture and tradition were affirmed as equal authorities in religious matters; only the church could interpret Scripture. Both

faith and good works were declared necessary for salvation. The seven sacraments, the Catholic doctrine of transubstantiation (the belief that bread and wine are miraculously transformed into the body and blood of Jesus during the Eucharist—a belief rejected by the Protestant reformers), and clerical celibacy were all upheld. Belief in purgatory and in the efficacy of indulgences was strengthened, although the hawking of indulgences was prohibited.

After the Council of Trent, the Roman Catholic church possessed a clear body of doctrine and a unified church under the acknowledged supremacy of the popes who had triumphed over bishops and councils. The Roman Catholic church had become one Christian denomination among many with an organizational framework and doctrinal pattern that would not be significantly altered until the Second Vatican Council four hundred years later. With a new spirit of confidence, the Catholic church entered a militant phase, as well prepared as the Calvinists to do battle for the Lord. An era of religious warfare was about to unfold.

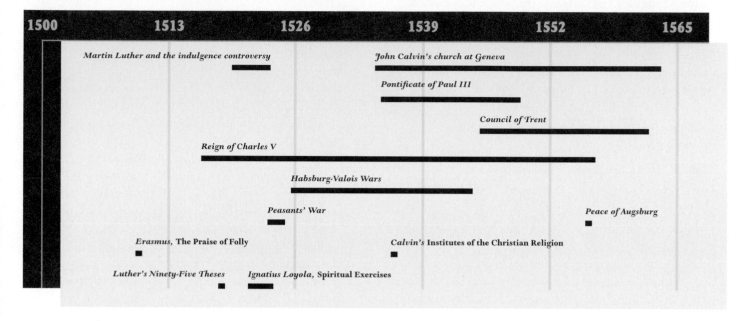

| 1500 | 1513 | 1526 | 1539 | 1552 | 1565 |

Martin Luther and the indulgence controversy

John Calvin's church at Geneva

Pontificate of Paul III

Council of Trent

Reign of Charles V

Habsburg-Valois Wars

Peasants' War

Peace of Augsburg

Erasmus, **The Praise of Folly**

Calvin's **Institutes of the Christian Religion**

Luther's Ninety-Five Theses

Ignatius Loyola, **Spiritual Exercises**

Conclusion

When the Augustinian monk Martin Luther posted his theses on indulgences, few people suspected that they would eventually split Europe apart along religious lines. But the yearning for reform of the church and meaningful religious experience caused a seemingly simple dispute to escalate into a powerful movement. Clearly, the papacy and other elements in the Catholic church underestimated the strength of Martin Luther's ideas and the desire for religious change.

Although Luther believed that his revived Christianity, based on his interpretation of the Bible, would be acceptable to all, others soon appeared who interpreted the Bible in yet other different ways. Protestantism fragmented into various sects, which, though united in their dislike of Catholicism, were themselves divided over the interpretation of the sacraments and religious practices. As reform ideas spread, religion and politics became ever more intertwined. Political support played a crucial role in the spread of the Reformation.

Although Lutheranism was legally acknowledged in the Holy Roman Empire by the Peace of Augsburg in 1555, it had lost much of its momentum and outside of Scandinavia had scant ability to attract new supporters. Its energy was largely replaced by the new Protestant form of Calvinism, which had a clarity of doctrine and a fervor that made it attractive to a whole new generation of Europeans. But while Calvinism's vigor enabled it to expand across Europe, Catholi-cism was also experiencing its own revival and emerged as a militant faith, prepared to do combat for the souls of the faithful. An age of religious passion would, tragically, be followed by an age of religious warfare.

Notes

1. Desiderius Erasmus, *The Paraclesis*, in John Olin, ed., *Christian Humanism and the Reformation: Selected Writings of Erasmus*, 3d ed. (New York, 1987), p. 101.

2. John P. Dolan, ed., *The Essential Erasmus* (New York, 1964), p. 149.

3. Quoted in Alister E. McGrath, *Reformation Thought: An Introduction* (Oxford, 1988), p. 72.

4. Quoted in E. G. Rupp and Benjamin Drewery, eds., *Martin Luther* (New York, 1970), p. 50.

5. Quoted in Roland Bainton, *Here I Stand: A Life of Martin Luther* (New York, 1950), p. 144.

6. Quoted in De Lamar Jensen, *Reformation Europe* (Lexington, Mass., 1981), p. 83.

7. John Calvin, *Institutes of the Christian Religion*, trans. John Allen (Philadelphia, 1936), vol. 1, p. 228; vol. 2, p. 181.

8. Quoted in Roland Bainton, *Women of the Reformation in Germany and Italy* (Boston, 1971), p. 154.

9. Quoted in Bonnie S. Anderson and Judith P. Zinsser, *A History of Their Own: Women in Europe from Prehistory to the Present* (New York, 1988), vol. 1, p. 259.

10. Quoted in John A. Phillips, *Eve: The History of an Idea* (New York, 1984), p. 105.

Suggestions for Further Reading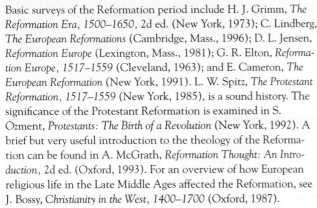

Basic surveys of the Reformation period include H. J. Grimm, *The Reformation Era, 1500–1650*, 2d ed. (New York, 1973); C. Lindberg, *The European Reformations* (Cambridge, Mass., 1996); D. L. Jensen, *Reformation Europe* (Lexington, Mass., 1981); G. R. Elton, *Reformation Europe, 1517–1559* (Cleveland, 1963); and E. Cameron, *The European Reformation* (New York, 1991). L. W. Spitz, *The Protestant Reformation, 1517–1559* (New York, 1985), is a sound history. The significance of the Protestant Reformation is examined in S. Ozment, *Protestants: The Birth of a Revolution* (New York, 1992). A brief but very useful introduction to the theology of the Reformation can be found in A. McGrath, *Reformation Thought: An Introduction*, 2d ed. (Oxford, 1993). For an overview of how European religious life in the Late Middle Ages affected the Reformation, see J. Bossy, *Christianity in the West, 1400–1700* (Oxford, 1987).

The development of humanism outside Italy is examined in C. G. Nauert Jr., *Humanism and the Culture of Renaissance Europe* (Cambridge, 1995). The best general biography of Erasmus is still R. Bainton, *Erasmus of Christendom* (New York, 1969), although the shorter works by J. K. Sowards, *Desiderius Erasmus* (Boston, 1975), and J. McConica, *Erasmus* (Oxford, 1991), are also good.

The Reformation in Germany can be examined in H. Holborn, *A History of Modern Germany: The Reformation* (New York, 1959), still an outstanding survey of the entire Reformation period in Germany, and J. Lortz, *The Reformation in Germany*, trans. R. Walls, 2 vols. (New York, 1968), a detailed Catholic account. The classic account of Martin Luther's life is R. Bainton, *Here I Stand: A Life of Martin Luther* (New York, 1950). More recent works include H. A. Oberman, *Luther* (New York, 1992); W. von Loewenich, *Martin Luther: The Man and His Work* (Minneapolis, 1986); and J. M. Kittelson, *Luther the Reformer: The Story of the Man and His Career* (Minneapolis, 1986). On the Peasants' War, see especially P. Blickle, *The Revolution of 1525: The German Peasants' War from a New Perspective* (Baltimore, Md., 1981). The spread of Luther's ideas in Germany can be examined in B. Moeller, *Imperial Cities and the Reformation* (Durham, N.C., 1982); S. Ozment, *The Reformation in the Cities* (New Haven, Conn., 1975); and R. Po-Chia Hsia, ed., *The German People and the Reformation* (Itaca, N.Y., 1988).

The best account of Ulrich Zwingli is G. R. Potter, *Zwingli* (Cambridge, 1976), although W. P. Stephens, *Zwingli* (Oxford, 1994), is an important study of the man's ideas.

The most comprehensive account of the various groups and individuals who are called Anabaptists is G. H. Williams, *The Radical Reformation*, 2d ed. (Kirksville, Mo., 1992). Other valuable studies include C. P. Clasen, *Anabaptism: A Social History, 1525–1618* (Ithaca, N.Y., 1972), and M. Mullett, *Radical Religious Movements in Early Modern Europe* (London, 1980).

Two worthwhile surveys of the English Reformation are A. G. Dickens, *The English Reformation*, 2d ed. (New York, 1989), and G. R. Elton, *Reform and Reformation: England, 1509–1558* (Cambridge, Mass., 1977). Good biographies of the leading personalities of the age include J. J. Scarisbrick, *Henry VIII* (Berkeley, Calif., 1968); J. Ridley, *Thomas Cranmer* (Oxford, 1962); and D. M. Loades, *The Reign of Mary Tudor* (London, 1979). Other specialized works on the period include the controversial classic by G. R. Elton, *The Tudor Revolution in Government*, 2d ed. (Cambridge, 1973), and D. Knowles, *Bare Ruined Choirs: The Dissolution of the English Monasteries* (New York, 1976).

On John Calvin, see A. McGrath, *A Life of John Calvin: A Study in the Shaping of Western Culture* (Cambridge, Mass., 1990), and W. J. Bouwsma, *John Calvin* (New York, 1988). The best account of Calvin's work in Geneva is W. Monter, *Calvin's Geneva* (New York, 1967).

On the impact of the Reformation of the family, see J. F. Harrington, *Reordering Marriage and Society in Reformation Germany* (New York, 1995). M. E. Wiesner's *Working Women in Renaissance Germany* (New Brunswick, N.J., 1986) covers primarily the sixteenth century. There is also a good collection of essays in S. Marshall, ed., *Women in Reformation and Counter-Reformation Europe: Public and Private Worlds* (Bloomington, Ind., 1989).

A good introduction to the Catholic Reformation can be found in the beautifully illustrated brief study by A. G. Dickens, *The Counter-Reformation* (New York, 1969). Also valuable is M. R. O'Connell, *The Counter-Reformation, 1559–1610* (New York, 1974). On Loyola, see P. Caravan, *Ignatius Loyola: A Biography of the Founder of the Jesuits* (San Francisco, 1990), and W. W. Meissner, *Ignatius of Loyola: The Psychology of a Saint* (New Haven, Conn., 1994). The work by J. O'Malley, *The First Jesuits* (Cambridge, Mass., 1995), offers a clear discussion of the founding of the Jesuits.

 For additional reading, go to InfoTrac College Edition, your online research library at http://web1.infotrac-college.com

Enter the search term *Reformation* using the Subject Guide.

Enter the search terms *Counter-Reformation* using the Subject Guide.

Enter the search terms *Martin and Luther not King* using Key Terms.

Enter the search terms *John Calvin* using the Subject Guide.

CHAPTER

14

Discovery and Crisis in the Sixteenth and Seventeenth Centuries

CHAPTER OUTLINE

- An Age of Discovery and Expansion
- Politics and the Wars of Religion in the Sixteenth Century
- Economic and Social Crises
- Seventeenth-Century Crises: War and Rebellions
- Culture in a Turbulent World
- Conclusion

FOCUS QUESTIONS

- Why did Europeans begin to amass overseas empires during the sixteenth century, and what effects did this experience have on both the Europeans and conquered peoples?
- What role did religion play in the European wars of the sixteenth century and the Thirty Years' War of the seventeenth century?
- How did the religious policy, the foreign policy, and the governments of Philip II of Spain and Elizabeth I of England differ?
- What economic and social crises did Europe experience between 1560 and 1650?
- How did the turmoil in Europe between 1560 and 1650 contribute to the witchcraft craze and to the artistic and intellectual developments of the period?

B Y THE MIDDLE of the sixteenth century, it was apparent that the religious passions of the Reformation era had brought an end to the religious unity of medieval Europe. The rift between Catholics and Protestants was instrumental in fueling a series of wars that dominated much of European history between 1560 and 1650. The struggles fought in Germany at the beginning of the seventeenth century (known as the Thirty Years' War) were especially brutal and devastating. When the Catholic general Johann Tilly captured Neubrandenburg, his forces massacred the city's three thousand defenders. A month later, the army of the

Protestant leader Gustavus Adolphus retaliated by slaughtering the entire garrison of two thousand men at Frankfurt-an-der-Oder. Noncombatants suffered as well, as is evident from the contemporary description by Otto von Guericke of the sack of Magdeburg. Once the city had been captured, Tilly's forces were let loose: "Then there was nothing but beating and burning, plundering, torture, and murder." All the buildings were looted of anything valuable, and then the city was "given over to the flames, and thousands of innocent men, women, and children, in the midst of a horrible noise of heartrending shrieks and cries, were tortured and put to death in so cruel and shameful a manner that no words would suffice to describe." Thus "in a single day this noble and famous city, the pride of the whole country, went up in fire and smoke, and the remnant of its citizens, with their wives and children, were taken prisoners and driven away by the enemy."

The wars worsened the economic and social crises that were besetting the continent. The fact that Europe unrelentingly suffered wars, rebellions, constitutional crises, economic depression, social disintegration, a witchcraft craze, and demographic perturbations between 1560 and 1650 has led some historians to speak of those ninety years as an age of crisis in European life.

Crisis, however, often creates opportunities, and nowhere is that more apparent than in the geographical discoveries that made this an era of European expansion into new worlds. Although the discovery of new territories began before the sixteenth century, it was not until the sixteenth and seventeenth centuries that Europeans began to comprehend the significance of their discoveries and to exploit them for material gain.

◆ An Age of Discovery and Expansion

Never has the dynamic and even ruthless energy of Western civilization been more apparent than in its expansion into the rest of the world. By the sixteenth century, the Atlantic seaboard had become the center of a commercial activity that raised Portugal and Spain and later the Dutch Republic, England, and France to prominence. The age of expansion was a crucial factor in the European transition from the agrarian economy of the Middle Ages to a commercial and industrial capitalistic system. Expansion also led Europeans into new and lasting contacts with non-European peoples that inaugurated a new age of world history.

※ The Motives

Europeans had long been attracted to lands outside of Europe. Indeed, a large body of fantasy literature about "other worlds" blossomed in the Middle Ages. In *The Travels of John Mandeville* in the fourteenth century, the author spoke of lands (which he had never seen) filled with precious stones and gold. Other lands were more frightening, "where the folk be great giants of twenty-eight foot long, or thirty foot long. . . . And they eat more gladly man's flesh than any other flesh," as well as lands farther north full of "cruel and evil women. And they have precious stones in their eyes. And they be of that kind that if they behold any man with wrath they slay him at once with the beholding."[1] Other writers spoke of mysterious Christian kingdoms: the magical kingdom of Prester John in Africa and a Christian community in southern India that was supposedly founded by Thomas, the apostle of Jesus.

Although Muslim control of Central Asia cut Europe off from the countries farther east, the Mongol conquests in the thirteenth century had reopened the doors. The most famous medieval travelers to the East were the Polos of Venice. Niccolò and Maffeo, merchants from Venice, accompanied by Niccolò's son Marco, undertook the lengthy journey to the court of the great Mongol ruler Kublai Khan (1259–1294) in 1271. An account of Marco's experiences, the *Travels*, proved to be the most informative of all the descriptions of Asia by medieval European travelers. Others followed the Polos, but in the fourteenth century, the conquests of the Ottoman Turks and then the breakup of the Mongol Empire reduced Western traffic to the East. With the closing of the overland routes, a number of people in Europe became interested in the possibility of reaching Asia by sea to gain access to the spices and other precious items of the region. Christopher Columbus had a copy of Marco Polo's *Travels* in his possession when he began to envision his epoch-making voyage across the Atlantic Ocean.

An economic motive thus loomed large in Renaissance European expansion. Merchants, adventurers, and government officials had high hopes of finding precious metals and new areas of trade. Many European explorers and conquerors did not hesitate to express their desire for material gain. One Spanish conquistador explained that he and his kind went to the New World to "serve God and His Majesty, to give light to those who were in darkness, and to grow rich, as all men desire to do."[2]

This statement expresses another major reason for the overseas voyages—religious zeal. Hernán Cortés, the conqueror of Mexico, asked his Spanish rulers if it was not their duty to ensure that the native Mexicans "are introduced into and instructed in their holy Catholic faith."[3] Spiritual and secular affairs were closely intertwined in the sixteenth century. No doubt grandeur and glory as well as plain intellectual curiosity and spirit of adventure also played some role in European expansion.

If "God, glory, and gold" were the motives, what made the voyages possible? First of all, the expansion of Europe was connected to the growth of centralized monarchies during the Renaissance. By the second half of the fifteenth century, European monarchies had increased both their authority and their resources and were in a position to turn their energies beyond their borders. At the same time, by the end of the fifteenth century, European states had achieved a level of wealth and technology that enabled them to undertake a regular series of voyages beyond Europe. Cartography had developed to the point that Europeans possessed fairly accurate maps of the known world. Moreover, Europeans had developed remarkably seaworthy ships and reliable navigational aids, such as the compass and astrolabe (an instrument used to determine the position of heavenly bodies).

❀ The Development of a Portuguese Maritime Empire

Portugal took the lead in exploring the coast of Africa under the leadership of Prince Henry the Navigator (1394–1460), who sought to discover a Christian kingdom that would serve as an ally against the Muslims, to acquire trade opportunities for Portugal, and to extend Christianity. Beginning in 1419, Portuguese fleets began probing southward along the western coast of Africa. After Henry's death in 1460, there was a hiatus in Portuguese exploration, but the Portuguese gradually crept down the African coast until Bartholomeu Dias finally rounded the Cape of Good Hope on the southern tip of Africa in 1488 (see Map 14.1). Ten years later, a fleet under the command of Vasco da Gama rounded the cape and stopped at several ports controlled by Muslim merchants along the coast of East Africa. Then da Gama's fleet crossed

the Arabian Sea and reached the port of Calicut on the southwestern coast of India, on May 18, 1498. On arriving in Calicut, da Gama announced to his surprised hosts that he had arrived in search of "Christians and spices." He did not find the first, but he did find the second. Although he lost two ships en route, da Gama's remaining vessels returned to Europe with their holds filled with ginger and cinnamon, a cargo that earned the investors a profit of several thousand percent. Da Gama's successful voyage marked the beginning of an all-water trade route to India. By 1501, annual Portuguese fleets to India were making serious inroads into the Mediterranean trade of the Venetians and Turks.

Under the direction of officials known as viceroys, Portugal now created an overseas empire. Most important of the viceroys was Alfonso d'Albuquerque (c. 1462–1515), a tough nobleman who took the lead in establishing a ring of commercial-military bases centered at Goa, an island off the Malabar Coast of India. The Portuguese also reached beyond India by taking the island of Macao at the mouth of the Pearl River in China. The Portuguese empire remained a limited one of enclaves or trading posts on the coasts of India and China. The Portuguese did not have the power, the people, or the desire to colonize the Asian regions.

Why were the Portuguese so successful? Basically their success was a matter of guns and seamanship. Portuguese fleets, which began to arrive in Indian waters with regularity by the end of the sixteenth century, were heavily armed and were able not only to intimidate but also to inflict severe defeats if necessary on local naval and land forces. By no means did the Portuguese possess a monopoly on the use of firearms and explosives, but their effective use of naval technology, heavy guns, and tactics gave them a military superiority over lightly armed rivals that they were able to exploit until the arrival of other European forces—the English, Dutch, and French—in the seventeenth century.

❀ Voyages to the New World

While the Portuguese sought access to the spice trade of the Indies by sailing eastward through the Indian Ocean, the Spanish attempted to reach the same destination by sailing westward across the Atlantic. Although the Spanish came to overseas discovery and exploration after the initial efforts of Henry the Navigator, their greater resources enabled them to estab-

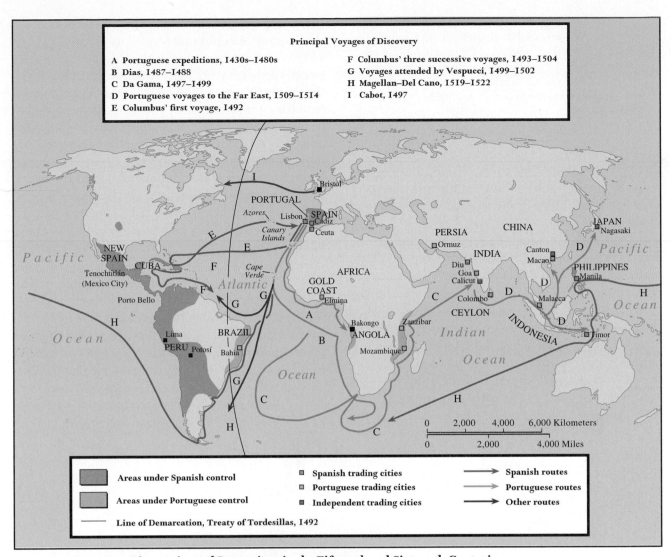

Principal Voyages of Discovery

A Portuguese expeditions, 1430s–1480s
B Dias, 1487–1488
C Da Gama, 1497–1499
D Portuguese voyages to the Far East, 1509–1514
E Columbus' first voyage, 1492

F Columbus' three successive voyages, 1493–1504
G Voyages attended by Vespucci, 1499–1502
H Magellan–Del Cano, 1519–1522
I Cabot, 1497

Areas under Spanish control
Areas under Portuguese control
Line of Demarcation, Treaty of Tordesillas, 1492

Spanish trading cities
Portuguese trading cities
Independent trading cities

Spanish routes
Portuguese routes
Other routes

MAP 14.1   European Discoveries and Possessions in the Fifteenth and Sixteenth Centuries.

lish a far grander overseas empire of a nature quite different from the Portuguese empire.

An important figure in the history of Spanish exploration was an Italian known as Christopher Columbus (1451–1506). Knowledgeable Europeans were aware that the world was round but had little understanding of its circumference or the extent of the continent of Asia. Convinced that the circumference of the earth was less than contemporaries believed and that Asia was larger than people thought, Columbus felt that Asia could be reached by sailing west instead of going around Africa. After being rejected by the Portuguese, he persuaded Queen Isabella of Spain to finance his exploratory expedition.

With three ships, the *Santa Maria, Niña,* and *Pinta,* manned by ninety men, Columbus set sail for the Atlantic on August 3, 1492. On October 12, he made landfall in the Bahamas and then went on to explore the coastline of Cuba and the northern shores of Hispaniola (present-day Haiti and the Dominican Republic). Columbus believed that he had reached Asia, and in his reports to Queen Isabella, he reassured her of his eventual success in finding gold as well as the golden opportunity to convert the natives to Christianity:

These islands are very green and fertile and the breezes are very soft, and it is possible that there are in them many things, of which I do not know, because I did not wish to delay in finding gold, by discovering and going about many islands. And since these men give these signs that they wear it on their arms and legs, and it is gold because I showed them some pieces of gold which I have, I cannot fail, with the aid of Our Lord, to find the place whence it comes.

... So your Highness should resolve to make them Christians, for I believe that, if you begin, in a little while you will achieve the conversion of a great number of peoples to our holy faith, with the acquisition of great lordships and riches and all their inhabitants for Spain. For without a doubt there is a very great amount of gold in these lands.[4]

In three subsequent voyages (in 1493, 1498, and 1502), Columbus sought in vain to find a route through the outer lands to the Asian mainland. In his four voyages, Columbus reached all the major islands of the Caribbean and the mainland of Central America.

Although Columbus clung to his belief that he had reached Asia until his death, other explorers soon realized that he had discovered a new frontier altogether. State-sponsored explorers joined the race to the New World. A Venetian seaman, John Cabot, explored the New England coastline of the Americas under a license from King Henry VII of England. The continent of South America was discovered accidentally by the Portuguese sea captain Pedro Cabral in 1500. Amerigo Vespucci, a Florentine, accompanied several voyages and wrote a series of letters describing the geography of the New World. The publication of these letters led to the use of the name "America" (after Amerigo) for the new lands.

The first two decades of the sixteenth century witnessed numerous overseas voyages that explored the eastern coasts of both North and South America.

Perhaps the most dramatic of these expeditions was the journey of Ferdinand Magellan (1480–1521) in 1519. After passing through the Straits named after him at the bottom of South America, he sailed across the Pacific Ocean and reached the Philippines (named after King Philip of Spain by Magellan's crew), where he met his death at the hands of the natives. Although only one of his original fleet of five ships survived and returned to Spain, Magellan's name is still associated with the first known circumnavigation of the earth.

The newly discovered territories were referred to as the New World, although they already possessed flourishing civilizations populated by millions of people when the Europeans arrived. But the Americas were completely new to the Europeans, who quickly saw opportunities for conquest and exploitation. The Spanish, in particular, were interested because in 1494 the Treaty of Tordesillas had divided up the newly discovered world into separate Portuguese and Spanish spheres of influence. Hereafter the route east around the Cape of Good Hope was to be reserved for the Portuguese while the route across the Atlantic (except for the eastern hump of South America) was assigned to Spain.

THE CARAVEL, WORKHORSE OF THE AGE OF EXPLORATION. Prior to the fifteenth century, most European ships were either small craft with lateen sails used in the Mediterranean or slow, unwieldy square-rigged vessels operating in the North Atlantic. By the sixteenth century, European naval architects had begun to build ships that combined the maneuverability and speed offered by lateen sails with the carrying capacity and seaworthiness of the square-riggers. Shown here is a representation of Christopher Columbus' flagship *Santa Maria*, which took part in the first Spanish voyage across the Atlantic Ocean.

✳ The Spanish Empire in the New World

The Spanish conquistadors were hardy individuals motivated by a typical sixteenth-century blend of glory, greed, and religious crusading zeal. Although sanctioned by the Castilian crown, these groups were financed and outfitted privately, not by the government. Their superior weapons, organizational skills, and determination brought the conquistadors incredible success. They also benefited from rivalries among the native peoples.

In 1519, a Spanish expedition under the command of Hernán Cortés landed at Veracruz, on the Gulf of Mexico. He marched to the city of Tenochtitlan (see the box on p. 286) at the head of a small contingent of troops (550 soldiers and 16 horses), and as he went, he made alliances with city-states that had tired of the oppressive rule of the Aztecs. Especially important was Tlaxcala, a state that the Aztecs had not

been able to conquer. In November, Cortés arrived at Tenochtitlán, where he received a friendly welcome from the Aztec monarch Moctezuma (often called Montezuma). At first, Moctezuma believed that his visitor was a representative of Quetzalcoatl, the god who had departed from his homeland centuries before and had promised that he would return. Riddled with fears, Moctezuma offered gifts of gold to the foreigners and gave them a palace to use while they were in the city.

But tensions eventually erupted between the Spaniards and the Aztecs. The Spanish took Moctezuma hostage and began to pillage the city. In the fall of 1520, one year after Cortés had arrived, the local population revolted and drove the invaders out. Many of the Spanish were killed, but the Aztecs soon experienced new disasters. As one Aztec related: "At about the time that the Spaniards had fled from Mexico, there came a great sickness, a pestilence, the smallpox." Many Aztecs fell sick and died. Meanwhile,

THE SLAUGHTER OF THE AZTECS. Fearful of growing Aztec resistance, the Spaniards responded by slaughtering many Aztecs. This sixteenth-century watercolor shows the massacre of Aztecs at Cholula, carried out on the orders of Cortés.

The Spanish Conquistador: Cortés and the Conquest of Mexico

Hernán Cortés was a minor Spanish nobleman who came to the New World in 1504 to seek his fortune. Contrary to his superior's orders, Cortés waged an independent campaign of conquest and overthrew the Aztec empire of Mexico (1519–1521). Cortés wrote a series of five reports to Emperor Charles V to justify his action. The second report includes a description of Tenochtitlán, the capital of the Aztec empire. The Spanish conquistador and his men were obviously impressed by this city, awesome in its architecture yet built by people who lacked European technology, such as wheeled vehicles and tools of hard metal.

✳ Cortés' Description of Tenochtitlán

The great city Tenochtitlán is built in the midst of this salt lake, and it is two leagues from the heart of the city to any point on the mainland. Four causeways lead to it, all made by hand and some twelve feet wide. The city itself is as large as Seville or Córdoba. The principal streets are very broad and straight, the majority of them being of beaten earth, but a few and at least half the smaller thoroughfares are waterways along which they pass in their canoes. Moreover, even the principal streets have openings at regular distances so that the water can freely pass from one to another, and these openings which are very broad are spanned by great bridges of huge beams, very stoutly put together, so firm indeed that over many of them ten horsemen can ride at once. Seeing that if the natives intended any treachery against us they would have every opportunity from the way in which the city is built, for by removing the bridges from the entrances and exits they could leave us to die of hunger with no possibility of getting to the mainland, I immediately set to work as soon as we entered the city on the building of four brigs, and in a short space of time had them finished, so that we could ship three hundred men and the horses to the mainland whenever we so desired.

The city has many open squares in which markets are continuously held and the general business of buying and selling proceeds. One square in particular is twice as big as that of Salamanca and completely surrounded by arcades where there are daily more than sixty thousand folk buying and selling. Every kind of merchandise such as may be met with in every land is for sale there, whether of food and victuals, or ornaments of gold and silver, or lead, brass, copper, tin, precious stones, bones, shells, snails and feathers; limestone for building is likewise sold there, stone both rough and polished, bricks burnt and unburnt, wood of all kinds and in all stages of preparation. . . . There is a street of herb-sellers where there are all manner of roots and medicinal plants that are found in the land. There are houses as it were of apothecaries where they sell medicines made from these herbs, both for drinking and for use as ointments and salves. There are barbers' shops where you may have your hair washed and cut. There are other shops where you may obtain food and drink. . . .

Finally, to avoid prolixity [wordiness] in telling all the wonders of this city, I will simply say that the manner of living among the people is very similar to that in Spain, and considering that this is a barbarous nation shut off from a knowledge of the true God or communication with enlightened nations, one may well marvel at the orderliness and good government which is everywhere maintained.

The actual service of Moctezuma and those things which call for admiration by the greatness and state would take so long to describe that I assure your Majesty I do not know where to begin with any hope of ending. For as I have already said, what could there be more astonishing than that a barbarous monarch such as he should have reproductions made in gold, silver, precious stones, and feathers of all things to be found in his land, and so perfectly reproduced that there is no goldsmith or silversmith in the world who could better them, nor can one understand what instrument could have been used for fashioning the jewels; as for the featherwork its like is not to be seen in either wax or embroidery; it is so marvelously delicate.

Cortés received fresh soldiers from his new American allies; the state of Tlaxcala alone provided fifty thousand warriors. After four months, the city capitulated. And then the destruction began. The Aztecs' pyramids, temples, and palaces were leveled to the ground, and the stones were used to build Spanish government buildings and churches. The rivers and canals were filled in. The mighty Aztec empire on mainland Mexico was no more. Between 1531 and 1550, the Spanish consolidated their control of northern Mexico.

The Inca empire high in the Peruvian Andes was still flourishing when the first Spanish expeditions arrived in the area. In December 1530, Francisco Pizarro landed on the Pacific coast of South America with a small band of about 180 men, but like Cortés, he had steel weapons, gunpowder, and horses, none of which were familiar to his hosts. Pizarro was also lucky because the Inca empire had already succumbed to an epidemic of smallpox. Like the Aztecs, the Incas had no immunities to European diseases, and all too soon, smallpox was devastating entire villages. Even the Inca emperor was a victim, bringing even more good fortune for Pizarro. Upon the emperor's death, two sons claimed the throne, leading to a civil war. Pizarro took advantage of the situation by taking Atahualpa, whose forces had just defeated his brother's, captive. Armed only with stones, arrows, and light spears, Inca soldiers provided little challenge to the charging horses of the Spanish, let alone their guns and cannons. After executing Atahualpa, Pizarro and his soldiers, aided by their Inca allies, marched on Cuzco and captured the Inca capital. By 1535, Pizarro had established a capital at Lima for a new colony of the Spanish empire.

ADMINISTRATION OF THE SPANISH EMPIRE

Spanish policy toward the Indians of the New World was a combination of confusion, misguided paternalism, and cruel exploitation. While the conquistadors made decisions based on expediency and their own interests, Queen Isabella declared the Indians subjects of Castile and instituted the Spanish *encomienda,* a system that permitted the conquering Spaniards to collect tribute from the natives and use them as laborers. In return, the holders of an *encomienda* were supposed to protect the Indians, pay them wages, and supervise their spiritual needs. Three thousand miles from Spain, Spanish settlers largely ignored their government and brutally used the Indians to pursue their own economic interests. Indians were put to work on plantations and in the lucrative gold and silver mines. Forced labor, starvation, and especially disease took a fearful toll of Indian lives. With little or no natural resistance to European diseases, the Indians of America were ravaged by the smallpox, measles, and typhus brought by the explorers and conquistadors. At least half of the native population died of European diseases. On Hispaniola alone, out of an initial population of one hundred thousand natives when Columbus arrived in 1493, only three hundred Indians survived by 1570.

In the New World, the Spanish developed an administrative system based on viceroys. Spanish possessions were initially divided into two major administrative units: New Spain (Mexico, Central America, and the Caribbean islands), with its center at Mexico City, and Peru (western South America), governed by a viceroy in Lima. Each viceroy served as the king's chief civil and military officer and was aided by advisory groups called *audiencias,* which also functioned as supreme judicial bodies.

By papal agreement, the Catholic monarchs of Spain were given extensive rights over ecclesiastical affairs in the New World. They could nominate church officials, build churches, collect fees, and supervise the affairs of the various religious orders who sought to Christianize the heathen. Catholic monks had remarkable success in converting and baptizing hundreds of thousands of Indians in the early years of the conquests. Soon after the missionaries came the establishment of dioceses, parishes, schools, and hospitals—all the trappings of a European society.

☀ The Impact of European Expansion

The arrival of the Europeans had an enormous impact on both the conquerors and the conquered. The native American civilizations, which had their own unique qualities and a degree of sophistication rarely appreciated by the conquerors, were virtually destroyed, and the native populations were ravaged by diseases introduced by the Europeans. Ancient social and political structures were ripped up and replaced by European institutions, religion, language, and culture.

For some Europeans, expansion abroad in the sixteenth century also brought hopes for land, riches, and social advancement. One Spaniard commented in 1572 that many "poor young men" left Spain for Mexico, where they might hope to acquire landed estates and "call themselves gentlemen." Although some wives accompanied their husbands abroad, many ordinary European women found new opportunities for marriage in the New World because of the lack of white women. Indeed, as one commentator bluntly put it, even "a whore, if handsome, can make a wife for some rich planter."[5] In the violence-prone world of early Spanish America, a number of women also found themselves rich after their husbands were killed unexpectedly. In one area of Central America, women owned about 25 percent of the landed estates by 1700.

European expansion also affected the conquerors in the economic arena. Wherever they went in the New World, Europeans sought to find sources of gold and silver. One Aztec commented that the Spanish conquerors "longed and lusted for gold. Their bodies swelled with greed, and their hunger was ravenous; they hungered like pigs for that gold."[6] Rich silver deposits were found and exploited in Mexico and southern Peru (modern Bolivia). When the mines at Potosí in Peru were opened in 1545, the value of precious metals imported into Europe quadrupled. It has been estimated that between 1503 and 1650, some 16 million kilograms (over 35 million pounds) of silver and 185,000 kilograms (400,000 pounds) of gold entered the port of Seville, triggering a price revolution that reverberated throughout the Spanish economy.

But gold and silver were only two of the products that became part of the exchange between the New World and the Old. Europeans brought their horses and sheep and also took up the cultivation of wheat. Into Seville flowed sugar, dyes, cotton, vanilla, and hides from livestock raised on the grass-covered plains of South America. New agricultural products such as potatoes, coffee, corn, and tobacco were also imported. Because of its trading posts in Asia, Portugal soon challenged the Italian states as the chief entry point of the eastern trade in spices, jewels, silks, carpets, ivory, leather, and perfumes, although the Venetians clung tenaciously to the spice trade until they lost out to the Dutch in the seventeenth century. Economic historians believe that the increase in the volume and area of European trade as well as the rise in liquid capital due to this expansion were crucial factors in producing a new era of commercial capitalism that represented the first step toward the global economy we know today.

European expansion, which was in part a product of European rivalries, also deepened those rivalries and increased the tensions among European states.

Bitter conflicts arose over the cargoes coming from the New World and Asia. Although the Spanish and Portuguese entered the competition first, the Dutch, French, and English soon became involved on a large scale and by the seventeenth century were challenging the Portuguese and Spanish monopolies.

◆ Politics and the Wars of Religion in the Sixteenth Century

By the middle of the sixteenth century, Calvinism and Catholicism had become militant religions dedicated to spreading the word of God as they interpreted it. Although this religious struggle for the minds and hearts of Europeans is at the heart of the religious wars of the sixteenth century, economic, social, and political forces also played important roles in these conflicts. Of the sixteenth-century religious wars, none were more momentous or shattering than the French civil wars known as the French Wars of Religion.

❈ The French Wars of Religion (1562–1598)

Religion was at the heart of the French civil wars of the sixteenth century. The growth of Calvinism led to persecution by the French kings but did little to stop the spread of Calvinism. Huguenots (as the French Calvinists were called) came from all layers of society: artisans and shopkeepers hurt by rising prices and a rigid guild system, merchants and lawyers in provincial towns whose local privileges were tenuous, and members of the nobility. Possibly 40 to 50 percent of the French nobility became Huguenots, including the house of Bourbon, which stood next to the Valois dynasty in the royal line of succession and ruled the southern French kingdom of Navarre. The conversion of so many nobles made the Huguenots a potentially dangerous political threat to monarchical power. Though the Calvinists constituted only about 7 percent of the population, they were a strong-willed and well-organized minority.

The Catholic majority greatly outnumbered the Calvinist minority. The Valois monarchy was staunchly Catholic, and its control of the Catholic church gave it little incentive to look favorably on Protestantism. At the same time, an extreme Catholic party—known as the ultra-Catholics—favored strict opposition to the Huguenots and were led by the Guise family. Possessing the loyalty of Paris and large sections of northern and northwestern France, they could recruit and pay for large armies and received support abroad from the papacy and Jesuits who favored their noncompromising Catholic position.

The religious issue was not the only factor that contributed to the French civil wars. Towns and provinces, which had long resisted the growing power of monarchical centralization, were only too willing to join a revolt against the monarchy. This was also true of the nobility, and the fact that so many of them were Calvinists created an important base of opposition to the crown. The French Wars of Religion, then, based a major constitutional crisis for France and temporarily halted the development of the French centralized territorial state. The claim of the ruling dynasty of the state to a person's loyalties was temporarily superseded by loyalty to one's religious belief. For thirty years, battles raged in France between Catholic and Calvinist parties, who obviously considered the unity of France less important than religious truth. But there also emerged in France a group known as the *politiques* who placed politics before religion and believed that no religious truth was worth the ravages of civil war. The *politiques* ultimately prevailed, but not until both sides had become exhausted by bloodshed.

Finally, in 1589, Henry of Navarre, the political leader of the Huguenots and a member of the Bourbon dynasty, succeeded to the throne as Henry IV (1589–1610). Realizing, however, that he would never be accepted by Catholic France, Henry took the logical way out and converted to Catholicism. With his coronation in 1594, the Wars of Religion finally came to an end. The Edict of Nantes in 1598 solved the religious problem by acknowledging Catholicism as the official religion of France while guaranteeing the Huguenots the right to worship and to enjoy all political privileges, including the holding of public offices.

❈ Philip II and the Cause of Militant Catholicism

The greatest advocate of militant Catholicism in the second half of the sixteenth century was King Philip II of Spain (1556–1598), the son and heir of Charles V. Philip's reign ushered in an age of Spanish greatness, both politically and culturally. Philip's first major goal was to consolidate and secure the lands he had inherited from his father. These included Spain, the Netherlands, and possessions in Italy and the New World. For Philip, this meant strict conformity to Catholicism, enforced by aggressive use of the Spanish Inquisition, and the establishment of strong monarchical authority. Establishing this authority was not an easy task because Philip had inherited a governmental structure in which each of the various states and territories of his empire stood in an individual relationship to the king. Philip did manage, however, to expand royal power by making the monarchy less dependent on the traditional landed aristocracy.

Crucial to an understanding of Philip II is the importance of Catholicism to the Spanish people and their ruler. Driven by a heritage of crusading fervor, the Spanish had little difficulty seeing themselves as a nation of people divinely chosen to save Catholic Christianity from the Protestant heretics. Philip II, the "Most Catholic King," became the champion of Catholicism throughout Europe, a role that led him to spectacular victories and equally spectacular defeats. Spain's leadership of a "holy league" against Turkish encroachments in the Mediterranean resulted in a stunning victory over the Turkish fleet in the Battle of Lepanto in 1571. But Philip's attempt to crush the revolt in the Netherlands and his tortured policy with England's Queen Elizabeth led to his greatest misfortunes.

❈ The Revolt of the Netherlands

As one of the richest parts of Philip's empire, the Spanish Netherlands was of great importance to the "Most Catholic King." Philip's attempt to strengthen his control in the Netherlands, which consisted of seventeen provinces (modern Netherlands, Belgium, and Luxembourg), soon led to a revolt. The nobles, who stood to lose the most politically if their jealously guarded privileges and freedoms were weakened, strongly opposed Philip's efforts. Resentment against Philip was also aroused by the collection of taxes when the residents of the Netherlands realized that these revenues were being used for Spanish interests. Finally, religion became a major catalyst for rebellion when Philip attempted to crush Calvinism. Violence erupted in 1566, when Calvinists—especially nobles—began to destroy statues and stained-glass windows in Catholic churches. Philip responded by sending the duke of Alva with ten thousand veteran Spanish and Italian troops to crush the rebellion.

But the revolt became organized, especially in the seven northern provinces where the Dutch, under the leadership of William of Nassau, the prince of

❊ CHRONOLOGY

The Wars of Religion in the Sixteenth Century

The French Wars of Religion	1562–1598
Coronation of Henry IV	1594
Edict of Nantes	1598
Outbreak of revolt in the Netherlands	1566
Battle of Lepanto	1571
Spanish Armada	1588
Twelve-year truce (Spain and the Netherlands)	1609
Independence of the United Provinces	1648

❊ The England of Elizabeth

After the death of Queen Mary in 1558, her half-sister Elizabeth, the daughter of Henry VIII and Anne Boleyn, ascended the throne of England. During Elizabeth's reign, England rose to prominence as the relatively small island kingdom became the leader of the Protestant nations of Europe, laid the foundations for a world empire, and experienced a cultural renaissance.

Intelligent, cautious, and self-confident, Elizabeth moved quickly to solve the difficult religious problem she inherited from her half-sister. Elizabeth's religious policy was based on moderation and compromise. The Catholic laws of Mary's reign were repealed, and a new Act of Supremacy designated Elizabeth as "the only supreme governor" of both church and state. The church service used during the reign of Edward VI was revised to make it more acceptable to Catholics. The Church of England under Elizabeth was basically Protestant, but of a moderate sort that kept most people satisfied in the second half of the sixteenth century.

Caution, moderation, and expediency also dictated Elizabeth's foreign policy. Fearful of other countries' motives, Elizabeth realized that war could be

Orange, offered growing resistance. The struggle dragged on for decades until 1609, when a twelve-year truce ended the war, virtually recognizing the independence of the northern provinces. These seven northern provinces, which began to call themselves the United Provinces of the Netherlands in 1581, soon emerged as the Dutch Republic, although the Spanish did not formally recognize them as independent until 1648. The ten southern provinces remained a Spanish possession (see Map 14.2).

MAP 14.2   The Height of Spanish Power Under Philip II.

PROCESSION OF QUEEN ELIZABETH I. Intelligent and learned, Elizabeth was familiar with Latin and Greek and spoke several European languages. Served by able administrators, she ruled for nearly forty-five years and generally avoided open military action against any major power. Her participation in the revolt of the Netherlands, however, brought England into conflict with Spain. This picture, painted near the end of her reign, shows the queen on a ceremonial procession.

disastrous for her island kingdom and her own rule. While encouraging English piracy and providing clandestine aid to French Huguenots and Dutch Calvinists to weaken France and Spain, Elizabeth pretended complete aloofness and avoided alliances that would force her into war with any major power. Gradually, however, Elizabeth was drawn into conflict with Spain. After years of resisting the idea of invading England as too impractical, Philip II of Spain was finally persuaded to do so by advisers who assured him that the people of England would rise against their queen when the Spaniards arrived. Moreover, Philip was easily convinced that the revolt in the Netherlands would never be crushed as long as England provided support for it. In any case, a successful invasion of England would mean the overthrow of heresy and the return of England to Catholicism, surely an act in accordance with the will of God. Philip therefore ordered preparations for an armada (fleet of warships) to spearhead the invasion of England in 1588.

The armada proved a disaster. The Spanish fleet that finally set sail had neither the ships nor the troops that Philip had planned to send. A conversation between a papal emissary and an officer of the Spanish fleet before the armada departed reveals the fundamental flaw:

> "And if you meet the English armada in the Channel, do you expect to win the battle?"
>
> "Of course," replied the Spaniard.
>
> "How can you be so sure?" [asked the emissary]
>
> "It's very simple. It is well known that we fight in God's cause. So, when we meet the English, God will surely

arrange matters so that we can grapple and board them, either by sending some strange streak of weather, or, more likely, just by depriving the English of their wits. If we can come to close quarters, Spanish valor and Spanish steel (and the great masses of soldiers we shall have on board) will make our victory certain. But unless God helps us by a miracle the English, who have faster and handier ships than ours, and many more long-range guns, and who know their advantage just as well as we do, will never close with us at all, but stand aloof and knock us to pieces with their culverins, without our being able to do them any serious hurt. So," concluded the captain, and one fancies a grim smile, "we are sailing against England in the confident hope of a miracle."[7]

The hoped-for miracle never materialized. The Spanish fleet, battered by a number of encounters with the English, sailed back to Spain by a northward route around Scotland and Ireland where it was further battered by storms. Although the English and Spanish would continue their war for another sixteen years, the defeat of the Spanish Armada guaranteed for the time being that England would remain a Protestant country. Although Spain made up for its losses within a year and a half, the defeat was a psychological blow to the Spaniards.

◆ Economic and Social Crises

The period of European history from 1560 to 1650 witnessed severe economic and social crises as well as political upheaval. The inflation-fueled prosperity of the sixteenth century showed signs of slackening by the beginning of the seventeenth century. Economic contraction began to be evident in some parts of Europe by the 1620s. In the 1630s and 1640s, as imports of silver from the Americas declined, economic recession intensified, especially in the Mediterranean area. The industrial and financial center of Europe in the Renaissance, Italy was now becoming an economic backwater. Spain's economy was also seriously failing by the 1640s.

Population trends of the sixteenth and seventeenth centuries also reveal Europe's worsening conditions. The sixteenth century was a period of expanding population, possibly related to a warmer climate and increased food supplies. It has been estimated that the population of Europe increased from 60 million in 1500 to 85 million by 1600, the first major recovery of European population since the devastation of the Black Death in the mid-fourteenth century. However, records also indicate a leveling off of the population by 1620 and even a decline by 1650, especially in central and southern Europe. Europe's longtime adversaries—war, famine, and plague—continued to affect population levels. Another "little ice age" after the middle of the sixteenth century, when average temperatures fell, affected harvests and gave rise to famines. These economic problems created social tensions that were also evident in the witchcraft craze.

✳ The Witchcraft Craze

Hysteria over witchcraft affected the lives of many Europeans in the sixteenth and seventeenth centuries. Witchcraft trials were prevalent in England, Scotland, Switzerland, Germany, some parts of France and the Low Countries, and even New England in America.

Witchcraft was not a new phenomenon in the sixteenth and seventeenth centuries. Its practice had been part of traditional village culture for centuries, but it came to be viewed as both sinister and dangerous when the medieval church began to connect witches to the activities of the devil, thereby transforming witchcraft into a heresy that had to be extirpated. After creation of the Inquisition in the thirteenth century, people were accused of a variety of witchcraft practices and, following the biblical injunction, "Thou shalt not suffer a witch to live," were turned over to secular authorities for burning at the stake or, in England, hanging.

What distinguished witchcraft in the sixteenth and seventeenth centuries from these previous developments was the increased number of trials and executions of presumed witches. Perhaps more than a hundred thousand people were prosecuted throughout Europe on charges of witchcraft. As more and more people were brought to trial, the fear of witches as well as the fear of being accused of witchcraft escalated to frightening proportions. Although larger cities were affected first, the trials spread to smaller towns and rural areas as the hysteria persisted well into the seventeenth century (see the box on p. 293).

The accused witches usually confessed to a number of practices, most often after intense torture. But even when people confessed voluntarily, certain practices stand out. Many said that they had sworn allegiance to the devil and attended sabbats, nocturnal gatherings where they feasted, danced, and even copulated with the devil in sexual orgies. More common, however, were admissions of using evil incantations and special ointments and powders to wreak havoc on neighbors by killing their livestock, injuring their children, or raising storms to destroy their crops.

A number of contributing factors have been suggested to explain why the witchcraft craze became so widespread in the sixteenth and seventeenth centuries. Religious uncertainties clearly played some part. Many witchcraft trials occurred in areas where Protestantism had been recently victorious or in regions, such as southwestern Germany, where Protestant-Catholic controversies still raged. As religious passions became inflamed, accusations of being in league with the devil became common on both sides. Recently, however, historians have emphasized the importance of social conditions, especially the problems of a society in turmoil, in explaining the witchcraft hysteria. At a time when the old communal values that stressed working together for the good of the community were disintegrating, property owners became more fearful of the growing numbers of poor among them and transformed them psychologically into agents of the devil. Old women were particularly susceptible to suspicion. Many of them, no longer the recipients of the local charity found in traditional society, may even have tried to survive by selling herbs, potions, or secret remedies for healing. When problems arose—and there were many in this crisis-laden period—these same people were the most likely scapegoats.

That women should be the chief victims of witchcraft trials was hardly accidental. Nicholas Rémy, a witchcraft judge in France in the 1590s, found it "not unreasonable that this scum of humanity, i.e., witches, should be drawn chiefly from the feminine sex."[8] To another judge, it came as no surprise that witches would confess to sexual experiences with Satan: "The

A Witchcraft Trial in France

Persecutions for witchcraft reached their high point in the sixteenth and seventeenth centuries when tens of thousands of people were brought to trial. In this excerpt from the minutes of a trial in France in 1652, we can see why the accused witch stood little chance of exonerating herself.

The Trial of Suzanne Gaudry

28 May, 1652. . . . Interrogation of Suzanne Gaudry, prisoner at the court of Rieux. . . . [During interrogations on May 28 and May 29, the prisoner confessed to a number of activities involving the devil.]

❋ *Deliberation of the Court—June 3, 1652*

The undersigned advocates of the Court have seen these interrogations and answers. They say that the aforementioned Suzanne Gaudry confesses that she is a witch, that she had given herself to the devil, that she had renounced God, Lent, and baptism, that she has been marked on the shoulder, that she has cohabited with the devil and that she has been to the dances, confessing only to have cast a spell upon and caused to die a beast of Philippe Cornié. . . .

❋ *Third Interrogation—June 27*

The prisoner being led into the chamber, she was examined to know if things were not as she had said and confessed at the beginning of her imprisonment.

—Answers no, and that what she has said was done so by force.

Pressed to say the truth, that otherwise she would be subjected to torture, having pointed out to her that her aunt was burned for this same subject.

—Answers that she is not a witch. . . .

She was placed in the hands of the officer in charge of torture, throwing herself on her knees, struggling to cry, uttering several exclamations, without being able, nevertheless to shed a tear. Saying at every moment that she is not a witch.

❋ *The Torture*

On this same day, being at the place of torture.

This prisoner, before being strapped down, was admonished to maintain herself in her first confessions and to renounce her lover.

—Says that she denies everything she has said, and that she has no lover. Feeling herself being strapped down, says that she is not a witch, while struggling to cry . . . and upon being asked why she confessed to being one, said that she was forced to say it.

Told that she was not forced, that on the contrary she declared herself to be a witch without any threat.

—Says that she confessed it and that she is not a witch, and being a little stretched [on the rack] screams ceaselessly that she is not a witch. . . .

Asked if she did not confess that she had been a witch for twenty-six years.

—Says that she said it, that she retracts it, crying that she is not a witch.

Asked if she did not make Philippe Cornié's horse die, as she confessed.

—Answers no, crying Jesus-Maria, that she is not a witch.

The mark having been probed by the officer, in the presence of Doctor Bouchain, it was adjudged by the aforesaid doctor and officer truly to be the mark of the devil.

Being more tightly stretched upon the torture-rack, urged to maintain her confessions.

—Said that it was true that she is a witch and that she would maintain what she had said.

Asked how long she has been in subjugation to the devil.

—Answers that it was twenty years ago that the devil appeared to her, being in her lodgings in the form of a man dressed in a little cow-hide and black breeches. . . .

❋ *Verdict*

July 9, 1652. In the light of the interrogations, answers and investigations made into the charge against Suzanne Gaudry, . . . seeing by her own confessions that she is said to have made a pact with the devil, received the mark from him, . . . and that following this, she had renounced God, Lent, and baptism and had let herself be known carnally by him, in which she received satisfaction. Also, seeing that she is said to have been a part of nocturnal carols and dances.

For expiation of which the advice of the undersigned is that the office of Rieux can legitimately condemn the aforesaid Suzanne Gaudry to death, tying her to a gallows, and strangling her to death, then burning her body and burying it here in the environs of the woods.

Devil uses them so, because he knows that women love carnal pleasures, and he means to bind them to his allegiance by such agreeable provocations."[9] Of course, not only witch hunters held such low estimates of women. Most theologians, lawyers, and philosophers in early modern Europe maintained a belief in the natural inferiority of women, making it plausible to them that they would be more susceptible to witchcraft.

By the mid-seventeenth century, the witchcraft hysteria began to subside. The destruction of the religious wars had at least forced people to accept a grudging toleration, causing religious passions to subside. Moreover, as governments began to stabilize after the period of crisis, fewer magistrates were willing to accept the unsettling and divisive conditions generated by the trials of witches. Finally, by the end of the seventeenth and beginning of the eighteenth centuries, more and more people were questioning altogether their old attitudes toward religion and found it especially contrary to reason to believe in the old view of a world haunted by evil spirits.

◆ Seventeenth-Century Crises: War and Rebellions

Although many Europeans responded to the upheavals of the second half of the sixteenth century with a desire for peace and order, the first fifty years of the seventeenth century continued to be a period of crisis. A devastating war that affected much of Europe and rebellions seemingly everywhere protracted an atmosphere of disorder and violence.

✶ The Thirty Years' War (1618–1648)

Religion, especially the struggle between militant Catholicism and militant Calvinism, certainly played an important role in the outbreak of the Thirty Years' War, often called the "last of the religious wars." As the war progressed, however, it became increasingly clear that secular, dynastic-nationalist considerations were far more important.

The Thirty Years' War began in 1618 in the Germanic lands of the Holy Roman Empire as a struggle between Catholic forces, led by the Habsburg Holy Roman Emperors and Protestant—primarily Calvinist—nobles in Bohemia who rebelled against Habsburg authority. What began as a struggle over religious issues soon became a wider conflict determined by political motivations as both minor and major European powers—Denmark, Sweden, France, and Spain—made the war a Europe-wide struggle (see Map 14.3). The conflict between the Bourbon dynasty of France and the Habsburg dynasties of Spain and the Holy Roman Empire for European leadership was an especially important factor. Nevertheless, most of the battles were fought on German soil, with devastating results for the German people (see the box on p. 296).

The war in Germany was officially ended by the Peace of Westphalia in 1648. What were the results of this "basically meaningless conflict," as one historian has called it? The Peace of Westphalia ensured that all German states, including the Calvinist ones, were free to determine their own religion. The major contenders gained new territories, and one of them, France, emerged as the dominant nation in Europe. The more than three hundred states that made up the Holy Roman Empire were virtually recognized as independent states, because each received the power to conduct its own foreign policy; this brought an end to the Holy Roman Empire as a political entity and ensured German disunity for another two hundred years. The Peace of Westphalia also made it clear that religion and politics were now separate worlds. The pope was completely ignored in all decisions at Westphalia, and political motives became the guiding forces in public affairs as religion moved closer to becoming primarily a matter of personal conviction and individual choice.

The economic and social effects of the Thirty Years' War on Germany are still debated. An older view pictured a ruined German economy and a decline in German population from 21 to 13 million between 1600 and 1650, but more recent opinions have estimated that Germany's population grew from 16 to 17 million while a redistribution of economic activity rather than an overall decline took place. Both views contain some truth. Some areas of Germany were completely devastated while others remained relatively untouched and even experienced economic growth. In any case, the Thirty Years' War was undoubtedly the most destructive conflict Europeans had yet experienced.

✶ Rebellions

Before, during, and after the Thirty Years' War, a series of rebellions and civil wars stemming from the discontent of both nobles and commoners rocked the domestic stability of many European governments. To

MAP I4.3   **Europe During the Thirty Years' War.**

strengthen their power, monarchs attempted to extend their authority at the expense of traditional powerful elements who resisted the rulers' efforts. At the same time, to fight their battles, governments increased taxes and created such hardships that common people also rose in opposition.

Between 1590 and 1640, peasant and lower-class revolts occurred in central and southern France, Austria, and Hungary. In the decades of the 1640s and 1650s, even greater unrest occurred. Portugal and Catalonia rebelled against the Spanish government in 1640. The common people in Naples and Sicily revolted against both the government and the landed nobility in 1647. Russia, too, was rocked by urban uprisings in 1641, 1645, and 1648. Nobles rebelled in France from 1648 to 1652 to halt the growth of royal power. The northern states of Sweden, Denmark,

and Holland also were not immune from upheavals involving clergy, nobles, and mercantile groups. Even relatively stable Switzerland had a peasant rebellion in 1656. By far the most famous and widest-ranging struggle, however, was the civil war and rebellion in England, commonly known as the English Revolution (see Chapter 15).

◆ Culture in a Turbulent World

Art and literature passed through two major stylistic stages between the Renaissance and 1650. These changes were closely linked to the religious, political, and intellectual developments of the period.

The Face of War in the Seventeenth Century

The Thirty Years' War was the most devastating war Europeans had experienced. Destruction was especially severe in Germany. We have a firsthand account of the face of war in Germany from a picaresque novel called Simplicius Simplicissimus, *written by Jakob von Grimmelshausen. The author's experiences as a soldier in the Thirty Years' War gave his descriptions of the effect of the war on ordinary people a certain vividness and reality. This selection describes the fate of a peasant farm, an experience all too familiar to thousands of German peasants between 1618 and 1648.*

❋ Jakob von Grimmelshausen, Simplicius Simplicissimus

The first thing these horsemen did in the nice back rooms of the house was to put in their horses. Then everyone took up a special job, one having to do with death and destruction. Although some began butchering, heating water, and rendering lard, as if to prepare for a banquet, others raced through the house, ransacking upstairs and down; not even the privy chamber was safe, as if the golden fleece of Jason might be hidden there. Still others bundled up big packs of cloth, household goods, and clothes, as if they wanted to hold a rummage sale somewhere. What they did not intend to take along they broke and spoiled. Some ran their swords into the hay and straw, as if there hadn't been hogs enough to stick. Some shook the feathers out of beds and put bacon slabs, hams, and other stuff in the ticking, as if they might sleep better on these. Others knocked down the hearth and broke the windows, as if announcing an everlasting summer. They flattened out copper and pewter dishes and baled the ruined goods. They burned up bedsteads, tables, chairs, and benches, though there were yards and yards of dry firewood outside the kitchen. Jars and crocks, pots and casseroles all were broken, either because they preferred their meat broiled or because they thought they'd eat only one meal with us. In the barn, the hired girl was handled so roughly that she was unable to walk away, I am ashamed to report. They stretched the hired man out flat on the ground, stuck a wooden wedge in his mouth to keep it open, and emptied a milk bucket full of stinking manure drippings down his throat; they called it a Swedish cocktail. He didn't relish it and made a very wry face. By this means they forced him to take a raiding party to some other place where they carried off men and cattle and brought them to our farm. Among these were my father, mother, and [sister] Ursula.

Then they used thumbscrews, which they cleverly made out of their pistols, to torture the peasants, as if they wanted to burn witches. Though he had confessed to nothing as yet, they put one of the captured hayseeds in the bake-oven and lighted a fire in it. They put a rope around someone else's head and tightened it like a tourniquet until blood came out of his mouth, nose, and ears. In short, every soldier had his favorite method of making life miserable for peasants, and every peasant had his own misery. My father was, as I thought, particularly lucky because he confessed with a laugh what others were forced to say in pain and martyrdom. No doubt because he was the head of the household, he was shown special consideration; they put him close to a fire, tied him by his hands and legs, and rubbed damp salt on the bottoms of his feet. Our old nanny goat had to lick it off and this so tickled my [father] that he could have burst laughing. This seemed so clever and entertaining to me—I had never seen or heard my [father] laugh so long—that I joined him in laughter, to keep him company or perhaps to cover up my ignorance. In the midst of such glee he told them the whereabouts of hidden treasure much richer in gold, pearls, and jewelry than might have been expected on a farm.

I can't say much about the captured wives, hired girls, and daughters because the soldiers didn't let me watch their doings. But I do remember hearing pitiful screams from various dark corners and I guess that my mother and our Ursula had it no better than the rest.

✳ Art: Mannerism and the Baroque

The artistic Renaissance came to an end when a new movement called Mannerism emerged in Italy in the 1520s and 1530s. The age of the Reformation had brought a revival of religious values accompanied by much political turmoil. Especially in Italy, the worldly enthusiasm of the Renaissance gave way to anxiety, uncertainty, suffering, and a yearning for spiritual experience. Mannerism reflected this environment in its deliberate attempt to break down the High Renaissance principles of balance, harmony, and moderation. Italian Mannerist painters deliberately distorted the rules of proportion by portraying elongated figures that conveyed a sense of suffering and a strong emotional atmosphere filled with anxiety and confusion.

Mannerism spread from Italy to other parts of Europe and perhaps reached its apogee in the work of El Greco (1541–1614). Doménikos Theotocópoulos (called "the Greek"—El Greco) was from Crete, but after studying in Venice and Rome, he moved in the 1570s to Spain, where he became a church painter in Toledo. El Greco's elongated figures, portrayed in unusual shades of yellow and green against an eerie background of turbulent grays, reflect well the artist's desire to create a world of intense emotions.

EL GRECO, *LAOCOÖN*. **Mannerism reached high expression in the work of El Greco. Born in Crete, trained in Venice and Rome, and settling finally in Spain, El Greco worked as a church painter in Toledo. Pictured here is his version of the *Laocoön*, a famous piece of Hellenistic sculpture that had been discovered in Rome in 1506. The elongated, contorted bodies project a world of suffering, while the somber background scene of the city of Toledo adds a sense of terror and doom.**

Mannerism was eventually replaced by a new movement—the Baroque—that dominated the artistic world for another century and a half. The Baroque began in Italy in the last quarter of the sixteenth century and spread to the rest of Europe. Baroque artists sought to harmonize the classical traditions of Renaissance art with the intense religious feelings fostered by the revival of religion in the Reformation. Although Protestants were also affected, the Baroque was most wholeheartedly embraced by the Catholic reform movement, as is evident at the Catholic courts, especially those of the Habsburgs in Madrid, Prague, Vienna, and Brussels. Eventually the Baroque style spread to all of Europe and Latin America.

In large part, Baroque art and architecture reflected the search for power that was characteristic of much of the seventeenth century. Baroque churches and palaces featured richly ornamented facades, sweeping staircases, and an overall splendor that were meant to impress people. Kings and princes wanted other kings and princes as well as their subjects to be in awe of their power. The Catholic church, which commissioned many new churches, wanted people to see the triumphant power of the Catholic faith.

Baroque painting was known for its use of dramatic effects to heighten emotional intensity. This style was especially evident in the works of the Flemish painter Peter Paul Rubens (1577–1640), a prolific artist and an important figure in the spread of the Baroque from Italy to other parts of Europe. In his artistic masterpieces, bodies in violent motion, heavily fleshed nudes, a dramatic use of light and shadow, and rich sensuous pigments converge to show intense emotions. The restless forms and constant movement blend together into a dynamic unity.

Perhaps the greatest figure of the Baroque was the Italian architect and sculptor Gian Lorenzo Bernini (1598–1680), who completed Saint Peter's basilica and designed the vast colonnade enclosing the piazza in front of it. Action, exuberance, profusion, and dramatic effects mark his work in the interior of Saint Peter's, where Bernini's *Throne of St. Peter* hovers in midair, held by the hands of the four great doctors of the Catholic church. Above the chair, rays of golden light drive a mass of clouds and angels toward the spectator.

PETER PAUL RUBENS, *THE LANDING OF MARIE DE' MEDICI AT MARSEILLES*. **The Fleming Peter Paul Rubens played a key role in spreading the Baroque style from Italy to other parts of Europe. In *The Landing of Marie de' Medici at Marseilles*, Rubens made a dramatic use of light and color, bodies in motion, and luxurious nudes to heighten the emotional intensity of the scene. This was one of a cycle of twenty-one paintings dedicated to the queen mother of France.**

ARTEMISIA GENTILESCHI, *JUDITH BEHEADING HOLOFERNES.* Artemisia Gentileschi painted a series of pictures portraying scenes from the lives of courageous Old Testament women. In this painting, a determined Judith, armed with her victim's sword, struggles to saw off the head of Holofernes. Gentileschi realistically and dramatically shows the bloody nature of Judith's act.

Less well known than the male artists who dominated the seventeenth-century art world in Italy but prominent in her own right was Artemisia Gentileschi (1593–1653). Born in Rome, she studied painting under her father's direction. In 1616, she moved to Florence and began a successful career as a painter. At the age of twenty-three, she became the first woman to be elected to the Florentine Academy of Design. Although she was known internationally in her day as a portrait painter, her fame now rests on a series of pictures of heroines from the Old Testament, including Judith, Esther, and Bathsheba. Most famous is her *Judith Beheading Holofernes*, a dramatic rendering of the biblical scene in which Judith slays the Assyrian general Holofernes in order to save her besieged town from the Assyrian army.

※ A Golden Age of Literature: England and Spain

Periods of crisis often produce great writing, and so it was of this age, which was characterized by a golden age of theater. In both England and Spain, writing for the stage reached new heights between 1580 and 1640. The golden age of English literature is often called the Elizabethan era because much of the English cultural flowering of the late sixteenth and early sev-

enteenth centuries occurred during the reign of Queen Elizabeth. Elizabethan literature exhibits the exuberance and pride associated with English exploits at the time (see the box on p. 300). Of all the forms of Elizabethan literature, none expressed the energy and intellectual versatility of the era better than drama. Of all the dramatists, none is more famous than William Shakespeare (1564–1614).

Shakespeare was the son of a prosperous glovemaker from Stratford-upon-Avon. When he appeared in London in 1592, Elizabethans were already addicted to the stage. By 1576, two professional theaters run by actors' companies were in existence. Elizabethan theater became a tremendously successful business. In or near London, four to six theaters were open six afternoons a week. London theaters ranged from the Globe, which was a circular unroofed structure holding three thousand spectators, to the Blackfriars, which was roofed and held only five hundred. In the former, the admission charge of only a penny or two enabled even the lower classes to attend, while the higher prices charged in the latter attracted the well-to-do. Elizabethan audiences varied greatly, consisting as they did of nobles, lawyers, merchants, and even vagabonds—putting pressure on playwrights to write works that pleased all.

William Shakespeare: In Praise of England

William Shakespeare is one of the most famous playwrights of the Western world. He was a universal genius, outclassing all others in his psychological insights, depth of characterization, imaginative skills, and versatility. His historical plays reflected the patriotic enthusiasm of the English in the Elizabethan era, as this excerpt from Richard II illustrates.

❋ William Shakespeare, Richard II

This royal throne of kings, this sceptered isle,
This earth of majesty, this seat of Mars,
This other Eden, demi-Paradise,
This fortress built by Nature for herself
Against infection and the hand of war,
This happy breed of men, this little world,
This precious stone set in the silver sea,
Which serves it in the office of a wall
Or as a moat defensive to a house
Against the envy of less happier lands—

This blessed plot, this earth, this realm, this England,
This nurse, this teeming womb of royal kings,
Feared by their breed and famous by their birth,
Renowned for their deeds as far from home,
For Christian service and true chivalry,
As is the sepulcher in stubborn Jewry [the Holy
   Sepulcher in Jerusalem]
Of the world's ransom, blessed Mary's Son—
This land of such dear souls, this dear dear land,
Dear for her reputation through the world,
Is now leased out, I die pronouncing it,
Like a tenement or pelting farm.
England, bound in with the triumphant sea,
Whose rocky shore beats back the envious siege
Of watery Neptune, is now bound in with shame,
With inky blots and rotten parchment bonds.
That England, what was wont to conquer others,
Hath made a shameful conquest of itself.
Ah, would the scandal vanish with my life,
How happy then were my ensuing death!

Shakespeare was a "complete man of the theater." Although best known for writing plays, he was also an actor and a shareholder in the chief performing company of the time, the Lord Chamberlains' Company, which played in theaters as diverse as the Globe and the Blackfriars. Shakespeare has long been recognized as a universal genius. He was a master of the English language, but this technical proficiency was matched by an incredible insight into human psychology. Whether in his tragedies or comedies, Shakespeare exhibited a remarkable understanding of the human condition.

The theater was one of the most creative forms of expression during Spain's golden century. The first professional theaters created in Seville and Madrid in the 1570s were run by actors' companies as in England. Soon a public playhouse could be found in every large town, including Mexico City in the New World. Touring companies brought the latest Spanish plays to all parts of the Spanish empire.

Beginning in the 1580s, the agenda for playwrights was set by Lope de Vega (1562–1635). Like Shakespeare, he was from a middle-class background. He was an incredibly prolific writer; almost one-third of his fifteen hundred plays survive. They have been characterized as witty, charming, action-packed, and realistic. Lope de Vega made no apologies for the fact that he wrote his plays to please his audiences. In a treatise on drama written in 1609, he stated that the foremost duty of the playwright was to satisfy public demand. He remarked that if anyone thought he had written his plays for fame, "undeceive him and tell him that I wrote them for money."

One of the crowning achievements of the golden age of Spanish literature was the work of Miguel de Cervantes (1547–1616), whose *Don Quixote* has been acclaimed as one of the great literary works of all time. Each of the two main figures of this work personifies a side of the Spanish character. The knight Don Quixote from La Mancha is the visionary who is so involved in his lofty ideals that he is oblivious to the hard realities around him. To him, for example, windmills appear as four-armed giants. In contrast, the knight's fat and earthy squire, Sancho Panza, is the rationalist who cannot get his master to see the realities in front of him. But after adventures that take them to all parts of Spain, each comes to see the value of the other's perspective. We are left with Cervantes' conviction that idealism and realism, visionary dreams and the hard work of reality, are both necessary to the human condition.

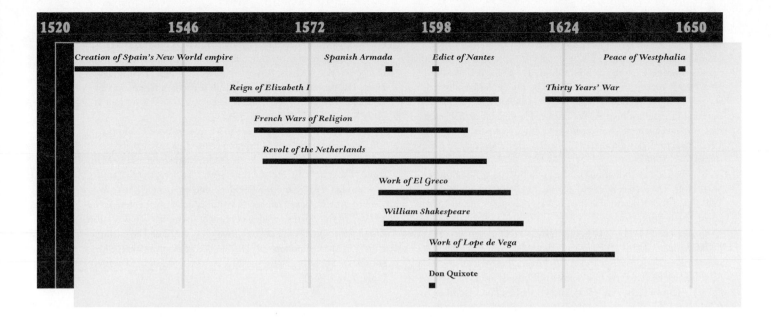

1520	1546	1572	1598	1624	1650

Creation of Spain's New World empire

Spanish Armada

Edict of Nantes

Peace of Westphalia

Reign of Elizabeth I

Thirty Years' War

French Wars of Religion

Revolt of the Netherlands

Work of El Greco

William Shakespeare

Work of Lope de Vega

Don Quixote

Conclusion

Between 1560 and 1650, Europe attempted to adjust to a whole range of change-laden forces. Populations contracted as economic expansion gave way to economic recession. The discovery of new trade routes to the East and the "accidental" discovery of the Americas led Europeans to venture outside the medieval world in which they had been enclosed for virtually a thousand years. The conquest of the Americas brought out the worst and some of the best of European civilization. The greedy plundering of resources and the brutal enslavement and virtual annihilation of millions of New World inhabitants were hardly balanced by attempts to create new institutions, convert the natives to Christianity, and foster the rights of the indigenous peoples.

In the sixteenth century, the discoveries made little impact on Europeans preoccupied with the problems of dynastic expansion and, above all, religious division. It took one hundred years of religious warfare complicated by serious political, economic, and social issues—the worst series of wars and civil wars since the collapse of the Roman Empire in the west—before Europeans finally admitted that they would have to tolerate different ways of worshiping God. That men who were disciples of the Apostle of Peace would kill each other—often in brutal and painful fashion—aroused skepticism about Christianity itself. As one German writer put it in 1650: "Lutheran, popish, and Calvinistic, we've got all these beliefs here; but there is some doubt about where Christianity has got to." It is surely no accident that the search for a stable, secular order of politics and for order in the universe through natural laws played such important roles in the seventeenth century. The religious wars of the sixteenth and seventeenth centuries opened the door to the secular perspectives that have characterized modern Western civilization.

Notes

1. Quoted in J. R. Hale, *Renaissance Exploration* (New York, 1968), p. 32.
2. Quoted in J. H. Parry, *The Age of Reconnaissance: Discovery, Exploration, and Settlement, 1450 to 1640* (New York, 1963), p. 33.
3. Quoted in Richard B. Reed, "The Expansion of Europe," in Richard De Molen, ed., *The Meaning of the Renaissance and Reformation* (Boston, 1974), p. 308.
4. Quoted in Mary B. Campbell, *The Witness and the Other World: Exotic European Travel Writing, 400–1600* (Ithaca, N.Y., 1991), p. 197.
5. Quoted in G. V. Scammell, *The First Imperial Age: European Overseas Expansion, c. 1400–1715* (London, 1989), p. 62.
6. Miguel Leon-Portilla, ed., *The Broken Spears: The Aztec Account of the Conquest of Mexico* (Boston, 1969), p. 51.
7. Quoted in Garrett Mattingly, *The Armada* (Boston, 1959), pp. 216–217.
8. Quoted in Joseph Klaits, *Servants of Satan: The Age of the Witch Hunts* (Bloomington, Ind., 1985), p. 68.
9. Ibid.

Suggestions for Further Reading

General works on the period from 1560 to 1650 include C. Wilson, *The Transformation of Europe, 1558–1648* (Berkeley, Calif., 1976), and R. Bonney, *The European Dynastic States, 1494–1660* (Oxford, 1991).

The best general accounts of European discovery and expansion are G. V. Scammell, *The First Imperial Age: European Overseas Expansion, c. 1400–1715* (London, 1989); J. H. Parry, *The Age of Reconnaissance: Discovery, Exploration, and Settlement, 1450 to 1650* (New York, 1963); and B. Penrose, *Travel and Discovery in the Renaissance, 1420–1620* (New York, 1962). On the medieval background to European expansion, see J. R. S. Phillips, *The Medieval Expansion of Europe* (New York, 1988). On European perceptions of the world outside Europe, see M. B. Campbell, *The Witness and the*

Other World: Exotic European Travel Writing, 400–1600 (Ithaca, N.Y., 1991). On Columbus, see the brief biography by J. S. Collis, *Christopher Columbus* (London, 1976), and F. Fernandez-Armesto, *Columbus* (New York, 1991). The impact of expansion on European consciousness is explored in J. H. Elliott, *The Old World and the New, 1492–1650* (Cambridge, 1970). The human and ecological effects of the interaction of New World and Old World cultures are examined thoughtfully in A. W. Crosby, *The Columbian Exchange: Biological and Cultural Consequences of 1492* (Westport, Conn., 1972), and *Ecological Imperialism: The Biological Expansion of Europe* (New York, 1986).

For good introductions to the French Wars of Religion, see M. P. Holt, *The French Wars of Religion, 1562–1629* (Cambridge, 1995), and R. J. Knecht, *The French Wars of Religion, 1559–1598,* 2d ed. (New York, 1996).

Two good histories of Spain in the sixteenth century are J. Lynch, *Spain, 1516–1598: From Nation-State to World Empire* (Cambridge, Mass., 1994), and A. W. Lovett, *Early Habsburg Spain* (Oxford, 1986). The best biographies of Philip II are P. Pierson, *Philip II of Spain* (London, 1975), and G. Parker, *Philip II,* 3d ed. (Chicago, 1995). On the revolt of the Netherlands, see the classic work by P. Geyl, *The Revolt of the Netherlands, 1555–1609* (London, 1962), and the more recent work of G. Parker, *The Dutch Revolt* (London, 1977).

Elizabeth's reign can be examined in two good biographies: C. Haigh, *Elizabeth I,* 2d ed. (New York, 1998), and W. T. MacCaffrey, *Elizabeth I* (London, 1993). The classic on the Spanish Armada is the beautifully written work *The Armada* by G. Mattingly (Boston, 1959).

The classic study on the Thirty Years' War is C. V. Wedgwood, *The Thirty Years' War* (Garden City, N.Y., 1961), but it needs to be supplemented by G. Parker, ed., *The Thirty Years' War,* 2d ed.

(London, 1997); R. G. Asch, *The Thirty Years' War: The Holy Roman Empire and Europe, 1618–1648* (New York, 1997); and the brief study by S. J. Lee, *The Thirty Years' War* (London, 1991).

The story of the witchcraft craze can be examined in three modern works: J. Klaits, *Servants of Satan: The Age of the Witch Hunts* (Bloomington, Ind., 1985); J. B. Russell, *A History of Witchcraft* (London, 1980); and B. P. Levack, *The Witch-Hunt in Early Modern Europe* (London, 1987).

For a brief, readable guide to Mannerism, see L. Murray, *The Late Renaissance and Mannerism* (New York, 1967). For a general survey of Baroque culture, see M. Mainstone and L. Mainstone, *The Cambridge Introduction to Art: The Seventeenth Century* (Cambridge, 1981), and J. S. Held, *Seventeenth- and Eighteenth-Century Art: Baroque Painting, Sculpture, Architecture* (New York, 1971). On the Spanish golden century of literature, see R. O. Jones, *The Golden Age: Prose and Poetry,* which is vol. 2 of *The Literary History of Spain* (London, 1971). The literature on Shakespeare is enormous. For a biography, see A. L Rowse, *The Life of Shakespeare* (New York, 1963).

For additional reading, go to InfoTrac College Edition, your online research library at http://web1.infotrac-college.com

Enter the search terms *Vasco da Gama* using Key Terms.

Enter the search terms *Christopher Columbus* using the Subject Guide.

Enter the search terms *Thirty Years' War* using Key Terms.

Enter the search terms *Elizabeth I* using Key Terms.

15

Response to Crisis: State Building and the Search for Order in the Seventeenth Century

FOCUS QUESTIONS

- What was absolutism in theory, and how did its actual practice in France reflect or differ from the theory?
- What developments enabled Brandenburg-Prussia, Austria, and Russia to emerge as major powers in the seventeenth century?
- What were the main issues in the struggle between king and Parliament in seventeenth-century England, and how were they resolved?
- What theories of government were proposed by Thomas Hobbes and John Locke, and how did their respective theories reflect concerns and problems of the seventeenth century?
- What role did the Netherlands play in the political, economic, and artistic life of the seventeenth century?

T HE AGE OF CRISIS *from 1560 to 1650 was accompanied by a decline in religious orientation and a growing secularization that affected both the political and the intellectual worlds of Europe. Some historians like to speak of the seventeenth century as a turning point in the evolution of a modern state system in Europe. The ideal of a united Christian Europe, which had become increasingly unattainable, gave way to the practical realities of a system of secular states in which reason of state took precedence over the salvation of subjects' souls. These states had emerged and begun their development during the Middle Ages, but medieval ideas about statehood had been couched in religious terms. By the seventeenth century, the credibility of Christianity had been so weakened in the religious wars that more and more Europeans came to think of politics in secular terms.*

One of the responses to the crises of the seventeenth century was a search for order. As the internal social and political rebellions and revolts died down, it became apparent that the privileged classes of society—the aristocrats—remained in control, although the various states exhibited important differences in political forms. The most general trend saw an extension of monarchical power as a stabilizing force. This development, which historians have called absolutism or absolute monarchy, was most evident in France during the flamboyant reign of Louis XIV, regarded by some as the perfect embodiment of an absolute monarch. In his memoirs, the duc de Saint-Simon, who had firsthand experience of French court life, said that Louis was "the very figure of a hero, so imbued with a natural but most imposing majesty that it appeared even in his most insignificant gestures and movements." The king's natural grace gave him a special charm as well: "He was as dignified and majestic in his dressing gown as when dressed in robes of state, or on horseback at the head of his troops." His life was orderly: "Nothing could be regulated with greater exactitude than were his days and hours." His self-control was impeccable: "He did not lose control of himself ten times in his whole life, and then only with inferior persons." But even absolute monarchs had imperfections, and Saint-Simon had the courage to point them out: "Louis XIV's vanity was without limit or restraint," which led to his "distaste for all merit, intelligence, education, and, most of all, for all independence of character and sentiment in others," as well as his "mistakes of judgment in matters of importance."

But absolutism was not the only response to crisis in the seventeenth century. Other states, such as England, reacted differently to domestic crisis, and another very different system emerged where monarchs were limited by the power of their representative assemblies. Absolute and limited monarchy were the two poles of seventeenth-century state building.

◆ The Practice of Absolutism: Western Europe

Absolute monarchy or absolutism meant that the sovereign power or ultimate authority in the state rested in the hands of a king who claimed to rule by divine right—that kings received their power from God and were responsible to no one (including parliaments) except God. But what did sovereignty mean? The late-sixteenth-century political theorist Jean Bodin believed that sovereign power consisted of the authority to make laws, tax, administer justice, control the state's administrative system, and determine foreign policy. These powers made a ruler sovereign.

✳ France and Absolute Monarchy

France during the reign of Louis XIV (1643–1715) has traditionally been regarded as the best example of the practice of absolute monarchy in the seventeenth century. French culture, language, and manners reached into all levels of European society. French diplomacy and wars shaped the political affairs of western and central Europe. The court of Louis XIV seemed to be imitated everywhere in Europe. Of course, the stability of Louis' reign was magnified by the instability that had preceded it.

The fifty years of French history before Louis XIV came to power were a time in which royal and ministerial governments struggled to avoid the breakdown of the state. The line between order and anarchy was often a thin one. The situation was especially complicated by the fact that in 1610 and 1643, when Louis XIII and Louis XIV, respectively, succeeded to the throne, they were only boys, leaving the government dependent on royal ministers. Two especially competent ministers played crucial roles in maintaining monarchical authority.

Cardinal Richelieu, Louis XIII's chief minister from 1624 to 1642, initiated policies that eventually strengthened the power of the monarchy. By eliminating the political and military rights of the Huguenots while preserving their religious ones, Richelieu transformed the Huguenots into more reliable subjects. Richelieu acted more cautiously in "humbling the pride of the great men," the important French nobility. He understood the influential role played by the nobles in the French state. The dangerous ones were those who asserted their territorial independence when they were excluded from participating in the central government. Proceeding slowly but determinedly, Richelieu developed an efficient network of spies to uncover noble plots and then crushed the conspiracies and executed the conspirators, thereby eliminating a major threat to royal authority.

When Louis XIV succeeded to the throne in 1643 at the age of four, Cardinal Mazarin, the trained successor of Cardinal Richelieu, dominated the government. An Italian who had come to France as a papal legate and then became naturalized, Mazarin attempted to carry on Richelieu's policies until his death in 1661. The most important event during Mazarin's rule was the Fronde, a revolt led primarily by nobles who wished to curb the centralized administrative power being built up at the expense of the provincial nobility. The Fronde was crushed by 1652, and with its end, a vast number of French people concluded that the best hope for stability in France lay in the crown. When Mazarin died in 1661, the greatest of the seventeenth-century monarchs, Louis XIV, took over supreme power.

THE REIGN OF LOUIS XIV (1643–1715)

The day after Cardinal Mazarin's death, Louis XIV, at the age of twenty-three, expressed his determination to be a real king and the sole ruler of France:

> Up to this moment I have been pleased to entrust the government of my affairs to the late Cardinal. It is now time that I govern them myself. You [secretaries and ministers of state] will assist me with your counsels when I ask for them. I request and order you to seal no orders except by my command. . . . I order you not to sign anything, not even a passport . . . without my command; to render account to me personally each day and to favor no one.[1]

His mother, who was well aware of Louis' proclivity for fun and games and getting into the beds of the maids in the royal palace, laughed aloud at these words. But Louis was quite serious.

Louis proved willing to pay the price of being a strong ruler (see the box on p. 306). He established a conscientious routine from which he seldom deviated, but he did not look on his duties as drudgery because he judged his royal profession to be "grand, noble, and delightful." Eager for glory (in the French sense of achieving what was expected of one in an important position), Louis created a grand and majestic spectacle at the court of Versailles. Consequently, Louis and his court came to set the standard for monarchies and aristocracies all over Europe. The great French writer Voltaire dubbed the period from 1661 to 1715 the "Age of Louis XIV," and historians have tended to call it that ever since.

Although Louis may have believed in the theory of absolute monarchy and consciously fostered the myth of himself as the Sun King, the source of light

LOUIS XIV. **Louis XIV was determined to be the sole ruler of France. He eliminated the threat of the high nobility by removing them from the royal council and replacing them with relatively new aristocrats whom he could dominate. This portrait by Hyacinth Rigaud captures the king's sense of royal dignity and grandeur.**

for all of his people, historians are quick to point out that the realities fell far short of the aspirations. Despite the centralizing efforts of Cardinals Richelieu and Mazarin, France still possessed a bewildering system of overlapping authorities in the seventeenth century. Provinces had their own regional courts, their own local Estates, their own sets of laws. Members of the high nobility with their huge estates and clients among the lesser nobility still exercised much authority. Both towns and provinces possessed privileges and powers seemingly from time immemorial that they would not easily relinquish.

One of the keys to Louis' power was that he was able to restructure the central policy-making machinery of government because it was part of his own court

Louis XIV: Kingly Advice

Throughout his reign, Louis XIV was always on stage, acting the role of the wise "Grand Monarch." In 1661, after he became a father, Louis began his Memoirs for the Dauphin, *a frank collection of precepts for the education of his oldest son and heir to the throne. He continued to add to the* Memoirs *over the next twenty years.*

❋ *Louis XIV,* **Memoirs for the Dauphin**

Kings are often obliged to do things which go against their inclinations and offend their natural goodness. They should love to give pleasure and yet they must often punish and destroy persons on whom by nature they wish to confer benefits. The interest of the state must come first. One must constrain one's inclinations and not put oneself in the position of berating oneself because one could have done better in some important affair but did not because of some private interest, because one was distracted from the attention one should have for the greatness, the good and the power of the state. Often there are troublesome places where it is difficult to make out what one should do. One's ideas are confused. As long as this lasts, one can refrain from making a decision. But as soon as one has fixed one's mind upon something which seems best to do, it must be acted upon. This is what enabled me to succeed so often in what I have done. The mistakes which I made, and which gave me infinite trouble, were the result of the desire to please or of allowing myself to accept too carelessly the opinions of others. Nothing is more dangerous than weakness of any kind whatsoever. In order to command others, one must raise oneself above them and once one has heard the reports from every side one must come to a decision upon the basis of one's own judgment, without anxiety but always with the concern not to command anything which is of itself unworthy either of one's place in the world or of the greatness of the state. Princes with good intentions and some knowledge of their affairs, either from experience or from study and great diligence in making themselves capable, find numerous cases which instruct them that they must give special care and total application to everything. One must be on guard against oneself, resist one's own tendencies, and always be on guard against one's own natural bent. The craft of a king is great, noble and delightful when one feels worthy of doing well whatever one promises to do. But it is not exempt from troubles, weariness and worries. Sometimes uncertainty causes despair, and when one has spent a reasonable time in examining an affair, one must make a decision and take the step which one believes to be best. When one has the state in view, one works for one's self. The good of the one constitutes the glory of the other. When the former is fortunate, eminent and powerful, he who is the cause thereof becomes glorious and consequently should find more enjoyment than his subjects in all the pleasant things of life for himself and for them. When one has made a mistake, it must be corrected as soon as possible, and no other consideration must stand in the way, not even kindness.

and household. The royal court located at Versailles was an elaborate structure that served three purposes simultaneously: it was the personal household of the king, the location of central governmental machinery, and the place where powerful subjects came to find favors and offices for themselves and their clients, as well as the main arena where rival aristocratic factions jostled for power. The greatest danger to Louis' personal rule came from the very high nobles and princes of the blood (the royal princes) who considered it their natural function to assert the policy-making role of royal ministers. Louis eliminated this threat by removing them from the royal council, the chief administrative body of the king and overseer of the central machinery of government, and enticing them to his court where he could keep them preoccupied with court life and out of politics. Instead of the high nobility and royal princes, Louis relied for his ministers on nobles who came from relatively new aristocratic families. His ministers were expected to be subservient; said Louis, "I had no intention of sharing my authority with them."

Louis' domination of his ministers and secretaries gave him control of the central policy-making machinery of government and thus authority over the traditional areas of monarchical power: the formulation of foreign policy, the making of war and peace, the assertion of the secular power of crown against any religious authority, and the ability to levy taxes to fulfill these functions. However, Louis had considerably less success with the internal administration of the kingdom. The traditional groups and institutions of French society—the nobles, officials, town councils, guilds, and representative Estates in some provinces—were simply too powerful for the king to have direct control over the lives of his subjects. As a result, the control of the central government over the provinces and the people was carried out largely by careful bribery of the important people to see that the king's policies were executed.

The maintenance of religious harmony had long been considered an area of monarchical power. The desire to keep it led Louis to pursue an anti-Protestant policy, aimed at converting the Huguenots to Catholicism. In October 1685, Louis issued the Edict of Fontainebleau. In addition to revoking the Edict of Nantes, the new edict provided for the destruction of Huguenot churches and the closing of their schools. Although forbidden to leave France, it is estimated that 200,000 Huguenots left for shelter in England, the United Provinces, and the German states.

The cost of building palaces, maintaining his court, and pursuing his wars made finances a crucial issue for Louis XIV. He was most fortunate in having the services of Jean-Baptiste Colbert (1619–1683) as controller-general of finances. Colbert sought to increase the wealth and power of France through mercantilism, a set of principles that dominated economic thought in the seventeenth century. According to the mercantilists, the prosperity of a nation depended on a plentiful supply of bullion or gold and silver. For this reason, it was desirable to achieve a favorable balance of trade in which goods exported were of greater value than those imported, promoting an influx of gold and silver payments that would increase the quantity of bullion. To encourage exports, governments should stimulate and protect export industries and trade by granting trade monopolies, encouraging investment in new industries through subsidies, and improving transportation systems by building roads, bridges, and canals. By placing high tariffs on foreign goods, they could be kept out of the country and prevented from competing with domestic industries. Colonies were also deemed valuable sources of raw materials and mar-

PALACE OF VERSAILLES. Louis XIV spent untold sums of money on the construction of a new royal residence at Versailles. The enormous palace also housed the members of the king's government and served as home for thousands of French nobles. As the largest royal residence in Europe, Versailles impressed foreigners and became a source of envy for other rulers.

kets for finished goods. As a system of economic principles, mercantilism focused on the role of the state, believing that state intervention in some aspects of the economy was desirable for the sake of the national good.

Colbert was an avid practitioner of mercantilism. To decrease the need for imports and increase exports, he founded new luxury industries and granted special privileges, including tax exemptions, loans, and subsidies to individuals who established new industries. To improve communications and the transportation of goods internally, he built roads and canals. To decrease imports directly, Colbert raised tariffs on foreign manufactured goods and created a merchant marine to carry French goods.

Both the increase in royal power that Louis pursued and his desire for military glory led the king to develop a professional army numbering 100,000 men in peacetime and 400,000 in time of war. Louis made war an almost incessant activity of his reign. To achieve the prestige and military glory befitting the Sun King as well as to ensure the domination of his Bourbon dynasty over European affairs, Louis waged

MAP 15.1   Territories Won in the Wars of Louis XIV.

four wars between 1667 and 1713 (see Map 15.1). His ambitions roused much of Europe to form coalitions to prevent destruction of the European balance of power Bourbon hegemony would cause. Although Louis added some territory to France's northeastern frontier and established a member of his own Bourbon dynasty on the throne of Spain, he also left France impoverished and surrounded by enemies.

✲ The Decline of Spain

At the beginning of the seventeenth century, Spain possessed the most populous empire in the world, controlling almost all of South America and a number of settlements in Asia and Africa. To most Europeans, Spain still seemed the greatest power of the age, but the reality was quite different. The treasury was empty;

Philip II went bankrupt in 1596 from excessive expenditures on war, and his successor did the same in 1607 by spending a fortune on his court. The armed forces were obsolescent, the government was inefficient, and the commercial class was weak in the midst of a suppressed peasantry, a luxury-loving class of nobles, and an oversupply of priests and monks. Spain continued to play the role of a great power, but appearances were deceiving.

During the reign of Philip III (1598–1621), many of Spain's weaknesses became all too apparent. Interested only in court luxury or miracle-working relics, Philip III allowed his first minister, the greedy duke of Lerma, to run the country. The aristocratic Lerma's primary interest was accumulating power and wealth for himself and his family. As important offices were filled with his relatives, crucial problems went unsolved.

At first, the reign of Philip IV (1621–1665) seemed to offer hope for a revival of Spain's energies, especially in the capable hands of his chief minister, Gaspar de Guzman, the count of Olivares. This clever, hardworking, and power-hungry statesman dominated the king's every move and worked to revive the interests of the monarchy. A flurry of domestic reform decrees, aimed at curtailing the power of the church and the landed aristocracy, was soon followed by a political reform program whose purpose was to further centralize the government of all Spain and its possessions in monarchical hands. All of these efforts met with little real success, however, because both the number (estimated at one-fifth of the population) and power of the Spanish aristocrats made them too strong to curtail in any significant fashion.

At the same time, most of the efforts of Olivares and Philip were undermined by their desire to pursue Spain's imperial glory and by a series of internal revolts. Spain's involvement in the Thirty Years' War led to a series of frightfully expensive military campaigns that led to internal revolts and years of civil war. Unfortunately for Spain, the campaigns also failed to produce victory. As Olivares wrote to King Philip IV, "God wants us to make peace; for He is depriving us visibly and absolutely of all the means of war."[2] The defeats in Europe and the internal revolts of the 1640s ended any illusions about Spain's greatness. The actual extent of its economic difficulties is still debated, but there is no question about its foreign losses. Dutch independence was formally recognized by the Peace of Westphalia in 1648, and the Peace of the Pyrenees with France in 1659 meant the surrender of certain border regions, such as the Catalonian province of Roussillon, to France.

◆ Absolutism in Central and Eastern Europe

During the seventeenth century, a development of great importance for the modern Western world took place in central and eastern Europe, the appearance of three new powers: Prussia, Austria, and Russia.

✳ *The German States*

The Peace of Westphalia, which officially ended the Thirty Years' War in 1648, left each of the more than three hundred German states comprising the Holy Roman Empire virtually autonomous and sovereign. Of these states, two emerged in the seventeenth and eighteenth centuries as great European powers.

✿ THE RISE OF BRANDENBURG-PRUSSIA

The development of Brandenburg as a state was largely the story of the Hohenzollern dynasty. By the seventeenth century, the dominions of the house of Hohenzollern, now called Brandenburg-Prussia, consisted of three disconnected masses in western, central, and eastern Germany (see Map 15.2).

MAP 15.2   The Growth of Brandenburg-Prussia.

Absolutism in Western Europe

France	
Louis XIII	1610–1643
Cardinal Richelieu as chief minister	1624–1642
Ministry of Cardinal Mazarin	1642–1661
Fronde	1648–1652
Louis XIV	1643–1715
Edict of Fontainebleau	1685
Spain	
Philip III	1598–1621
Philip IV	1621–1665

The foundation for the Prussian state was laid by Frederick William the Great Elector (1640–1688). Realizing that Brandenburg-Prussia was a small, open territory with no natural frontiers for defense, Frederick William built a competent and efficient standing army. By 1678, he possessed a force of forty thousand men that absorbed more than 50 percent of the state's revenues. To sustain the army and his own power, Frederick William established the General War Commissariat to levy taxes for the army and oversee its growth and training. The Commissariat soon evolved into an agency for civil government as well. Directly responsible to the elector, the new bureaucractic machine became his chief instrument to govern the state. Many of its officials were members of the Prussian landed aristocracy, the Junkers, who also served as officers in the all-important army.

Frederick William was succeeded by his son Frederick III (1688–1713), who made one significant contribution to the development of Prussia. In return for his commitment to aid the Holy Roman Emperor in a war against Spain, he received the title of king in Prussia in 1701. Elector Frederick III was transformed into King Frederick I, and Brandenburg-Prussia became simply Prussia. In the eighteenth century, Prussia emerged as a great power on the European stage.

❀ The Emergence of Austria

The Austrian Habsburgs had long played a significant role in European politics as Holy Roman Emperors. By the end of the Thirty Years' War, the Habsburg hopes of creating an empire in Germany had been dashed. In the seventeenth century, the house of Austria made a difficult transition; the German Empire was lost, but a new empire was created in eastern and southeastern Europe.

The nucleus of the new Austrian Empire remained the traditional Austrian hereditary possessions: Carinthia, Carniola, Styria, and Tyrol (see Map 15.3). To these had been added the kingdom of Bohemia and parts of northwestern Hungary in the sixteenth century. In the seventeenth century, Leopold I (1658–1705) encouraged the eastward movement of the Austrian Empire, but he was sorely challenged by the revival of Turkish power. Having moved into Transylvania, the Turks eventually pushed westward and laid siege to Vienna in 1683. A European army, led by the Austrians, counterattacked and decisively defeated the Turks in 1687. Austria took control of Hungary, Transylvania, Croatia, and Slovenia, thus establishing an Austrian Empire in southeastern Europe. At the end of the War of Spanish Succession (1702–1713), Austria gained possession of the Spanish Netherlands and received formal recognition of its occupation of the Spanish possessions in Italy (Milan, Mantua, Sardinia, and Naples), thus making Austria the dominant power in divided Italy. By the beginning of the eighteenth century, the house of Austria had acquired a new empire of considerable size.

The Austrian monarchy, however, never became a highly centralized, absolutist state, primarily because it contained so many different national groups. The Austrian Empire remained a collection of territories held together by a personal union. The Habsburg emperor was archduke of Austria, king of Bohemia, and king of Hungary. Each of these areas, however, had its own laws, Estates-General, and political life. The landed aristocrats throughout the empire were connected by a common bond of service to the house of Habsburg, as military officers or government bureaucrats, but there was no common sentiment to tie the regions together. By the beginning of the eighteenth century, Austria was a populous empire in central Europe of great potential military strength.

❀ Russia: From Fledgling Principality to Major Power

A new Russian state had emerged in the fifteenth century under the leadership of the principality of Moscow and its grand dukes. In the sixteenth century,

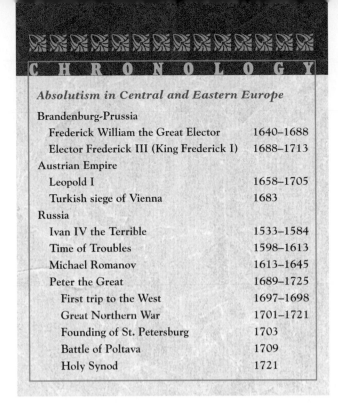
autocracy of the tsar by crushing the power of the Russian nobility, known as the boyars. Ivan's dynasty came to an end in 1598 and was followed by a resurgence of aristocratic power in a period of anarchy known as the Time of Troubles. It did not end until the Zemsky Sobor, or national assembly, chose Michael Romanov in 1613 as the new tsar, beginning a dynasty that lasted until 1917.

In the seventeenth century, Muscovite society was highly stratified. At the top was the tsar, who claimed to be a divinely ordained autocratic ruler. Russian society was dominated by an upper class of landed aristocrats who, in the course of the seventeenth century, managed to bind their peasants to the land. An abundance of land and a shortage of peasants made serfdom desirable to the landowners, who sustained a highly oppressive system. Townspeople were also controlled. Many merchants were not allowed to move from their cities without government permission or to sell their businesses to anyone outside their class. In the seventeenth century, merchant and peasant revolts as well as a schism in the Russian Orthodox church created very unsettled conditions. In the midst of these political and religious upheavals, Russia was experiencing more frequent contacts with the West and Western ideas were beginning to penetrate a few Russian circles. At the end of the seventeenth century,

Ivan IV the Terrible (1533–1584), who was the first ruler to take the title of tsar (Russian word "Caesar"), expanded the territories of Russia eastward, after finding westward expansion blocked by the powerful Swedish and Polish states. Ivan also extended the

MAP 15.3 The Growth of the Austrian Empire.

Peter the Great noticeably accelerated this westernizing process.

❧ THE REIGN OF PETER THE GREAT (1689–1725)

Peter the Great was an unusual character. A strong man, towering 6 feet 9 inches tall, Peter was coarse in his tastes and rude in his behavior. He enjoyed a low kind of humor—belching contests and crude jokes—and vicious punishments—flogging, impalings, and roastings (see the box on p. 313). Peter received a firsthand view of the West when he made a trip there in 1697–1698 and returned to Russia with a firm determination to westernize or Europeanize Russia. Perhaps too much has been made of Peter's desire to westernize a "backward country." Peter's policy of Europeanization was largely technical. He admired European technology and gadgets and desired to transplant these to Russia. Only this kind of modernization could give him the army and navy he needed to make Russia a great power.

PETER THE GREAT. Peter the Great wished to westernize Russia, especially in the realm of technical skills. His foremost goal was the creation of a strong army and navy in order to make Russia a great power. A Dutch painter created this portrait of the armored tsar during his visit to the West in 1697.

As could be expected, one of his first priorities was the reorganization of the army and the creation of a navy. Employing both Russians and Europeans as officers, he conscripted peasants for twenty-five-year stints of service to build a standing army of 210,000 men. Peter has also been given credit for forming the first Russian navy.

Peter reorganized the central government, partly along Western lines. In 1711, he created a senate to supervise the administrative machinery of state while he was away on military campaigns. In time, the Senate became something like a ruling council, but its ineffectiveness caused Peter to borrow the Western institution of "colleges," or boards of administrators entrusted with specific functions, such as foreign affairs, war, and justice. To impose the rule of the central government more effectively throughout the land, Peter divided Russia into eight provinces and later, in 1719, into fifty. Although he hoped to create a "police state," by which he meant a well-ordered community governed in accordance with law, few of his bureaucrats shared his concept of honest service and duty to the state. Peter hoped for a sense of civic duty, but his own forceful personality created an atmosphere of fear that prevented it.

To satisfy his insatiable need of money for an army and navy that absorbed as much as four-fifths of the state revenue, Peter adopted Western mercantilistic policies to stimulate economic growth. He tried to increase exports and develop new industries while exploiting domestic resources like the iron mines in the Urals. But his military needs were endless, and he came to rely on the old expedient of simply raising taxes, imposing additional burdens on the hapless peasants who were becoming ever more oppressed in Peter's Russia.

Peter also sought to gain state control of the Russian Orthodox church. In 1721, he abolished the position of patriarch and created a body called the Holy Synod to make decisions for the church. At its head stood a procurator, a layman who represented the interests of the tsar and assured Peter of effective domination of the church.

Immediately upon returning from his first trip to the West in 1698, Peter began to introduce Western customs, practices, and manners into Russia. He ordered the preparation of the first Russian book of etiquette to teach Western manners. Among other things, it pointed out that it was not polite to spit on the floor or scratch oneself at dinner. Because Westerners did not wear beards or the traditional long-skirted coat, Russian beards had to be shaved

Peter the Great Deals with a Rebellion

During his first visit to the West in 1697–1698, Peter received word that the Streltsy, an elite military unit stationed in Moscow, had revolted against his authority. Peter hurried home and crushed the revolt in a very savage fashion. This selection is taken from an Austrian account of how Peter dealt with the rebels.

❈ Peter and the Streltsy

How sharp was the pain, how great the indignation, to which the tsar's Majesty was mightily moved, when he knew of the rebellion of the Streltsy, betraying openly a mind panting for vengeance! He was still tarrying at Vienna, quite full of the desire of setting out for Italy; but, fervid as was his curiosity of rambling abroad, it was, nevertheless, speedily extinguished on the announcement of the troubles that had broken out in the bowels of his realm. Going immediately to Lefort . . . , he thus indignantly broke out: "Tell me, Francis, how I can reach Moscow by the shortest way, in a brief space, so that I may wreak vengeance on this great perfidy of my people, with punishments worthy of their abominable crime. Not one of them shall escape with impunity. Around my royal city, which, with their impious efforts, they planned to destroy, I will have gibbets and gallows set upon the walls and ramparts, and each and every one of them will I put to a direful death." Nor did he long delay the plan for his justly excited wrath; he took the quick post, as his

ambassador suggested, and in four weeks' time he had got over about three hundred miles without accident, and arrived the 4th of September, 1698,—a monarch for the well deposed, but an avenger for the wicked.

His first anxiety after his arrival was about the rebellion—in what it consisted, what the insurgents meant, who dared to instigate such a crime. And as nobody could answer accurately upon all points, and some pleaded their own ignorance, others the obstinacy of the Streltsy, he began to have suspicions of everybody's loyalty. . . . No day, holy or profane, were the inquisitors idle; every day was deemed fit and lawful for torturing. There was as many scourges as there were accused, and every inquisitor was a butcher. . . . The whole month of October was spent on lacerating the backs of culprits with the knout and with flames; no day were those that were left alive exempt from scourging or scorching; or else they were broken upon the wheel, or driven to the gibbet, or slain with the ax. . . .

To prove to all people how holy and inviolable are those walls of the city which the Streltsy rashly meditated scaling in a sudden assault, beams were run out from all the embrasures in the walls near the gates, in each of which two rebels were hanged. This day beheld about two hundred and fifty die that death. There are few cities fortified with as many palisades as Moscow has given gibbets to her guardian Streltsy.

and coats shortened, a reform Peter personally enforced at court by shaving off his nobles' beards and cutting their coats at the knees with his own hands. Outside the court, the edicts were enforced by barbers and tailors planted at town gates with orders to cut the beards and cloaks of all who entered or left. Anyone who failed to conform was to be "beaten without mercy."

One group of Russians benefited greatly from Peter's cultural reforms—women. Having watched women mixing freely with men in Western courts, Peter shattered the seclusion of upper-class Russian women and demanded that they remove the traditional veils that covered their faces. Peter also decreed that social gatherings be held three times a week in

the large houses of St. Petersburg where men and women could mix for conversation, card games, and dancing, which Peter had learned in the West. The tsar also now insisted that women could marry of their own free will.

The object of Peter's domestic reforms was to make Russia into a great state and military power. His primary goal was to "open a window to the west," meaning an ice-free port easily accessible to Europe. This could only be achieved on the Baltic, but at that time the Baltic coast was controlled by Sweden, the most important power in northern Europe. Desirous of these lands, Peter, with the support of Poland and Denmark, attacked Sweden in the summer of 1700, believing that the young king of Sweden, Charles XII, could easily be defeated. Charles, however, proved to be a brilliant general. He smashed the Danes, flattened the Poles, and, with a well-disciplined force of only eight thousand men, routed the Russian army of forty thousand at the Battle of Narva (1700). The Great Northern War (1701–1721) soon ensued.

But Peter fought back. He reorganized his army along Western lines and at the Battle of Poltava in July 1709 decisively defeated Charles's army. Although the war dragged on for another twelve years, the Peace of Nystadt in 1721 gave formal recognition to what Peter had already achieved: the acquisition of Estonia, Livonia, and Karelia (see Map 15.4). Sweden became a second-rate power while Russia was now the great European state Peter had wanted. Already in 1703, in these northern lands on the Baltic, Peter had begun the construction of a new city, St. Petersburg, his window to the west and a symbol that Russia was looking westward to Europe. The lives of thousands of peasants were lost during its construction. Finished during Peter's lifetime, St. Petersburg remained the Russian capital until 1917.

Peter modernized and westernized Russia to the extent that it became a great military power and, by his death in 1725, an important member of the European state system. But his policies were also detrimental to Russia. Westernization was a bit of a sham, because Western culture reached only the upper classes while the real object of the reforms, the cre-

ation of a strong military, only added more burdens to the masses of the Russian people. The forceful way in which Peter the Great brought westernization led his people to distrust Europe and Western civilization.

❋ *The Limits of Absolutism*

In recent decades, historical studies of local institutions have challenged the traditional picture of absolute monarchs. It is misleading to think that these rulers actually controlled the lives of their subjects. In 1700, government for most people still meant the local institutions that affected their lives: local courts, local tax collectors, and local organizers of armed forces. Kings and ministers might determine policies and issue guidelines, but they still had to function through local agents and had no guarantee whatever that their wishes would be carried out. A mass of urban and provincial privileges, liberties, and exemptions (including from taxation) and a whole host of corporate bodies and interest groups—provincial and national Estates, clerical officials, officeholders who had bought or inherited their positions, and provincial nobles—limited what monarchs could achieve. The most successful rulers were not those who tried to destroy the old system but rather those like Louis XIV who knew how to use the old system to their advantage. Above all other considerations stood the

MAP 15.4   The Expansion of Russia.

landholding nobility. Everywhere in the seventeenth century, the landed aristocracy played an important role in the European monarchical system. As military officers, judges, officeholders, and landowners in control of vast, untaxed estates, their power remained immense. In some places, their strength even put severe limits on how effectively monarchs could rule.

◆ Limited Monarchy: The Dutch Republic and England

Almost everywhere in Europe in the seventeenth century, kings and their ministers were in control of central governments. But not all European states followed the pattern of absolute monarchy. In western Europe, two great states—the Dutch Republic and England—successfully resisted the power of hereditary monarchs.

※ *The Golden Age of the Dutch Republic*

The seventeenth century has often been called the golden age of the Dutch Republic as the United Provinces held center stage as one of Europe's great powers. Like France and England, the United Provinces was an Atlantic power, underlining the importance of that shift of political and economic power in the seventeenth century from the Mediterranean Sea to the countries on the Atlantic seaboard. As a result of the sixteenth-century revolt of the Netherlands, the seven northern provinces, which began to call themselves the United Provinces of the Netherlands in 1581, became the core of the modern Dutch state. The new state was officially recognized by the Peace of Westphalia in 1648.

With independence came internal dissension. There were two chief centers of political power in the new state. Each province had an official known as a stadholder who was responsible for leading the army and maintaining order. Beginning with William of Orange and his heirs, the house of Orange occupied the stadholderate in most of the seven provinces and favored the development of a centralized government with themselves as hereditary monarchs. The States General, an assembly of representatives from every province, opposed the Orangist ambitions and advocated a decentralized or republican form of government. For much of the seventeenth century, the republican forces were in control. But in 1672, burdened with war against both France and England, the United Provinces allowed William III (1672–1702) of the house of Orange to establish a monarchical regime. However, his death in 1702 without direct heirs enabled the republican forces to gain control once more. The Dutch Republic would not be seriously threatened again by the monarchical forces.

Underlying Dutch prominence in the seventeenth century was its economic prosperity, fueled by the role of the Dutch as carriers of Europe trade. But war proved disastrous to the Dutch Republic. Wars with France and England placed heavy burdens on Dutch finances and manpower. English shipping began to challenge what had been Dutch commercial supremacy, and by 1715, the Dutch were experiencing a serious economic decline.

※ *England and the Emergence of Constitutional Monarchy*

One of the most prominent examples of resistance to absolute monarchy came in seventeenth-century England where king and Parliament struggled to determine the role each should play in governing the nation. But the struggle over this political issue was complicated by a deep and profound religious controversy. Along with the victory of Parliament came the foundation for constitutional monarchy by the end of the seventeenth century.

✖ REVOLUTION AND CIVIL WAR

With the death of Queen Elizabeth in 1603, the Tudor dynasty became extinct, and the Stuart line of rulers was inaugurated with the accession to the throne of Elizabeth's cousin, King James VI of Scotland, who became James I (1603–1625) of England. Although used to royal power as king of Scotland, James understood little about the laws, institutions, and customs of the English. He espoused the divine right of kings—the belief that kings receive their power directly from God and are responsible to no one except God. This viewpoint alienated Parliament, which had grown accustomed under the Tudors to act on the premise that monarch and Parliament together ruled England as a "balanced polity." Parliament expressed its displeasure with James's claims by refusing his requests for additional monies needed by the king to meet the increased cost of government. Parliament's power of the purse proved to be its trump card in its relationship with the king.

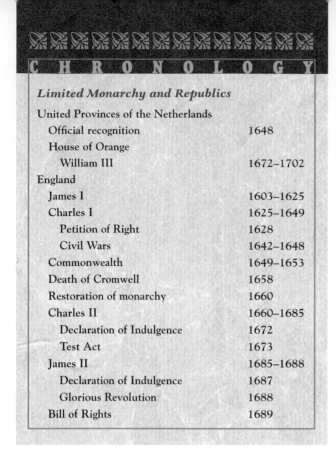

Some members of Parliament were also alienated by James's religious policy. The Puritans—Protestants within the Anglican church inspired by Calvinist theology—wanted James to eliminate the episcopal system of church organization used in the Church of England (in which the bishop or *episcopos* played the major administrative role) in favor of a Presbyterian model (used in Scotland and patterned after Calvin's church organization in Geneva, where ministers and elders—also called presbyters—played an important governing role). James refused because he realized that the Anglican church, with its bishops appointed by the crown, was a major support of monarchical authority. But the Puritans were not easily cowed and added to the rising chorus of opposition to the king. Many of England's gentry, mostly well-to-do landowners below the level of the nobility, had become Puritans, and these Puritan gentry not only formed an important and substantial part of the House of Commons, the lower house of Parliament, but also held important positions locally as justices of the peace and sheriffs. It was not wise to alienate them.

The conflict that began during the reign of James came to a head during the reign of his son Charles I (1625–1649). In 1628, Parliament passed a petition of right that the king was supposed to accept before being granted any taxes. This petition prohibited taxes without Parliament's consent, arbitrary imprisonment, the quartering of soldiers in private houses, and the declaration of martial law in peacetime. Although he initially accepted it, Charles later reneged on the agreement because of its limitations on royal power. In 1629, Charles decided that because he could not work with Parliament, he would not summon it to meet. From 1629 to 1640, Charles pursued a course of "personal rule," which forced him to find ways to collect taxes without Parliament's cooperation. These expedients aroused opposition from middle-class merchants and landed gentry who believed the king was attempting to tax without Parliament's consent.

The king's religious policy also proved disastrous. The attempt of Charles to impose more ritual on the Anglican church struck the Puritans as a return to Catholic popery. Charles's efforts to force them to conform to his religious policies infuriated the Puritans, thousands of whom abandoned England for the "howling wildernesses" of America.

Grievances mounted until England finally slipped into a civil war (1642–1648) that was won by the parliamentary forces. Most important to Parliament's success was the creation of the New Model Army by Oliver Cromwell, the only real military genius of the war. The New Model Army was composed primarily of more extreme Puritans known as the Independents, who, in typical Calvinist fashion, believed they were doing battle for the Lord. It is striking to read in Cromwell's military reports such statements as "Sir, this is none other but the hand of God; and to Him alone belongs the glory."

Between 1648 and 1660, England faced a trying situation. After the execution of Charles I on January 30, 1649, Parliament abolished the monarchy and the House of Lords and proclaimed England a republic or commonwealth. But Cromwell and his army, unable to work effectively with Parliament, dispersed it by force. As the members of Parliament departed in April 1653, Cromwell shouted after them: "It's you that have forced me to do this, for I have sought the Lord night and day that He would slay me rather than put upon me the doing of this work." With the certainty of one who is convinced he is right, Cromwell had destroyed both king and Parliament.

Finally, Cromwell dissolved Parliament and divided the country into eleven regions, each ruled by a major general who served virtually as a military governor. Unable to establish a constitutional basis for a

OLIVER CROMWELL. Oliver Cromwell was a dedicated Puritan who formed the New Model Army and defeated the forces supporting King Charles I. Unable to work with Parliament, he came to rely on military force to rule England. Cromwell is pictured here in 1649, on the eve of his military campaign in Ireland.

working government, Cromwell had resorted to military force to maintain the rule of the Independents, ironically using even more arbitrary policies than those of Charles I.

Oliver Cromwell died in 1658. After floundering for eighteen months, the military establishment decided that arbitrary rule by the army was no longer feasible and reestablished the monarchy in the person of Charles II (1660–1685), the son of Charles I. The restoration of the Stuart monarchy ended England's time of troubles, but it was not long before England experienced yet another constitutional crisis.

❊ Restoration and a Glorious Revolution

The restoration of the monarchy and the House of Lords did not mean that the work of the English Revolution was undone. Parliament kept much of the power it had won, arbitrary courts were still abolished,

Parliament's role in government was acknowledged, and the necessity for its consent to taxation was accepted. Yet Charles continued to push his own ideas, some of which were clearly out of step with many of his subjects.

Charles was sympathetic to and perhaps even inclined to Catholicism. Moreover, Charles's brother James, heir to the throne, did not hide the fact that he was a Catholic. Parliament's suspicions were therefore aroused in 1672 when Charles took the audacious step of issuing a declaration of indulgence that suspended the laws that Parliament had passed against Catholics and Puritans after the restoration of the Anglican church as the official church of England. Parliament would have none of it and induced the king to suspend the declaration. Propelled by strong anti-Catholic sentiment, Parliament then passed the Test Act of 1673, specifying that only Anglicans could hold military and civil offices.

The accession of James II (1685–1688) to the crown virtually guaranteed a new constitutional crisis for England. An open and devout Catholic, his attempt to further Catholic interests made religion once more a primary cause of conflict between king and Parliament. In 1687, James issued a declaration of indulgence that suspended all laws that excluded Catholics and Puritans from office. Parliamentary outcries against James's policies stopped short of rebellion because members knew that he was an old man and his successors were his Protestant daughters Mary and Anne, born to his first wife. But on June 10, 1688, a son was born to James II's second wife, also a Catholic. Suddenly the specter of a Catholic hereditary monarchy loomed large. A group of prominent English noblemen invited the Dutch chief executive, William of Orange, husband of James's daughter Mary, to invade England. William and Mary raised an army and invaded England while James, his wife, and their infant son fled to France. With almost no bloodshed, England had undergone its "Glorious Revolution," not over the issue of whether there would be monarchy but rather over who would be monarch.

The events of late 1688 constituted only the initial stage of the Glorious Revolution. In January 1689, Parliament offered the throne to William and Mary, who accepted it along with the provisions of a bill of rights (see the box on p. 318). The Bill of Rights affirmed Parliament's right to make laws and levy taxes and made it impossible for kings to oppose or do without Parliament by stipulating that standing armies could be raised only with the consent of Parliament.

The Bill of Rights

In 1688, the English experienced yet another revolution, a bloodless one in which the Stuart king James II was replaced by Mary, James's daughter, and her husband, William of Orange. After William and Mary had assumed power, Parliament passed a bill of rights that specified the rights of Parliament and laid the foundation for a constitutional monarchy.

❋ *The Bill of Rights*

Whereas the said late King James II having abdicated the government, and the throne being thereby vacant, his Highness the prince of Orange (whom it has pleased Almighty God to make the glorious instrument of delivering this kingdom from popery and arbitrary power) did (by the device of the lords spiritual and temporal, and diverse principal persons of the Commons) cause letters to be written to the lords spiritual and temporal, being Protestants, and other letters to the several counties, cities, universities, boroughs, and Cinque Ports, for the choosing of such persons to represent them, as were of right to be sent to parliament, to meet and sit at Westminster upon the two and twentieth day of January, in this year 1689, in order to such an establishment as that their religion, laws, and liberties might not again be in danger of being subverted; upon which letters elections have been accordingly made.

And thereupon the said lords spiritual and temporal and Commons, pursuant to their respective letters and elections, being now assembled in a full and free representation of this nation, taking into their most serious consideration the best means for attaining the ends aforesaid, do in the first place (as their ancestors in like case have usually done), for the vindication and assertion of their ancient rights and liberties, declare:

1. That the pretended power of suspending laws, or the execution of laws, by regal authority, without consent of parliament is illegal.

2. That the pretended power of dispensing with the laws, or the execution of law by regal authority, as it has been assumed and exercised of late, is illegal.

3. That the commission for erecting the late court of commissioners for ecclesiastical causes, and all other commissions and courts of like nature, are illegal and pernicious.

4. That levying money for or to the use of the crown by pretense of prerogative, without grant of parliament, for longer time or in other manner than the same is or shall be granted, is illegal.

5. That it is the right of the subjects to petition the king, and all commitments and prosecutions for such petitioning are illegal.

6. That the raising or keeping a standing army within the kingdom in time of peace, unless it be with consent of parliament, is against law.

7. That the subjects which are Protestants may have arms for their defense suitable to their conditions, and as allowed by law.

8. That election of members of parliament ought to be free.

9. That the freedom of speech, and debates or proceedings in parliament, ought not to be impeached or questioned in any court or place out of parliament.

10. That excessive bail ought not to be required, nor excessive fines imposed, nor cruel and unusual punishments inflicted.

11. That jurors ought to be duly impaneled and returned, and jurors which pass upon men in trials for high treason ought to be freeholders.

12. That all grants and promises of fines and forfeitures of particular persons before conviction are illegal and void.

13. And that for redress of all grievances, and for the amending, strengthening, and preserving of the laws, parliament ought to be held frequently.

The rights of citizens to petition the sovereign, keep arms, have a jury trial, and not be subject to excessive bail were also confirmed. The Bill of Rights helped fashion a system of government based on the rule of law and a freely elected Parliament, thus laying the foundation for a constitutional monarchy.

The Bill of Rights did not settle the religious questions that had played such a large role in England's troubles in the seventeenth century. The Toleration Act of 1689 granted Puritan Dissenters the right of free public worship (Catholics were still excluded). Although the Toleration Act did not mean complete religious freedom and equality, it marked a departure in English history because few people would ever again be persecuted for religious reasons.

Many historians have viewed the Glorious Revolution as the end of the seventeenth-century struggle between king and Parliament. By deposing one king and establishing another, Parliament had destroyed the divine-right theory of kingship (William was, after all, king by grace of Parliament, not God) and confirmed its right to participate in the government. Parliament did not have complete control of the government, but it now had an unquestioned right to participate in affairs of state. During the next century, it would gradually prove to be the real authority in the English system of constitutional monarchy.

❋ Responses to Revolution

The English revolutions of the seventeenth century prompted very different responses from two English political thinkers, Thomas Hobbes and John Locke. Thomas Hobbes (1588–1679), who lived during the English Civil War, was alarmed by the revolutionary upheavals in his contemporary England. His name has since been associated with the state's claim to absolute authority over its subjects, which he elaborated in his major treatise on political thought known as the *Leviathan*, published in 1651.

Hobbes claimed that in the state of nature, before society was organized, human life was "solitary, poor, nasty, brutish, and short." Humans were guided not by reason and moral ideals but by animalistic instincts and a ruthless struggle for self-preservation. To save themselves from destroying each other (the "war of every man against every man"), people contracted to form a commonwealth, which Hobbes called "that great Leviathan (or rather, to speak more reverently, that mortal god) to which we owe our peace and defense." This commonwealth placed its collective power in the hands of a sovereign authority, preferably a single ruler, who served as executor, legislator, and judge. This absolute ruler possessed unlimited power. In Hobbes's view, subjects may not rebel; if they do, they must be suppressed.

John Locke (1632–1704), author of a political work called *Two Treatises of Government*, viewed the exercise of political power quite differently from Hobbes and argued against the absolute rule of one man. Like Hobbes, Locke began with the state of nature before human existence became organized socially. But unlike Hobbes, Locke believed that humans lived then in a state of equality and freedom rather than a state of war. In this state of nature, humans had certain inalienable natural rights—to life, liberty, and property. Like Hobbes, Locke did not believe that all was well in the state of nature. Since there was no impartial judge in nature, people found it difficult to protect these natural rights. So they mutually agreed to establish a government to ensure the protection of their rights. This agreement established mutual obligations: government would protect the rights of people, and the people would act reasonably toward their government. But if a government broke this agreement—if a king, for example, failed to live up to his obligation to protect the natural rights or claimed absolute authority and made laws without the consent of the community—the people might form a new government. For Locke, however, the community of people was primarily the landholding aristocracy who were represented in Parliament, not the landless masses. Locke was hardly an advocate of political democracy, but his ideas proved important to both the Americans and the French in the eighteenth century and were used to support demands for constitutional government, the rule of law, and the protection of rights.

◆ Economic Trends in the Seventeenth Century

The seventeenth century was marked by economic contraction, although conditions varied by country or region. Trade, industry, and agriculture all felt the pinch of a depression, which some historians believe bottomed out between 1640 and 1680. Translated into everyday life, for many people the economic contraction of the seventeenth century meant scarce food, uncertain employment, and high rates of taxation.

Population was also affected. Based on the birthrate of the seventeenth century, demographers would expect the European population to have doubled every twenty-five years. In reality, the population either declined or increased only intermittently as a result of a variety of factors. Infant mortality rates were high, 30 percent in the first year of life and 50 percent before the age of ten. Epidemics and famines were again common experiences in European life. The last great epidemic of bubonic plague spread across Europe in the middle and late years of the seventeenth century. The Mediterranean region suffered from 1646 to 1657, when the plague killed off 130,000 persons in

Naples alone. In 1665, it struck England and devastated London, killing 20 percent of its population.

❋ Overseas Trade and Colonies

As we saw in our discussion of Colbert's policies in France, one of the principles of mercantilism was a high regard for colonies as sources of raw materials and markets for finished goods. Mercantilist theory on the role of colonies was matched in practice by Europe's overseas expansion. With the development of colonies and trading posts in the Americas and the East, Europeans entered an age of international commerce in the seventeenth century. We should remember, however, that local, regional, and intra-European trade still dominated. About one-tenth of English and Dutch exports were shipped across the Atlantic; slightly more went to the East. What made the transoceanic trade rewarding, however, was not the volume but the value of its goods. Dutch, English, and French merchants were bringing back products that were still consumed largely by the wealthy but were beginning to make their way into the lives of artisans and merchants. Pepper and spices from the Indies, West Indian and Brazilian sugar, and Asian coffee and tea were becoming more readily available to European consumers. The first coffee and tea houses opened in London in the 1650s and spread rapidly to other parts of Europe.

In 1600, much overseas trade was still carried by the Spanish and Portuguese, who alone possessed colonies of any significant size. But war and steady pressure from their Dutch and English rivals eroded Portuguese trade in both the West and the East. The Spanish also maintained an enormous South American empire, but Spain's importance as a commercial power declined rapidly in the seventeenth century.

The Dutch became a major economic power in the seventeenth century. The Dutch East India Company, formed in 1602 to exploit the riches of the East, gradually took control of most of the Portuguese bases in the East and opened trade with China and Japan. Its profits were spectacular in the first ten years. The Dutch West India Company, created in 1621, was less successful. One of its projects was the North American colony of New Netherlands, which stretched from the mouth of the Hudson River as far north as Albany. In 1664, the English seized New Netherlands and renamed it New York, and the Dutch West India Company soon went bankrupt.

The Dutch overseas trade and commercial empire faced two major rivals in the seventeenth century—the English and the French. The English had founded their own East India Company in 1601 and proceeded to create a colonial empire in the New World along the Atlantic seaboard of North America. French commercial companies in the East experienced much difficulty. Though due in part to a late start, the problems of the French also demonstrated the weakness of a commerce dependent on political rather than economic impetus (see the box on p. 321). The East India Companies set up by Henry IV and Richelieu all failed. The French had greater success in North America, where in 1663 Canada was made the property of the crown and administered like a French province. But the French failed to provide adequate men or money, allowing their continental wars to take precedence over the conquest of the North American continent. Already in 1713, by the Treaty of Utrecht, the French began to cede some of their American possessions to their English rival.

◆ The World of European Culture

The seventeenth century witnessed remarkable talent. In addition to the intellectuals responsible for the Scientific Revolution (see Chapter 16), the era was blessed with a number of prominent thinkers, artists, and writers.

❋ Art: French Classicism and Dutch Realism

In the second half of the seventeenth century, France replaced Italy as the cultural leader of Europe. Rejecting the Baroque style as overly showy and passionate, the French remained committed to the classical values of the High Renaissance. French late classicism, with its emphasis on clarity, simplicity, balance, and harmony of design, was, however, a rather austere version of the High Renaissance style. Its triumph reflected the shift in seventeenth-century French society from chaos to order. While rejecting the emotionalism and high drama of the Baroque, French classicism continued the Baroque's conception of grandeur in the portrayal of noble subjects, especially those from classical antiquity.

The supremacy of Dutch commerce in the seventeenth century was paralleled by a brilliant flowering of Dutch painting. Wealthy patricians and

West Meets East: An Exchange of Royal Letters

Economic gain was not the only motivation of Western rulers who wished to establish a European presence in the East. In 1681, King Louis XIV of France wrote a letter to the king of Tonkin asking permission for Christian missionaries to proselytize in Vietnam. The king of Tonkin politely declined the request.

✻ A Letter to the King of Tonkin

Most high, most excellent, most mighty and most magnanimous Prince, our very dear and good friend, may it please God to increase your greatness with a happy end!

We hear from our subjects who were in your Realm what protection you accorded them. We appreciate this all the more since we have for you all the esteem that one can have for a prince as illustrious through his military valor as he is commendable for the justice which he exercises in his Realm. . . . Since the war which we have had for several years, in which all of Europe had banded together against us, prevented our vessels from going to the Indies, at the present time, when we are at peace after having gained many victories and expanded our Realm through the conquest of several important places, we have immediately given orders to the Royal Company to establish itself in your kingdom as soon as possible. . . . We have given orders to have brought to you some presents which we believe might be agreeable to you. But the one thing in the world which we desire most, both for you and for your Realm, would be to obtain for your subjects who have already embraced the law of the only true God of heaven and earth, the freedom to profess it, since this law is the highest, the noblest, the most sacred and especially the most suitable to have kings reign absolutely over the people.

We are even quite convinced that, if you knew the truths and the maxims which it teaches, you would give first of all to your subjects the glorious example of embracing it. We wish you this incomparable blessing together with a long and happy reign, and we pray God that it may please Him to augment your greatness with the happiest of endings.

Your very dear and good friend,
Louis

✻ Answers from the King of Tonkin to Louis XIV

The King of Tonkin sends to the King of France a letter to express to him his best sentiments. . . . Your communication, which comes from a country which is a thousand leagues away, and which proceeds from the heart as a testimony of your sincerity, merits repeated consideration and infinite praise. Politeness toward strangers is nothing unusual in our country. There is not a stranger who is not well received by us. How then could we refuse a man from France, which is the most celebrated among the kingdoms of the world and which for love of us wishes to frequent us and bring us merchandise? These feelings of fidelity and justice are truly worthy to be applauded. As regards your wish that we should cooperate in propagating your religion, we do not dare to permit it, for there is an ancient custom, introduced by edicts, which formally forbids it. Now, edicts are promulgated only to be carried out faithfully; without fidelity nothing is stable. How could we disdain a well-established custom to satisfy a private friendship? . . . This then is my letter. We send you herewith a modest gift which we offer you with a glad heart.

This letter was written at the beginning of winter and on a beautiful day.

---

burghers of Dutch urban society commissioned works of art for their guild halls, town halls, and private dwellings. Following the wishes of these patrons, Dutch painters became primarily interested in the realistic portrayal of secular, everyday life. This interest in painting scenes of everyday life is evident in the work of Judith Leyster (c. 1609–1660), who established her own independent painting career, a remarkable occurrence in seventeenth-century Europe. Leyster became the first woman member of the painting guild of St. Luke in Haarlem, which enabled her to set up her own workshop and take on three male pupils. Musicians playing their instruments, women sewing, children laughing while playing games, and actors performing

JUDITH LEYSTER, *SELF-PORTRAIT.* **Although Judith Leyster was a well-known artist to her Dutch contemporaries, her fame diminished soon after her death. In the late nineteenth century, however, a Dutch art historian rediscovered her work. In her *Self-Portrait*, painted in 1635, she is seen pausing in her work in front of one of the scenes of daily life that made her such a popular artist in her own day.**

are the subjects of Leyster's portraits. But she was also capable of introspection, as is evident in her *Self-Portrait*.

The finest example of the golden age of Dutch painting was Rembrandt van Rijn (1606–1669). Although Rembrandt shared the Dutch predilection for realistic portraits, he became more introspective as he grew older. He refused to follow his contemporaries, whose pictures were largely secular in subject matter; half of his paintings focused on scenes from biblical tales. Since the Protestant tradition of hostility to religious pictures had discouraged artistic expression, Rembrandt stands out as the one great Protestant painter of the seventeenth century.

❋ The Theater: The Triumph of French Neoclassicism

As the great age of theater in England and Spain was drawing to a close around 1630, a new dramatic era began to dawn in France that lasted into the 1680s. Unlike Shakespeare in England and Lope de Vega in Spain, French playwrights wrote more for an elite

REMBRANDT VAN RIJN, *SYNDICS OF THE CLOTH GUILD.* **The Dutch experienced a golden age of painting during the seventeenth century. The burghers and patricians of Dutch urban society commissioned works of art, and these quite naturally reflected the burghers' interests, as this painting by Rembrandt illustrates.**

audience and were forced to depend on royal patronage. Louis XIV used theater as he did art and architecture—to attract attention to his monarchy. French dramatists cultivated a classical style that emphasized the clever, polished, and correct over the emotional and imaginative. Many of the French works of this period derived their themes and plots from Greek and Roman sources.

Jean-Baptiste Molière (1622–1673) enjoyed the favor of the French court and benefited from the patronage of the Sun King. He wrote, produced, and acted in a series of comedies that often satirized the religious and social world of his time. In *The Misanthrope*, he mocked the corruption of court society, while in *Tartuffe*, he ridiculed religious hypocrisy. Molière's satires, however, sometimes got him into trouble. The Paris clergy did not find *Tartuffe* funny and had it banned for five years. Only the protection of Louis XIV saved Molière from more severe harassment.

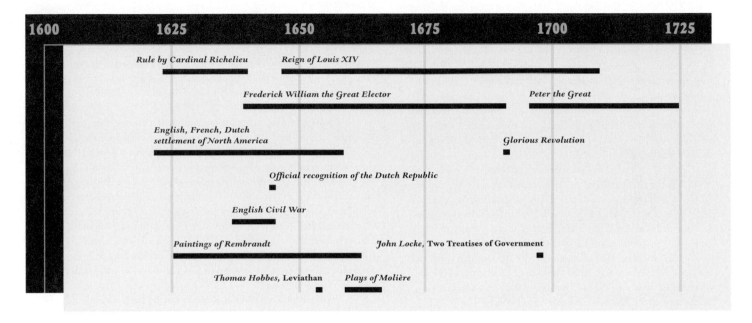

| 1600 | 1625 | 1650 | 1675 | 1700 | 1725 |

Rule by Cardinal Richelieu

Reign of Louis XIV

Frederick William the Great Elector

Peter the Great

English, French, Dutch settlement of North America

Glorious Revolution

Official recognition of the Dutch Republic

English Civil War

Paintings of Rembrandt

John Locke, Two Treatises of Government

Thomas Hobbes, Leviathan

Plays of Molière

Conclusion

To many historians, the seventeenth century has assumed extraordinary proportions. The divisive effects of the Reformation had been assimilated and the concept of a united Christendom, held as an ideal since the Middle Ages, had been irrevocably destroyed by the religious wars, making possible the emergence of a system of nation-states in which power politics took on increasing significance. The growth of political thought focusing on the secular origins of state power reflected the changes that were going on in seventeenth-century society.

Within those states, there slowly emerged some of the machinery that made possible a growing centralization of power. In those states called absolutist, strong monarchs, with the assistance of their aristocracies, provided the leadership for greater centralization. But in England, where the landed aristocracy gained power at the expense of the monarchs, the foundations were laid for a constitutional government in which Parliament provided the focus for the institutions of centralized power. In all the major European states, a growing concern for power and dynastic expansion led to larger armies and greater conflict. War remained an endemic feature of Western civilization.

But the search for order and harmony continued, evident in art and literature. At the same time, although it would be misleading to state that Europe had become a secular world, it is fair to say that religious preoccupations and values were losing ground to secular considerations. The seventeenth century was a transitional period to a more secular spirit that has characterized modern Western civilization until the present. No stronger foundation for this spirit could be found than in the new view of the universe that was created by the Scientific Revolution of the seventeenth century, and it is to that story that we now turn.

Notes

1. Quoted in John B. Wolf, *Louis XIV* (New York, 1968), p. 134.
2. Quoted in J. H. Elliott, *Imperial Spain, 1469–1716* (New York, 1963), p. 338.

Suggestions for Further Reading

In addition to the general works listed in Chapter 14, see also D. H. Pennington, *Europe in the Seventeenth Century*, 2d ed. (New York, 1989); T. Munck, *Seventeenth Century Europe, 1598–1700* (London, 1990); and R. S. Dunn, *The Age of Religious Wars, 1559–1715*, 2d ed. (New York, 1979).

For brief accounts of seventeenth-century French history, see R. Briggs, *Early Modern France, 1560–1715* (Oxford, 1977), and J. B. Collins, *The State in Early Modern France* (Cambridge, 1995). A solid and very readable biography of Louis XIV is J. B. Wolf, *Louis XIV* (New York, 1968). For a brief study, see P. R. Campbell, *Louis XIV, 1661–1715* (London, 1993). Also of value are the works by O. Bernier, *Louis XIV* (New York, 1988), and P. Goubert, *Louis XIV and Twenty Million Frenchmen*, trans. A. Carter (New York, 1970). A now classic work on life in Louis XIV's France is W. H. Lewis, *The Splendid Century* (Garden City, N.Y., 1953). Well-presented summaries of revisionist views on Louis's monarchical power are R. Mettam, *Power and Faction in Louis XIV's France* (Oxford, 1988), and W. Beik, *Absolutism and Society in Seventeenth Century France* (Cambridge, 1985). C. W. Cole, *Colbert and a Century of French Mercantilism*, 2 vols. (London, 1939), is still the fundamental study.

Good general works on seventeenth-century Spanish history include J. Lynch, *Spain Under the Habsburgs*, 2d ed. (New York, 1981), and the relevant sections of J. H. Elliott, *Imperial Spain, 1469–1716* (New York, 1963; rev. ed. 1977). The important minister Olivares is examined in J. H. Elliott, *The Count-Duke of Olivares: The Statesman in an Age of Decline* (London, 1986).

An older but still valuable survey of the German states in the seventeenth century can be found in H. Holborn, *A History of Modern Germany, 1648–1840* (London, 1965). An important recent work is M. Hughes, *Early Modern Germany, 1477–1806* (Philadelphia, 1992). On the creation of an Austrian state, see R. J. W. Evans, *The Making of the Habsburg Monarchy, 1550–1700* (Oxford, 1979), and C. Ingrao, *The Habsburg Monarchy, 1618–1815* (Cambridge, 1994). The older work by F. L. Carsten, *The Origins of Prussia* (Oxford, 1954), remains an outstanding study of early Prussian history.

On Russian history before Peter the Great, see the classic work by V. O. Klyuchevsky, *A Course in Russian History: The Seventeenth Century* (Chicago, 1968). Works on Peter the Great include L. Hughes, *Russia in the Age of Peter the Great* (New Haven, Conn., 1998); M. S. Anderson, *Peter the Great*, 2d ed. (New York, 1995); and the massive popular biography by R. K. Massie, *Peter the Great* (New York, 1980).

Good general works on the period of the English Revolution include M. A. Kishlansky, *A Monarchy Transformed* (London, 1996); G. E. Aylmer, *Rebellion or Revolution? England, 1640–1660*

(New York, 1986); and A. Hughes, *The Causes of the English Civil War* (New York, 1991). On the war itself, see R. Ashton, *The English Civil War: Conservatism and Revolution, 1604–1649* (London, 1976). On Oliver Cromwell, see R. Howell Jr., *Cromwell* (Boston, 1977), and P. Gaunt, *Oliver Cromwell* (Cambridge, Mass., 1996). For a general survey of the post-Cromwellian era, see J. R. Jones, *Country and Court: England, 1658–1714* (London, 1978). A more specialized study is W. A. Speck, *The Revolution of 1688* (Oxford, 1988). On Charles II, see the scholarly biography by R. Hutton, *Charles II* (Oxford, 1989). Locke's political ideas are examined in J. H. Franklin, *John Locke and the Theory of Sovereignty* (London, 1978). On Thomas Hobbes, see D. D. Raphael, *Hobbes* (London, 1977).

On the United Provinces, there is a valuable but very lengthy study by J. Israel, *The Dutch Republic: Its Rise, Greatness, and Fall* (New York, 1995). See also the short but sound introduction by K. H. D. Haley, *The Dutch in the Seventeenth Century* (London, 1972). Of much value is S. Schama, *The Embarrassment of Riches: An Interpretation of Dutch Culture in the Golden Age* (New York, 1987).

On the economic side of the seventeenth century, there are the three volumes by F. Braudel, *Civilization and Capitalism in the 15th to 18th Century*, which obviously cover much more than just the seventeenth century: *The Structures of Everyday Life* (London, 1981), *The Wheels of Commerce* (London, 1982), and *The Perspective of the World* (London, 1984). Two single-volume comprehensive surveys are J. de Vries, *The Economy of Europe in an Age of Crisis* (Cambridge, 1976), and R. S. Duplessis, *Transitions to Capitalism in Early Modern Europe* (Cambridge, 1997). On overseas trade and colonial empires, see C. R. Boxer, *The Dutch Seaborne Empire, 1600–1800* (New York, 1965), and R. Davis, *English Overseas Trade, 1500–1700* (London, 1973).

French theater and literature are examined in A. Adam, *Grandeur and Illusion: French Literature and Society, 1600–1715*, trans. J. Tint (New York, 1972). For an examination of French and Dutch art, see A. Merot, *French Painting in the Seventeenth Century* (New Haven, Conn., 1995), and S. Slive, *Dutch Painting, 1600–1800* (New Haven, Conn., 1993).

 For additional reading, go to InfoTrac College Edition, your online research library at http://web1.infotrac-college.com

Enter the search terms *Louis XIV* using Key Terms.

Enter the search terms *Peter the Great* using Key Terms.

Enter the search terms *Oliver Cromwell* using Key Terms.

Enter the search term *mercantilism* using the Subject Guide.

CHAPTER

16

Toward a New Heaven and a New Earth: The Scientific Revolution and the Emergence of Modern Science

CHAPTER OUTLINE

- Background to the Scientific Revolution
- Toward a New Heaven: A Revolution in Astronomy
- Advances in Medicine
- Women in the Origins of Modern Science
- Toward a New Earth: Descartes, Rationalism, and a New View of Humankind
- Science and Religion in the Seventeenth Century
- The Spread of Scientific Knowledge
- Conclusion

FOCUS QUESTIONS

- What developments during the Middle Ages and Renaissance contributed to the Scientific Revolution of the seventeenth century?
- What did Copernicus, Kepler, Galileo, and Newton contribute to a new vision of the universe, and how did it differ from the Ptolemaic conception of the universe?
- What role did women play in the Scientific Revolution?
- What problems did the Scientific Revolution present for organized religion, and how did both the church and the emerging scientists attempt to solve these problems?
- How were the ideas of the Scientific Revolution disseminated, and what impact did they have on society?

*I*N ADDITION TO POLITICAL, *economic, social, and intellectual crises, the seventeenth century witnessed an intellectual one. The Scientific Revolution questioned and ultimately challenged conceptions and beliefs about the nature of the external world and reality that had crystallized into a rather strict orthodoxy by the Late Middle Ages. Derived from the works of ancient Greeks and Romans and grounded in Christian thought, the medieval worldview had become almost overpowering. But the breakdown of Christian unity during the Reformation and the subsequent religious wars had created an environment in which Europeans became more* comfortable with challenging both the ecclesiastical and political realms. Should it surprise us that a challenge to intellectual authority soon followed?

The Scientific Revolution taught Europeans to view the universe and their place in it in a new way. The shift from an earth-centered to a sun-centered cosmos had an emotional as well as intellectual effect on those who understood it. Thus the Scientific Revolution, popularized in the eighteenth-century Enlightenment, stands as the major force in the transition to the largely secular, rational, and materialistic perspective that has defined the modern Western mentality since its full acceptance in the nineteenth and twentieth centuries.

The transition to a new worldview, however, was far from easy. In the seventeenth century, the Italian scientist Galileo, an outspoken advocate of the new worldview, found that his ideas were strongly opposed by the authorities of the Catholic church. Galileo's position was clear: "I hold the sun to be situated motionless in the center of the revolution of the celestial bodies, while the earth rotates on its axis and revolves about the sun." Moreover, "nothing physical that sense-experience sets before our eyes . . . ought to be called in question (much less condemned) upon the testimony of biblical passages." But the church had a different view, and in 1633, Galileo, now sixty-eight and in ill health, was called before the dreaded Inquisition in Rome. He was kept waiting for two months before he was tried and found guilty of heresy and disobedience. Completely shattered by the experience, he denounced his errors: "With a sincere heart and unfeigned faith I curse and detest the said errors and heresies contrary to the Holy Church." Legend holds that when he left the trial rooms, Galileo muttered to himself: "And yet it does move!" In any case, Galileo had been silenced, but his writings remained, and they began to spread through Europe. The actions of the Inquisition had failed to stop the spread of the new ideas of the Scientific Revolution.

In one sense, the Scientific Revolution was not a revolution. It was not characterized by the explosive change and rapid overthrow of traditional authority that we normally associate with the word revolution. The Scientific Revolution did overturn centuries of authority, but only in a gradual and piecemeal fashion. Nevertheless, its results were truly revolutionary. The Scientific Revolution was a key factor in setting Western civilization on its modern secular and material path.

◆ Background to the Scientific Revolution

To say that the Scientific Revolution brought about a dissolution of the medieval worldview is not to say that the Middles Ages was a period of scientific ignorance. Many educated Europeans took an intense interest in the world around them since it was, after all, "God's handiwork" and therefore an appropriate subject for study. Late medieval scholastic philosophers had advanced mathematical and physical thinking in many ways, but the subjection of these thinkers to a strict theological framework and their unquestioning reliance on a few ancient authorities, especially Aristotle and Galen, limited where they could go. Many "natural philosophers," as medieval scientists were known, preferred refined logical analysis to systematic observations of the natural world. A number of changes and advances in the fifteenth and sixteenth centuries may have played a major role in helping "natural philosophers" abandon their old views and develop new ones.

The Renaissance humanists mastered both Greek and Latin and made available new works of Ptolemy and Archimedes as well as Plato. These writings made it apparent that even the unquestioned authorities of the Middle Ages, Aristotle and Galen, had been contradicted by other thinkers. The desire to discover which school of thought was correct stimulated new scientific work that sometimes led to a complete rejection of the classical authorities.

Renaissance artists have also been credited with making an impact on scientific study. Their desire to imitate nature led them to rely on a close observation of nature. Their accurate renderings of rocks, plants, animals, and human anatomy established new standards for the study of natural phenomena. At the same time, the "scientific" study of the problems of perspective and correct anatomical proportions led to new insights. "No painter," one Renaissance artist declared, "can paint well without a thorough knowledge of geometry."[1]

Technical problems, such as calculating the tonnage of ships accurately, also served to stimulate scientific activity because they required careful observation and accurate measurements. Then, too, the invention of new instruments and machines, such as the telescope and microscope, often made new scientific discoveries possible. Above all, the printing press had an indirect but crucial role in spreading innovative ideas quickly and easily.

Mathematics, so fundamental to the scientific achievements of the sixteenth and seventeenth centuries, was promoted in the Renaissance by the rediscovery of the works of ancient mathematicians and the influence of Plato, who had emphasized the importance of mathematics in explaining the universe. Applauded as the key to navigation, military science, and geography, mathematics was also regarded as the key to understanding the nature of things. According to Leonardo da Vinci, since God eternally geometrizes, nature is inherently mathematical: "Proportion is not only found in numbers and measurements but also in sounds, weights, times, positions, and in whatsoever power there may."[2] Copernicus, Kepler, Galileo, and Newton were all great mathematicians who believed that the secrets of nature were written in the language of mathematics.

Another factor in the origins of the Scientific Revolution may have been magic. Renaissance magic was the preserve of an intellectual elite from all of Europe. By the end of the sixteenth century, Hermetic magic had become fused with alchemical thought into a single intellectual framework. This tradition believed that the world was a living embodiment of divinity. Humans, who it was believed also had that spark of divinity within, could use magic, especially mathematical magic, to understand and dominate the world of nature or employ the powers of nature for beneficial purposes. Was it Hermeticism, then, that inaugurated the shift in consciousness that made the Scientific Revolution possible, since the desire to control and dominate the natural world was a crucial motivating force in the Scientific Revolution? Scholars debate the issue, but histories of the Scientific Revolution frequently overlook the fact that the great names we associate with the revolution in cosmology—Copernicus, Kepler, Galileo, and Newton—all had a serious interest in Hermetic ideas and the fields of astrology and alchemy. The mention of these names also reminds us of one final consideration in the origins of the Scientific Revolution: it resulted largely from the work of a handful of great intellectuals.

◆ Toward a New Heaven: A Revolution in Astronomy

The greatest achievements in the Scientific Revolution of the sixteenth and seventeenth centuries came in the fields most dominated by the ideas of the Greeks—astronomy, mechanics, and medicine. The cosmological views of the Late Middle Ages had been built on a synthesis of the ideas of Aristotle, Claudius Ptolemy (the greatest astronomer of antiquity who lived in the second century A.D.), and Christian theology. In the resulting Ptolemaic or geocentric conception, the universe was seen as a series of concentric spheres with a fixed or motionless earth as its center. Composed of material substance, the earth was imperfect and constantly changing. The spheres that surrounded the earth were made of a crystalline, transparent substance and moved in circular orbits around the earth. Circular movement, according to Aristotle, was the most "perfect" kind of motion and hence appropriate for the "perfect" heavenly bodies thought to consist of a nonmaterial, incorruptible "quintessence." These heavenly bodies, pure orbs of light, were embedded in the moving, concentric spheres, and in 1500 the number of known spheres was ten. Working outward from the earth, eight spheres contained the moon, Mercury, Venus, the sun, Mars, Jupiter, Saturn, and the fixed stars. The ninth sphere imparted to the eighth sphere of the fixed stars its motion, while the tenth sphere was frequently described as the prime mover that moved itself and imparted motion to the other spheres. Beyond the tenth sphere was the Empyrean Heaven—the location of God and all the saved souls. This Christianized Ptolemaic universe, then, was finite. It had a fixed outer boundary in harmony with Christian thought and expectations. God and the saved souls were at one end of the universe, while humans were at the center. They had been given power over the earth, but their real purpose was to achieve salvation.

✳ *Copernicus*

In May 1543, shortly before his death, Nicolaus Copernicus (1473–1543), who had studied mathematics and astronomy first at Krakow in his native Poland and later at the Italian universities of Bologna and Padua, published his famous book *On the Revolutions of the Heavenly Spheres*. Copernicus was not an accomplished observational astronomer and relied for his data on the records of his predecessors. But he was a mathematician who felt that Ptolemy's geocentric system was too complicated and failed to accord with the observed motions of the heavenly bodies (see the box on p. 330). Copernicus hoped that his heliocentric (sun-centered) conception would offer a more accurate explanation.

Copernicus argued that the universe consisted of eight spheres with the sun motionless at the center and the sphere of the fixed stars at rest in the eighth sphere. The planets revolved around the sun in the order of Mercury, Venus, the earth, Mars, Jupiter, and Saturn. The moon, however, revolved around the earth. Moreover, according to Copernicus, what appeared to be the movement of the sun and the fixed stars around the earth was really explained by the daily rotation of the earth on its axis and the journey of the earth around the sun each year.

The heliocentric theory had little immediate impact; most people were not yet ready to accept Copernicus' thinking. But doubts about the Ptolemaic system were growing. The next step in destroying the geocentric conception and supporting the Copernican system was taken by the German scientist Johannes Kepler.

❋ Kepler

The work of Johannes Kepler (1571–1630) illustrates well the narrow line that often separated magic and science in the early Scientific Revolution. An avid astrologer, Kepler possessed a keen interest in Hermetic thought and mathematical magic. In a book

written in 1596, he elaborated on his theory that the universe was constructed on the basis of geometric figures, such as the pyramid and the cube. Believing that the harmony of the human soul (a divine attribute) was mirrored in the numerical relationships existing between the planets, he focused much of his attention on discovering the "music of the spheres." Kepler was also a brilliant mathematician and astronomer who took a post as imperial mathematician to Emperor Rudolf II. Using the detailed astronomical data of his predecessor, Kepler derived laws of planetary motion that confirmed the heliocentric theory. In his first law, he contradicted Copernicus by showing that the orbits of the planets around the sun were not circular but elliptical, with the sun at one focus of the ellipse rather than at the center.

Kepler's work effectively eliminated the idea of uniform circular motion as well as the idea of crystalline spheres revolving in circular orbits. The basic structure of the traditional Ptolemaic system had been destroyed, and people had been freed to think in new ways of the paths of planets revolving around the sun. By the end of Kepler's life, the Ptolemaic system was rapidly losing ground to the new ideas. Important questions remained unanswered, however. What were the planets made of? And how does one explain

MEDIEVAL CONCEPTION OF THE UNIVERSE. As this sixteenth-century illustration shows, the medieval cosmological view placed the earth at the center of the universe, surrounded by a series of concentric spheres. The earth was imperfect and constantly changing, whereas the heavenly bodies that surrounded it were perfect and incorruptible. Beyond the tenth and final sphere was heaven, where God and all the saved souls were located.

motion in the universe? It was an Italian scientist who achieved the next important breakthrough to a new cosmology by answering the first question.

✳ *Galileo*

Galileo Galilei (1564–1642) taught mathematics, first at Pisa and later at Padua, one of the most prestigious universities in Europe. Galileo was the first European to make systematic observations of the heavens by means of a telescope, thereby inaugurating a new age in astronomy. He had heard of a Flemish lens grinder who had created a "spyglass" that magnified objects seen at a distance and soon constructed his own. Instead of peering at terrestrial objects, Galileo turned his telescope to the skies and made a remarkable series of discoveries: mountains on the moon, four moons revolving around Jupiter, the phases of Venus, and sunspots. Galileo's observations seemed to destroy yet another aspect of the traditional cosmology in that the universe seemed to be composed of a material substance similar to that of earth rather than an ethereal or perfect and unchanging substance.

Galileo's revelations, published in the *The Starry Messenger* in 1610, stunned his contemporaries and probably did more to make Europeans aware of the new picture of the universe than the mathematical theories of Copernicus and Kepler (see the box on p. 331). But even in the midst of his newfound acclaim, Galileo found himself increasingly suspect by the authorities of the Catholic church. The Roman Inquisition (or Holy Office) of the Catholic church condemned Copernicanism and ordered Galileo to abandon the Copernican thesis. The report of the Inquisition ran: "The doctrine that the sun was the center of the world and immovable was false and absurd, formally heretical and contrary to Scripture, whereas the doctrine that the earth was not the center of the world but moved, and has further a daily motion, was philosophically false and absurd and theologically at least erroneous."[3] It is apparent from the Inquisition's response that the church attacked the Copernican system because it threatened not only Scripture but also the entire prevailing conception of the universe. The heavens were no longer a spiritual world but a world of matter. Humans were no longer at the center, and God was no longer in a specific place. The new system raised such uncertainties that it seemed prudent simply to condemn it. In 1633, Galileo was found guilty of teaching the condemned Copernician system and was forced to recant his errors.

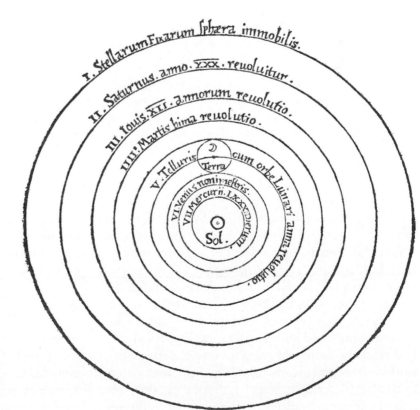

THE COPERNICAN SYSTEM.
The Copernican system was presented in *On the Revolutions of the Heavenly Spheres*, published shortly before Copernicus' death. As shown in this illustration from the first edition of the book, Copernicus maintained that the sun was the center of the universe and that the planets, including the earth, revolved around it. Moreover, the earth rotated daily on its axis.

On the Revolutions of the Heavenly Spheres

Nicolaus Copernicus began a revolution in astronomy when he argued that the sun and not the earth was at the center of the universe. Expecting controversy and scorn, Copernicus hesitated to publish the work in which he put forth his heliocentric theory. He finally relented, however, and managed to see a copy of it just before he died.

✳ *Nicolaus Copernicus,* On the Revolutions of the Heavenly Spheres

For a long time, then, I reflected on this confusion in the astronomical traditions concerning the derivation of the motions of the universe's spheres. I began to be annoyed that the movements of the world machine, created for our sake by the best and most systematic Artisan of all, were not understood with greater certainty by the philosophers, who otherwise examined so precisely the most insignificant trifles of this world. For this reason I undertook the task of rereading the works of all the philosophers which I could obtain to learn whether anyone had ever proposed other motions of the universe's spheres than those expounded by the teachers of astronomy in the schools. And in fact first I found in Cicero that Hicetas supposed the earth to move. Later I also discovered in Plutarch that certain others were of this opinion. I have decided to set his words down here, so that they may be available to everybody:

> Some think that the earth remains at rest. But Philolaus the Pythagorean believes that, like the sun and moon, it revolves around the fire in an oblique circle. Heraclides of Pontus and Ecphantus the Pythagorean make the earth move, not in a progressive motion, but like a wheel in a rotation from the west to east about its own center.

Therefore, having obtained the opportunity from these sources, I too began to consider the mobility of the earth. And even though the idea seemed absurd, nevertheless I know that others before me had been granted the freedom to imagine any circles whatever for the purpose of explaining the heavenly phenomena. Hence I thought that I too would be readily permitted to ascertain whether explanations sounder than those of my predecessors could be found for the revolution of the celestial spheres on the assumption of some motion of the earth.

Having thus assumed the motions which I ascribe to the earth later on in the volume, by long and intense study I finally found that if the motions of the other planets are correlated with the orbiting of the earth, and are computed for the revolution of each planet, not only do their phenomena follow therefrom but also the order and size of all the planets and spheres, and heaven itself is so linked together that in no portion of it can anything be shifted without disrupting the remaining parts and the universe as a whole. . . .

Hence I feel no shame in asserting that this whole region engirdled by the moon, and the center of the earth, traverse this grand circle amid the rest of the planets in an annual revolution around the sun. Near the sun is the center of the universe. Moreover, since the sun remains stationary, whatever appears as a motion of the sun is really due rather to the motion of the earth.

The condemnation of Galileo by the Inquisition seriously hampered further scientific work in Italy, which had been at the forefront of scientific innovation. Leadership in science now passed to the northern countries, especially England, France, and the Dutch Netherlands. By the 1630s and 1640s, no reasonable astronomer could overlook that Galileo's discoveries combined with Kepler's mathematical laws had made nonsense of the Ptolemaic-Aristotelian world system and clearly established the reasonableness of the Copernican model. Nevertheless, the problem of explaining motion in the universe and tying together the ideas of Copernicus, Galileo, and Kepler had not yet been solved. This would be the work of an Englishman who has long been considered the greatest genius of the Scientific Revolution.

✳ *Newton*

Born in the English village of Woolsthorpe, Isaac Newton (1642–1727) showed little promise until he attended Cambridge University. In 1669, he accepted a chair of mathematics at the university. During an intense period of creativity from 1684 to 1686, he wrote

The Starry Messenger

The Italian Galileo Galilei was the first European to use a telescope to make systematic observations of the heavens. His observations, as reported in The Starry Messenger *in 1610, stunned European intellectuals by revealing that the celestial bodies were not perfect and immutable, as had been believed, but were apparently composed of material substance similar to the earth. In this selection, Galileo describes how he devised a telescope and what he saw with it.*

✸ *Galileo Galilei,* The Starry Messenger

About ten months ago a report reached my ears that a certain Fleming had constructed a spyglass by means of which visible objects, though very distant from the eye of the observer, were distinctly seen as if nearby. Of this truly remarkable effect several experiences were related, to which some persons gave credence while others denied them. A few days later the report was confirmed to me in a letter from a noble Frenchman at Paris, Jacques Badovere, which caused me to apply myself whole-heartedly to inquire into the means by which I might arrive at the invention of a similar instrument. This I did shortly afterwards, my basis being the theory of refraction. First I prepared a tube of lead, at the ends of which I fitted two glass lenses, both plane on one side while on the other side one was spherically convex and the other concave. Then placing my eye near the concave lens I perceived objects satisfactorily large and near, for they appeared three times closer and nine times larger than when seen with the naked eye alone. Next I constructed another one, more accurate, which represented objects as enlarged more than sixty times. Finally, sparing nei-

ther labor nor expense, I succeeded in constructing for myself so excellent an instrument that objects seen by means of it appeared nearly one thousand times larger and over thirty times closer than when regarded without natural vision.

It would be superfluous to enumerate the number and importance of the advantages of such an instrument at sea as well as on land. But forsaking terrestrial observations, I turned to celestial ones, and first I saw the moon from as near at hand as if it were scarcely two terrestrial radii. After that I observed often with wondering delight both the planets and the fixed stars, and since I saw these latter to be very crowded, I began to seek (and eventually found) a method by which I might measure their distances apart. . . .

Now let us review the observations made during the past two months, once more inviting the attention of all who are eager for true philosophy to the first steps of such important contemplations. Let us speak first of that surface of the moon which faces us. For greater clarity I distinguish two parts of this surface, a lighter and a darker; the lighter part seems to surround and to pervade the whole hemisphere, while the darker part discolors the moon's surface like a kind of cloud, and makes it appear covered with spots. . . . From observation of these spots repeated many times I have been led to the opinion and conviction that the surface of the moon is not smooth, uniform, and precisely spherical as a great number of philosophers believe it (and the other heavenly bodies) to be, but is uneven, rough, and full of cavities and prominences, being not unlike the face of the earth, relieved by chains of mountains and deep valleys.

his major work, *Mathematical Principles of Natural Philosophy*, known simply as the *Principia* by the first word of its Latin title. In this work, Newton spelled out the mathematical proofs demonstrating his universal law of gravitation. Newton's work was the culmination of the theories of Copernicus, Kepler, and Galileo. While each had undermined some part of the Ptolemaic-Aristotelian cosmology, no one until Newton had pieced together a coherent synthesis for a new cosmology.

In the first book of the *Principia*, Newton defined the basic concepts of mechanics by elaborating the

three laws of motion: every object continues in a state of rest or uniform motion in a straight line unless deflected by a force, the rate of change of motion of an object is proportional to the force acting on it, and to every action there is always an equal and opposite reaction. In Book Three, Newton applied his theories of mechanics to the problems of astronomy by demonstrating that these three laws of motion govern the planetary bodies as well as terrestrial objects. Integral to his whole argument was the universal law of gravitation to explain why the planetary bodies did

ff in straight lines but continued in elliptical
about the sun. In mathematical terms, New-
n explained that every object in the universe was
attracted to every other object with a force (gravity)
that is directly proportional to the product of their
masses and inversely proportional to the square of the
distances between them.

The implications of Newton's universal law of
gravitation were enormous, even if it took another
century before they were widely recognized. Newton
had demonstrated that one universal law, mathemat-
ically proved, could explain all motion in the universe.
The secrets of the natural world could be known by
human investigations. At the same time, the Newtonian synthesis created a new cosmology in which the
world was seen largely in mechanistic terms. The universe was one huge, regulated, and uniform machine
that operated according to natural laws in absolute
time, space, and motion. Although Newton believed

that God was "everywhere present" and acted as the
force that moved all bodies on the basis of the laws he
had discovered, later generations dropped his spiritual
assumptions. Newton's world-machine, conceived as
operating absolutely in space, time, and motion, dominated the modern worldview until the twentieth century, when the Einsteinian revolution based on a
concept of relativity superseded the Newtonian mechanistic concept.

Newton's ideas were soon accepted in England
but were resisted on the Continent, and it took much
of the eighteenth century before they were generally
accepted everywhere in Europe. They were also reinforced by developments in other fields, especially
medicine.

◆ **Advances in Medicine**

Although the Scientific Revolution of the sixteenth
and seventeenth centuries is associated primarily with
the dramatic changes in astronomy and mechanics
that precipitated a new perception of the universe, a
third field that had been dominated by Greek thought
in the Late Middle Ages, medicine, also experienced
a transformation. Late medieval medicine was dominated by the teachings of the Greek physician Galen,
who had lived in the second century A.D.

Galen's influence on the medieval medical world
was pervasive in anatomy, physiology, and disease.
Galen had relied on animal, rather than human, dissection to arrive at a picture of human anatomy that
was quite inaccurate in many instances. Even when
Europeans began to practice human dissection in the
Late Middle Ages, instruction in anatomy still relied
on Galen. While a professor read a text of Galen, an
assistant dissected a cadaver for illustrative purposes.
Physiology, or the functioning of the body, was also
dominated by Galenic hypotheses, including the belief
that there were two separate blood systems, one controlling muscular activities and containing bright red
blood moving upward and downward through the
arteries, the other governing the digestive functions
and containing dark red blood that ebbed and flowed
in the veins.

Two major figures are associated with the
changes in medicine in the sixteenth and seventeenth
centuries: Andreas Vesalius and William Harvey. The
new anatomy of the sixteenth century was the work of
the Belgian Andreas Vesalius (1514–1564). His study
of medicine at Paris involved him in the works of
Galen, the great ancient authority. Especially impor-

ISAAC NEWTON. Pictured here is a portrait of Isaac
Newton by Godfrey Kneller. With a single law of
universal gravitation, Newton was able to explain all
motion in the universe. His great synthesis of the work
of his predecessors created a new picture of the universe,
one in which the universe was viewed as a great machine
operating according to natural laws.

tant to him was a recently discovered text of Galen, *On Anatomical Procedures*, that led Vesalius to emphasize practical research as the principal avenue for understanding human anatomy.

After receiving a doctorate in medicine at the University of Padua in 1536, he accepted a position there as professor of surgery. In 1543, he published his masterpiece, *On the Fabric of the Human Body*. This book was based on his Paduan lectures, in which he deviated from traditional practice by personally dissecting a body to illustrate what he was discussing. Vesalius's anatomical treatise presented a careful examination of the individual organs and general structure of the human body. The book would not have been feasible without the artistic advances of the Renaissance and the technical developments in the art of printing. Together, these advances made possible the creation of illustrations superior to any hitherto produced.

Vesalius' hands-on approach to teaching anatomy enabled him to overthrow some of Galen's most glaring errors. He did not hesitate, for example, to correct Galen's assertion that the great blood vessels originated from the liver since his own observations made it clear that they came from the heart. Nevertheless, Vesalius still clung to a number of Galen's erroneous assertions, including the Greek physician's ideas on the ebb and flow of two kinds of blood in the veins and arteries. It was not until William Harvey's work on the circulation of the blood that this Galenic misperception was corrected.

Englishman William Harvey (1578–1657) attended Cambridge University and later Padua, where he earned a doctorate of medicine in 1602. His reputation rests on his book *On the Motion of the Heart and Blood,* published in 1628. Although questions had been raised in the sixteenth century about Galen's physiological principles, no major challenge to his system had emerged. Harvey's work, based on meticulous observations and experiments, led him to reject the ancient Greek's contentions. Harvey demonstrated that the heart was the beginning point of the circulation of blood in the body, that the same blood flows in both veins and arteries, and that the blood makes a complete circuit as it passes through the body. Although Harvey's work dealt a severe blow to Galen's theories, his ideas did not begin to achieve general recognition until the 1660s, when the capillaries, which explained how the blood passed from the arteries to the veins, were discovered. Harvey's theory of the circulation of the blood laid the foundation for modern physiology.

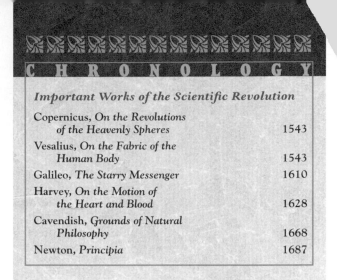

◆ Women in the Origins of Modern Science

During the Middle Ages, except for members of religious orders, women who sought a life of learning were severely hampered by the traditional attitude that a woman's proper role was as a daughter, wife, and mother. But in the late fourteenth and early fifteenth centuries, new opportunities for elite women emerged as enthusiasm for the new secular learning called humanism encouraged Europe's privileged and learned men to encourage women to read and study classical and Christian texts. The ideal of a humanist education for some of the daughters of Europe's elite persisted into the seventeenth century.

Much as they were drawn to humanism, women were also attracted to the Scientific Revolution. Unlike females educated formally in humanist schools, women attracted to science had to obtain a largely informal education. European nobles had the leisure and resources that gave them easy access to the world of learning. This door was also open to noblewomen who could participate in the informal scientific networks of their fathers and brothers. One of the most prominent female scientists of the seventeenth century, Margaret Cavendish (1623–1673), came from an aristocratic background. Cavendish was not a popularizer of science for women but a participant in the crucial scientific debates of her time. Despite her achievement, however, she was excluded from membership in the Royal Society (see "The Spread of Scientific Knowledge" later in the chapter), although she was once allowed to attend a meeting. She wrote a number of works on scientific matters, including *Observations upon Experimental Philosophy* and

MARGARET CAVENDISH. Shown in this portrait is Margaret Cavendish, the duchess of Newcastle. Her husband, thirty years her senior, encouraged her to pursue her literary interests. In addition to scientific works, she wrote plays, an autobiography, and a biography of her husband titled *The Life of the Thrice Noble, High and Puissant Prince William Cavendish, Duke, Marquess and Earl of Newcastle*. The autobiography and biography led one male literary critic to call her "a mad, conceited and ridiculous woman."

Grounds of Natural Philosophy. In these works, she did not hesitate to attack what she considered the defects of the rationalist and empiricist approaches to scientific knowledge and was especially critical of the growing belief that humans through science were the masters of nature: "We have no power at all over natural causes and effects . . . for man is but a small part. . . . His powers are but particular actions of Nature. and he cannot have a supreme and absolute power."[4]

As an aristocrat, the duchess of Cavendish was a good example of the women in France and England who worked in science. Women interested in science who lived in Germany came from a different background. There the tradition of female participation in craft production enabled some women to become involved in observational science, especially astronomy. Between 1650 and 1710, one in every seven German astronomers was a woman.

The most famous of the female astronomers in Germany was Maria Winkelmann (1670–1720). She was educated by her father and uncle and received advanced training from a nearby self-taught astronomer. Her opportunity to practice came when she married Gottfried Kirch, Germany's foremost astronomer. She became his assistant at the astronomical observatory operated in Berlin by the Academy of Science. She made some original contributions, including a hitherto undiscovered comet, as her husband related:

> Early in the morning (about 2:00 A.M.) the sky was clear and starry. Some nights before, I had observed a variable star, and my wife (as I slept) wanted to find and see it for herself. In so doing, she found a comet in the sky. At which time she woke me, and I found that it was indeed a comet. . . . I was surprised that I had not seen it the night before.[5]

When her husband died in 1710, she applied for a position as assistant astronomer for which she was highly qualified. As a woman—with no university degree—she was denied the post by the Berlin Academy, which feared that it would establish a precedent if it hired a woman ("mouths would gape").

Winkelmann's difficulties with the Berlin Academy reflect the obstacles women faced in being accepted in scientific work, which was considered a male preserve. Although there were no formal statutes excluding women from membership in the new scientific societies, no woman was invited to join either the Royal Society of England or the French Academy of Sciences until the twentieth century. All of these women scientists were exceptional women because a life devoted to any kind of scholarship was still viewed as at odds with the domestic duties women were expected to perform.

The nature and value of women had been the subject of an ongoing, centuries-long debate. Male opinions in the debate were largely a carryover from medieval times and were not favorable. Women were portrayed as inherently base, prone to vice, easily swayed, and "sexually insatiable." Hence men needed to control them. Learned women were viewed as having overcome female liabilities to become like men. One man in praise of a woman scholar remarked that her writings were so good that you "would hardly believe they were done by a woman at all."

In the seventeenth century, women joined this debate by arguing against the distorted images of women held by men. They argued that women also had rational minds and could grow from education. Further, since most women were pious, chaste, and

The "Natural" Inferiority of Women

Despite the shattering of old views and the emergence of a new worldview in the Scientific Revolution of the seventeenth century, attitudes toward women remained tied to traditional perspectives. In this selection, the philosopher Benedict de Spinoza argues for the "natural" inferiority of women to men.

✵ *Benedict de Spinoza,* A Political Treatise

But, perhaps, someone will ask, whether women are under men's authority by nature or institution. For if it has been by mere institution, then we had no reason compelling us to exclude women from government. But if we consult experience itself, we shall find that the origin of it is in their weakness. For there has never been a case of men and women reigning together, but wherever on the earth men are found, there we see that men rule, and women are ruled, and that on this plan, both sexes live in harmony. But on the other hand, the Amazons, who are reported to have held rule of old, did not suffer men to stop in their country, but reared only their female children, killing males to whom they gave

birth. But if by nature women were equal to men, and were equally distinguished by force of character and ability, in which human power and therefore human right chiefly consist; surely among nations so many and different some would be found, where both sexes rule alike, and others, where men are ruled by women, and so brought up, that they can make less use of their abilities. And since this is nowhere the case, one may assert with perfect propriety, that women have not by nature equal right with men: but that they necessarily give way to men, and that thus it cannot happen, that both sexes should rule alike, much less that men should be ruled by women. But if we further reflect upon human passions, how men, in fact, generally love women merely from the passion of lust, and esteem their cleverness and wisdom in proportion to the excellence of their beauty, and also how very ill-disposed men are to suffer the women they love to show any sort of favor to others, and other facts of this kind, we shall easily see that men and women cannot rule alike without greater hurt to peace.

---

temperate, there was no need for male authority over them. These female defenders of women emphasized education as the key to women's ability to move into the world. How, then, did the era of the Scientific Revolution affect this debate over the nature of women? As an era of intellectual revolution in which traditional authorities were being overthrown, we might expect significant change in men's views of women. But by and large, instead of becoming an instrument for liberation, science was used to find new support for the old, traditional views about a woman's "true place" in the scheme of things. New views were used to perpetrate old stereotypes about women.

An important project in the new anatomy of the sixteenth and seventeenth centuries was the attempt to illustrate the human body and skeleton. For Vesalius, the portrayal of physical differences between males and females was limited to external bodily form (the outlines of the body) and the sexual organs. Vesalius saw no difference in skeletons and portrayed them as the same for men or women. It was not until the eighteenth century, in fact, that a new anatomy finally pre-

vailed. Drawings of female skeletons between 1730 and 1790 varied, but females tended to have a larger pelvic area, and in some instances, female skulls were portrayed as smaller than those of males. Eighteenth-century studies on the anatomy and physiology of sexual differences provided "scientific evidence" to reaffirm the traditional inferiority of women. The larger pelvic area "proved" that women were meant to be childbearers, and men's larger skull "demonstrated" the superiority of the male mind. Male-dominated science had been used to "prove" male social dominance.

Overall, the Scientific Revolution reaffirmed traditional ideas about women's nature. Male scientists used the new science to spread the view that women were inferior by nature, subordinate to men, and suited by nature to play a domestic role as nurturing mothers. The widespread distribution of books ensured the continuation of these ideas (see the box above). Jean de La Bruyère, the seventeenth-century French moralist, was typical when he remarked that an educated woman was like a gun that was a collector's item

---

"which one shows to the curious, but which has no use at all, any more than a carousel horse."[6]

◆ Toward a New Earth: Descartes, Rationalism, and a New View of Humankind

The fundamentally new conception of the universe contained in the cosmological revolution of the sixteenth and seventeenth centuries inevitably had an impact on the Western view of humankind. Nowhere is this more evident than in the work of the Frenchman René Descartes (1596–1650), an extremely important figure in Western history. Descartes began by reflecting the doubt and uncertainty that seemed pervasive in the confusion of the seventeenth century and ended with a philosophy that dominated Western thought until the twentieth century.

The starting point for Descartes' new system was doubt, as he explained at the beginning of his

DESCARTES WITH QUEEN CHRISTINA OF SWEDEN. René Descartes was one of the primary figures in the Scientific Revolution. Claiming to use reason as his sole guide to truth, Descartes posited a sharp distinction between mind and matter. He is shown here, standing to the right of Queen Christina of Sweden. The queen had a deep interest in philosophy and invited Descartes to her court.

most famous work, *Discourse on Method*, written in 1637:

> From my childhood I have been familiar with letters; and as I was given to believe that by their means a clear and assured knowledge can be acquired of all that is useful in life, I was extremely eager for instruction in them. As soon, however, as I had completed the course of study, at the close of which it is customary to be admitted into the order of the learned, I entirely changed my opinion. For I found myself entangled in so many doubts and errors that, as it seemed to me, the endeavor to instruct myself had served only to disclose to me more and more of my ignorance.[7]

Descartes decided to set aside all that he had learned and begin again. One fact seemed beyond doubt—his own existence:

> But I immediately became aware that while I was thus disposed to think that all was false, it was absolutely necessary that I who thus thought should be something; and noting that this truth *I think, therefore I am*, was so steadfast and so assured that the suppositions of the skeptics, to whatever extreme they might all be carried, could not avail to shake it, I concluded that I might without scruple accept it as being the first principle of the philosophy I was seeking.[8]

With this emphasis on the mind, Descartes asserted that he would accept only things that his reason said were true.

From his first postulate, Descartes deduced an additional principle, the separation of mind and matter. Descartes argued that since "the mind cannot be doubted but the body and material world can, the two must be radically different." From this came an absolute dualism between mind and matter, or what has also been called Cartesian dualism. Using mind or human reason, the path to certain knowledge, and its best instrument, mathematics, humans can understand the material world because it is pure mechanism, a machine that is governed by its own physical laws because it was created by God—the great geometrician.

Descartes' conclusions about the nature of the universe and human beings had important implications. His separation of mind and matter allowed scientists to view matter as dead or inert, as something that was totally separate from themselves and could be investigated independently by reason. The split between mind and body led Westerners to equate their identity with mind and reason rather than with the whole organism. Descartes has rightly been called the father of modern rationalism. His books were placed on the papal Index of Forbidden Books and condemned by many Protestant theologians. The radical Cartesian split between mind and matter, and between mind and body, had devastating implications not only for traditional religious views of the universe but also for how Westerners viewed themselves.

◆ Science and Religion in the Seventeenth Century

In Galileo's struggle with the Holy Office of the Catholic church, we see the beginning of the conflict between science and religion that has marked the history of modern Western civilization. Since time immemorial, theology had seemed to be the queen of the sciences. It was natural that the churches would continue to believe that religion was the final measure of everything. To the emerging scientists, however, it often seemed that theologians knew not of what they spoke. These "natural philosophers" then tried to draw lines between the knowledge of religion and the knowledge of "natural philosophy" or nature. Galileo had clearly felt that it was unnecessary to pit science against religion when he wrote that

> in discussions of physical problems we ought to begin not from the authority of scriptural passages, but from sense-experiences and necessary demonstrations; for the holy Bible and the phenomena of nature proceed alike from the divine word, the former as the dictate of the Holy Ghost and the latter as the observant executrix of God's commands. It is necessary for the Bible, in order to be accommodated to the understanding of every man, to speak many things which appear to differ from the absolute truth so far as the bare meaning of the words is concerned. But Nature, on the other hand, is inexorable and immutable; she never transgresses the laws imposed upon her, or cares a whit whether her abstruse reasons and methods of operation are understandable to men.[9]

To Galileo, it made little sense for the church to determine the nature of physical reality on the basis of biblical texts that were subject to radically divergent interpretations. The church, however, decided otherwise in Galileo's case and lent its great authority to one scientific theory, the Ptolemaic-Aristotelian cosmology, no doubt because it fit so well with its own philosophical views of reality. But the church's decision had tremendous consequences. For educated individuals, it established a dichotomy between scientific investigations and religious beliefs. As the scientific beliefs triumphed, it became almost inevitable that religious beliefs would suffer, leading to a growing secularization in European intellectual life—precisely what the church had hoped to combat by opposing Copernicanism. Many seventeenth-century intellectuals were both religious and scientific and believed that the implications of this split would be tragic. Some believed that the split was largely unnecessary, while others felt the need to combine God, humans, and a mechanistic universe into a new philosophical synthesis. One individual, Pascal, illustrates how one European intellectual responded to the implications of the cosmological revolution of the seventeenth century.

Blaise Pascal (1623–1662) was a French scientist who sought to keep science and religion united. Pascal had a brief but checkered career. He was an accomplished scientist and a brilliant mathematician who excelled at both the practical (he invented a calculating machine) and the abstract (he devised a theory of probability and did work on conic sections). After a profound mystical vision on the night of November 23, 1654, which assured him that God cared for the human soul, he devoted the rest of his life to religious matters. He planned to write an "apology for the Christian religion" but died before he could do so. He did leave a set of notes for the larger work, however, which in published form became known as *Pensées* or *Thoughts*.

In the *Pensées*, Pascal tried to convert rationalists to Christianity by appealing to both their reason and their emotions. Humans were, he argued, frail creatures, often deceived by their senses, misled by reason, and battered by their emotions. And yet they were beings whose very nature involved thinking: "Man is but a reed, the weakest in nature; but he is a thinking reed."[10]

Pascal was determined to show that the Christian religion was not contrary to reason: "If we violate the principles of reason, our religion will be absurd, and it will be laughed at."[11] Christianity, he felt, was the only religion that recognized people's true state of being as both vulnerable and great. To a Christian, a human being was both fallen and at the same time God's special creation. But it was not necessary to emphasize one at the expense of the other—to view humans as only rational or only hopeless. Pascal even had an answer for skeptics in his famous wager: God is a reasonable bet; it is worthwhile to assume that God exists. If he does, we win all; if he does not, we lose nothing.

Despite his own background as a scientist and mathematician, Pascal refused to rely on the scientist's world of order and rationality to attract people to God: "If we submit everything to reason, there will be no mystery and no supernatural element in our religion." In the new cosmology of the seventeenth century, "finite man," Pascal believed, was lost in the new infinite world, a realization that frightened him: "The

Pascal: "What Is a Man in the Infinite?"

Perhaps no intellectual in the seventeenth century gave greater expression to the uncertainties generated by the cosmological revolution than Blaise Pascal. Himself a scientist, Pascal's mystical vision of God's presence caused him to pursue religious truths with a passion. His work, the Pensées, *consisted of notes for a larger, unfinished work justifying the Christian religion. In this selection, Pascal presents his musings on the human place in an infinite world.*

✺ *Blaise Pascal*, Pensées

Let man then contemplate the whole of nature in her full and exalted majesty. Let him turn his eyes from the lowly objects which surround him. Let him gaze on that brilliant light set like an eternal lamp to illumine the Universe; let the earth seem to him a dot compared with the vast orbit described by the sun, and let him wonder at the fact that this vast orbit itself is no more than a very small dot compared with that described by the stars in their revolutions around the firmament. But if our vision stops here, let the imagination pass on; it will exhaust its powers of thinking long before nature ceases to supply it with material for thought. All this visible world is no more than an imperceptible speck in nature's ample bosom. No idea approaches it. We may extend our conceptions beyond all imaginable space; yet produce only atoms in comparison with the reality of things. It is an infinite sphere, the center of which is everywhere, the circumference nowhere. In short, it is the greatest perceptible mark of God's almighty power that our imagination should lose itself in that thought.

Returning to himself, let man consider what he is compared with all existence; let him think of himself as lost in his remote corner of nature; and from this little dungeon in which he finds himself lodged—I mean the Universe—let him learn to set a true value on the earth, its kingdoms, and cities, and upon himself. What is a man in the infinite? . . .

For, after all, what is a man in nature? A nothing in comparison with the infinite, an absolute in comparison with nothing, a central point between nothing and all. Infinitely far from understanding these extremes, the end of things and their beginning are hopelessly hidden from him in an impenetrable secret. He is equally incapable of seeing the nothingness from which he came, and the infinite in which he is engulfed. What else then will he perceive but some appearance of the middle of things, in an eternal despair of knowing either their principle or their purpose? All things emerge from nothing and are borne onward to infinity. Who can follow this marvelous process? The Author of these wonders understands them. None but He can.

---

eternal silence of those infinite spaces strikes me with terror" (see the box above). The world of nature, then, could never reveal God: "Because they have failed to contemplate these infinites, men have rashly plunged into the examination of nature, as though they bore some proportion to her. . . . Their assumption is as infinite as their object." A Christian could only rely on a God who through Jesus cared for human beings. In the final analysis, after providing reasonable arguments for Christianity, Pascal came to rest on faith. Reason, he believed, could take people only so far: "The heart has its reasons of which the reason knows nothing." As a Christian, faith was the final step: "The heart feels God, not the reason. This is what constitutes faith: God experienced by the heart, not by the reason."[12]

In retrospect, it is obvious that Pascal failed to achieve his goal. Increasingly, the gap between science and traditional religion grew wider as Europe continued along its path of secularization. Of course, traditional religions were not eliminated, nor is there any evidence that churches had yet lost their numbers. That would happen later. Nevertheless, more and more of the intellectual, social, and political elites began to act on the basis of secular rather than religious assumptions.

◆ The Spread of Scientific Knowledge

During the seventeenth century, scientific learning and investigation began to increase dramatically. Major universities in Europe established new chairs of science, especially in medicine. Royal and princely patronage

---

of individual scientists became an international phenomenon. Of great importance to the work of science, however, was the creation of a scientific method and new learned societies that enabled the new scientists to communicate their ideas to each other and to disseminate them to a wider, literate public.

❋ The Scientific Method

In the course of the Scientific Revolution, attention was paid to the problem of establishing the proper means to examine and understand the physical realm. This creation of a scientific method was crucial to the evolution of science in the modern world. Curiously enough, it was an Englishman with few scientific credentials who attempted to put forth a new method of acquiring knowledge that made an impact on English scientists in the seventeenth century and other European scientists in the eighteenth century. Francis Bacon (1561–1626), a lawyer and lord chancellor, rejected Copernicus and Kepler and misunderstood Galileo. And yet in his unfinished work *The Great Instauration* (*The Great Restoration*), he called for his contemporaries "to commence a total reconstruction of sciences, arts, and all human knowledge, raised upon the proper foundations." Bacon did not doubt humans' ability to know the natural world, but he believed that they had proceeded incorrectly: "The entire fabric of human reason which we employ in the inquisition of nature is badly put together and built up, and like some magnificent structure without foundation."[13]

Bacon's new foundation—a correct scientific method—was to be built on inductive principles. Rather than beginning with assumed first principles from which logical conclusions could be deduced, he urged scientists to proceed from the particular to the general. From carefully organized experiments and systematic, thorough observations, correct generalizations could be developed. Bacon was clear about what he believed his method could accomplish. His concern was more for practical than for pure science. He stated that "the true and lawful goal of the sciences is none other than this: that human life be endowed with new discoveries and power." He wanted science to contribute to the "mechanical arts" by creating devices that would benefit industry, agriculture, and trade. Bacon was prophetic when he said that "I am laboring to lay the foundation, not of any sect or doctrine, but of human utility and power." And how would this "human power" be used? To "conquer nature in action."[14] The control and domination of nature became a central proposition of modern science and

the technology that accompanied it. Only in the twentieth century did some scientists ask whether this assumption might not be at the heart of the modern ecological crisis.

Descartes proposed a different approach to scientific methodology by emphasizing deduction and mathematical logic. Descartes believed that one could start with self-evident truths, comparable to geometrical axioms, and deduce more complex conclusions. His emphasis on deduction and mathematical order complemented Bacon's stress on experiment and induction. It was Newton who synthesized them into a single scientific methodology by uniting Bacon's empiricism with Descartes's rationalism. This scientific method began with systematic observations and experiments, which were used to arrive at general concepts. New deductions derived from these general concepts could then be tested and verified by precise experiments.

❋ The Scientific Societies

The first of the scientific societies appeared in Italy, but those of England and France were ultimately of more significance. The English Royal Society evolved out of informal gatherings of scientists at London and Oxford in the 1640s, although it did not receive a formal charter from King Charles II until 1662. The French Royal Academy of Sciences also arose out of informal scientific meetings in Paris during the 1650s. In 1666, Louis XIV bestowed on the group a formal recognition. The French Academy received abundant state support and remained under government control; its members were appointed and paid salaries by the state. In contrast, the Royal Society of England received little government encouragement, and its fellows simply co-opted new members.

Early on, both the English and French scientific societies formally emphasized the practical value of scientific research. The Royal Society created a committee to investigate technological improvements for industry; the French Academy collected tools and machines. This concern with the practical benefits of science proved short lived, however, as both societies came to focus their primary interest on theoretical work in mechanics and astronomy. The construction of observatories at Paris in 1667 and at Greenwich, England, in 1675 greatly facilitated research in astronomy by both groups. While both the English and French societies made useful contributions to scientific knowledge in the second half of the seventeenth century, their true significance arose from their example that science should proceed along the lines of a cooperative venture.

LOUIS XIV AND COLBERT VISIT THE ACADEMY OF SCIENCES. In the seventeenth century, individual scientists received royal and princely patronage, and a number of learned societies were established. In France, Louis XIV, urged on by his minister Colbert, gave formal recognition to the French Academy in 1666. In this painting by Henri Testelin, Louis XIV is shown seated, surrounded by Colbert and members of the French Royal Academy of Sciences.

✳ Science and Society

The importance of science in the history of modern Western civilization is usually taken for granted. But how did science become such an integral part of Western culture in the seventeenth and early eighteenth centuries? Recent research has stressed that one cannot simply assert that people perceived that science was a rationally superior system. An important social factor, however, might help explain the relatively rapid acceptance of the new science.

It has been argued that the literate mercantile and propertied elites of Europe were attracted to new science because it offered new ways to exploit resources for profit. Some of the early scientists made it easier for these groups to accept the new ideas by demonstrating how the ideas could be applied directly to specific industrial and technological needs. Galileo, for example, consciously sought an alliance between science and the material interests of the educated elite when he assured his listeners that the science of mechanics would be quite useful "when it becomes necessary to build bridges or other structures over water, something occurring mainly in affairs of great importance." At the same time, Galileo stressed that science was fit for the "minds of the wise" and not for "the shallow minds of the common people." This made science part of the high culture of Europe's wealthy elites at a time when that culture was being increasingly separated from the popular culture of the lower classes.

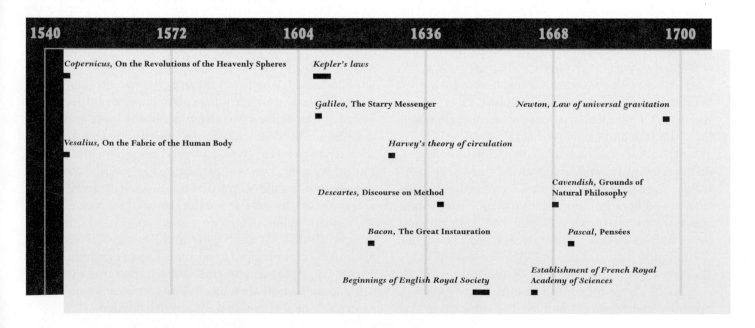

1540	1572	1604	1636	1668	1700
Copernicus, On the Revolutions of the Heavenly Spheres		Kepler's laws			
		Galileo, The Starry Messenger		Newton, Law of universal gravitation	
Vesalius, On the Fabric of the Human Body			Harvey's theory of circulation		
		Descartes, Discourse on Method		Cavendish, Grounds of Natural Philosophy	
		Bacon, The Great Instauration		Pascal, Pensées	
		Beginnings of English Royal Society		Establishment of French Royal Academy of Sciences	

Conclusion

The Scientific Revolution represents a major turning point in modern Western civilization. In the Scientific Revolution, the Western world overthrew the medieval, Ptolemaic-Aristotelian worldview and arrived at a new conception of the universe: the sun at the center, the planets as material bodies revolving around the sun in elliptical orbits, and an infinite rather than finite world. With the changes in the conception of heaven came changes in the conception of earth. The work of Bacon and Descartes left Europeans with the separation of mind and matter and the belief that by using only reason, they could in fact understand and dominate the world of nature. The development of a scientific method furthered the work of scientists, and the creation of scientific societies and learned journals spread its results. Although traditional churches stubbornly resisted the new ideas and a few intellectuals pointed to some inherent flaws, nothing was able to halt the replacement of the traditional ways of thinking by new ways that created a more fundamental break with the past than that represented by the breakup of Christian unity in the Reformation.

The Scientific Revolution forced Europeans to change their conception of themselves. At first, some were appalled and even frightened by its implications. Formerly, humans on earth had been at the center of the universe. Now the earth was only a tiny planet revolving around a sun that was itself only a speck in a boundless universe. Most people remained optimistic despite the apparent blow to human dignity. After all, had Newton not demonstrated that the universe was a great machine governed by natural laws? Newton had found one—the universal law of gravitation. Could others not find other laws? Were there not natural laws governing every aspect of human endeavor that could be found by the new scientific method? Thus the Scientific Revolution leads us logically to the age of the Enlightenment of the eighteenth century.

Notes

1. Quoted in Alan G. R. Smith, *Science and Society in the Sixteenth and Seventeenth Centuries* (London, 1972), p. 59.
2. Edward MacCurdy, *The Notebooks of Leonardo da Vinci* (London, 1948), vol. 1, p. 634.
3. Quoted in John H. Randall, *The Making of the Modern Mind* (Boston, 1926), p. 234.
4. Quoted in Londa Schiebinger, *The Mind Has No Sex? Women in the Origins of Modern Science* (Cambridge, Mass., 1989), pp. 52–53.
5. Ibid., p. 85.
6. Quoted in Phyllis Stock, *Better than Rubies: A History of Women's Education* (New York, 1978), p. 16.
7. René Descartes, *Philosophical Writings*, ed. and trans. Norman K. Smith (New York, 1958), p. 95.
8. Ibid., pp. 118–119.
9. Stillman Drake, ed. and trans., *Discoveries and Opinions of Galileo* (New York, 1957), p. 182.
10. Pascal, *Pensées*, trans. J. M. Cohen (Harmondsworth, England, 1961), p. 100.
11. Ibid., p. 31.
12. Ibid., pp. 52–53, 164, 165.
13. Francis Bacon, *The Great Instauration*, trans. Jerry Weinberger (Arlington Heights, Ill., 1989), pp. 2, 8.
14. Ibid., pp. 2, 16, 21.

Suggestions for Further Reading

Four general surveys of the entire Scientific Revolution are A. G. R. Smith, *Science and Society in the Sixteenth and Seventeenth Centuries* (London, 1972); J. R. Jacob, *The Scientific Revolution: Aspirations and Achievements, 1500–1700* (Atlantic Highlands, N.J., 1998); S. Shapin, *The Scientific Revolution* (Chicago, 1996); and J. Henry, *The Scientific Revolution and the Origins of Modern Science* (New York, 1997). Also of much value is A. G. Debus, *Man and Nature in the Renaissance* (Cambridge, 1978), which covers the period from the mid-fifteenth through the mid-seventeenth centuries. On the relationship of magic to the beginnings of the Scientific Revolution, see the pioneering works by F. Yates, *Giordano Bruno and the Hermetic Tradition* (New York, 1964) and *The Rosicrucian Enlightenment* (London, 1975).

A good introduction to the transformation from the late medieval to the early modern worldview is A. Koyré, *From the Closed World to the Infinite Universe* (New York, 1958). Also still of value is A. Koestler, *The Sleepwalkers: A History of Man's Changing Vision of the Universe* (New York, 1959). On the important figures of the revolution in astronomy, see E. Rosen, *Copernicus and the Scientific Revolution* (New York, 1984); M. Sharratt, *Galileo: Decisive Innovator* (Oxford, 1994); S. Drake, *Galileo, Pioneer Scientist* (Toronto, 1990); M. Casper, *Johannes Kepler*, trans. C. D. Hellman (London, 1959), the standard biography; and R. S. Westfall, *The Life of Isaac Newton* (New York, 1993). On Newton's relationship to alchemy, see M. White, *Isaac Newton: The Last Sorcerer* (Reading, Mass., 1997).

The standard biography of Vesalius is C. D. O'Malley, *Andreas Vesalius of Brussels, 1514–1564* (Berkeley, Calif., 1964). The work of Harvey is discussed in G. Whitteridge, *William Harvey and the Circulation of the Blood* (London, 1971). A good general account of the development of medicine can be found in W. P. D. Wightman, *The Emergence of Scientific Medicine* (Edinburgh, 1971).

The importance of Francis Bacon in the early development of science is underscored in P. Zagorin, *Francis Bacon* (Princeton, N.J., 1998). A good introduction to the work of Descartes can be found in G. Radis-Lewis, *Descartes: A Biography* (Ithaca, N.Y., 1998).

For histories of the scientific academies, see R. Hahn, *The Anatomy of a Scientific Institution: The Paris Academy of Sciences, 1666–1803* (Berkeley, Calif., 1971), and M. Purver, *The Royal Society, Concept and Creation* (London, 1967).

On the subject of women and early modern science, see the comprehensive and highly informative work by L. Schiebinger,

The Mind Has No Sex? Women in the Origins of Modern Science (Cambridge, Mass., 1989). See also C. Merchant, *The Death of Nature: Women, Ecology, and the Scientific Revolution* (San Francisco, 1980). The social and political context for the triumph of science in the seventeenth and eighteenth centuries is examined in M. Jacobs, *The Cultural Meaning of the Scientific Revolution* (New York, 1988) and *The Newtonians and the English Revolution, 1689–1720* (Ithaca, N.Y., 1976).

 For additional reading, go to InfoTrac College Edition, your online research library at http://web1.infotrac-college.com

Enter the search term *Copernicus* using Key Terms.

Enter the search terms *Galileo not Jupiter* using Key Terms.

Enter the search terms *Isaac Newton* using Key Terms.

Enter the search terms *Rene Descartes* using Key Terms.

Glossary

absolutism   a form of government where the sovereign power or ultimate authority rested in the hands of a monarch who claimed to rule by divine right and was therefore responsible only to God.

Agricultural (Neolithic) Revolution   the shift from hunting animals and gathering plants for sustenance to producing food by systematic agriculture that occurred gradually between 10,000 and 4000 B.C. (the Neolithic or "New Stone" Age).

agricultural revolution   the application of new agricultural techniques that allowed for a large increase in productivity in the eighteenth century.

anarchism   a political theory that holds that all governments and existing social institutions are unnecessary and advocates a society based on voluntary cooperation.

anti-Semitism   hostility toward or discrimination against Jews.

appeasement   the policy, followed by the European nations in the 1930s, of accepting Hitler's annexation of Austria and Czechoslovakia in the belief that meeting his demands would assure peace and stability.

Arianism   a Christian heresy that taught that Jesus was inferior to God. Though condemned by the Council of Nicaea in 325, Arianism was adopted by many of the Germanic peoples who entered the Roman Empire over the next centuries.

aristocracy   a class of hereditary nobility in medieval Europe; a warrior class who shared a distinctive lifestyle based on the institution of knighthood, although there were social divisions within the group based on extremes of wealth.

Ausgleich   the "Compromise" of 1867 that created the dual monarchy of Austria-Hungary. Austria and Hungary each had its own capital, constitution, and legislative assembly, but were united under one monarch.

authoritarian state   a state that has a dictatorial government and some other trappings of a totalitarian state, but does not demand that the masses be actively involved in the regime's goals as totalitarian states do.

auxiliaries   troops enlisted from the subject peoples of the Roman Empire to supplement the regular legions composed of Roman citizens.

balance of power   a distribution of power among several states such that no single nation can dominate or interfere with the interests of another.

benefice   in the Christian church, a position, such as a bishopric, that consisted of both a sacred office and the right of the holder to the annual revenues from the position.

bicameral legislature   a legislature with two houses.

Black Death   the outbreak of plague (mostly bubonic) in the mid-fourteenth century that killed from 25 to 50 percent of Europe's population.

Blitzkrieg   "lightning war." A war conducted with great speed and force, as in Germany's advance at the beginning of World War II.

Bolsheviks   a small faction of the Russian Social Democratic Party who were led by Lenin and dedicated to violent revolution; seized power in Russia in 1917 and were subsequently renamed the Communists.

boyars   the Russian nobility.

Brezhnev Doctrine   the doctrine, enunciated by Leonid Brezhnev, that the Soviet Union had a right to intervene if socialism was threatened in another socialist state; used to justify the use of Soviet troops in Czechoslovakia in 1968.

caliph   the secular leader of the Islamic community.

capital   material wealth used or available for use in the production of more wealth.

cartel   a combination of independent commercial enterprises that work together to control prices and limit competition.

Cartesian dualism   Descartes' principle of the separation of mind and matter (and mind and body) that enabled scientists to view matter as something separate from themselves that could be investigated by reason.

chansons de geste   a form of vernacular literature in the High Middle Ages that consisted of heroic epics focusing on the deeds of warriors.

chivalry   the ideal of civilized behavior that emerged among the nobility in the eleventh and twelfth centuries under the influence of the church; a code of ethics knights were expected to uphold.

Christian (northern) humanism   an intellectual movement in northern Europe in the late fifteenth and early sixteenth centuries that combined the interest in the classics of the Italian Renaissance with an interest in the sources of early Christianity, including the New Testament and the writings of the church fathers.

civic humanism   an intellectual movement of the Italian Renaissance that saw Cicero, who was both an intellectual and a statesman, as the ideal and held that humanists should be involved in government and use their rhetorical training in the service of the state.

civil rights the basic rights of citizens including equality before the law, freedom of speech and press, and freedom from arbitrary arrest.

Cold War the ideological conflict between the Soviet Union and the United States after World War II.

collective farms large farms created in the Soviet Union by Stalin by combining many small holdings into one large farm worked by the peasants under government supervision.

collective security the use of an international army raised by an association of nations to deter aggression and keep the peace.

coloni free tenant farmers who worked as sharecroppers on the large estates of the Roman Empire (singular: *colonus*).

common law law common to the entire kingdom of England; imposed by the king's courts beginning in the twelfth century to replace the customary law used in county and feudal courts that varied from place to place.

commune in medieval Europe, an association of townspeople bound together by a sworn oath for the purpose of obtaining basic liberties from the lord of the territory in which the town was located; also, the self-governing town after receiving its liberties.

conciliarism a movement in fourteenth- and fifteenth-century Europe that held that final authority in spiritual matters resided with a general church council, not the pope; emerged in response to the Avignon papacy and the Great Schism and used to justify the summoning of the Council of Constance (1414–1418).

condottieri leaders of bands of mercenary soldiers in Renaissance Italy who sold their services to the highest bidder (singular: *condottiere*).

conquistadors "conquerors." Leaders in the Spanish conquests in the Americas, especially Mexico and Peru, in the sixteenth century.

conscription a military draft.

conservatism an ideology based on tradition and social stability that favored the maintenance of established institutions, organized religion, and obedience to authority and resisted change, especially abrupt change.

consuls the chief executive officers of the Roman Republic. Two were chosen annually to administer the government and lead the army in battle.

consumer society a term applied to Western society after World War II as the working classes adopted the consumption patterns of the middle class and installment plans, credit cards, and easy credit made consumer goods such as appliances and automobiles widely available.

Continental System Napoleon's effort to bar British goods from the Continent in the hope of weakening Britain's economy and destroying its capacity to wage war.

cosmopolitanism the quality of being sophisticated and having wide international experience.

cottage industry a system of textile manufacturing in which spinners and weavers worked at home in their cottages using raw materials supplied to them by capitalist entrepreneurs.

cultural relativism the belief that no culture is superior to another because culture is a matter of custom, not reason, and derives its meaning from the group holding it.

cuneiform "wedge-shaped." A system of writing developed by the Sumerians that consisted of wedge-shaped impressions made by a reed stylus on clay tablets.

decolonization the process of becoming free of colonial status and achieving statehood; occurred in most of the world's colonies between 1947 and 1962.

deism belief in God as the creator of the universe who, after setting it in motion, ceased to have any direct involvement in it and allowed it to run according to its own natural laws.

demesne the part of a manor retained under the direct control of the lord and worked by the serfs as part of their labor services.

depression a very severe, protracted economic downturn with high levels of unemployment.

destalinization the policy of denouncing and undoing the most repressive aspects of Stalin's regime; begun by Nikita Khrushchev in 1956.

détente the relaxation of tension between the Soviet Union and the United States that occurred in the 1970s.

dialectic logic, one of the seven liberal arts that made up the medieval curriculum. In Marxist thought, the process by which all change occurs through the clash of antagonistic elements.

Diaspora the scattering of Jews throughout the ancient world after the Babylonian captivity in the sixth century B.C.

dictator in the Roman Republic, an official granted unlimited power to run the state for a short period of time, usually six months, during an emergency.

diocese the area under the jurisdiction of a Christian bishop; based originally on Roman administrative districts.

direct representation a system of choosing delegates to a representative assembly in which citizens vote directly for the delegates who will represent them.

divination the practice of seeking to foretell future events by interpreting divine signs, which could appear in various forms, such as in entrails of animals, in patterns in smoke, or in dreams.

divine-right monarchy a monarchy based on the belief that monarchs receive their power directly from God and are responsible to no one except God.

domino theory the belief that if the Communists succeeded in Vietnam, other countries in Southeast and East Asia would also fall (like dominoes) to communism; a justification for the U.S. intervention in Vietnam.

dualism the belief that the universe is dominated by two opposing forces, one good and the other evil.

dynastic state a state where the maintenance and expansion of the interests of the ruling family is the primary consideration.

economic imperialism the process in which banks and corporations from developed nations invest in underdeveloped regions and establish a major presence there in the hope of making high profits; not necessarily the same as colonial expansion in that businesses invest where they can make a profit, which may not be in their own nation's colonies.

empiricism the practice of relying on observation and experiment.

enclosure movement in the eighteenth century, the fencing in of the old open fields, combining many small holdings into larger units that could be farmed more efficiently.

encyclical a letter from the pope to all the bishops of the Roman Catholic church.

enlightened absolutism an absolute monarchy where the ruler follows the principles of the Enlightenment by introducing reforms for the improvement of society, allowing freedom of speech and the press, permitting religious toleration, expanding education, and ruling in accordance with the laws.

Enlightenment an eighteenth-century intellectual movement, led by the philosophes, that stressed the application of reason and the scientific method to all aspects of life.

entrepreneur one who organizes, operates, and assumes the risk in a business venture in the expectation of making a profit.

Epicureanism a philosophy founded by Epicurus in the fourth century B.C. that taught that happiness (freedom from emotional turmoil) could be achieved through the pursuit of pleasure (intellectual rather than sensual pleasure).

equestrians a group of extremely wealthy men in the late Roman Republic who were effectively barred from high office, but sought political power commensurate with their wealth; called equestrians because many had gotten their start as cavalry officers (*equites*).

ethnic cleansing the policy of killing or forcibly removing people of another ethnic group; used by the Serbs against Bosnian Muslims in the 1990s.

eucharist a Christian sacrament in which consecrated bread and wine are consumed in celebration of Jesus' Last Supper; also called the Lord's Supper or communion.

evolutionary socialism a socialist doctrine espoused by Eduard Bernstein who argued that socialists should stress cooperation and evolution to attain power by democratic means rather than by conflict and revolution.

fascism an ideology or movement that exalts the nation above the individual and calls for a centralized government with a dictatorial leader, economic and social regimentation, and forcible suppression of opposition; in particular, the ideology of Mussolini's Fascist regime in Italy.

feminism the belief in the social, political, and economic equality of the sexes; also, organized activity to advance women's rights.

fief a landed estate granted to a vassal in exchange for military services.

Final Solution the physical extermination of the Jewish people by the Nazis during World War II.

folk culture the traditional arts and crafts, literature, music, and other customs of the people; something that people make, as opposed to modern popular culture, which is something people buy.

free trade the unrestricted international exchange of goods with low or no tariffs.

general strike a strike by all or most workers in an economy; espoused by Georges Sorel as the heroic action that could be used to inspire the workers to destroy capitalist society.

gentry well-to-do English landowners below the level of the nobility; played an important role in the English Civil War of the seventeenth century.

geocentric theory the idea that the earth is at the center of the universe and that the sun and other celestial objects revolve around the earth.

glasnost "openness." Mikhail Gorbachev's policy of encouraging Soviet citizens to openly discuss the strengths and weaknesses of the Soviet Union.

good emperors the five emperors who ruled from 96 to 180 (Nerva, Trajan, Hadrian, Antoninus Pius, and Marcus Aurelius), a period of peace and prosperity for the Roman Empire.

Great Schism the crisis in the late medieval church when there were first two and then three popes; ended by the Council of Constance (1414–1418).

guest workers foreign workers working temporarily in European countries.

guild an association of people with common interests and concerns, especially people working in the same craft. In medieval Europe, guilds came to control much of the production process and to restrict entry into various trades.

gymnasium in classical Greece, a place for athletics; in the Hellenistic Age, a secondary school with a curriculum centered on music, physical exercise, and literature.

heliocentric theory the idea that the sun (not the earth) is at the center of the universe.

Hellenistic literally, "to imitate the Greeks"; the era after the death of Alexander the Great when Greek culture spread into the Near East and blended with the culture of that region.

helots   serfs in ancient Sparta, who were permanently bound to the land that they worked for their Spartan masters.

heresy   the holding of religious doctrines different from the official teachings of the church.

Hermeticism   an intellectual movement beginning in the fifteenth century that taught that divinity is embodied in all aspects of nature; included works on alchemy and magic as well as theology and philosophy. The tradition continued into the seventeenth century and influenced many of the leading figures of the Scientific Revolution.

hetairai   highly sophisticated courtesans in ancient Athens who offered intellectual and musical entertainment as well as sex.

hieroglyphics   a highly pictorial system of writing used in ancient Egypt.

high culture   the literary and artistic culture of the educated and wealthy ruling classes.

Holocaust   the mass slaughter of European Jews by the Nazis during World War II.

hoplites   heavily armed infantry soldiers used in ancient Greece in a phalanx formation.

Huguenots   French Calvinists.

humanism   an intellectual movement in Renaissance Italy based upon the study of the Greek and Roman classics.

iconoclasm   an eighth-century Byzantine movement against the use of icons (pictures of sacred figures), which was condemned as idolatry.

ideology   a political philosophy such as conservatism or liberalism.

imperium   "the right to command." In the Roman Republic, the chief executive officers (consuls and praetors) possessed the *imperium*; a military commander was an *imperator*. In the Roman Empire, the title *imperator*, or emperor, came to be used for the ruler.

indirect representation   a system of choosing delegates to a representative assembly in which citizens do not choose the delegates directly but instead vote for electors who choose the delegates.

individualism   emphasis on and interest in the unique traits of each person.

indulgence   the remission of part or all of the temporal punishment in purgatory due to sin; granted for charitable contributions and other good deeds. Indulgences became a regular practice of the Christian church in the High Middle Ages, and their abuse was instrumental in sparking Luther's reform movement in the sixteenth century.

infanticide   the practice of killing infants.

inflation   a sustained rise in the price level.

intendants   royal officials in seventeenth-century France who were sent into the provinces to execute the orders of the central government.

intervention, principle of   the idea, after the Congress of Vienna, that the great powers of Europe had the right to send armies into countries experiencing revolution to restore legitimate monarchs to their thrones.

isolationism   a foreign policy in which a nation refrains from making alliances or engaging actively in international affairs.

jihad   "striving in the way of the Lord." In Islam, the practice of conducting raids against neighboring peoples, which was an expansion of the Arab tradition of tribal raids against their persecutors.

joint-stock company   a company or association that raises capital by selling shares to individuals who receive dividends on their investment while a board of directors runs the company.

joint-stock investment bank   a bank created by selling shares of stock to investors. Such banks potentially have access to much more capital than do private banks owned by one or a few individuals.

justification of faith   the primary doctrine of the Protestant Reformation; taught that humans are saved not through good works, but by the grace of God, bestowed freely through the sacrifice of Jesus.

laissez-faire   "to let alone." An economic doctrine that holds that an economy is best served when the government does not interfere but allows the economy to self-regulate according to the forces of supply and demand.

latifundia   large landed estates in the Roman Empire (singular: *latifundium*).

lay investiture   the practice in which a layperson invested a bishop with the symbols of both his temporal office and his spiritual office; led to the Investiture Controversy, which was ended by compromise in the Concordat of Worms in 1122.

Lebensraum   "living space." The doctrine, adopted by Hitler, that a nation's power depends on the amount of land it occupies; thus, a nation must expand to be strong.

legitimacy, principle of   the idea that after the Napoleonic wars peace could best be reestablished in Europe by restoring legitimate monarchs who would preserve traditional institutions; guided Metternich at the Congress of Vienna.

Leninism   Lenin's revision of Marxism that held that Russia need not experience a bourgeois revolution before it could move toward socialism.

liberal arts   the seven areas of study that formed the basis of education in medieval and early modern Europe. Following Boethius and other late Roman authors, they consisted of grammar, rhetoric, and dialectic or logic (the *trivium*) and arithmetic, geometry, astronomy, and music (the *quadrivium*).

liberalism an ideology based on the belief that people should be as free from restraint as possible. Economic liberalism is the idea that the government should not interfere in the workings of the economy. Political liberalism is the idea that there should be restraints on the exercise of power so that people can enjoy basic civil rights in a constitutional state with a representative assembly.

limited liability the principle that shareholders in a joint-stock corporation can be held responsible for the corporation's debts only up to the amount they have invested.

limited (constitutional) monarchy a system of government in which the monarch is limited by a representative assembly and by the duty to rule in accordance with the laws of the land.

mandates a system established after World War I whereby a nation officially administered a territory (mandate) on behalf of the League of Nations. Thus, France administered Lebanon and Syria as mandates, and Britain administered Iraq and Palestine.

manor an agricultural estate operated by a lord and worked by peasants who performed labor services and paid various rents and fees to the lord in exchange for protection and sustenance.

Marshall Plan the European Recovery Program, under which the United States provided financial aid to European countries to help them rebuild after World War II.

Marxism the political, economic, and social theories of Karl Marx, which included the idea that history is the story of class struggle and that ultimately the proletariat will overthrow the bourgeoisie and establish a dictatorship en route to a classless society.

mass education a state-run educational system, usually free and compulsory, that aims to ensure that all children in society have at least a basic education.

mass leisure forms of leisure that appeal to large numbers of people in a society including the working classes; emerged at the end of the nineteenth century to provide workers with amusements after work and on weekends; used during the twentieth century by totalitarian states to control their populations.

mass politics a political order characterized by mass political parties and universal male and (eventually) female suffrage.

mass society a society in which the concerns of the majority—the lower classes—play a prominent role; characterized by extension of voting rights, an improved standard of living for the lower classes, and mass education.

materialism the belief that everything mental, spiritual, or ideal is an outgrowth of physical forces and that truth is found in concrete material existence, not through feeling or intuition.

mercantilism an economic theory that held that a nation's prosperity depended on its supply of gold and silver and that the total volume of trade is unchangeable; therefore, advocated that the government play an active role in the economy by encouraging exports and discouraging imports, especially through the use of tariffs.

Mesolithic Age the period from 10,000 to 7000 B.C., characterized by a gradual transition from a food-gathering/hunting economy to a food-producing economy.

metics resident foreigners in ancient Athens; not permitted full rights of citizenship but did receive the protection of the laws.

militarism a policy of aggressive military preparedness; in particular, the large armies based on mass conscription and complex, inflexible plans for mobilization that most European nations had before World War I.

ministerial responsibility a tenet of nineteenth-century liberalism that held that ministers of the monarch should be responsible to the legislative assembly rather than to the monarch.

Modernism the new artistic and literary styles that emerged in the decades before 1914 as artists rebelled against traditional efforts to portray reality as accurately as possible (leading to Cubism and Abstract Expressionism) and writers explored new forms.

monotheistic/monotheism having only one god; the doctrine or belief that there is only one god.

mutual deterrence the belief that nuclear war could best be prevented if both the United States and the Soviet Union had sufficient nuclear weapons so that even if one nation launched a preemptive first strike, the other could respond and devastate the attacker.

mystery religions religions that involve initiation into secret rites that promise intense emotional involvement with spiritual forces and a greater chance of individual immortality.

nationalism a sense of national consciousness based on awareness of being part of a community—a "nation"—that has common institutions, traditions, language, and customs and that becomes the focus of the individual's primary political loyalty.

nationalities problem the dilemma faced by the Austro-Hungarian Empire in trying to unite a wide variety of ethnic groups including, among others, Austrians, Hungarians, Poles, Croats, Czechs, Serbs, Slovaks, and Slovenes in an era when nationalism and calls for self-determination were coming to the fore.

nationalization the process of converting a business or industry from private ownership to government control and ownership.

nation in arms the people's army raised by universal mobilization to repel the foreign enemies of the French Revolution.

nation-state a form of political organization in which a relatively homogeneous people inhabits a sovereign state, as opposed to a state containing people of several nationalities.

NATO the North Atlantic Treaty Organization; a military alliance formed in 1949 in which the signatories (Belgium, Canada, Denmark, France, Great Britain, Iceland, Italy, Luxembourg, the Netherlands, Norway, Portugal, and the United States) agreed to provide mutual assistance if any one of them was attacked; later expanded to include other nations.

natural laws a body of laws or specific principles held to be derived from nature and binding upon all human society even in the absence of positive laws.

natural rights certain inalienable rights to which all people are entitled; include the right to life, liberty, and property, freedom of speech and religion, and equality before the law.

natural selection Darwin's idea that organisms that are most adaptable to their environment survive and pass on the variations that enabled them to survive, while other, less adaptable organisms become extinct; "survival of the fittest."

Nazi New Order the Nazis' plan for their conquered territories; included the extermination of Jews and others considered inferior, ruthless exploitation of resources, German colonization in the east, and the use of Poles, Russians, and Ukrainians as slave labor.

Neoplatonism a revival of Platonic philosophy. In the third century A.D., a revival associated with Plotinus; in the Italian Renaissance, a revival associated with Marsilio Ficino who attempted to synthesize Christianity and Platonism.

New Economic Policy a modified version of the old capitalist system introduced in the Soviet Union by Lenin in 1921 to revive the economy after the ravages of the civil war and war communism.

new imperialism the revival of imperialism after 1880 in which European nations established colonies throughout much of Asia and Africa.

new monarchies the governments of France, England, and Spain at the end of the fifteenth century, where the rulers were successful in reestablishing or extending centralized royal authority, suppressing the nobility, controlling the church, and insisting upon the loyalty of all peoples living in their territories.

nobiles "nobles." The small group of families from both patrician and plebeian origins who produced most of the men who were elected to office in the late Roman Republic.

nominalism a school of thought in medieval Europe that, following Aristotle, held that only individual objects are real and that universals are only names created by humans.

nuclear family a family group consisting only of father, mother, and children.

old regime/old order the political and social system of France in the eighteenth century before the Revolution.

oligarchy rule by a few.

optimates "best men." Aristocratic leaders in the late Roman Republic who generally came from senatorial families and wished to retain their oligarchical privileges.

orders/estates the traditional tripartite division of European society based on heredity and quality rather than wealth or economic standing, first established in the Middle Ages and continuing into the eighteenth century; traditionally consisted of those who pray (the clergy), those who fight (the nobility), and those who work (all the rest).

organic evolution Darwin's principle that all plants and animals have evolved over a long period of time from earlier and simpler forms of life.

Paleolithic Age the period of human history when humans used simple stone tools (c. 2,500,000–10,000 B.C.).

pantheism a doctrine that equates God with the universe and all that is in it.

paterfamilias the dominant male in a Roman family whose powers over his wife and children were theoretically unlimited, though they were sometimes circumvented in practice.

patriarchal/patriarchy a society in which the father is supreme in the clan or family; more generally, a society dominated by men.

patriarchal family a family in which the husband/father dominates his wife and children.

patricians great landowners who became the ruling class in the Roman Republic.

patronage the practice of awarding titles and making appointments to government and other positions to gain political support.

Pax Romana "Roman peace." A term used to refer to the stability and prosperity that Roman rule brought to the Mediterranean world and much of western Europe during the first and second centuries A.D.

Pentateuch the first five books of the Hebrew Bible (Genesis, Exodus, Leviticus, Numbers, and Deuteronomy).

perestroika "restructuring." A term applied to Mikhail Gorbachev's economic, political, and social reforms in the Soviet Union.

permissive society a term applied to Western society after World War II to reflect the new sexual freedom and the emergence of a drug culture.

Petrine supremacy the doctrine that the bishop of Rome—the pope—as the successor of Saint Peter (traditionally considered the first bishop of Rome) should hold a preeminent position in the church.

phalanx a rectangular formation of tightly massed infantry soldiers.

philosophes intellectuals of the eighteenth-century Enlightenment who believed in applying a spirit of rational criticism to all things, including religion and politics, and who focused on improving and enjoying this world, rather than on the afterlife.

plebeians the class of Roman citizens who included nonpatrician landowners, craftspeople, merchants, and small farmers in the Roman Republic. Their struggle for equal rights with the patricians dominated much of the Republic's history.

pluralism the practice in which one person holds several church offices simultaneously; a problem of the late medieval church.

pogroms organized massacres of Jews.

polis an ancient Greek city-state encompassing both an urban area and its surrounding countryside; a small but autonomous political unit where all major political and social activities were carried out in a central location.

political democracy a form of government characterized by universal suffrage and mass political parties.

politiques a group who emerged during the French Wars of Religion in the sixteenth century; placed politics above religion and believed that no religious truth was worth the ravages of civil war.

polytheistic/polytheism having many gods; belief in or the worship of more than one god.

popular culture as opposed to high culture, the unofficial, written and unwritten culture of the masses, much of which was passed down orally; centers on public and group activities such as festivals. In the twentieth century, refers to the entertainment, recreation, and pleasures that people purchase as part of mass consumer society.

populares "favoring the people." Aristocratic leaders in the late Roman Republic who tended to use the people's assemblies in an effort to break the stranglehold of the *nobiles* on political offices.

popular sovereignty the doctrine that government is created by and subject to the will of the people, who are the source of all political power.

praetorian guard the military unit that served as the personal bodyguard of the Roman emperors.

predestination the belief, associated with Calvinism, that God, as a consequence of his foreknowledge of all events, has predetermined those who will be saved (the elect) and those who will be damned.

price revolution the dramatic rise in prices (inflation) that occurred throughout Europe in the sixteenth and early seventeenth centuries.

primogeniture an inheritance practice in which the eldest son receives all or the largest share of the parents' estate.

principate the form of government established by Augustus for the Roman Empire; continued the constitutional forms of the Republic and consisted of the *princeps* ("first citizen") and the senate, although the *princeps* was clearly the dominant partner.

proletariat the industrial working class. In Marxism, the class who will ultimately overthrow the bourgeoisie.

Puritans English Protestants inspired by Calvinist theology who wished to remove all traces of Catholicism from the Church of England.

querelles des femmes "arguments about women." A centuries-old debate about the nature of women that continued during the Scientific Revolution as those who argued for the inferiority of women found additional support in the new anatomy and medicine.

rationalism a system of thought based on the belief that human reason and experience are the chief sources of knowledge.

realism in medieval Europe, the school of thought that, following Plato, held that the individual objects we perceive are not real but merely manifestations of universal ideas existing in the mind of God. In the nineteenth century, a school of painting that emphasized the everyday life of ordinary people, depicted with photographic realism.

Realpolitik "politics of reality." Politics based on practical concerns rather than theory or ethics.

real wages/income/prices wages/income/prices that have been adjusted for inflation.

reason of state the principle that a nation should act on the basis of its long-term interests and not merely to further the dynastic interests of its ruling family.

relativity theory Einstein's theory that holds, among other things, that (1) space and time are not absolute but are relative to the observer and interwoven into a four-dimensional space-time continuum and (2) matter is a form of energy ($E = mc^2$).

relics the bones of Christian saints or objects intimately associated with saints that were considered worthy of veneration.

Renaissance the "rebirth" of classical culture that occurred in Italy between c. 1350 and c. 1550; also, the earlier revivals of classical culture that occurred under Charlemagne and in the twelfth century.

rentier a person who lives on income from property and is not personally involved in its operation.

reparations payments made by a defeated nation after a war to compensate another nation for damage sustained as a result of the war; required from Germany after World War I.

revisionism a socialist doctrine that rejected Marx's emphasis on class struggle and revolution and argued instead that workers should work through political parties to bring about gradual change.

revolution a fundamental change in the political and social organization of a state.

revolutionary socialism the socialist doctrine espoused by Georges Sorel who held that violent action was the only way to achieve the goals of socialism.

rhetoric the art of persuasive speaking; in the Middle Ages, one of the seven liberal arts.

sacraments rites considered imperative for a Christian's salvation. By the thirteenth century consisted of the eucharist or Lord's Supper, baptism, marriage, penance, extreme unction, holy orders, and confirmation of children; Protestant reformers of the sixteenth century generally recognized only two—baptism and communion (the Lord's Supper).

salons gatherings of philosophes and other notables to discuss the ideas of the Enlightenment; so-called from the elegant drawing rooms (salons) where they met.

sans-culottes the common people who did not wear the fine clothes of the upper classes (sans-culottes means "without breeches") and played an important role in the radical phase of the French Revolution.

satrap/satrapy a governor with both civil and military duties in the ancient Persian Empire, which was divided into satrapies, or provinces, each administered by a satrap.

scholasticism the philosophical and theological system of the medieval schools, which emphasized rigorous analysis of contradictory authorities; often used to try to reconcile faith and reason.

scientific method a method of seeking knowledge through inductive principles; uses experiments and observations to develop generalizations.

Scientific Revolution the transition from the medieval worldview to a largely secular, rational, and materialistic perspective; began in the seventeenth century and was popularized in the eighteenth.

secularization the process of becoming more concerned with material, worldly, temporal things and less with spiritual and religious things.

self-determination the doctrine that the people of a given territory or a particular nationality should have the right to determine their own government and political future.

senate/senators the leading council of the Roman Republic; composed of about 300 men (senators) who served for life and dominated much of the political life of the Republic.

serf a peasant who is bound to the land and obliged to provide labor services and pay various rents and fees to the lord; considered unfree but not a slave because serfs could not be bought and sold.

skepticism a doubtful or questioning attitude, especially about religion.

Social Darwinism the application of Darwin's principle of organic evolution to the social order; led to the belief that progress comes from the struggle for survival as the fittest advance and the weak decline.

socialism an ideology that calls for collective or government ownership of the means of production and the distribution of goods.

social security/social insurance government programs that provide social welfare measures such as old age pensions and sickness, accident, and disability insurance.

Socratic method a form of teaching that uses a question-and-answer format to enable students to reach conclusions by using their own reasoning.

Sophists wandering scholars and professional teachers in ancient Greece who stressed the importance of rhetoric and tended toward skepticism and relativism.

soviets councils of workers' and soldiers' deputies formed throughout Russia in 1917; played an important role in the Bolshevik Revolution.

sphere of influence a territory or region over which an outside nation exercises political or economic influence.

Stoicism a philosophy founded by Zeno in the fourth century B.C. that taught that happiness could be obtained by accepting one's lot and living in harmony with the will of God, thereby achieving inner peace.

subinfeudation the practice in which a lord's greatest vassals subdivided their fiefs and had vassals of their own, and those vassals, in turn, subdivided their fiefs and so on down to simple knights whose fiefs were too small to subdivide.

suffrage the right to vote.

suffragists those who advocate the extension of the right to vote (suffrage), especially to women.

surplus value in Marxism, the difference between a product's real value and the wages of the worker who produced the product.

syncretism the combining of different forms of belief or practice, as, for example, when two gods are regarded as different forms of the same underlying divine force and are fused together.

tariffs duties (taxes) imposed on imported goods; usually imposed both to raise revenue and to discourage imports and protect domestic industries.

tetrarchy rule by four; the system of government established by Diocletian (284–305) in which the Roman Empire was divided into two parts, each ruled by an "Augustus" assisted by a "Caesar."

theocracy a government ruled by a divine authority.

three-field system in medieval agriculture, the practice of dividing the arable land into three fields so that one could lie fallow while the others were planted in winter grains and spring crops.

tithe a tenth of one's harvest or income; paid by medieval peasants to the village church.

Torah the body of law in Hebrew Scripture, contained in the Pentateuch (the first five books of the Hebrew Bible).

totalitarian state a state characterized by government control over all aspects of economic, social, political, cultural, and intellectual life, the subordination of the individual to the state, and insistence that the masses be actively involved in the regime's goals.

total war warfare in which all of a nation's resources, including civilians at home as well as soldiers in the field, are mobilized for the war effort.

trade union an association of workers in the same trade, formed to help members secure better wages, benefits, and working conditions.

transubstantiation a doctrine of the Roman Catholic church that teaches that during the eucharist the substance of the bread and wine is miraculously transformed into the body and blood of Jesus.

trench warfare warfare in which the opposing forces attack and counterattack from a relatively permanent system of trenches protected by barbed wire; characteristic of World War I.

trivium **and** ***quadrivium*** together formed the seven liberal arts that were the basis of medieval and early modern education. Grammar, rhetoric, and dialectic or logic made up the *trivium;* arithmetic, geometry, astronomy, and music made up the *quadrivium.*

Truman Doctrine the doctrine, enunciated by Harry Truman in 1947, that the United States would provide economic aid to countries that said they were threatened by Communist expansion.

tyrant/tyranny in an ancient Greek *polis* (or an Italian city-state during the Renaissance), a ruler who came to power in an unconstitutional way and ruled without being subject to the law.

uncertainty principle a principle in quantum mechanics, posited by Heisenberg, that holds that one cannot determine the path of an electron because the very act of observing the electron would affect its location.

unconditional surrender complete, unqualified surrender of a belligerent nation.

utopian socialists intellectuals and theorists in the early nineteenth century who favored equality in social and economic conditions and wished to replace private property and competition with collective ownership and cooperation; deemed impractical and "utopian" by later socialists.

vassal a person granted a fief, or landed estate, in exchange for providing military services to the lord and fulfilling certain other obligations such as appearing at the lord's court when summoned and making a payment on the knighting of the lord's eldest son.

vernacular the everyday language of a region, as distinguished from a language used for special purposes. For example, in medieval Paris, French was the vernacular, but Latin was used for academic writing and for classes at the University of Paris.

volkish thought the belief that German culture is superior and that the German people have a universal mission to save Western civilization from inferior races.

war communism Lenin's policy of nationalizing industrial and other facilities and requisitioning the peasants' produce during the civil war in Russia.

War Guilt Clause the clause in the Treaty of Versailles that declared that Germany (and Austria) were responsible for starting World War I and ordered Germany to pay reparations for the damage the Allies had suffered as a result of the war.

Warsaw Pact a military alliance, formed in 1955, in which Albania, Bulgaria, Czechoslovakia, East Germany, Hungary, Poland, Romania, and the Soviet Union agreed to provide mutual assistance.

welfare state a social/political system in which the government assumes the primary responsibility for the social welfare of its citizens by providing such things as social security, unemployment benefits, and health care.

wergeld "money for a man." In early Germanic law, a person's value in monetary terms, which was paid by a wrongdoer to the family of the person who had been injured or killed.

world-machine Newton's conception of the universe as one huge, regulated, and uniform machine that operated according to natural laws in absolute time, space, and motion.

ziggurat a massive stepped tower upon which a temple dedicated to the chief god or goddess of a Sumerian city was built.

Zionism an international movement that called for the establishment of a Jewish state or a refuge for Jews in Palestine.

Zoroastrianism a religion founded by the Persian Zoroaster in the seventh century B.C.; characterized by worship of a supreme god Ahuramazda who represents the good against the evil spirit, identified as Ahriman.

al-Abbas, Abu   al-AH-bus, AH-boo

Abbasid   AB-uh-sid *or* a-BA-sid

Adenauer, Konrad   AD-n'our-er

aediles   EE-diles

Aeolians   ee-OH-lee-uns

Aeschylus   ESS-kuh-lus

Afrikaners   a-fri-KAH-ners

Agincourt   AJ-in-kor

Ahuramazda   ah-HOOR-ah-MAHZ-duh

Akhenaton   ah-kuh-NAH-tun

Akkadians   a-KAY-dee-uns

Albigensians   al-bi-GEN-see-uns

d'Albret, Jeanne   dahl-BRAy, ZHAHN

Albuquerque, Afonso de   AL-buh-kur-kee, ah-FON-soh d'

Alcibiades   al-suh-BY-uh-deez

Alcuin   AL-kwin

Aliz, Ramiz   AL-ee-uh, ra-MEEZ

Allah   AH-luh *or* AL-uh

Amenhotep   ah-mun-HOE-tep

Andreotti, Giulio   ahn-dray-AH-tee, JOOL-yoh

Andropov, Yuri   an-DROP-ov, YOOR-ee

Anjou   AN-joo

Antigonid   an-TIG-oh-nid

Antigonus Gonatus   an-TIG-oh-nus goh-NAH-tus

Antiochus   an-TIE-uh-kus

Antonescu, Ion   An-tuh-NES-koo, YON

Antoninus Pius   an-toh-NIGH-nus PIE-us

apella   a-PELL-uh

Apollonius   ap-uh-LOH-nee-us

Aquinas, Thomas   uh-KWIGH-nus

aratrum   a-RA-trum

Archimedes   are-kuh-MEE-deez

Argonautica   ARE-guh-NOT-i-kuh

Aristarchus   ar-is-TAR-kus

Aristotle   ar-i-STAH-tul

Arsinoë   ar-SIN-oh-ee

artium baccalarius   are-TEE-um back-uh-LAR-ee-us

artium magister   are-TEE-um ma-GIS-ter

Ashkenazic   ash-kuh-NAH-zic

Ashurnasirpal   ah-shoor-NAH-suh-pul

asiento   a-SEE-en-toh

assignat   as-seen-YAH *or* AS-sig-nat

Assyrians   uh-SEER-ee-uns

Atahualpa   ah-tuh-WALL-puh

Attalid   AT-a-lid

audiencias   ah-DEE-en-CEE-ahs

Augustine   AW-gus-STEEN

Avicenna   av-i-SEN-uh

Avignon   ah-veen-YONE

Auschwitz-Birkenau   OUSH-vitz-BUR-kuh-now

Ausgleich   OUS-glike

Babeuf, Gracchus   bah-BUHF, GRAK-us

Bach, Johann Sebastian   BAHK, yoh-HAHN suh-BASS-chen

Bakunin, Michael   ba-KOO-nin

Balboa, Vasco Nuñez de   bal-BOH-uh, VASH-koh NOON-yez duh

Ballin, Albert   BAHLL-een

Barbarossa   bar-buh-ROH-suh

Bastille   ba-STEEL

Bayle, Pierre   BAYL, PYER

Beauvoir, Simone de   boh-VWAH, see-MOAN duh

Bebel, August   BAY-bul

Beccaria, Cesare   bek-KAH-ree-uh, CHAY-zahr-ay

Beguines   bi-GEENS

Belisarius   bell-i-SAR-ee-us

benefice   BEN-uh-fiss

Bergson, Henri   BERG-son, AWN-ree

Bernini, Gian Lorenzo   bur-NEE-nee, JAHN loh-RENT-soh

Bernstein, Eduard   BURN-stine, AY-doo-art

Blitzkrieg   BLITZ-kreeg

Blum, Léon   BLOOM, LAY-OHN

Boccaccio, Giovanni   boh-KAH-chee-oh, joe-VAHN-nee

Bodichon, Barbara   BOH-duh-chon

Boer   BOHR

Boethius   boh-EETH-ee-us

Boleyn, Anne   BUH-lin

Bólívar, Simón   BOH-luh-VAR, see-MOAN

Bologna   buh-LOHN-yuh

Bossuet, Jacques   baw-SWAY, ZHAHK

Bottai, Giuseppe   BOT-tah, joo-ZEP-pay

Botticelli, Sandro   BOT-i-CHELL-ee, SAHN-droh

Boulanger, Georges   boo-lahn-ZHAY, ZHORZH

Bracciolini, Poggio   braht-choh-LEE-nee, POD-joh

Brahe, Tycho BRAH, TIE-koh
Bramante, Donato brah-MAHN-tee, doe-NAY-toe
Brandt, Willy BRAHNT, VIL-ee
Brétigny bray-tee-NYEE
Brezhnev, Leonid BREZH-nef, lyi-on-YEET
Briand, Aristide bree-AHN, a-ree-STEED
Brunelleschi, Filippo BROO-nuh-LES-kee, fee-LEEP-poe
Brüning, Heinrich BROO-ning, HINE-rik
Bulganin, Nilolai bul-GAN-in, nyik-uh-LYE
Bund deutscher Mädel BUNT DOICHer MAIR-del
Burschenschaften BOOR-shen-shaft-un
Calais ka-LAY
Caligula ka-LIG-yuh-luh
caliph/caliphate KAY-lif/KAY-li-FATE
Calonne, Charles de kah-LAWN, SHARL duh
Cambyses kam-BY-seez
Camus, Albert kuh-MOO, al-BEAR
Canaanites KAY-nuh-nites
Capet/Capetian ka-PAY or KAY-put/kuh-PEE-shun
Caraffa, Gian Pietro kah-RAH-fuh, JAHN PYEE-troh
carbonari kar-buh-NAH-ree
Carolingian kar-oh-LIN-jun
carruca ca-ruh-kuh
Carthage/Carthaginian KAR-thij/KAR-thuh-JIN-ee-un
Cassiodorus kass-ee-oh-DOR-us
Castlereagh, Viscount KAS-ul-RAY
Catharism KA-tha-ri-zem
Catullus ka-TULL-us
Cavendish, Margaret KAV-un-dish
Cavour, Camillo di ka-VOOR, kah-MIL-oh
Ceausescu, Nicolai chow-SHES-koo, nee-koh-LYE
cenobitic sen-oh-BIT-ik
Cèzanne, Paul say-ZAN
Chaeronea ker-oh-NEE-uh
Chaldean kal-DEE-un
chanson de geste shahn-SAWN duh ZHEST
Charlemagne SHAR-luh-mane
Chateaubriand, François-René de shah-TOH-bree-AHN, FRAN-swah-ruh-NAY duh
Chernenko, Konstantin cher-NYEN-koh, kon-stunTEEN
Chiang Kai-Shek CHANG KIGH-shek
Chrétien de Troyes KRAY-tee-ahn duh TRWAH
Cicero SIS-uh-roh
ciompi CHOM-pee
Cistercians si-STIR-shuns
Claudius KLAW-dee-us
Cleisthenes KLISE-thuh-neez
Clemenceau, Georges klem-un-SOH, ZHORZH
Clovis KLOH-vis
Codreanu, Corneliu kaw-dree-AH-noo, kor-NELL-yoo

colonus kuh-LOH-nus
Columbanus kol-um-BAHN-us
comitia centuriata kuh-MISH-ee-uh sen-TYOO-ree-ah-tuh
Commodus KOM-uh-dus
Comnenus kom-NEE-nus
Comte, Auguste KOHNT
concilium plebis con-CIL-ee-um PLE-bis
Concordat of Worms kon-KOR-dat of WURMZ or VAWRMZ
Condorcet, Marie-Jean de kawn-dar-SAY, mur-REE-ZHAHN duh
condottieri kon-dah-TEE-AIR-ee
consul KON-sul
Contarini, Gasparo kahn-tuh-REE-nee, Gahs-pah-roh
conversos kon-VAIR-sohs
Copernicus, Nicolaus koh-PURR-nuh-kus, nee-koh-LAH-us
Corinth KOR-inth
corregidores kor-REG-uh-DOR-ays
Cortés, Hernán kor-TEZ, er-NAHN
Corvinus, Matthias kor-VIE-nus, muh-THIGH-us
Courbet, Gustave koor-BAY, guh-STAWV
Crassus KRASS-us
Crécy kray-SEE
Crédit Mobilier kred-EE mohb-eel-YAY
Croesus KREE-sus
Danton, Georges dahn-TAWN, Zhorzh
Darius duh-RYE-us
dauphin DAW-fin
David, Jacques-Louis dah-VEED, ZHAHK-LWEE
Debussy, Claude de-BYOO-see, KLODE
Decameron di-KAM-uh-run
Deffand, marquise du di-FAHN, mar-KEEZ doo
de Gaulle, Charles duh GOLL, SHARL
Delacroix, Eugène del-uh-KWAW, yoo-ZHAHN
Demosthenes di-MOSS-thuh-neez
Denikin, Anton dyi-NYEE-kin, an-TAWN
Descartes, René day-KART, ruh-NAY
Diaghilev, Sergei dee-AHG-uh-lef, syir-GYAY
Dias, Bartholomeu DEE-us, bar-too-loo-MAY
Diaspora die-AS-pur-uh
Diderot, Denis DEE-duh-roh, duh-NEE
Diocletian die-uh-KLEE-shun
Disraeli, Benjamin diz-RAY-lee
Dollfuss, Engelbert DOLL-foos
Domesday Book DOOMZ-day
Domitian doh-MISH-un
Donatus/Donatist doh-NAY-tus/DOH-nuh-tist
Dorians DOR-ee-uns
Dostoevsky, Fyodor DOS-tuh-YEF-skee, FYOD-ur
Douhet, Giulio doo-EE, JOOL-yoh
Dreyfus, Alfred DRY-fus

Dubcek, Alexander   DOOB-chek
Duma   DOO-muh
Dürer, Albrecht   DOO-er, AWL-brekt
ecclesia   eh-KLEE-zee-uh
Eckhart, Meister   EK-hart, MY-ster
encomienda   en-koh-mee-EN-dah
Engels, Friedrich   ENG-ulz, FREE-drik
Entente Cordiale   ahn-TAHNT kor-DYALL
Epaminondas   i-PAM-uh-NAHN-dus
ephor   EF-or
Epicurus/Epicureanism   EP-i-KYOOR-us/EP-i-kyoo-
   REE-uh-ni-zem
equestrians   i-KWES-tree-uns
equites   EK-wuh-tays
Erasistratus   er-uh-SIS-truh-tus
Erasmus, Desiderius   i-RAZZ-mus, des-i-DIR-ee-us
Eratosthenes   er-uh-TOSS-thuh-neez
eremitical   air-uh-MITT-i-cul
d'Este, Isabella   ES-tay
Erhard, Ludwig   AIR-hart
Etruscans   i-TRUSS-kuhns
Euclid   YOO-klid
Euripides   yoo-RIP-i-deez
exchequer   EX-chek-ur
fasces   FASS-eez
Fascio di Combattimento   FASH-ee-oh di
   com-BATT-ee-men-toh
Fatimid   FAT-i-mid
Fedele, Cassandra   FAY-del-ee
Feltre, Vittorino da   FELL-tree, vee-tor-EE-noh dah
Ficino, Marsilio   fee-CHEE-noh, mar-SIL-ee-oh
Flaubert, Gustave   floh-BEAR, guh-STAWV
Fleury, Cardinal   floe-REE
Fontainebleau   FAWN-tin-BLOW
Fontenelle, Bernard de   fawnt-NELL, Ber-nar duh
Fouquet, Nicolas   foo-KAY, nee-KOH-lah
Frequens   FREE-kwens
Friedan, Betty   fri-DAN
Frimaire   free-MARE
Fronde   FROND
Führerprinzip   FYOOR-ur-PRIN-tseep
gabelle   gah-BELL
Gama, Vasco da   GAM-uh, VASH-koh duh
Gamond, Zoé Gatti de   gah-MAHN, zaw-ay
   GAHT-tee duh
Garibaldi, Giuseppe   gar-uh-BAWL-dee, joo-ZEP-pay
Gasperi, Alcide de   GAHS-pe-ree, awl-CHEE-day de
Gaugamela   gaw-guh-MEE-luh
Gentileschi, Artemisia   jen-tul-ESS-kee, are-tee-
   MISS-ee-uh
gerousia   juh-ROO-see-uh
Gierek, Edward   GYER-ek
Gilgamesh   GILL-guh-mesh

Giolitti, Giovanni   joh-LEET-tee, joe-VAHN-nee
Giotto   JAW-toh
Girondins   juh-RAHN-dins
glasnost   GLAZ-nohst
Gleichschaltung   GLIKE-shalt-ung
Goebbels, Joseph   GUHR-bulz
Gomulka, Wladyslaw   goh-MOOL-kuh, vla-DIS-lawf
gonfaloniere   gon-fa-loh-NEE-ree
Gorbachev, Mikhail   GOR-buh-chof, meek-HALE
Gracchus, Tiberius and Gaius   GRAK-us,
   tie-BIR-ee-us and GAY-us *or* GUY-us
grandi   GRAHN-dee
Grieg, Edvard   GREEG, ED-vart
Groote, Gerard   GROH-tuh
Gropius, Walter   GROH-pee-us, VAHL-ter
Grossdeutsch   gross-DOICH
Guicciardini, Francesco   gwee-char-DEE-nee,
   frahn-CHASE-koh
Guizot, François   gee-ZOH, FRAN-swah
Gustavus Adolphus   gus-STAY-vus a-DOLF-us
Guzman, Gaspar de   goos-MAHN, gahs-PAR day
Habsburg   HAPS-burg
Hadrian   HAY-dree-un
Hagia Sophia   HAG-ee-uh soh-FEE-uh
hajj   HAJ
Hammurabi   ham-uh-RAH-bee
Handel, George Friedrich   HAN-dul
Hannibal   HAN-uh-bul
Hanukkah   HAH-nuh-kuh
Hardenberg, Karl von   HAR-d'n-burg
Harun al-Rashid   huh-ROON al-ra-SHEED
Hatshepsut   hat-SHEP-soot
Haussmann, Baron   HOUS-mun
Havel, Vaclav   HAH-vuhl, VAHT-slaf
Haydn, Franz Joseph   HIDE-n, FRAHNTS
hegemon   HEJ-uh-mon
Heisenberg, Werner   HIGH-zun-burg, VUR-nur
Hellenistic   hell-uh-NIS-tik
helots   HELL-uts
hermandades   er-mahn-DAHDH-ays
Herodotus   hi-ROD-oh-tus
Herophilus   hi-ROF-uh-lus
Herzen, Alexander   HER-tsun
Herzl, Theodor   HERT-sul, TAY-oh-dor
Hesiod   HEE-see-ud
Heydrich, Reinhard   HIGH-drik, RINE-hart
hieroglyph   HIGH-ur-oh-glif
Hildegard of Bingen   HILL-duh-gard of BING-en
Hitler Jugend   JOO-gunt
Ho Chi Minh   HOE CHEE MIN
Höch, Hannah   HOKH
Hohenstaufen   HOE-un-SHTAU-fun

Hohenzollern HOE-un-ZAHL-lurn
d'Holbach, Paul awl-BAHK
Honecker, Erich HOE-nuh-ker
hoplites HOP-lites
Horace HOR-us
Horthy, Miklós HOR-tee, MIK-lohsh
Hoxha, Enver HAW-jah
Huguenots HYOO-guh-nots
Husák, Gustav HOO-sahk, guh-STAHV
Ibn Sina ib-en SEE-nuh
Ignatius of Loyola ig-NAY-shus of loi-OH-luh
Il Duce eel DOO-chay
imperator im-puh-RAH-tor
imperium im-PIER-ee-um
intendant in-TEN-duhnt
Isis EYE-sis
Issus ISS-us
ius gentium YOOS GEN-tee-um
Jacobin JAK-uh-bin
Jacquerie zhah-KREE
Jagiello yah-GYELL-oh
Jahn, Friedrich Ludwig YAHN, FREE-drik
Jaruzelski, Wojciech yahr-uh-ZEL-skee, VOI-chek
Jaurés, Jean zhaw-RESS, ZHAHN
jihad ji-HAHD
Judaea joo-DEE-uh
Judas Maccabaeus JOO-dus mak-uh-BEE-us
Jung, Carl YOONG
Junkers YOONG-kers
Jupiter Optimus Maximus JOO-pi-ter OPP-tuh-mus MAK-suh-mus
Justinian juh-STIN-ee-un
Juvenal JOO-vuh-nul
Kádár, János KAY-dahr, YAHN-us
Kadinsky, Vasily kan-DIN-skee, vus-YEEL-yee
Karlowitz KARL-oh-vitz
Kaunitz, Wenzel von KOU-nits, VENT-sul
Kerensky, Alexander kuh-REN-skee
Keynes, John Maynard KAYNZ
Khrushchev, Nikita KROOSH-chef, nuh-KEE-tuh
Kleindeutsch kline-DOICH
Kohl, Helmut KOLE, HELL-mut
koiné koi-NAY
Kolchak, Alexander KAWL-chok
Kollantai, Alexandra kawl-un-TIE
Kosciuszko, Thaddeus kos-ee-US-koh, tah-DE-us
Kossuth, Louis KOSS-ooth
kouros KOO-raws
Kraft durch Freude CRAFT durch FROI-duh
Kristallnacht KRIS-tal-NAHCHT
Krupp, Alfred KROOP
Kuchuk-Kainarji koo-CHOOK-kigh-NAR-jee

kulaks koo-LAKS
kulturkampf kool-TOOR-kahmf
Kun, Béla KOON, Bay-luh
Lafayette, marquis de lah-fee-ETTE, mar-KEE duh
laissez-faire les-ay-FAIR
Lamarck, Jean-Baptiste luh-MAHRK, ZHAHN-buh-TEEST
Lancaster LAN-kas-ter
latifundia lat-uh-FUN-dee-uh
Latium LAY-shee-um
Laurier, Wilfred LAWR-ee-ay
Lebensraum LAY-benz-room
Lespinasse, Julie de les-peen-AHS
Le Tellier, François Michel luh tel-YAY, FRAN-swah-mee-SHELL
Lévesque, René luh-VEK, ruh-NAY
Leyster, Judith LE-ster
Liebenfels, Lanz von LEE-bun-felz, LAHNZ
Liebknecht, Karl LEEP-knekt
Liebknecht, Wilhelm LEEP-knekt, VIL-helm
Lionne, Hugues de LYAWN, UGH
List, Friedrich LIST, FREE-drik
Liszt, Franz LIST, FRAHNZ
Livy LIV-ee
Lucretius loo-KREE-shus
Luddites LUD-ites
Ludendorff, Erich LOOD-un-dorf
Lueger, Karl LOO-ger
Luftwaffe LUFT-vaf-uh
Luxemburg, Rosa LUK-sum-burg
Machiavelli, Niccolò mak-ee-uh-VELL-ee, nee-koh-LOH
Magna Graecia MAG-nuh GREE-shuh
Magyars MAG-yars
Maistre, Joseph de MES-truh
Malleus Maleficarum mall-EE-us mal-uh-FIK-ar-um
al-Ma'mun al-MAH-moon
Manetho MAN-uh-THOH
Mao Zedong mau zee-DONG
Marcus Aurelius MAR-kus au-REE-lee-us
Marcuse, Herbert mar-KOO-zuh
Marie Antoinette muh-REE an-twuh-NET
Marius MAR-ee-us
Marsiglio of Padua mar-SIL-ee-oh of PA-juh-wuh
Masaryk, Thomas MAS-uh-rik
Matteotti, Giacomo mat-ee-OH-tee, Jahk-oh-moh
Mazarin maz-uh-RAN
Mazzini, Giuseppe maht-SEE-nee, joo-ZEP-pay
Meiji MAY-jee
Mein Kampf mine KAHMF
Melanchthon, Philip muh-LANGK-thun
Menander me-NAN-der
Mendeleyev, Dmitri men-duh-LAY-ef, di-MEE-tri

Merian, Maria Sibylla MARE-ee-un
Mesopotamia mess-oh-poh-TAME-ee-uh
Messiaen, Olivier me-SYAHN, O-LEEV-yay
Metaxas, John me-TAK-sus
Metternich, Klemens von MET-er-nik, KLAY-mens
Michel, Louise mee-SHELL
Michelangelo my-kell-AN-juh-loh
Mieszko MYESH-koh
Millet, Jean-François mi-LAY, ZHAHN-FRAN-swah
Milošević, Slobodan mi-LOH-suh-vik, SLOW-buh-dan
Miltiades mil-TIE-uh-deez
Mirandola, Pico della muh-RAN-duh-luh, PEE-koh DELL-uh
missi dominici MISS-ee doe-MIN-ee-chee
Moctezuma mahk-tuh-ZOO-muh
Mohács MOH-hach
Moldavia mahl-DAY-vee-uh
Molière, Jean-Baptiste mole-YAIR, ZHAHN-buh-TEEST
Moltke, Helmuth von MOLT-kuh, HELL-mut fahn
Monet, Claude moh-NAY, KLODE
Montaigne, Michel de mahn-TANE, mee-SHELL duh
Montefeltro, Federigo da mahn-tuh-FELL-troh, fay-day-REE-goh dah
Montesquieu MONT-ess-skyoo
Montessori, Maria mon-ti-SOR-ee
Morisot, Berthe mor-ee-ZOH, BERT
Muawiyah moo-AH-wee-yah
Mühlberg mool-BERK
Muhammad moe-HA-mud
Müntzer, Thomas MOON-tsur
Muslim MUZ-lum
Mutsuhito moo-tsoo-HEE-toe
Mycenaean my-suh-NEE-un
Nabonidas na-bun-EYE-dus
Nagy, Imry NAHJD, IM-re
Navarre nuh-VARR
Nebuchadnezzar neb-uh-kad-NWZZ-ar
Nero NEE-roh
Nerva NUR-vuh
Neumann, Balthasar NOI-mahn, BAHL-tah-zar
Neumann, Solomon NOI-mahn
Nevsky, Alexander NEW-skee
Newcomen, Thomas new-KUH-mun
Ngo Dinh Diem NGOH din dee-EM
Nietzsche, Friedrich NEE-chuh, FREE-drik
Nimwegen NIM-vay-gun
Ninhursaga nin-HUR-sah-guh
Nogaret, William de noh-guh-RAY
Nogarola, Isotta NOH-guh-roll-uh, eye-SOT-tuh
Novalis, Friedrich noh-VAH-lis, FREE-drik
Novotny, Antonin noh-VOT-nee, AN-ton-yeen

Nystadt nee-STAHD
Octavian ok-TAY-vee-un
Odoacer oh-doh-AY-ser
optimates opp-tuh-MAH-tays
Osiris oh-SIGH-ris
Ovid OV-id
Paleologus pay-lee-OHL-uh-gus
papal curia PAY-pul KOOR-ee-uh
Papen, Franz von PAH-pun, FRAHNTZ fahn
Paracelsus par-uh-SELL-sus
Parlement par-luh-MAHN
Pascal, Blaise pass-KAL, BLEZ
paterfamilias pay-ter-fuh-MILL-ee-us
Pentateuch PEN-tuh-tuke
Pepin PEP-in
perestroika pair-ess-TROY-kuh
Pergamum PURR-guh-mum
Pericles PER-i-kleez
perioeci per-ee-EE-sie
Pétain, Henri pay-TAN, AHN-ree
Petrarch PE-trark
Petronius pi-TROH-nee-us
philosophe fee-luh-ZAWF
Phoenicians fi-NISH-uns
Photius FOH-shus
Picasso, Pablo pi-KAW-soh
Pilsudski, Joseph peel-SOOT-skee
Pisistratus pi-SIS-truh-tus
Pissaro, Camille pi-SARR-oh, kah-MEEYL
Pizarro, Francesco pi-ZARR-oh, frahn-CHASE-koh
Planck, Max PLAHNK
Plantagenet plan-TA-juh-net
Plato PLAY-toe
Plautus PLAW-tus
Poincaré, Raymond pwan-kah-RAY, re-MOAN
polis POE-lis
politiques puh-lee-TEEKS
Polybius poe-LIB-ee-us
Pombal, marquis de pom-BAHL, mar-KEE duh
Pompadour, madame de POM-puh-door, muh-DAM duh
Pompey POM-pee
pontifex maximus PON-ti-feks MAK-suh-mus
populares POP-yoo-lar-ays
populo grasso POP-uh-loh GRAH-soh
Poussin, Nicholas poo-SAN, NEE-kaw-lah
Praecepter Germaniae PREE-sep-ter ger-MAN-ee-eye
praetor PREE-ter
princeps PRIN-seps
Procopius proh-KOH-pee-us
procurator PROK-yuh-ray-ter
Ptolemy/Ptolemaic TOL-uh-mee/TOL-uh-MAY-ik

Pugachev, Emelyan POO-guh-choff, yim-yil-YAHN
Punic PYOO-nik
Pyrrhus/Pyrrhic PIR-us/PIR-ik
quaestors KWES-ters
Quetzelcoatl ket-SAHL-koh-ATE-ul
Quran kuh-RAN
Racine, Jean-Baptiste ra-SEEN, ZHAHN-buh-TEEST
al-Rahman, Abd al-RAH-mun, abd
Ramesses RAM-i-seez
Raphael RAFF-ee-ul
Rasputin rass-PYOO-tin
Realpolitik ray-AHL-poe-li-teek
Reichsrat RIKES-raht
Rembrandt van Rijn REM-brant vahn RINE
Renan, Ernst re-NAHN
Ricci, Matteo REECH-ee, mah-TAY-oh
Richelieu RISH-uh-loo
Rilke, Rainer Maria RILL-kuh, RYE-ner
risorgimento ree-SOR-jee-men-toe
Robespierre, Maximilien ROHBZ-pee-air,
    mak-SEE-meel-yahn
Rococo ro-KOH-koh
Röhm, Ernst RURM
Roon, Albrecht von ROHN AHL-brekt
Rousseau, Jean-Jacques roo-SOH ZHAHN-ZHAHK
Rurik ROOR-ik
Ryswick RIZ-wik
Sacrosancta sak-roh-SANK-tuh
Saint-Just san-ZHOOST
Saint-Simon, Henri de san-see-MOAN, AHN-ree duh
Sakharov, Andrei SAH-kuh-rof, ahn-DRAY
Saladin SAL-uh-din
Sallust SALL-ust
Samnites SAM-nites
San Martín, José de san mar-TEEN, hoe-Say day
Sartre, Jean-Paul SAR-truh, ZHAHN-PAUL
satrap/satrapy SAY-trap/SAY-truh-pee
Satyricon SAY-tir-ee-kon
Schaumburg-Lippe SHAHM-berkh-LI-puh
Schleswig-Holstein SCHLES-vig-HOLE-stine
Schlieffen, Alfred von SHLEE-fun
Schmidt, Helmut SHMIT, HELL-mut
Schönberg, Arnold SHURN-burg, ARR-nawlt
Schönerer, George von SHURN-er-er, ZHORSH
Schuschnigg, Karl von SHOOSH-nik
Schutzmannschaft SHOOTS-mun-shaft
Scipio Africanus SI-pee-oh af-ri-KAY-nus
Scipio Aemilianus SI-pee-oh i-mill-ee-AY-nus
scriptoria skrip-TOR-ee-uh
Sejm SAME
Seleucus/Seleucid si-LOO-kus/si-LOO-sid
Seljuk Turks SELL-juke

Seneca SEN-i-kuh
Sephardic suh-FAR-dik
Septimius Severus sep-TIM-ee-us se-VIR-us
Sforza, Ludovico SFORT-zuh, loo-doe-VEE-koh
Sieveking, Amalie SEEVE-king
Sieyès, Abbé sye-YES, a-BAY
signoria seen-YOOR-ee-uh
Socrates SOK-ruh-teez
Solon SOH-lun
Solzhenitsyn, Alexander SOLE-zhuh-NEET-sin
Sophocles SOF-uh-kleez
Sorel, Georges sah-RELL, ZHORZH
Spartacus SPAR-tuh-kus
Speer, Albert SHPIER
Speransky, Michael spyuh-RAHN-skee
Spinoza, Benedict de spi-NOH-zuh
squadristi sqah-DREES-tee
Staël, Germaine de STAWL, ZHER-men duh
Stein, Heinrich von STINE, HINE-rik
Stoicism STOH-i-siz-um
Stolypin, Peter stuh-LEE-pyin
Stravinsky, Igor struh-VIN-skee, EE-gor
Stresemann, Gustav SHTRAY-zuh-mahn, GUS-tahf
Struensee, John Frederick SHTROO-un-zay
Sulla SULL-uh
Sumerians soo-MER-ee-uns
Suppiluliumas suh-pil-oo-LEE-uh-mus
Suttner, Bertha von ZOOT-ner
Taafe, Edward von TAH-fuh
Tacitus TASS-i-tus
taille TAH-yuh or TIE
Talleyrand, Prince TAL-ee-ran
Tauler, Johannes TOU-ler, yoh-HAHN-us
Tenochtitlán tay-NAWCH-teet-LAWN
Tertullian tur-TULL-yun
Theocritus thee-OCK-ri-tus
Theodora thee-uh-DOR-uh
Theognis thee-OGG-nus
Thermidor ter-mee-DOR
Thermopylae thur-MOP-uh-lee
Thiers, Adolphe tee-ER, a-DOLF
Thucydides thoo-SID-uh-deez
Thutmosis thoot-MOH-sus
Tiberius tie-BIR-ee-us
Tiepolo, Giovanni Battista tee-AY-puh-loh,
    joe-VAHN-ee baht-TEES-tah
Tiglath-pileser TIG-lath-puh-LEE-zur
Tirpitz, Admiral von TUR-puts
Tito TEE-toh
Tlaxcala tlah-SKAHL-uh
Torah TOR-uh
Tordesillas tor-duh-SEE-yus

Trajan TRAY-jun
Trevithick, Richard TREV-uh-thik
Tristan, Flora TRIS-tun
Tyche TIE-kee
Ulbricht, Walter UL-brikt, VAHL-ter
Umayyads oo-MY-ads
Unam Sanctam OON-ahm SANK-tahm
universitas yoo-ni-VER-si-tahs
Valois VAL-wah
van Eyck, Jan van IKE
van Gogh, Vincent van GOE
Vasa, Gustavus VAH-suh, gus-STAY-vus
Vega, Lope de VAY-guh, LOH-pay day
Vendée vahn-DAY
Venetia vuh-NEE-shee-uh
Vesalius, Andreas vi-SAY-lee-us, ahn-DRAY-us
Vespasian ves-PAY-zhun
Vespucci, Amerigo ves-POO-chee, ahm-ay-REE-goe
Vichy VISH-ee
Vierzenheiligen feer-tsun-HILE-i-gun
Virchow, Rudolf FEER-koh, roo-DOLF
Virgil VUR-jul
Volkschulen FOLK-shool-un
Voltaire vole-TAIR
von Bora, Katherina BOR-uh
Wagner, Richard VAHG-ner, RIK-art
Walesa, Lech va-WENZ-uh, LEK
Wallachia wah-lay-KEE-uh
Wallenstein, Albrecht von WOLL-un-stine, AWL-brekt
Watteau, Antoine wah-TOE, AHN-twahn

Wannsee VAHN-say
Weizsäcker, Richard von VITS-zek-er, RIK-art
wergeld wur-GELD
Windischgrätz, Alfred vin-dish-GRETS
Winkelmann, Maria VING-kul-mun
Witte, Sergei VIT-uh, syir-GYAY
Worms, Edict of WURMZ *or* VAWRMZ
Wyclif, John WIK-lif
Xavier, Francis ZAY-vee-ur
Xerxes ZURK-seez
Xhosa KOH-suh
Ximenes hee-MAY-nus
Yahweh YAH-wah
Yeats, William Butler YATES
Yeltsin, Boris YELT-sun
yishuv Yish-uv
Zemsky Sobor ZEM-skee SOH-bur
zemstvos ZEMPST-voh
Zeno ZEE-noh
Zeus ZOOS
Zhivkov, Todor ZHEV-kof, toh-DOR
ziggurat ZIG-guh-rat
Zimmermann, Domenikus TSIM-ur-mahn,
    doe-MEE-nee-kus
Zinzendorf, Nikolaus von ZIN-zun-dorf,
    nee-koh-LAH-us
Zola, Emile ZOH-luh, ay-MEEL
zollverein TSOL-fuh-rine
Zoroaster ZOR-oh-as-ter

Index

Note: Page references in *italics* indicate map or figure.

A

al-Abbas, Abu, 168
Abbasid dynasty, 168, 169, 184–86
Abortion, 157
Absolutism, 303–15
    in central and eastern Europe in 17th century, 309–14
    culture in age of, in 17th century, 320–23
    Dutch republic in age of, in 17th century, 315
    economic trends in age of, in 17th century, 319–20
    England as constitutional monarchy in age of, 315–17
    in France and Spain of western Europe in 17th century, 304–9
    limits of, 314–15
    theory of, 304
Abu Bakr, 147
Achaemenid dynasty, Persian, 37
Actium, Battle of (31 B.C.), 103
Act of Supremacy of 1534 (England), 271, 290
Address to the Nobility of the German National (Luther), 265
Adoration of the Magi (Dürer), *252*
Aeneid (Virgil), 113
Aeolian Greeks, 48
Aeschylus, 58
Agamemnon, 47
Agincourt, Battle of (1415), 222
Agriculture
    ancient Egyptian, 14, 17
    Assyrian, 36
    European, in High Middle Ages, 173–75
    European manorial system of Middle Ages, 163–64
    Hellenistic, 74
    Mesopotamian, 7
    Neolithic, in Europe, 3–5
    Roman, 99, 113
Ahuramazda (deity), 39, 41, 121
Ain Ghazal (Jordan), 5
Akhenaton (Egyptian king), 20

Akkadians, 8
Alaric (king of Visigoths), 125, 129
Alberti, Leon Battista, 236
Albigensians, persecution of, 183
Albuquerque, Alfonso de, 282
Alcoholic beverage consumption
    in Early Middle Ages, 158
    in High Middle Ages, 175
Alexander VI (pope), 244, 257
Alexander the Great, 67–72
    conquests of, 67, 69–70, 71
    Hellenistic civilization disseminated by, 77–81
    Hellenistic kingdoms united by, 72–76
    legacy of, 70–72
Alexandria (Egypt), 69, 76–77, 112
Alexius I Comnenus (Byzantine emperor), 186
Alfonso X (king of Castile), 210
Ali (son-in-law of Muhammad), 147, 148
Allah (deity), 145
Amenhotep IV (Egyptian king), 20
Amish, 271
Amores (Ovid), 114, 115
Amorite dynasty, 8
Anabaptists, 270–71, 273
Anatomy, advances in study of human, 332–33
Angles, 132, 138
Anglican Church. *See* Church of England
Anglo-Saxon kingdom (England), 132–33
    Christian conversion of, 138
    Viking invasion of, 161
Annals (Tacitus), 116
Antapodosis (Liudprand), 165
Anthony, Saint, 136
Antigonid dynasty (Macedonia), 72
Antioch (Syria), 112
Antiochus IV (Seleucid dynasty), 81
Anti-Semitism in Middle Ages, 184, 218
Antony, Mark (Roman triumvirate), 99, 103
Aquinas, Thomas, 184
Arabs, 145
    as inheritors of Greco-Roman culture, 169–70

Aragon, Spanish kingdom of, 209
Archbishop, Christian church, 180
    of Canterbury, 206, 271
Archimedes, 78
Architecture
    Baroque, 298
    Byzantine empire, 143, *144*
    castles in Middle Ages, 175–76
    classical Greek, 58–59
    Egyptian, 18–19
    Gothic, 204–5
    Hellenistic, 77
    Islamic, *169*
    Mesopotamian, 7
    Neolithic European megaliths, 26–27
    Persian, 39
    Renaissance, *249*
    Roman, 93, 98
    Romanesque, 203–4
Arianism, 131, 132, 135
Aristarchus of Samos, 78
Aristocracy. *See also* Elites, European
    Greek, 49
    of High Middle Ages, 175–78
    lords and vassals in Middle Ages, 162–63
    Renaissance, 238, 239
    Roman, 87, 99, 116–17
    Russian boyars, 212, 311
Aristophanes, 58
Aristotle, 50, 78, 170, 200, 202
    cosmological and astronomical views of, 327
    political and social ideas of, 61
Armada, English defeat of Spanish, 291
Arrian, 71
Arsinoë II (queen of Egypt), 75
Art
    Assyrian, *34, 36*
    Baroque, 298–99
    Byzantine, *143*
    Dutch realism in 17th century, 320–23
    effect of Black Death on, in Late Middle Ages, 231–32
    Egyptian, *18,* 19–20, *21*
    French classicism in 17th century, 320
    Greek, *47, 50, 60, 63*
    Greek classical ideal, 58–60
    Hellenistic, 77